Feature	How to Get There	Feature	How to Get There
Double-Sided Printing (non-duplex)	F5 OO	Generate Auto-References	Ctrl+F9
Draft view	Ctrl+F5	Go To	Ctrl+G
Drag-and-Drop	Select, drag (or Ctrl+drag), release	Grammar	Alt+Shift+F1
		Graphics (show/hide)	Alt+V G
Draw	Alt+G D (or double-click a Figure box)	Graphics Box	Alt+G then F, T, Q, or C
E-mail	Alt+F M	Graphics Box (edit)	Shift+F11
Embed (object)	Alt+I J		
Endnote	Alt+I F	Graphics Line (custom)	Alt+G L
Envelope	Alt+L V	Graphics Line (edit)	Alt+G N (or double-click line)
Equations	Alt+G Q		
Exit Document	Ctrl+F4	Graphics Line (horizontal)	Ctrl+F11
Exit WordPerfect	Alt+F4		
Export Text	F3 Alt+T	Graphics Line (vertical)	Ctrl+Shift+F11
Fax	F5 S (select fax driver), then P		
		Graphics Styles	Alt+G G
Figure (retrieve)	Alt+G F	Hanging Indent	Ctrl+F7
File (insert)	Alt+I I	Hard Page Break	Ctrl+↵
File Management	Ctrl+O or F3 or F4	Hard Space	Ctrl+space
File Name (insert in text)	Alt+I OF	Headers	Alt+L H, A or B
		Help	Alt+H or F1 or Shift+F1
Files (default location)	Alt+F E Alt+F ↵		
		Hidden Text (show/hide)	Alt+V X
Find	F2		
Find Next	Shift+F2	Hide/Show Bars	Alt+Shift+F5
Find Previous	Alt+F2	Hide Text*	F9 Alt+E
Floating cell	F12 Alt+F	Hypertext	Alt+T H
Flush Right (all lines)	Ctrl+R	Hyphenation	Alt+L LE
		Import Text	Ctrl+O or Alt+I I
Flush Right (line)	Alt+F7	Indent	F7
Font	F9	Index	Alt+T X
Footers	Alt+L H, F or O	Indexer (QuickFinder)	Alt+F Q
Footnote	Alt+I F		
Force Odd/Even Page	Alt+L PF	Info (document)	Alt+F I
		Info (WP)	Alt+H A
Full Justification (all lines)	Alt+L JA	Initial Codes Style	Alt+L DS
		Initial Font	F9 Alt+T or Alt+L DF
Full Justification (paragraph)	Ctrl+J	Insert/Typeover	Ins
		Italics	Ctrl+I

For every kind of computer user, there is a SYBEX book.

All computer users learn in their own way. Some need straightforward and methodical explanations. Others are just too busy for this approach. But no matter what camp you fall into, SYBEX has a book that can help you get the most out of your computer and computer software while learning at your own pace.

Beginners generally want to start at the beginning. The **ABC's** series, with its step-by-step lessons in plain language, helps you build basic skills quickly. Or you might try our **Quick & Easy** series, the friendly, full-color guide.

The **Mastering** and **Understanding** series will tell you everything you need to know about a subject. They're perfect for intermediate and advanced computer users, yet they don't make the mistake of leaving beginners behind.

If you're a busy person and are already comfortable with computers, you can choose from two SYBEX series—**Up & Running** and **Running Start**. The **Up & Running** series gets you started in just 20 lessons. Or you can get two books in one, a step-by-step tutorial and an alphabetical reference, with our **Running Start** series.

Everyone who uses computer software can also use a computer software reference. SYBEX offers the gamut—from portable **Instant References** to comprehensive **Encyclopedias**, **Desktop References**, and **Bibles**.

SYBEX even offers special titles on subjects that don't neatly fit a category—like **Tips & Tricks**, the **Shareware Treasure Chests**, and a wide range of books for Macintosh computers and software.

SYBEX books are written by authors who are expert in their subjects. In fact, many make their living as professionals, consultants or teachers in the field of computer software. And their manuscripts are thoroughly reviewed by our technical and editorial staff for accuracy and ease-of-use.

So when you want answers about computers or any popular software package, just help yourself to SYBEX.

For a complete catalog of our publications, please write:

SYBEX Inc.
2021 Challenger Drive
Alameda, CA 94501
Tel: (510) 523-8233/(800) 227-2346 Telex: 336311
Fax: (510) 523-2373

SYBEX is committed to using natural resources wisely to preserve and improve our environment. As a leader in the computer book publishing industry, we are aware that over 40% of America's solid waste is paper. This is why we have been printing the text of books like this one on recycled paper since 1982.

This year our use of recycled paper will result in the saving of more than 15,300 trees. We will lower air pollution effluents by 54,000 pounds, save 6,300,000 gallons of water, and reduce landfill by 2,700 cubic yards.

In choosing a SYBEX book you are not only making a choice for the best in skills and information, you are also choosing to enhance the quality of life for all of us.

Mastering
WordPerfect 6 for
Windows
Special Edition

Mastering
WordPerfect® 6 for
Windows™
Special Edition

ALAN SIMPSON

SYBEX®

San Francisco • Paris • Düsseldorf • Soest

DEVELOPMENTAL EDITOR: Steve Lipson
EDITORS: Doug Robert, Sarah Wadsworth
TECHNICAL EDITOR: Maryann Brown
BOOK DESIGNER: Suzanne Albertson
CHAPTER ART: Charlotte Carter
SCREEN GRAPHICS: John Corrigan
TYPESETTERS: Len Gilbert, Deborah Maizels, Ann Dunn, Alissa Feinberg
PRODUCTION ASSISTANTS: Kristin Amlie, Elisabeth Dahl
INDEXER: Ted Laux
COVER DESIGNER: Ingalls + Associates
COVER PHOTOGRAPHER: Mark Johann
COVER PHOTO ART DIRECTION: Ingalls + Associates

Screen reproductions produced with Collage Complete.

Collage Complete is a trademark of Inner Media Inc.

SYBEX is a registered trademark of SYBEX Inc.

TRADEMARKS: SYBEX has attempted throughout this book to distinguish proprietary trademarks from descriptive terms by following the capitalization style used by the manufacturer.

SYBEX is not affiliated with any manufacturer.

Every effort has been made to supply complete and accurate information. However, SYBEX assumes no responsibility for its use, nor for any infringement of the intellectual property rights of third parties which would result from such use.

Library of Congress Card Number: 93-85950
ISBN: 0-7821-1382-6

Manufactured in the United States of America
10 9 8 7 6 5 4 3

To the million or so of you who bought my previous WordPerfect book. This one's for you. (My wife thanks you too. She gets the money.)

ACKNOWLEDGMENTS

THANKS to Elizabeth Olson, my #1 perfection-demanding, co-authoring sidekick on this ambitious project.

Thanks to Martha Mellor who, as always, fielded problems and made cool heads prevail through yet another stress-ridden time.

Thanks to everyone at SYBEX who changed this book from my original WordPerfect manuscript into the beautiful finished product you're now holding in your hands. In particular, thanks to Steve Lipson, Developmental Editor; Doug Robert and Sarah Wadsworth, Editors; Len Gilbert, Deborah Maizels, Ann Dunn, and Alissa Feinberg, Typesetters; Kristin Amlie, Production Assistant; John Corrigan, who produced the screen graphics; Charlotte Carter, Production Artist; and Michelle Khazai, Kathleen Lattinville and David Krassner for their valuable assistance as the deadlines loomed.

Also at SYBEX, thanks to Rodnay, Alan, Rudy, Barbara, and Dianne, for giving me the opportunity.

Thanks to WordPerfect Corporation for creating the best word processing program in the universe. And for supporting me and my work.

Thanks to Bill Gladstone and the gang at Waterside Productions, my literary agency. It's been over a decade now, gang.

Thanks to John Vorhaus-rhymes-with-(never mind), writing instructor extraordinaire. Your two-day seminar at UCSD Extension taught me to lighten up and enjoy my work once again.

And of course, thanks to Susan, Ashley, and Alec, for cutting Daddy loose for a few weeks, to pound the keyboard night and day. Again.

Contents

AT A GLANCE

CONTENTS

PART FOUR   MANAGING (AND SIMPLIFYING) YOUR WORK

PART FIVE   **OFFICE TOOLS**

INTRODUCTION

FIRST of all, thanks for buying this book. If you just borrowed it from someone else, then thanks for giving it a chance.

Who This Book Is For

Who is this book for? You. That is, this book is for every WordPerfect user, from the absolute beginner to the experienced WordPerfect wizard who wants to take full advantage of everything WordPerfect has to offer. Here's a little guidance on how to get started with this book, depending on which of those two types of people you are.

Road Map for Beginners

If you're new to WordPerfect, you might want to take this route to get up to speed in a jiffy:

- The five quick hands-on lessons in Chapter 1 will teach all you need to know about creating, printing, saving, retrieving, and editing documents with WordPerfect.

- Read Chapters 2 through 4 to get a broader, and deeper, understanding of the features you learned about in Chapter 1.

- Later, when you're working on your own, if you feel stuck, lost, or confused, look to Appendix C for quick first aid to common problems.

Road Map for Experienced Users

If you're already a WordPerfect wizard, but you've recently upgraded to (or are considering upgrading to) Version 6.0 for Windows, try this route:

- Browse through Appendix B for a quick overview of Version 6.0's best new features.

- Skim through the first three chapters, if you wish. And take a close look at Chapter 4. There you'll learn about some great updates to the graphical interface and other hot new features.

Road Map for Everyone

Once you've gotten your bearings, use the book to find answers to questions, and solutions to problems, as they arise. No, I *don't* expect you to read this entire book. Nobody (except an author like me) needs to know *everything* about WordPerfect.

After all, if you don't use equations in your documents, why learn about equations? If you have no interest in desktop publishing, why read Part Six? On the other hand, if you know the basics already, and you enjoy being creative, you certainly wouldn't want to miss Part Six.

Features and Structure of This Book

This book has one goal: to make the time you spend at the keyboard with WordPerfect as productive and enjoyable as possible. This book about WordPerfect is loaded with information. And here's how that information is organized to help you get to what you need, when you need it.

Glossary, Table of Contents, Index

Like any useful book, this one has a Table of Contents up front and an index at the back to help you look up the information you need. I've also added a glossary to the back of the book, so you can look up any unfamiliar terms you might come across.

Step-by-Step Instructions

Within each chapter, I typically describe a feature by first identifying it with a heading, such as "Starting WordPerfect." That's usually followed by a brief description of the feature. The description, in turn, is usually followed by step-by-step instructions for using the feature.

When you're in a hurry, feel free to skip the paragraph under the heading, and jump right to step 1 to put that feature to work.

"Fast Tracks"

"Fast Tracks" at the beginning of each chapter summarize the main features discussed in the chapter. Use these for an overview of things to come, or as reminders after you've learned about a feature and just need a quick nudge on how to get to it.

First Aid for Common Problems

I've summarized the most common day-to-day problems and confusions in Appendix C. There you can look up a problem and find a solution in a hurry. If that doesn't do the trick, you can always use the index or Table of Contents to find more in-depth information about a way to solve the problem.

Quick Reference Charts

There's a lot of quick-reference type information inside the front and back covers of this book. If you just need to remember how to get to a particular feature, you may be able to find the answer right there inside the covers.

For beginners, I offer some simplified reference charts near the end of Chapter 1. Feel free to make copies and keep them near your keyboard for quick reminders on using the meat-and-potatoes features of WordPerfect.

Notes, Tips, and Warnings

My Notes and Tips provide references to related topics, shortcuts, good ideas, and tips on using the feature in conjunction with other features.

The Warnings point out actions that, if taken carelessly, might not be too easy to "undo" (such as deleting your entire document from disk!). Think of a warning as a way of saying "Hmmm…. I better think before I act here."

Sample Documents

Sometimes the best way to learn something new is to look at something someone else has created and then find out how they did it. Because of that, this book is loaded with sample documents. You'll find everything from your basic business letter to professional-quality newsletters.

If you'd like to see some of the more advanced and particularly fancy sample documents I've dished up for you, thumb through Chapters 5, 7, and 25–28.

If you did just go and peek at those sample documents, you may be thinking "I could never do *that* one." *Au contraire!* If *I* can do it, *you* can do it. It's simply a matter of knowing which features to use and when to use them. And that, ultimately, is *really* what this book is all about.

Perhaps I should mention that I typed all the text in this entire book with WordPerfect before sending it to the publisher. And, except for a little custom artwork here and there, I created virtually all of the sample documents in this book with WordPerfect, too.

I did take the liberty of using fonts and clip art beyond those that come with the WordPerfect program. I did so under the assumption that if you'll be creating more advanced documents, you probably will use additional fonts and clip art. Chapter 10 explains how to expand your font collection. Chapter 25 talks about expanding your clip art collection. It's remarkably inexpensive to do these days. So it's pretty hard to resist!

Installing/Upgrading to Version 6.0

If you (or someone else) hasn't already installed WordPerfect on your computer, you'll need to do so before you can do anything in this book. Refer to Appendix A for installation instructions.

About WordPerfect Interim Releases

WordPerfect occasionally puts out *interim releases* of their products. These interim releases fix minor bugs or improve features as users offer up their suggestions.

An interim release has the same version number as the initial release. If you want to be sure that you're always using the latest and greatest release, you can contact WordPerfect's Software Subscription Service to learn about the various programs they have for keeping you up to date. The phone number is (800) 282-2892.

Additional Support

Part of the success WordPerfect has enjoyed stems from the fact that they're serious about offering telephone support to their customers. WordPerfect Corporation phone numbers for answers to specific questions are listed below:

Orders	(800) 321-4566
Installation	(800) 228-7610
Equations/Graphics/Sound/Tables	(800) 228-8720
Macros/Merges	(800) 228-2021
Laser/PostScript Printers	(800) 228-2803
Dot Matrix/Other Printers	(800) 228-6646
Networks	(800) 228-8807
All Other Features	(800) 228-9907

There's also the monthly magazine titled *WordPerfect for Windows Magazine*. For more information, contact

WP for Windows Magazine
Circulation Department
270 West Center Street
Orem, UT 84057-9927
Voice: (800) 228-9626

A Pep Talk for the Technically Timid

One last pep talk for those of you who are still feeling a little skittish. Keep in mind that like everything else in life, from driving a car to skiing down a mountain, WordPerfect is only confusing and intimidating when you're at the very bottom of the learning curve—that disorienting time when you're struggling to get your bearings and figure out how to work the darn thing.

WordPerfect is not an evil menace. Nor is it solely for the use of Nobel prize–winning scholars and assorted geniuses. Nope. It's a writing tool that *everyone* can use. I promise you: Once you get a little time "behind the wheel," the fear and intimidation will melt away, as it does in *every* endeavor we humans undertake. So do what I always do: Quit worrying and start *enjoying* yourself already!

PART ONE

The Least You Need to Know...

CHAPTER

1

WordPerfect in an Evening!

IF YOU'RE new to WordPerfect, probably the first thing you want to know is "how do I work this pup?" At the very least, you might want to type up a letter or memo without getting totally lost. In this chapter we'll go through five quick lessons that will teach you how to do just that. You can probably complete these lessons in an evening, which is a lot better than spending weeks fumbling around in the dark.

Notice I said you can *probably* complete the lessons in an evening. If you can't type worth beans, it might take you a little longer. But don't worry. We'll let you know when a good time to take a break comes up, so you can resume your lessons at a later time. Try to give yourself at least a half hour of free time, without distractions, to get through the first few lessons.

If you're an experienced WordPerfect user, you'll probably scoff at most of the material in this chapter—too easy! Not to worry. There's plenty of more advanced stuff later in the book.

Learning about Windows

If this is your first experience using a Windows program, you might need to back up a bit and learn some basic Windows skills. Here are some quick ways to get started:

- Go through the interactive tutorial that comes with Windows. Run Windows at the DOS command prompt (type **win** then press the ↵ key), then choose Help from the Program Manager menu bar (hold down the Alt key, type the letter **h**, then release both keys). Next, choose Windows Tutorial from the menu that appears (type the letter **w**). Follow the instructions on the screen.

- If time permits, refer to the often-neglected *Microsoft Windows User's Guide* and *Getting Started with Microsoft Windows* manuals that came with your Windows package. Or, you can purchase a third-party book, such as my own *Windows 3.1 Running Start,* also published by SYBEX.

You should know how to work the mouse, and you should understand some basic Windows terminology, before beginning these lessons. If you have difficulty with some of the terms, you can refer to the Glossary near the end of this book. Or, read through Chapters 2–4 for more detailed background information, then come back and try the hands-on lessons.

Lesson 1: Getting Started

HANDS ON!

In this lesson, you'll learn how to start Windows and WordPerfect for Windows. First, you'll need to turn on your printer, screen, and computer in the usual manner (switch all the "off" switches to "on" or from 0 to 1). If your computer is set up to start Windows automatically when you turn it on, skip to the next section, "Starting WordPerfect for Windows," now.

On most computers, you'll be greeted with the DOS command prompt, usually **C>** or **C:\>**. If the MS-DOS Shell or some other shell program appears instead, exit the shell. For example, to exit the MS-DOS shell, you would press Alt+F4 (hold down the Alt key, tap F4, then release both keys). If you're using some other shell and you aren't sure how to exit, please refer to the shell program's documentation or ask your local guru for help.

N O T E

Alt+F4 is an example of a *combination keystroke.* See "Key+Key Combination Keystrokes," later in this chapter, to learn more about combination keystrokes.

When the DOS prompt appears, type **win** and press the ↵ (Enter) key. If you get the message "Bad command or file name," try switching to Windows' home directory before starting Windows. Here are the steps:

1. Type **c:** and press ↵.
2. Type **cd \windows** and press ↵.
3. Type **win** and press ↵.

If this still doesn't work, either Windows isn't installed on your disk, or you need to ask your local computer ace for appropriate startup instructions for your computer.

If all works well, you should be taken to the Windows Program Manager, which looks something like Figure 1.1. If the Program Manager appears as a tiny icon near the lower-left corner of the screen, *double-click* that icon to open the window.

FIGURE 1.1

The Windows Program Manager window

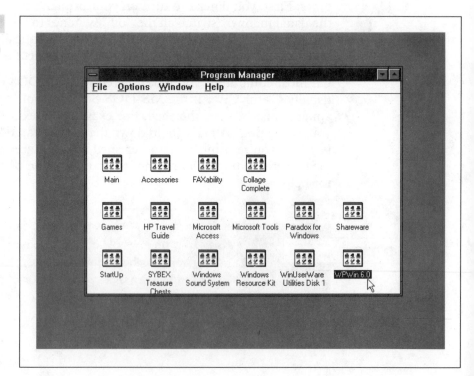

Starting WordPerfect for Windows

HANDS ON!

Once you've got the Windows Program Manager running, look for a group window named *WPWin 6.0.* This window might be open or closed, but it should be there somewhere. If you can't find the WPWIN 6.0 window, WordPerfect for Windows may not be installed on your computer. Appendix A explains how to install the program.

Now, follow these steps to start WordPerfect for Windows:

1. If the WPWin 6.0 group window is closed, double-click it. Or, press Ctrl+F6 (hold down the Ctrl key, tap F6, then release both keys) until the WPWin 6.0 group icon is highlighted, then press ↵. When the WPWin 6.0 group window is open, you'll see the icons for several WordPerfect for Windows programs.

2. Double-click the WPWin 6.0 icon (shown at left). Or use the arrow keys to highlight that icon, then press ↵.

You should see a fancy graphic of a pen tip announcing that WordPerfect 6.0 is starting up. That's followed by the WordPerfect application window, shown in Figure 1.2. Don't worry if your screen doesn't match Figure 1.2 exactly. As you'll learn in Chapter 4, there are many ways to customize the appearance of WordPerfect's screen to get exactly the look and tools you want.

TIP

A quick way to start WordPerfect for Windows on most computers is to type *win wpwin* and press ↵ at the DOS prompt.

If at any time you're not sure whether you're in or out of WordPerfect, just look at the title bar at the top of the screen. It should say "WordPerfect" (a dead giveaway!).

FIGURE 1.2

The WordPerfect for Windows document window, ready for you to begin typing

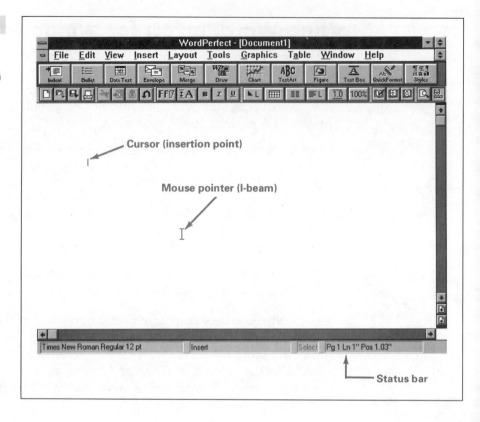

The Document Window

When you first start WordPerfect for Windows, your screen will look something like Figure 1.2. The large blank area is where you'll do your typing and editing (it's like a blank sheet of paper). This area is the *document window* (also called the *Edit screen*). Notice the *status bar* at the bottom of the screen. Initially, the status bar shows the following information in the lower-right corner:

Pg 1 Ln 1" Pos 1"

That just tells you where the *cursor* (the blinking vertical marker) is positioned on the page. As you type and move the cursor through your document, the status bar will change to reflect the cursor's current position. You may also notice the *mouse pointer* (also called the *I-beam*) on your screen. The mouse pointer moves in whatever direction you move the mouse. It can be used in a variety of ways, as I'll discuss in upcoming lessons.

Lesson 2: Typing with WordPerfect

Typing with WordPerfect is practically identical to typing on a typewriter, except that you type on a screen before you print on paper (it's much easier to make changes when you type on a screen first). But there are a few special circumstances to keep in mind when typing with WordPerfect:

- You can back up and correct your text on the spot by pressing the Backspace key. (The Backspace key usually has a ← symbol on it, and it's usually located above the ↵ key.)

- If you type *John Smith* and it comes out as *jOHN sMITH*, your Caps Lock key is on. Press the Caps Lock key once, then press Backspace until you've erased all the mistyped text. Then type the text again.

- When you're typing a paragraph with WordPerfect, *don't* press ↵ to end each line. Instead, just keep typing off the right edge of the screen, and let WordPerfect break the line for you.

- When typing 1 (one) and zero (0) with WordPerfect, you need to use the 1 and 0 keys above the letters on the keyboard. Don't use the letters "l" and "o".

Key+Key Combination Keystrokes

Sometimes you'll need to press *combination keystrokes* to make WordPerfect do what you want. You'll know when you need to press a combination keystroke when you see a plus sign between two keys, like this: *key+key*.

To press a combination keystroke, *hold down* the first key, *tap* the second key, then *release* the first key. Don't try to press both keys at once, don't type the plus sign, and don't press the second key first. For example, to press Ctrl+F1, hold down the Ctrl (Control) key, press and release the *function key* labeled F1 (usually found at the top or left side of your keyboard), then release the Ctrl key.

You're Never Stuck

Contrary to what you might feel from time to time, you're rarely ever "stuck" in WordPerfect. When you think you're stuck or lost, try choosing the Close or Cancel button—whichever one appears—until you get back to familiar territory. (In fact, if you pressed Ctrl+F1 in the preceding section, you can now click <u>C</u>lose or press Alt+C to get rid of the *dialog box* that popped up on your screen.) In a dialog box that has a Cancel button, you can also press the Esc key (Escape) to cancel the dialog box.

If you ever feel stuck in a pull-down menu, you can just press Escape until you've cleared the menu (or menus) from the screen or click outside the pull-down menu.

Typing a Letter

HANDS ON!

OK, let's get to work by typing the letter shown in Figure 1.3.

1. Type **Wanda Bea Tuna** (if it comes out as *wANDA...*, your Caps Lock key is on, as explained earlier).

2. Press ↵ to end that line and move to the next line.

3. Type **123 Oak Tree Lane** and then press ↵ to move to the next line.

FIGURE 1.3

The sample letter you'll be typing in this lesson

```
Wanda Bea Tuna
123 Oak Tree Lane
Hollywood, CA  91234

Dear Ms. Tuna:

     Rumor has it that you're an expert on TV script writing.
Therefore, I'm hoping you can answer a simple question for me.
Why is it that actors and actresses never say "Goodbye" before
hanging up the phone? I always say Goodbye (or at least 'kay-
bye). Why don't you make the actors do that to, you know, make
it more realistic like? This has always puzzled me, and drives me
crazy becuase I can't stop noticing it.

Thanks in advance for your reply:



Willie B. Goode
```

4. Type **Hollywood, CA 91234** and press ↵ twice (once to end the line, then again to insert a blank line).

5. Type **Dear Ms. Tuna:** and press ↵ twice.

Now you should see something like this on your screen:

Wanda Bea Tuna
123 Oak Tree Lane
Hollywood, CA 91234

Dear Ms. Tuna:

Don't worry if it's not perfect. I'll show you how to make corrections later.

Typing Paragraphs

When you're typing a paragraph that's longer than a single line, don't press ↵ at the end of each line. Just type right off the edge of the screen and let WordPerfect *word-wrap* the line for you.

WARNING

If you *do* press ↵ at the end of each line and you make changes to the paragraph later, WordPerfect won't be able to reformat the paragraph on its own. This can be a major pain.

1. Press the Tab key (usually to the left of the Q) to indent about half an inch. (Don't use the spacebar to indent, or you may end up with an incorrectly aligned document.)

2. Type the paragraph below (including mistakes) as though it were one long line. Don't worry if the paragraph wraps differently on your screen—just don't press ↵.

Rumor has it that you're an expert on TV script writing. Therefore, I'm hoping you can answer a simple question for me. Why is it that actors and actresses never say "Goodbye" before hanging up the phone? I always say Goodbye (or at least 'kay-bye). Why don't you make the actors do that to, you know, make it more realistic like? This has always puzzled me, and drives me crazy because I can't stop noticing it.

3. After you've typed the whole paragraph, press ↵ twice (once to end the paragraph, a second time to put in a blank line).

4. Type **Thanks in advance for your reply:** and then press ↵ about five times to insert some blank lines where your signature will go.

5. Type your own name, or **Willie B. Goode**, or whatever you want.

Now your letter should look something like the one in Figure 1.3.

What Happens to Text at the Top?

We'll keep this sample document short, just to make life easy. But don't think you're limited to typing only as much as there's space for on the screen. You can type as much text as you want. In fact, I typed this whole book using WordPerfect!

As you type off the bottom of the screen, some text will scroll up out of view, off the top of the screen. The text isn't gone for good; it's just out of our way for now. As you'll learn in Chapter 2, you can scroll up and down through the entire document using either your mouse or the keyboard.

Lesson 3: Printing and Saving Your Document

HANDS ON!

Assuming your printer is turned on, hooked up, and online (according to the manufacturer's instructions), you can now print a copy of the letter that's on your screen. Follow these steps:

1. If the *menu bar* isn't visible, press Escape. The menu bar appears as a row of commands across the top of the screen, like this:

    File   **Edit**   **View**   **Insert**   **Layout**   **Tools**   **Graphics**   **Table**   **Window**   **Help**

2. Click on the **File** option or press Alt+F. A *drop-down menu* (also called a *pull-down menu*) will appear.

3. Type the letter **p** to choose the Print option. You'll be taken to the Print dialog box. (The name of the dialog box always appears centered at the top of the box.)

4. Type the letter **p** to choose the Print button (or click that button with your mouse).

TIP

The section titled "Using a Mouse" in Chapter 2 defines basic mouse terminology and explains how to use the mouse in more detail.

After a brief delay, the printed letter should roll out of your printer. It will probably have 1-inch margins, which is the default margin size for all WordPerfect documents. (You'll learn how to change the margins in your document in Chapter 5.)

Saving Your Work

HANDS ON!

In the best of all worlds, your letter would be perfect just as it is and wouldn't need any more work. But in real life, we often need to go back and change things. Therefore, you'll want to *save* a copy of most documents you create.

WARNING

Right now the letter on your screen is in *memory*, or RAM (Random Access Memory). Anything in memory is wiped out the moment you turn off the computer or leave WordPerfect for Windows. That's why you always want to save your work before calling it quits.

When you save a document, you store a copy of it on disk with a *file name* that you can remember. That way, you can find the document when you need it later. Follow these steps:

1. Once again, click on File or press Alt+F to pull down the File menu.

2. Type **s** or click on the Save option to choose Save.

3. Now you need to enter a file name. The basic rule of thumb is that the file name can be no longer than eight characters, followed by a period, followed by an extension up to three letters long, such as MYLETTER.WPD or SPAREME.WPD. If you can't think up a good name right now, type **myfirst** (without any period at the end).

4. Press ⏎ or choose OK by clicking the OK button with your mouse.

You might see a message like this:

> File C:\WPWIN60\WPDOCS\MYFIRST.WPD already exists. Do you want to replace it?

This message means that a file with the name you chose already exists on disk. If it's just an earlier version of the same file, or you're *certain* that the file contains no vital information, choose Yes (by typing **y**) to replace that file with what's on your screen right now. Otherwise, choose No (by typing **n**), then type a different file name and press ⏎.

Be aware that if you don't add an extension to the file name WordPerfect will automatically add the extension .WPD (for "WordPerfect Document"). Thus, if you named your file MYFIRST, its actual name on disk will be MYFIRST.WPD.

Exiting Gracefully

HANDS ON!

You always want to *exit* WordPerfect for Windows, and Windows itself, before you turn off your computer. Forgetting to do so is the leading cause of corrupted files, lost work, and *misocomputerism* (my term for "hatred of computers"). Exiting is easy—you just have to remember to do it!

1. Press Alt+F or click on the File option to open the File menu.

2. Click on Exit, or type **x** to choose that command.

3. If you haven't saved this document (or you haven't saved your latest changes), you'll see a dialog box like this:

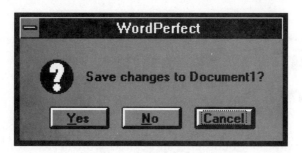

- If you want to save your changes, choose <u>Y</u>es (by typing **y**). Now, type in a file name as described under "Saving Your Work," above. If WordPerfect asks you about replacing the previous copy, you can choose <u>Y</u>es (by typing **y**).

- If you don't want to save your changes for some reason, choose <u>N</u>o (by typing **n**).

You'll be returned to the Windows Program Manager. The document you created in this lesson is safely stored on disk under the file name you assigned to it (for example, MYFIRST.WPD).

WARNING

Contrary to what you may have heard, pressing Ctrl+Alt+Del (*rebooting*) is *not* a graceful way to exit a program. Rebooting can result in lost work and corrupted files.

Exiting Windows

You also must exit Windows before turning off the computer. To do so, just press Alt+F4, or choose <u>F</u>ile then E<u>x</u>it Windows from the Program Manager menu bar. Choose OK (or press ↵) when you get a message saying that this will end your Windows session. You'll be returned to the DOS command prompt, which means it's safe to turn off your computer.

Now is the perfect time to take a break if you need one. Just pick up with Lesson 4 whenever it's convenient and you have half an hour or so of free time.

Lesson 4: Opening Your Document

So far, you've started WordPerfect for Windows, created, printed, and saved a document, and exited WordPerfect for Windows. Now, let's suppose that after reading through the printed copy of your letter, you decide to make some changes to it. Since you created the document in WordPerfect for Windows, you'll first need to get WordPerfect up and running again so you can *open* your document.

Starting WordPerfect (Again)

HANDS ON!

Start Windows and WordPerfect for Windows again, as explained earlier in this chapter. If you're starting from the DOS prompt, you may be able to start WordPerfect for Windows with one simple command: Type **win wpwin** and press ↵. You should see WordPerfect's opening graphic followed by the now-familiar blank document window.

Opening a Document

Now that WordPerfect is up and running again, how do you open the document you created earlier? Easy: Choose File ➤ Open by following these steps:

1. Make sure the menu bar is visible. If it's not, press Escape.

2. Press Alt+F or click on File to choose File.

3. Type **o** or click on <u>O</u>pen to choose Open. You'll be taken to the Open File dialog box, which looks something like this:

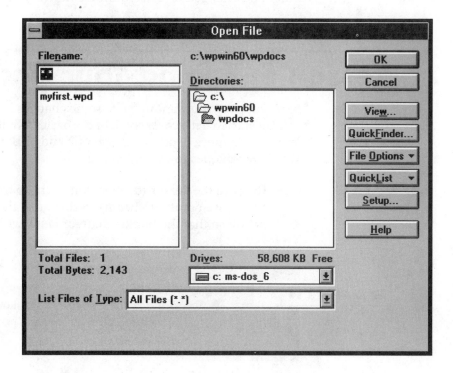

4. Here you can tell WordPerfect which file to open using any of the methods below:

- Type in the name you entered in Lesson 2. Remember, it will have a .WPD extension if you didn't add your own extension. For example, if you originally named the file MYFIRST, you would type **myfirst.wpd**. Press ↵ after typing the full file name.

- Or, just double-click the name of the file you want to open. Its name should be listed in the left side of the dialog box.

- You can also use the standard Windows methods for selecting a different drive and directory in the Open File dialog box. See Chapter 20 or your Windows manual for details.

The document should appear on the screen looking exactly like it did when you last saved it (unless, of course, somebody else used the computer and changed or deleted the document).

Lesson 5: Editing Your Document

Now, suppose you want to make some changes to your document. Before you get started, let's cover some of the basics. We'll discuss all of these topics in much more depth in Chapters 2 and 3. But for now, here are some simple techniques to get you going:

- To move the cursor to where you want to make a change, move the mouse pointer (I-beam) to that area, then click the left mouse button so that the blinking cursor lands where you want.

WARNING Remember that anything you type will appear at the cursor position—*not* at the position of the I-beam. To move the cursor to the I-beam, just click the left mouse button before you start typing.

- You can use the →, ←, ↑, ↓, Home, and End keys to move the cursor. The Num Lock key must be turned off if you want to use the arrow and other special keys on the numeric keypad.

- To get to the bottom of the document, press Ctrl+End. To move down from there, you must press ↵ rather than ↓ (the ↓ key and the other arrow keys only move the cursor through *existing* text, including blank lines, not past the end of the text).

- To delete characters and spaces, and to unbreak accidentally broken lines, use the Backspace key or the Del (Delete) key. The Backspace key deletes characters to the left of the cursor; the Del key deletes characters to the right of the cursor.

- If you make a mistake and want to "undo" your most recent change, press Ctrl+Z.

- To add text to the document, move the cursor to where you want to add text and start typing. If the new text *replaces* existing text, but you want to *insert* new text, press Ctrl+Z, then press the Ins (Insert) key once to switch to Insert mode before you start typing the new text.

That, in a nutshell, is how you edit with WordPerfect. Let's give it a whirl so you can see these keys and techniques in action.

Figure 1.4 shows a copy of the original letter, marked up with some changes and corrections that need to be made. You probably could make the changes on your own, simply by experimenting with the keys and techniques I just summarized. But I'll take you through it step-by-step.

FIGURE 1.4

The sample letter marked up with some corrections

```
                        ←——— Insert date

Wanda Bea Tuna
123 Oak Tree Lane
Hollywood, CA  91234

Dear Ms. Tuna:
                                    ↓ world-renowned
←—— Rumor has it that you're an∧expert on TV script writing.
Therefore, I'm hoping you can answer a simple question for me.
Why is it that actors and actresses never say "Goodbye" before
hanging up the phone? I always say Goodbye (or at least 'kay-
bye) ⌐Why don't you make the actors do that to, you know, make
it more realistic like? This has always puzzled me, and drives me
crazy because I can't stop noticing it.

Thanks in advance for your reply:



Willie B. Goode
```

Inserting the Current Date

HANDS ON!

First, let's insert the date and a blank line at the top of the page. Here's a shortcut for typing the current date:

1. Move the cursor to the top of the document (press Ctrl+Home).

2. Now, instead of typing the date yourself, just press Ctrl+D.

3. Press ↵ three times to place the date on a line by itself and insert two blank lines.

The date that appears is your computer's *system date*. (You'll learn more about this date shortcut in Chapter 4.)

Un-Indenting a Paragraph

Some people like to indent the first line of every paragraph. Others prefer to put a blank line between each paragraph and not indent. It's a free country. You can do whatever you want. But for the sake of our example, let's use the latter method.

First, since you're near the top of the document, delete the indent:

1. Using your mouse or arrow keys, move the cursor to the beginning of the line that starts with "Rumor has it," like this:

   | Rumor has it...

2. Press the Del key.

WordPerfect removes the indentation in one quick stroke. If you indented with spaces instead of tabs, you'll need to press Delete once for each space.

Adding Words to a Sentence

Next, insert the words "world-renowned" and change the "an" in front of expert to "a":

1. Use the arrow keys or your mouse to move the cursor to the *n* in "an," like this:

   you're a|n expert

2. Press the Del key to delete the *n*.

3. Press the spacebar to insert a space. (If the text didn't move to the right when you typed the space, you're in Typeover mode. Press the Ins key once to switch to Insert mode, and press the spacebar again.)

4. Type **world-renowned** and notice how WordPerfect automatically squeezes the text in, moving the words around to reformat the rest of the paragraph as necessary.

Splitting the Paragraphs

Now let's split the big paragraph into two where I've marked it with a paragraph symbol (¶) back in Figure 1.4:

1. Position the cursor just after the period following "'kay-bye)":

   'kay-bye).| Why

2. Press ↵ twice: once to break the line, a second time to insert a blank line.

3. Press the Del key to delete the blank space at the start of the paragraph.

TIP   If you ever break a line accidentally, you can just press Backspace once or twice to rejoin the lines.

Deleting Text

Next it's time to get rid of the unnecessary words in the penultimate (don't you love that word?) sentence. This is an easy one:

1. Use the mouse or arrow keys to move the cursor to the comma after "do that to":

   to|, you know,

2. Press Delete 11 times, and watch it gobble up those characters on the screen.

3. Now position the cursor just after the word "realistic". (This may be at the end of the line if the word "like" is on the next line.)

   realistic| like?

4. Press Delete five times to delete the five characters to the right of the cursor.

Correcting a Misspelling

Now we just have to change "becuase" to "because":

1. Use your mouse or arrow keys to move the cursor to the *u* in "becuase":

   becluase

2. Type **a**.

3. Press → to move over the letter *u*.

4. Press the Del key to delete the old letter *a*.

That was easy enough. You see, editing in WordPerfect is simply a matter of putting the cursor where you want to make a change, then typing the change (or deleting text, pressing ↵, or whatever else it takes).

Now your letter should look something like the example shown in Figure 1.5. (It may look a little different because different printers use different *fonts*. I'll discuss fonts in Chapter 6.)

FIGURE 1.5

The sample letter after making all the changes and corrections shown in Figure 1.4

```
July 10, 1993

Wanda Bea Tuna
123 Oak Tree Lane
Hollywood, CA  91234

Dear Ms. Tuna:

Rumor has it that you're a world-renowned expert on TV script
writing. Therefore, I'm hoping you can answer a simple question
for me. Why is it that actors and actresses never say "Goodbye"
before hanging up the phone? I always say Goodbye (or at least
'kay-bye).

Why don't you make the actors do that to make it more realistic?
This has always puzzled me, and drives me crazy because I can't
stop noticing it.

Thanks in advance for your reply:


Willie B. Goode
```

Saving Your Recent Changes

HANDS ON!

Keep in mind that whatever you're looking at on the screen is the *copy* of the document that's in memory (RAM). The copy that's on the disk is the original copy. That original version "knows" nothing of the changes you've been making since you reopened the document.

To save your changes, you need to save the entire document again. This replaces the previous copy on disk with the updated copy you've been working on. Here's the quick and easy way to do it: Press Ctrl+S.

As long as you've already saved the document and given it a name, Word-Perfect won't bother to ask you for a new name. Instead, it will flash the familiar Windows hourglass to let you know that it's saving the current copy to disk.

You can print a copy of the current version of the document using the same technique you used to print the first copy. (Wanna take the short-cut? Press Ctrl+P, or press F5 then **p**.)

This concludes our hands-on lessons. Now you can exit WordPerfect using the same technique you used to exit earlier in this chapter. (Here's another shortcut: If you don't want to go through the menus, just press Alt+F4 to exit WordPerfect.)

Learning the Rest

Believe it or not, what you've learned in these few lessons could very well be most of what you really need to know to get along with WordPerfect. "So then," you might ask, "why are there about a jillion more pages after this one?" Good question.

The answer is that WordPerfect is a big program with lots of options. (Note the word "options"—as in "not mandatory.") You may find some of those options extremely handy from time to time. So this book is here to help when your work requirements, curiosity, or creative desires go beyond the basics you've already learned.

Finding What You Need

When you're learning to use WordPerfect, you need to know what's available, and you need answers to questions and solutions to problems as they arise. Otherwise, you'll end up doing everything the hard way. Therefore, I suggest the following approach for using the rest of this book:

- Browse through the Table of Contents at the start of this book to get a general idea of what's in WordPerfect and what's in this book.

- Work through Part One of this book (Chapters 1–4). Part One covers the meat-and-potatoes of WordPerfect and explains all the things you should know by the time you read later chapters.

- When you have a specific problem or question, you might want to check WordPerfect's online Help first, since it's right there on your screen. Or, check the index at the back of this book. Chances are, you'll find the answer you're looking for soon enough.

- Browse through this book and look at the pictures to get some ideas or learn new tricks. The sample documents were created with the very same WordPerfect program you're using. Of course, I did use fonts and clip art that I purchased separately, but the samples are WordPerfect documents nonetheless.

- Last, but not least, read the Introduction at the front of this book. Many people skip introductions because they think they're just so much blathering. But in this kind of book, we authors generally use the Introduction to explain how the book is organized and how to use it effectively.

The Five Commandments of WordPerfect

If you're new to WordPerfect, you might want to make a photocopy of Figure 1.6 and keep it near your computer. Then you can refer to it for quick reminders on the most important aspects of WordPerfect 6 for Windows.

FIGURE 1.6

The Five Command-
ments of WordPerfect

Five Commandments of WordPerfect

I. Thou shalt start WordPerfect *to create or edit a document, by typing win wpwin↵ at the DOS prompt. Or, on my computer – Chapter 2*

II. Thou shalt position the cursor *using arrow keys or mouse button <u>before</u> typing or deleting text – Chapter 3*

III. Thou shalt not press ↵ when typing a paragraph *until you get to the very end of that paragraph – Chapter 2*

IV. Thou shalt not use the spacebar to indent. *Better to use Tab, Indent (F7), Center (Shift+F7), Flush Right (Alt+F7) and so forth – Chapter 5*

V. Thou shalt save thy work often *using File ▸ Save or Ctrl+S. And thou also shalt remember to exit WordPerfect using File ▸ Exit or Alt+F4 before turning off the computer – Chapter 3*

```
                              from Alan Simpson's
                     Mastering WordPerfect 6.0 for Windows
```

WordPerfect Survival Guide

Inside the front and back covers of this book, you'll find a quick reference to all of WordPerfect's many features. But if you're just getting started, you might prefer to use the handy Survival Guide shown in Figure 1.7. This Survival Guide highlights the most frequently used stuff. Many of the features listed in Figure 1.7 go beyond what we've covered in this chapter. When you need more information about one of these features, just look it up in the index at the back of this book.

	Feature	Shortcut or Menu Sequence
B	Boldface	CTRL + B
	Center	SHIFT + F7
	Columns	Layout ▸ Columns
	Envelope	Layout ▸ Envelope
	Erase	DEL or ←
	Escape	ESC
	Exit WP	ALT + F4 or File ▸ Exit
	Flush-Right	ALT + F7
&	Font	F9 or Layout ▸ Font
	Full Justify	CTRL + J
i	Help/Coach	F1 or Help ▸ Coach
	Indent	F7
	Indent All	CTRL + SHIFT + F7
	Indent First	TAB
I	Italic	CTRL + I
	Left Justify	CTRL + L
	Line Spacing	Layout ▸ Line ▸ Spacing

FIGURE 1.7

WordPerfect 6 for Windows Survival Guide: The Most Frequently Used Keys and Techniques (continued)

Feature	*Shortcut or Menu*
Margins	CTRL + F8
Move/Copy	Drag and Drop (Chapter 2)
New Doc.	CTRL + N
Open Doc.	CTRL + O
Print Doc.	F5 ▸ Print
Save Doc.	CTRL + S
Search	F2 or Edit ▸ Find
Select Text	Drag or Edit ▸ Select
Special Char.	CTRL + W
Speller	Tools ▸ Speller
Start WP	(from DOS) **win wpwin** ↵
Tables	Table ▸ Create
Undelete	CTRL + SHIFT + Z
Underline	CTRL + U
Undo	CTRL + Z or Edit ▸ Undo
Window	Window ▸ (option)
Zoom	View ▸ Zoom

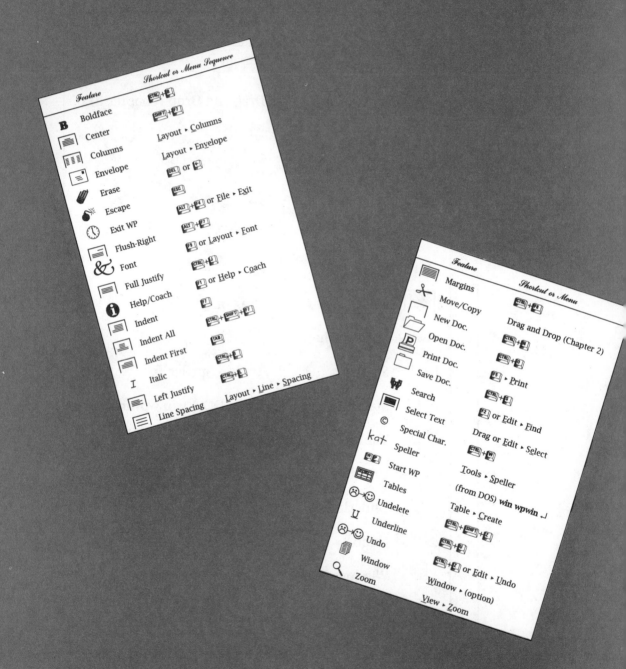

CHAPTER

2

Getting Around in WordPerfect

fast TRACK

To start WordPerfect for Windows (on most computers)   32

type **win wpwin** and press ↵ at the DOS command prompt. Or, from Windows, double-click the *WPWin 6.0* icon in the *WPWin 6.0* group window.

To press a *key+key* combination   34

such as Alt+F1, hold down the first key, press the second key, then release both keys.

To click (select) an item on your screen   36

use your mouse to move the mouse pointer to the item. Then press and release (click) the active mouse button (typically, the button on the left).

To choose menu commands   37

click options with your mouse. To open a menu using the keyboard, hold down the Alt key while typing the underlined letter in the menu name (Alt+<u>letter</u>). Then, to choose a command, type the underlined letter of the command you want.

To use dialog boxes   42

click the option you want to change, or hold down the Alt key while typing the underlined letter of the option you want (Alt+<u>letter</u>). To activate dialog box selections, choose OK. To cancel dialog box selections, choose Cancel or press Escape.

To switch between Draft, Page, and Two-Page views   **49**

choose <u>V</u>iew and then choose the view you want. To switch to Page view quickly, press Alt+F5. To switch to Draft view quickly, press Ctrl+F5.

To get help   **52**

with the current task, press F1 or choose the Help button in a dialog box. For general help, choose <u>H</u>elp ➤ <u>C</u>ontents from the menu or click the <u>C</u>ontents button in any Help window. To "point-and-click" for help, press Shift+F1, then click on whatever you want help with. For online coaching, choose <u>H</u>elp ➤ C<u>o</u>ach.

To exit the Help system   **55**

double-click the Control-menu box in the Help window or choose <u>F</u>ile ➤ E<u>x</u>it.

To exit WordPerfect for Windows   **55**

choose <u>F</u>ile ➤ E<u>x</u>it or press Alt+F4.

IN THIS chapter and the next, we'll look at basic skills and options for using WordPerfect for Windows. Here I'll explain in more detail some of the techniques you might have already tried out in Chapter 1. I'll also present some new techniques and options, and teach you how to get around in (and get along with) WordPerfect for Windows.

Starting WordPerfect

If you took the guided tour in Chapter 1, you've already figured out how to start WordPerfect for Windows. Here's a quick review of the standard routine:

1. Turn on your computer, monitor, and printer.

2. When you get to the DOS command prompt (typically **C>** or **C:\>**), type **win** and press ↵ to start Windows.

3. If the Program Manager appears as an icon on your screen, double-click it with your mouse or press ↵. This will open the Program Manager window.

4. If the WPWin 6.0 group window isn't open, double-click its icon or press Ctrl+F6 until you highlight the name *WPWin 6.0*, then press the ↵ key.

5. In the WPWin 6.0 group window, double-click the WPWin 6.0 icon, or highlight the WPWin 6.0 icon using the arrow keys and press ↵.

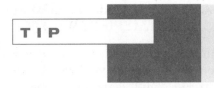

TIP On many computers, you can start Windows and WordPerfect for Windows in one fell swoop. At the DOS prompt, type *win wpwin* and press ↵.

That's all there is to it. You should see the WordPerfect 6.0 pen graphic momentarily as the program loads, followed by the WordPerfect application window.

If these steps give you trouble, it may be that the startup procedures on your particular network or computer are different. Ask your local computer guru for advice.

Backup File Exists: Rename, Open, Delete, Huh?

Sometimes after starting WordPerfect, you'll see a message asking if you want to Rename, Open, or Delete a backup file that's still hanging around. This message means that you (or somebody else, or some*thing* else—like a power outage) turned the computer off before exiting WordPerfect for Windows. And, WordPerfect automatically saved *some* of your work before that improper exit occurred.

NOTE While it's true that WordPerfect automatically backs up your work every 10 minutes or so, don't rely on that as an excuse for not saving your work and exiting properly. See Chapter 19 for more on automatic backups.

You can see what's in that saved file by choosing Open (just type the letter **o** or click the Open button with your mouse).

Opening a Document at Startup

If you want to start WordPerfect for Windows from DOS and open a previously saved file in one fell swoop, you can follow the **win wpwin** command with a space and the name of the file you want to edit. For example, the command **win wpwin myfirst.wpd** starts Windows and WordPerfect for Windows and opens the document named MYFIRST.WPD (if it exists).

It's not necessary to open a document right at startup, however. Once you're in WordPerfect you can open any document you want by choosing File then Open, or by pressing Ctrl+O. You'll learn more about this in Chapter 3.

Using Your Keyboard

This section offers a quick tour of the computer keyboard. The keyboard is divided into several areas: the function keys, typing keys, numeric keypad, and cursor-movement keys. Figure 2.1 illustrates some common computer keyboards.

Figure 2.1 also points out the locations of the ↵ (Enter), Tab, Backspace, Esc, and Shift keys. The quick tour in Chapter 1 gave you some practice using the keyboard and explained how to use ↵, Escape, Num Lock, Caps Lock, Shift, Tab, and Backspace while editing a document. Be aware that different keyboards use different symbols for some keys. For example, the ↵ key is sometimes labeled "Enter" or "Return."

All the computer's keys are *typematic*. This means you can repeat a keystroke simply by holding down the key. You can see this for yourself by holding down any letter key on the keyboard for a few seconds. To erase the letters you typed, hold down the Backspace key until all the letters have been deleted.

Key+Key Combination Keystrokes

When you see two keystrokes separated by a plus sign (+), you need to *hold down the first key, tap the second key, then release the first key.* These *combination keystrokes* can often be used as shortcuts to the menus. For example, to press Alt+F1 (the shortcut for starting the Thesaurus), you would hold down the first key (Alt), tap the second key (the F1 function key), then release both keys. Don't try to press the two keys at the same moment.

FIGURE 2.1

Popular computer keyboards

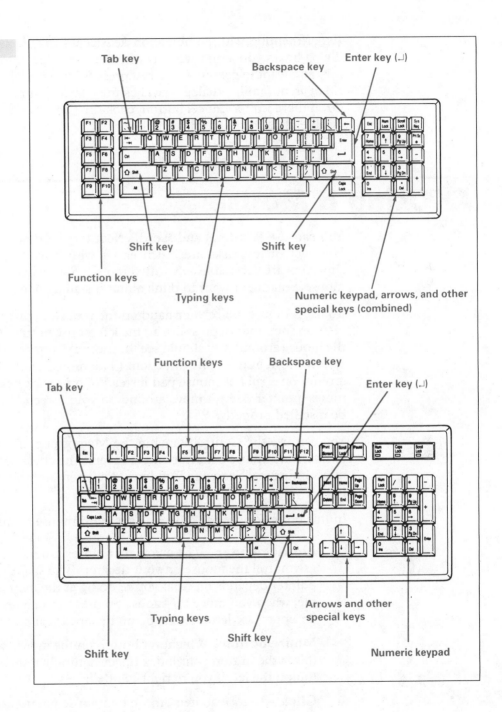

Experimenting with combination keystrokes may bring up menus and dialog boxes you aren't familiar with yet. If you get into unfamiliar territory and want to get out again, just press Escape to clear the menu. To get rid of an unfamiliar dialog box, click the Cancel button (or press Escape). Or, if there isn't a Cancel button, click the Close button, press Alt+C, or double-click the Control-menu box.

Using a Mouse

You can use Windows and WordPerfect for Windows without a mouse. However, many tasks are much easier with a mouse, and some super shortcuts are accessible *only* with a mouse. So if you don't already have a mouse, you might want to think about installing one on your system.

To use a mouse, place your hand on the mouse so that your index finger rests on (but doesn't press down) the left mouse button. As you slowly roll the mouse around, you should see the mouse pointer on your WordPerfect screen move in the same direction. (The mouse works best if you roll it around on a rubber mouse pad instead of on a slick desk surface.) If the mouse pointer doesn't move around on your screen, the mouse may not be installed properly.

You can use the Control Panel in the Main group of Program Manager to fine-tune mouse behavior and to reverse the effect of the left and right mouse buttons. See your Windows documentation for details on these topics.

In this book, I'll use the following standard mouse terminology:

Mouse pointer   The arrow that moves around on the screen as you roll the mouse on your desktop. The shape of the mouse pointer depends on what you're doing at the moment. For example, when you move the mouse pointer through text, it resembles an uppercase letter I (this pointer shape is called an *I-beam*).

Mouse button   Whichever button on the mouse works. Typically this is the button your index finger naturally rests upon—the button on the left if you're right-handed.

Click   To *click* an item, move the mouse pointer to that item on the screen, and then press and release the mouse button.

Double-click   To *double-click* an item, move the mouse pointer to the item on the screen, and then press and release the mouse button twice in rapid succession, as fast as you can: *click click!*

Drag   To *drag* an item on the screen, move the mouse pointer to the item, *hold down* the mouse button, roll the mouse to some other location on the screen, then release the mouse button.

Right-click   To *right-click* an item, move the mouse pointer to the item and click the button on the right if you normally use the left mouse button; click the button on the left if you normally use the right mouse button.

The Windows tutorial mentioned under "Learning about Windows" in Chapter 1 demonstrates how to use a mouse and lets you practice the techniques described above.

Using the Menus

Like menus in a restaurant, the *menus* in WordPerfect present you with choices. The options on the menus (called *commands*) tell WordPerfect to do something. The *menu bar* displays commands across the top of the WordPerfect screen, like this:

File   Edit   View   Insert   Layout   Tools   Graphics   Table   Window   Help

Using menus in WordPerfect for Windows is exactly the same as using menus in any other Windows application. You can choose commands using either the mouse or the keyboard. The tour in Chapter 1 gave you practice using both methods, but I'll summarize them here just for fun.

Choosing Menu Commands

To choose menu commands with the **mouse,** follow these steps:

1. If the menu bar isn't already visible, press Escape.

2. Click whichever command you want to choose.

If you make a mistake and want to back up, click the mouse in an empty area of the document window.

To choose menu commands with the **keyboard**, follow these steps:

1. If the menu bar isn't already visible, press Escape.

2. Use one of the methods below to open a menu.

   - Hold down the Alt key and type the underlined letter of the option you want. For example, you can press Alt+F to open the File menu.

   - Press Alt, use the ← or → keys to highlight the option you want, then press ↵ or ↓.

3. Use any of these techniques to choose a command from an opened menu:

   - Type the underlined letter in the option name.
   - Use the ↓, ↑, →, and ← keys to highlight the option you want, then press ↵.

If you make a mistake and want to back up, press the Esc or Alt key.

Changing Your Mind

When you're first learning to use WordPerfect, you may choose commands that lead you to menus or dialog boxes that you don't understand. To back up into familiar territory, try any of the following techniques:

- Press and release the Alt key to deactivate the menus.

- Press Escape until you return to familiar territory.

- If your selection opened a dialog box that includes a Cancel button, press Escape or click Cancel.

- If your selection opened a dialog box that includes a Close button, click Close, press Alt+C, or double-click the Control-menu box.

What's on the Menu?

When you open a menu, it will look something like the example shown below:

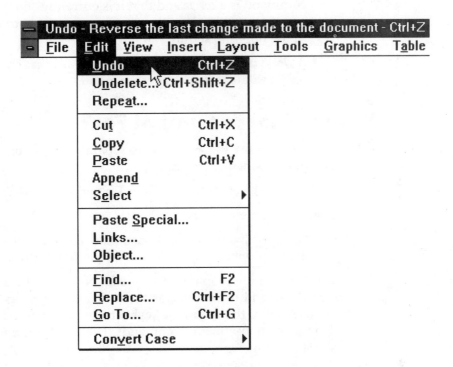

Menus also provide information about what the currently highlighted option does, alternative shortcuts, and what to expect next.

- The **description** in the title bar at the top of the window tells you what the highlighted command is for. As you scroll through the menu (by pressing the arrow keys or dragging the mouse pointer through the options), you can look to the title bar for a quick reminder of the highlighted command's purpose.

- The ... **symbol** next to a command tells you that choosing a command will take you to a dialog box.

- A **key name** (such as F2) or a combination keystroke (such as Ctrl+Z) next to a command is the shortcut for choosing that command. Thus, you can press Ctrl+Z instead of choosing Undo from the Edit menu.

- **Dimmed commands** on the menu aren't relevant to the current situation and can't be selected.

- A **check mark** (✓) to the left of a command tells you that the command is a *toggle* and that it is currently "on." Toggle commands can either be *on* or *off*. Choosing the command changes it to the opposite setting.

- A ➤ **symbol** next to a command means that choosing the command will take you to another menu.

What's That ➤ Symbol For?

In this book I use the ➤ symbol to separate a series of commands you select from the menus. For example,

Choose Insert ➤ Date ➤ Date Text or press Ctrl+D

means the same thing as

Open the Insert menu, choose Date, then choose Date Text from the next menu. If you prefer, you can press Ctrl+D as a shortcut.

The shortcut notation is easier to read. Note that the underlined letter in each command is the same as the *hotkey* that appears in the menu. You can use any of the mouse or keyboard methods described earlier in this chapter to choose menu commands. Feel free to use whichever method is best for you.

If you just did those menu commands listed above, you inserted the current date into your document. You can choose Edit ➤ Undo or press Ctrl+Z to undo the change.

Right-Clicking and QuickMenus

Those of you who have always wondered why only one of the buttons on your mouse seems important will be pleased to know that WordPerfect now takes advantage of both the left and right mouse buttons.

The left mouse button plays its usual role—choosing menu and dialog box commands, positioning the cursor, and so forth. Clicking the right mouse button will take you to a QuickMenu: a small menu that's relevant to whatever you happen to be doing at the moment. For example, if you right-click while the mouse pointer is somewhere near the middle of a page, you'll be taken to a QuickMenu like the one shown in Figure 2.2. Figure 2.2 also points out other areas of the screen that you can right-click to get to a QuickMenu.

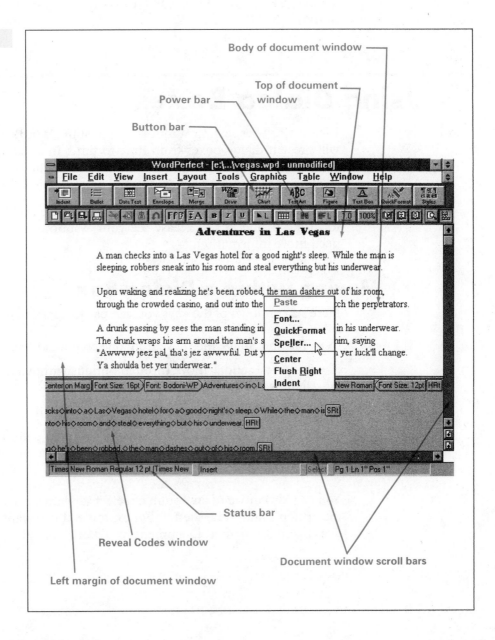

When the QuickMenu appears, you can choose options from it in the usual manner. For example, you can right-click an area, and then click on the command you want in the QuickMenu.

If you open a QuickMenu by accident and you don't want to make a selection from it, just click anywhere outside the menu (using the left mouse button).

Using Dialog Boxes

Like any self-respecting Windows application, WordPerfect for Windows will present dialog boxes from time to time. In a dialog box, you "complete the dialog" by making choices and then choosing OK. Figure 2.3 shows a sample dialog box with some *controls* pointed out.

The next few sections present the easiest mouse and keyboard methods for using dialog boxes. Please see your Windows documentation if you need more information.

Moving within a Dialog Box

Here's a rundown of the keys you can use to navigate within a dialog box:

- Tab and Shift+Tab move from one command (control) to the next.
- →, ←, ↑, and ↓ move through options within a group (if the highlight is within a group).
- The spacebar toggles a check box on and off.
- The ↵ key selects the currently highlighted command button—usually the OK button, which saves the current settings and closes the dialog box.

You can also move to an option or select it by pressing Alt while you type the option's underlined letter. For example, if you want to move to or select the option named Document, you'd press Alt+D.

FIGURE 2.3

A sample dialog box

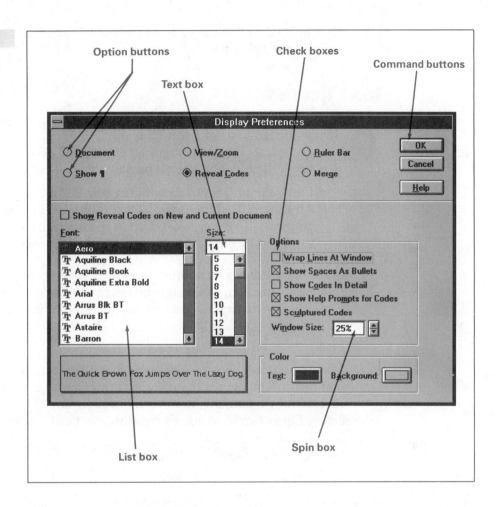

When the cursor is *not* in a text box, you can usually move to or select a different option by typing just the option's underlined letter (for example, **D** for Document). If the cursor is in a text box, you need to hold down Alt while typing the underlined letter (for example, **Alt+D**).

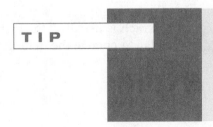

TIP

If a dialog box is covering an essential part of the screen, simply drag the title bar of the dialog box to a new location. Or, press Alt+spacebar to open the Control menu, type *m*, use your arrow keys to reposition the box, and press ↵.

Now let's take a look at some of the specific types of controls that might appear in a dialog box.

Text Boxes

A *text box* accepts text or a number. Use one of the methods below to change the contents of a text box:

- Click the text box, then type new text or change existing text.
- Press Tab or Shift+Tab until the text box is highlighted, or press Alt+<u>letter</u>. Then, to *replace* the contents of the text box, just type your text. To *change* the contents, position the cursor using the ← or → key or your mouse, then type your text.

Many of the editing techniques described in Chapter 3—such as selecting (blocking), inserting, deleting, and overwriting text—work when you're in a text box, as do keys such as Home and End. If in doubt, try it out.

Entering Measurements

Many text boxes allow you to enter measurements. Though I'll often say that measurements are in *inches,* you can choose a different unit of measurement by typing the number followed by one of the letters or symbols below. For example, to enter a measurement of 10 points, you'd type **10p**.

LETTER OR SYMBOL	MEANING
″ or i	inches
c	centimeters
m	millimeters
p	points
w	1200ths of an inch

If you omit the letter or symbol following the measurement, WordPerfect will use the default unit of measurement (which is usually ″ for inches). You can choose <u>F</u>ile ➤ P<u>r</u>eferences ➤ <u>D</u>isplay to change the default unit of measurement (Chapter 19).

Option Buttons

Option buttons represent mutually exclusive options. You can select only one option in a group. To choose an option button, use any of the methods below:

- Click the option button.
- Press Alt+<u>letter</u>.
- Press Tab or Shift+Tab until you reach the group that contains the option button, then press ↑, ↓, ←, or → to select the button you want.

Check Boxes

A *check box* can have one of two possible values: *selected* (the check box contains an ×) or *deselected* (the check box does not contain an ×). You can select or deselect as many check boxes in a group as you wish. Use any of these methods:

- Click the check box.
- Press Alt+<u>letter</u>.
- Press Tab or Shift+Tab until the check box option is highlighted, then press the spacebar.

Spin Boxes

A *spin box* is similar to a text box that contains a number. Here are two ways to work a spin box:

- Click the ▲ button to increase the value in the box; click the ▼ button to decrease the value.
- Press Tab or Shift+Tab until you highlight the number in the spin box, or press Alt+<u>letter</u>. Then type a new number.

NOTE

If pressing Alt+<u>letter</u> doesn't highlight the number in the spin box, press Tab and then type a new number.

Drop-Down Lists

Some text boxes include a *drop-down list* button, as shown at left. You either type an entry into the text box or choose an option from the drop-down list. Use either of the methods below to open a drop-down list:

- Click the drop-down list button or click in the text box.

- Press Tab or Shift+Tab until the text box is highlighted, or press Alt+<u>letter</u>. Then press ↓.

Once the list appears, you can use the PgUp, PgDn, ↑, and ↓ keys to scroll through the list. To select a highlighted item from the list, click it or press ↵. (You can also use scroll bars to scroll through the list, as described a bit later.)

TIP   In some lists, you can type the first letter(s) of an item in the list to highlight that item quickly.

Pop-Up Lists

Command buttons that have up- and down-pointing triangles on them are called *pop-up lists*. To activate a pop-up list, use one of the following methods:

- Click the pop-up list button, *keep the mouse button depressed*, drag the highlight to the option you want, then release the mouse button.

- Press Tab or Shift+Tab until the option is highlighted, or press Alt+<u>letter</u>. Press Alt+↓ to open the list, then click on the item you want or type the item's underlined letter.

Drop-Down Menus

Command buttons marked with a small ▼ display *drop-down menus*. To open the menu, use either of the methods below:

- Click the command button.
- Press Tab or Shift+Tab until the button is highlighted, or press Alt+<u>letter</u>. Then press Alt+↓.

Once the menu is open, you select options just as you would for any normal menu: Click on the item you want, type the option's underlined letter, or press the ↑ and ↓ keys until the option is highlighted and press ↵.

Scroll Bars

Scroll bars let you scroll to areas that aren't currently visible on the screen. To use a scroll bar, pick one of the following techniques:

- Click the ↑ button at the top of the scroll bar to scroll up one line at a time; click the ↓ button at the bottom of the scroll bar to scroll down one line at a time.
- Drag the *scroll box* (the movable box between the ↑ and the ↓ symbols) up or down the bar.
- Click the portion of the scroll bar above or below the scroll box to scroll one "boxful" at a time.

NOTE If you're using the keyboard, use the PgUp, PgDn, arrow, and other cursor-movement keys (described in Chapter 3) to move around in a list or document.

Scroll bars appear within dialog boxes automatically. But scroll bars for the entire document appear only if the Horizo<u>n</u>tal and <u>V</u>ertical options are selected (checked) in the Display Preferences dialog box (see Chapters 3 and 4).

Commands...

Any command in a dialog box that's followed by ... leads to another dialog box. To select that command...

- Click the command.
- Press Alt+<u>letter</u>.
- Press Tab or Shift+Tab until the option you want is highlighted, then press ⏎.

Command Buttons

Command buttons make things happen. They're simple to operate, using any of these methods:

- Click the command button you want.
- Press Tab or Shift+Tab until the button you want is highlighted, then press ⏎.
- Press Alt+<u>letter</u> (if the button has an underlined letter).

Typically, you can press Escape as a shortcut to choosing the Cancel command button, or press ⏎ to choose the OK command button.

Saving and Abandoning Dialog Box Selections

Most dialog boxes have an OK command button and/or a Cancel command button. Here's the difference between these buttons:

OK If you choose OK, choices you made in the dialog box will be activated, and WordPerfect will proceed with the initial command.

Cancel The Cancel button lets you "bail out" of a dialog box without activating any changes. (Some dialog boxes use a <u>C</u>lose button in place of Cancel.)

TIP

If you ever get confused while using a dialog box (or you get to a dialog box that you don't understand), use the Cancel button (or Esc key) or Close button to back out gracefully.

Draft, Page, and Two-Page Views or Modes

You can view and edit your documents in any one of three different modes: Draft, Page, and Two-Page. Figures 2.4, 2.5, and 2.6 show the same document displayed in these three modes. (You'll learn how to add headers, footers, page numbers, graphics, and other items to your documents in later chapters.)

FIGURE 2.4

A sample document in Draft mode. This display mode doesn't show top and bottom margins, page headers, footers, watermarks, or page numbers.

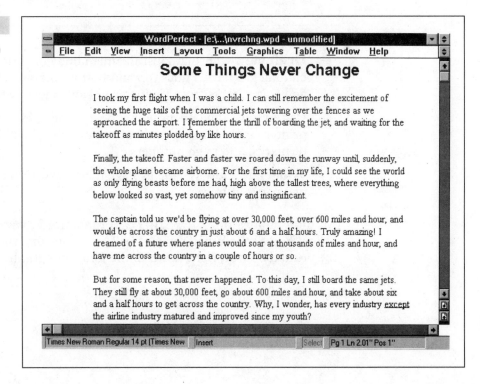

FIGURE 2.5

A sample document in Page mode. The top margin and page header are visible in this mode.

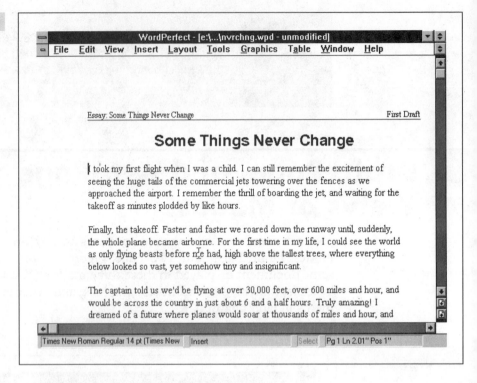

Draft view Displays just the main body of your document, including graphics. Hides top and bottom margins, headers, footers, and watermarks from view, so you can concentrate on the text.

Page view The document appears exactly as it will look when printed, including top and bottom margins, headers, footers, watermarks, and page numbers.

Two-Page view Same as Page mode, except that you can see two pages at once.

All three modes offer *WYSIWYG* (pronounced "wizzy wig," short for "What You See Is What You Get"). This means that the screen looks like the printed output, right down to the fonts and graphics.

FIGURE 2.6

A sample document in Two-Page mode. Two full pages, including margins, headers, and footers, are visible.

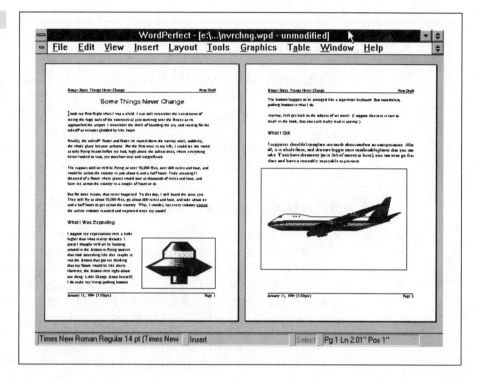

Switching Views

It's easy to switch from one mode to another. Just use the techniques below:

- Choose View from the menu bar, then choose Draft, Page, or Two-Page—whichever you prefer.
- To switch to Page mode quickly, press Shift+F5.
- To switch to Draft view quickly, press Ctrl+F5.

What Happened to View Document?

If you've used earlier versions of WordPerfect, you might recall the *View Document* or *Print Preview* mode, where you could zoom in and out to view your document as it would be printed. Happily, WordPerfect 6.0 doesn't need such a mode, because the screen *always* shows the document as it will appear when printed. You can still zoom in and out, as you'll learn in Chapter 4.

Getting Instant Help

While this book is stuffed full of information about WordPerfect for Windows, it isn't your *only* source. In fact, WordPerfect makes available tons of information right on your screen. The trick is knowing where to find the information you're looking for. WordPerfect for Windows' Help system works just like Help in most Windows applications. Let's take a quick look at what it can do.

Getting Context-Sensitive Help

A good starting point for quick information is to press the F1 key or choose the Help button in a dialog box. This will bring up *context-sensitive* Help. Context-sensitive Help provides help with whatever you were doing when you pressed F1. If you have a document open but you're not actually doing anything with it, you'll be taken to the Help Contents, which is a Table of Contents for WordPerfect's Help system.

When you've gotten the information you need from the Help screen and you're ready to return to whatever you were doing before you pressed F1,

- Double-click the Control-menu box in the upper-left corner of the Help window.
- Or, choose File ➤ Exit from the Help window's menu bar.

Getting "What Is?" Help

If you're curious about what purpose some item on your screen serves, you can use "What Is?" help to find out:

1. Press Shift+F1. The mouse pointer changes to the icon shown at left.

2. Using your mouse, point to the item you're curious about, then click the left mouse button.

When you've finished reading the Help message, choose File ➤ Exit from the Help menu to return to your document.

Getting More General Help

If the context-sensitive Help screen doesn't give you the information you're looking for, or you're not even sure how to start getting help, you can go to the Help Contents using either of these techniques:

- If you haven't already entered the Help system, press F1 or choose <u>H</u>elp ➤ <u>C</u>ontents from the menu bar.

- If you're already in a Help window, choose the <u>C</u>ontents command button near the top of the Help window.

You'll see the Help Contents window shown in Figure 2.7.

Notice that the Help Contents window contains underlined words and a number of command buttons. The underlined words are called *jump*

FIGURE 2.7

The Help Contents window is a good place to start when you're looking for information.

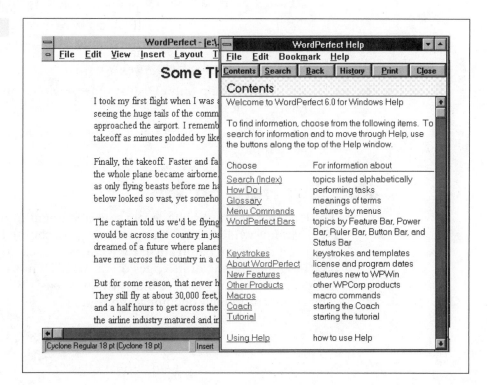

words because they lead to other topics. Here's how to choose a jump word:

- Click the jump word.
- Or, press the Tab or Shift+Tab keys to highlight the jump word you want, then press ⏎.

After choosing a jump word, you'll be taken to the next Help screen. From there, you can choose another jump word to keep going, or you can choose any of the command buttons along the top of the Help window. These command buttons are available:

Contents   Displays the Help Contents.

Search   Lets you search for a topic by keyword or phrase.

Back   Backs up to the previous topic you viewed.

History   Displays a list of topics that you've viewed in sequential order.

Print   Prints the currently displayed Help topic.

Close   Closes the Help window

<<   (macro help only) Displays the previous topic in a group of related topics.

>>   (macro help only) Displays the next topic in a group of related topics.

Keeping Help on Top

The Help window normally covers your document. If you'd like to see the Help window while you're editing a document, choose Help ➤ Always On Top from the menu bar in any Help window. You can then resize the window by dragging any of its edges or corners. To move the window, drag its title bar. Again, if you need help with these basic Windows skills, please refer to your Windows documentation.

Exiting Help

When you're ready to exit the Help window, use any of these methods to return to your document:

- Click the Close button at the top of the Help window.
- Double-click the Control-menu box in the upper-left corner of the Help window.
- Choose File ➤ Exit from the Help window's menu bar.
- If you chose Help ➤ Always On Top (described above), click anywhere on the Help window (just to be sure that you don't exit WordPerfect accidentally). Then press Alt+F4.

Built-In Coaches

WordPerfect's *coaches* will guide you through every step of an operation— just like a patient flesh-and-blood teacher. They'll even demonstrate an operation (just choose the Show Me button when it's available) and then let you do it yourself.

To use a coach, choose Help ➤ Coach from the pull-down menus. Highlight the coach you want from the list that appears, choose OK, and follow the instructions. You'll be an expert in no time flat!

Checking the Version Number

This book is specifically about Version 6 of WordPerfect for Windows. If the information in this book seems totally wrong, make sure that you're actually using Version 6 of WordPerfect for Windows. It's easy to find out: choose Help ➤ About WordPerfect from the menu bar. Choose OK or press ↵ to leave the About WordPerfect dialog box.

Don't Shut Down Yet!

Before turning off your computer, you must exit WordPerfect for Windows, save any unsaved work (if prompted), and then exit Windows. If you forget to do this, you might lose your current work.

To exit WordPerfect properly and keep those precious documents safe, follow the steps below:

1. Choose File ➤ Exit or press Alt+F4.

2. If WordPerfect prompts you, choose Yes to save any open documents that haven't been saved since you last changed them. (See Chapter 3 for more information on saving documents and assigning valid file names.)

3. When you return to the Windows Program Manager, choose File ➤ Exit Windows (or press Alt+F4) and choose OK. You'll be returned to the DOS command prompt.

4. If your computer is connected to a network, your network administrator might request that you always log off before turning off your computer. Ask the administrator for the logging-off command.

In this chapter I've covered some of the basics of getting along with WordPerfect for Windows. Next, we'll look at techniques for opening, editing, printing, and saving documents.

File   Edit   View   Insert   Layout   Tools   Graphics   Table   Window   Help

---

Some Things Never Change

I took my first flight when I was a child. I can still remember the excitement of seeing the huge tail of the commercial jet towering over the fence as we approached the airport. I remember the thrill of boarding the jet, and waiting for the take-off as minutes plodded by like hours.

Finally, the take-off! Faster and faster we roared down the runway until, suddenly, the whole plane became airborne. For the first time in my life, I could see the world as only flying beings before me had, high above the tallest trees, where everything below looked so tiny, yet somehow tidy and insignificant.

The captain told us we'd be flying above 30,000 feet, over 500 miles an hour, and would be across the country in just about 5 and a half hours. Truly amazing! I dreamed of a future where planes would zoom at thousands of miles an hour, and have me across the country in a couple of hours or so.

But for some reason, that never happened. To this day, I still board the same jets. They still fly at about 30,000 feet, go about 500 miles an hour, and take about six and a half hours to get across the country. Why, I wonder, has every industry except the airline industry matured and improved since my youth?

What I Was Expecting

I suppose my expectations were a little higher than what reality dictated. I guess I thought we'd all be buzzing around in the heavens in flying saucers that look something like this; maybe it was the heavens that got me thinking that my future would be like this. However, the heavens were right about

---

one thing. Like Change herself, I do make my living pushing buttons. The buttons happen to be arranged like a typewriter keyboard. But nonetheless, pushing buttons is what I do.

Anyway, let's get back to the subject of air travel. (I suppose this text is now so small in the book, that you can't really read it anyway.)

What I Got

I suppose I shouldn't complain too much about modern air transportation. After all, it is a little faster, and there are bigger more comfortable planes than you can take. If you have the money (or so little of money to burn), you can even go first class and have a reasonably enjoyable experience.

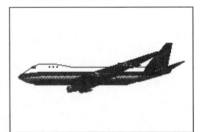

CHAPTER

3

Opening, Editing, Printing, and Saving

fast TRACK

To copy selected text   **83**

> hold down the Ctrl key while you drag the text to its new position. Or, choose Edit ➤ Copy (or press Ctrl+C). Then move the cursor to the new position and choose Edit ➤ Paste (or press Ctrl+V).

To undo a recent move, copy, or other change   **87**

> choose Edit ➤ Undo or press Ctrl+Z.

To delete text, lines, or spaces   **88**

> use the Del and Backspace keys. You can use Ctrl+Backspace to delete words. Use Ctrl+Del to delete the rest of a line.

To "undelete" text   **88**

> choose Edit ➤ Undelete, or press Ctrl+Shift+Z. If necessary, choose Next or Previous (up to two times) and choose Restore when the text you want to undelete reappears.

To print the document that's currently on your screen   **90**

> choose File ➤ Print ➤ Print or press Ctrl+P.

To save your work   **93**

> choose File ➤ Save or press Ctrl+S. (Do this often!) To save your work and exit WordPerfect, choose File ➤ Exit or press Alt+F4. Choose Yes if prompted to save any previously unsaved work.

IN CHAPTER 1 you learned the basics of creating, printing, and saving a document. In this chapter, we'll get into these topics in more depth and broaden your knowledge of typing and editing in WordPerfect.

Opening a Document

When you want to work on a document that you've previously saved and closed, you first need to open that document. There are several ways to do this, as you'll learn in the sections that follow.

Opening a Recent Document

If you've edited and saved a document recently, chances are you can use this simple procedure to open it:

1. Choose File from the menu bar.

2. At the bottom of the menu, you'll see a list of the four most recently saved files. If the file you want to open is in that list, just click on its name, or type the number next to it.

If the file you want to open isn't in the list of recently saved files, you can press the Alt key, and use the method described below to open the file.

Opening Any Document

When you need to open a file that you haven't used in a while, you may need to dig a little deeper for it. This section explains how.

1. Choose File ➤ Open, press Ctrl+O, or click the Open button in the power bar (shown at left). You'll see the Open File dialog box, shown in Figure 3.1.

TIP If the (optional) power bar isn't visible, you can choose View ➤ Power Bar to bring it out of hiding. You'll learn more about the power bar in Chapter 4.

2. In the Filename text box, type the name of the file exactly as you typed it when you first saved it (for example, type **myfirst.wpd**). Then press ⏎ or choose OK. Or, if you can see the file name in the list at the left side of the dialog box, simply double-click the file name.

FIGURE 3.1

The Open File dialog box

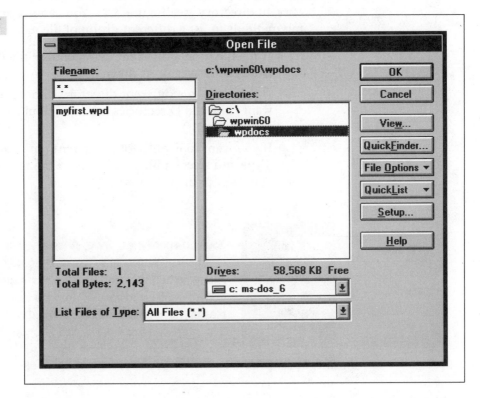

Assuming you've spelled the file name correctly (don't worry about upper- and lowercase letters), and assuming nobody has deleted or moved the file, the document should appear on your screen, ready for editing.

"But My File Isn't There!"

Sometimes you might go to open a file, only to discover that WordPerfect can't find it. In some cases, you may merely have misspelled the file name. In that case, just try again, making sure to spell the file name correctly.

In other cases, the file you're looking for might be on a *drive* and/or *directory* other than the one you're searching. If you want to look around for the missing file, follow the steps below (assuming you're at the document window and haven't opened any dialog boxes yet).

1. Choose File ➤ Open or use one of the shortcuts described above.

2. The list below the Filename text box initially shows all files in the current directory (see Figure 3.1). You can use any of the following methods to list a different group of file names:

   - If the file is on a different drive, choose the drive you want from the Drives drop-down list.

   - If the file is in a different directory, choose the directory you want from the Directories list (e.g., double-click the directory you want).

   - If you want to list files of a different type, select List Files Of Type and select a file type. Choose the top entry in the list if you want to display all files (*.*).

TIP

You can specify the drive, directory, and file type all at once. Simply type the path name into the Filename text box and press ↵. For example, typing c:\wpwin60\wpdocs\e*.* into the box would list all files in the \WPWIN60\WPDOCS directory on drive C that start with the letter E. See Chapter 20 for more about file names and path names.

3. When the list displays the name of the file you want to open, choose the file:

- Double-click the file name you want.
- Or, press Tab or Shift+Tab until the highlight lands in the Filename list. Use the arrow keys to highlight the file you want, or type the first few characters of the file name. Then choose OK or press ↵.

If you have problems opening a file, or you see a "Read-Only" message in the title bar, see "File Problems" in Appendix C. Chapter 20 explains more about working with files and describes other options you can choose in the Open File dialog box.

How Are Open, New, and Insert Different?

WordPerfect actually has three commands that let you open or create files. Here are the main differences among those commands:

File ➤ New (or Ctrl+N) Opens a new, blank document window. Use this command to create a document from scratch in a new window.

File ➤ Open (or Ctrl+O) Copies a saved document from disk into a new document window. The file is not combined with any other open documents.

TIP I'll talk about the File ➤ Template command in Chapters 4 and 20.

Insert➤ File Copies a saved document from the disk into the *current* document at the place where the cursor was positioned when you chose the command. Use Insert ➤ File to combine two documents. The Insert File dialog box works just like the Open File dialog box described above.

If you start to lose track of which documents are open, you can choose Window ➤ Cascade to *cascade*, or stagger, the windows and see all their titles. I'll talk more about managing document windows in Chapter 4.

Peeking into an Unopened File

Sometimes you'll want to take a quick peek at a file without actually opening it. WordPerfect makes this easy. Any time a dialog box includes a View button (as in Figure 3.1), you can choose that button to open the Viewer window. With the Viewer open, you can...

- Highlight or click on a file in the list of file names, then look at the Viewer window to see what's inside the file.

- Move, resize, maximize, or restore the Viewer window.

- Click on the Viewer window, or press Alt+F6 to activate the window (the Viewer's title bar will be highlighted when the Viewer window is active). Then scroll through the text or search for text using Find (F2). (Chapter 9 explains the Find feature.)

- When you're done using the Viewer window, you can close it. (Double-click the Control-menu box in the Viewer window. Or, highlight or click the Viewer window's title bar and press Alt+F4.)

To display the Viewer window (shown in Figure 3.2), I chose File ➤ Open, clicked the View button, and then clicked the name of a file I had saved previously (MYFIRST.WPD).

The View button appears in several dialog boxes, including Open File (File ➤ Open), Insert File (Insert ➤ File), Save As (File ➤ Save As), and Insert Image (Graphics ➤ Figure). You'll learn more about the Viewer in Chapter 20.

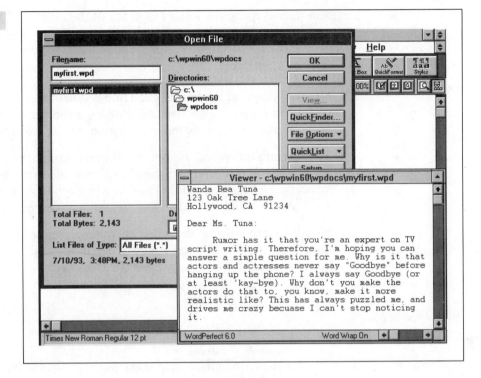

FIGURE 3.2

Choosing the View button in a dialog box opens the Viewer window.

Typing with WordPerfect

Typing with WordPerfect is much like typing with a typewriter. Below are a few differences to keep in mind:

- With WordPerfect, you set the margins using Layout ➤ Margins, as discussed in Chapter 5. Don't try to create margins by typing spaces or using tabs.

- If you want to indent or center a single line of text, *don't* use the spacebar. Instead use Tab, Center (Shift+F7), Flush Right (Alt+F7), or other indenting commands (see Chapter 5).

- As you type past the right margin on your screen, WordPerfect automatically *word-wraps* text to the next line. You should press the ↵ key only to end a short line that doesn't reach the right margin, to end a paragraph, or to add blank lines.

- Avoid using the letter *l* in place of the number *1*, and avoid using the letter *o* in place of the number *0*. These characters aren't the same to a computer, nor do they look the same when printed by most printers.

Not pressing ↵ at the end of each line is one of the toughest things for experienced typists to get used to. But it's important to press ↵ only when appropriate. Otherwise, making changes to the text later will be a hassle.

To illustrate this point, Figure 3.3 shows a sample printed business letter typed with WordPerfect. Figure 3.4 shows the same letter, with symbols indicating where you would press ↵ while typing that document. (The ↵ symbols normally won't show up on your screen or on the printed copy.)

Notice that to insert a blank line between paragraphs, you need only press the ↵ key. If you press the ↵ key accidentally and insert too many blank lines, you can use the Backspace (or Del) key to delete the line(s).

FIGURE 3.3

A sample business letter

```
August 7, 1993


Sidney R. Jackson, M.D.
Bayside Medical Group
5231 East Statton Drive, Suite 106
Los Angeles, CA 92312


Dear Dr. Jackson:

The update on your insurance policy is as follows. I am including
a letter from the Regional Manager of Farmstead regarding the
information specific to your occupational and medical concerns.
Pending receipt of a referral letter from your previous doctor,
this letter serves as an important part of your policy and should
be safeguarded with your other documents.

I have turned over your policy to a full-time insurance agent,
Bastien Cole. He will be able to serve you more adequately and
provide the detailed information you may need for your specific
problems. This will also allow me to relinquish my commissions in
order to better serve you in a consultant capacity. In the
meantime, however, you do have coverage in effect.

As indicated earlier by phone, I will be out of town for the next
three weeks. Should you have any questions, please feel free to
leave a message for me at my Florida office. I will be in contact
with them daily for messages. Rest assured that I hope to
continue to be of service to you.

Sincerely,



Edna R. Jones, M.D.

ERJ:ess

cc: Bastien Cole
```

FIGURE 3.4

The ⏎ symbols show when you would press the ⏎ key while typing the letter—at the ends of short lines, at the ends of paragraphs, and wherever you want a blank line to appear.

```
August 7, 1993 ⏎
⏎
⏎
Sidney R. Jackson, M.D. ⏎
Bayside Medical Group ⏎
5231 East Statton Drive, Suite 106 ⏎
Los Angeles, CA 92312 ⏎
⏎
⏎
Dear Dr. Jackson: ⏎
⏎
The update on your insurance policy is as follows. I am including
a letter from the Regional Manager of Farmstead regarding the
information specific to your occupational and medical concerns.
Pending receipt of a referral letter from your previous doctor,
this letter serves as an important part of your policy and should
be safeguarded with your other documents. ⏎
⏎
I have turned over your policy to a full-time insurance agent,
Bastien Cole. He will be able to serve you more adequately and
provide the detailed information you may need for your specific
problems. This will also allow me to relinquish my commissions in
order to better serve you in a consultant capacity. In the
meantime, however, you do have coverage in effect. ⏎
⏎
As indicated earlier by phone, I will be out of town for the next
three weeks. Should you have any questions, please feel free to
leave a message for me at my Florida office. I will be in contact
with them daily for messages. Rest assured that I hope to
continue to be of service to you. ⏎
⏎
Sincerely, ⏎
⏎
⏎
⏎
⏎
Edna R. Jones, M.D. ⏎
⏎
ERJ:ess ⏎
⏎
cc: Bastien Cole ⏎
```

TIP

If you import a non-WordPerfect file that's formatted with ⏎ characters at the end of each line, you may be able to use WordPerfect's Find And Replace feature to fix things up (see Chapter 9).

Moving the Cursor

When you want to make changes to text that you've already typed onto the screen, the first thing you need to do is move the blinking cursor to wherever you want to make the change. You can use either the mouse or the keyboard to position the cursor, but you can position it only within existing text. More on this in a moment.

Using the Mouse

Remember that typing takes place at the cursor—*not* at the position of the mouse pointer. Therefore, you must position the mouse pointer and then *click* to move the cursor to a particular spot in the document before you begin typing. (It's easy to forget this little tidbit and wind up adding or deleting text at the wrong place!)

You can also use the mouse and the scroll bars to scroll up, down, left, and right through your document. If the scroll bars aren't visible, choose File ➤ Preferences ➤ Display, check Vertical and Horizontal, and choose OK then Close. The scroll bars will appear at the right and bottom edges of your document.

If your document is several pages long, you can click the tiny page icons in the vertical scroll bar at the right edge of the document window to scroll from page to page.

Using the Keyboard

You can also use the cursor-positioning keys listed in Table 3.1 to move the cursor within text. Remember, if you want to use the keys on the numeric keypad, Num Lock must be turned off.

Repeating a Keystroke

You can repeat any keystroke simply by holding the key down for a while. However, if you'd like to repeat a keystroke, a menu selection, or even the

TABLE 3.1: Keys for Positioning the Cursor

TO MOVE...	USE THIS KEY...
Right one character	→
Left one character	←
Up one line	↑
Down one line	↓
Next word	Ctrl+→
Previous word	Ctrl+←
Start of line	Home
End of line	End
Next paragraph	Ctrl+↓
Previous paragraph	Ctrl+↑
Top of screen	PgUp
Bottom of screen	PgDn
Next page	Alt+PgDn
Previous page	Alt+PgUp
Top of document (under codes)	Ctrl+Home
Top of document (above codes)	Ctrl+Home Ctrl+Home
End of document	Ctrl+End
To a specific position, page, bookmark, or table cell	Ctrl+G
To a specific character, word, or phrase	F2 (see Chapter 9)
To a QuickMark bookmark	Ctrl+Q (see Chapter 9)

click of a button on a button bar a specific number of times, follow these steps:

1. Choose Edit ➤ Repeat. You'll see this dialog box:

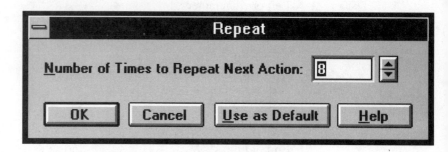

2. If you want to change the number of times to repeat, type a number in the Number Of Times To Repeat Next Action text box. If you'd like WordPerfect to display this number automatically the next time you repeat an action, choose Use As Default.

3. Choose OK or press ↵.

4. Press any cursor-positioning key (to move the cursor the specified number of times) or character (to repeat the character). Or choose a menu option or click a button on one of the button bars to take an action repeatedly. (This technique might not work for every command or button.)

Suppose you're working in a large document, and you want to move the cursor down 20 pages. Rather than pressing Alt+PgDn twenty times, you could just choose Edit ➤ Repeat, type **20** and choose OK, then press Alt+PgDn.

Jumping to a Specific Place

Another way to move the cursor in your document is to use the Go To command:

1. Choose Edit ➤ Go To or press Ctrl+G to open a Go To dialog box like the one shown below. (You can also right-click a scroll bar and choose GoTo from the Quick Menu.)

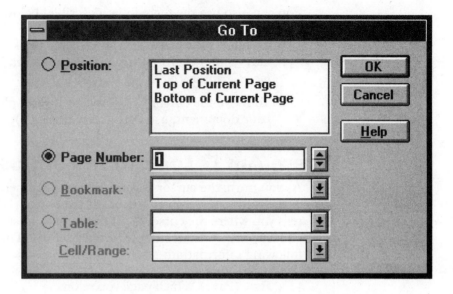

2. Now do any of the following:

- To go to a specific position in the document, choose Position and select an option from the Position list.
- To go to a specific page, choose Page Number and type in a page number.
- To go to a bookmark (Chapter 9), choose Bookmark and select the bookmark you want.
- To go to a specific table and cell (Chapter 7), choose Table then select the table and cell or the range.

3. Choose OK or press ↵.

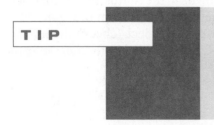

TIP

To move the cursor back to wherever you just came from, press Ctrl+G (to choose Go To), press Alt+P (to choose Position), and press ↵. This is handy for getting right back where you were if you press a cursor-positioning key accidentally.

Special Ways to Position the Cursor

You can also use the techniques described below to position the cursor:

- To mark your place with an invisible bookmark, press Ctrl+Shift+Q. To return to that bookmark later, press Ctrl+Q (see Chapter 9).

- To move the cursor to a character, word, phrase, or code within your document, use Find (see Chapter 9).

Where Am I? Look to the Status Bar!

`Pg 1 Ln 1" Pos 1"`   As you move the cursor around in your document, the position indicator in the right edge of the *status bar* at the bottom of the document window tells you where the cursor is. (If the status bar isn't visible at the moment, choose View ▶ Status Bar from the menus). The status bar includes the following information:

Pg (Page) Which page you're on.

Ln (Line) How far down the cursor is from the top of the page.

Pos (Position) How far the cursor is from the left edge of the page.

> **TIP**
>
> To open the Go To dialog box in a hurry, double-click the position indicator in the status bar.

By default, WordPerfect leaves a 1-inch margin around your document. So when you're at the very top of a new document, the status bar will usually show **Pg 1 Ln 1″ Pos 1″**. Chapter 5 explains how to change the margin widths at any time.

To customize the information shown in the status bar, right-click anywhere on the status bar and choose Preferences from the QuickMenu, or choose File ▶ Preferences ▶ Status Bar. Select (check) the information you want to include and choose OK. See Chapter 19 for more information.

Inserting and Replacing Text

When editing a document, you can choose between two modes of adding text: *Insert mode* and *Typeover mode*. In Insert mode, new text is inserted between existing characters. Suppose you move the cursor to the letter P in the word "WordPerfect." Then, in Insert mode, you type **XXX**. Those three letters would be inserted into the text, like this: **WordXXXPerfect**.

If you put the cursor on the letter P and typed **XXX** in Typeover mode, those three letters would *type over* (overwrite) three existing letters, like this: **WordXXXfect**.

Switching between Insert and Typeover Modes

Normally, WordPerfect is in Insert mode. To switch to Typeover mode, press the Ins (Insert) key once. The message "Typeover" will appear in the status bar.

The Insert key acts as a *toggle*. This means that to switch from Typeover mode back to Insert mode, you just press Ins again. The message in the status bar will change to "Insert." You can also switch between the two modes by double-clicking the Typeover or Insert message in the status bar.

You might be surprised to discover that the Backspace key operates differently in Insert mode and Typeover mode. In Insert mode, pressing Backspace deletes the character to the left of the cursor and drags all characters to the right of the cursor along with it, filling in any "holes" that would otherwise be left by the deleted text. In Typeover mode, the Backspace key deletes the character to the left of the cursor, but doesn't drag any characters with it.

Inserting Text, Spaces, and Blank Lines

To insert text, spaces, or blank lines in a document, follow these steps:

1. Move the cursor to the place where you want to insert text, spaces, or blank lines.

2. Make sure you're in Insert mode.

3. Type as you normally would:

- To insert a blank space, press the spacebar.
- To insert text, just type it.
- To insert a blank line or to break a line into two pieces, press ↵.

If you make mistakes while inserting new text, you can correct them using Backspace, Delete, or Undo (which is described later in this chapter).

Splitting and Joining Lines and Paragraphs

You might accidentally press ↵ in the middle of a line, causing the line to split in two, like two separate paragraphs. If this happens, just move the cursor to the start of the lower line and press Backspace. Or, move the cursor to the end of the top line and press Delete. This deletes the *hard return* ([HRt]) code that's splitting the line. (You'll learn more about hidden codes in Chapter 4.)

To split one paragraph into two, move the cursor to the place where you want to make the split. Then press ↵ once or twice, and, if you wish, press Tab to indent. If you go too far, just use the Backspace key to back up.

Selecting (Blocking) Text

Sometimes, you don't want to work with individual letters and characters. Instead, you want to work with a phrase, sentence, paragraph, or some other large chunk of text. When you want to do something to a chunk of text, you must first *select* (or "block") the text. You can select any amount of text from a single character, to an entire document, and any amount of text in between.

Once selected, the text appears highlighted (in reverse colors) on your screen, as in the example shown in Figure 3.5. Once you've selected a chunk of text, you can move it, copy it, change its appearance, delete it, print it, save it to a separate file... whatever! I'll summarize the things you can do with selected text later in this chapter.

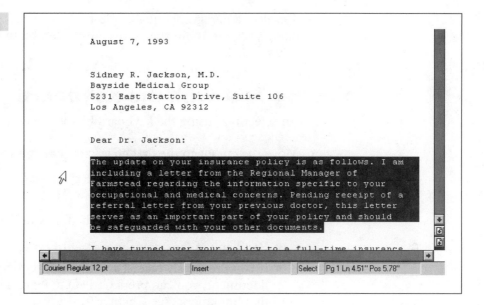

Selecting Text with a Mouse

To select text using a mouse, follow the steps below:

1. Move the mouse pointer to the first character of text that you want to select.

2. Hold down the mouse button and drag the pointer to the last character that you want to select.

3. When the text you want to work with is selected (highlighted), release the mouse button.

Here are some shortcuts for selecting text with a mouse:

- To select a word, double-click anywhere in that word.

- To select many lines at once quickly, move the mouse pointer into the left margin area. The pointer will change to an arrow (as shown in Figure 3.5). Now hold down the mouse button and drag the pointer up or down to select the lines you want.

- To select a sentence, triple-click anywhere in that sentence. Or, move the pointer to the left margin area and click the mouse.

- To select a paragraph, quadruple-click anywhere in that paragraph. Or, move the pointer to the left margin area and double-click.

Selecting Text with the Keyboard

You can select text using the keyboard by following the steps below:

1. Move the cursor to the first character that you want to select.

2. Press F8 (or double-click the "Select" message in the status bar). The "Select" message will darken.

3. Extend the selection using any of the following methods:

   - Press any of the cursor-movement keys listed in Table 3.1.
   - If you previously placed a Ctrl+Shift+Q bookmark in your document, you can press Ctrl+Q to extend the selection to that bookmark (see Chapter 9).
   - You can use Find (F2) to extend the selection to a specific word, phrase, or formatting code (see Chapter 9).

Here's another way to select text with the keyboard:

1. Move the cursor to the first character that you want to select.

2. Hold down the Shift key while pressing any of the cursor-movement keys listed in Table 3.1.

Regardless of whether you use the mouse or the keyboard to select text, the text will appear highlighted on the screen, and the status bar will display the "Select" message (usually just to the left of the position indicator).

Selecting Large Blocks

Here are some tips to keep in mind when you're selecting a large block of text:

- If you're using the mouse and the selection gets to the top or bottom edge of the screen, just keep dragging the pointer off the edge of the screen. Text will scroll into the selection area until you release the mouse button.

- If you run out of desk space while rolling the mouse, keep the mouse button depressed, lift the mouse and reposition it, then resume rolling the mouse.

- You can combine mouse techniques with keyboard cursor-movements. For instance, you can start by dragging with the mouse, then hold down the Shift key and use the cursor-movement keys to finish selecting the text.

Deselecting and Reselecting Text

If you've made a mess of the selection job or you just change your mind, it's easy to deselect the text:

- Click anywhere within the document.
- Or press F8.
- Or double-click the Select message in the status bar.
- Or release the Shift key (if you're holding it down) and press a cursor-movement key.

Suppose you deselected some selected text accidentally, and you want to reselect the same text. That's easy too:

1. Choose Edit ➤ Go To (or press Ctrl+G or double-click the position indicator in the status bar).

2. Double-click Reselect Last Selection in the Position list, or highlight that option and choose OK or press ↵.

Shortcuts for Selecting Text

Here are some shortcuts for selecting the sentence or paragraph or page that the cursor is in, or the entire document. Move the cursor anywhere into the sentence, paragraph, page, or document that you want to select. Then...

- Choose Edit ➤ Select, and choose the amount of text you want to select: Sentence, Paragraph, Page, or All.

- Or, move the mouse pointer to the left of the text you want to select, click the right mouse button, and choose the option that describes what you want to do: Select S̲entence, Select P̲aragraph, Select P̲a̲ge, or Select A̲ll.

Things You Can Do with Selected Text

Once you've selected a chunk of text and the "Select" message darkens in the status bar, you can do all kinds of things with that text. In this chapter I'll discuss moving, copying, deleting, and changing the case (upper- vs. lower-) of blocked text.

Table 3.2 lists operations you can perform on selected text, together with cross-references to where in the book those operations are covered in more detail. Many of the features listed in Table 3.2 are also available on the button bar, power bar, and QuickMenu.

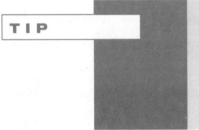

TIP

To display the button bar or power bar, choose V̲iew, then choose B̲utton Bar or P̲ower Bar (as appropriate). To open the QuickMenu options for selected text, right-click the selected text. QuickMenus are described in Chapter 2. You'll learn more about the button bar and power bar in Chapter 4.

TABLE 3.2: Things You Can Do with Selected Text

ACTION	MENU CHOICES	SHORTCUT KEY	CHAPTER
Add to Clipboard	E̲dit ➤ Appen̲d		3
Alphabetize/sort	T̲ools ➤ S̲ort	Alt+F9	22
Boldface	L̲ayout ➤ F̲ont ➤ B̲old	Ctrl+B	6
Bookmark (create)	I̲nsert ➤ Bookmark ➤ Cre̲ate	Ctrl+Shift+Q	9

TABLE 3.2: Things You Can Do with Selected Text (continued)

ACTION	MENU CHOICES	SHORTCUT KEY	CHAPTER
Center	Layout ➤ Line ➤ Center or Layout ➤ Justification ➤ Center	Shift+F7 or Ctrl+E	5
Change appearance	Layout ➤ Font	F9	6
Change case	Edit ➤ Convert Case	Ctrl+K	3
Change size	Layout➤ Font	F9	6
Comment	Insert ➤ Comment ➤ Create		4
Copy to Clipboard	Edit ➤ Copy	Ctrl+C or Ctrl+Ins	3
Copy within the document	Edit ➤ Copy, then Edit ➤ Paste	Ctrl+C then Ctrl+V, or press Ctrl while dragging	3
Delete		Delete or Backspace	3
Envelope (create)	Layout ➤ Envelope		8
Find/replace	Edit ➤ Find or Edit ➤ Replace	F2 or Ctrl+F2	9
Flush right	Layout ➤ Line ➤ Flush Right or Layout ➤ Justification ➤ Right	Alt+F7 or Ctrl+R	5
Grammar check	Tools ➤ Grammatik	Alt+Shift+F1	12

TABLE 3.2: Things You Can Do with Selected Text (continued)

ACTION	MENU CHOICES	SHORTCUT KEY	CHAPTER
Italicize	Layout ➤ Font ➤ Italic	Ctrl+I	6
Margins (change)	Layout ➤ Margins	Ctrl+F8	5
Move to Clipboard	Edit ➤ Cut	Ctrl+X or Shift+Del	3
Move within current document	Edit ➤ Cut, then Edit ➤ Paste	Ctrl+X then Ctrl+V, or drag with mouse	3
Print	File ➤ Print ➤ Print	Ctrl+P	3, 10
Protect	Layout ➤ Page ➤ Keep Text Together ➤ Keep Selected Text Together on Same Page		8
Quick Format	Layout ➤ Quick Format		5
Save	File ➤ Save	Ctrl+S	3
Spell check	Tools ➤ Speller	Ctrl+F1	11
Style	Layout ➤ Styles	Alt+F8	17
Table (Convert to)	Table ➤ Create	F12	7
Underline	Layout➤ Font ➤ Underline	Ctrl+U	6

Moving and Copying Text (Cut-and-Paste)

Moving text around and copying text are two of the most common editing operations. Suppose you're typing a list of names and addresses of people who live in the same neighborhood. You could avoid needless retyping by copying the street address, city, state, and zip code from one person's entry to the next. Or, you could save those typing fingers by copying certain passages of text, such as standard paragraphs, from one document to another.

The basic steps for moving and copying are practically identical. The only difference between the two operations is that *moving* text takes it from one place and puts it in another. *Copying* leaves the text in its original position and places a copy of that text in a new location.

For example, in the passage below, I've selected the third sentence within a paragraph.

> Organization is the lion's share of clear writing. Within each section, every paragraph needs a strong topic sentence that tells the reader what the rest of the paragraph is about. Every chapter should be broken into sections and subsections that not only flow smoothly from beginning to end, but also make it easy for the reader to find information as needed. And of course, even the words within each sentence must be organized for easy reading and crystal clarity.

Once the text is selected, I can choose Edit ➤ Cut (or press Ctrl+X) to cut the sentence, moving it into the Clipboard. (The Clipboard is a place in memory that holds the text until you cut or copy some *other* chunk of text, or you exit Windows.) Then, I can place the cursor at the beginning of the second sentence, and choose Edit ➤ Paste (or press Ctrl+V). The selected sentence is now the second, rather than third, sentence in the paragraph, as shown on the next page.

NOTE   When selecting a sentence, be sure to include the space that follows the period.

Organization is the lion's share of clear writing. Every chapter should be broken into sections and subsections that not only flow smoothly from beginning to end, but also make it easy for the reader to find information as needed. Within each section, every paragraph needs a strong topic sentence that tells the reader what the rest of the paragraph is about. And of course, even the words within each sentence must be organized for easy reading and crystal clarity.

Copying text is a handy way to avoid typing repetitive text. For example, while typing the list of names and addresses below, I selected a portion of the last line.

Neighborhood Watch
Anderson, J.A., 123 Oak St., Glendora, CA 91740
Jest, Shirley U., 124 Oak St., Glendora, CA 91740
Hartunian, Willie P, 127 Oak St., Glendora, CA 91740
Anderson, J.A., 229 Oak St., Glendora, CA 91740

Then I chose Edit ➤ Copy (or pressed Ctrl+C) to copy the selected text into the Clipboard. Next, I pressed the End key, then ↵ to move down a line. Finally, I selected Edit ➤ Paste (or pressed Ctrl+V), and a copy of that selected text appeared on the new line. I can now type in the name and street number for the next person in the list without retyping the street name, city, and so forth.

Neighborhood Watch
Anderson, J.A., 123 Oak St., Glendora, CA 91740
Jest, Shirley U., 124 Oak St., Glendora, CA 91740
Hartunian, Willie P, 127 Oak St., Glendora, CA 91740
Anderson, J.A., 229 Oak St., Glendora, CA 91740
Oak St., Glendora, CA 91740

To move or copy text, follow these steps:

1. Select the text you want to move or copy, as described earlier in this chapter.

   - To *move* the text, choose Edit ➤ Cut, press Ctrl+X (or Shift+Del), or click the Cut button in the power bar (shown at left). Or, right-click the selected text and choose Cut from the QuickMenu.

   - To *copy* the text, choose Edit ➤ Copy, press Ctrl+C (or Ctrl+Ins), or click the Copy button in the power bar (shown at left). Or, right-click the selected text and choose Copy from the QuickMenu.

2. Move the cursor to where you want to place the cut or copied text.

3. Choose Edit ➤ Paste, press Ctrl+V (or Shift+Ins), or click the Paste button in the power bar (shown at left). Or, right-click near the middle of the editing window and choose Paste from the QuickMenu.

N O T E   You're not restricted to moving and copying text only. You can also move and copy hidden formatting codes and graphics.

Moving and Copying with Drag-and-Drop

Many Windows applications offer a feature called *drag-and-drop*. Word-Perfect for Windows is no slouch in this department. With drag-and-drop, you simply use your mouse to drag selected text where you want it and drop it into place. Here's how to do it:

1. Select the text you want to move or copy.

2. Click and hold down the mouse button anywhere on the selected text.

   - If you want to *move* the text, drag the text to its new spot.

- If you want to *copy* the text, hold down the Ctrl key while you drag the text to its new spot.

The text will remain selected after the move or copy. You can deselect it by pressing F8, clicking the mouse, or pressing a cursor-movement key.

Moving and Copying across Documents

As soon as you choose Edit ➤ Cut or Edit ➤ Copy (or equivalent shortcut keys, power buttons, or QuickMenu options), a copy of the selected text is placed in the Windows Clipboard. Although you can't see the Clipboard while you're in WordPerfect, it's useful to remember that it contains a copy of whatever you last cut or copied.

Why is this useful? Well, you might want to do some of these clever things:

- Choose File ➤ New (Ctrl+N) to create a new empty document, then choose Edit ➤ Paste (Ctrl+V) to copy text from the Clipboard into that new document.

- Choose File ➤ Open (Ctrl+O) to open a previously saved document, position the cursor in that document, then use Edit ➤ Paste to paste in text from the Clipboard.

- Use the Window menu (Chapter 4) to switch to a different open document, then choose Edit ➤ Paste to paste in the text.

So you see, once you've cut or copied text using Edit ➤ Cut or Edit ➤ Copy, you can place the cursor anywhere you want and choose Edit ➤ Paste (or press Ctrl+V) to paste in the text. You can even select Edit ➤ Paste a bunch of times to keep pasting in multiple copies of the same text. Just remember that when you exit Windows, the Clipboard will be emptied.

Appending to the Clipboard

Normally, text that you move or copy to the Clipboard *replaces* whatever was there before. If you'd like to *add* more text to the Clipboard without deleting what's already there, just select the text you want to add, then choose Edit ➤ Append. WordPerfect will copy the selected text to the Clipboard, below whatever you placed there previously.

Saving the Clipboard Contents

If you want to save a copy of the Clipboard contents for future sessions in WordPerfect for Windows, you must save it to a file:

1. Select the text you want to store. (If that text is in the Clipboard but not on your screen, choose Edit ➤ Paste then select the text to store.)

 2. Choose File ➤ Save, press Ctrl+S, or click the Save button in the power bar (shown at left).

3. Choose OK or press ↵.

4. Type the name for this file (for example, CLIPBRD) and choose OK or press ↵.

If a file with the name you specified already exists and you don't mind overwriting (replacing) that file, choose Yes. If you don't want to replace an existing file, choose No and enter a different file name.

NOTE   If you want to copy the text for use with a different program, see the section on exporting text in Chapter 33.

Anytime later, you can open the CLIPBRD file (or whatever file contains the Clipboard contents) using File ➤ Open. Select all of its text, and re-copy that text into the Clipboard. Or, you can place the cursor where you want the contents of the CLIPBRD file to appear, then choose Insert ➤ File to retrieve the contents of that CLIPBRD file.

Undoing Major Boo-Boos

If you really mess up, you can undo your most recent action, including moving or copying text. The catch is that you must undo it right away!

 To undo your most recent action, choose Edit ➤ Undo, press Ctrl+Z, or click the Undo button in the power bar (shown at left).

Deleting Text

Table 3.3 shows many ways to delete text. As you can see, deleting text is easy. Keep in mind that you can delete any chunk of text simply by selecting that text as described earlier and pressing the Del (or Backspace) key.

TABLE 3.3: Different Ways to Delete Text

TO DELETE	MOVE CURSOR TO	AND PRESS
Break at end of a line	End of upper line	Delete
Character/space at cursor	Character	Delete
Character/space left of cursor	Next character	Backspace
Word	Word	Ctrl+Backspace
Blank line	Start of blank line	Delete or Backspace
Rest of line	Start of deletion point	Ctrl+Del
Rest of page	Start of deletion point	Ctrl+Shift+Del
Rest of document	Start of deletion	Shift+Ctrl+End Delete
Selected text	Selected text	Delete or Backspace

Undeleting Deleted Text

If you delete a chunk of text accidentally, you can follow these steps to "undelete" it:

1. Choose Edit ➤ Undelete or press Ctrl+Shift+Z.

2. The deleted text reappears, highlighted on the screen.

- If the highlighted text is what you want to undelete, choose <u>R</u>estore.

- If the highlighted text isn't what you want to undelete, choose <u>N</u>ext or <u>P</u>revious. When the text you want to undelete appears on the screen, choose <u>R</u>estore.

- If you don't find the text you want to undelete within three tries, choose Cancel or press Escape to give up.

The Undelete command can "remember" no more than your last three deletions. So if you don't find the text you want to undelete after choosing <u>N</u>ext or <u>P</u>revious twice, you're plain out of luck (unless you recently saved the file, as I'll explain later in this chapter).

Undo vs. Undelete

Now, you may be wondering what the difference is between Undo and Undelete. There are several differences:

- Undelete "remembers" up to your last three deletions. Undo only remembers your (one) most recent action.

- Undelete can only "undo" a deletion. Undo can undo almost any action, including moving, copying, and changing case.

- Undelete puts recovered text at the current cursor position. Undo puts recovered text back in its original spot.

TIP

Another way to move text, graphics, and hidden codes is to delete whatever you want to move, then move the cursor to the new location and undelete it.

Switching Case

WordPerfect lets you change the case of selected text between upper- and lowercase or to initial capital letters. Here's how:

1. Select the text you want to change.

2. Choose Edit ➤ Convert Case.

3. Choose Lowercase, Uppercase, or Initial Capitals, depending on how you want the results to be formatted:

   THIS IS UPPERCASE
   this is lowercase
   And This Is Initial Caps

Choose Edit ➤ Undo (Ctrl+Z) if you change your mind and want to revert to the original case.

If you'd like to toggle quickly between uppercase and lowercase, select the text and press Ctrl+K. Each time you press Ctrl+K, WordPerfect will toggle the selected text to a different case. Try it!

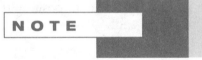

NOTE With a sentence selected, Ctrl+K toggles between all caps and lowercase with initial word capped.

Printing Your Document

You can print the document that you're currently working on by following these simple steps:

1. Choose File ➤ Print, press F5, or click the Print button in the power bar (shown at left).

2. Choose Print or type **p**.

3. Wait a few seconds.

After a brief delay, the printer should kick in. (If the printer refuses to co-operate, please refer to Chapter 10, as well as to "Printer Problems" in Appendix C.)

TIP

Want a shorter shortcut for printing your document? Just press Ctrl+P. You'll learn how to print multiple copies, choose from several installed printers, and use other printing options in Chapter 10.

Your printed document will have 1-inch margins all the way around (these don't appear on the document window in Draft mode). The 1-inch margins are the default margins, which WordPerfect uses for every printed document. The term *default* refers to any setting that you do not alter. You can change the default margins if you wish (see Chapter 5).

Saving Your Work

It's important to understand that any recent work you've done on open documents is stored in memory (RAM) only. If you turn off your computer without saving those documents, you'll lose all the work you've done. Ouch!

When you save a WordPerfect document, it is stored as a file on your disk. Individual files are often stored in groups, called *directories*. No two files in the same directory can have the same name.

If you're not familiar with drives, directories, and files, don't sweat it right now. You can learn the details at your leisure by referring to Chapter 20 or to an introductory DOS book.

Naming Documents

Before saving a document for the first time, you need to think up a file name that conforms to the following rules:

- The name can be up to eight characters long and may contain letters, numbers, or a mixture of the two.

- You can follow the file name with a period and an *extension* up to three characters long. The period that separates the file name from the extension is the only period allowed in the file name.

- If you omit the period and extension, WordPerfect will assign the extension .WPD automatically. If you type the file name and a period, but no extension (as in **myfile.**), WordPerfect will save the file without an extension.

- Neither the name nor the extension can contain blank spaces. If you want to separate characters in the file name, use an underscore character or a hyphen (MY_FILE.WPD or MY-FILE.WPD).

- You cannot use the following characters in a file name:

  * ? + = [ ] : ; " / \ | > <

- File names are not case-sensitive. Therefore, SMITH.WPD, Smith.Wpd, and smith.wpd are all the same file name.

TIP

Try to assign descriptive file names that will make it easy to find the file again in the future. For example, the file name XXX tells you nothing about the contents of that file. But the file name SMITH.WPD tells you that the file contains something about somebody named Smith—perhaps a letter to that person.

Table 3.4 gives some examples of valid and invalid file names.

TABLE 3.4: Examples of Valid and Invalid File Names

FILE NAME	VALID/INVALID
LETTER	Valid
LETTER.1	Valid
SMITH.LET	Valid
1991TAX.QT1	Valid
QTR_1.WPD	Valid

TABLE 3.4: Examples of Valid and Invalid File Names (continued)

FILE NAME	VALID/INVALID
MyLetter.wpd	Valid
QTR 1.WPD	Invalid (contains a blank space)
QTR1.W PD	Invalid (extension contains a blank space)
12.1.91.WPD	Invalid (too many periods)
MYFIRSTLETTER.TXT	Invalid (too long, will be converted to MYFIRSTL.TXT)
WON'T.WPD	Invalid (contains a punctuation mark)

Saving for the First Time

A new document that's never been saved has no file name. Its document window will display the name *Document* followed by a number (for example, *Document1*). To save a document that hasn't been saved before, follow the steps below:

1. Choose File ➤ Save, press Ctrl+S, or click the Save button in the power bar (shown at left).

2. Type a valid file name, then choose OK. (Include or choose a path, as discussed in Chapter 20, if you wish.)

A copy of the document will remain on your screen for editing, and the document will be copied to disk.

TIP

If you press Ctrl+Shift+Q to place a QuickMark just before you save the file, you can then use Ctrl+Q to return to that place after you reopen the file (see Chapter 9).

Saving Recent Changes

Once you've saved a file and given it a name, it's easy to save your changes as you go along. In particular, you might find it useful to save your file...

- Just after doing something that was tough.
- Just before trying something you think is risky.
- Every 5 minutes or so, regardless of what you're doing.

To save the file, just choose File ➤ Save or press Ctrl+S. You'll see the famous Windows hourglass icon as WordPerfect updates the copy of your file on disk to match the current copy in memory.

Saving with a Different Name

If you want to keep the previously saved copy of your document on disk and save the current document in a new, separate file, proceed as follows:

1. Choose File ➤ Save As or press F3.

2. Type in a new (different) file name for the copy that's currently on your screen.

3. Choose OK.

Any additional changes you make to the document and save will be saved under this new file name only. The previous version of the document will remain unchanged under its original file name.

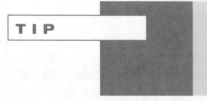

TIP

The Save As dialog box works almost like the Open File dialog box shown in Figure 3.1. This makes it easy to navigate through the file system and view files before saving your document.

Closing a Document Window

To close the document you're working on (and save it if you wish) without leaving WordPerfect, just follow these steps:

1. Choose File ➤ Close or press Ctrl+F4.

2. If you've made changes to the document but haven't saved them yet, you'll be asked if you want to save the current version. Choose Yes (unless you've made a mess of this copy and would prefer to keep the last copy you saved).

Creating a New Document Window

 If you want to create a new document without closing the one that's currently open on your screen, choose File ➤ New, press Ctrl+N, or click the New Document button in the power bar (shown at left). Then you can use commands and shortcuts on the Window menu to switch among open documents (see Chapter 4).

Throwing Away Bad Work

You should always save your work just before trying something risky. Why? Because if the risky action involves several steps and really makes a mess of things, the Undo feature won't be much help in restoring your document to its pristine state.

But if you save the document using File ➤ Save just before the foul-up, you can always "undo" by replacing the messed-up copy on your screen with the good copy you saved just before the screw-up. Here's how it works:

1. Use File ➤ Save (Ctrl+S) to save the file just *before* trying that risky procedure.

2. Do the procedure. If you do more harm than good, choose File ➤ Close (Ctrl+F4) to close this copy of the file.

3. When asked about saving, choose No.

4. Use File ➤ Open (Ctrl+O) to reopen the copy of the file you saved just before the foul-up.

The trick, of course, is remembering *always* to save your work just *after* you complete a job successfully and just *before* you try something that might mess things up royally.

Saving and Exiting All at Once

You always want to exit WordPerfect for Windows (and Windows) before you turn off your computer, just to make sure that you haven't left any work behind in memory (RAM). To exit WordPerfect, follow these steps:

1. Choose File ➤ Exit or press Alt+F4.

2. If there's any unsaved work in memory, WordPerfect will give you a chance to save that work. You'll see a dialog box like this one:

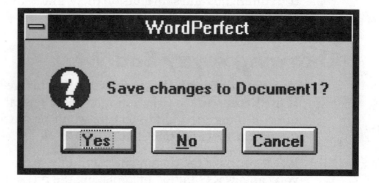

- If you want to save the unsaved file, choose Yes.
- If you don't want to save the unsaved file, choose No.
- If you change your mind about exiting altogether, choose Cancel to stay in WordPerfect.

This chapter has covered things you need to know in order to edit text quickly and easily. In the next chapter, you'll learn ways to get the most out of WordPerfect, including some terrific tools and super shortcuts.

CHAPTER

4

Getting the Most from WordPerfect

fast TRACK

To zoom in for a close-up or out for an arm's-length view of your document   **111**

> choose a magnification from the Zoom button on the power bar, or choose View ➤ Zoom and select a magnification.

To open multiple documents simultaneously   **112**

> choose File ➤ Open for each document you want to open.

To make it easier to switch among various open documents   **112**

> choose Window, then choose Cascade or Tile.

To reveal the hidden codes within your document   **119**

> choose View ➤ Reveal Codes or press Alt+F3.

Use document comments   **129**

> (Insert ➤ Comment) to include notes to yourself or others within a document.

To insert the current date into a document   **134**

> without actually typing the date, choose Insert ➤ Date, then choose either Date Text for a date that never changes or Date Code for a date that always reflects the current system date.

To choose a template that establishes the initial document format and other settings   **137**

> choose File ➤ Template (or press Ctrl+T), highlight or click the template you want, and choose OK.

NOW THAT you know most of what you really *need* to know, we can start looking at some optional techniques that will make your time spent at the keyboard a little more productive. In this chapter, we'll focus on the many tools that you can turn on and off at will and use at your convenience to get your work done as quickly and efficiently as possible.

Belly Up to the Bars

WordPerfect offers several optional tools and bars: the button bar, power bar, ruler bar, and so forth. All are easy to use, and you can turn them on and off at your convenience. What's more, you can customize most of the bars, and you can even create your own menu bars and button bars. I'll explain how later in this chapter.

Turning Bars On and Off

You can turn the bars on or off by following these steps:

1. To turn a bar on or off, choose Yiew (or press Alt+V).

2. Choose the bar you want to turn on or off (that is, Button Bar, Power Bar, Ruler Bar, or Status Bar).

3. Repeat steps 1 and 2 to turn as many bars on or off as you wish.

What's That Button For?

The buttons on the button bar and power bar have icons on them that represent what the button is for. If you want details about what a particular button does, just move the mouse pointer to the button. The title bar at the top of the screen will describe the button that the mouse pointer is currently resting on. (If you want to activate the button, just click the mouse while it's on the button.)

Hiding and Redisplaying the Bars

One disadvantage to having all the bars on your screen is that there's less room to view your text. To hide all the bars in a flash, follow these steps:

1. Choose View ➤ Hide Bars (or press Alt+Shift+F5).

2. Choose OK.

This turns off all bars, even the menu bar. Of course, once you've turned off all the bars, you won't be able to see options from the menu. No problem. To redisplay any bars that were previously visible, press Escape or Alt+Shift+F5. Or press Alt+V and choose Hide Bars.

In the next sections, I'll discuss each of the bars (except the menu bar, which I described in Chapter 2).

Using the Button Bar

The button bar gives you quick access to frequently used features, macros (discussed in Chapter 18), and other button bars. To choose a button on the button bar, just click the button you want to activate. If there are more buttons on the bar than will fit across the screen, you can scroll the hidden buttons into view by clicking the ▲ or ▼ buttons on the button bar.

Choosing a Button Bar

WordPerfect comes with about a dozen button bars for you to choose from. You can add buttons to the predefined button bars or create button bars of your own, as described later in this chapter. Selecting the button bar you want to use is a snap:

- If the button bar is visible, right-click it and choose the button bar you want from the QuickMenu that appears.

If no button bar is visible on the screen, you can do this instead:

1. Choose File ➤ Preferences and double-click Button Bar. You'll see the Button Bar Preferences dialog box:

2. Double-click the button bar you want, or highlight it and choose Select.

3. Choose Close.

Positioning the Button Bar

You can move the button bar to any spot on the screen and customize its appearance by following the steps below:

1. Choose File ➤ Preferences and double-click Button Bar, or right-click the button bar and choose Preferences from the QuickMenu.

2. Choose Options to open the Button Bar Setup dialog box shown below:

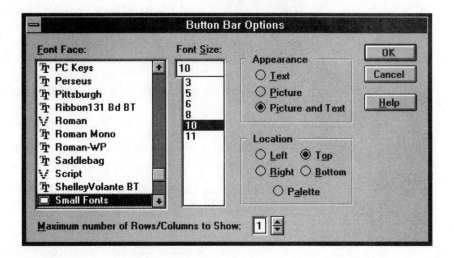

3. Choose the Location you want: Left, Top, Right, Bottom, or Palette (choosing Palette converts the button bar to a free-floating dialog box).

4. If you chose a location other than Palette in step 3, you can choose Maximum Number Of Rows/Columns To Show and specify the number of rows or columns you want.

5. If you wish, choose the Font Face and Font Size you want for the text that appears on each button (fonts are discussed in Chapter 6).

6. If you wish, choose the Appearance you want for the buttons: Text (no icon), Picture (icon only), or Picture And Text (both text and icon).

7. When you're done, choose OK, then choose Close as necessary to work your way back to the document window.

The button bar will have its new appearance, location, and shape.

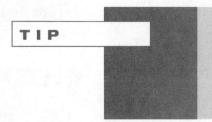

T I P When the button bar is displayed as a palette, you can drag its title bar to move it, drag any portion of its border to resize it, and double click its Control-menu box to remove the button bar from the screen. Choosing View ➤ Button bar will redisplay the button bar window.

You can also reposition the button bar by dragging it on the screen:

1. If necessary, choose View ➤ Button Bar to display the button bar.

2. Move the mouse pointer to an empty spot in the button bar. The pointer will change to a hand icon (shown at left).

3. Hold down the mouse button and drag the outline of the button bar. The button bar outline will change shape as you move it.

   - To display the buttons in a single row or column, drag the outline to the top, bottom, left, or right edge of the screen.
   - To display the buttons in a floating palette, drag the outline to the middle of the screen.

4. When the outline is where you want it, release the mouse button.

I'll explain how to add new buttons to the button bar a little later in this chapter.

Using the Power Bar

The power bar provides shortcuts to the menu commands. If the power bar is hidden, you can choose View ➤ Power Bar to display it. You can move the mouse pointer to any button on the power bar and look to the title bar at the top of the window to see a description of that button.

You can use the power buttons in any of four ways:

- **Click** the button once to select a feature. On the default power bar, this works for New Document, Open, Save, Print, Cut, Copy,

Paste, Undo, Bold Font, Italic Font, Underline Font, Speller, The-saurus, Grammatik, Page Zoom Full, and View Button Bar.

- **Double-click** the button to open a dialog box related to the fea-ture. You can double-click these buttons: Font Face, Font Size, Tab Set, Table Quick Create, Columns Define, Line Spacing, and Zoom.

- **Click and drag** to display a pull-down menu. Keep the mouse button depressed, scroll to the option you want, then release the mouse button. This method works with Font Face, Font Size, Tab Set, Table Quick Create, Columns Define, Justification, Line Spac-ing, and Zoom.

- **Right-click** anywhere on the power button to choose between customizing the power bar (Preferences) and hiding the bar (Hide Power Bar). To bring a hidden power bar back into view, choose View ➤ Power Bar.

Using the Ruler Bar

You can use the ruler bar to set tabs, margins, paragraph format, table col-umn widths, and multicolumn widths in a jiffy (features you'll learn about in upcoming chapters). The ruler bar doesn't have any buttons to click. Instead, you drag the markers around to reset margins, tabs, and column widths. You can also double-click certain spots on the ruler bar to set mar-gins, change ruler display options, and set tabs. You'll learn more about this versatile tool in Chapters 5, 7, and 27.

Using the Status Bar

The status bar, at the bottom of the screen, provides information about what you're doing and offers quick ways to activate certain features. To select a feature in the status bar, double-click an area on the bar. For ex-ample, double-clicking the current font name (if it's visible) in the status bar takes you to the Font dialog box (discussed in Chapter 6).

Using the Feature Bars

Feature bars pop up only when they're needed to provide shortcuts for specific WordPerfect features. For example, when you choose Insert ➤ Comment ➤ Create, the feature bar shown below pops up:

The buttons on this bar make it easy to edit a document comment (you'll learn more about this feature later in the chapter). To use a button in a feature bar, click the button you want, or hold down the Alt and Shift keys while you press the underlined letter in the button name. For example, you can select the Close button by clicking it or by pressing Alt+Shift+C.

The following buttons appear in every feature bar:

?   Click this button if you want to select a different feature bar or choose menu options instead of clicking buttons on the feature bar. Right-click this button if you want to select a different feature bar or get help.

Close   Choose this button when you're done using the feature bar and want to return to the normal document window.

Customizing the Bars

As you gain experience with WordPerfect, and discover which features you use the most, you can customize the various bars to give yourself quick access to those features. You can also create new menu bars or button bars of your own.

You can customize all bars except feature bars. Of course, the specific steps depend on which bar you're customizing. The best way to learn how to customize a bar is simply to try it. Here are the basic steps to follow to customize most bars:

1. Do one of the following to open the Preferences dialog box for the bar you want to customize:

   - Choose File ➤ Preferences, then double-click the icon for the bar you want to change.
   - Right-click the bar and choose Preferences.

2. Depending on which bar you chose, the Preferences dialog box that appears will include some (or most) of the command buttons described below:

   Create To create a new menu bar or button bar, choose Create, type in a name for the bar, select a template (if you wish), and choose OK. Continue with step 3. (You'll learn more about templates later in this chapter, and in Chapter 20.)

   Edit To change an existing menu bar or button bar, highlight the bar you want to change and choose Edit. Continue with step 3.

   Copy To copy a menu bar or button bar to another template, choose Copy. Choose the template to copy from, the bar(s) you want to copy, and the template to copy to. Then choose Copy.

   Delete To delete a menu bar or button bar, highlight the bar you want to delete, choose Delete, then choose Yes to confirm the deletion.

   Default To return the status bar or power bar to the default ("factory") settings, choose Default. This option is helpful if you've messed up the bar and want to restore its original arrangement.

   Fonts To customize the fonts and sizes offered on the Font Face and Font Size buttons of the power bar, choose Fonts. Then select (check) or deselect the fonts and sizes you want, or choose the Select button in the Power Bar Font/Size Lists dialog box to select or deselect many options at once. Choose OK.

Options   To customize the appearance of the button bar, power bar, or status bar, choose Options. Then select the options you want and choose OK.

3. Follow the screen prompts and customize the bar to your heart's content. Each time you make a change, WordPerfect will display the updated bar. If you need extra help, press the F1 key or choose the Help button.

4. When you're done customizing, choose OK or Close until you work your way back to the document window.

The Screen: Have It Your Way

There's almost no limit to the ways in which you can personalize your WordPerfect for Windows screen. The easiest way to find out what's available is to go to the Preferences dialog box and experiment with some of the options. Here's how to get started:

1. Choose File ➤ Preferences.

2. Double-click the first option, Display. You'll see the Display Preferences dialog box, shown in Figure 4.1.

3. In the top part of the dialog box, choose the part of the screen you want to customize: Document, Show ¶, View/Zoom, Reveal Codes, Ruler Bar, or Merge. The options shown in the dialog box will change to reflect your selection.

4. Select the display options you want. (If you're not sure what an option does, you can choose the Help button or press F1 to get information.

5. When you're finished making changes, choose OK or press ↵ then choose Close (if necessary).

FIGURE 4.1

The Display Preferences dialog box

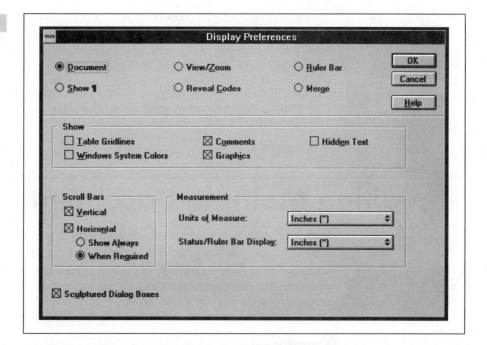

TIP

Here's a quicker way to do the first three steps listed above: Move the mouse pointer to the part of the screen you want to customize, right-click the mouse, then choose Preferences from the QuickMenu that appears.

Remember that if you make a change then decide you don't like it, you can just repeat the steps needed to get to the Preferences dialog box and "undo" any of your prior selections.

Zooming In and Out

You can zoom in for a closer look at any portion of your document or zoom out for an arm's-length view at any time. Here's how:

- Click the Zoom button in the power bar (shown at left) and drag the highlight down to select a magnification from the list.

- Double-click the Zoom button in the power bar or choose View ➤ Zoom to open the Zoom dialog box. Choose a preset magnification or specify a magnification (between 25% and 400%) in the Other text box. Choose OK or press ↵.

- To see the entire page, click the Page Zoom Full button in the power bar (shown at left). Click the Page Zoom Full button again to return to the previous magnification.

Editing Multiple Documents

WordPerfect 6 lets you edit up to nine documents at a time. This is particularly handy when you need to move and copy text across several documents. Each open document is placed in its own document window. You can size the document window to fill the entire editing portion of your screen, or only part of your screen.

NOTE

Most of the commands on the Window menu don't do much unless you have several documents open at once. You can use File ➤ Open to open existing documents and File ➤ New to create a new document in its own document window.

Managing Document Windows

Managing multiple windows in WordPerfect is the same as managing multiple windows in any other Windows application. Figure 4.2 illustrates the basic anatomy of a window. As you can see from the list below, you can do just about anything you want with a window.

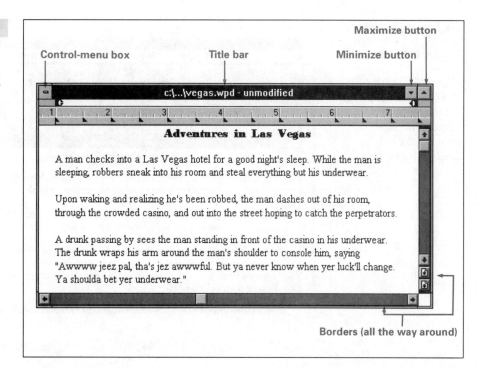

FIGURE 4.2

These tools let you size, move, and close the document window.

- **To arrange multiple document windows** in an overlapping format, where one window is on top and the titles of the other windows are visible, choose <u>W</u>indow ➤ <u>C</u>ascade (see Figure 4.3).

- **To arrange multiple document windows** in a tiled format, where the windows do not overlap, choose <u>W</u>indow ➤ <u>T</u>ile.

- **To expand** a window to its maximum size, click the window's Maximize button (▲) or double-click its title bar.

- **To restore** a window to its previous size after maximizing it, click the window's Restore button (the Restore button has a ▲ and a ▼ on it and appears in place of the Maximize button when the window is maximized).

- **To switch to** a specific document window, choose <u>W</u>indow and choose the window you want from the lower portion of the menu.

- **To switch to** the next document window, press Ctrl+F6.

- **To reduce** a window to an icon, click the window's Minimize button (▼).

Multiple documents, named BROCHURE.WPD, MYFIRST.WPD, and VEGAS.WPD, in a cascaded arrangement like stacked sheets of paper

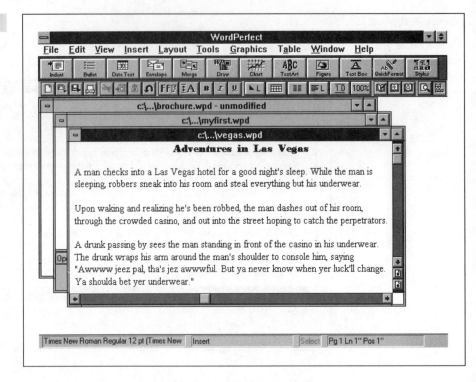

- **To open** a minimized window, double-click the window's icon or click the icon and choose <u>R</u>estore.

- **To close** a window, double-click its Control-menu box or switch to the window and press Ctrl+F4. If you've changed the document recently, you'll have a chance to save your work before the window closes. (Watch the screen for prompts about saving your changes!)

- **To move** a window, drag it by its title bar.

- **To bring a window to the front**, so that it's not covered by other windows, click its title bar.

- **To size** a window, drag its left, right, top, or bottom border. Drag the corners to size the window diagonally.

TIP The Control menu also includes options for managing a window. To open the Control menu, click it. Or switch to the appropriate window and press Alt+- (Alt+hyphen). Then choose the option you want.

The scroll bars along the right and bottom edges of the document window appear only if the Scroll Bars options are selected in the Display Preferences dialog box (File ➤ Preferences ➤ Display).

About the Active Window

Even though you can have several documents open at once, you can edit only one at a time. That is, the cursor can be in only one document at a time. The document that the cursor is in is called the *active window*.

You can tell at a glance which window on your screen is active by looking for the following clues:

- The active window is always on top of other open windows.

- The cursor appears only in the active window.

- The title bar of the active window is colored or shaded differently from the other windows.

Uncovering Hidden Windows

When you have lots of document windows open, the windows may stack up and cover one another. Don't worry about it. You can easily get them into shape using any of these techniques:

- If at least part of the window that you want to use is visible, click anywhere on that window to bring it to the top.

- Choose Window ➤ Cascade to stack all the open windows neatly. Choose Window ➤ Tile to display all the open windows at once.

- To switch to a different window, choose Window and click the name of the window or type its document window number. To switch to the next window, press Ctrl+F6.

Don't forget that all those open documents are in memory, not necessarily on disk. Therefore, you must be sure to save *all* your work when you exit WordPerfect (*before* you turn off your computer). When you choose File ➤ Exit (or press Alt+F4), WordPerfect will prompt you to save any unsaved work in each window.

Moving and Copying Text between Documents

It's easy to move and copy text from one open document to another. Just use the cut-and-paste technique described in Chapter 3. That is, select the text you want to move or copy and choose Edit ➤ Copy (Ctrl+C) or Edit ➤ Cut (Ctrl+X). Then, switch to the document you want to put the text into, move the cursor to the place where you want the text to appear, and choose Edit ➤ Paste (Ctrl+V).

Minimizing Window and File Confusion

Remember that each document window represents one file. To avoid confusion about how commands on the File menu relate to document windows, keep in mind the following points:

- File ➤ New (Ctrl+N) creates a new, empty document window (think of it as a clean sheet of paper). Other windows remain open but are behind this new window.

- File ➤ Open (Ctrl+O) opens a previously saved document in its own document window. This new window will probably cover other document windows.

- Insert ➤ File pulls a copy of a previously saved file into the *current* document window at the cursor position, combining the two documents into one.

- File ➤ Save (Ctrl+S) saves the document in the active window with its existing file name (if it has one) or a name you specify (if it isn't named yet).

- File ➤ Save As (F3) saves the document in the active window with a different file name.

- File ➤ Close (Ctrl+F4) saves and closes the active document window without closing other document windows or exiting WordPerfect.

- File ➤ Exit (Alt+F4) gives you a chance to save any changes in all open, modified document windows, then exits WordPerfect.

Viewing Several Parts of a Document at Once

Suppose you're working in a large document and you want to view page 5 and page 20 at the same time. Maybe you'd even like to move or copy text from one page to the other.

With WordPerfect for Windows you can easily open two or more copies of the same document at once. Just use File ➤ Open (up to nine times!) to open additional copies of the active document.

To prevent you from changing different copies of the same document accidentally, the title bar of some copies will show "(Read-Only)" next to the document name. To avoid confusion and to keep one copy of the document fully up to date, edit *only* the copy that *does not* show "(Read-Only)" in the title bar. (If you do edit a read-only copy then try to save those changes, WordPerfect will ask that you give this copy of the document a new name.)

Cut-and-Paste with Multiple Views of a Single Document

If you have two or more copies of a single document open, and you want to move or copy text within that document, first go to the window that displays "(Read-Only)" in the title bar (in other words, make the read-only copy the active document window). Select the text you want to move or copy, then choose Edit ➤ Cut (to move text) or Edit ➤ Copy (to copy text).

Next, switch to the original version of your document (the one that doesn't display "(Read-Only)" in the title bar). Scroll to the place where you want to put the text and choose Edit ➤ Paste. Works like a charm!

Just be careful to keep track of which copy of the document is in which window. Once again, to avoid confusion, always cut or copy *from* a read-only window *to* the original document window. That way you'll know which window contains the latest version of the document.

Saving Your Workspace

WordPerfect normally displays an empty document window when you fire up the program. If you like, you can have WordPerfect "remember" which files you were working on and how they were arranged on-screen when you last exited the program. Then, when you start WordPerfect again, those files will be reopened and arranged automatically. This is called "saving the workspace." Here's how to do it:

1. Choose File ➤ Preferences and double-click Environment.

2. Choose the option you want from the Save Workspace area near the lower-left corner of the dialog box. Your options are as follows:

   Always   Always save the current workspace when you exit WordPerfect.

   Never   Never save the workspace when you exit WordPerfect. (This is the default setting.)

   Prompt on Exit   Prompt for permission to save the workspace when you exit WordPerfect. The workspace is saved only if you answer Yes to the prompt.

3. Choose OK then Close.

WordPerfect will now use whichever workspace-saving method you chose in step 2.

Revealing the Hidden Codes

All the formatting features that you use in a WordPerfect document, including hard returns (when you press ↵), page breaks, and the many formatting features you'll learn about in future chapters, are controlled by *codes* within the document. These codes are hidden initially to make your document look normal as you type and make changes. If your screen were cluttered with a bunch of strange-looking codes, your work would be much more complicated.

However, you can use these hidden codes to your advantage, particularly when you get into WordPerfect's more advanced features. For this reason, WordPerfect lets you view the codes so that you can see what's going on behind the scenes.

Turning Reveal Codes On and Off

To display the hidden codes, you need to open the Reveal Codes window. Choose View ➤ Reveal Codes or press Alt+F3. Your document window will split into two sections. The upper part shows the regular text. The lower part shows the same text with the codes revealed.

Codes in the Reveal Codes window usually appear as gray buttons with black text. In this book, I'll show codes enclosed in square brackets, like this: [HRt]. Figure 4.4 illustrates several codes, including [Open Style: InitialStyle], [Hd Center on Marg], [Font:…], and [HRt] codes. We'll talk about the purpose of each of the various codes as we go along in this book.

In Reveal Codes, the cursor appears as a small solid box. The cursor is in exactly the same position in the Reveal Codes window and in the upper portion of the document window. In Figure 4.1, the cursor is positioned right after the [Open Style: InitialStyle] code at the top of the document (a code you'll learn to change in Chapter 19).

When you're done using the Reveal Codes window, you can close it. Choose View ➤ Reveal Codes or press Alt+F3 (the same thing you do to open it). Or, right-click in the Reveal Codes window and choose Hide Reveal Codes.

Practical Uses of Hidden Codes

Every code plays some role in WordPerfect. For example, a hard-return code, [HRt], tells WordPerfect to end the current line and start a new line. In the normal text portion of the screen (the upper portion of the split window), you see only the short line of text; but in the Reveal Codes window you actually see the [HRt] code. If you were to move the cursor just

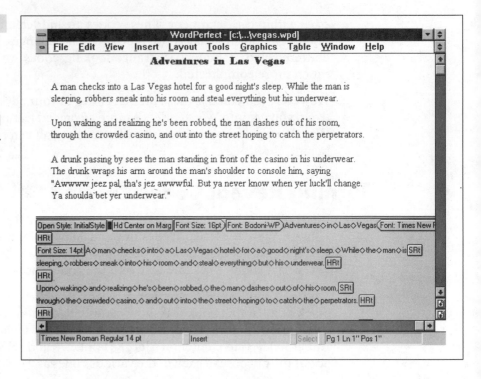

to the left of that hidden code and press Delete, the [HRt] code would disappear, and the line would be joined to the line below it in the regular text window.

It's possible to edit and format a document without *ever* looking at hidden codes. However, as you start doing more refined work, you'll probably find Reveal Codes to be an indispensable aid in formatting and troubleshooting your documents. Future chapters provide more specific information, but for now I'll give you some general guidelines for using Reveal Codes effectively.

About Single Codes

Most features in WordPerfect are controlled by a single code, such as [HRt] or [SRt] (hard return and soft return). In addition, there are dozens of single codes that affect *formatting*, for example, line spacing and justification (Chapter 5).

Single formatting codes affect text from the cursor position to the end of your document, or until you change the formatting feature again. For example, if you change the line spacing from 1 to 2 in the middle of your document, WordPerfect will insert a [Ln Spacing:2.0] code at the cursor position. That new line spacing will be effective to the end of the document, unless WordPerfect encounters a different line spacing code later.

NOTE   Certain codes appear in a shortened form in Reveal Codes. For example, the line spacing code initially appears as [Ln Spacing]. The code will expand fully (for example, to [Ln Spacing:2.0]) when you click on it or move the cursor just to the left of the code in Reveal Codes. To display expanded codes at all times, select (check) the Show Codes In Detail option in the Display Preferences dialog box (which is described later in the chapter).

Suppose you want to change the line spacing in a chunk of text, not in the entire document. You *could* set the line spacing at the beginning of the passage, then reset it to another value at the end of the passage. But here's an easier way:

1. Select (block) the text you want to format.

2. Set the formatting feature you want. (For example, choose Layout ➤ Line ➤ Line Spacing, type **2**, and choose OK.)

Assuming that your document started out single-spaced, and you double-spaced the selected text, WordPerfect would insert two codes in your document—one at the beginning of the block and one at the end of the block—something like this:

[Ln Spacing:2.0]double-spaced text would be here…**[HRt]**
[Ln Spacing:1.0]single-spaced text would be here…

The first code says "start this formatting feature here." The second code says "return to the original formatting here."

Paired Codes

Some formatting features, such as boldface and italics, are controlled by *paired codes*. For example, suppose you boldface a block of text (Chapter 6), so that the text appears in boldface on the normal (upper) screen. On the Reveal Codes (lower) screen, the hidden codes that cause the text to appear boldfaced would look like this:

[Bold]This text is boldfaced**[Bold]**, and this is not.

Here WordPerfect is using paired codes to activate and deactivate a specific feature, boldface type. In paired codes, the starting code turns the feature on. The ending code turns the feature off. When you print or view the sentence shown above, it appears partly boldface, partly normal, like this:

This text is boldfaced, and this is not.

About Hard and Soft Codes

In most cases, codes are inserted in a document when you press some key (such as ↵) or choose a formatting feature (such as boldface). In other cases, codes are inserted automatically, behind the scenes. For example, when you're typing a paragraph and you type past the right margin, Word-Perfect inserts a soft-return code ([SRt]) at the end of the upper line. This code tells WordPerfect and your printer to end the line there and resume text on the next line.

In general, codes that you insert yourself are called *hard codes*, and codes that WordPerfect inserts for you are called *soft codes*. (The distinction between hard and soft codes varies slightly, but this definition is sufficient for our purposes right now.)

NOTE You can't delete soft codes that WordPerfect puts in automatically, such as soft return codes ([SRt]).

Positioning the Cursor in Reveal Codes

When Reveal Codes is on, you can use the mouse and cursor-movement keys to move the cursor about in either the upper or lower window. It's generally easiest to use the upper (normal) text window to get the cursor into the right ballpark. Then you can zero in on a particular code on the lower screen using the arrow keys or mouse.

You can also use the Find feature to locate a specific code in Reveal Codes (see Chapter 9).

You can delete, move, or insert codes in the Reveal Codes window using the same techniques that you use with regular text. WordPerfect also offers some special shortcuts for working with codes. In the next few sections, I'll describe the general techniques for editing codes.

What Do the Hidden Codes Mean?

It's by no means necessary to memorize, or even understand, the role of every code in order to use WordPerfect successfully. In most cases, you can guess what a code does simply by looking at its name in the Reveal Codes window. If you're ever curious about the meaning of a code, simply move the mouse pointer to the code, then look to the title bar near the top of the screen for a brief explanation of the code.

If the title bar doesn't show the description of the code that the mouse pointer is currently on, select Show Help Prompts for Codes in the Display Preferences dialog box, as discussed under "Customizing the Reveal Codes Window," later in this chapter.

Deleting Codes

If you're having a problem with the format of your document, you can sometimes fix the problem simply by removing the code that's activating a feature you no longer want to use. Deleting a code is the same as deleting any other character on the screen:

1. If you haven't already done so, turn on Reveal Codes (Alt+F3).

2. Move the cursor just to the left of the code you want to delete in the Reveal Codes window, or click on the code, and press Delete. Or, move the cursor just to the right of the problem code and press Backspace.

Here's an even easier way to delete a code whenever the Reveal Codes window is open: Move the mouse pointer to the code you want to delete, drag the code anywhere outside of the Reveal Codes window, and release the mouse button. What could be easier?

Of course, you might delete a code by accident. No big deal. Typically you can just use Edit ➤ Undo (Ctrl+Z) to undo the change.

Deleting one code in a paired-code set, such as [Bold]…[Bold], automatically deletes the other code. To undo a paired-code deletion, you must use Edit ➤ Undo or Ctrl+Z (not Edit ➤ Undelete).

Deleting Codes without Reveal Codes

When Reveal Codes is turned off, you can still delete many codes using the standard text-deletion techniques. For example, if you move the cursor to a blank line and press Delete, WordPerfect will delete the hard-return code ([HRt]) that's causing the blank line. Similarly, if you select a section of text and then delete it, any codes that were in that selected text will also be deleted, whether or not Reveal Codes is on.

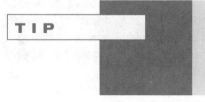

TIP

If you want to delete all instances of a particular code in a document (for example, delete all the codes for boldface), you can use the Replace feature, which is discussed in Chapter 9.

On the other hand, there are certain codes that WordPerfect won't delete when Reveal Codes is off. For example, if you're deleting individual characters with the Del or Backspace key and you get to boldfaced text, WordPerfect won't delete the [Bold] code. It's as though WordPerfect thinks, "Since you can't see the hidden codes right now, I'll assume you want to delete the text, not the codes." But when Reveal Codes is on, WordPerfect seems to think, "Since you *can* see the codes now, and you pressed Delete or Backspace while a code was highlighted, I'll assume you want to delete that code."

Deleting Codes the Old Way

The fact that WordPerfect won't delete certain codes when Reveal Codes is turned off is something you can change. In older versions of WordPerfect, the program would ask for permission before deleting a code with Reveal Codes turned off. If you'd like WordPerfect to behave this way, follow the steps below:

1. Choose File ➤ Preferences and double-click Environment.

2. Select (check) Confirm Deletion Of Codes, Stop Insertion Point At Hidden Codes.

3. Choose OK or press ↵, then choose Close.

Once you've completed these steps, if the cursor happens to be on a code when you press Backspace or Delete, a dialog box will ask if you want to delete the code. Choose Yes to delete the code. Otherwise, choose No and the code will be retained. Remember, the dialog box will appear only if Reveal Codes is turned off. When Reveal Codes is on, WordPerfect assumes that you want to delete the code.

Moving and Copying Codes

When you move or copy selected text that contains codes, the codes within the selection are moved or copied along with the text. Rarely will you need to move or copy a single code or set of codes.

But then again, there's always that once-in-a-while situation where it would be really handy just to move or copy a group of existing codes, rather than going through all the menu commands to put them into the document from scratch. This is especially true for pictures, lines, and other graphic elements that are stored as codes in your document (you'll learn about these later on). The next few sections explain how to move and copy codes.

Moving a Single Code

The easiest way to move a single (unpaired) code is to delete it, then undelete it in some new place:

1. If you haven't done so yet, activate Reveal Codes (Alt+F3).

2. Click on the code, or move the cursor just to the left of the code you want to move.

3. Press Delete to delete the code.

4. Move the cursor to the new location for the code.

5. Choose Edit ➤ Undelete (or press Ctrl+Shift+Z).

6. Choose Restore. The code is inserted at the new cursor position.

You cannot move or copy only one code in a set of paired codes.

Moving or Copying Several Codes

To move or copy several single codes, or paired codes and the text they enclose, proceed as follows:

1. If you haven't done so, turn on Reveal Codes.

2. Click on the code, or move the cursor just to the left of the first code that you want to move or copy.

3. Press F8 or double-click "Select" in the status bar, then use the arrow keys to extend the selection so that all the codes you want to move or copy are highlighted. Be sure to move the cursor one character or code *past* the last code that you want to include in the selection.

4. If you want to move the codes, choose Edit ➤ Cut (Ctrl+X). To copy the codes, choose Edit ➤ Copy (Ctrl+C).

5. Move the cursor to the new position for the codes and choose Edit ➤ Paste (Ctrl+V).

The text and codes will appear in the new location.

Here are some points to keep in mind:

- The paragraph may reformat immediately after you paste the codes, so don't be surprised if text moves right away. WordPerfect might also rearrange the codes after you paste them in.

- It's impossible to move or copy only one code of a paired code or move a pair of codes without the text that's between them. You'll have to insert or delete text between the codes, or just delete the codes and start over.

- It takes a little time to master the art of juggling text and codes. Be patient and give yourself time.

The Case of the Slippery Code

Some codes are specifically designed to format an entire page. Others format just a paragraph or line. If you don't place these codes at the beginning of the appropriate page or paragraph, WordPerfect will automatically move the code to the spot that's "most likely" to be correct. For example, it might shoot the code over to the start of a paragraph, or even to the top of a page. In addition, WordPerfect reduces "code clutter" by deleting any nearby codes that would compete with and cancel out the new one.

For example, let's say there's a [Ln Spacing:2.0] code for double-spacing at the start of a paragraph. You move the cursor anywhere in that paragraph, change the line spacing to 3, and guess what happens? You've got it! WordPerfect not only puts the [Ln Spacing:3.0] code at its (most likely) proper position—the start of the paragraph—it also *deletes* the old [Ln Spacing:2.0] code from the beginning of the paragraph.

NOTE If you've used an older version of WordPerfect, you may recognize this as the "Auto Code Placement" feature. In WordPerfect version 5.x, you could turn Auto Code Placement on or off. In WordPerfect 6, this feature is always on.

This "slippery code" feature affects only those codes that apply specifically to paragraphs and pages. If you want a simple rule of thumb to follow, remember these points:

- Layout ➤ Line and Layout ➤ Paragraph codes generally move to the start of the paragraph.
- Layout ➤ Page codes move to the top of the page.

Presto Change Code!

One of WordPerfect's best new features is its ability to change a code simply by double-clicking it. For example, double-clicking a [Ln Spacing] code in the Reveal Codes window instantly opens the Line Spacing dialog box, where you can change the Line Spacing on the spot. Not too shabby!

Customizing the Reveal Codes Window

As with so many of WordPerfect's features, the Reveal Codes window is easy to customize. Just follow the steps below:

1. Right-click in the Reveal Codes window and choose Preferences. Or, choose File ➤ Preferences and double-click Display, then choose Reveal Codes. Figure 4.5 shows the Display Preferences dialog box that appears.

2. Choose the options you want from the dialog box. For information on what each option is for, simply press F1 or click the Help button in the dialog box, or press Shift+F1 and click on the option you're curious about.

3. When you're finished selecting options, choose OK or press ↵.

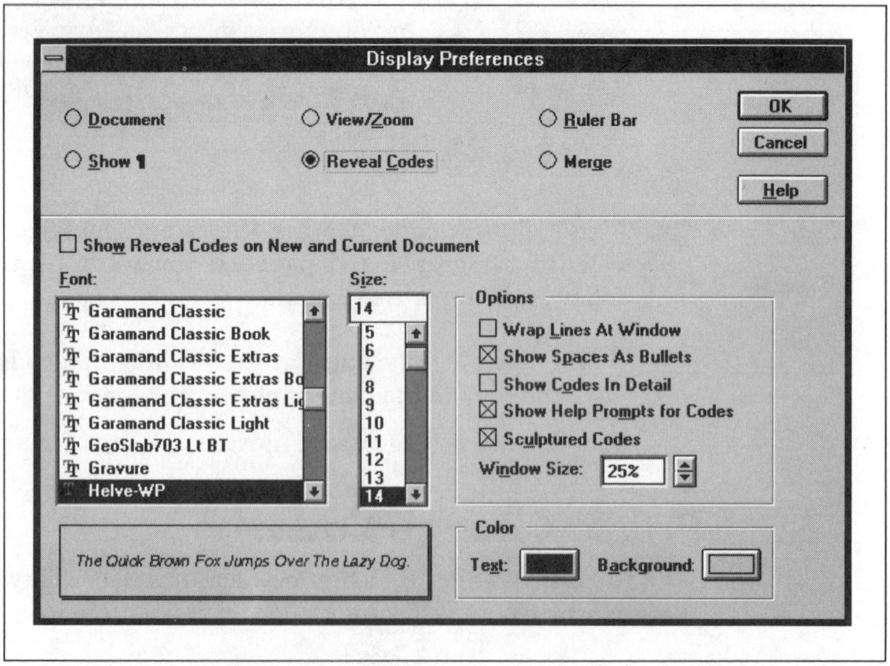

FIGURE 4.5

The Display Preferences dialog box for Reveal Codes lets you customize the Reveal Codes window.

TIP

Reveal Codes will be much easier to use if you select (check) the options Wrap Lines At Window, Show Spaces As Bullets, Show Help Prompts For Codes, and Sculptured Codes in the Display Preferences dialog box.

Notice that the Display Preferences dialog box in Figure 4.5 allows you to define the default size for the Reveal Codes window. You can temporarily adjust the size of the Reveal Codes window without going into the Display Preferences dialog box. To do this, move the mouse pointer to the divider at the top of the Reveal Codes window (the pointer will change to a two-headed vertical arrow). Drag the divider up to make the Reveal Codes window larger, or down to make it smaller, then release the mouse button.

Using Document Comments

As you're working in a document, you may want to use *document comments* to add reminder notes to yourself. If you work in a group, you might want to write comments to the editor, writer, or other group members.

 Document comments and text will appear in a shaded box in Draft view. In Page or Two-Page view, comments are marked with an icon in the left margin (shown at left). To view the comment text, simply click the icon. To hide the comment, click the icon a second time.

Figure 4.6 shows an example in Page mode after I clicked the comment icon in the left margin. Document comments never appear on the printed copy of the document, so you can always review a clean copy of the text without being distracted by the comments.

To add a comment to a document, follow the steps below:

1. Move the cursor to a section of text near where you want the comment to appear. Then do one of the following:

   • Choose Insert ➤ Comment ➤ Create.

To display the document comment, I clicked the comment icon in the left margin. In Reveal Codes, only the [Comment] code appears.

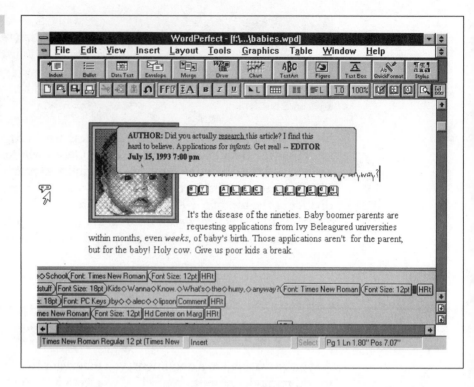

- Move the mouse pointer to the far-left margin (the pointer will change to an arrow shape), then right-click and choose Comment from the QuickMenu.

An empty comment-editing window will open, and the Comment feature bar will appear at the top of the window. (A sample Comment feature bar appeared earlier in this chapter, in the section titled "Using the Feature Bar.")

2. Type your comment, using the standard editing keys to make changes and corrections. Keep the comment short—half a page or so at most. Here are some other things you can do while typing comments:

   - Use many of the formatting features described in this book.
   - Click the Initials or Name button in the feature bar to insert the user Initials or Name at the cursor position (see "Customizing Document Comments," below).

- Click the Date or Time button in the feature bar to insert the system date or time at the cursor position.
- Click the Next or Previous button in the feature bar to edit the next or previous comment (if any) in the document.

3. Click the Close button in the feature bar (or press Alt+Shift+C or Ctrl+F4) when you've finished typing the comment.

A comment box or icon will appear in your document. (If it doesn't, see "Hiding and Displaying Document Comments," later in this chapter.) In Page or Two-Page view, you'll need to click the comment icon in the left margin to see the comment text.

Changing a Document Comment

Changing the text within a document comment is easy:

1. To open the comment-editing window, use any of these methods:

- Move the cursor to just below the comment you want to change. If you want, you can use Find (F2) to locate the [Comment] code (see Chapter 9). Then choose Insert ➤ Comment ➤ Edit.
- Double-click the comment icon or comment box in the document window.
- Point to the comment icon or box with your mouse, right-click, and choose Edit from the QuickMenu.
- Double-click the [Comment] code in the Reveal Codes window.

2. Make whatever changes you wish, then click the Close button in the feature bar or press Alt+Shift+C.

Moving, Copying, and Deleting a Comment

Each document comment you create is placed in a hidden [Comment] code at the cursor position. To move, copy, or delete a [Comment] code (and the comment itself), use the techniques described in the Reveal Codes section earlier in this chapter.

You can delete all the comments in a document in one step by using the Replace feature to replace all the [Comment] codes with "nothing" (see Chapter 9).

Converting Text to a Comment

You can convert any text in a document to a comment. This might come in handy if, say, you can't decide whether or not to leave a particular passage in text, but you don't want to delete it altogether. Just follow these steps:

1. Select the text that you want to convert to a comment.

2. Choose Insert ➤ Comment ➤ Create. Or, move the mouse pointer to the far-left margin (the pointer changes to an arrow), then right-click and choose Comment from the QuickMenu.

The selected text is removed from the regular text and converted to a comment.

Converting a Comment to Text

If you want to convert a comment to normal text within the document, follow these steps:

1. Move the cursor just below the comment you want to convert to text.

2. Choose Insert ➤ Comment ➤ Convert To Text.

The text within the comment is converted to normal text, and the [Comment] code is removed. If necessary, you can add spaces or hard returns (press ↵) to blend the text with existing text.

Hiding and Displaying Document Comments

If you want to hide document comments on the screen so that you can focus on the regular text, follow these steps:

1. Choose File ➤ Preferences and double-click Display, or right-click one of the scroll bars in the document window and choose Preferences from the QuickMenu.

2. Deselect Comments in the Display Preferences dialog box, then choose OK (and Close if necessary).

To take the comments back out of hiding, repeat step 1 above, select (check) Comments, then choose OK (and Close).

TIP

WordPerfect also lets you create hidden text, which you can either show or hide (Layout ➤ Font ➤ Hidden). If the hidden text is showing, you can print it. (See Chapter 6.)

Customizing Document Comments

In documents that contain comments from several different people, it's nice to know, with one quick glance, whom the comment is from. (That way you can decide whether to bother reading it.) WordPerfect's User Information feature (User Info For Comments And Summary) lets you define the initials that appear in a comment icon, the color of the comment icon or box, and the text that WordPerfect inserts when you click the Initials and Name buttons in the Comment feature bar. Here's how to customize the User Information:

1. Choose File ➤ Preferences and double-click Environment.

2. In the User Information area of the Environment Preferences dialog box, do any of the following:

   • Choose Name, then type the name you want WordPerfect to insert when you click the Name button in the Comment feature bar.

   • Choose Initials, then type the initials you want to appear in the comment icon and when you click the Initials button.

   • Click the button next to User Color, then click the color you want to use as the background for new comments.

3. Choose OK or press ↵, then choose Close.

Your changes will affect new comments that you create (existing comments will be unaffected).

The Dating Game

A simple, though handy, feature of WordPerfect is its ability to *date-stamp* a document. You can include two types of date stamps in your document:

Date Text   Types the current date (the date never changes).

Date Code   Places a [Date] code that appears as the current system date (the date automatically changes when the system date changes).

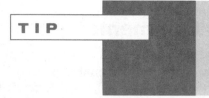

TIP

The *system date* is determined by your computer's system clock. If necessary, you can correct the date and time using the Date/Time option in the Windows Control Panel (see your Windows manual).

You might want to use Date Text when typing a letter, since you probably won't want the date in the letter to change. On the other hand, you might prefer to insert the Date Code in a page header or footer in your document (see Chapter 8). That way, when you print the document, the top or bottom of each page will show when that copy was printed.

Inserting the Date

Follow these steps to use WordPerfect's shortcut for typing a date:

1. Move the cursor to wherever you want the date to appear.

2. Do one of the following, depending on which type of date you want to insert:

   - To insert the date text, choose Insert ➤ Date ➤ Date Text, or press Ctrl+D, or click the Date Text button on the WordPerfect button bar.

   - To insert the date code, choose Insert ➤ Date ➤ Date Code or press Ctrl+Shift+D.

The date will appear at the cursor position.

Changing the Date Format

If you want to display the date in a format other than the one WordPerfect uses, follow these steps:

1. Move the cursor to where the new date format should take effect. Usually, this will be the start of the document (in which case, just press Ctrl+Home).

2. Choose Insert ➤ Date ➤ Date Format.

3. Choose the format you want (or the one that most closely matches the format you want) from the options shown below:

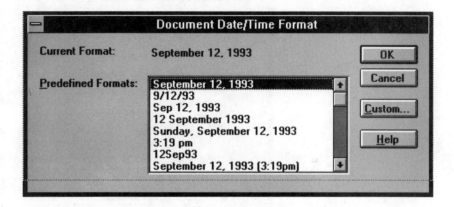

4. If you want to customize the format to suit your needs, choose Custom and then use the Custom Document Date/Time Format dialog box to make changes. (If you need help with this, just click the Help button or press F1.)

5. Choose OK to return to the document.

Only dates that you put into the document *after* changing the format and *past* the hidden [Date Fmt] code will appear in the new format. Use Reveal Codes, if necessary, to locate the [Date Fmt] code and to delete (or move) any previous [Date] codes. For best results, just put the [Date Fmt] code at the top of the document.

Instant Document Statistics

Do you want some quick statistics on your document, such as the number of words, lines, or sentences? That's easy:

1. Choose File ➤ Document Info. You'll get a complete run-down of characters, words, and so forth in the current document, as in the example shown below:

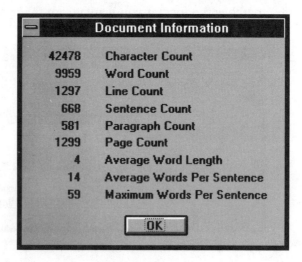

	Document Information
42478	Character Count
9959	Word Count
1297	Line Count
668	Sentence Count
581	Paragraph Count
1299	Page Count
4	Average Word Length
14	Average Words Per Sentence
59	Maximum Words Per Sentence

OK

2. After reviewing the information, choose OK or press ↵ to return to your document.

Using Document Templates

Every time you create a new document, you're actually using a *template* to set up all the format and screen settings for the document. Templates make it easy to establish a consistent look for your document and consistent behavior for WordPerfect. You can use any of WordPerfect's built-in templates or create templates of your own.

N O T E   If you don't choose a template, you'll get the *standard* WordPerfect template, which sets up a blank document window. In general, I'll assume that you're using the standard template for your documents.

Choosing a Template

To choose a template, follow these steps:

1. Choose File ➤ Template or press Ctrl+T to open the Templates dialog box shown below:

2. If you'd like to preview a template before selecting it, choose View to open the Viewer window.

3. Highlight or click on the template you want. If a description has been defined for the template, it will appear in the Description box. If you've opened the Viewer window, it will show a sample of the highlighted template.

4. When you've highlighted the template you want, choose OK or press ↵.

5. WordPerfect may display a message about personalizing your templates. Choose OK to clear the message, then fill in the Enter Your Personal Information dialog box that appears next. When you're done filling in the information, choose OK.

TIP   If you know which template you want, you can select it quickly by pressing Ctrl+T and double-clicking the appropriate template name.

A new document window will open. It will include any text, formatting settings, menus, button bars, macros, and other elements that were defined for the template.

Creating Your Own Templates

WordPerfect comes with many handy templates, which you can customize if you wish. You can also create, edit, and delete templates of your own (using the Options button in the Templates dialog box). Please see Chapter 20 for more information on this topic.

In this chapter we've looked at some handy general-purpose tools that can make your time at the keyboard easier and more productive. Next, we'll look at ways to control spacing, alignment, and indenting in your documents.

PART TWO

... and the Start of Everything Else

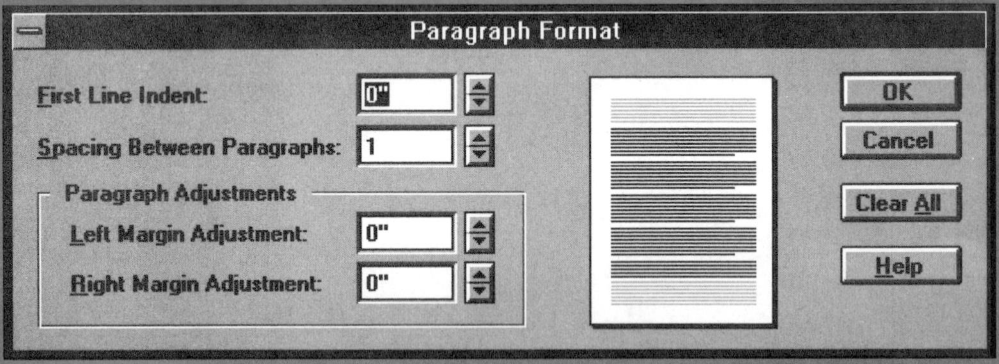

Paragraph Format
First Line Indent:
0"
Spacing Between Paragraphs:
1
Paragraph Adjustments
Left Margin Adjustment:
0"
Right Margin Adjustment:
0"
OK
Cancel
Clear All
Help

CHAPTER

5

Spacing, Aligning, and Indenting Text

fast TRACK

To change the tab stops   **160**

> position the cursor or select a block of text. Turn on the ruler bar, and use click, right-click, and drag techniques to set the tabs. Alternatively, you can set tabs by choosing options from the Tab Set dialog box (Layout ➤ Line ➤ Tab Set).

To insert hard tabs or hard tabs with dot leaders, without changing the tab stops   **173**

> choose Layout ➤ Line ➤ Other Codes, select the hard tab option you want and choose Insert. Use this method instead of pressing Tab before typing the text or number you want to align.

To create flush-right or centered dot leaders without changing the tab stops   **178**

> press Alt+F7 twice where you want the flush-right dot leaders to start. Or, press Shift+F7 twice to insert dot leaders in front of centered text.

To "quick-format" other text with the same fonts or paragraph styles used at the cursor position   **180**

> place the cursor in text that has the font or paragraph style you want to copy. Choose Layout ➤ QuickFormat, select the formatting option you want, and choose OK. Use your mouse to highlight the text you want to quick-format, then release the mouse button to reformat the text. When you're done with QuickFormat, choose Layout ➤ QuickFormat again.

TYPING and writing usually involve more than just short lines and paragraphs. You also need to space, justify, indent, and align text. As you'll discover in this chapter, WordPerfect offers more flexibility for these tasks than even the most sophisticated typewriter. Here's just one small example: On a typewriter, you must set your tab stops before you start to type. But with WordPerfect, you can change the tab stops *after* you've typed your text, and your text will adjust instantly to the new settings. And that's just the beginning!

Getting Started

All the formatting features discussed in this chapter insert hidden codes into your document. For most features, you can do either of the following:

- Position the cursor at a specific place in your document, and then choose a formatting option. Your changes will affect existing text beyond the cursor or new text that you type past the cursor.

- Or, select the text that you want to format, and then choose a formatting option. Your changes will affect only the selected text.

When you choose a formatting option, WordPerfect automatically inserts the appropriate hidden codes into your document. In most cases, the code will be placed exactly at the cursor position. But in other cases, the code will automatically be moved to the beginning of the page, or the beginning of the paragraph (if that placement makes the most sense). If you want to watch WordPerfect place codes in the document, just turn on Reveal Codes (press Alt+F3, as discussed in Chapter 4).

As you work with the formatting features described in this chapter, keep these additional points in mind:

- Double-clicking a formatting code in the Reveal Codes window often takes you directly to a dialog box where you can change the settings for that code.

- The ruler bar and your mouse offer the easiest way to change margins, tab stops, and other settings that indent text in paragraphs. To display the ruler bar, choose View ➤ Ruler Bar or press Alt+Shift+F3. Or, choose Set Tabs from the pull-down menu on the Tab Set button in the power bar (shown at left).

- If you make a mistake and discover it immediately, choose Edit ➤ Undo or press Ctrl+Z to undo the change.

- The *Layout* button bar offers push-button shortcuts for the tab setting, indenting, and text justification features discussed in this chapter. The *WordPerfect* button bar includes buttons for indent, the Bullets & Numbers feature, and QuickFormat. (See Chapter 4 and Figure 5.6.)

Changing Line Spacing

Suppose you've typed a single-spaced document, only to discover that you should have double-spaced it. That's no problem. Simply follow the steps below to change the line spacing to any measurement you wish:

1. Move the cursor to the paragraph or line where you want to change the line spacing (or where you're about to type new text). Or, select the text that should have the new line spacing.

2. Choose Layout ➤ Line ➤ Spacing.

3. Type the new line spacing amount. You can enter whole numbers or fractions (up to two decimal places).

4. Choose OK or press ⏎.

As an alternative to steps 2–4 above, you can choose a line spacing option from the Line Spacing button in the power bar. Figure 5.1 illustrates four types of line spacing.

FIGURE 5.1

Text set with single (1), double (2), one-and-a-quarter (1.25), and one-and-a-half (1.5) line spacing

Single spacing

This paragraph uses the default single spacing. To change the line spacing, position the cursor wherever you want to change the spacing (either before or after typing the text), or select text. Choose Layout ▸ Line ▸ Spacing. Then type a number and press ↵. You can also change line spacing by double-clicking an existing [Ln Spacing:...] code in Reveal Codes.

Double spacing

This paragraph uses double spacing (2). To select double spacing, position the

cursor wherever you want to start double spacing (either before or after typing

the text), or select text. Choose Layout ▸ Line ▸ Spacing, type **2** and press ↵.

One-and-a-quarter spacing

You can enter fractions when you define the line spacing. For example, this text uses one-and-a-quarter (1.25) spacing. WordPerfect lets you set the line spacing to just about any number — you're not at all limited to 1, 1.5, and 2.

One-and-a-half spacing

In this example, the text uses one-and-a-half (1.5) spacing. As you can see, WordPerfect line spacing can be as flexible (and varied) as you want it to be.

NOTE

If your printer prints at double the space you've requested, chances are the Auto LineFeed or Auto LF setting on your printer is turned on. Consult your printer manual to learn how to turn this switch off.

Adjusting the Space between Paragraphs

Many people like to type text so that a blank line appears between paragraphs. One way to accomplish this is to press ⏎ twice after each paragraph. If you want more control over how much space WordPerfect puts between each paragraph, follow these steps:

1. Move the cursor to where you want the spacing changes to begin, or select the paragraphs you want to adjust.

2. Choose Layout ➤ Paragraph ➤ Format ➤ Spacing Between Paragraphs.

3. Type the number of lines that should appear between paragraphs. For example, type **2** to place a blank line between paragraphs. Type **2.5** to add a blank line plus half a line between paragraphs.

4. Choose OK or press ⏎.

Changing the Margins

WordPerfect places a default 1-inch margin around every printed page of your document. This is illustrated in Figure 5.2. However, you can change the margins at any time, either before or after typing the document.

TIP

You don't need to change the margins to indent a block of text. You can use the Indent feature instead, as discussed later in this chapter.

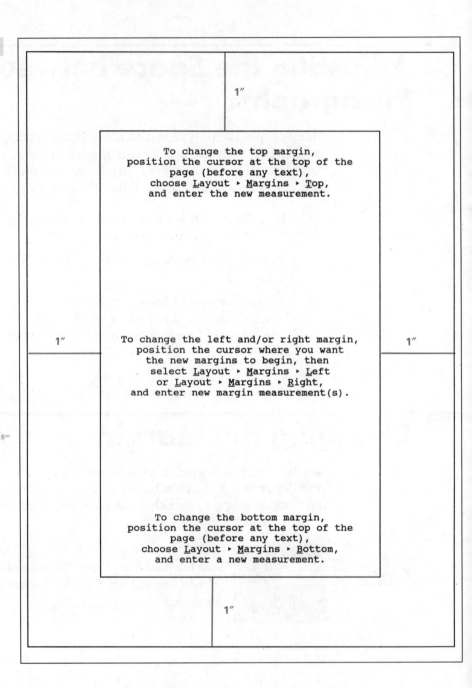

1″

1″   1″

To change the top margin,
position the cursor at the top of the
page (before any text),
choose Layout ▸ Margins ▸ Top,
and enter the new measurement.

To change the left and/or right margin,
position the cursor where you want
the new margins to begin, then
select Layout ▸ Margins ▸ Left
or Layout ▸ Margins ▸ Right,
and enter new margin measurement(s).

To change the bottom margin,
position the cursor at the top of the
page (before any text),
choose Layout ▸ Margins ▸ Bottom,
and enter a new measurement.

1″

Using the Margins Dialog Box

To change the margins in a document, follow these steps:

1. Position the cursor where you want the new margins to start (press Ctrl+Home to change margins for the entire document). Or, select a block of text to change margins in that block only.

2. Select Layout ➤ Margins (or press Ctrl+F8). Or, right-click near the top or middle of the ruler bar and choose Margins. Or, click the Margins button in the Layout button bar.

3. Select the margin you want to change (Left, Right, Top, or Bottom).

4. Type a measurement for the margin, such as **2** for 2 inches or **1.5** for $1\frac{1}{2}$ inches. You can specify up to two decimal places (for example, 1.25, 2.75).

5. Repeat steps 3 and 4 until you've changed all the settings you want.

6. Choose OK or press ↵.

WordPerfect will automatically reformat all text below the cursor (or the text you selected) to fit in the new margins. You may want to click the Page Zoom Full button in the power bar to quickly verify your new settings.

Setting Margins with the Ruler Bar

The ruler bar provides an even easier way to change the left and right margins. Here's how to use it:

1. Turn on the ruler bar if you haven't already done so (Alt+Shift+F3).

2. Position the cursor where you want the new margins to take effect, or select a block of text that you want to reformat with new margins.

3. Use your mouse to drag the left or right margin marker in the ruler bar to a new position. The left and right margin markers look like this:

4. Release the mouse button when the marker is positioned properly.

The tips below will help you set perfect margins every time:

- As you drag, the exact position of the marker will appear at the right edge of the status bar; a broken vertical line (called a *ruler guide*) will show where the marker is with respect to the text in your document.

- While you're dragging the marker, you can return it to its original position. Drag the mouse pointer up to the top of the document window (until the ruler guide disappears), then release the mouse button. The margin for the marker you were dragging will remain unchanged.

Minimum Margin Widths

Laser printers and other printers that feed paper from a tray do so with small wheels that pull the paper by its edges through the printer. The outer edges of the page are called the "dead zone" because the printer cannot print there. If text were printed within the dead zone, the small wheels would probably smudge the printed text.

You can't set the margins to a value that falls within the dead zone. For example, if you try to set the margins to 0″, WordPerfect will automatically increase your margin measurement to compensate for the dead zone. Typically the minimum value falls between 0.20 and 0.30 inches.

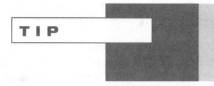

T I P

If you have problems printing text within the margins, the paper may simply be misaligned in your printer. See Chapter 10 for some tips.

Justifying Text

WordPerfect offers five ways to align (or *justify*) text. These are Left, Full, Center, Right, and All. Figure 5.3 illustrates and describes each type of justification.

Justifying text is a lot easier than justifying your expense account. Here's how to do it:

1. Position the cursor where you want the justification to take effect, or select the block of text you want to justify.

2. Choose <u>L</u>ayout ➤ <u>J</u>ustification. You'll see a menu of justification options and their shortcut keys.

3. Select a justification style (<u>L</u>eft, C<u>e</u>nter, <u>R</u>ight, <u>F</u>ull, or <u>A</u>ll).

You can also choose a justification by clicking appropriate buttons in the Layout button bar.

N O T E

WordPerfect can also center text vertically between the top and bottom margins. You'll learn about this type of centering in Chapter 8.

If you change your mind and want to use another kind of justification, you can do any of the following:

- Open Reveal Codes (Alt+F3) and delete the [Just] code that you inserted.

Full Justification (Ctrl+J)
With full justification, both the left and right margins are smooth. Full justification is one of the hallmarks of documents created with a word processor instead of a typewriter. To smooth out the the left and right margins, WordPerfect must add space between words and letters. This can make the text look "gappy," and even produce rivers of white space running down the page in large documents.

A l l   J u s t i f i c a t i o n
All justification is a lot like full justification, where both the left and right margins are smooth. However, unlike plain old full justification, the <u>all</u> flavor tries to spread out short lines as well. This can look very strange, but there must be some good
r e a s o n   t o   u s e   i t .

Left Justification (Ctrl+L)
Left justification produces a ragged-right margin, as in this example. This method creates a more personalized "hand-typed" look. Because left justification doesn't add extra spaces just to make text reach the right margin, words and letters appear without extra gaps, and rivers of white space are never a problem. Many people prefer left-justified documents because they tend to be easier on the eyes.

Center Justification (Ctrl+E)

Self-Centered Text in a Cockeyed World
by
Ann E. Buddee

August 18, 1994

Right Justification (Ctrl+R)

Rightly Justified, Inc.
1234 Walla Walla Lane
P.O. Box 1234
Cucamonga, CA 91234

- Change the newly added justification to another kind of justification.

- Switch to another kind of justification later in your document.

Centering or Right-Justifying a Line

Here's a quick way to center or right-align a single short line of text:

1. Position the cursor where you're about to type the short line or at the start of the line if you've already typed it.

2. Do one of the following:

   - To **center** the line, right-click the mouse in the document window and choose Center, or press Shift+F7.

   - To **right-justify** the line, right-click the mouse in the document window and choose Flush Right, or press Alt+F7.

3. If you haven't done so yet, type the short line of text and press ↵. If you've already typed a short line, press the End key, then press ↓ or ↵.

Indenting Paragraphs

As Figure 5.4 illustrates, there are many ways to indent paragraphs in WordPerfect. To indent a single paragraph:

1. Move the cursor to the place where you'll start typing your paragraph. If you've already typed the paragraph, move the cursor to the first character in the paragraph.

2. Depending on what you want, do one of the following:

   - To indent the **first line** of the paragraph, press Tab.

    - To indent the **entire left side** of the paragraph, press F7 or choose Layout ➤ Paragraph ➤ Indent. Or, click the Indent button (shown at left) in the WordPerfect or Layout button bar.

   - To create a **double indent** or what some people might call a "centered indent" (in that both the left and right sides of the paragraph are indented by equal amounts), press

FIGURE 5.4

A document with various indents and outdents

Indenting with Tab

   To indent the first line of a paragraph, just press Tab before typing the first line. That's how you'd do it on a typewriter, and that's how I did it at the beginning of this paragraph. Of course, if you've already typed the entire paragraph, *then* decide to indent the first line, you can just move the cursor to the start of that line and press Tab.

Indenting with Indent (F7)

   To indent the entire left margin of a paragraph, move the cursor to the beginning of the paragraph you want to indent (or to where you're about to type a paragraph). Now press F7 as many times as you need to get the indentation level you want. WordPerfect will indent the entire left margin of that paragraph, like it did for this one. (Here, I pressed F7 twice and then typed the paragraph.)

Indenting with Double Indent (Ctrl+Shift+F7)

   To indent both the left and right margins, move the cursor to the beginning of the paragraph you want to indent (or to where you're about to type a paragraph). Now press Ctrl+Shift+F7 as many times as you need to get the indentation level you want. This technique is great for long passages of quoted text.

Hanging Indent (Ctrl+F7)

To indent all the lines *beneath* the first line in a paragraph, move the cursor to the beginning of that paragraph (or to where you're about to start typing that paragraph). Press Ctrl+F7.

Margin Release (outdenting) into the Left Margin (Shift+Tab)

To hang the first line of a paragraph out into the margin, move the cursor to the beginning of that paragraph (or to where you're about to start typing that paragraph). Press Shift+Tab.

Ctrl+Shift+F7 or choose Layout ➤ Paragraph ➤ Double Indent. Or, click the Double Indent button in the Layout button bar.

- To create a **hanging indent** (where the first line of the paragraph hangs out and the remaining lines are indented), press Ctrl+F7. Or select Layout ➤ Paragraph ➤ Hanging Indent. Or, click the Hanging Indent button in the Layout button bar.

- To hang the first line of a paragraph into the left margin, press Shift+Tab or choose <u>L</u>ayout ➤ P<u>a</u>ragraph ➤ <u>M</u>argin Release at the beginning of the line. (Shift+Tab is sometimes called *back tab* or *hard back tab* because it inserts a [Hd Back Tab] code into your document.)

3. Repeat step 2 as often as you wish to deepen the indent or outdent.

4. If you haven't typed the paragraph yet, go ahead and do so now. Then press ↵.

Regardless of how you indent or outdent a paragraph, you can change your mind and un-indent or un-outdent the text later by removing the hidden codes. If you want to change the *amount* of indentation (or out-dentation), you'll need to change the tab stops, as described later in this chapter.

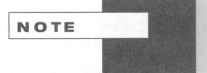

NOTE   The indenting described above applies only to the current paragraph. When you end the paragraph (press ↵), the indenting ends as well.

Indenting Many Paragraphs

The indent features discussed in the previous section affect one paragraph only. If you'd like to indent several paragraphs at once, follow these steps:

1. Move the cursor to where you want paragraph indenting to start, or select the paragraphs you want to indent.

2. Choose <u>L</u>ayout ➤ P<u>a</u>ragraph ➤ <u>F</u>ormat. Or, right-click the top or middle of the ruler bar and choose Paragraph <u>F</u>ormat. Either way, you'll open the Paragraph Format dialog box shown at the top of the next page.

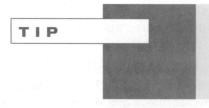

Paragraph Format

First Line Indent: `0"`

Spacing Between Paragraphs: `1`

Paragraph Adjustments

Left Margin Adjustment: `0"`

Right Margin Adjustment: `0"`

OK   Cancel   Clear All   Help

3. Select any of the following options:

> **First Line Indent**   Indents the first line of subsequent paragraphs or the selected paragraphs.
>
> **Left Margin Adjustment**   Indents the left margin for subsequent paragraphs or the selected paragraphs.
>
> **Right Margin Adjustment**   Indents the right margin for subsequent paragraphs or the selected paragraphs.

4. Specify a new setting. To indent from the margin, enter a positive measurement. To outdent *into* the margin, enter a negative measurement. For example, entering **.5** as the Left Margin Adjustment moves the paragraph to the right by $1/2$ inch. Entering **−.5** moves the paragraph $1/2$ inch into the left margin.

TIP

The small sample page in the Paragraph Format dialog box will reflect the settings you've chosen so far. Look at the sample page for a preview of how the text will reformat when you're done using the dialog box.

5. Repeat steps 3 and 4 until you're done, then choose OK or press ↵.

You can also use the ruler bar to *change* these paragraph format settings. Follow these steps:

1. Turn on the ruler bar (Alt+Shift+F3).

2. Move the cursor to where you want the changes to start, or select the paragraphs you want to change.

3. Use your mouse to drag the First Line Indent, Left Margin Adjust, or Right Margin Adjust marker in the ruler bar to a new position. The markers are the small triangles shown below:

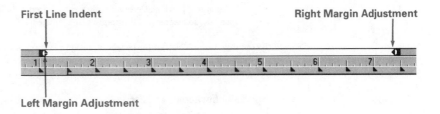

4. Release the mouse button when the marker is positioned properly.

The tips discussed under "Setting Margins with the Ruler Bar," earlier in the chapter, apply here as well.

Typing Lists

Everyone needs to type a simple list from time to time. Figure 5.5 shows several examples of short lists, and also explains a little bit about how I typed each list.

Typing a Simple List

Follow these steps to type a simple list:

1. If you want to indent the item number or bullet, press Tab until you've indented as far as you want.

2. Type the item number or letter.

FIGURE 5.5

Several types of lists

Numbered List

1. To type this simple numbered list, I typed **1.** then pressed F7 to indent one tab stop, and then typed this text.

2. I pressed ↵ twice after typing the first item, then typed **2.** and pressed F7 before typing this item in the list.

Bulleted List

*   To type this bulleted list, I chose Insert ▸ Bullets & Numbers, the Small Bullet option, then OK. Then I just typed this text.
*   Every time I press ↵ after typing an item in the list, WordPerfect automatically inserts the bullet for me.
*   After typing this line, I pressed ↵ then chose Insert ▸ Bullets & Numbers, then <None>, then OK, so that the text that follows isn't bulleted

By the way, to double-space the list above, just move the cursor to the top of the list. Choose Layout ▸ Paragraph ▸ Format and change the Spacing Between Paragraphs to whatever setting to 2 (or whatever spacing you want.)

Special Characters In List

☐   You're not limited to letters, bullets and numbers in a list. Here, the first item is marked with a small box, as when you want to type a check list.
☞   Here I've used a pointing hand as the first character in the list.
✔   To learn more about these special characters, please see Chapter 6.

Changing the Gap

1   To change the gap between the character that identifies each item in the list and the text that follows that character.
2   Move the cursor to above the list, and change the tab stop that separates the item from the text.
3   In this example, I reduced the space between the number and the text that follows it by reducing the gap from .5" to .25". The next section explains how to change tab stops.

3. Press F7 or Ctrl+Shift+F7 (to indent the text from both sides).

4. Type the text of the item and press ↵ (press ↵ twice if you want to place a blank line between items).

That takes care of the first list item. Now simply repeat the above steps for the remaining items in your list.

Typing a Bulleted or Numbered List

Here's an easy way to type a list in which items are marked with bullets, numbers, roman numerals, or letters:

1. Choose Insert ➤ Bullets & Numbers, or click the Bullets & Numbers button on the WordPerfect Button bar, to get to the dialog box shown below.

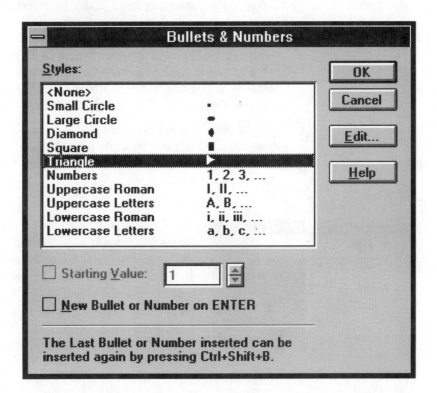

2. Highlight the character you want to put at the start of the item. (If you choose a number, roman numeral, or letter, WordPerfect will increment markers automatically when you add a list item and decrement markers when you delete an item.)

3. If you want a new bullet or number to appear when you press ↵, select New Bullet Or Number On ENTER.

4. If necessary, select Starting **V**alue and enter a different starting number for the first marked item.

5. Choose OK.

6. Type the text of the item and press ↵. (If you didn't select **N**ew Bullet Or Number On ENTER in step 3, you can add a blank line by pressing ↵ a second time.)

Now, to type the remaining items in the list, use either of the methods below:

- If you selected **N**ew Bullet Or Number On ENTER in step 3 above, type the next item and press ↵. Repeat this step until you've typed all the items. When you're done, choose **I**nsert ➤ Bullets & **N**umbers, select <None> in the **S**tyles list, and choose OK.

- If you didn't select **N**ew Bullet Or Number On ENTER in step 3, press Ctrl+Shift+B, type the next item, and press ↵ (twice if you want a blank line between items). Repeat this step until you've typed all the items.

TIP

Pressing ↵ twice in a "Bullets & Numbers" list where you've selected **N**ew Bullet Or Number On ENTER adds an extra marker character. To add blank lines in this type of list, finish typing the list. Then select the text in the list, choose **L**ayout ➤ **P**aragraph ➤ Format ➤ **S**pacing Between Paragraphs, type 2, and choose OK.

Setting Tab Stops

WordPerfect automatically sets tab stops every half inch, starting at the left edge of the page. That's why all indents and outdents created with the Tab, Shift+Tab, F7, and Ctrl+Shift+F7 keys are initially in half-inch increments. You can change the tab stops either before or after you've typed your text, or in a selected block of text. (Just in case you're not a typist, a *tab stop* is the place where the cursor stops when you press Tab or indent.)

NOTE　Tab stops offer the best way to control the amount of indenting and outdenting. However, other methods—including *tables* (Chapter 7) and *columns* (Chapter 27) may be easier when you want to align text in columns.

Types of Tab Alignment

The *ruler bar* shows the current tab positions and alignments for whatever text the cursor is in at the moment. It also offers the easiest way to add, change, or delete tab stops. At each tab stop, you can change both the position and alignment of text. Your alignment options are as follows:

Left　Text typed at the tab setting is left-aligned at the tab stop. (This is the default method.)

Center　Text is centered at the tab stop.

Right　Text is right-aligned at the tab stop.

Decimal　Text is aligned on a decimal point or some other character.

Dot Leader　Empty space to the left of the tab stop is filled with dots. You can use dot leaders with any of the tab settings above.

Figures 5.6 through 5.8 illustrate various tab settings. The triangles on the ruler bar show the position and alignment of each tab stop. (Margin markers on the ruler bar show the location of the left and right margins. Earlier in this chapter you learned how to drag the margin markers to change the margins in a document.)

Setting Tab Stops with the Ruler Bar

Setting tabs is simple if you have a mouse:

1. If you haven't already done so, turn on the ruler bar (View ➤ Ruler Bar or Alt+Shift+F3).

2. Position the cursor at the start of the text where you want to change the tab settings, or select text to limit your changes to the selected text.

FIGURE 5.6

The ruler bar indicates the current tab and margin settings. (This figure also illustrates the Layout button bar.)

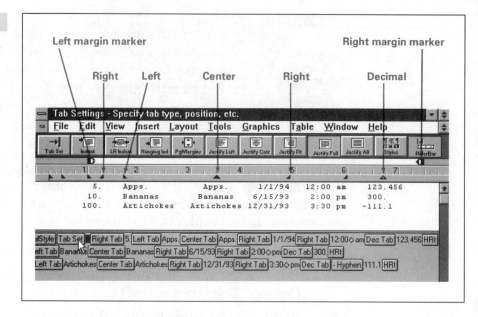

FIGURE 5.7

Text under two center-aligned tab stops

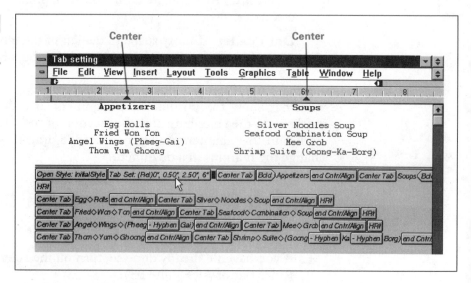

FIGURE 5.8

Text with left tab stops, and right tab stops with dot leaders

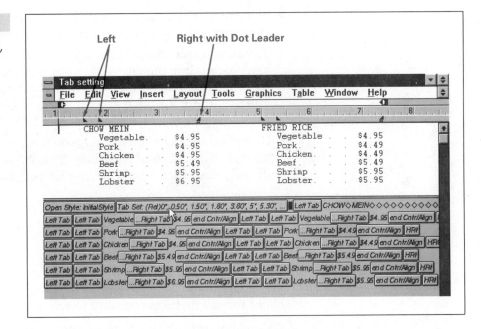

3. Use any of the techniques below to add, change, or delete tab settings. Each time you make a change, tabbed text below the current cursor position (or within selected text) will reformat instantly to reflect the new tab settings. This makes it easy to play with the settings until they're just right.

- **To delete a tab stop**, drag the tab marker below the ruler bar and release the mouse button.

- **To delete all tab stops**, right-click the bottom of the ruler bar and choose Clear All Tabs. Or, choose Clear All Tabs from the pull-down menu displayed when you click and hold on the Tab Set button in the power bar.

- **To select a tab type** (alignment), right-click the bottom of the ruler bar (where the tab markers are) and select a tab type from the QuickMenu. Or, select a tab type from the pull-down menu displayed when you click and hold on the Tab Set button in the power bar. Your choices are Left, Center, Right, Decimal, ...Left, ...Center, ...Right, and ...Decimal.

- **To set a new tab stop**, select the tab type you want (as described just above), then click on the ruler bar where you want the new tab to appear.

- **To change the type** of an existing tab stop, delete the tab stop, then set a new tab stop (as described just above).

- **To move a tab stop**, drag it to a new position on the ruler bar. As you drag the tab marker, the right edge of the status bar will show the exact tab position. A *ruler guide* will also indicate where the tab marker is with respect to the text in your document.

- If, while dragging a tab marker, you want to return the marker to its **original position**, drag the marker up above the ruler bar, then release the mouse button.

If you find yourself changing formats frequently, you might be pleased to know that you can select several tab markers at a time to work with:

- **To select several tab markers at once,** hold down the Shift key, move the mouse pointer to an empty spot just to the left of the first tab marker you want to select, then drag across the ruler to highlight the tab markers you want to select.

- **To delete several tab markers at once,** select the tab markers as described just above, drag the selected tab markers down below the ruler bar, then release the mouse button and the Shift key.

- **To move several tab markers at once,** select the tab markers as described just above, drag the selected tab markers across the ruler bar to their new position, then release the mouse button and the Shift key.

- **To copy several tab markers to a new position** on the ruler bar, hold down Ctrl and Shift while selecting multiple tab markers. While still pressing Ctrl and Shift, drag the selected tab markers across the ruler bar to their new position, then release the mouse button and the Ctrl and Shift keys.

Customizing the Ruler Bar

If you want to customize the appearance and behavior of the ruler bar, follow the steps below:

1. Right-click the ruler bar and choose Preferences. Or, choose File ➤ Preferences and double-click Display, then choose Ruler Bar.

2. In the Display Preferences dialog box, select (or deselect) any of the options listed below:

Show Ruler on New and Current Document   When deselected (the default setting), you must turn the ruler bar on manually. Select (check) this option if you want the ruler bar to appear automatically when you open a document.

Tabs Snap to Ruler Bar Grid   When selected (the default setting), tab stops position automatically to the ruler grid lines. Grid lines are set every .1 centimeter (about .06 inch). Deselect this option if you want to place tab stops to an exact position, without having them snap to the ruler grid.

Show Ruler Bar Guides   When selected (the default setting), ruler guides will appear when you drag the margin and tab stop markers. Deselect the option to hide the ruler guides.

Sculptured Ruler Bar   When selected (the default setting), the ruler bar has a sculptured appearance. When deselected, the ruler bar is flat.

3. Choose OK or press ↵, then choose Close (if necessary).

Initially, the ruler bar is marked in inches. To change the units of measure for the ruler bar, choose File ➤ Preferences, double-click Display, and choose Document. Use the Status Bar/Ruler Display pop-up list button to select a unit of measure. Choose OK or press ↵, then choose Close.

Setting Tabs without a Mouse

The Tab Set dialog box shown in Figure 5.9 provides another way to set tabs, and it's especially useful if you don't have a mouse. Here's how to get to and use the Tab Set dialog box.

1. Position the cursor at the start of the text where you want to change the tab settings, or select text to limit changes to a block.

2. Use any of these techniques to open the Tab Set dialog box:

- Choose Layout ➤ Line ➤ Tab Set.
- Right-click the ruler bar and choose Tab Set.

FIGURE 5.9

The Tab Set dialog box. Position the cursor to where you want new tab stops to take effect. Then choose Layout ➤ Line ➤ Tab Set to get here.

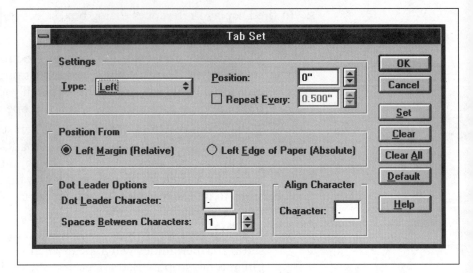

- Double-click a tab marker in the ruler bar.
- Double-click the Tab Set button in the power bar.
- Click the Tab Set button in the Layout button bar.

3. Use any of the tab setting techniques below. In general, you can do the tasks in any order you wish.

- **To choose how you want to position tabs,** as discussed in a moment, choose either Left Margin (Relative) or Left Edge Of Paper (Absolute).

- **To delete all tab stops,** choose the Clear All button.

- **To delete one tab stop,** choose Position and type the position of the tab stop you want to delete. Then choose the Clear button.

- **To set default tab stops** (left tab stops every one-half inch), choose the Default button.

- **To select a tab type** (alignment), choose a tab type from the Type pop-up list button. Your choices are Left, Center, Right, Decimal, Dot Left, Dot Center, Dot Right, and Dot Decimal.

- **To set equally spaced tab stops,** select the tab type you want to repeat (as described just above). Choose Position and type in the position for the first tab stop. Select Repeat Every, press Tab, and type the distance you want between tabs. Choose the Set button.

- **To set one tab stop,** select the tab type you want (as described above). Choose Position and type in the position for the new tab stop. Make sure Repeat Every is *not* selected. Choose the Set button.

- **To change the type** of an existing tab stop, follow the procedure for setting one tab stop at the position of the tab stop you want to change (as described just above).

- **To move a tab stop,** delete the tab stop, then set a new tab stop at the spot you want.

T I P

In the Position text box, you can enter whole numbers, decimals (for example, 3.25), or fractions (for example, 3 1/4).

4. When you're finished making changes, choose OK.

If you need additional help with setting tabs, remember to choose that good old Help button while you're working in the Tab Set dialog box.

About Relative and Absolute Measurements

While you're in the Tab Set dialog box described in the previous section, you can choose either absolute or relative measurements when you set or change the tab stops. With *relative* measurement, WordPerfect always measures tab stops from the left margin. In other words, the tab stops "float" with the left margin. Suppose that you've set relative tab stops every $1/2$ inch and then you move the left margin $1/4$ inch to the right. All tab stops will automatically move $1/4$ inch to the right. This way, the first tab stop remains the same relative distance from the left margin.

When you use *absolute* measurement, WordPerfect measures tab stops from the left edge of the *page*, independent of the left margin. Unlike relative tabs, absolute tab stops don't float with the left margin.

Generally speaking, *relative* tab stops are the easiest to get along with because the indent keys always have the same effect, no matter where you've set the left margin. However, if you're working with graphics and multicolumn layouts (see Part Six in this book), absolute tab measurements may be better, since they let you control exactly where each tab stop is.

Changing the Dot Leader

The default style for dot leaders is to use periods separated by a space. But, you can choose any dot leader character and spacing you wish:

1. Place the cursor wherever you want the changes to take effect, or select a block of text to limit your changes to that block.

2. Use any technique given in the previous section to open the Tab Set dialog box. (For example, choose Layout ➤ Line ➤ Tab Set.)

3. In the Dot Leader Character text box, type any keyboard character. Or, to insert a special *WordPerfect Character*, press Ctrl+W, choose a Character Set, select any WordPerfect Character from the Characters list, and choose Insert And Close. (Chapter 6 explains how to enter WordPerfect Characters.)

4. In the Spaces Between Characters text box, type the number of spaces that should appear between each dot leader character.

5. Choose OK or press ↵.

The new dot leader character will affect dot-leader tab stops, text that you center by pressing Shift+F7 twice, and text that you right-align by pressing Alt+F7 twice.

Using Tab Stops

When you're ready to use the tab stops you've set, return to the document window. Then press Tab, Shift+Tab (to back-tab), F7 (to indent), Ctrl+F7 (to set a hanging indent), or Ctrl+Shift+F7 (to double-indent) to make the cursor jump to the next tab stop of the type indicated. Until you press one of those keys, the tab stop does nothing. For example, in Figure 5.8 I didn't get dot leaders until I pressed Tab after typing the Chow Mein entry.

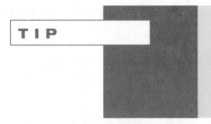

If you'd like to see invisible tab, space, and hard returns in your document window, choose <u>V</u>iew ➤ <u>S</u>how ¶ or press Ctrl+Shift+F3. Tabs, for example, will appear as → characters. Use the same commands (or shortcut keys) to hide the symbols again.

When Pressing Tab Doesn't Insert Tabs

When you work with text that's already tabbed into place, remember these important points:

- When you're in Insert mode, pressing the Tab key inserts another tab code in the text. If pressing Tab doesn't move the cursor, it's possible that no more tab settings remain on the line.

- When the tab stop you want to jump to is very close to the current cursor position, the cursor does not move any appreciable distance.

- When you're in Typeover mode, pressing Tab simply moves the cursor to the next tab stop without inserting a tab code.

Therefore, when you edit text that's already aligned on tab stops, you might want to press the Insert key to switch to Typeover mode. Then you can press Tab or Shift+Tab to move from column to column without inserting extra tabs and back tabs (which would move the text out of alignment). Of course, you can also use the mouse or the arrow keys to position the cursor without inserting unwanted tabs.

Fixing Alignment Errors

Beware of these tab-alignment bugaboos:

- Lines between the columns are wavy instead of straight.

- Columns are misaligned because of missing or extra tab-alignment codes.

- Columns are misaligned because the text is wider than the columns themselves.

- Columns are misaligned because of extra space(s) at the beginning or end of the text.

In the next few sections, we'll look at ways to avoid these pitfalls.

TIP Use the Tables feature (Chapter 7) or Columns feature (Chapter 27) to avoid alignment maladies.

Fixing Wavy Columns

Figure 5.10 shows an example of printed text that should be evenly spaced in columns but is wavy instead. This problem often occurs when you use blank spaces instead of tabs to separate columns. Columns aligned by spaces look especially bad when you use proportionally spaced fonts (Chapter 6), such as the CG Times font in Figure 5.10.

FIGURE 5.10

Wavy columns caused by using spaces instead of tabs to separate columns

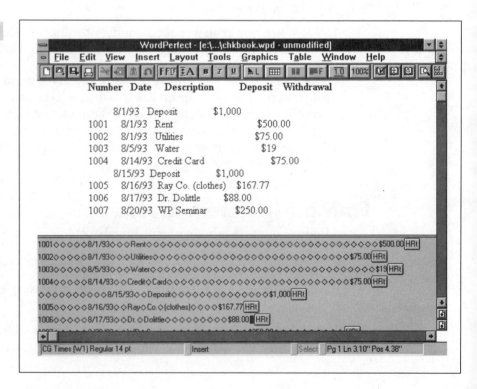

To fix the problem, replace each group of blank spaces with a tab, and then set proper tab stops. (Or start all over and use the Tables or Columns features.)

Fixing Misaligned Columns

Another common problem occurs when most of the text lines up neatly into columns but occasionally goes out of whack. This is illustrated by Strappman's street address and phone number in Figure 5.11.

If you look at the Reveal Codes screen in Figure 5.11, you'll notice two [Left Tab] codes in front of Strappman's address. The extra code pushes the address out to the second tab stop. The simplest solution is to remove one of the tabs in front of the address.

FIGURE 5.11

Columns are mis-aligned because I added an extra tab.

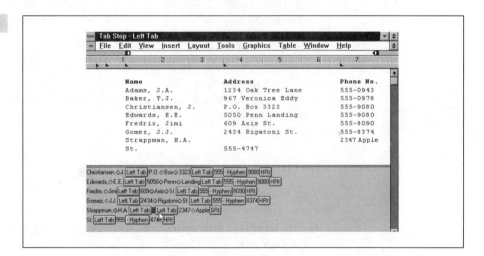

The alignment problem in Figure 5.12 looks a lot like the extra tab problem in Figure 5.11. However, if you look at the Reveal Codes screen, you'll see that *every* address has only one tab code in front of it. So, if there aren't any extra tab codes, what's causing some addresses to shoot over to the third column?

The answer is that some names in the first column are simply too wide for that column. Because the name in the first column extends *past* the first tab stop, the next tab code in that column forces the address out to the third column. This tab is ignored, and is converted to an [Ignore Tab] code.

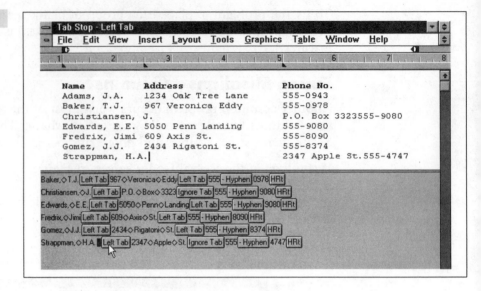

To clear up this mess, you'll need to change the tab stops at the start of the list so that the first column is wide enough to hold the longest name. After you adjust the tab settings, the [Ignore Tab] codes will be converted to normal tabs (such as [Left Tab]). (See the section on "Refining Tab Stops" later in this chapter.)

Checking the Tab-Stop Codes

When you change the tab stops, be sure to position the cursor immediately to the *right* of the existing [Tab Set] code you want to change. That way WordPerfect will adjust the existing [Tab Set] code rather than creating a new one.

If you're having trouble with tab stops, use Reveal Codes to see if multiple [Tab Set] codes appear anywhere before the problem area. Then delete the extra codes that follow the one you want to use. (See Chapter 4 for more on using Reveal Codes.)

Fixing Back-Tab Errors

If you press Shift+Tab when the cursor is in the middle of a line of text, your text may disappear. This happens because the back-tabbed text overwrites existing text. To remedy the problem, go to the Reveal Codes screen and delete the [Hd Back Tab] code in the text. (Or, if you catch the problem right away, press Ctrl+Z or Backspace.)

Similarly, if you move text into the left margin inadvertently or you change your mind about typing text in the left margin, use Reveal Codes to delete the [Hd Back Tab] code that's pushing the text into the margin.

Aligning Text "On the Fly"

In this section I'll show you some quick ways to force any type of tab stop to behave as a left-aligned, decimal-aligned, center-aligned, right-aligned, or dot-leader tab stop. You'll also learn a trick for adding dot leaders to centered or flush-right text. These shortcuts let you align text without changing the tab settings. Before we get to the shortcuts, however, I need to explain the difference between hard and soft tabs.

Hard Tabs vs. Soft Tabs

Soft tabs are the "natural" tabs you get when you press the Tab key. They are called "soft tabs" because they will change automatically if you change the tab stop alignment on the ruler bar or in the Tab Set dialog box. For example, if you change a center-aligned tab stop to a right-aligned tab stop, WordPerfect will automatically convert any [Center Tab] codes at that tab stop to [Right Tab] codes.

Hard tabs, on the other hand, *never* adjust to changes in the tab stops. On the Reveal Codes screen, hard tabs appear with the word *Hd* preceding the tab type (for example, [Hd Center Tab]).

NOTE   WordPerfect inserts a hard back-tab code ([Hd Back Tab]) when you press Shift+Tab or choose Layout ➤ Paragraph ➤ Back Tab.

Entering a Hard Tab

The example in Figure 5.13 shows the effects of using hard tabs to temporarily override the normal tab-alignment settings on the ruler. In the figure, the tab stops are left-aligned at 1.5" and 3.25", and right-aligned

FIGURE 5.13

In this example, I used a hard right tab with dot leader to enter the job titles in the second and third lines of the phone list.

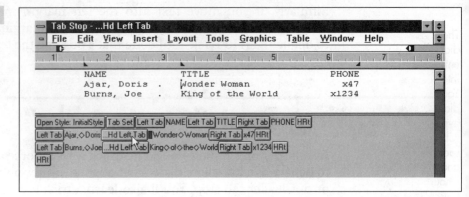

at 6.5″. I typed the first line normally (pressing Tab before NAME, TI-TLE, and PHONE and pressing ↵ at the end of the line).

On the second line I pressed Tab and typed **Ajar, Doris**. Then, instead of pressing Tab again, I used the steps given just below to insert a hard left tab with dot leader at the next tab stop. One more press of the Tab key brought me to the right-aligned tab stop at 6.5″. There I typed **x47** and pressed ↵. I used the same basic procedure to type the third line.

Here are the steps to follow if you want to align text in a jiffy—without changing the tab settings:

1. If necessary, press Tab (or type text) until the cursor is at (or slightly past) the tab stop that's just ahead of the spot where you want to align your text on the fly.

2. Choose Layout ➤ Line ➤ Other Codes to open the Other Codes dialog box shown in Figure 5.14.

3. Select the type of tab you want. You can choose any option from the Hard Tab Codes area or the Hard Tab Codes With Dot Leaders area of the dialog box.

4. Choose Insert or press ↵.

5. Type the text.

The text you typed will have the type of alignment you chose in step 3 above.

FIGURE 5.14

The Other Codes dialog box lets you enter a hard tab code into your document. You can also use this dialog box to insert hyphenation codes (Chapter 16) and hard spaces (Chapter 8), and to change the "thousands separator" (described in the next section).

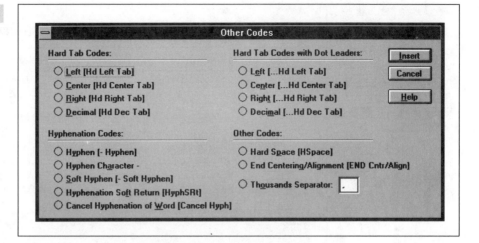

Changing the Decimal Alignment Character

In general, dates, times, and numbers that have the same number of decimal places (or no decimal places) look fine when you right-align them (see Figure 5.15).

FIGURE 5.15

Examples of right-aligned text

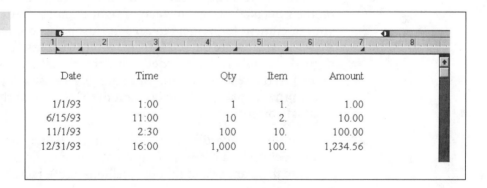

However, if you right-align numbers that have different numbers of decimal places, the decimal points won't line up vertically (see the left column in Figure 5.16).

FIGURE 5.16

Right-aligned numbers, American-style numbers aligned on decimal points, and European-style numbers aligned on commas

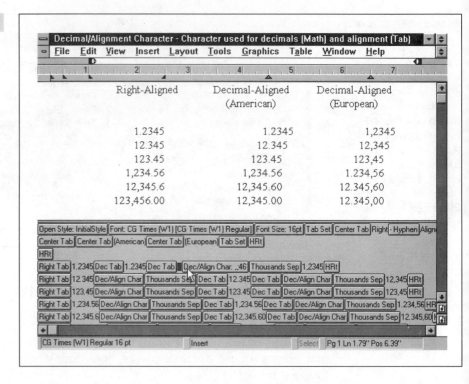

To fix the problem of uneven alignment, you need to align the numbers on their decimal points, instead of right-aligning them. (If you're writing your document for readers in certain European countries, you would use a *comma* to separate decimals from whole numbers. Therefore you would align the numbers on the decimal comma rather than on the decimal point.) In the second column of Figure 5.16 I used decimal alignment to line up the numbers. In the last column I've aligned the numbers on the decimal comma.

As you can see, WordPerfect allows you to change the decimal character from a period to a comma. It also lets you change the character used to separate thousands (and millions, billions, etc.). Here's how to change the decimal alignment character and thousands separator.

1. Position the cursor where the new decimal alignment character should take effect, or select text to limit your changes to the selected block.

2. Open the Tab Set dialog box (Layout ➤ Line ➤ Tab Set).

3. In the Character text box, type the character you want to use for aligning the numbers. For example, type a comma to use the European way.

4. Choose OK or press ↵.

To change the thousands separator character, follow these steps:

1. Position the cursor where the new thousands separator should take effect, or select text to limit your changes to the selected block.

2. Choose Layout ➤ Line ➤ Other Codes to open the Other Codes dialog box shown in Figure 5.14.

3. In the Thousands Separator text box, type the character you want to use for the thousands separator. For example, type a period to use the European way.

4. Choose Insert or press ↵.

TIP

You can use any character, including special characters described in Chapter 6, for decimal alignment and thousands separation.

You can use this technique for numbers that you've decimal-aligned with tab stops on the tab ruler or on the fly with the Other Codes dialog box. To return to American-style decimal alignment, repeat the steps above wherever you want to resume that style.

If you want to use two different decimal-alignment or thousands separator characters in side-by-side columns, you'll need to change the characters before each number. In the Reveal Codes part of the screen in Figure 5.16, you can see that the first tab stop is right-aligned [Right Tab] and the next two are decimal-aligned [Dec Tab].

To switch between aligning on a period and a comma in the two right-hand columns, I had to redefine the decimal-alignment and thousands separator characters several times (notice the many [Dec/Align Char] and [Thousands Sep] codes in the Reveal Codes window). If you need to use many unusual alignments like this, you're better off using the Tables feature (see Chapter 7).

Creating Dot Leaders "On the Fly"

You can also add dot leaders in front of a centered line or flush-right line without changing the tab settings. This is very handy for simple two-column lists like this:

```
Ajar, Doris . . . . . . . . . . . . . . . . . . . . .x47
Burns, Joe. . . . . . . . . . . . . . . . . . . .x1234
```

To use this shortcut for flush-right lines, type the text in the first column, and press Alt+F7 twice. (For a centered line, type the text in the first column, and press Shift+F7 twice.) Then type the text in the second column. To narrow the gap between the two columns, simply adjust the left and right margins.

TIP To remove the dot leaders, delete the [...Hd Flush Right] or [...Hd Center on Marg] code on the Reveal Codes screen, then press Alt+F7 (for flush right) or Shift+F7 (for centering).

Moving, Copying, and Deleting Tabular Columns

The tables feature (Chapter 7) really is the easiest way to create multi-column tables. But suppose you've used tabs instead. Now you decide to move, copy, or delete a particular column. Do you have to type everything over again? Of course not! You can do this by selecting the column.

NOTE It's easy to convert tabular text to a table, and then arrange the table columns in any order (Chapter 7). You can also sort or alphabetize rows of text into alphabetical order (Chapter 22).

Unfortunately, selecting columns can be tricky, so I recommend that you save your document before attempting this. Here are the general steps:

1. Save your document by choosing File ➤ Save (or pressing Ctrl+S) just in case you do more harm than good.

2. Move the cursor to the top left character in the column you want to move, copy, or delete.

3. Select text up to and including the last character in the column. Initially, the selection covers text in adjacent columns, as shown below:

```
Name                     Address              Phone No.
Adams, J.A.              1234 Oak Tree Lane    555-0943
Baker, T.J.             967 Veronica Eddy     555-0978
Christiansen, J.        P.O. Box 3323         555-9080
Edwards, E.E.           5050 Penn Landing     555-9080
Fredrix, Jimi           609 Axis St.          555-8090
Gomez, J.J.             2434 Rigatoni St.     555-8374
Strappman, H.A.         2347 Apple St.        555-4747
```

4. Select Edit ➤ Select ➤ Tabular Column. Now only one column is selected, as shown below:

```
Name                     Address              Phone No
Adams, J.A.             1234 Oak Tree Lane    555-0943
Baker, T.J.             967 Veronica Eddy     555-0978
Christiansen, J.        P.O. Box 3323         555-9080
Edwards, E.E.           5050 Penn Landing     555-9080
Fredrix, Jimi           609 Axis St.          555-8090
Gomez, J.J.             2434 Rigatoni St.     555-8374
Strappman, H.A.         2347 Apple St.        555-4747
```

5. If you want to delete the column, press the Del key and you're done. If you want to move or copy the column, move the mouse pointer to the selected text and right-click, or pull down the Edit menu. To *move*, choose Cut. To *copy*, choose Copy.

6. If you're moving or copying, place the cursor where you want the top left corner of the moved or copied column to appear. Choose Edit ➤ Paste or press Ctrl+V.

You may need to adjust the tab stops to get exactly the effect you want after you delete or rearrange a column. Just use the general technique described earlier in "Refining Tab Stops."

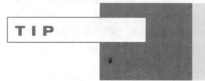

TIP After selecting the column in step 4 above, you can use the drag-and-drop techniques discussed in Chapter 3 to move or copy it.

Undoing a Botched Move, Copy, or Delete

If you make more of a mess than an improvement, and you'd like to undo the whole operation, just choose Edit ➤ Undo or press Ctrl+Z. If you chose Cut, you'll also need to place the cursor where the top left corner of that column belongs and choose Edit ➤ Paste (or press Ctrl+V).

Here's another way to recover if you saved your file first: Choose File ➤ Close ➤ No. Then choose File ➤ Open (or press Ctrl+O), type the file name, and press ↵ to retrieve the file in the state it was in before you made your changes.

"Quick-Formatting" Your Document

WordPerfect offers several ways to format documents consistently. Perhaps the easiest method is QuickFormat. As its name implies, QuickFormat lets you quickly format text in your document—with the same fonts and paragraph styles that are already in effect elsewhere. Here's how to use it:

1. Place the cursor in text that has the font or paragraph style you want to copy.

2. Choose Layout ➤ QuickFormat. Or, right-click and choose QuickFormat, or click the QuickFormat button in the WordPerfect button bar (shown at left).

3. Choose the options you want from the QuickFormat dialog box that appears. Your options are:

> **Fonts and Attributes**   Copy only the fonts and print attributes to other text. (You'll learn about these topics in Chapter 6).

> **Paragraph Styles**   If the paragraph you're copying from is formatted with any paragraph styles, WordPerfect will copy those styles only. If the paragraph isn't formatted with any paragraph styles, this option has no effect. Paragraph styles are discussed in Chapter 17.

> **Both**   Copy the fonts, attributes, and paragraph styles to other text.

4. Choose OK or press ↵.

5. Use your mouse to select the text you want to quick-format. When you release the mouse button, WordPerfect will copy the appropriate formatting codes from the original text to the selected text. Repeat this step until you've selected and reformatted as many portions of text as you want.

6. To turn off QuickFormat, simply repeat step 2.

Keep in mind that WordPerfect accomplishes a QuickFormat by *copying* codes from the original text into the selected text. For example, if you asked QuickFormat to copy fonts and attributes from a boldfaced paragraph, WordPerfect would insert [Bold] codes around the text you selected in step 5 above.

There's one potential catch to this technique: If you later change the fonts and attributes of the original paragraph, WordPerfect *will not* adjust the other text that you quick formatted using the Fonts And Attributes or Both option.

By contrast, if you used a *Paragraph style* to format the original paragraph, and later changed that style, any paragraphs quick formatted with the Paragraph Styles or Both option will be adjusted accordingly. You'll learn more about the wonders of styles in Chapter 17.

WordPerfect's justification, indentation, and alignment techniques range from simple tabs to fancy indentations and every possible kind of text alignment. In the next chapter, you'll find out how to spruce up your documents with fonts, borders, and special characters.

Courier 12 cpi Courier Italic 12 cpi
Courier Bold 12 cpi
Times Roman, 12 pt. *Times Roman Italic, 12 pt.*
Times Roman Bold, 12 pt.
Helvetica, 18 pt. **Helvetica Bold, 18 pt.**

Bodoni-WP, 24 pt.

Broadway-WP, 24 pt.

Brush Script-WP 18 pt

Century-WP, 14 pt. *Century-WP Italic, 14 pt.*

Chili Pepper 24 pt.

Commercial Script-WP, 24pt

Cooper Black-WP, 18 pt.

Eurostile-WP, 24 pt.

Hobo-WP, 36 pt.

Kidstuff, 48 pt.

Wingdings 18 pt. (below)

You Are Hereby Invited
to Attend a Black Tie Affair...

Mastery of WordPerfect:
Taking WP to an Art Form

12:00 Friday, June 24
1234 New Age Way
Higher Being, CA 91234

CHAPTER

6

Fonts, Borders, and Special Characters

f a s t **TRACK**

To hide text   **206**

> select the text you want to hide, then choose Layout ➤ Font
> or press F9. Choose Hidden, then choose OK. At the docu-
> ment window, you can then choose View ➤ Hidden Text to
> display, or hide, that text. Your current selection also affects
> the printed copy of the document.

To type a special character   **207**

> choose Insert ➤ Character or press Ctrl+W, choose a charac-
> ter set and character, and choose Insert And Close.

To draw a custom horizontal or vertical graphic line   **214**

> position the cursor and choose Graphics ➤ Custom Line, and
> define your line from the options given. After choosing OK to
> return to the document, you can further refine the line by
> sizing and positioning it with the mouse (click the line first to
> select it).

To draw borders around paragraphs   **217**

> move the cursor to the first paragraph to be bordered or select
> several paragraphs. Choose Layout ➤ Paragraph ➤ Border/Fill.
> Define the border from the options given, then choose OK.

To change the print color of text   **220**

> choose Layout ➤ Font and then make your color selections
> from the Color Options area of the Font dialog box.

CHANGING the size and appearance of text, adding a few lines and borders, and perhaps a few special characters, is easy to do, and can add a real professional touch to your document. For example, take a look at the portion of a sample résumé in Figure 6.1, which uses only a standard typewriter font. Compare that to Figure 6.2, which uses the kinds of WordPerfect features we'll be discussing in this chapter.

A plain document, without special fonts, lines, or characters

```
                            Wanda Bea Starr

184 Wingit St.        Lake Meyer, CO.  93415        (319) 555-0938


OBJECTIVE             Produce word processing and desktop
                      publishing documents on a freelance basis.

EDUCATION             Bachelor of Arts, Business Administration,
                      State University of Colorado, Denver, 1980.

EXPERIENCE            Sole Proprietor, Wanda Bea Starr Word
                      Processing, Sturgeon Pond, Colorado to Present

                      Freelance secretary and home-based word
                      processing services.
                         Secretary for small office of architects
                         Freelance secretary for various offices
                         as temporary help
```

FIGURE 6.2

The document in Figure 6.1, spruced up with new fonts, lines, and special characters

Wanda Bea Starr

| 184 Wingit St | Lake Meyer, CO 93415 | (319)555-0938 |

OBJECTIVE   Produce word processing and desktop publishing documents on a freelance basis.

EDUCATION   Bachelor of Arts, Business Administration, State University of Colorado, Denver, 1980.

EXPERIENCE   **Sole Proprietor,** *Wanda Bea Starr Word Processing,* Sturgeon Pond, Colorado.   1985 to Present

Freelance secretary and home-based word processing services.

✓ Secretary for small office of architects
✓ Freelance secretary for various offices as temporary help

Before You Read This Chapter...

Up to this point, every WordPerfect feature that I've described will work like a charm regardless of what type of printer you're using. But now we've come to a point where certain features I'll talk about aren't really WordPerfect features at all. Instead, they're printer-specific features that WordPerfect can use if (and only if) your printer can produce them.

If you try to use a special feature that isn't available with your printer, WordPerfect will ignore your request, making you feel as though *you've* done something wrong. If you cannot find a particular font that you'd like to use, most likely that font isn't built into your printer or it's not available in the current font collection. So if you start feeling confused about fonts, remember...

- In *this* chapter, I'll talk about fonts that have already been installed and are ready for use in WordPerfect.

- In Chapter 10 I'll discuss ways to expand your collection of fonts and install them for use with WordPerfect.

About Fonts

Unless you're already familiar with computers or typesetting, the term *font* may be new to you. A font is basically a combination of three things:

- A *typeface* (sometimes called a *typestyle* or a *face*)
- A *weight,* such as **boldface,** *italic,* or roman, or other attribute as described under "Changing the Appearance of Text" later in this chapter.
- A size, measured in *points* or characters per inch (abbreviated *cpi*)

Figure 6.3 shows examples of various fonts.

Proportional vs. Monospaced Fonts

Most fonts are either proportionally spaced, or monospaced, as defined below:

Monospace   Every character takes up the same amount of space (for example, an *i* is just as wide as a *w).*

Proportional spacing   Every character takes up only the space it needs (an *i* takes up less space than a *w).*

Figure 6.4 illustrates this with a string of the letters *i* and *w* in a monospaced font (Courier) and a proportionally spaced font (Times). The letters are the same width in the monospaced font, but the *i* is narrower than the *w* in the proportional font. This packs the letters together more tightly.

Because each character in a monospaced font takes up the same amount of space, its size can be measured in characters per inch (*cpi*). Two common Courier sizes are *pica* (10 cpi) and *elite* (12 cpi). Proportionally spaced fonts can't really be measured in characters per inch because the characters are different widths. These fonts are measured in terms of *height* instead. The unit of measurement for the height of a character is the *point.* One point is about 1/72 of an inch.

Courier 12 cpi *Courier Italic 12 cpi*
Courier Bold 12 cpi
Times Roman, 12 pt. *Times Roman Italic, 12 pt.*
Times Roman Bold, 12 pt.
Helvetica, 18 pt. **Helvetica Bold, 18 pt.**

Bodoni-WP, 24 pt.

Broadway-WP, 24 pt.

Brush Script-WP 18pt

Century-WP, 14 pt. *Century-WP Italic, 14 pt.*

Chili Pepper 24 pt.

Commercial Script-WP, 24pt

Cooper Black-WP, 18 pt.

Eurostile-WP, 24 pt.

Hobo-WP, 36 pt.

Kidstuff, 48 pt.

Wingdings 18 pt. (below)

N O T E

A 10-cpi monospaced font is about the same size as a 12-point proportional font.

FIGURE 6.4

Monospaced and proportionally spaced fonts compared

```
iwiwiwiwiwiw
```
In a monospaced font, like Courier, every letter is the same width.

iwiwiwiwiwiw

In a proportionally spaced font, like Times, each letter uses only the space it needs.

Serif vs. Sans-Serif Fonts

A *serif* is the little curlicue, or tail, at the top and bottom of each letter. For example, Times Roman (refer back to Figure 6.3) is a Serif font. Serif fonts are often used for small- to medium-size print because the serifs help your eyes move through the text and read more easily.

Sans-serif fonts, like Helvetica, have no curlicue, and are generally used for large text—from the headlines in newspapers to the messages on street signs (as a glance at any road sign will prove).

Decorative Fonts

Decorative fonts aren't particularly easy to read (especially in smaller sizes), but they look nice and can be used to create a mood. Examples abound, from the elegance of an invitation to the zaniness of a humorous greeting card. Figures 6.5 and 6.6 show some examples using decorative fonts.

FIGURE 6.5

An elegant decorative font adds to the formality of this document.

*You Are Hereby Invited
to Attend a Black Tie Affair...*

**Mastery of WordPerfect:
Taking WP to an Art Form**

*12:00 Friday, June 24
1234 New Age Way
Higher Being, CA 91234*

Scalable vs. Non-Scalable Fonts

Some fonts are *scalable*, which means that you can choose a size, such as 10.5 points, on the fly. Most modern graphic fonts, including the popular TrueType and PostScript fonts, are scalable. WordPerfect can tell whether a font is scalable, and it lets you choose a size for the font as soon as you've chosen the typeface.

Non-scalable fonts cannot be sized on the fly. They are available in predetermined sizes only: 10 point, 12 point, etc. When using a non-scalable font, you choose the size and typeface in a single step. WordPerfect won't let you set an in-between size, such as 11 points, for a non-scalable font.

FIGURE 6.6

Informal, child-like fonts create a casual, unintimidating look. The cartoon face is in a graphic User box (see Chapter 25).

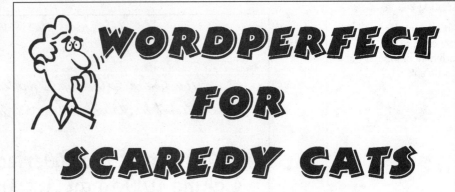

WORDPERFECT FOR SCAREDY CATS

Getting Started

Start your computer (yikes!), get to the DOS command prompt (huh?), type **win wpwin** and press ↵. No, you can't just type **wordperfect** instead. Yes, you do have to press ↵ after you type **win wpwin**.

Getting A Clue

Find someone who has a clue on how to work this thing. If that person is too busy / expensive / cranky / malodorous / nonexistent for you, get rid of them. Fumble around. Ignore everything on your screen.

Giving Up

When you've had enough, turn off your computer. Do something else.

Choosing a Font

Fortunately, using fonts in WordPerfect is easier than getting through all the terminology. Here's how to pick a font for any text in your document:

NOTE

If you have several printers attached to your computer, keep in mind that each might have its own unique fonts. WordPerfect comes with a handy macro named ALLFONTS to create a document that shows you all fonts available for the current printer. See Chapter 18. (See Chapter 10 to learn how to select another printer.)

1. Move the cursor to wherever you want to switch to the new font. This can be either before existing text or at the point where you want to start typing new text. To change the font for a portion of existing text, select that text.

2. Choose Layout ➤ Font, or press F9. A dialog box like the one shown in Figure 6.7 will appear. (The fonts listed will depend on which fonts you've purchased and installed on your computer, as discussed in Chapter 10.)

NOTE

You can also get to the Font dialog box by double-clicking the Font Face or Font Size buttons in the power bar, or by clicking the Font button in the Font button bar.

3. If you want to change the typeface, choose a font from the Font Face list, either by clicking or by using the arrow keys. You can quickly jump to a font name by typing the first few characters in the font name.

4. If you want to change the font size, choose a size from the Font Size list, or type a size into the Font Size text box.

FIGURE 6.7

The Font dialog box lets you choose a font and other text attributes. Choose Layout ➤ Font or press F9 to get to this dialog box.

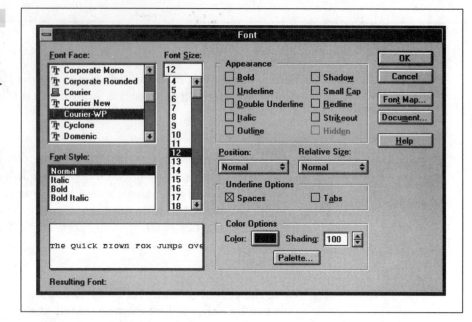

5. If you wish, you can choose style, appearance, position, and other options described later in this chapter.

6. When you're done making your selections, choose OK to return to your document.

If you selected text, or placed the cursor in front of existing text in step 1, the font change will be readily apparent on your screen. Any new text that you start typing will appear in the font you selected.

But It Didn't Work!

If you change the font in a document and nothing seems to happen, there's probably a competing [Font] code right after the code you just inserted. To fix this problem, you need to delete the old font code, as discussed under "Deleting Codes" in Chapter 4.

Font Shortcuts

If the power bar is turned on (View ➤ Power Bar), you can use the Font Face and Font Size buttons shown below to select a font and size without going through the menus. There's also a Font button bar that you can use to get quick access to font options (right-click the button bar, then choose Font).

Using Relative Font Sizes

If you want to change only the size of the current font, it's not necessary to choose a different font. You can just choose a new size in relation to the current size. Here's one advantage to using a relative size: If you change the point size of the current font, all text that is sized relatively to that font will also be resized, automatically.

For example, WordPerfect's "fine" font is a relative size that's usually 60% of the *base font* size (the current size). Thus, when the base font is 10 points, fine text will be 6 points in size. If you double the base font size to 20 points, WordPerfect will automatically double the fine text as well, to 12 points.

TIP

If you want to use fonts consistently with the various design elements in your document (heads, subheads, body text, etc.) you should definitely know about *styles* (see Chapter 17).

Figure 6.8 shows examples of the relative sizes available to you. Each size is a percentage of the current base-font size.

If your printer has scalable fonts, WordPerfect will calculate the relative type size mathematically, since anything goes with scalable fonts. If your printer doesn't offer scalable fonts, WordPerfect will select the font that best approximates the size you've requested. Therefore, if your printer has a limited selection of fonts, the sizes available may not match WordPerfect's predefined percentages.

FIGURE 6.8

Examples of sizes
in relation to a
16-point font

Base Font: Times Roman 16pt

This ends with a ^{superscript}

This ends with a _{subscript}

This is Fine Size

This is Small Size

This is Normal Size

This is Large Size

This is Very Large

This is Extra Large

Changing the Relative Size or Position

To change the relative size of text, follow the steps below:

1. Select the text that you want to change. Or, if you haven't typed the text yet, place the cursor where you want to start typing in the new size.

2. Go to the Font dialog box (choose Layout ➤ Font or press F9).

3. Choose appropriate options from the Position and Relative Size pop-up lists.

If you didn't select text in step 1, type the new text now. Press → when you're ready to start typing normal-sized text again. Like many formatting features, relative sizes are controlled by paired codes, such as [Ext Large]. Only text between the two codes is sized according to the selection.

Changing the Size Ratios

The ratios of relative text sizes aren't etched in granite; they are simply the defaults that WordPerfect uses for convenience. You may want to specify a different ratio—for example, to make your superscripts and sub-scripts a little smaller or to make your extra-large sizes a little larger. You can change the relative-size ratios by following these steps:

1. Choose File ➤ Preferences and double-click the Print icon. You'll be taken to the Print Preferences dialog box shown below.

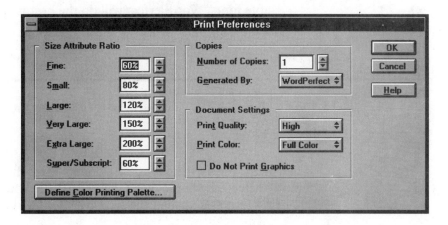

2. Change the ratios near the left side of the dialog box, as appropriate, then choose OK and Close to return to your document.

Be aware that changing the size ratio affects the entire current document, as well as any other documents that use relative sizing.

Troubleshooting Problems with Relative Sizing

If you open a document and the relative font sizes look out of whack, you may need to troubleshoot the situation. Here's how:

- If you use multiple printers, be sure to select the correct printer for that document (File ➤ Select Printer).

- Repeat the steps given above ("Changing the Size Ratios") to check the relative size ratios. If necessary, change the ratios.

- Use Reveal Codes to check the positions of font and size codes. Only the text between the starting and ending codes will appear in the specified size.

- Remember that if the currently selected printer doesn't have scalable fonts, WordPerfect will do the best it can to size the text to the proportions you've defined.

Changing the Document's Initial Font

Normally, the starting font for a document is the default font for the currently selected printer (see Chapter 10). If you want to use a different starting font (also called the *base font*), follow these steps:

1. Choose Layout ➤ Document ➤ Initial Font or click the Initial Font button in the Font dialog box. The Document Initial Font dialog box appears.

2. Choose a Font Face, Font Size, and Font Style, then choose OK.

Changing the Appearance of Text

You don't have to choose a new font to change the appearance of text. You can change the *appearance attributes* of text to get any weight (for example, boldfaced, italicized) or other appearance shown below.

Regular **Bold** <u>Underline</u>
<u>Double Underline</u>
Italic Outline **Shadow** Sᴍᴀʟʟ
Cᴀᴘ Redline S̶t̶r̶i̶k̶e̶o̶u̶t̶

Be aware, however, that not all printers and fonts support the full range of appearances. For example, Redline and Shadow tend to look different on different printers. Outline appearance is generally available only on later-model laser printers. You may need to experiment to find out how the various appearances will look when you print them. The steps for changing the appearance of text are nearly identical to those for changing the relative size:

1. Select the text you want to change, or, if you haven't typed that text yet, place the cursor where you plan to type the text.

2. Choose Layout ➤ Font, and then select whatever attributes you want from the Appearance section of the dialog box. Or, if the power bar is visible, you can just use the Bold, Italic, and Underline buttons, shown below, as a quick shortcut to the most commonly used appearances.

3. If you selected text in step 1, you're done. Otherwise, type the new text, and press → when you want to start typing normal text without the attributes again.

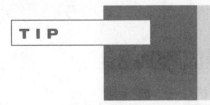

TIP

Other shortcuts for changing the text appearance include Ctrl+B (Bold), Ctrl+I (Italic), and Ctrl+U (Underline). The Font button bar also offers shortcuts for appearances.

Pressing → in the last step above moves the cursor past the last ending code for the appearance, so that any new text you type returns to the original appearance. (You can see the codes that control the text appearance in Reveal Codes. Only text between the codes will have the requested appearance.)

TIP

You can combine sizes, appearances, and fonts however you wish, to come up with whatever appearance appeals to you. If you're interested in creating dramatic special effects with your text, see Chapter 28.

Undoing Size and Appearance Changes

To undo a size or appearance change immediately, just choose Edit ➤ Undo or press Ctrl+Z. Or, if you've made more changes since the size/appearance change, move the cursor to where you want to undo the change, turn on Reveal Codes, and delete any codes that you no longer want.

You can also remove a size or appearance change by selecting the text, choosing Layout ➤ Font, and deselecting any Appearance options that you want to get rid of.

Underlining Spaces and Tabs

The Underline and Double Underline appearances normally underline words *and* the blank spaces between words. But you can choose whether to have WordPerfect underline spaces and tabs. Figure 6.9 shows examples of your options, where tabs are used to separate Name, Address, and City, and spaces separate City, State, and Zip.

FIGURE 6.9

Underlining methods,
available for both
single underlining and
double-underlining

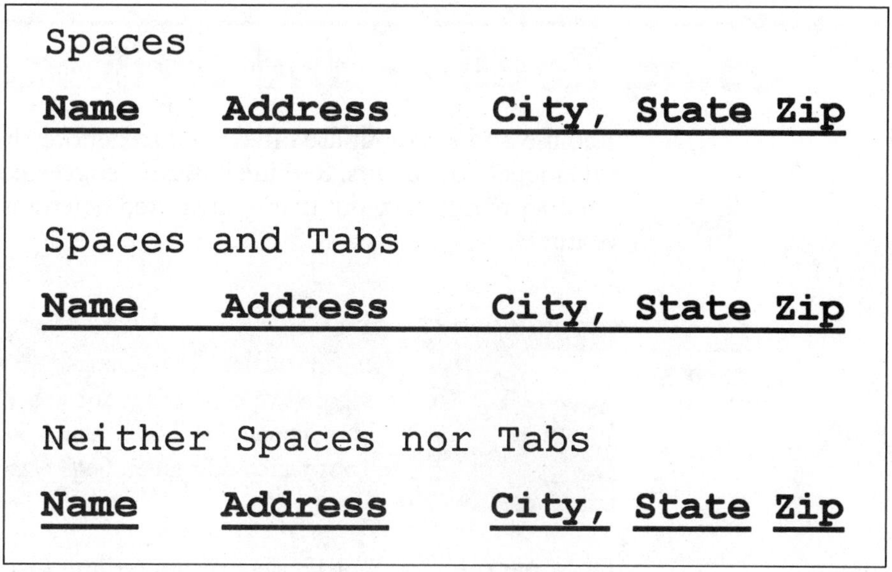

```
Spaces

Name      Address          City, State Zip


Spaces and Tabs

Name      Address          City, State Zip


Neither Spaces nor Tabs

Name      Address          City, State Zip
```

To choose an underlining method, follow these steps:

1. Move the cursor to the first character or blank space where you want to change the underlining method, or select the text where you want to change the underlining method.

2. Choose Layout ➤ Font or press F9 to get to the Font dialog box.

3. In the Underline Options area you can choose which characters you want included in the underlines (Spaces, Tabs, both, or neither) by selecting the check boxes for the characters you do want underlined, and deselecting (clearing) the check boxes for the characters you don't want underlined.

4. Choose OK to return to your document.

All underlined and double-underlined text past the cursor will have the new underlining method.

Using Redline and Strikeout

Redline and strikeout are often used to denote changes in contracts and other legal documents. Redline indicates suggested additions to the original document; strikeout marks suggested deletions. Figure 6.10 shows an example.

NOTE
You can use the File ➤ Compare Document command to compare two copies of a document and automatically add redline and strikeout based on the differences between each document. See Chapter 31.

On some printers, WordPerfect prints redline text as a grayed shade. On other printers, redline text appears with a shaded background or with dots beneath the characters. On color printers, redline text is printed in red.

FIGURE 6.10

Redline and strikeout in a sample paragraph

THE PURCHASE PRICE INCLUDES: All tacked down carpeting, ~~all existing window treatments,~~ all existing window and door screens, all built-in appliances, all ~~fixtures,~~ shrubs, trees and items permanently attached to the real property, all window treatments excluding the wooden louvers in the dining room, and all fixtures excluding chandelier in the dining room. Pool and spa equipment is also to be included.

Special Techniques for Redline and Strikeout

You can change the appearance of redline text if you wish. To do so, choose Layout ➤ Document ➤ Redline Method. Here's a summary of the redline options available to you:

Printer Dependent   Redline is printed as specified by your printer.

Mark Left Margin   Redline text is marked by a character in the left margin.

Mark Alternating Margins   Redline text is marked by a character in the left margin on even-numbered pages and a character in the right margin on odd-numbered pages.

Mark Right Margin   Redline text is marked by a character in the right margin.

Redline Character   If you chose any of the margin options just above, you can also define your own redline character. Initially, it's a vertical bar (|). But you can delete that character from the Redline Character text box, (with the usual Del key), then type any character you want, or use Ctrl+W to select a special character.

Use as Default   If you click this button, all future documents will use the redline method you've chosen here. If you don't click this button, only the current document will use the redline method you've selected here.

When you've finished defining your redline method, choose OK to return to your document.

Removing Redline Markings and Strikeout Text

WordPerfect lets you remove all the redline markings and strikeout text from a document with a single command. This is useful when you want to print a final draft of a document, after you're certain that you no longer need the redline markings or the text that has been struck out. Follow these steps:

1. Choose File ➤ Compare Document ➤ Remove Markings.

2. Choose whether you want to remove both redline markings and strikeout text or just the strikeout text.

3. Choose OK.

If you want to leave the original copy of the document with redlines and strikeout still intact, save this copy of the document with a new file name using the File ➤ Save As command.

Using Hidden Text

Chapter 4 explained how you could use *document comments* (Insert ➤ Comment) to write notes to yourself or to someone else who might be reviewing your document. Document comments appear in framed boxes or as icons in the left margin of your document when viewed on screen. However, they don't print unless you convert them to text.

Hidden text offers a flexible alternative to document comments. Like document comments, hidden text is useful for questions, messages, and comments. However, hidden text offers these advantages over document comments:

- You can show or hide hidden text. When you show the text, it appears both on screen and in your printed document. When you hide the text, it's invisible on the screen and in printouts.

- You can include text, fonts, attributes, lines, graphics—*anything*—between the hidden text codes.

- When hidden text is visible, WordPerfect treats it like any other information in your document. When it's invisible, it's just that—completely invisible. To mark text as hidden:

  1. Move the cursor to where you're about to type hidden text, or select existing text that you want to hide.

2. Choose <u>L</u>ayout ➤ <u>F</u>ont, then select Hidd<u>e</u>n in the Appearance section of the Font dialog box.

3. Choose OK to return to the document window.

Hiding/Displaying Hidden Text

Once you've defined some text as hidden, you can choose whether you really want it hidden, or whether you want to see and print it. Just choose <u>V</u>iew ➤ Hidden Te<u>x</u>t to either show (✓) or hide (no checkmark) the hidden text. Your selection affects both the screen and printed copies of the document.

T I P

To change the default setting for showing/hiding hidden text, choose <u>F</u>ile ➤ Pref<u>e</u>rences ➤ <u>D</u>isplay ➤ <u>D</u>ocument. Then, in the Show group, check the Hidd<u>e</u>n Text box if you want that text to be visible by default.

WordPerfect places hidden text in a [Hidden] code, which you can see in Reveal Codes. If you've selected <u>V</u>iew ➤ Hidden Te<u>x</u>t, you can edit the hidden text if necessary. To return hidden text to its normal (visible) self, simply delete its [Hidden] code in Reveal Codes.

Typing Special Characters

You can type all the letters, numbers, and punctuation marks needed for most documents right from your keyboard. However, many situations call for special characters, such as bullets, copyright symbols (for example, © and ™), foreign currency signs, and the ↑, ↓, ←, →, and ↵ characters used in this book.

WordPerfect offers over 1400 special characters, including foreign-language characters and scientific symbols, and several mathematical equations and foreign alphabets. When you want to type a special character that isn't on the keyboard:

1. Move the cursor to the place where you want to type the special character.

2. Choose Insert ➤ Character or press Ctrl+W. The WordPerfect Characters dialog box appears:

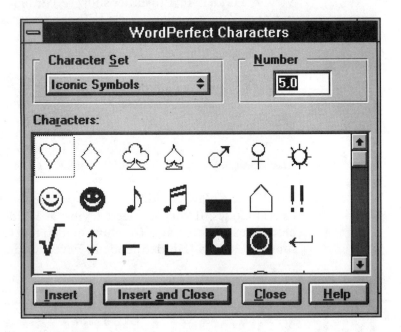

TIP

If you know the two-letter shortcut or the number code of the character you want, you can type that two-letter shortcut or number (including the comma) under Number in the dialog box, then press ↵.

3. Optionally, to choose a different character set, choose Character Set and then select one of the set names in the pop-up list.

4. In the Characters list, click on or highlight a character you want to insert.

5. Choose Insert <u>A</u>nd Close if you just want to insert one character. Or, choose <u>I</u>nsert to insert the character and also select more characters to insert.

The special character you selected will appear in the document window. When you move the cursor to that character, you can see the character and its code in the Reveal Codes window, like this:

[©:4,23]

Figure 6.11 shows some of the more commonly used special characters and the codes used to type each one. You can tell which character set each special character belongs to by the first number in the code, as follows:

4   Typographic Symbols

5   Iconic Symbols

6   Math/Scientific

Shortcuts for Commonly Used Special Characters

WordPerfect offers yet another shortcut for typing some special characters. You can use a two-letter code in place of the two-number code. To use a two-letter shortcut, press Ctrl+W then type the two-character combination shown to the right of each special character in Figure 6.12. For example, to type a large bullet, you can press Ctrl+W, then type ** and press ↵.

TIP

When typing a list, you can easily insert a bullet (or number) in front of each item using the <u>I</u>nsert ➤ Bullets & <u>N</u>umbers commands, as discussed under "Typing Lists" in Chapter 5.

FIGURE 6.11

Examples of special characters not found on the keyboard, but available after you choose Insert ➤ Character or press Ctrl+W.

Bullets		Fractions		General	
•	4,0	½	4,17	'	4,27
o	4,1	¼	4,18	'	4,28
■	4,2	¾	4,25	'	4,29
·	4,3	⅓	4,64	"	4,30
○	4,37	⅔	4,65	"	4,31
□	4,38	⅛	4,66	"	4,32
●	4,44	⅜	4,67	–	4,33
o	4,45	⅝	4,68	—	4,34
■	4,46	⅞	4,69	†	4,39
■	4,47			‡	4,40
□	4,48	**Graphics**		™	4,41
□	4,49	♥	5,0	SM	4,42
☞	5,43	♦	5,1	℞	4,43
☜	5,22	♣	5,2	…	4,56
✓	5,51	♠	5,3	℅	4,73
□	5,24	♂	5,4	‰	4,75
⊠	5,25	♀	5,5	№º	4,76
		☼	5,6	°	6,36
		☺	5,7	★	6,112
Currency		☻	5,8	►	6,27
£	4,11	☹	5,26	◄	6,28
¥	4,12	☎	5,30	▲	6,29
Pt	4,13	☼	5,31	▼	6,30
ƒ	4,14	⌛	5,32		
¢	4,19			**Keyboard**	
¤	4,24	**General**		↵	5,20
$	4,57	¶	4,5	→	6,21
₣	4,58	§	4,6	←	6,22
₢	4,59	®	4,22	↑	6,23
₠	4,60	©	4,23	↓	6,24
₤	4,61				

FIGURE 6.12

Two-letter shortcuts for frequently used special characters

Bullets		Foreign		General	
·	*	é	e'	«	<<
•	**	¡	!!	»	>>
o	*o	¿	??	©	co
O	*O	å	ao	®	ro
Currency		**Math**		™	tm
¢	c/	±	+-	SM	sm
ƒ	f-	≥	>=	–	n-
£	L-	≤	<=	—	m-
¥	Y=	≡	==	¶	P|

Fractions

½ /2

¼ /4

This is the | (vertical bar) character, found on the same key as the backslash on most keyboards.

Wingdings, Dingbats, and Extras

Some fonts don't contain any letters, or they contain letters plus a variety of small icons. Fonts with names like Zingbats, Wingdings, Dingbats, Symbols, and Extras often fall into this category.

After choosing such a font, just typing upper and lowercase letters (and numbers) might display the special characters you're looking for. If not, the special characters might be in one of the WordPerfect character sets. To be sure, you can print out all the characters in a font, as discussed next.

Viewing All the Character Sets in a Font

To view all the character sets for any font, you can open the file named CHARMAP.WPD file that came with your WordPerfect program. (Usually, this file is stored in the directory C:\WPC20.) Near the top of that document, choose the font you're interested in. Then print the document with Graphics Quality set to High. (It might take a while!)

When you're done printing, choose File ➤ Close ➤ No.

The file named CHARACTR.DOC (usually in the C:\WPC20 directory) also lists all the characters available. In addition to showing the character and its number code, this file lists each character's English name. For example, the entry for the # character looks like this:

    0,35   #   (Number/Pound)

Because the CHARCTR.DOC file is nearly sixty pages long, you might not want to print it.

Sizing Special Characters

The size of the current font determines the size of special characters. For example, Figure 6.13 uses a pointing hand (special character 5,43 from the Iconic Symbols) next to text. In the first item, the hand is the same size as the text. In the second item, the hand is Very Large Size. In the third item, the hand is Extra Large size. (Normally, that would make the hand point "over" the accompanying text. But I used the Advance feature described in Chapter 28 to move the hand down a few points, to better align it with text to the right.)

FIGURE 6.13

Examples of special characters in different sizes

☞ Hand is same size as the font

☞ Hand is Very Large size

☞ Hand is Extra Large, advanced down

Printing Two Characters in One Space

If you can't find a special character or symbol that you need, you may be able to create it by typing two or more characters in a single space using the Overstrike feature. Here's how:

1. Move the cursor to the spot where you want to type multiple characters.

2. Choose Layout ➤ Typesetting ➤ Overstrike. The dialog box below will appear on your screen:

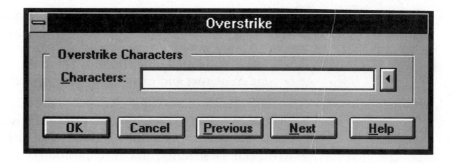

3. If you wish, you can click the small button to the right of the Characters text box (or press F4), and select an option to insert formatting codes into the overstrike.

4. Type the characters that you want to overstrike. For example, typing **O/** will produce a slashed O in the document.

5. Choose OK when you're done.

The characters appear in the same space in the document window. In Reveal Codes, the characters are displayed in an [Ovrstk] code.

Changing or Deleting an Overstrike

To delete an overstrike character altogether, turn on Reveal Codes and delete the [Ovrstk] code.

To change an overstrike character, double-click its code in Reveal Codes. Or, position the cursor near the overstrike, choose Layout ➤ Typesetting ➤ Overstrike, then choose Previous or Next as appropriate until the overstrike you want to edit appears in the text box. Make your changes using the standard editing techniques. (If you make a mistake, you can click the Reset button to restore the previously saved characters to the text box.) Choose OK to save your changes.

Adding Graphic Lines

Lines provide a simple way to spruce up and organize a document. There are actually several ways to add lines to a document:

- You can use the Underline and Double Underline appearances to underline text and/or spaces and tabs, as described earlier in this chapter.

- You can use the Graphic Lines feature, discussed in the following section, to draw horizontal and vertical lines. You can control the thickness, shading, and exact position of graphic lines.

- To draw lines *around* text and graphics, you can use the Graphic Borders feature described later in this chapter.

- The *Tables* feature (Chapter 7) also lets you place lines around text and graphics.

- You can use WordPerfect's *Draw* feature to draw lines of any size and shape. Additionally, the *Chart* feature makes it easy to display and print line graphs of tabular data. (See Chapter 26.)

I discussed underlining text earlier in this chapter. We'll look next at techniques for adding horizontal and vertical graphic lines to your documents.

Drawing Graphic Lines

Adding horizontal or vertical graphic lines to a document is fairly easy:

- To create a vertical line between the left and right margins, move the cursor to where you want the line to appear, and choose Graphics ➤ Horizontal Line or press Ctrl+F11.

- To draw a vertical line down the left margin, that runs from the top margin to the bottom margin, choose Graphics ➤ Vertical Line or press Ctrl+Shift+F11.

- To draw a horizontal or vertical line anywhere else on the page, or to change the thickness or length of the line, put the cursor where you want the line to begin. Then choose Graphics ➤ Custom Line to open the Create Graphics Line dialog box shown in Figure 6.14.

FIGURE 6.14

The Create Graphics Line dialog box lets you create any line you wish. Choose Graphics ➤ Custom Line to get to this dialog box.

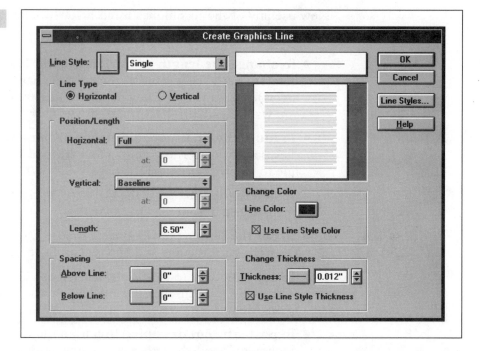

If you opted to create a custom line, you can now define the Line Style, Line Type (Horizontal or Vertical), Position/Length, and so forth, as shown in the dialog box. The sample line and page in the dialog box shows you how the line will look on the printed page. So feel free to experiment until the line looks just right. Then choose OK to return to the document window.

Changing a Line

When you put a line in your document, WordPerfect inserts a [Graph Line] code in your document, which displays the line.

You can change the appearance of the line in many ways. To begin, click the line so it has sizing handles (little squares), as shown here:

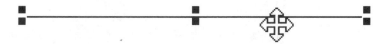

Now use any of the techniques listed below to make changes to the selected line:

- **To change the length or thickness** of the line, move the mouse pointer to any sizing handle (the pointer changes to a two-headed arrow), and drag that sizing handle to the length and/or thickness you want.

- **To move the line**, move the mouse pointer inside the sizing handles, so the pointer turns into a four-headed arrow. Then drag the line to a new position on the page.

- **To delete the line**, press the Del key. Or, right-click the line and choose Delete from the QuickMenu.

- **To cut the line** to the Clipboard, choose Edit ➤ Cut (Ctrl+X). Or, right-click the line and choose Cut from the QuickMenu.

- **To copy the line** to the Clipboard, choose Edit ➤ Copy (Ctrl+C). Or, right-click the line and choose Copy from the QuickMenu.

- **To paste the cut or copied line** from the Clipboard into your document, move the cursor to the new position for the line in your document, then choose Edit ➤ Paste (Ctrl+V).

- **To change the line's appearance** (in the dialog box you used to create the line), do any of the following: Right-click the line you want to change and choose the Edit option from the QuickMenu. Or, double-click the [Graph Line] code for the line you want to change. Or, choose Graphics ➤ Edit Line to edit the line nearest the current cursor position. Or, double-click the line. When the Edit Graphics Line dialog box appears, make whatever changes you wish, and choose OK.

Do remember that for documents requiring many lines, like the examples shown near the end of Chapter 7, it's much easier to use the Tables feature than the graphic lines discussed here.

Drawing Borders around Pages and Paragraphs

Another way to add lines to a document is by drawing *borders* around text. You can draw lines around the entire page, around all paragraphs, or around specific paragraphs.

Drawing Borders around Paragraphs

To draw borders around paragraphs, follow the steps below:

1. Type the paragraph(s) that you want to draw borders around. Then...

   - If you want to put a border around specific paragraphs, select those paragraphs.

   - If you want to put a border around a paragraph, or around a paragraph and all subsequent paragraphs, move the cursor to anywhere within the first paragraph you want bordered.

2. Choose Layout ➤ Paragraph ➤ Border/Fill. You'll see the Paragraph Border dialog box:

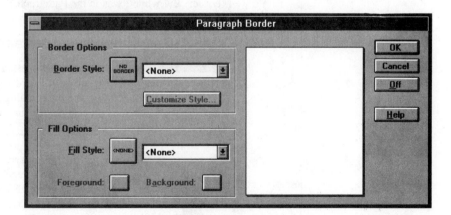

- Choose a border style from the <u>B</u>order Style drop-down list or button.
- If you want to make a fancier border, select a border style other than <None>, and choose <u>C</u>ustomize Style. Then you can experiment with the options in the Customize Border dialog box to change the color, corners, drop shadow, spacing, and other characteristics of the border (see Figure 6.15). This dialog box is easy to experiment with, because the sample border within the box instantly shows you how the border will look as you make selections. Choose OK after customizing the border.
- If you want to shade the paragraph(s), choose <u>F</u>ill Style, then select one of the available fill styles.
- If you want to put a border around the current paragraph only, select (check) Apply Border To Current Paragraph

FIGURE 6.15

Examples of various paragraph border styles, as well as a simple page border.

This paragraph has a single-line border. After typing all the paragraphs on this page, I selected this paragraph. I chose <u>L</u>ayout ▸ <u>P</u>aragraph ▸ <u>B</u>order/Fill, selected Single from the list of <u>B</u>order Style options, and chose OK.

This paragraph has a fancy border. I followed the same basic steps as in the previous paragraph to create this border. But while I was in the Paragraph Border dialog box, I selected this fancier border (Gray Mat) from the <u>B</u>order Style button.

This border shows a drop shadow. I used the <u>C</u>ustomize Style button in the Paragraph Border dialog box to add it. (Be aware that you can also put text in graphics boxes, as discussed in Chapter 25.)

To put the border around the page, I chose <u>L</u>ayout ▸ <u>P</u>age ▸ <u>B</u>order/Fill and picked Single from the list of <u>B</u>order Style options. I then chose OK. The arrow is a piece of clip art (see Chapter 25).

Only. If you want to put a border around the current paragraph and all subsequent paragraphs, deselect this option. (The setting doesn't matter if you selected paragraphs in step 1.)

3. When you've finished defining your border, choose OK to return to your document.

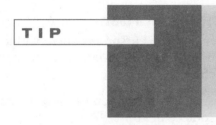

TIP If you find that you need to add text below a bordered paragraph, but you can't get the cursor out of the borders, choose Layout ➤ Paragraph ➤ Border/Fill ➤ Off. Later, you can repeat the steps given above to put borders around whichever paragraphs you wish.

Changing or Deleting Paragraph Borders

To change a paragraph border, move the cursor anywhere within the border, and choose Layout ➤ Paragraph ➤ Border/Fill. You'll be returned to the dialog box that you used to create the border.

Like most things in WordPerfect, paragraph borders are controlled by hidden codes. This means you can delete a paragraph border by deleting the [Para Border] code at the beginning of the bordered paragraph. You can also delete paragraph borders as follows: Put the cursor in a bordered paragraph, or select one or more bordered paragraphs. Choose Layout ➤ Paragraph ➤ Border/Fill. If you didn't select text, check or clear the Apply Border To Current Paragraph Only box, as appropriate. Then choose Off.

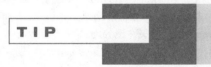

TIP You can use the Find feature described in Chapter 9 to search for [Para Border] codes.

Drawing Page Borders

To draw a border around the current page:

1. Place the cursor anywhere on the page that you want to put a border around.

2. Choose Layout ➤ Page ➤ Border/Fill.

3. As with paragraph borders, you can choose a border style, customize that style, and choose a fill Style. You can also decide whether to apply the border to the current page only, or to the current and all subsequent pages.

4. Choose OK.

Changing or Deleting a Page Border

To change the current page border, put the cursor anywhere within the border and choose Layout ➤ Page ➤ Border/Fill. Make your changes in the dialog box that appears, then choose OK.

To delete *all* the page borders in your document, you can just delete the [Pg Border] codes, using Reveal Codes (Alt+F3).

To turn off page bordering at a specific place in your document, move the cursor to the first page you want unbordered. Then choose Layout ➤ Page ➤ Border/Fill. Select or deselect the Apply Border To Current Page Only check box, as appropriate. Then choose Off.

Then choose Layout ➤ Page ➤ Border/Fill. Select or deselect the Apply Border to Current Page Only check box, as appropriate. Then choose Off.

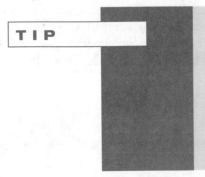

TIP

WordPerfect comes with a snazzy macro named PGBORDER. This macro can set up a fancy page border on the current page, using a page-sized graphics Figure box that's anchored to the page. To place the fancy border on every page, or on alternating pages, create a header (Layout ➤ Header/Footer). Then, while editing the header, play the PGBORDER macro. See Chapters 8 (headers), 18 (macros), and 25 (graphics boxes).

Coloring Your Text

If you're lucky enough to own a color printer, you can easily add color to your printed text. But even if you don't own a color printer, your local print shop or service bureau can probably print your documents in color for you. To color your text:

1. Place the cursor where you want the color to start, or select the text you want to color.

2. Choose Layout ➤ Font (or press F9) then click the Color button in the Font dialog box. A color palette appears on the screen.

3. Click the color you want, or use the arrow keys to move the selector to the color you want and then press ↵.

4. If you want to change the shade, set the Shading option to the appropriate percentage. The higher the number (for example, 100%), the darker the color. Note that the Resulting Font box shows the current shading.

5. Choose OK to return to the document window. If you selected text in step 1, the color will be reversed until you turn off the selection (just click any other text in your document, or press an arrow key).

Text colors are controlled by [Color] codes, which you can see in Reveal Codes. You can move or delete these codes like any other codes (see Chapter 4).

Printing in Color

When you're ready to print your document in color, choose File ➤ Print. In the Print dialog box, choose Print Color, then Full Color. Then choose Print to start printing the document.

Different printers will interpret different colors and gray shades differently. Therefore, you may need to experiment to find just the right shades for your printer.

In this chapter you've learned about a number of techniques for sprucing up the appearance of a document. In the next chapter, you'll learn about one of WordPerfect's most powerful (yet also one of the easiest) tools for organizing text in columns—the Tables feature.

AUGUST 1994

Sun	Mon	Tue	Wed	Thu	Fri	Sat
	1	2	3	4	5	6
7	8	9	10	11	12	13
14	15	16	17	18	19	20
21	22	23	24	25	26	27
28	29	30	31			

CHAPTER

7

Creating Dazzling Tables

f a s t TRACK

WORDPERFECT'S Tables feature is one of its best for organizing text and graphic images on a page. In its simplest usage, the Tables feature is handy for creating small tables like the example shown in Figure 7.1.

What most people don't realize, however, is that the Tables feature is great for just about any document that's formatted into columns and rows. You can even use the Tables feature—instead of a stand-alone spreadsheet package—to calculate formulas and do fancy arithmetic, calendar, financial, logical, and text operations! (See Chapter 24.)

In fact, tables are perfect for producing almost any type of multiple-column documents, *except* those with newspaper-style columns. For those types of documents, you'll probably prefer to use the Columns feature, discussed in Chapter 27.

Destination	Arrives	Ticket Price
Oceanside	8:30 am	$12.50
San Clemente	9:00 am	$17.50
Santa Ana	10:00 am	$37.50
Anaheim	10:30 am	$40.00
Los Angeles	11:45 am	$55.00
Malibu	1:00 pm	$70.00

Hidden Advantages of Tables

Figure 7.2 shows an example of how you might use the Tables feature to create a multicolumn document. You can see the first draft of an itinerary, in which the Tables feature was used to organize some of the text into columns.

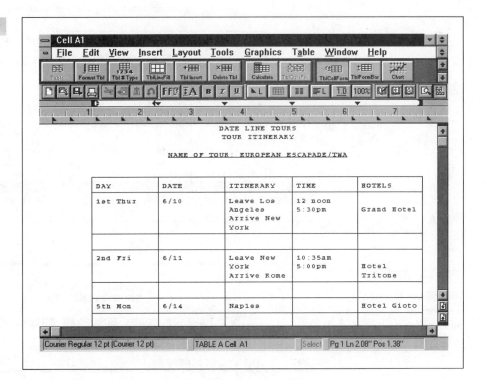

You can widen or narrow columns and join and split cells at any time to get the appearance you want. Text within each cell will automatically wrap to fit the cell, and you can see your changes right on the screen as you make them. Figure 7.3 shows the sample itinerary after column widths within the table have been adjusted to accommodate the text inside the cells.

When you're done adjusting column widths and cells, you can easily change or remove any of the lines in the table. For example, Figure 7.4 shows the completed itinerary after removing most of the lines from the table. Text is placed neatly into columns, without the clutter of lines.

FIGURE 7.3

The second draft of the itinerary, after changing some column widths

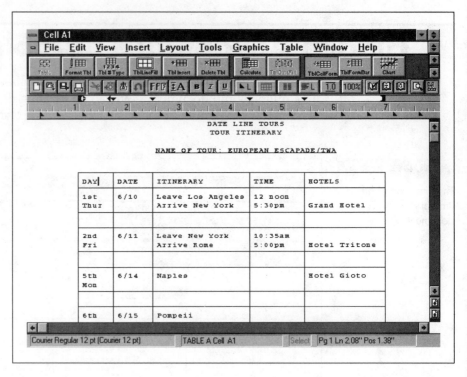

FIGURE 7.4

The sample itinerary with most of the lines removed

DATE LINE TOURS
TOUR ITINERARY

NAME OF TOUR: EUROPEAN ESCAPADE/TWA

DAY	DATE	ITINERARY	TIME	HOTELS
1st Thur	6/10	Leave Los Angeles Arrive New York	12 noon 5:30pm	Grand Hotel
2nd Fri	6/11	Leave New York Arrive Rome	10:35am 5:00pm	Hotel Tritone
5th Mon	6/14	Naples		Hotel Gioto
6th Tue	6/15	Pompeii		

Tables Terminology

The Tables feature uses some terminology that comes from spreadsheet applications. A table consists of *rows* and *columns*. The place where a row and a column meet is a *cell* (see Figure 7.5).

Each cell has an *address* that indicates its position in the table. Whenever the cursor is inside the table, the address of the current cell appears on the status line as you move the cursor from cell to cell. The cell address also appears in the WordPerfect title bar when you move the mouse pointer to a cell. Table columns are named alphabetically from left to right, and the rows are numbered from top to bottom. So the cell in the upper-left corner is always cell A1, the cell to the right of that is cell B1, and so forth. Beneath cell A1 are cells A2, A3, etc.

FIGURE 7.5

Columns, rows, and a cell in a table

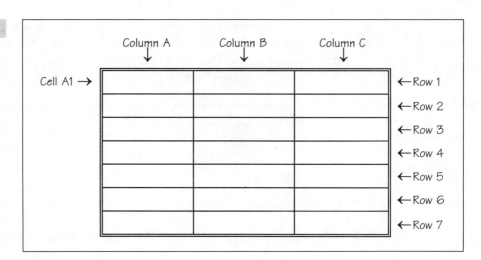

Creating a Table

To create a table, move the cursor to wherever you want to put the table. Then, you have a choice of approaches...

- Choose Table ➤ Create or press F12, specify the number of rows and columns you want (you can change your mind later if need be), and choose OK.

- Or, if the Table button bar is visible, click the Table Create button shown at left, specify the number of rows and columns you want, then choose OK.

TIP The Tables button bar will appear automatically if you display any button bar (View ➤ Button Bar) and then move the cursor into a table. The previously selected button bar will reappear when you move the cursor out of the table again. To display the Tables button bar when the cursor isn't in a table, right click the current button bar and choose Tables.

- Or, click the Table Quick Create button (shown at left) in the power bar, and drag to highlight as many rows and columns as you want (as below). Then release the mouse button. (If the power bar isn't visible, choose View ➤ Power Bar.)

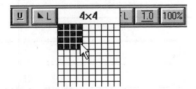

The table will appear in your document, initially empty.

Moving through a Table

You can move the cursor to any cell within the table by using your mouse to click the cell you want to move the cursor to. You can also use the keys listed in Table 7.1 to move around the table.

TABLE 7.1: Keys used to move the cursor through a table

TO MOVE	PRESS
One Cell Right	Tab or Alt+→
One Cell Left	Shift+Tab or Alt+←
One Cell Down	Alt+↓
One Cell Up	Alt+↑
First cell in row	Home, Home
Last cell in row	End, End
Top of multi-line cell	Alt+Home
Bottom of multi-line cell	Alt+End

Typing and Editing Table Text

Once you've created an empty table, it's easy to type and edit text in it. Just move the cursor to whichever cell you want to type in or change, and type or edit your text normally. If you type more text than will fit into the cell, the text will word-wrap, and the entire row will be a line taller. (As you'll see shortly, you can change the column width later, as necessary, to prevent word wrapping, as I did for Figures 7.2 and 7.3.)

When Your Entry Changes...

If you type an entry that looks like a formula (that is, it contains numbers and mathematical symbols like + - / *), WordPerfect may assume it is a formula, and do the math as soon as you move the cursor out of the cell. For example, if you type in the date 12/31/94 WordPerfect will display 0, or perhaps 0.004118..., the result of dividing 12 by 31 by 94. Similarly, if you type in a number such as 1,234.56 WordPerfect might display the number as 1234.56. There are two possible reasons for this sudden change:

- *Cell Formula Entry mode may be turned on.* When Cell Formula Entry mode is on, WordPerfect automatically does calculations if you enter numbers (or text that can be interpreted as numbers, such as 12/31/94) into a cell, and then move the cursor to another cell. When this mode is off, WordPerfect will treat numbers as normal text. To turn Cell Formula Entry mode on or off, choose Table ➤ Cell Formula Entry, or click the Cell Formula Entry button in the Tables button bar. This is a toggle option. When Cell Formula Entry is selected (checked) the mode is on. When it's deselected (unchecked), the mode is off. (There's more about formulas in Chapter 24.)

- *The cell you're typing in may be preformatted to display numbers in a certain way.* If you run into problems with this sort of thing, refer to "Changing Appearances and Alignment" later in the chapter for ways to change the appearance of the entry. But just for the sake of example, let's take a look at some of your formatting options right now:

  - If you use Table ➤ Number Type to format the cell containing the 12/31/94 date to the Text type, the date will appear as 12/31/94 (though if you've already typed in the date, you'll need to *delete* your entry first and retype the correct entry).

  - If you set the Number Type of a cell to Date/Time, then type in 12/31/94, your entry will be converted to *December 31, 1994* (or whatever custom format you define).

  - If you set the Number Type of a cell to Accounting, then type a number like 12345.67, WordPerfect will automatically convert that to $12,345.67.

NOTE After typing your entry into a cell, move the cursor to a different cell to see the formatting changes.

Removing Extra Blanks in a Row

One common, pesky mishap occurs when you inadvertently press ⏎ after typing text in a table. There's no harm in doing this, but it does cause the current row to double in height. You probably won't want this extra blank space across the row. So to get rid of it, press Backspace. Or, if you've already moved the cursor elsewhere, go back to the offending cell, turn on Reveal Codes, and delete the [HRt] code at the end of the cell's text.

Tabbing and Indenting within a Table

When the cursor is in a table, the Tab and Shift+Tab keys move it around the table. If you want to indent, you can use options on the Layout ➤ Line menu or the shortcut keys listed in Table 7.2. (See Chapters 5 and 6 for more information about alignment, tabs, and dot leaders.)

TABLE 7.2: Keys used for indenting within a table cell

TO INSERT A	PRESS
Tab	Ctrl+Tab
Center	Shift+F7
Center with Dot Leader	Shift+F7, Shift+F7
Flush Right	Alt+F7
Flush Right with Dot Leader	Alt+F7, Alt+F7
Indent	F7
Double-Indent	Ctrl+Shift+F7
Hanging Indent	Ctrl+F7

Selecting Cells

You can select a group of cells that you want to reformat or change. The basic techniques for selecting cells are the same as for selecting text outside of a table:

- Move the mouse pointer to the first cell you want to select, hold down the mouse button, and drag until the cells you want to select are highlighted.

- Or, move the cursor to the first cell you want to select, hold down the Shift key, and use the keys listed back in Table 7.1 to extend the highlight through the cells you want to work with.

If you need to start over, just click any cell or press any arrow key without holding down the Shift key.

Selection Shortcuts

Here are some shortcuts for selecting an entire row, column, or table:

- **To select a cell or a row,** move the mouse pointer to any vertical line until the cell pointer changes to a single-headed, horizontal arrow. Then click once to select the cell, or double-click to select the entire row.

- **To select a cell or a column,** move the mouse pointer to any horizontal line, until it turns to a vertical, single-headed arrow. Then click to select the cell, or double-click to select the entire column.

- **To select all the cells in the table,** move the mouse pointer to any line in the table, so that it looks like a horizontal or vertical arrow (← or ↑). Then triple-click the mouse button.

If you make a mistake, just click anywhere in the table, or press any arrow key, to undo the selection.

Selecting a Cell vs. Selecting Its Contents

When you're selecting table contents, you can either choose the entire cell, or just a portion of the cell's contents. For example, in the left side of the example below, the entire cell is selected. In the right side of the example, only certain words within the cell are selected. You can use the mouse and Shift+arrow keys to make either type of selection.

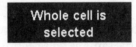

Any formatting you select affects only the selected text. For example, if you were to click the Bold Font button on the power bar after selecting the entire cell, the entire cell contents would be boldfaced. However, if you were to activate boldface with just a portion of the text selected, *only* that selected text will be boldfaced.

Resizing Columns

One of the best advantages of WordPerfect's tables is that you can interactively resize the columns until the text within each column fits best, as in the examples you saw in Figures 7.2 through 7.4. To change the width of a column, follow the steps below:

1. Using your mouse, move the mouse pointer to a column line until the pointer changes to the two-headed crosshairs shown at left.

2. Hold down the mouse button, drag the dashed line that appears to whatever width you want the column to be, then release the mouse button.

TIP   If the ruler bar is on, you can also drag the ▼ above the ruler marks to change the width of a column.

Sizing Columns to a Specific Width

If you want to set a column or group of columns to a specific width, such as 2.5 inches, follow these steps:

1. Move the cursor to the column you want to resize. If you want to set several adjacent columns to the same size, select those columns.

2. Choose Table ➤ Format or click the Table Format button in the Tables button bar. The Format dialog box appears.

3. Choose Column in the top set of option buttons.

4. Under Column Width, choose Width and type in the width in inches (for example, **1.25** for 1.25 inches).

5. If you want the column widths to remain fixed (so that the column isn't resized to accommodate changes to *other* columns), select (check) Fixed Width.

6. Choose OK to return to the document window.

Be aware that you cannot widen the table beyond the width that the current margins allow. For instance, if you're using 1-inch margins on paper that's $8\frac{1}{2}$ inches wide, the combined widths of all the columns in your table cannot exceed $6\frac{1}{2}$ inches.

TIP

Throughout this chapter I'll generally send you through a menu sequence starting with the Table command. However, you can get to a QuickMenu that offers many of the same commands. Just put the cursor into any table cell, then click the right mouse button! (The Tables button bar also offers shortcuts for most Table menu options.)

Changing the Size of a Table

WordPerfect lets you change the size of any table, even if you've already filled in many of the cells. The next few sections explain how to insert and delete rows and columns.

Inserting Rows and Columns

To insert a single row into a table, move the cursor to where you want to insert a new row. Then ...

- To insert a row *above* the current row, press Alt+Ins.

- To put the new row *below* the current row, press Alt+Shift+Ins.

To insert columns or multiple rows, move the cursor to wherever you want to insert rows or columns within the table. Then ...

1. Choose Table ➤ Insert. You'll see this dialog box:

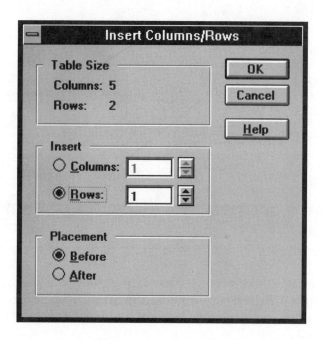

2. Choose either Rows (to insert rows) or Columns (to insert columns). Then, type in the number of rows or columns you want to insert.

3. Choose whether you want these new rows or columns to be placed Before or After the current row or column.

4. Choose OK.

You can use blank rows and columns to add space between rows and columns, if you wish. For example, Figure 7.6 shows a portion of a document

FIGURE 7.6

A blank column and blank rows used for extra spacing in a table

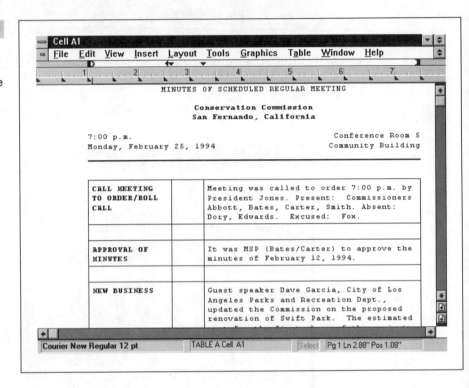

with a blank column separating the two columns containing text. Figure 7.7 shows the same document with the lines removed. The blank column and blank rows become extra blank space in the finished document.

Deleting Rows, Columns, and Text

To quickly delete a row from the table, move the cursor to the row you want to remove, then press Alt+Del. If you change your mind, choose Edit ➤ Undo or press Ctrl+Z.

To delete columns or multiple rows, follow the steps below:

1. Move the cursor to the row or column you want to delete, or select the rows or columns you want to delete.

FIGURE 7.7

The table shown in
Figure 7.6 with the
lines removed

```
            MINUTES OF SCHEDULED REGULAR MEETING

                    Conservation Commission
                   San Fernando, California

7:00 p.m.                                    Conference Room 5
Monday, February 25, 1994                    Community Building
_____


CALL MEETING          Meeting was called to order 7:00 p.m. by
TO ORDER/ROLL         President Jones. Present:  Commissioners
CALL                  Abbott, Bates, Carter, Smith. Absent:
                      Dory, Edwards.  Excused:  Fox.


APPROVAL OF           It was MSP (Bates/Carter) to approve the
MINUTES               minutes of February 12, 1994.


NEW BUSINESS          Guest speaker Dave Garcia, City of Los
                      Angeles Parks and Recreation Dept.,
                      updated the Commission on the proposed
                      renovation of Swift Park.  The estimated
                      cost for the first phase of the project
                      is $2.9 million, to include enhancement
                      of the existing parking lot.
```

2. Press Del or click the Table Delete button on the Table button
bar, or choose Table ➤ Delete. You'll see this dialog box (however,
there won't be any spin boxes to specify how many rows/columns to
delete if you already selected the rows or columns you want to delete):

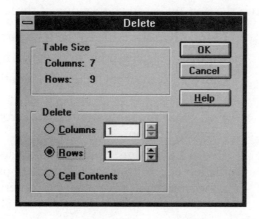

- To delete the column(s), choose Columns.
- To delete the row(s), choose Rows.
- If you *didn't* already select the row(s) and/or column(s) you want to delete, type in the number of rows or columns you want to delete.
- If you just want to empty the selected cells of their current contents, without destroying the cells, choose Cell Contents.

3. Choose OK to return to the document.

As usual, you can press Ctrl+Z if you change your mind.

Positioning the Table on the Page

By default, WordPerfect makes the table as wide as your margins will allow. If you make the table narrower than that, you can pick a position on the page by following these steps:

1. Move the cursor into the table, and choose Table ➤ Format, or click the Table Format button in the Tables button bar (if it's available).

2. In the top row of option buttons, choose Table.

3. Under Table Position near the lower left corner of the dialog box, use the pop-up list to choose one of these options:

Left   Align the table to the left margin.

Right   Align the table to the right margin.

Center   Center the table between the left and right margins.

Full   Size the table so it extends from the left margin to the right margin.

From Left Edge   Set the table a specific distance from the left edge of the page. If you choose this option, enter a measurement. (For example, entering **.5** will put the left edge of the table one half inch from the left edge of the page.)

4. Choose OK.

More Accurate Table Positioning

If you want text to wrap around a table, or to put two tables side-by-side on the page, you need to put the table(s) in a graphics box. Similarly, when using tables in a multicolumn layout, you may find it easiest to position the table on the page if you use graphics boxes.

If you want to ensure that a small table is never split across two pages in your document, your best bet, once again, is to place the table in a graphics box. See Chapters 25 and 27 for more information.

Managing Lines and Cells

Learning how to manage cells and the lines that separate them is quick and easy, and also your best tool for creativity when it comes to using the Tables feature.

Joining Cells

To *join* cells means to remove the boundaries (lines) between them. You can join any number of adjacent cells into a single cell. Just follow these steps:

1. Select the cells you want to join.

2. Choose Table ➤ Join ➤ Cell.

If you're not happy with the results, press Ctrl+Z. Figure 7.8 shows an example of cells in the top row of a table before, during, and after joining cells and centering text within the cell. In this figure, shading indicates selected (highlighted) cells. Of course, this is just one example; you can join *any* group of adjacent cells in a table. You'll see additional examples later in this chapter.

FIGURE 7.8

Joining cells to create
a table title

Train Schedule		
Destination	**Arrives**	**Price**
Oceanside	8:30 am	$12.50
San Clemente	9:00 am	$17.50
Santa Ana	10:00 am	$37.50

Step 1: Select the cells to join using your mouse or using Shift plus the cursor-movement keys. Here, I've selected all the cells across row 1.

Train Schedule		
Destination	**Arrives**	**Price**
Oceanside	8:30 am	$12.50
San Clemente	9:00 am	$17.50
Santa Ana	10:00 am	$37.50

Step 2: Choose Table ➤ Join ➤ Cell. The lines separating the cells are removed.

Train Schedule		
Destination	**Arrives**	**Price**
Oceanside	8:30 am	$12.50
San Clemente	9:00 am	$17.50
Santa Ana	10:00 am	$37.50

Step 3: If you wish, choose Table ➤ Format ➤ Cell, then choose Justification ➤ Center (and Bold if you want) to center the title. Choose OK when done.

If you join cells that already contain text, the text will be separated by [Hd Tbl Tab] codes. If you don't want the text to be separate, go back to the normal document editing mode and use Reveal Codes to delete the unwanted codes.

Splitting Cells

Splitting cells is the opposite of joining them. Rather than removing the boundaries between cells, splitting adds boundaries. You can use this feature to break a cell down into more cells, or to resplit cells you've joined. Here's how:

1. If you want to split several cells, select those cells. Otherwise, just move the cursor to the cell you want to split.

2. Choose Table ➤ Split ➤ Cell. You'll see this dialog box:

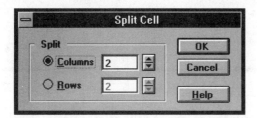

3. Choose Columns or Rows, depending on whether you want to split the cell into columns or rows.

4. Enter the number of columns or rows you want to split the cell into, then choose OK.

If you're not happy with the results, press Ctrl+Z.

Changing the Lines in a Table

To change, add, or remove table lines, follow these steps:

1. If you want to change the lines for a single cell, move the cursor to that cell. If you want to change the lines for several cells, select those cells.

2. Choose Table ➤ Lines/Fill, or press Shift+F12, or click the Lines/Fill button in the Tables button bar, to get to the Table Lines/Fill dialog box shown in Figure 7.9.

FIGURE 7.9

The Table Lines/Fill dialog box lets you control the lines in a table. Choose Table ➤ Lines/Fill, or press Shift+F12 to get to this dialog box.

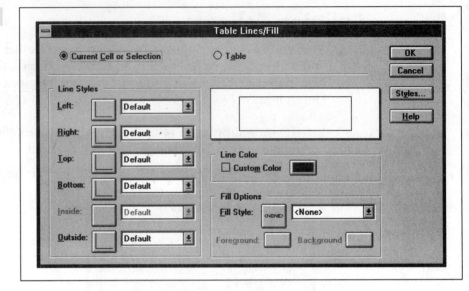

3. If you want to change the current cell, or selected cells only, choose Current Cell Or Selection from the option buttons at the top of the dialog box. If you want to define the lines for the entire table, choose the Table.

Now you can choose Line Styles, Line Color, Fill Options, and Fill Styles to your heart's content. The small sample table in the dialog box reflects your current choices, so feel free to experiment until you get exactly the look you want. Choose OK when you're done.

Shading and Patterning Cells

Shading is a really great way to add pizzazz to a table. Shading can be a nice alternative to lines as well, as illustrated in Figure 7.10.

To shade a cell, or group of cells, in a table:

1. Move the cursor to the cell you want to shade, or select the cells you want to shade.

2. Choose Table ➤ Lines/Fill (or press Shift+F12).

3. If you want to shade the current cell or selected cells, choose Current Cell Or Selection. If you want to shade the entire table, choose Table.

FIGURE 7.10

Shading used as an
alternative to lines

Milk	A	B$_1$	B$_2$	B$_6$	B$_{12}$
		Vitamin (mg)			
Whole	307	0.093	0.395	0.102	0.871
Lowfat (2%)	500	0.095	0.403	0.105	0.888
Skim	500	0.088	0.343	0.098	0.926
Buttermilk	81	0.083	0.377	0.083	0.537
Condensed	1004	0.275	1.270	0.156	1.360
Evaporated	306	0.059	0.398	0.063	0.205
Chocolate	302	0.092	0.405	0.100	0.835

4. Click the button next to Fill Style, or the drop-down list next to the text box, and then choose the fill shade/pattern you want.

5. Optionally, use the Foreground and Background buttons to choose colors for the table (the sample table in the dialog box shows your current color combination).

6. Choose OK to return to the document.

Formatting the Table's Contents

You can also format the text within your table, using fonts, appearances, and all the other techniques described throughout this book. You can format text within a cell, or you can format a single cell, a group of cells, a column, or several columns in a single operation. The table shown in Figure 7.11 was created using several formatting techniques.

Figure 7.12 shows how the table in Figure 7.11 looked before splitting some cells and removing the default inside and outside lines. But as you can see, I've also used fonts and such to further spruce up the table. (I'll explain how I did the white text on a black background a little later in the chapter.)

	Eastern	Central	Mountain	Pacific
Registration	10:00 am	9:00 am	8:00 am	7:00 am
Conference Starts	10:30 am	9:30 am	8:30 am	7:30 am
Conference Ends	6:30 am	5:30 am	4:30 am	3:30 am

FEB 25 1994

FEB
25
1994

	Eastern	Central		Mountain	Pacific
Registration	10:00 am	9:00 am		8:00 am	7:00 am
Conference Starts	10:30 am	9:30 am		8:30 am	7:30 am
Conference Ends	6:30 am	5:30 am		4:30 am	3:30 am

The first thing to understand about formatting the contents of cells is which of your selections take precedence over others:

- Any format options that you assign by choosing Table ➤ Format ➤ Table will affect the entire table. However…

- Any formatting you do by choosing Table ➤ Format ➤ Column or Table ➤ Format ➤ Row will override formatting changes you made to the table as a whole.

- Furthermore, if you start out by selecting a cell or group of cells, and then choose Table ➤ Format ➤ Cell, any formatting changes you make will override changes you made at the Table, Row, or Column level.

- Finally, if you select a portion of text within a cell, and change its format, only that selected portion of text will be formatted, and will override formats defined at the Table, Row, Column, and Cell levels.

In other words, when you're formatting a table, you might want to get the general format at the Table level first. Then, you may wish to align text at the Column level. Finally, do your more specific cell-by-cell formatting last.

Using Fonts in a Table

Changing fonts in a table is similar to changing fonts elsewhere in a document. When you first start typing in a table, the text will appear in whatever font happens to be selected at the moment. Here's how to start:

- To change the font for all the cells in the table, move the cursor to the start of the first cell.
- To change the font of all the cells beyond a particular cell, move the cursor to wherever you want the new font to begin.
- To change the font of a particular cell or group of cells, select those cell(s).
- To change the font of text within a cell, select the specific text you want to change.

Then choose your font through the normal means. That is, choose Layout ➤ Font or press F9, and pick your font face, size, and any other options, as discussed in Chapter 6. Then choose OK to return to your document.

The [Font] codes that control the font appearance are stored within their cells; they are readily visible when Reveal Codes is on. As usual, you can change the font by deleting the appropriate [Font] codes.

Changing Appearances and Alignment

You can change the appearance and alignment of your text at the cell, column, or table level. That is:

1. If you want to change the entire table, put the cursor anywhere within the table. If you want to change a column, put the cursor in the column you want to change. If you want to change a single cell, put the cursor in that cell. Or to change several cells, select those cells.

2. Use any of the following methods to get to the Format dialog box: Choose Table ➤ Format, press Ctrl+F12, click the Table Format

button in the Tables button bar, or right-click the table and choose Format from the QuickMenu that appears.

3. From the option buttons at the top of the Format dialog box, choose the level you want to change—Cell, Column, or Table. (I'll explain the Row option later in the chapter.) The dialog box will change to reflect the level you selected. It includes options for altering the alignment, appearance, and size of text, among other options.

4. Now, do any of the following:

- To change the **alignment**, choose one of the options from the Justification pop-up list, as illustrated below.

Left	Right	Center	Full	A l l	Decimal
Hello	Hello	Hello	Hello	H e l l o	Hello
1/1/94	1/1/94	1/1/94	1/1/94	1 / 1 / 9 4	1/1/94
123.45	123.45	123.45	123.45	1 2 3 . 4 5	123.45
1,234.56	1,234.56	1,234.56	1,234.56	1,234.56	1,234.56

- To change the **appearance**, choose any combination of options from the Appearance group.
- To change the **relative text size**, choose any option(s) from the Position and Size pop-up lists.

5. Choose OK when you're done.

Remember, if you want to change the size or appearance of text within a single cell, you should select the text you want to alter. Then make your changes through the standard Layout ➤ Font commands.

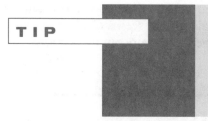

T I P When you set the Justification to <u>F</u>ull, only lines that end with a soft return ([SRt] code) are fully justified. Short lines that end with a hard return [HRt] are *not* fully justified. If you set the Justification to <u>A</u>ll, every line in the cell will be fully justified.

If It Doesn't Work...

If nothing seems to happen, it's probably because the cell(s) have already been formatted at some "deeper" level. For example, suppose you italicize the contents of a cell using the Ctrl+I shortcut. Then you "unitalicize" all the text in that column. That one cell will still be italicized because it was formatted at a deeper level. To unitalicize that one cell, you'd need to turn on Reveal Codes and delete the [Italc] code within the cell. Or, alter that cell, using T<u>a</u>ble ➤ F<u>o</u>rmat ➤ C<u>e</u>ll.

Changing the Vertical Alignment

You can also decide how you want WordPerfect to align the text *vertically* within each row, as illustrated below.

Top	Bottom	Center	
Hello			This cell has
		Hello	enough text to
	Hello		fill three lines.

To vertically align text in cells,

1. Move to the cell, or select the cells, you want to vertically align.

2. Choose T<u>a</u>ble ➤ F<u>o</u>rmat ➤ C<u>e</u>ll.

3. Using the pop-up list next to the <u>V</u>ertical Alignment option, choose a vertical alignment option, then choose OK.

The cell's contents will be aligned with respect to the top and bottom margins defined in the cell. If the alignment seems off, you might need to change the cell margins as described in the upcoming sections.

Changing the Margins inside a Cell

By default, WordPerfect leaves a small margin inside each table cell to prevent the text within the cell from touching the neighboring line. You can change those margins if you wish, as described in the next sections.

Changing the Left and Right Margins

To change the left and right margins within cells:

1. If you want to change the margins for the entire table, just move the cursor anywhere into the table. If you want to change the margins of a particular column (or columns) only, move the cursor to the appropriate column, or select the columns you want to change.

2. Choose Table ➤ Format.

3. To change the margins for the entire table, choose Table. To change the margins for the current column(s) only, choose Column.

4. In the Column Margins group, set the Left and Right options to the column widths you desire, then choose OK.

Changing the Top and Bottom Margins

Here's how to adjust the top and bottom margins in a row (or rows):

1. Put the cursor into the row, or select the rows, in which you want to change top and bottom margins.

2. Choose Table ➤ Format ➤ Row.

3. Use the Top and Bottom options near the bottom of the dialog box to set the margins within the cells, then choose OK.

Locking In the Row Height

You can also decide how tall you want a row to be, and whether or not you want it to wrap into multiple lines when there's more text than can fit into the cell. To do so, complete steps 1–2 from the previous section to get to the Format dialog box for rows. Then...

- If you *don't* want text to wrap to two or more lines within a row, change the Lines Per Row setting from Multi Line to Single Line.

- If you want WordPerfect to calculate the row height automatically, leave the Row Height setting on Auto. Otherwise, choose Fixed and type in a fixed row height for the row or rows.

Choose OK when you're done to return to your document.

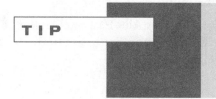

TIP   The narrow rows in the progress chart in Figures 7.16 and 7.17 near the end of this chapter have a small, fixed row height, and serve as blank lines between other rows.

Repeating a Table Header on Multiple Pages

A *table header* is a row or group of rows that is repeated when the table occupies more than one page. The table header will appear at the *top* of the table on every page that the table appears on. This is most useful for showing the top row of column titles or heads on every page of your table. To create header row(s):

1. Move the cursor into the top row of the table. If you want to use multiple rows as header rows, select those rows.

2. Choose Table ➤ Format ➤ Row.

3. Select (check) Header Row, then choose OK to return to the document window.

If you change your mind later, just repeat the steps above, but clear (deselect) the Header Row option in step 3.

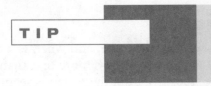

TIP

Once you define a header row in a table, WordPerfect won't rearrange that row when you sort or alphabetize the table (see Chapter 22). A very handy little bonus!

Changing the Appearance of Numbers

You can format the numbers in a table so they're all shown in accounting format (for example, $1,234.56), or Scientific format (−1.23e+03), or whatever best serves your needs. To do so:

1. Move the cursor into the table. If you want to change the number format of a specific column, move the cursor into that column. If you want to change the format of a specific cell, move the cursor into that cell. If you want to change the number format of a group of columns or cells, select those columns or cells.

2. Choose Table ➤ Number Type or press Alt+F12 or click the Table Number Type button on the Tables button bar to get to the Number Type dialog box shown below:

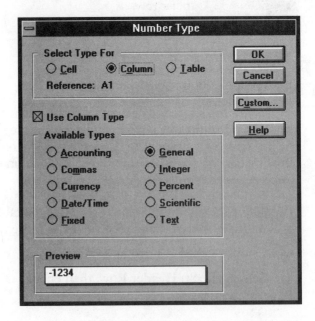

3. Choose how much of the table you want to format: Cell, Column, or Table.

4. Choose a format from the Available Types. The Preview window near the bottom of the dialog box gives you an example of a number displayed in the currently selected format.

5. If you want to refine the currently selected number type, choose the Custom button. You'll then see a dialog box that looks something like this (though the exact appearance of the dialog box depends on which type of number format you're customizing).

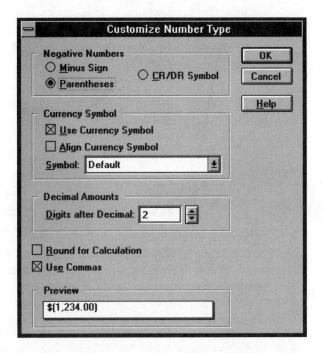

The options in this dialog box are summarized below:

Negative Numbers   You can use a minus sign, as in **–123.45,** or parentheses, as in **(123.45),** or a CR/DR Symbol (for credits/debits), as in **123.45 DR,** to display negative numbers.

Currency Symbol   If you want to display a currency symbol with the number, select (check) Use Currency Symbol. Then, if you want to align the currency symbol at the left edge of the column, select (check) A̲lign Currency Symbol. If you prefer to attach the currency symbol to the number, leave A̲lign Currency Symbol deselected. You can also choose a specific currency symbol from the S̲ymbol drop-down list.

D̲igits after Decimal   Enter the number of decimal places you want to display in each number. For example, for dollar amounts, you'd enter **2** if you want to show the pennies, or **0** if you're rounding off the pennies.

R̲ound for Calculation   No matter how many decimal places you decide to *show* in the number, the table will *store* all numbers to 15 decimal places of accuracy. This can lead to slight rounding errors when a table involves multiplication and addition (Chapter 24). To prevent rounding errors, choose the R̲ound For Calculation option.

Us̲e Commas   If you want to use comma separators for thousands (for example, 12,345.67) select Us̲e Commas. Otherwise, deselect this option. (Without the commas, that same number would look like this: 12345.67.)

After making your selections, choose OK twice to return to the document window.

Tips for Typing Negative Numbers

If you decimal-aligned or right-aligned numbers in a column, and also used parentheses to display negative numbers, you might find that either the numbers don't line up quite right, or the closing parenthesis gets bumped to the next line, as in the first two columns below.

Right- Aligned	Decimal Aligned	Decimal Aligned, 3 decimal digits
$1,234.56	$1,234.56	$1,234.56
$(1,234.56)	$(1,234.56)	$(1,234.56)
$(999.99)	$(999.99)	$(999.99)

You can fix this problem by choosing decimal alignment and adding an extra digit to the decimal portion of each number. Here's how:

1. Select the column(s) that have the misaligned numbers.

2. Choose Table ➤ Format ➤ Column.

3. Next to Justification choose Decimal Align.

4. Next to Digits After Decimal, add 1 to the number of digits currently shown (for example, type **3** if it was originally showing 2).

5. Choose OK to return to the document window.

If it doesn't work, make sure the column is wide enough to display the entire number. Also, don't forget that some previous formatting might be overriding your current selection. You can select the entire table by triple-clicking it. Then choose Table ➤ Format ➤ Cell ➤ Use Column Justification to make all the cells use the justification that's defined for the rest of the cells. Choose OK to return to your document.

Moving and Copying within a Table

To move or copy text in your table:

1. Select the text, cell(s), column(s), or row(s) that you want to move or copy.

2. If you want to copy, choose Edit ➤ Copy or press Ctrl+C. If you want to move, choose Edit ➤ Cut or press Ctrl+X. You'll be taken to a dialog box like this one:

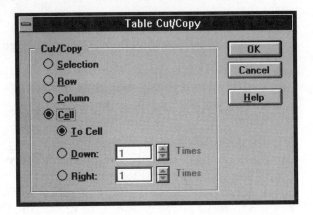

3. Choose the amount of text to copy. You can copy the current Selection only, the entire Row(s) or Column(s) you've selected (even if you haven't actually selected the entire row or column), or the currently selected Cell. (The Cell option isn't available if you've selected more than one cell.)

4. Choose OK.

5. Move the cursor to the destination for the cut or copied text, then choose Edit ➤ Paste or press Ctrl+V.

If you copied or moved a row, it will appear above the current row. Or, if you copied or moved a column, it's placed to the left of the column that the cursor is in.

For example, to move the second-to-last row or column to the end of the table, select the last row or column in your table (by double-clicking). Choose Edit ➤ Cut, then either Row or Column (depending on which you just selected). Choose OK, and the last row/column disappears from the table. Now choose Edit ➤ Paste or press Ctrl+V, and the missing row is re-inserted before the current row or column.

Copying or Moving into or out of Tables

You can use cut-and-paste to copy text into and out of tables. Remember that once you use Edit ➤ Copy or Edit ➤ Cut to copy or cut *any* text (whether it's in a table or not), that selected text stays in the Windows Clipboard. So you can actually move the cursor *anywhere*, and choose Edit ➤ Paste to then put that text anywhere in your document.

There's one gotcha in all of this, however: When you move or copy text from the document into a table, the entire selection tends to end up in a single cell. If you're thinking about moving a large amount of text into a table, your best bet might be to first *convert* that text itself to a table, as described a little later in this chapter.

Managing Tables

The remainder of this chapter discusses general topics concerning tables and how you can use tables in combination with other features of Word-Perfect. Chapter references to these related features are provided.

Hidden Codes for Tables

When you create a table, WordPerfect stores several hidden codes in the document, starting with [Tbl Def] and ending with [Tbl Off]. Between these, the [Row] codes mark the beginning of a new row in the table, and the [Cell] codes precede the contents of each cell. All these codes, of course, are visible on the Reveal Codes screen.

A cell cannot contain another table. That is, it can't contain [Tbl Def] and [Tbl Off] codes. It can, however, contain a code to display a *graphics box* that contains a table. So technically, it is possible to display a table within a table (though you may be hard-pressed to think of a practical reason for doing so).

Moving and Copying Entire Tables

Copying or moving a table is easy. First, select the entire table by triple-clicking one of the vertical or horizontal lines in the table, as described earlier in this chapter. Next, choose Edit ➤ Copy (Ctrl+C) or Edit ➤ Cut (Ctrl+X), depending on whether you want to copy or move the table. In the Table Cut/Copy dialog box, choose Selection and choose OK. Finally, position the cursor where you want the table to appear, and choose Edit ➤ Paste (Ctrl+V) to bring the table in to the current document. (You can also select the entire table and use drag and drop to move or copy it, as described in Chapter 3.)

Deleting a Table

To delete an entire table, select the entire table (for example, by triple-clicking any line within the table). Then press Del, choose Entire Table, and OK. If you change your mind, use Edit ➤ Undelete or Edit ➤ Undo to bring the table back.

Converting a Table to Text

If you wish, you can use the Tables feature to organize your text and then convert the table to standard text. This is sometimes handy for exporting a document to a typesetting machine or another word processor that cannot interpret WordPerfect codes. To convert a table to text:

1. Select the table. The easiest way to do this is to move the mouse pointer to any line within the table (so it becomes a single-headed arrow), then triple-click.

2. Press Del and you'll see the following dialog box.

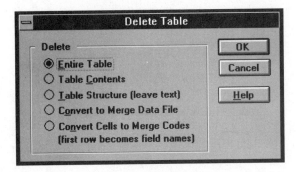

3. Choose **T**able Structure (Leave Text) then OK.

The columns in the remaining text will be separated by tabs, the rows separated by hard returns. You can change the tab stops, and add tabs as appropriate (Chapter 5) to better align the columns if need be. And, you can change the line spacing (**L**ayout ➤ **L**ine ➤ **S**pacing) to change the distance between rows if you like.

Converting Text to a Table

Let's suppose that you initially used tabs to type text into columns. But now that you know about the Tables feature, you would rather use that. Your best bet is to just convert the tabbed text to a table. Here's how:

1. Move the cursor to the first character of text that you want to put into a table.

2. Select the text you want to convert to a table, making sure to extend the selection to just before the last [HRt] code at the bottom of the text you want to convert.

3. Choose T**a**ble ➤ **C**reate, and you'll see the following dialog box.

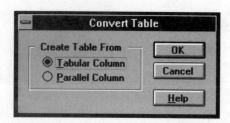

4. If you're creating the table from text organized with tabs, choose Tabular Column. If you formatted the text with parallel columns (discussed in Chapter 27), choose Parallel Column.

5. Choose OK.

The table will appear, and you can use the techniques described in this chapter to make changes, if you wish.

If your table comes out looking really screwy, you have two ways to fix it up. One method is to join or split cells as necessary (though doing so can be tedious). An easier method is to first convert the table back to text, using Edit ➤ Undo, or the steps given earlier in the section "Converting a Table to Text." Then adjust the tab settings and [Tab] codes (Chapter 5), so that only one tab code separates each column. After making these adjustments, you can convert the text to a table again (as discussed just above). But this time, you'll end up with neater rows and columns.

Joining Two Tables into One

If you create two separate tables, then decide to combine them into a single table, you can do so using the general cut-and-paste techniques to copy or move rows and columns from one table to the other.

If you specifically want to attach one table to the bottom of another table, here's a quick and easy way to do it:

1. Make sure both tables have an equal number of columns. (If necessary, use Table ➤ Insert ➤ Columns to insert as many columns as necessary into the smaller table.)

2. If necessary, move the lower table so that it's just beneath the upper table. (In Reveal Codes, you want the [Tbl Off] code that marks the end of the first table to be next to or above the [Tbl Def] code that starts the second table, with absolutely no other text or codes between them.)

3. Move the cursor into the top table, and choose Table ➤ Join ➤ Table.

That's all there is to it (as long as you followed the instructions to a tee)!

Splitting One Table into Two

To break a large table into two smaller ones, follow these steps:

1. Move the cursor into whatever row you want to become the first row of the new, separate table.

2. Choose Table ➤ Split ➤ Table.

You can add some space between the tables by moving the cursor to just between the [Tbl Off] code that ends the top table and the [Tbl Def] code that starts the second table, then press ↵ to insert blank lines.

Making More Room in a Table

If you simply cannot get enough room in a table to squeeze in all the text you need to, you can use any combination of the techniques described earlier in this chapter to make more room. For example, you can:

• Change the font to a smaller point size (see Chapter 6) just to the left of the [Tbl Def] code. The entire table will use the font, so more characters will fit into each cell. (Don't forget to reestablish your body text font for the rest of the document after you've finished creating the table.)

• Reduce the left and right margins just above the table so that you can widen the table.

• If your printer can do it, print the table sideways on the page by changing the paper size to landscape format (see Chapter 8). After you've changed the paper size, you can add more columns to the new page width or widen existing columns.

- Reduce the spacing within the table by changing cell margins, as described earlier in this chapter.

- Use the typesetting features described in Chapter 28 to reduce leading and word or letter spacing, as appropriate.

Printing White on Black

With most printers, you can use the Tables feature to display white text on a black background. But the only way to know for sure if your printer can do the job is simply to try it. Here's how:

1. Create your table, choose your fonts, type your text, and set your alignments as you normally would.

2. Select the text that you want printed in White, then choose Layout ➤ Font, click the Color button and pick the solid white color (usually at the upper right corner of the palette that appears).

3. Choose OK to return to your table. The text, being white-on-white, will now be visible only in Reveal Codes, but don't worry about that.

4. Now, to set the cell color to black, select the cells that you want to have a black background. (Those cells will still be selected if you didn't touch the mouse or keyboard after completing step 3.)

5. Choose Table ➤ Lines/Fill. Make sure that the Current Cell Or Selection option near the top of the dialog box is selected.

6. Next to the Fill Style option, use the button or drop-down list to choose a fill style, or the 100% Fill if you indeed want a solid black background.

7. Choose OK to return to your document.

Your best bet now would be to press any arrow key to deselect the current cell or cells to get an accurate view of how they look. To see how they'll look when printed, choose File ➤ Print ➤ Current Page ➤ Print.

Taking It to Extremes

The Tables feature is a great tool for typing text into tables. But as I've mentioned, it's really a great tool for organizing text and pictures in general, and you can be quite creative with your tables. The next few sections present some examples that you can use as food for thought in creating your own more advanced documents.

Calendar

Figure 7.13 shows a calendar that I created with WordPerfect. The picture at the top is in a graphics User box, as discussed in Chapter 25. (That particular picture is from the Data-Cal's SuperClips clip art collection.) To stretch AUGUST 1994, I set its justification to All (Layout ➤ Justification ➤ All).

The days of the month are in a table consisting of seven columns and six rows. The day names are in shaded cells with 20% shading. Each row below the day names has a fixed height of 1″. The cells after day 31 are joined using the Join technique described earlier in this chapter. And that's about all there is to it.

Organization Chart

Tables are a great way to create organization charts ("org charts"), like the one shown in Figure 7.14. Figure 7.15 shows the org chart after joining and filling cells but before removing any lines.

Notice in the bottom row of the org chart that you need to join a pair of cells to create one box. This is necessary to get the centered vertical line to come out of the top of the box. You also need at least one blank cell to separate each box.

Progress Chart

Figure 7.16 shows a progress chart created with the Tables feature. The chart is printed sideways on the page (landscape format), as discussed in Chapter 8. Figure 7.17 shows the chart before removing any lines from the table.

FIGURE 7.13

A calendar created
with the Tables feature

AUGUST 1994

Sun	Mon	Tue	Wed	Thu	Fri	Sat
	1	2	3	4	5	6
7	8	9	10	11	12	13
14	15	16	17	18	19	20
21	22	23	24	25	26	27
28	29	30	31			

FIGURE 7.14

An organization chart

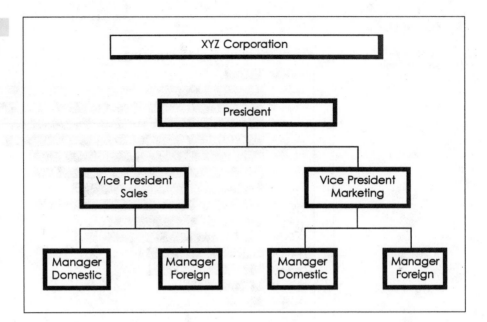

FIGURE 7.15

The org chart before
removing table lines

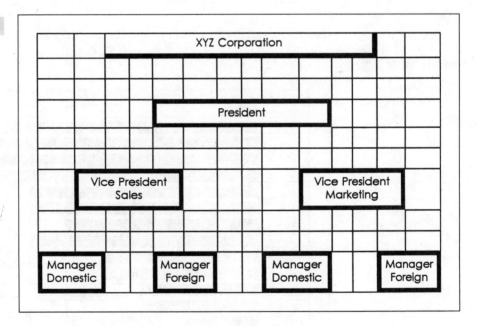

FIGURE 7.16

A progress chart
created with Tables

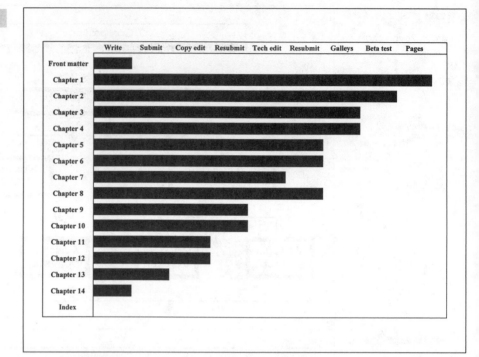

FIGURE 7.17

The progress chart
before removing table
lines

I used a couple of simple tricks to create the progress chart. First, I used Table ➤ Format ➤ Row to narrow every other row, starting at the second row, to a fixed height of 0.1″. This reduced the gap between the bars in the chart.

To draw each bar, I selected all the cells in a given row that I wanted to darken. Then I used Table ➤ Lines/Fill and set the Fill Style to 100% Fill, and the color to Black. I used a similar technique to fill the grayed cells with 20% Fill of Black. Then I removed most of the table lines, except for the outermost lines and the ones below row 1 and to the right of column A.

Fill-in Forms

Tables are also great for creating your own company fill-in forms, like the invoice shown in Figure 7.18. This invoice is actually a collection of three tables on a single page, as you can see in Figure 7.19. This latter figure shows the invoice after joining cells and filling them with text but before shading cells and removing table lines.

Actually, one of the trickiest parts of creating this form was getting the company name and address to align next to the table. To accomplish that, I put the text in a User box (see Chapter 25) that was anchored to the upper-right corner of the page with Wrapping Type set to No Wrap (Through).

Vertical Column Headings

Now, for the truly hard-core, Figure 7.20 shows an example with the column headings rotated 90 degrees. To create that one, I created an empty table with nine rows and eleven columns. I gave columns B through K a fixed width of 0.347″. Then, to put in the first sideways title, I moved the cursor to cell B1, and created a Text box. I set the font to about 10 points, and typed the text for the first title (*Full-Screen Capture* in this example). I then chose Content in the Graphics Box feature bar and selected 90 Degrees rotation. I changed the box Style to a borderless User box. Next, I changed the box Position to Treat Box As Character and positioned the box at the Bottom. I then changed its Size to a fixed height of 2 inches. You'll learn to do all this in Chapter 25.

Next, I printed the document with just that first title. I did so mainly because I discovered that what you see on the screen here doesn't necessarily match up with printed reality. After tweaking the cell margins and User-box spacing options until the sideways text was just the way I wanted

ABC Materials Supply
1200 "A" Avenue
North Shore, CA 93215
(619) 555-0123

Invoice No.:	
Customer No.:	

SHIP TO:	BILL TO:
Telephone:	Telephone:
Contact:	Contact:

DATE	SHIP VIA	F.O.B.	TERMS

ITEM NO.	QTY	DESCRIPTION	PRICE	AMOUNT
			SUBTOTAL:	
			TAX:	
			TOTAL:	

FIGURE 7.19

The fill-in form before removing lines from the three tables

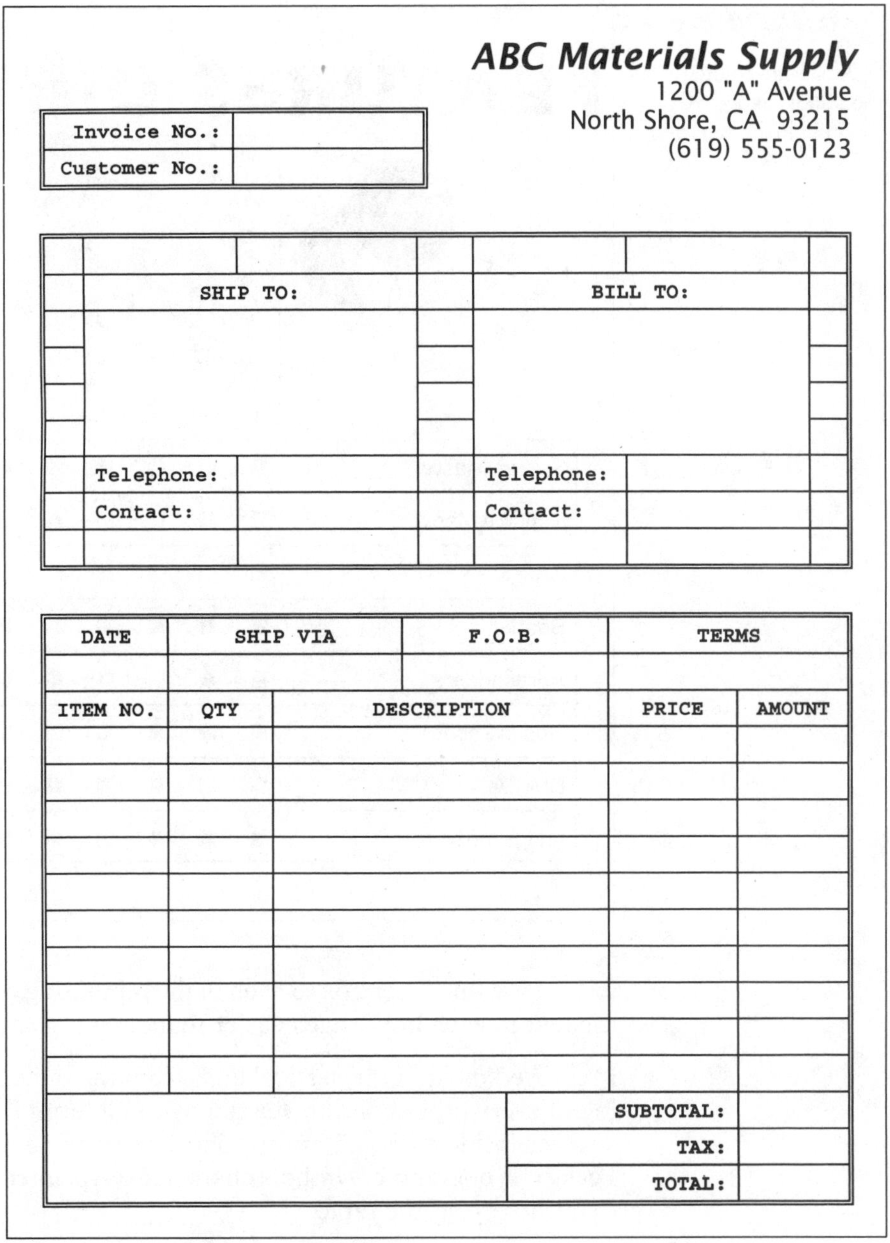

FIGURE 7.20

A table with column headings rotated 90 degrees in the top row

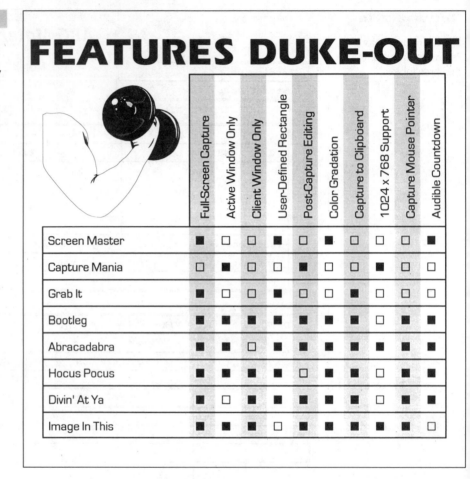

FEATURES DUKE-OUT

	Full-Screen Capture	Active Window Only	Client Window Only	User-Defined Rectangle	Post-Capture Editing	Color Gradation	Capture to Clipboard	1024 x 768 Support	Capture Mouse Pointer	Audible Countdown
Screen Master	■	□	□	■	□	■	□	□	□	■
Capture Mania	□	■	□	□	■	□	■	■	□	□
Grab It	■	□	□	■	□	■	■	□	□	■
Bootleg	■	■	■	■	■	■	■	□	■	■
Abracadabra	■	■	□	■	■	■	■	■	■	■
Hocus Pocus	■	■	■	■	□	■	■	□	■	■
Divin' At Ya	■	□	■	■	■	■	■	□	■	■
Image In This	■	■	■	□	■	■	■	■	■	□

it, I copied that User box to each of the remaining cells. Then, I just edited the text in each box (that's easier than creating each box from scratch).

I removed most of the vertical lines from the table, and I used 20% shading in every other column starting with Column B. The solid and empty squares inside each cell are special characters 38 and 46 from the WordPerfect Typographic Symbols character set, printed at a size slightly larger than the text in the table.

The graphic in cell A1 is in a graphics box. Like many examples in this book, that graphic comes from the Presentation Task Force clip art collection.

Desktop Publishing Examples

Figure 7.21 shows some examples of small tables used to create special desktop publishing effects. Figure 7.22 shows these same figures with the original inside (single) and outside (double) lines.

Here's a quick run-down on features used in these examples:

- The *WOW!* example is just a large font in cell A1 and a smaller font in cell B1. I adjusted the column widths to get the fit I wanted.

- In *So What Do You Think,* cell A1 contains small text that's centered vertically and right-aligned. Cell B1 contains large text that's bottom-aligned and fully justified. Cell C1 contains small text that's centered vertically and left-aligned.

- *Power Trip* started out as a table with three columns and three rows. After joining the cells in the bottom row, I put a picture into the cell using the graphics box tools (Chapter 25). Then I joined cells B1 and B2, put in the title, and changed and removed lines to form the frame. I also centered the title vertically and horizontally within the cell.

- *Western Regional Glass* started out as four rows and one column. After typing the text into each cell, I manually fixed the height of each row. Then I shaded cells A1 and A3 to 100% black, and changed the font color within cell A3 to white, as discussed earlier in this chapter. I controlled the spacing between letters and words using the letterspacing commands described in Chapter 28.

In this chapter we've covered most of the features of Tables. However, there is an entire math component that goes along with tables too. I'll talk about table math in Chapter 24. Next, however, let's take a look at some general page formatting techniques that you can use to get the format of your entire document well under control.

FIGURE 7.21

Some small desktop
publishing examples

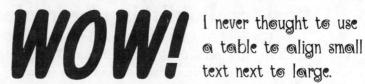

FIGURE 7.22

The examples shown in Figure 7.21 before removing all (or some) of the table lines.

File **Edit** **View** **Insert** **Layout** **Tools** **Graphics** **Table** **Window** **Help**

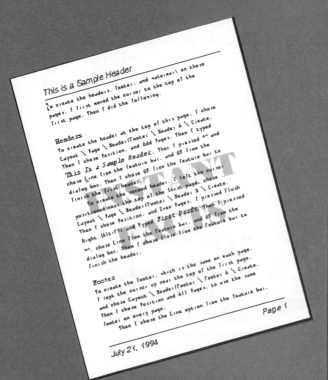

CHAPTER

8

Formatting Your Pages

fast **TRACK**

To keep words together on a line   **300**

insert a hard space (Ctrl+spacebar), instead of a regular space, between the words.

To select paper sizes other than 8.5"×11"   **301**

choose Layout ➤ Page ➤ Paper Size for standard papers. Choose Layout ➤ Labels for labels. Highlight the paper size you want to use and choose Select.

To create an envelope interactively   **303**

choose Layout ➤ Envelope and fill in the Envelope dialog box. Then, to print the envelope, choose Print Envelope. To insert the envelope contents into the current document, choose Append To Doc.

To type text on labels   **307**

move the cursor to the top of the document, choose Layout ➤ Labels, and choose your label size from the list that appears (either by double-clicking, or by highlighting and pressing ↵). When you return to the document window, type the contents of each label, followed by a hard page break (Ctrl+↵) when you want to move on to the next label.

IN THIS chapter you'll learn many ways to format documents that are longer than a single page. Among other things, you'll learn how to create title pages, number your pages, and use non-standard paper sizes such as envelopes and mailing labels. Here are some tips that will help you get the most out of page formatting:

- Most page-formatting features are available from the Layout menu. The Page button bar offers shortcuts for many of these same features. To switch to a different button bar, right-click the current button bar, and choose the name of the button bar you want to use.

- Page formatting changes are visible in Page view (Alt+F5) or Two-Page view (View ➤ Two Page), in Reveal Codes (Alt+F3), and when you print your document. They generally won't appear in Draft view (Ctrl+F5).

- To see hidden codes, turn on Reveal Codes (Alt+F3).

- To change a page formatting feature quickly, double-click its code in Reveal Codes. To delete a page formatting feature, delete its code in Reveal Codes.

- When you write documents that have long sections, consider placing each chapter or section in a separate file. The Styles (Chapter 17) and Master Document (Chapter 32) features can help you manage large documents.

Centering Text Vertically

Vertical centering is handy for centering text on title pages, brief letters or memos, and invitations. Figure 8.1 shows a sample title page that I've

FIGURE 8.1

A sample page with text centered horizontally (Layout ➤ Justification ➤ Center) and vertically (Layout ➤ Page ➤ Center ➤ Current Page)

```
                    ALL-AMERICAN LIFE

          A Flexible Premium Life Insurance Policy




                       Issued by:

               PREMIUM INSURANCE COMPANY
               1234 Avenue of the Americas
                 New York, NY  10019
                    (800)555-1234




            Supplement Dated August 30, 1994

                         to

            Prospectus Dated June 1, 1994
```

centered both horizontally and vertically. (I chose Layout ➤ Justification ➤ Center at the top of the page to center each line horizontally, as discussed in Chapter 5.) To center a page vertically:

1. Position the cursor on the page where vertical centering should start.

2. Choose Layout ➤ Page ➤ Center. Or, click the Center Page button in the Page button bar.

3. Now, do one of the following:

   • To center just the current page, choose Current Page.

   • To center the current page and all future pages until you turn off centering, choose Current And Subsequent Pages.

4. Choose OK or press ↵.

If you're just centering the current page, you should insert a *hard page break* (by pressing Ctrl+↵) after typing the last line of text on that page. For example, I pressed Ctrl+↵ after typing **June 1, 1994** in the example shown in Figure 8.1.

If you choose Current And Subsequent Pages, then later in the document decide not to vertically center text anymore, move the cursor to where you want to end vertical centering. Then choose Layout ➤ Page ➤ Center ➤ No Centering and choose OK.

Starting a New Page

Normally when you type a long document you can just let WordPerfect break pages automatically as you type. It does this by inserting a *soft page break* ([SPg]), which appears as a long horizontal divider across the document window, after you've filled one page and moved onto the next. The Pg indicator at the right edge of the status bar keeps you informed of which page you're on.

In some cases, however, you may want to force WordPerfect to start on a new page. A title page is a perfect example of a page where you typically want all the text on the page to be centered, then start the "real" text of the document on a new page. To force WordPerfect to start on a new page, you insert a *hard page break*. Here's how:

1. Position the cursor where you want to end the current page.

2. Press Ctrl+↵ or choose Insert ➤ Page Break.

WordPerfect will insert a [HPg] code, and you'll see a page divider where the page will break. As you move the cursor above or below the hard page break, the status bar will show which page the cursor is on.

Forcing an Odd or Even Page Number

You can also use the Force Page options to make sure that a certain page in a document has an odd page number (or, if you wish, an even page number) or starts on a new page. For example, you might want to start each chapter in a book with an odd-numbered page. Here's how to force an odd or even page number:

1. Place the cursor at the top of the page that you want to ensure is odd- or even-numbered.

2. Choose Layout ➤ Page ➤ Force Page, or click the Force Page button in the Page button bar.

3. Choose one of the following options:

    None   Turns off the Force Page feature (this is the default setting).

    Current Page Odd   Inserts a page break (if necessary) to start the following text on an odd page.

    Current Page Even   Inserts a page break (if necessary) to start the following text on an even page.

    New Page   Inserts a page break (if necessary) to start the following text on a new page.

4. Choose OK or press ↵.

Remember, the Force Page options don't insert a blank page, unless it's necessary to do so to get to an odd or even page number.

Automatic Page Numbering

You never need to type page numbers in a WordPerfect document, because you can instruct WordPerfect to number the pages for you automatically. This way you can guarantee that the page numbers will always be in proper sequence and in the right place on each page no matter how much text you add, change, or delete.

About Page Numbering Levels

You can use up to four numbering levels: page number, secondary page number, chapter number, and volume number. WordPerfect increments the page and secondary page numbers automatically. Chapter and volume page numbers stay the same unless you change them manually.

NOTE You can also use *counters* (Chapter 15) to count or number anything in your document manually. Like page numbers, counters can have several levels and can display numbers, letters, or roman numerals.

About Page Numbering Methods

WordPerfect usually keeps track of page numbers in sequence, starting with page 1, and displays the numbers using arabic numerals (*1, 2, 3, ...*). Sometimes, however, a different numbering method or starting page number might be better. This might be handy in a book or report that begins with a title page and other front matter that should be numbered with roman numerals (*i, ii, iii, iv, v, ...*).

You can use any of five numbering methods for each numbering level: Numbers (1, 2, 3, ...); Lowercase Letter (a, b, c, ...); Uppercase Letter (A, B, C, ...); Lowercase Roman (i, ii, iii, iv, v, ...); or Uppercase Roman (I, II, III, IV, V, ...).

Suppose you're working on Volume II of your life story, and you've finally made it to Chapter 5 (*My Life with Joe*). In this case, you might want to combine multilevel numbering with different numbering methods. The first page number of Chapter 5 might look like this:

Volume II ➤ Chapter 5 ➤ Page 1

Notice that I've used a volume number, chapter number, and page number in this example. The volume number is an uppercase roman numeral; the chapter and page numbers are arabic numerals.

In the next section, I'll explain how to use the automatic page numbering features. Later in this chapter, you'll learn how to set up *headers* and *footers* that display page numbers.

Numbering Pages Automatically

Follow these steps to turn on and customize automatic page numbering:

1. Move the cursor to the top of whichever page you want to be the first numbered page.

2. Choose Layout ➤ Page ➤ Numbering, or click the Page Numbering button in the Page button bar. This opens the Page Numbering dialog box (Figure 8.2).

FIGURE 8.2

The Page Numbering dialog box. Choose Layout ➤ Page ➤ Numbering to get here.

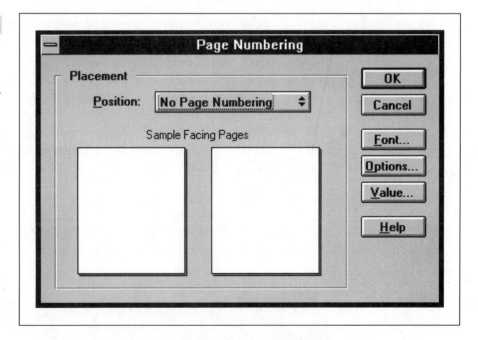

3. Open the Position pop-up list (shown below) and choose whichever position best describes where you want the page number to appear on the page. The Sample Facing Pages diagram at the bottom of the dialog box will reflect your choice.

```
√ No Page Numbering
  Top Left
  Top Center
  Top Right
  Alternating Top
  Bottom Left
  Bottom Center
  Bottom Right
  Alternating Bottom
```

4. If all you care about is the page numbers, you can choose OK now to return to your document, and skip the remaining options. Or, you can choose any of the following:

   Font Lets you change the font and appearance of the page number text. (See Chapter 6.)

   Options Lets you customize the page number format and text; select the numbering method for each level; and insert the formatted page number at the cursor position, as discussed in the next section.

   Value Lets you set page number values or insert page numbers (at any level) at the cursor position. More on this in a moment.

5. If you chose a button in step 4, choosing OK returns you to the Page Numbering dialog box so that you can choose more options if you wish. If you are finished with the dialog box, choose OK again to return to your document.

TIP   See Chapter 31 for a way to create dual page numbers, such as *Page 2 of 20.*

Remember that page numbers will appear in the Page view and Two Page views, and on the printed document. But the page numbers are invisible in Draft view.

Setting the Numbering Method and Text

Choosing the Options button in the Page Numbering dialog box will take you to the Page Numbering Options dialog box shown in Figure 8.3, where you can format the page number. As you define the appearance of your page numbers using the Format And Accompanying Text text box, and the Insert button, the Sample Facing Pages diagram at the bottom of the dialog box will present an example of your current format.

To define the appearance of your page numbers, you can type text, blanks, or WordPerfect Characters (Ctrl+W) in the Format And Accompanying Text text box. You can also insert a page number, secondary number, and so forth, as necessary, by choosing an option from the list displayed by the Insert button. For example, if you type **Page** followed by a blank space

FIGURE 8.3

You can use the Page Numbering Options dialog box to set the page numbering method for each level of page number, to customize the page number text, and to insert the page number format at the cursor position.

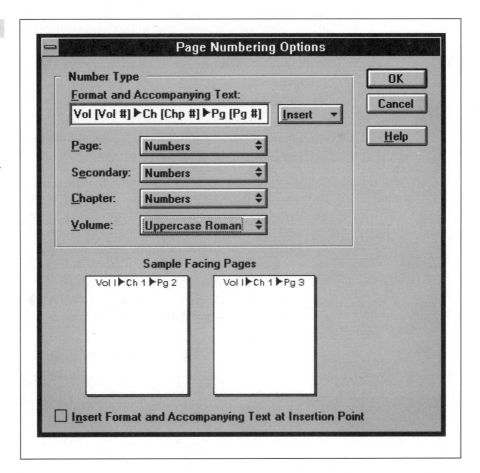

in the text box, then choose Page Number from the Insert button's list, the text box will contain:

Page [Pg #]

where [Pg #] just shows you where the page number will appear in the document. So on page 3 the page number would actually look like this:

Page 3

A fancy entry, like this:

Vol [Vol #], Chapter [Chp #], Page [Pg #]

would look like this (on page 3 of Chapter 5 in Volume II):

Vol II, Chapter 5, Page 3

You can choose the numbering method for each page numbering level. For example, to set the numbering method for chapter number, click the button next to Chapter and select the numbering method you want. When you're done making your selections, choose OK twice to return to the document window.

Changing the Page Number

You can choose the Value button in the Page Numbering dialog box to manually set page numbers at each level. This button takes you to the Numbering Value dialog box (Figure 8.4).

Notice that the dialog box is divided into four areas with three options each. The areas are Page Settings, Secondary Settings, Chapter Settings, and Volume Settings. Your options for each area are summarized just below:

New ... Number   Lets you set a new Page, Secondary page, Chapter, or Volume number. For example, if you want the third page in a document (after the title page and a blank page) to be numbered 1, set the New Page Number value to 1 on that page. Subsequent pages will be numbered 2, 3, 4, and so forth.

Increase/Decrease Existing ... Number   Lets you increment or decrement the page number that appears in the "New ... Number" text box. The values shown in the Increase/Decrease text boxes are *intervals*, not numbers. For example, if you are on page 3 of a document, and set the Increase/Decrease interval to −2, the page number that's printed on the page would be 1.

You can use the Numbering Value dialog box to manually set the page number for each level of page number, to increase or decrease an existing page number, and to display the page number for any level at the cursor position.

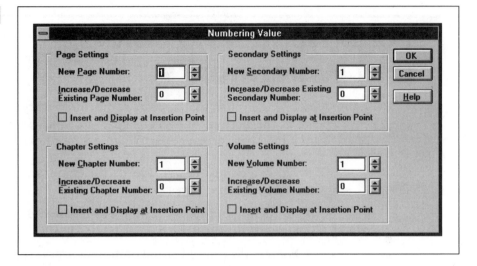

After setting all the options you want, choose OK as necessary to return to the document window.

Inserting a Page Number in Text

You can insert the current formatted page number, or any individual component of the page number, anywhere in your text (including headers and footers). Here are the steps:

1. Position the cursor where you want the number to appear.

2. Choose Layout ➤ Page ➤ Numbering.

3. Now do one of the following:

   - To insert **a single component,** choose Value, then select (check) the Insert And Display At Insertion Point option for the level (or levels) you want to display.

   - To insert **the entire formatted page number,** choose Options, then select Insert Format And Accompanying Text At Insertion Point.

4. Choose OK or Close to return to the document window.

Page Headers, Footers, and Watermarks

A *page header* is text that appears at the top of every page. A *page footer* appears at the bottom of every page. A *watermark* appears wherever you want it to appear on every page. Figure 8.5 shows some examples, where:

- *This is a Sample Header* and its underline are Header A, printed on odd-numbered pages.

- *First Draft* and its underline are Header B, printed on even-numbered pages.

- Footer A is printed at the bottom of every page, and includes codes for displaying the current date and page number.

- *INSTANT FACTS* is in Watermark A, and is printed on every page.

Because headers, footers, and watermarks all display text repeatedly throughout the document, I'll just refer to them all as *repeating elements* throughout most of this chapter. Here are some other useful things to remember about repeating elements:

- You only have to create the repeating elements once. From that point on, WordPerfect will print them on every page (or alternating pages, if you request it), regardless of whether you add or delete paragraphs.

- Repeating elements can include any text as well as WordPerfect Characters (Ctrl+W), page numbers, the current date/time and file name, graphic lines and boxes, boldface, italics, centering, and other formatting features.

- Two different repeating elements of *each* type (thus two headers, two footers, and two watermarks) can be active at any given place in your document. For example, you could show Header A on even-numbered pages and Header B on odd-numbered pages.

- Normally, WordPerfect leaves 0.167 inches of space between the header or footer and the body text. You can adjust this default spacing if you wish.

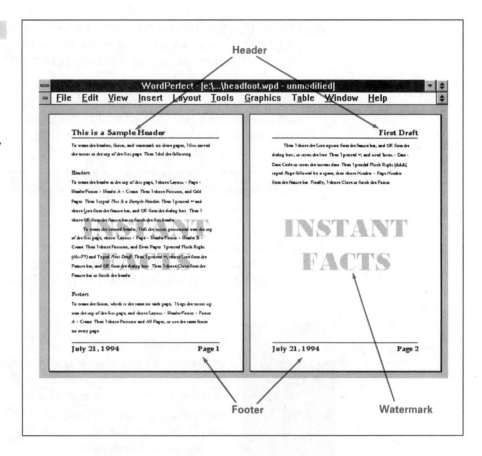

FIGURE 8.5

A sample document in Two Page view with page header, footer, and watermark. This example uses different headers, one for even-numbered pages, and one for odd-numbered pages.

Creating a Repeating Element

Follow these steps to create a repeating element:

1. Place the cursor near the top of the page that you want the header, footer, or watermark to appear on.

2. Do either of the following:

   - Choose Layout, then either Header/Footer or Watermark.
   - Or, if you're in Page view or Two Page view, right-click in the header or footer area of the page and choose either Header/Footer or Watermark from the QuickMenu.

3. From the dialog box that appears, choose the repeating element (A or B) you want to create. For example, choose Header A in the Headers/Footers dialog box if you want to create Header A.

4. Choose Create. An editing window will open and the title bar will remind you about which repeating element you're editing. You'll also see a feature bar with several buttons, similar to the example below for the headers and footers repeating elements:

5. Choose the Placement button in the feature bar, then select the pages where you want the repeating element to appear. Your options are Odd Pages, Even Pages, or Every Page. Choose OK.

NOTE

When you edit a header or footer in Page and Two Page view, the text of your document will still be visible (though you may need to use the scroll bars). You can switch to Draft view (choose View ➤ Draft) to hide that additional text. You can also use Alt+F3 to turn on Reveal Codes so that you can see any codes in your header/footer/watermark.

6. Enter the text, graphics, lines, and characters for the repeating element using standard WordPerfect techniques or the buttons in the feature bar. (There's more about editing just below.)

7. When you're done editing, choose the Close button in the feature bar (the feature bar will disappear). Or, click in the document text, outside of the header or footer (the feature bar will remain on screen).

The buttons in the feature bar make it easy to dress up your repeating element in step 6 above. Here's a summary of what they do:

Distance   (headers and footers only) Lets you change the distance between the document text and the header or footer.

Figure (watermarks only) Lets you insert a graphic stored on disk at the cursor position. See Chapters 25 and 28 for more about graphics.

File (watermarks only) Lets you insert a text file stored on disk at the cursor position.

Line (headers and footers only) Lets you create a horizontal or vertical graphic line at the cursor position (see Chapter 25). To add a simple line, click the Line button, choose Horizontal or Vertical, and choose OK.

Next Lets you edit the next repeating element of the same type (for example, the next Header A if you're editing Header A), if one exists.

Number (headers and footers only) Lets you insert the current Page Number, Secondary Number, Chapter Number, or Volume Number at the cursor position.

Previous Lets you edit the previous repeating element of the same type (for example, the previous Header A if you're editing Header A), if one exists.

Changing a Repeating Element

It's easy to change an existing repeating element without retyping it:

1. Position the cursor just to the right of the repeating element you want to change (turning on Reveal Codes will help).

2. Use any of the techniques below to open the editing window for the repeating element:

   - Choose Layout, then either Header/Footer or Watermark. Select the repeating element you want to change (for example, Header A) and choose Edit.
   - If you're in Page view or Two Page view, right-click in the header or footer area of the page and choose either Header/Footer or Watermark from the QuickMenu. Select the element you want and choose Edit.
   - If you want to edit the header or footer in Page view or Two Page view, click anywhere inside the header or footer you want to change.

TIP　If the feature bar isn't visible and you want to display it, right-click in the header or footer editing window, and choose Feature Bar from the QuickMenu.

3. Edit the repeating element as desired.

4. When you're done making changes, choose Close from the feature bar. Or, click anywhere in the document window (outside of the header or footer).

NOTE　When you edit a repeating element, WordPerfect searches backward from the current cursor position and lets you edit whichever code it finds first.

The section "Turning Off the Page Formatting" later in this chapter explains how to suppress, or turn off, repeating elements.

Perfecting Repeating Elements

Here are some tips and tricks that will help you create perfect repeating elements.

- To get a **bird's-eye view** of all your repeating elements at once, use Two Page view (View ➤ Two Page).

- You can insert the **current date and time** (Insert ➤ Date), **file name** (Insert ➤ Other ➤ Filename), or **path and file name** (Insert ➤ Other ➤ Path And Filename) into a repeating element while you're creating or editing that element.

- Headers and footers are never printed within the top and bottom margins. **To extend the header or footer into a margin**, move the cursor to the left of the codes that define the header and footer. Then use Layout ➤ Margins to reduce the height of the top and bottom margins. For example, in Figure 8.5 earlier, I set the top margin to .5″ and the bottom margin to .75″.

- To **move a repeating element to a different page**, turn on Reveal Codes. Then use techniques discussed in Chapter 3 to move the code to the top of the page where you want the repeating element to begin.

- To **prevent repeating elements from printing on top of one another**, align text in each repeating element so that printing won't overlap. For example, left align the text in one header and right-align text in another. Or, press ↵ several times at the beginning of a watermark to prevent it from printing in the same place as the header.

- To **prevent repeating elements from overlapping automatic page numbers**, align all the text so that repeating elements and page numbers don't cancel each other out. For instance, you might need to adjust the alignment if you've set up automatic page numbering at the top center of the page, and the page number appears on the same spot as your headers and watermarks.

- If your headers or footers include page numbers, **turn off automatic page numbering** for pages that use those headers or footers. Otherwise, the page number will appear twice on each page: once in the position set by the automatic page numbering and again in the header or footer.

- To **position watermarks vertically on the page**, press ↵ as many times as necessary. Or, use the Advance feature (Chapter 28) to place text in a watermark anywhere on the page. While creating the *INSTANT FACTS* watermark back in Figure 8.5, for example, I chose Layout ➤ Typesetting ➤ Advance ➤ From Top Of Page, and set the vertical distance to about 5.5″. I also used Layout ➤ Justification ➤ Center to center the text horizontally. I made sure the text, INSTANT FACTS, came after the [Just: Center] and [VAdv:...] codes in the watermark.

- To get **more control over a watermark**, choose Figure in the Watermark feature bar and put the watermark in a graphics box. A graphics box in a watermark is automatically centered on the page. You can use techniques discussed in Part Six to reposition the graphic, size it, replace the graphic image with text, and make other changes to the graphics box.

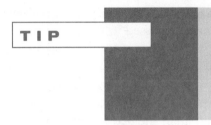

TIP

WordPerfect comes with a macro named WATERMRK, which can automatically create centered watermarks from a variety of predefined watermark graphics or from text that you type. See Chapter 18 for information on running a macro.

Turning Off Page Formatting

WordPerfect offers two ways to hide page formatting on a single page or on future pages without disrupting the page-numbering sequence or deleting the formatting code. This can be helpful on pages that display a full-page illustration or graph, or when you want to print an intentionally blank page.

...for This Page Only

You can turn off (suppress) automatic page numbering or repeating elements on the current page only. Here's how:

1. Move your cursor to the page where you want to suppress the feature.

2. Choose Layout ➤ Page ➤ Suppress, or click the Suppress button in the Page button bar. You'll see the Suppress dialog box, shown below.

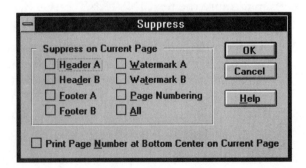

3. Select (check) whatever feature or features you want to suppress. Or, choose All to suppress all features at once.

4. If you've turned on automatic page numbering and want to print a page number at the bottom center of the page, select Print Page Number At Bottom Center On Current Page. (This option isn't available if you've suppressed Page Numbering.)

5. Choose OK or press ↵.

WordPerfect will hide the selected page-formatting feature or features on the current page only. To turn the suppressed features back on, move the cursor to the point where you want to resume the features, choose Layout ➤ Page ➤ Suppress, and deselect the appropriate check boxes, or remove the appropriate [Suppress] code in Reveal Codes.

...for Current and Future Pages

To turn off automatic page numbering on the current page and all pages that follow, follow the steps below:

1. Place the cursor on the page where you want to discontinue automatic numbering.

2. Choose Layout ➤ Page ➤ Numbering. Open the Position pop-up list and choose No Page Numbering.

3. Choose OK or press ↵.

Turning off repeating elements is just as easy:

1. Move the cursor just after the code for the feature you want to suppress.

2. Choose Layout ➤ Header/Footer or Layout ➤ Watermark. (Or right-click in the header or footer area of the page and choose Header/Footer or Watermark.)

3. Select the feature that you want to discontinue (for example, Header A), then choose Discontinue.

If you change your mind about discontinuing the feature, simply delete the appropriate [End ...] code (such as [End Header A]) in Reveal Codes.

Note that, if you turn off a repeating element on the same page where you defined it, WordPerfect will delete the code for the repeating element instead of inserting an [End ...] code.

Delaying Codes until Later Pages

You can insert formatting codes that won't take effect until a certain number of pages after the current page. This is like saying "make this new code take effect *n* pages after this one." This "Delay Codes" feature works with any open formatting code, including paper size, justification, line numbering, font, margins, headers, footers, watermarks, and so forth.

NOTE *Open codes affect the document from the cursor position to the end of the document, or until another code of the same type changes the format again.*

Delay Codes might come in handy if you're using *letterhead*—stationery with a custom logo—for your first page, and ordinary paper for the remaining pages. You could set the paper size for both kinds of paper at the start of your document (as described later in this chapter). First, you'd set the paper size for the letterhead paper. Then you'd use Delay Codes to make the paper size for normal paper take effect "one page from now"—that is, starting on the second page.

Follow these steps to delay a formatting code for a certain number of pages:

1. Place the cursor at the start of the document (or on the page where you want to start delaying codes).

2. Choose Layout ➤ Page ➤ Delay Codes.

3. Type the number of pages (from the current page) to delay the new codes that you'll be adding, and choose OK. For example, type 2 if you're on page 3 and you want the new codes to start taking effect on page 5. A Delay Codes editing window and feature bar (shown below) will appear.

4. Create the features you want to delay, just as you normally would when editing a document. Or, use the feature bar buttons to create a Figure, Paper Size, Header/Footer, or Watermark. Each time you finish setting up a feature, WordPerfect will add that feature's code to the Delay Codes editing window. (Turn on Reveal Codes to see it.)

5. When you're done entering codes to delay, choose the Close button in the feature bar.

WordPerfect will insert a [Delay:*n*] code, where *n* is the number you entered in step 3. Any page formatting codes that follow that [Delay] code will not take effect until the specified number of pages have passed.

To edit the [Delay] code, move the cursor to the top of your document, or to the hard page break where you entered the original codes that you now want to change. Now, simply repeat steps 1–5 above. Or, in Reveal Codes, double-click the [Delay:*n*] code you want to change and repeat steps 3–5. When you get to the Delay Codes editing window and turn on Reveal Codes, you'll see the codes you entered earlier. Change or delete them just as if you were editing a normal document, then choose Close.

Keeping Text Together

WordPerfect provides several ways to keep text together on a page or line:

Widow/Orphan Protection   I know this sounds like a social program. But in the word processing world, a *widow* occurs when the first line of a paragraph appears on the last line of a page. An *orphan* occurs when the last line of a paragraph appears on the first line of a new page. When widow and orphan protection is on,

WordPerfect avoids widows by moving the first line of a paragraph to the top of the next page. It avoids orphans by moving the next-to-last line of a paragraph to the top of the next page.

Block Protect Prevents selected passages of text, such as a quotation, sidebar, or columnar table, from being split across two pages.

Conditional End of Page Keeps a certain number of lines together on a page. For instance, in the example below, you'd probably want to keep the heading, blank line, and at least two lines in the paragraph together at the bottom of a page.

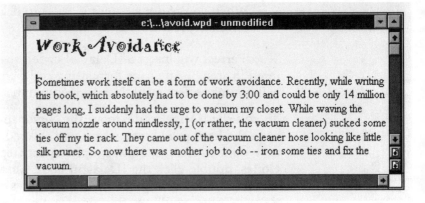

To keep text together on a page, follow these steps:

1. Position the cursor or select text as follows:

   - For widow/orphan protection or conditional end of page, position the cursor where you want the feature to take effect.
   - For block protection, select the text you want to keep together.

2. Choose Layout ➤ Page ➤ Keep Text Together, or click the Keep Text Together button in the Page button bar. You'll see the Keep Text Together dialog box shown below:

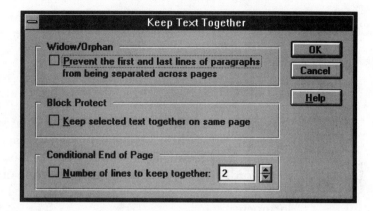

3. To turn a feature on, select (check) it in the dialog box. To turn the feature off, deselect it.

4. If you selected Number Of Lines To Keep Together in step 3, specify the number of lines you want to keep together. Be sure to include lines of text and any blank lines in between.

5. Choose OK or press ↵.

Why So Many Forms of Protection?

Perhaps you're wondering why WordPerfect has both Block Protect and Conditional End Of Page (perhaps not). At first glance, they seem to serve the same purpose. But, there *is* a subtle difference.

Block Protect places paired [Block Pro] codes around a protected block. Any changes that you make to the protected block, including new or deleted lines, will still keep the entire block protected.

On the other hand, Conditional End Of Page inserts only one hidden code, [Condl EOP:*n*]. This tells WordPerfect to skip to the next page if it doesn't have enough space to display at least *n* lines. Whether the text beneath the [Condl EOP] code grows or shrinks is irrelevant, because the idea is simply to keep a few lines from being split, not a whole body of text.

To turn off a "keep text together" feature, simply delete the appropriate code in Reveal Codes, or deselect the appropriate option in the Keep Text Together dialog box.

Keeping Words Together on a Line

You can prevent two words from being separated onto two lines by placing a *hard space* between the words. Suppose you're printing phone numbers with area codes, like *(415) 555-8233*. You could use a hard space to keep WordPerfect from placing the area code on one line and the rest of the phone number on the next line or page. To insert a hard space in your document:

1. Position the cursor where you would normally press the spacebar to separate words. If you've already typed the words, delete the space between them.

2. Press Ctrl+spacebar, or Choose Layout ➤ Line ➤ Other Codes ➤ Hard Space [HSpace], then choose Insert or press ↵.

Although the hard space looks like any other blank space in the document window, a peek at Reveal Codes will show the hidden [HSpace] code.

Printing on Nonstandard Page Sizes

WordPerfect assumes that you'll print documents on the *standard* page size, which is $8\frac{1}{2}''\times11''$ in the United States. But some documents use pages of other sizes. Legal documents, for example, require $8\frac{1}{2}''\times14''$ paper. Labels are only a few inches wide and high. And many preprinted forms, such as invoices and packing slips, use unusual paper sizes as well.

Whether you can print text on nonstandard page sizes depends largely on your printer. For instance, most laser printers require a special sheet feeder for legal-size paper. Many dot-matrix and other tractor-fed printers cannot print sideways on the page unless the platen (the paper roller) is wide enough to accommodate 11-inch wide paper. Laser printers can print sideways on a page even though the paper is fed normally.

NOTE If you have trouble with techniques in this section, you should study printing in general (see Chapter 10) and perhaps consult your printer's manual to learn more about your printer.

Selecting a Paper Size

Most printers come with a set of predefined paper sizes. To use one of those sizes:

1. If you've installed multiple printers for WordPerfect, select the one you want to use (choose File ➤ Select Printer).

2. Move the cursor to the top of the page that should use the new paper size.

3. Choose Layout ➤ Page ➤ Paper Size, or click the Paper Size button in the Page button bar. This opens the Paper Size dialog box shown in Figure 8.6. (The paper sizes displayed depend on your printer and the paper sizes you've created.)

4. Highlight the page size you want, as listed under Paper Definitions. As you scroll through the list with your arrow keys, WordPerfect will display a small example of the currently highlighted paper size in the Orientation portion of the dialog box. If you don't see the paper size you need, you can add it as described later in this chapter.

5. Choose Select, or double-click the paper name you want.

NOTE WordPerfect offers some special, and quite fun, ways to set up labels and envelopes. I'll get to those topics a bit later in the chapter.

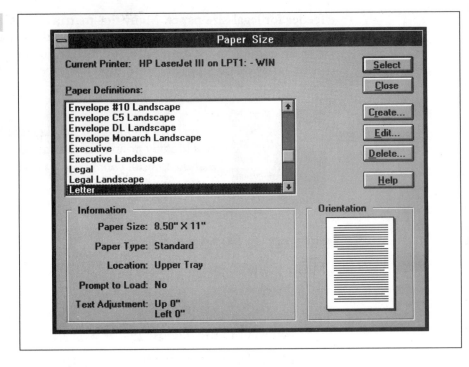

Printing Sideways on the Page

Most documents use *portrait* printing, so-called because the text appears vertically (the way artists usually paint portraits). Sometimes, however, you'll want to print a document sideways. Sideways printing is often called *landscape* printing, because the text or graphic appears horizontally across the page (the way artists usually paint landscapes).

TIP WordPerfect's built-in landscape paper sizes all have the word *Landscape* in their names.

Landscape printing is handy for many types of documents, particularly large, lengthy tables. How you print sideways on a standard-size page depends on what kind of printer you have. Here are the basic steps:

1. Select the landscape paper size, as described earlier. This is usually named *Letter Landscape*.

2. Now, insert the paper as follows:

- If you're using a *laser printer*, insert the paper normally. The laser printer will print sideways on the page even though you feed the page into the printer normally.

- If you're using a nonlaser printer, you'll probably need to feed the paper into the printer sideways. You can't do it unless the platen is wide enough to accommodate the page. Not every printer has a platen that wide.

3. Choose File ➤ Print ➤ Print or press Ctrl+P to print your document.

Printing on Letterhead

Most businesses use letterhead stock to print letters. Typically, you'll print only the first page of a multipage letter on letterhead; the remaining pages are printed on plain sheets. To accommodate the letterhead on the first page, it's usually necessary to add extra space before the first line of text.

To do this, just measure the distance from the top of the letterhead page to where you want the first line of text to begin (for example, let's say it's about 2.5 inches from the top of the page).

Before you start typing the first page of the letter, press ↵ until the Ln indicator in the status bar indicates that the cursor is somewhere near your measurement (in my example, I might press ↵ until the cursor gets to about 2.42 inches). Then, just start typing the letter on that line. When it comes time to print the letter, insert the letterhead stock into the printer normally, and print.

Printing on Envelopes

Printing envelopes in older versions of WordPerfect was a clunky job. But not any more, thanks to the snazzy envelope feature. Here's how it works:

1. Grab your envelopes. You'll need to know the size of the envelope, which usually is written on the box (of course, you can also measure it with a ruler).

2. If you wish, open the letter for the current envelope. To have WordPerfect use text from your letter as the mailing address for your envelope, select the text that you want to include.

3. Choose Layout ➤ Envelope, or click the Envelope button on the WordPerfect button bar. Up pops the Envelope dialog box shown in Figure 8.7. If you selected a mailing address in step 2, this will appear in the Mailing Addresses box. The Return Addresses box will contain the last return address you used.

4. Fill in the Return Addresses box with the address you want. You can use any technique described just below to manage return addresses. (Be sure to choose options in the left side of the dialog box.)

   - Accept the current return address.
   - Select an address from the drop-down list.
   - Select <New Address> from the drop-down list and type in a new address.
   - To add the current address to the drop-down list, choose the Add button.
   - To delete an address from the drop-down list, select that address from the drop-down list, choose the Delete button, and choose Yes.

FIGURE 8.7

The Envelope dialog box after typing in a return address and mailing address. (I selected Options ➤ Include USPS POSTNET Bar Code to get the POSTNET Bar Code text box.)

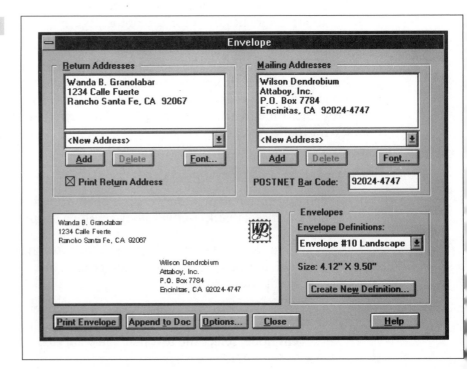

- To change the font for the address, choose the Font button and select a font (see Chapter 6).

- To print the return address on the envelope, select (check) Print Re*tu*rn Address. To hide the return address, deselect the option (useful with envelopes that already include the return address).

5. Fill in the *M*ailing Addresses box with the address you want. The procedure is basically the same as for filling in a return address (except that you choose options in the right side of the dialog box).

> **TIP**
>
> You can type normal keyboard characters or any WordPerfect Character (Ctrl+W) in the mailing or return address. Be sure to press ⏎ after typing each line.

6. If you wish, choose any of the options below:

- **To change the envelope size,** select a size from the En*ve*lope Definitions drop-down list.

- **To create a new envelope size,** choose Create Ne*w* Definition, specify the paper size options for an envelope, and choose OK. See "Adding a Paper Size" later in the chapter for details.

- **To print a POSTNET Bar Code** above the mailing address, choose *O*ptions, select (check) *I*nclude USPS POSTNET Bar Code, and choose OK. From now on (until you deselect the option), WordPerfect will retrieve the POSTNET Bar Code from the mailing address automatically.

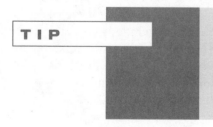

> **TIP**
>
> If the POSTNET Bar Code is blank or incorrect, try clicking in the POSTNET *B*ar Code text box (see Figure 8.7). You can edit the bar code if you wish. POSTNET Bar Codes must contain 5, 9, or 11 digits (for example, *92123* or *91234-1234*).

- **To change the position of the return or mailing addresses** on the envelope, choose Options, adjust the horizontal and vertical position of the appropriate address, and choose OK. WordPerfect will use the selected positions whenever you use the current envelope definition.

7. If you want to print your envelope immediately, choose Print Envelope. If you want to save the envelope information in the current document (without printing), choose Append To Doc.

If you chose to print your envelope in step 7, simply insert the envelope into the printer (according to your printer manual's instructions) and let WordPerfect do the rest. Figure 8.8 shows a sample printed envelope, with the appropriate POSTNET bar code.

FIGURE 8.8

An envelope printed with WordPerfect's envelope feature

```
Wanda B. Granolabar
1234 Calle Fuerte
Rancho Santa Fe, CA   92067




                              IlIuuIulIIIuuuIuIuIuIuIuIIuuIuIuIIuuIuuuIII

                              Wilson Dendrobium
                              Attaboy, Inc.
                              P.O. Box 7784
                              Encinitas, CA   92024-4747
```

TIP

You can manually insert the POSTNET code into your document. This might come in handy if you chose Append To Doc but forgot to include the POSTNET Bar Code. To add the bar code, position the cursor in your document, choose Insert ➤ Other ➤ Bar Code, type in a valid POSTNET Bar Code, and choose OK.

Creating information for several envelopes at once is a snap if you follow these steps:

1. Start from a clear document window.

2. Choose Layout ➤ Envelope, fill in the address information you want, and then choose Append To Doc (instead of Print Envelope).

3. Repeat step 2 for each envelope you want to print. WordPerfect will automatically add a hard page break between each envelope.

4. Save your file (just in case), then print it.

TIP

If you need to print envelopes or labels for mass mailings, you might want to take a look at the Merge feature (Chapter 21).

Printing on Labels

Most printers can print directly on labels, though you'll need to buy special *sheet-fed labels* that can tolerate high heat if you're using a laser printer. (Avery offers many laser printer labels.) Figure 8.9 shows some printed sheet labels.

FIGURE 8.9

Some printed sheet-fed labels. This is just an illustration to show how adjacent labels are arranged—the sheets are generally 11 inches long and can accommodate several rows of labels.

```
Mr. David E. Kenney
Attorney at Law
Crane and Fabian
123 Wilshire Blvd.
Los Angeles, CA  91234


Occupant
P.O. Box 123
123 A St.
Glendora, CA  91740


XYZ Corporation
P.O. Box 345
123 C. St.
Glendora, CA  91740
```

```
Shirleen Isagawa
123 Okinawa
Pindowa, Minowa  OUR2CL
Fiji


Miss Anna Jones
Design Consultant
P.O. Box 1234
17047 Sobre Los Cerros
Rancho Santa Fe, CA  92067


Dr. Wilma Rubble
Senior Staff Scientist
Rocket Propulsion Laboratories
P.O. Box 12345
7143 Technology Rd.
Pasadena, CA  91432
```

Dot-matrix and similar printers use *tractor-fed labels*. These are usually single-column labels, on long, continuous rolls (or connected sheets) of paper, with holes on both edges for feeding through the printer tractor. Figure 8.10 shows some printed tractor-fed labels. You can find both types of labels at most office supply or computer supply stores.

FIGURE 8.10

Some printed tractor-fed labels

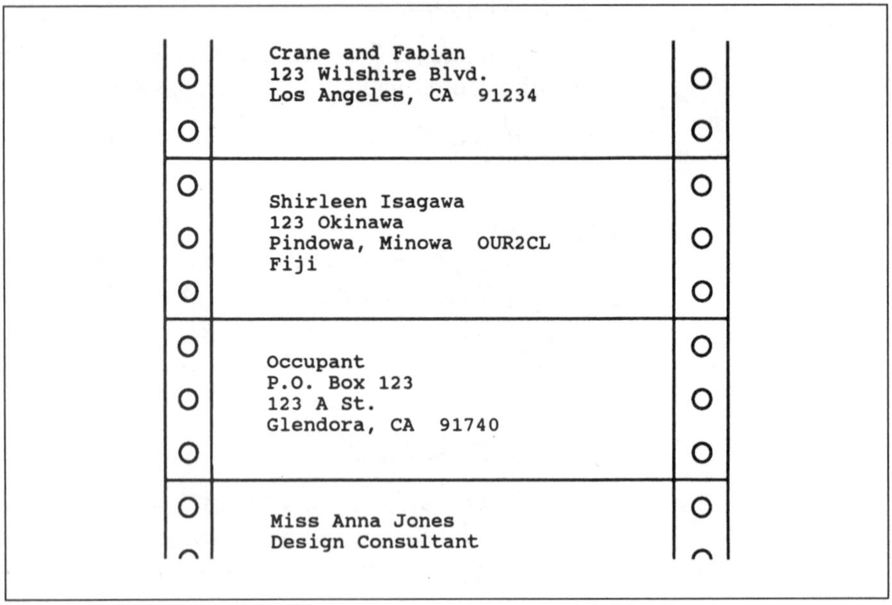

To print on labels, you must first select the appropriate label size. Word-Perfect makes this easy:

1. Place the cursor where you want the labels to start (usually at the top of the document).

2. Choose Layout ➤ Labels. You'll see the Labels dialog box, shown in Figure 8.11. (Notice the sample page of labels near the lower-right corner of the dialog box.)

3. Highlight the label you want in the Labels list and choose Select, or double-click the label name. If the label size you want isn't listed, you'll need to create it first (see "Creating a Paper Size for Labels," later in this chapter), then select the label name.

FIGURE 8.11

The Labels dialog box

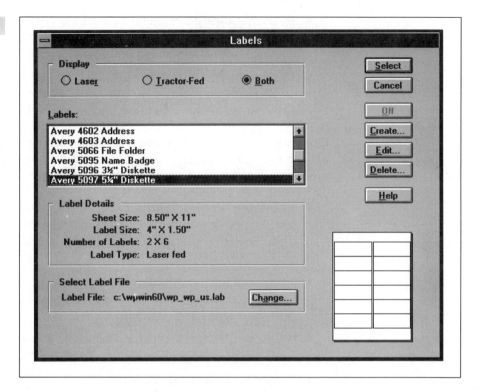

You've probably noticed that the Labels dialog box (Figure 8.11) has many options. Don't let that intimidate you; most of them are simple. Here are some tips to help you work your way through the label maze:

- To limit which labels appear in the list, choose Laser (to show laser labels only) or Tractor-Fed (to show tractor-fed labels only). To display both laser and tractor-fed labels, choose Both.

- The names in the Labels list correspond to the "official" label names that manufacturers use for their labels. You'll find those names on the box of labels. This list will also display the names of label formats that you've created.

- As you scroll through the Labels list with the arrow keys, the details about the highlighted label will appear in the Label Details area, along with a sample page of labels in the lower-right corner.

- To zoom quickly to a name in the Labels list, click anywhere in the list (or choose Labels), then start typing the name you want. WordPerfect will highlight the closest match in the list.

- The command buttons in the dialog box allow you to turn the label format Off; to Create, Edit, and Delete labels; to Change to a different file of label formats; and to get Help.

Once you've selected the paper size for printing on labels, you can think of each label as a "page" of text. Typing on individual labels is almost like typing on individual pages. Here are some tips:

- **To center text horizontally** on all the labels, choose Layout ➤ Justification ➤ Center (or press Ctrl+E) before you type the first label. To center a single line of text, press Shift+F7 at the beginning of the line.

- **To center text vertically** on all the labels, choose Layout ➤ Page ➤ Center ➤ Current And Subsequent Pages, and then OK *before* you type the first label.

- **When you're done typing a label,** you can press Ctrl+↵ to insert a hard page break and start a new "page" (label).

- **To see how your labels will look** when printed, switch to Page view (Alt+F5) or Two Page view (View ➤ Two Page).

Figure 8.12 shows some sample labels typed in the document window in Page view. The [Paper Sz/Type] and [Labels Form] codes in Reveal Codes set the label format, and the [Cntr Pgs] code centers each label vertically. Each label ends with a hard page break (Ctrl+↵).

When you're ready to print, load your labels into the printer. For a dot-matrix printer, position the paper so that the print head is where you want the first label to print. For a laser printer, simply load in the sheet labels. Then print normally.

If the text doesn't line up properly on each label, you may have misaligned the labels in your dot-matrix printer, or you may need to edit the label's paper size, as described later in this chapter.

FIGURE 8.12

Sample labels in the document window, with Reveal Codes on

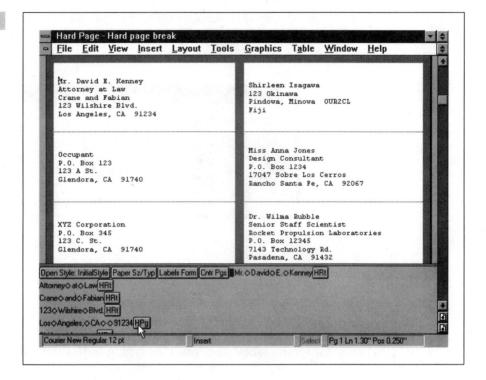

Subdividing the Page

WordPerfect offers another way, besides labels, to subdivide pages into rows and columns. This can be handy for setting up books and pamphlets (as described later), or other subdivided formats. Follow these steps to subdivide your pages:

1. Place the cursor on the page where you want to start subdividing the pages.

2. Choose Layout ➤ Page ➤ Subdivide Page to open the Subdivide Page dialog box.

3. Specify the Number Of Columns and Number Of Rows you want. The sample page in the dialog box will reflect your current choices, as shown below:

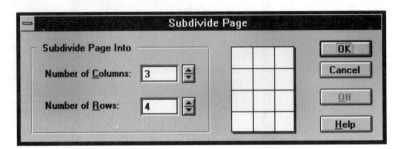

4. Choose OK.

Now type your text normally. You can let WordPerfect start new pages automatically when the page you're typing is filled, or you can press Ctrl+↵ to start a new page whenever you want. Any techniques that work for typing labels also work for typing onto subdivided pages.

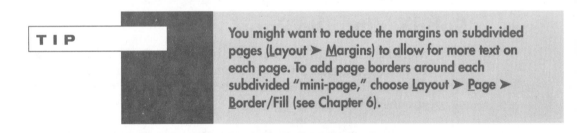

TIP

You might want to reduce the margins on subdivided pages (Layout ➤ Margins) to allow for more text on each page. To add page borders around each subdivided "mini-page," choose Layout ➤ Page ➤ Border/Fill (see Chapter 6).

Printing Booklets and Pamphlets

Surely you've seen examples of booklets and pamphlets. A booklet typically consists of 8.5x11 (or larger) sheets of paper folded in half and stapled on the fold. A pamphlet is basically the same thing, but folded lengthwise, to make a tall, thin multi-page document that fits in your pocket.

In the past, printing multipage booklets and pamphlets in WordPerfect was a major chore. That's true because it was so hard to figure out how to put pages into proper order for binding. But now you don't have to worry about pagination, thanks to a combination of the Subdivide Page and Print As Booklet features.

Preparing a Booklet or Pamphlet

If you want to set up a booklet (or pamphlet), you first need to choose a paper size and subdivide the page into two columns. Here are the steps.

1. Move the cursor to the very top of the document (press Ctrl+Home twice). Choose Layout ➤ Page ➤ Paper Size, and highlight the paper definition you want. For a standard pamphlet, choose a Letter size (8.5x11) definition. For a booklet, choose Letter Landscape (or another landscape definition). If your printer can't print on both sides (duplex), you'll need to pick a definition that has a paper location of *Manual Feed*. This will let you feed paper manually and print on the back side of the paper. (You'll learn how to create and edit paper definitions later in the chapter.) After highlighting the paper size you want, choose the Select button.

2. Choose Layout ➤ Page ➤ Subdivide Page, set the Number Of Columns to 2, and choose OK.

3. If you want smaller margins on each page, choose Layout ➤ Margins, set the margins, and choose OK. (In the example shown in Figure 8.13, I set all four margins to .5″.)

4. If you'd like to put borders around the pages, choose Layout ➤ Page ➤ Border/Fill. Then, using the drop-down list next to Border Style, choose Single and choose OK.

If you choose View ➤ Page or View ➤ Two Page, you'll get an idea of how your text will be placed on the page. Empty page divisions will be cross-hatched in gray.

Typing the Booklet or Pamphlet

You're now ready to start typing or editing your booklet or pamphlet. Typing a booklet or pamphlet is just like typing any other document, and you can use any features described in this book. When you fill a column, or insert a hard page break (Ctrl+↵), WordPerfect will jump to the next "page" automatically.

Figure 8.13 shows an example where I created a cover page, using the centering techniques described earlier in this chapter, followed by a blank page. (The figure is shown in Page view, with Zoom set to 50%.) To finish the booklet, I could press Ctrl+↵ to move the cursor onto the third page, and start typing the table of contents and the rest of the document.

FIGURE 8.13

After selecting a landscape paper size and subdividing the page into two columns, I can type a title page on the first page, and then press Ctrl+↵ to start the next page.

Printing the Booklet or Pamphlet

Follow these steps to print the subdivided document as a booklet or pamphlet:

1. Move the cursor to the top of the document (press Ctrl+Home), and choose Layout ➤ Page ➤ Binding. Set Duplexing to either From Short Edge (for a booklet) or From Long Edge (for a pamphlet). Choose OK to return to the document window.

2. Choose File ➤ Print ➤ Options, select Booklet Printing, and choose OK.

3. Choose Print to start printing.

4. If you chose a paper definition that requires manual feed, insert pages into the printer when prompted. To print on the back (second) side of the paper, feed the paper into the printer with the blank side up and top edge first (for pamphlets) or left edge first (for booklets). The top or left edge is where headings would appear if you printed them.

To turn off subdivided pages, move the cursor to the page where normal pages should begin, then choose Layout ➤ Page ➤ Subdivide Page ➤ Off.

When the printing is complete, you should be able to fold the pages in half and then staple them at the fold to create a properly ordered booklet.

Creating a New Paper Size

Most printers come with a wide range of predefined paper sizes. But if the paper size you need isn't available, you can create it. Here's how to create a paper size (other than labels—we'll get to labels a bit later).

1. If you've installed multiple printers for WordPerfect, select the printer first by choosing File ➤ Select Printer.

2. Choose the type of paper you're creating:

- **To create a paper size other than an envelope or label,** choose Layout ➤ Page ➤ Paper Size. If you'd like to base the new definition on one that's already in the Paper Definition list, highlight the existing definition. Choose Create. You'll see the Create Paper Size dialog box (see Figure 8.14).

- **To create an envelope,** choose Layout ➤ Envelope ➤ Create New Definition. The Create Envelope Definition dialog box is similar to Figure 8.14. However, it displays paper sizes for envelopes only, and initially selects Rotated Font and a Manual Feed paper location.

3. In the Paper Name text box, type a paper name (such as **Fancy Shmancy Paper**). This name will appear later in the list of available paper sizes. The name must not be the same as any other names in the list.

4. Choose any options you want, to define the paper size and type, as described below.

5. When you're done, choose OK. This brings you to the Paper Size (or Envelope) dialog box.

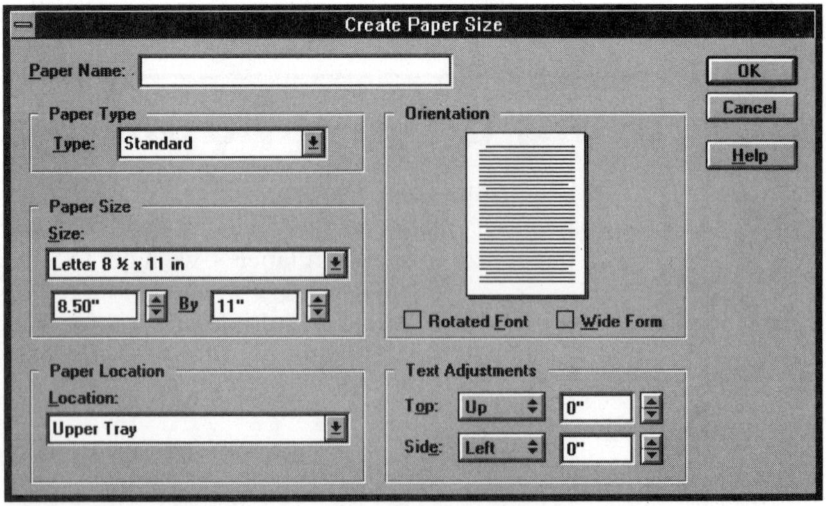

FIGURE 8.14

The Create Paper Size dialog box. Choose Layout ➤ Page ➤ Paper Size ➤ Create to get here.

6. Select your new definition, if you wish. Or choose <u>C</u>lose to exit the dialog box without selecting a paper or envelope size.

Here's a quick rundown of options available in the Create Paper Size and Create Envelope Definition dialog boxes:

Type   Lets you choose a basic *paper type*, which is purely a descriptive name. This name will appear in the Information area of the Paper Size dialog box.

Size   Lets you select the size of paper you'll be using. If you don't see the paper size you want, choose *User Defined Size* from the drop-down list. Press Tab and enter the measurement for the width. Press Tab again (or choose <u>B</u>y) and enter the measurement for the height.

Location   Lets you define where and how paper is loaded into the printer. The available options usually include Default (for the default bin) and Manual Feed. Choose *Default* if your printer can feed paper through a tractor or from the standard bin (sheet or envelope feeder) on a laser printer. Choose *Manual Feed* if you want to feed sheets or envelopes one at a time and have WordPerfect pause after printing each page.

Rotated <u>F</u>ont   Select (check) this option to get landscape (sideways) orientation on a page that is fed into the printer normally (that is, with the short edge first).

<u>W</u>ide Form   Select (check) this option to get landscape orientation on a page that is fed into the printer with the wide edge first. (Available only for printers with a wide bin or platen.)

Text Adjustments   This area lets you adjust where text prints on the page, without having to change the margins. Choose T<u>o</u>p if you want to move the text Up or Down. Choose Sid<u>e</u> if you want to move the text to the Left or Right. Initially, these settings are both 0″ (no text adjustment).

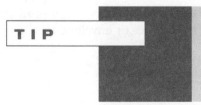

TIP Don't use text adjustments to *create* margins on your pages. Use them only to *adjust* the text when WordPerfect's margin measurements don't come out right on your printed pages.

Creating a New Label Size

If your label size doesn't appear in the labels list, you'll have to create it manually. Your first task is to get the exact measurements of your labels. Typically, these measurements are printed on the box containing the labels. (Some manufacturers even include instructions for creating label paper sizes in WordPerfect.)

If the measurements aren't handy, break out your faithful ruler and measure the labels yourself. Most important, you need to know the individual label's height and width. Figure 8.15 shows the measurements that Word-Perfect will ask you about.

FIGURE 8.15

Label measurements on sample labels

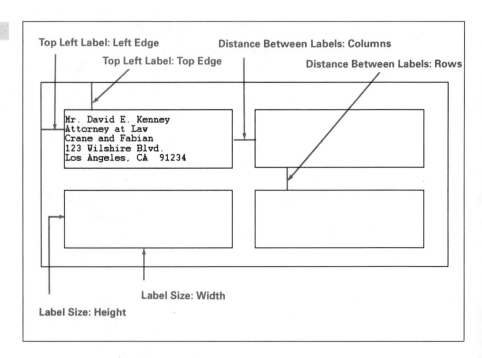

The procedures for defining *sheet* labels (those on separate sheets) and *tractor-fed* labels (those on a continuous roll, for nonlaser printers), vary slightly, as I'll discuss in a moment. But regardless of which type of label size you're creating, here's how to get started:

1. If necessary, use File ➤ Select Printer to select the printer you'll be using to print the labels. When you return to the document window...

2. Place the cursor where you want the new label size to take effect, if you wish.

3. Choose Layout ➤ Labels. If you'd like to base the new label definition on one that's already in the Labels list, highlight the existing definition. Choose Create. You'll see the Create Labels dialog box, shown in Figure 8.16.

4. Complete the dialog box, as described below.

5. When you have finished specifying the options you need, choose OK. This brings you to the Labels dialog box.

6. Select your new label size, if you wish. Or choose Cancel to exit the Labels dialog box without selecting a label size.

FIGURE 8.16

The Create Labels dialog box

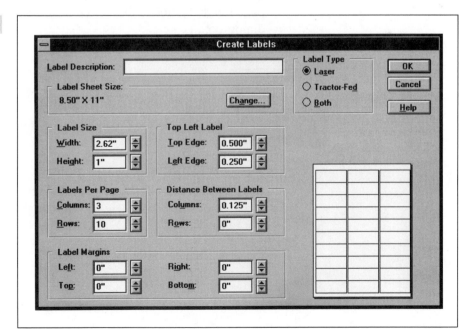

Here are the options available in the Create Labels dialog box. As you make changes, the sample label page at the lower-right corner of the dialog box will reflect your latest choices.

Label Description   The description that will appear in the Labels list. Each description must be unique.

Label Type   Determines which list or lists will display your new format in the Labels dialog box. (Choose La_s_er, Tractor-Fe_d_, or _B_oth.)

Cha_n_ge   Lets you select a paper size. Choose Cha_n_ge, then...

- If you're defining sheet labels for your _laser printer_, select Letter. This is the size of the entire sheet of labels.

- If you're defining _tractor-fed_ labels, select _C_reate. Type in a _P_aper Name. Choose _S_ize and set up a _User Defined_ size using the methods outlined earlier in "Adding a Paper Size." Set the width to the combined width of the labels (and any space between them). Set the height to the height of a single label. Let's suppose you're using two-across labels for a dot-matrix printer, and each label is 4″ wide and $1^{15}/_{16}$″ (1.938″) tall, with $^{1}/_{16}$″ (0.063″) space between each row of labels. For this example, you'd enter **8** as the page width and **2** as the page height. Choose OK twice to return to the Create Labels dialog box.

N O T E   You can enter measurements as decimal numbers (for example, .063) or as fractions (for example, 1/16). WordPerfect will round them off if necessary.

Label Size   Lets you specify the _W_idth and Height of a single label. _NOTE:_ For tractor-fed labels, include the distance between labels in the label width and height. For example, if labels are $2^{15}/_{16}$″ (2.938″) tall with $^{1}/_{16}$″ (0.063″) between each row, define the label height as **3**″.

Labels Per Page   Lets you specify the number of columns and rows in each sheet of labels.

- For Columns, enter the number of labels across the page.
- For Rows, the number depends on the type of labels you're defining. If you're defining sheet labels, enter the number of rows of labels on a sheet. *NOTE:* For tractor-fed labels, enter **1**.

Top Left Label   Lets you define the location of the first label. (If you're defining tractor-fed labels, you can set both measurements to **0** inches. However, before printing, you'll need to align the first label so that the print head is exactly where you want to print the first character.)

- For Top Edge, enter the measurement from the top of the page to the top of the first label.
- For Left Edge, enter the distance from the left edge of the page to the first label.

Distance Between Labels   The distance between labels isn't easy to measure exactly. Typically, it's 0 inches (no space), $\frac{1}{16}''$ (0.063''), $\frac{1}{8}''$ (0.125''), or perhaps $\frac{1}{4}''$ (0.25'').

- For Columns, type the distance between columns (the physical space between adjacent labels). If you're defining tractor-fed labels, enter this distance as **0**, regardless of the actual distance between two or more labels, since you already included the distance between tractor-fed labels when you specified the Width.
- For Rows, type in the distance between two rows. Again, for tractor-fed labels just type **0**, since you already included the distance between tractor-fed labels in your Height measurement.

Label Margins   The label margins are the spaces between the edges of the individual label and the text within the label. The Label Margins options let you specify the Left, Right, Top, and Bottom margins for a single label. Because typically you don't want WordPerfect to word-wrap the mailing label text, you should leave these settings at zero. However, you might want to adjust the label margins if:

- You think the text will be too close to the left edge of the label. Specify a small left margin (about **0.25"** or so).
- Your company's labels already include the company logo and return address.
- You're using $3\frac{1}{2}"$ disk labels. It's nice to leave a top margin of about **0.68"**. This prevents WordPerfect from printing on the part of the label that wraps to the back of the disk, and it helps you center text vertically on the front of the label.

N O T E The horizontal position of the tractors and vertical position of the print head on the first label affect where text appears on tractor-fed labels. WordPerfect doesn't know (or care) how you've aligned the labels in your printer; it just starts printing at the current print-head position.

When you are finished defining your labels, choose OK. This brings you to the Labels dialog box. Then select your new label size, if you wish. Or choose Cancel to exit the dialog box without selecting a label size.

Changing or Deleting a Paper Definition

Changing or deleting an existing paper, envelope, or label definition is easy. Just follow the steps below:

1. If necessary, choose File ➤ Select Printer to select the appropriate printer.

2. If your document uses the paper size you're about to change, place the cursor just after the existing [Paper Sz/Typ] code on the Reveal Codes screen, or delete the old code.

3. Choose Layout ➤ Page ➤ Paper Size (for normal paper and envelopes), or Layout ➤ Labels (for labels).

TIP Instead of doing steps 2 and 3 above, you can double-click the code you want to change in Reveal Codes.

4. Highlight the paper, label, or envelope size you want to change or delete. Then, do one of the following:

- If you want to *change* the highlighted definition, choose <u>E</u>dit. From here, the steps are the same as for defining a new paper size.

- If you want to *delete* the highlighted definition, choose <u>De</u>lete, then choose <u>Y</u>es when prompted.

5. Choose <u>C</u>lose to return to your document.

You've now explored dozens of ways to format your pages using centering, page numbering, headers, footers, watermarks, custom paper sizes, and other features. In the next chapter, we'll switch gears and talk about how to search for and replace text and codes in your document, mark your place so that you can return to it quickly and effortlessly, and quickly expand abbreviated text into a full word or phrase.

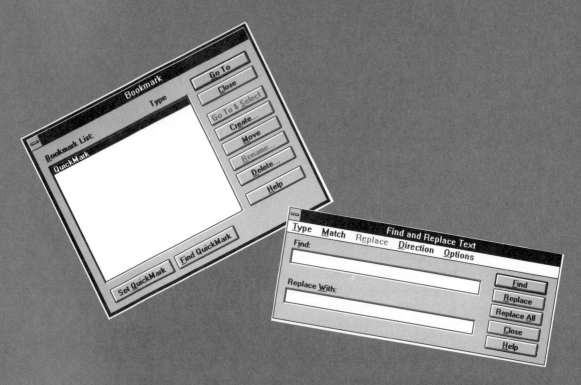

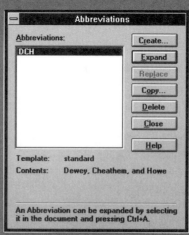

Finding, Replacing, and Marking Text

fast TRACK

HAVE YOU ever typed a long report only to discover consistent mistakes throughout? Maybe you typed *Dewey, Cheathem, and Nowe* instead of *Dewey, Cheathem, and Howe*. Perhaps you used Bodoni-WP Bold instead of CG Times (W1) Bold Italic. How do you fix a mess like this?

Or suppose you're working on a long document and need a caffeine fix. Wouldn't it be nice if you could mark your place with a "bookmark" and come back to the same spot later?

Finally, imagine that you need to type the same long text in various documents. If only WordPerfect could expand an easily typed abbreviation into that finger-twisting text....

Solving world-class problems like these is easy with WordPerfect.

Finding Text and Codes

The Find feature lets you locate a specific sequence of characters anywhere in your document. You tell WordPerfect what you're looking for, and WordPerfect finds it for you.

NOTE The text you're looking for is called the *search string*. The search string can include text, general codes (such as [Und On], [Und Off], and [HRt]), or a specific code (such as [Just:Left] or [Font:Stencil-WP]).

To do a search in the document you're currently viewing on the screen, follow the steps below:

1. Move the cursor where you want the search to start (for example, press Ctrl+Home to start searching at the top of the document). If you want to search only a specific portion of your document, select that portion.

2. Choose Edit ➤ Find, or press F2. You'll see the Find Text dialog box:

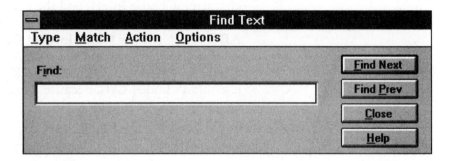

3. In the Find text box, specify the text and/or general codes you're looking for as described just below, then skip to step 5. Or, if you want to find a specific code, skip to step 4 now.

   - To search for a **word** or **phrase**, type that word or phrase in the Find text box.

   - To find **whole words only** (for example, you're looking for *cat* and don't want to come across *catalog* or *scat* along the way), choose Match ➤ Whole Word.

   - To search for words that match exactly in terms of **uppercase and lowercase** letters, choose Match ➤ Case.

   - *Note that you do not type codes into the Find text box.* To insert a **general code** (such as [HRt], [Und On], or [Left Tab]) into the search string, you must insert it from a list of codes. Position the cursor in the Find text box, then choose Match ➤ Codes. Choose the code you want to search for. (To get to the general vicinity of a code in the list, type the first few letters of the code you want, for example **left**. To limit the list to merge codes only, select Display Merge Codes Only.)

Double-click the code you want, or highlight the code and choose <u>I</u>nsert.

- To insert a **WordPerfect special character** in the search string, position the cursor in the F<u>i</u>nd text box, press Ctrl+W, and choose the character you want (see Chapter 6).

- To specify a **pattern of text** in the search string, position the cursor in the F<u>i</u>nd text box, and choose <u>M</u>atch ➤ C<u>o</u>des. Highlight the ★ (Many Char) code to match any number of characters, or the ? (One Char) code to match any single character. Choose <u>I</u>nsert, and the code will appear within brackets in the F<u>i</u>nd text box. For example, a search for **ABC CO[★ (Many Char)]** would find *ABC Company*, *ABC Co.*, *ABC Corp.*, and so forth. A search for **A[? (One Char)]C** would find *AAC, ABC, AXC*, and so on; however, it wouldn't find *AXXC*, because there are *two* letters, not one, between the A and C.

4. If you need to find a **specific code** (such as [Font:Stencil-WP] for the Stencil-WP font or [Just:Full] for full justification) instead of text or general codes, choose <u>T</u>ype ➤ <u>S</u>pecific Codes. Select the code you want to search for, then fill in the specific value you're looking for. (If you change your mind and want to find text instead, choose <u>T</u>ype ➤ Te<u>x</u>t and return to step 3.)

5. From the <u>A</u>ction menu, choose the action you want to take when WordPerfect finds a match:

- **To select** the text that's matched, choose <u>A</u>ction ➤ <u>S</u>elect Match. (This is the default.)

- **To position the cursor before** the text that's matched, choose <u>A</u>ction ➤ Position <u>B</u>efore.

- **To position the cursor after** the text that's matched, choose <u>A</u>ction ➤ Position <u>A</u>fter.

- **To extend the selection** to the next match, choose <u>A</u>ction ➤ <u>E</u>xtend Selection.

6. The search normally starts at the cursor position, or is limited to the selected text. Here's how to change this:

   - **To start at the top** of the document, choose Options ➤ Begin Find At Top Of Document.
   - **To start at the cursor,** search to the end, wrap to the start of the document, then search up to the cursor, choose Options ➤ Wrap At Beg./End Of Document.
   - **To exclude headers, footers, and other elements** that aren't part of the main body of your document, deselect Options ➤ Include Headers, Footers, etc. In Find. (This option is normally selected.)

NOTE   If you selected text in step 1, Options ➤ Limit Find Within Selection will be checked automatically. You can change this setting by checking any of the options listed in step 6 above.

7. To start the search, choose one of the following buttons:

   Find Next   Searches forward for the next match.

   Find Prev   Searches backward for the previous match.

If WordPerfect finds what you asked for, it will position the cursor according to your choice in step 5 above. If it doesn't find the search string, Find will display a "Not Found" message and the cursor won't move (choose OK or press ↵ to clear the message). In either case, the Find Text dialog box will remain on the screen.

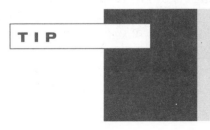

TIP   If Find didn't locate a match and you're sure the text you're looking for is somewhere in the document, make sure you've typed the search string correctly and selected (checked) the correct options on the Match and Options menus in the Find Text dialog box.

Here's what you can do next:

- **To repeat the search,** change any of the options or text (if necessary) then choose <u>F</u>ind Next or Find <u>P</u>rev again.

- **To switch to the document temporarily** (leaving the Find Text dialog box on-screen), simply click on the document window. When you're ready to find text again, click the Find Text dialog box.

- **To start editing** right at the cursor position and remove the dialog box from the screen, choose <u>C</u>lose.

Repeating a Find

If you've closed the Find Text dialog box, it's easy to repeat the Find. Here's what you can do:

- **To use the same search string and options** as for the previous Find, simply press Shift+F2. (The old search string and option settings are remembered until you change them or exit WordPerfect.)

- **To search backwards** for the same search string, press Alt+F2.

- **To use a different search string or options**, choose <u>E</u>dit ➤ <u>F</u>ind or press F2. WordPerfect will open the Find Text dialog box with the settings that you used last. You can change any settings you wish, then choose <u>F</u>ind Next or Find <u>P</u>rev as usual.

Replacing Text and Codes

WordPerfect's Replace feature lets you choose any sequence of characters or codes and change it to something else. (The replacement text or codes make up what is called the *replacement string*.) You can make changes selectively (one at a time), or globally. The term *global* refers to any operation that affects an entire document or an entire block of text within a document.

So what can you do with Replace? For starters, you could change every *aunt* in your document to *uncle*, every *red* to *blue*, every *night* to *day*. Want to delete all the underlining in your document? No problem. Simply replace the underline on ([Und On]) code with nothing.

T I P

The Styles feature (Chapter 17) offers a better and more reliable way to change the font appearance, headings, and other elements that are repeated through your document.

Replacing is almost identical to searching. However, because it can make significant changes to the document, you'd be wise to save your document *just before* performing the replace operation. That way, if you end up making a mess of things, you can just close the current copy of the document (using File ➤ Close ➤ No) *without* saving it, then reopen the good copy with the File ➤ Open command.

T I P

If you forget to save, Edit ➤ Undo (Ctrl+Z) can still bail you out *if* you don't make any other changes before you notice the damage that Replace has done.

Here's how to do a Replace:

1. Use File ➤ Save to save the document in its current state.

2. Move the cursor where you want the replacement to start (press Ctrl+Home to start at the top of the document). Or, select the text first to search and replace in the selected text only.

3. Choose Edit ➤ Replace or press Ctrl+F2. You'll see the Find And Replace Text dialog box:

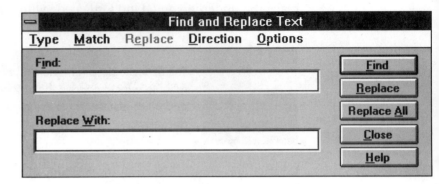

4. In the Find text box, specify the text and/or general codes you're looking for. Your options are the same as for step 3 of the "Finding Text and Codes" procedure above. (If you want to look for a specific code instead of text and general codes, skip to step 6 below.)

5. In the Replace With text box, specify the replacement text. If you want to delete the search string from the document, simply leave the Replace With text box blank. Skip to step 7.

6. If you want to change a specific code (such as Times New Roman Italic) to a different code (such as Univers (W1)) or delete it altogether, choose Type ➤ Specific Codes and select a code. Select the code you want to search for, then select the code you want to replace it with. (You can delete certain specific codes by checking the Replace With Nothing box.)

TIP   You can choose Type ➤ Text or Type ➤ Specific Codes anytime you need to clear out the existing text or codes and enter new ones.

7. Choose the search direction. Select either Direction ➤ Forward to search forward (the default), or Direction ➤ Backward to search backward.

8. The search normally starts at the cursor position, or is limited to the selected text; the replacement usually continues until all matches have been found. Here's how to change this:

- **To choose where the search will start** and how much text is searched, select items from the Options menu as explained in step 6 of the "Finding Text and Codes" procedure above.

- **To limit the number of changes made,** choose Options ➤ Limit Number Of Changes, type the maximum number of changes you want to allow, and choose OK.

9. When you're ready to do the replacement, choose any of the buttons described below:

> **Find**   Finds and highlights the next (or previous) match, *without* making any changes.
>
> **Replace**   Replaces one match of the search string, then highlights the next match.
>
> **Replace All**   Replaces all matches at once (up to the limit specified by Options ➤ Limit Number Of Changes in step 8).
>
> **Close**   Closes the Find and Replace dialog box without making more changes.

If WordPerfect couldn't find the search string, you'll see the message "Not found." Choose OK or press ↵ to clear the message.

Tips for Replacing Text and Codes

Here are some tips for making your replacements safer, faster, smarter, and more enjoyable:

- **To make replacements one at a time,** start by choosing the Find button (step 9). Then, if you want to replace the highlighted match, choose Replace. Otherwise, choose Find to skip this replacement and look for the next (or previous) match.

- If you realize, after doing a few individual Find and Replaces, that a **global replacement** is what you want to do, go ahead and choose Replace All to take care of the remaining matches in one quick step.

- **To save time and typing,** you might want to use abbreviations, like *ABC*, for longer names, like *ABC Corporation*, throughout your document. Then you can go back and replace all the *ABC*s with *ABC Corporation* using the Replace feature. Alternatively, you can use the Abbreviations feature described later in this chapter.

- **To edit your document** while the Find And Replace dialog box is on the screen, simply click on the document. When you're ready to continue the replacement, click on the Find And Replace dialog box.

- You can **replace text and paired codes** with different text and paired codes. For example to replace **this is bold** with this is underlined enter this search string into the Find text box:

  [Bold On]this is bold[Bold On]

  Then enter this replacement text into the Replace With text box:

  [Und On]this is underlined[Und Off]

  (Remember to use Match ➤ Codes to insert the codes shown in brackets.)

- **To delete text and/or general codes** throughout your document, specify the text or codes in the Find text box as usual, leave the Replace With text box empty, and choose Replace All. For example, you could strip out all the underlining by replacing the underline code, [Und On] or [Und Off], with nothing. (When you delete the starting or ending code of a paired code, WordPerfect deletes the other code automatically.)

Finding Your Place with Bookmarks

When WordPerfect loads a document, it places the cursor at the top of the first page. You may recall that you can press Ctrl+End to get to the end of the document quickly.

But what if it's a long document that's taken days or weeks to create, and you were last working on text in the middle of the document? How can you find where you left off? Or, what if you want to go back to a few juicy spots that you didn't quite finish during your last key-pounding session? How can you get to those spots without scrolling through page after page?

The answer is to insert a *bookmark* as a placeholder in the text. Then, when you need to locate your place again, simply use WordPerfect's bookmark feature to zoom back to that spot in a flash.

There are two kinds of bookmarks: *QuickMark bookmarks* and *named bookmarks*. Each document can have only one QuickMark bookmark, but as many named bookmarks as you want.

Here's the quick and easy way to create a QuickMark bookmark:

1. Before you move the cursor, press Ctrl+Shift+Q (*Q* as in *Quick-Mark*) or choose Insert ➤ Bookmark ➤ Set QuickMark. WordPerfect places a hidden [Bookmark] code at the cursor position.

2. Scroll through your document to your heart's content, or use Find if you like. When you're done looking around, press Ctrl+Q to return to your bookmark. It's that easy!

Setting a Bookmark Automatically

You can tell WordPerfect to set a QuickMark bookmark in your document automatically whenever you close the document. That way, whenever you open a document you can just press Ctrl+Q to get right back to where you left off.

Here's how to turn the automatic bookmark feature on:

1. Choose File ➤ Preferences and double-click Environment.

2. Select the Set QuickMark On Save check box (if it isn't already selected).

3. Choose OK, then choose Close.

The feature will stay on for all future documents unless you repeat the steps above and clear the × from the Set QuickMark On Save check box.

Putting Named Bookmarks in a Document

The QuickMark is not the only bookmark you can add to your document (though it's the only one that Ctrl+Q will find). You can put as many named bookmarks in your document as you wish. And you can move, delete, and rename existing bookmarks. Here's how to work with named bookmarks in WordPerfect:

1. If you're adding a new bookmark or you want to move an existing bookmark, move the cursor to where you want to put the bookmark.

2. If you wish, you can have the bookmark select text when you move back to it later by creating a *selected bookmark*. To do this, just select the text that you'll want to jump back to later.

3. Choose Insert ➤ Bookmark, or right-click a scroll bar on the document window and choose Bookmarks from the QuickMenu. You'll see the Bookmark dialog box (Figure 9.1).

FIGURE 9.1

The Bookmark dialog box lets you create, find, delete, and move bookmarks in a document. To get here, choose Insert ➤ Bookmark.

Bookmark	
Bookmark List: **Type**	Go To
QuickMark	Close
	Go To & Select
	Create...
	Move
	Rename...
	Delete...
	Help
Set QuickMark Find QuickMark	

4. Now you have several choices:

- **To create a new bookmark,** choose Create and type a unique name for your bookmark (something that will be easy to remember later). Choose OK. WordPerfect will insert a [Bookmark:*name*] code at the cursor position (where *name* is the name you assigned to the bookmark).

- **To return to a bookmark** that you created earlier, double-click its name or highlight its name and choose Go To. To return to a bookmark that you created with selected text, highlight the bookmark's name and choose Go To & Select.

- **To delete a bookmark** that you're not using anymore, highlight its name, then choose Delete and answer Yes when prompted for verification. (You can also delete a bookmark by deleting its [Bookmark] code in Reveal Codes.)

- **To move a bookmark** to the current cursor location in your document, highlight the bookmark's name and choose Move.

- **To rename a bookmark,** highlight the bookmark, choose Rename, type in (or edit) the name, and choose OK.

- **To highlight the name of a bookmark,** click in the Bookmark List (or press Alt+B) and type a few characters of the bookmark you want to find. WordPerfect will highlight the closest match as you type.

5. Choose Close, if necessary, to return to the document window.

TIP
You can get to the Bookmark dialog box in a hurry by double-clicking any [Bookmark] code in Reveal Codes.

Replacing Abbreviations Automatically

Suppose you work for the law firm of *Dewey, Cheathem, and Howe.* That finger-twister firm name isn't easy to type, especially if you have to do it often. However, it *is* easy to type the abbreviation **DCH**, or select it from a list and have WordPerfect *expand* it for you.

NOTE   The Abbreviations feature can be very useful for storing words and phrases you use frequently in your work. However, it may be just as easy to use the Find and Replace feature described earlier to expand abbreviated text.

Follow these steps to create an abbreviation:

1. Select the text that you want to abbreviate. For example, select *Dewey, Cheathem, and Howe* in your document.

2. Choose Insert ➤ Abbreviations, then choose Create from the Abbreviations dialog box.

3. Type a short name for the selected text (for example, **DCH**). Note that abbreviationos are case-sensitive. For example, *DCH* is different from *dch*.

4. Choose OK, then Close.

Once you've set up an abbreviation, you can insert the expanded form into your document. Proceed as follows:

1. Type the abbreviation exactly as you spelled it when you created the abbreviation.

2. Place the cursor in or just to the right of the abbreviated text.

3. Press Ctrl+A.

If you prefer to expand an abbreviation without typing it first, follow these steps:

1. Position the cursor where you want the full text to appear.

2. Choose Insert ➤ Abbreviations to open the Abbreviations dialog box:

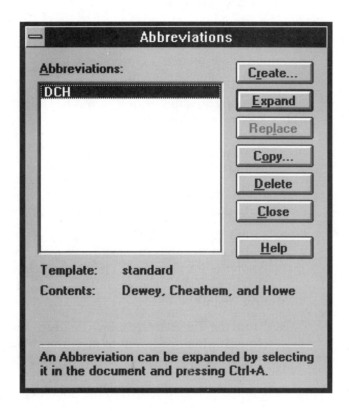

3. Double-click the abbreviation you want to expand, or highlight it and choose Expand. (In the example above, I highlighted *DCH*. Notice that the expanded text appears at the bottom of the dialog box next to the word *Contents*.)

The expanded abbreviation will appear at the cursor position.

N O T E WordPerfect comes with a macro, named EXPNDALL, that will expand all abbreviations in your document at once. See Chapter 18 to learn how to run a macro.

Deleting, Copying, and Replacing an Abbreviation

It's easy to delete an abbreviation if you no longer need it. Choose Insert ➤ Abbreviations, and highlight the abbreviation you want to delete. Now, choose Delete, answer Yes when asked for confirmation, and choose OK to return to your document.

You can copy an abbreviation to another document template if you wish. Here are the steps to follow:

1. Choose Insert ➤ Abbreviations ➤ Copy. The Copy Abbreviation dialog box will appear.

2. From the Template To Copy From drop-down list, select the template that contains the abbreviation you want to copy.

3. In the Select Abbreviation To Copy list, select the abbreviation(s) you want to copy. To select more than one abbreviation, hold down the Ctrl key while clicking each abbreviation you want. (To deselect an abbreviation, hold down Ctrl and click the abbreviation again.)

4. From the Template To Copy To drop-down list, select the template to which you want to copy the abbreviation.

5. Choose Copy.

6. Choose Close to return to the document window.

NOTE

Templates establish all the formatting and screen settings for a document. The *standard template* (a blank document) is selected for you automatically. However, you can choose from other built-in templates or make your own. See Chapters 4 and 20 for details.

You can also change the text associated with an existing abbreviation. Here are the steps to follow:

1. Select the new text for the expanded form of the abbreviation.

2. Choose Insert ➤ Abbreviations.

3. In the Abbreviations list, highlight the abbreviation you want to update.

4. Choose Replace and answer Yes when prompted for verification.

5. Choose Close to return to the document window.

In this chapter you've learned about four of WordPerfect's most indispensable workhorse tools: Find, Replace, Bookmarks, and Abbreviations. In Chapter 10 we'll switch gears and talk about how to master your printer and fonts. This is an important topic for anyone who wants to take full advantage of the printer's capabilities.

Indent

Ab
QuickFormat

Mastering Your Printer and Fonts

f a s t TRACK

To print multiple copies of a document   **354**

choose File ➤ Print ➤ Number Of Copies and enter the number of copies you want. Under Generated By, choose Word-Perfect if you want the copies to be collated, or choose Printer for faster printing with uncollated pages. Then choose Print.

To control print jobs   **355**

switch to the WP Print Process or Windows Print Manager window by pressing Alt+Tab. Then choose options you need to cancel, pause, or resume a print job.

To install graphics fonts   **367**

follow the font manufacturer's instructions for installing the fonts for use in Windows. (Most likely, you'll need to go through the Font utility in the Windows Control Panel.) That's all you need to do to make the fonts available in Word-Perfect for Windows.

YOU can print a copy of the document on your screen simply by going to the Print dialog box and choosing the Print button (or by pressing Ctrl+P). But as you'll see in this chapter, there are many things you can do to control your printer and maximize its speed. And you can expand your font collection in lots of ways to create ever more dazzling documents.

> **TIP**
> If you have problems with your printer or fonts, refer to Appendix C for quick tips on diagnosing and solving problems.

How to Print Documents

WordPerfect offers many ways to control the appearance of your printed document and the speed at which it prints. Let's take it from the top, step by step.

Step 1: Get Your Document Ready

If you have multiple documents open on your screen but want to print only one of them, make that document's window the active window. You can use the Window command on the menu bar to quickly switch to any open document.

Printing a Portion of Your Document

If you want to print only a portion of the document, select the portion you want to print (as discussed in Chapter 3). Or, if you want to print a single page, just move the cursor to the page you want to print.

Printing Several Documents

If you want to print several documents, including several documents that are currently open, your best bet is to save and close all the documents you want to print so that the copies on disk are up-to-date. Then you can choose File ➤ Open, and mark the files you want to print by holding down the Ctrl key as you click the names of files that you want to print. Finally, choose File Options ➤ Print, and follow the instructions on the screen.

Step 2: Get Your Printer Ready

Before you get started, take a quick glance at the printer and make sure it's turned on and is online. (See your printer manual if you need help.)

Tractor-Fed (Dot-Matrix) Printer

If you're using a tractor-fed (dot-matrix) printer, take a look at the position of the print head in relation to the page that's in the platen. (The *print head* does the actual printing. The *platen* is the roller that moves the paper through the printer.) If the print head isn't lined up near the top of a new page (or wherever you want to start printing on that page), turn the printer off, manually crank the paper into position, then turn the printer back on. Make sure the printer is online.

Sheet-Fed (Laser) Printer

If you're using a sheet-fed (laser) printer, chances are that you don't need to do anything at this point. But, if there's a partially printed page in the printer (and the form feed button is lit), you may want to eject that page from the printer using your printer's form feed button (according to the instructions in the manual).

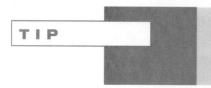

TIP To avoid having to reprint the document to fix simple spelling mistakes, run the document through the Speller (Ctrl+F1) just before printing it. (See Chapter 11.)

Step 3: Go to the Print Dialog Box

Next, you want to get to the Print dialog box. To do so, choose File ➤ Print, press F5, or click the Print button on the power bar. You'll be taken to the Print dialog box, shown in Figure 10.1. This dialog box is sort of like "command central" for telling WordPerfect exactly what you want to print and how to print it.

In the remaining steps, I'll assume you're in the Print dialog box.

FIGURE 10.1

The Print dialog box lets you tell WordPerfect what to print and how to print it. To get here, choose File ➤ Print or press F5.

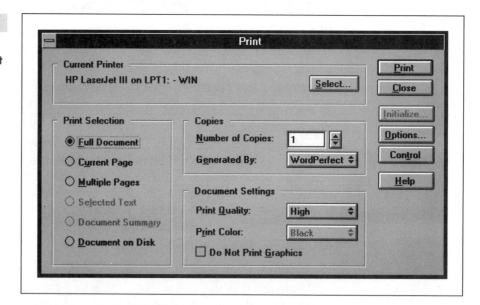

Step 4: Select Your Printer

If you've installed multiple printers for use in WordPerfect, take a look at the printer name under Current Printer. If that's not the printer you want to use, choose Select, then choose the name of the printer you want to use by double-clicking, or by highlighting and pressing ↵.

N O T E   Choosing Select from the Print dialog box is the same as choosing File ➤ Select Printer.

WordPerfect vs. Windows Drivers

You might notice that there are two drivers per printer: a WordPerfect driver, (marked with a *WP* icon), and a Windows driver (marked with the Windows 3.1 "flying window" icon), as in the example below.

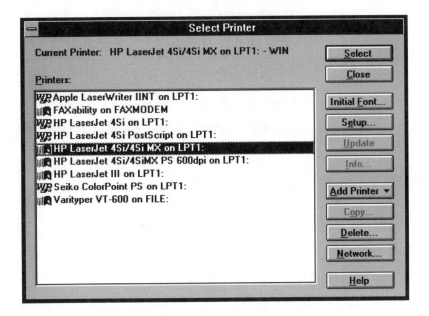

Unlike previous versions of WordPerfect, there's really no big difference between the two drivers. Both generally offer the same fonts and capabilities.

But if you work in a variety of platforms (for example, DOS, Windows, OS/2), you should use the WordPerfect driver to print your document—In fact, you should use it during general editing as well—to make the document more portable to other platforms. On the other hand, if you use Windows exclusively, you might as well just use the Windows printer driver.

Step 5: Tell It What to Print

Next, you want to tell WordPerfect exactly what you want to print, by using options in the Print Selection group of the Print dialog box. Your options are listed below:

Full Document Prints the entire document that's in the currently active document window.

Current Page Prints only the page that the cursor is on.

Multiple Pages Choose this option if you want to print only certain pages from the document, or if you want to use other special features described under "Printing Part of a Document" (following the Step 7 discussion below).

Selected Text This option will already be chosen if you selected text before coming to the Print dialog box. Otherwise it will be dimmed and unavailable.

Document Summary Choose this option if you want to print the document summary, described in Chapter 20. This option is available only if there's a document summary for the file.

Document On Disk Lets you print a document that's not open at the moment. After choosing this option, choose Print and specify the file name (or path and file name) of the document you wish to print.

Step 6: Tell It How to Print

There's a general rule of thumb that applies to most printers: *The lower the print quality you use, the worse the document looks, but the faster it prints.* For quick drafts of a document, you might want to try printing with a low print quality. To speed things along even more, you can mark the Do Not Print Graphics check box to print only the text.

If you have a color printer, and want to print in color, you can choose the Full Color option from the Print Color pop-up list.

Step 7: Start Printing

At this point, you can select other options described later in this chapter. But if you're ready to start printing, just click the <u>P</u>rint button. Depending on which options you chose in the previous steps, you may be prompted for additional information. When WordPerfect has all the information it needs, it creates a temporary file to print from (so that you can continue working), then starts actually printing the document after a short delay.

Printing Part of a Document

As mentioned under "Step 5: Tell WordPerfect What to Print," you can use the <u>M</u>ultiple Pages option in the Print dialog box to print a portion of the document. If you've selected that option, you'll be taken to the following dialog box after you click the <u>P</u>rint button to start printing.

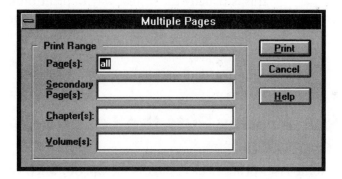

When specifying the pages to print, use a comma (,) to separate individual page numbers, and a hyphen (-) to specify a range. It is important to *always start with the earliest page number, and work your way toward the end.* For example, entering **3,5,15-20, 25-30** prints pages, 3, 5, 15 through 20, and 25 through 30. (Choose <u>H</u>elp if you need additional help.)

You can also define <u>S</u>econdary Page(s), <u>C</u>hapter(s), and <u>V</u>olume(s) to print, if you've defined such numbers in your pagination scheme (see Chapter 8 for more information). After defining your pages, choose <u>P</u>rint to proceed.

Printing Multiple Copies

Here's how to print several copies of a document:

1. In the Print dialog box, choose Number Of Copies.

2. Type in (or use the spin box arrows to indicate) the number of copies you want to print (for example, **3** for triplicate).

3. Choose Generated By and specify how you want the copies printed. Your options are as follows:

   WordPerfect   Though usually a little slower than the Printer option, this option has the advantage of collating the copies. For example, you'd get a complete copy of the document, then a second complete copy of the document, and so forth.

   Printer   If your printer can make the copies on its own, this is usually the fastest way to print multiple copies. However, the pages won't be collated. For example, you'd get three copies of page 1, then three copies of page 2, and so forth.

4. Click the Print button to proceed.

If Your Printer Puts the Last Page on Top

Some laser printers eject pages face-up. So, when your print job is done, the last page will be on the top, and the first page will be on the bottom.

To fix that, go to the Print dialog box (press F5), and then choose the Options button. Select the Print In Reverse Order (Back To Front) check box, choose OK, then choose Print.

Exiting while Printing

When you start printing a document, you'll see "Preparing Document for Printing." Once that message disappears, you can do anything else you wish in WordPerfect. You can even switch to another application or exit WordPerfect.

However, you cannot exit *Windows* until the print job is complete. If you try, you may see a message indicating that closing Print Manager will cancel all pending print jobs. To prevent that cancellation, choose Cancel.

Insider Printer Tips

Your printer documentation contains all the information about your particular printer. But WordPerfect Corporation might have some things to say about that particular printer as well. To find out what these are...

1. Choose File ➤ Select Printer.

2. Highlight the name of any WordPerfect printer driver, and click the Info button (if that button is dimmed, there is no additional information to view).

While you're in the Printer Information dialog box, you can choose Sheet Feeder, if it's available, to learn about sheet feeders (discussed a little later in this chapter) that WordPerfect can use. When you've finished reading, just choose Close, as usual, to work your way back to the document.

Controlling Print Jobs

Unlike DOS versions of WordPerfect, which have their own Control Printer screen, WordPerfect for Windows uses its own "Print Process," in conjunction with the Windows Print Manager, to manage print jobs. If you need to check up on, pause, or cancel a print job, you can do so by following these steps:

1. Press Alt+Tab until you get to the Print Manager or WP Print Process dialog box, then release the Alt and Tab keys.

2. If you're in the WordPerfect Print Job dialog box, you can cancel the print job by choosing Cancel Print Job.

3. If you get to the Windows Print Manager, you can choose Pause to pause the print job, then Resume when you're ready to start printing again.

N O T E

You can also reach the WordPerfect Print Job dialog box by pressing F5 in WordPerfect (to go to the Print dialog box) and then clicking the Control button (if it's not dimmed). And instead of pressing Alt+Tab to switch to the printer control applications, you can press Ctrl+Esc and double-click either *WordPerfect Print Job* or *Print Manager* in the Task List dialog box.

When you're in the Windows Print Manager dialog box, you can delete a print job by highlighting its name and choosing the <u>D</u>elete button. If you want to cancel all remaining print jobs, close the Print Manager window by double-clicking its Control-menu box, or by pressing Alt+F4. If you want to return to WordPerfect without canceling print jobs, just click the Minimize button in the Print Manager dialog box. Then press Alt+Tab, if necessary, to get back to WordPerfect.

For more information about the Windows Print Manager, please refer to your Windows documentation.

Printing on Both Sides of the Page

You may want to print your documents on both the front and back sides of the page, either for eventual binding or just to conserve paper. There are three ways to print back-to-back, as we'll discuss in the next three sections.

T I P

When you're printing back-to-back, you can use the Force feature to ensure that a particular page is odd- or even-numbered. See "Forcing an Odd or Even Page Number" in Chapter 8.

...with a Duplex Printer

If you have a *duplex printer* (one that can print on both sides of the page), like the LaserJet IID or LaserJet IIID, follow these steps to print on both sides of the page:

1. Move the cursor to the page where you want double-sided printing to begin in your document (for example, to the top of the first page if you want to print the entire document back-to-back).

2. Choose Layout ➤ Page ➤ Binding. You'll see this dialog box.

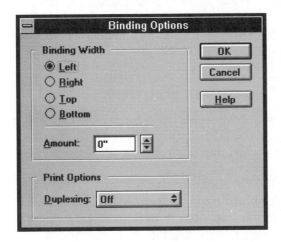

3. Use the Duplexing pop-up list button at the bottom of the dialog box to choose how you plan to bind the pages: along the Short Edge or along the Long Edge (see your printer manual for examples, if necessary).

4. If you wish, choose a Binding Width indicating which side of the page you want to leave extra space on (Left, Right, Top, or Bottom). Then indicate how much extra space you want for binding next to Amount (for example, .5 for half an inch).

N O T E The Binding amount is added to the margin. For example, if you put a .5" binding amount on the left side of the page, and you already have a one-inch margin, your actual left margin will be 1.5 inches.

5. Choose OK to return to your document. Then print with the usual File ➤ Print ➤ Print commands (or press F5 or Ctrl+P).

When you use this method to print back-to-back, WordPerfect inserts a [Dbl-Sided Print] code in your document (and also a [Binding Width] code if you change the default binding width). If you decide not to print back-to-back in the future, you can just remove those codes in Reveal Codes.

...with a Regular Printer

If you don't have a duplex printer, you can still print back-to-back by printing all the odd-numbered pages, then reloading the printed pages back into the printer, and printing all the even-numbered pages. To do so:

1. With your document on the screen, press Ctrl+End to move to the bottom of the document. Then check the number next to Pg in the status bar to determine how many pages are in the document. This step tells you whether the last page is odd or even—information you'll need in step 6 below.

2. Choose File ➤ Print ➤ Options.

3. Using the Print Odd/Even Pages pop-up list button, choose Odd.

4. Choose OK, then choose Print and wait for all the pages to be printed.

5. Remove the printed pages from the printer, and put them back in the printer bin. On most printers, you'll want the first page facing down so the back (blank side) of the last page is on top. The top of the pages should be aimed toward the printer.

6. If there is an odd number of pages in your document, remove the top page from the bin. (That will be the last printed page. You don't want to run it through the printer again.)

7. Choose File ➤ Print ➤ Options again.

8. Select (check) Print In Reverse Order (Back To Front).

9. Choose Even from the Print Odd/Even Pages pop-up list.

10. Choose OK, then choose Print.

N O T E The exact procedure for odd/even page printing might be different on your model of printer. Try the suggested steps on a short document (five pages should do it). If those steps don't work, you'll need to experiment until you find the right combination. Once you've worked out the details for your own printer, you could tape a reminder of the steps onto the printer.

Printing a Booklet or Pamphlet

Another way to print pages back-to-back, with any printer, is in booklet or pamphlet format, where you subdivide pages, print them, then fold and bind the pages in the center. This type of printing is discussed under "Printing Booklets and Pamphlets" in Chapter 8.

Printing One Page at a Time

If your printer or paper requires that you feed one sheet at a time, you might want to create a "manual feed" paper size. That way, you can just select that paper size whenever you need to print one page at a time.

To create such a paper size, start out by choosing Layout ➤ Page ➤ Paper Size, and then choose Create from the Paper Size dialog box. In the Paper Name text box, give the paper a name, such as **Manual Letter Size**. Choose your paper Type and Size, as discussed in Chapter 8. Under Location, choose Manual Feed. Then choose OK and Close to return to your document.

Whenever you want to print one page at a time in the future, just use this new paper size. That is, move the cursor to the top of the document (press Ctrl+Home). Then choose Layout ➤ Page ➤ Paper Size. Select the paper size you created in the previous paragraph by double-clicking or by high-lighting and pressing ↵. WordPerfect inserts a [Paper Sz/Type] code into your document (visible only in Reveal Codes of course).

Then, print your document normally (File ➤ Print ➤ Print). WordPerfect will pause for a new sheet of paper before printing each page. If your printer has a message window on it, the message will probably tell you when to feed a page.

"Printing to Disk"

Let's suppose you want to use somebody else's printer (and computer) to print a document. But that person doesn't have WordPerfect on their system. Can you still print your WordPerfect document on that system? The answer is Yes, if you print the document to disk first.

The first thing you need to do, on your own computer, is install a *printer driver* for the printer that you will be using to actually print the document. You can learn how to install a printer driver under "Adding a Printer" later in this chapter.

With the printer driver installed on your own computer, start WordPerfect and choose File ➤ Select Printer, and select the printer driver for the printer you'll actually be using to print the document (even though that printer might not actually be attached to your computer). In order to see exactly what the fonts and line breaks will look like when your document is eventually printed, you must use that printer driver while creating, editing, and saving your document.

The exact steps for printing to disk for later output on a different computer depend on whether you chose a WordPerfect or a Windows printer driver while creating your document.

...with a WordPerfect Printer Driver

If you're using a WordPerfect printer driver, and want to print to disk, follow these steps:

1. Choose File ➤ Select Printer and highlight the name of the WordPerfect printer driver that you'll be using to print the document later.

2. Choose S̲etup.

3. Under Destination, set the P̲ort option to F̲ile.

4. If you want WordPerfect to prompt you for a file name each time you print to disk in the future, leave the F̲ilename text box empty, and select (check) P̲rompt For Filename. If you want to use the same file name repeatedly in the future, enter that file name in the F̲ilename text box, and deselect the P̲rompt For Filename option.

5. Choose OK, then S̲elect, to return to your document.

6. Choose F̲ile ➤ P̲rint ➤ P̲rint or press Ctrl+P.

7. If you selected the Prompt For Filename option back in step 4, you'll see a dialog box asking for the name of the file to store the printed document in. Enter a valid DOS file name, such as **wpdriver.prn** and then choose OK.

Remember that *all* future documents that you print with the currently se-lected printer driver will be sent to a file, until you repeat the steps above and set the printer port back to L̲PT1 or whatever is appropriate for your system.

Now you can skip to the section titled "Printing the Disk File" later in this chapter for information on how to actually print that document you just sent to the disk.

...with a Windows Printer Driver

To print to disk using a Windows printer driver, you need to change the destination of that Windows driver to a file. Typically, you'll need to go through Windows to do this. You can refer to your Windows documenta-tion for more information, but here are the general steps, starting from WordPerfect:

1. Press Alt+Tab until you get to the Windows Program Manager.

2. Open the Main group, then double-click the Control Panel icon.

3. In the Control Panel, double-click the Printers icon.

4. Highlig̲ht the name of the printer you plan to print from, then choose C̲onnect.

5. Choose FILE: from the list of available ports, then choose OK.

6. Choose Close, and then close the Control Panel window and return to your WordPerfect document.

7. In WordPerfect, choose File ➤ Select Printer, highlight the printer you modified in step 4 (its name will likely end with ON FILE:) and choose Select.

8. Choose File ➤ Print ➤ Print or press Ctrl+P.

9. When prompted, type in a file name for the file you will be creating (for example, **windrive.prn**), then choose OK.

Remember, *all* future documents that you print with this printer will be sent to a file. To set the printer port back to LPT1 or whatever is appropriate for your system, repeat the first four steps above. In step 5, choose the port you want. Then repeat step 6.

Printing the Disk File

At this point, you should have already created your print file as discussed in one of the previous two sections. Now, to take that file to another computer and print it:

1. Copy the print file to a floppy disk (you can use DOS, the Windows File Manager, or WordPerfect to do so). If you can't find the file you printed to, go to the DOS command prompt and enter the command **dir *filename* /s** where *filename* is the filename and extension of the file you're looking for (for example, **windrive.prn**). Using the \ and /s as shown tells DOS to search all the directories on the disk. You can also use File ➤ Search in the Windows File Manager to locate files in any directory on the disk.

2. Start the computer that has the printer you want to use connected to it, and get to the DOS command prompt (typically *C:>*).

3. Put the floppy disk that contains the print file in drive A or B, and type the command:

   copy /b *drive:\filename port*

   where *drive* is the name of the floppy drive you put the disk in, *filename* is the name of the print file, and *port* is the port that the printer is connected to (typically LPT1 or PRN). For example, if the file you want to print is on the floppy in drive A, is named *wpdriver.prn*, and the printer is hooked to LPT1 on the current computer, the command to enter would be:

copy /b a:\wpdriver.prn lpt1

Don't forget to press ↵ after typing the command. After you see the message "One file(s) copied," the job is done.

If the last page doesn't print, eject the last page from the printer using the printer's form feed button or as instructed in the printer manual—or by typing **echo ^L > prn**↵ (you press Ctrl+L to type the ^L symbol).

Exporting to Another Program/Version

The techniques above create a "print file" that contains commands that are sent directly to the printer. You can't import that print file into another program. If you do want to print a copy of your document to disk for use with another program, or with an earlier version of WordPerfect, use File ➤ Save As rather than File ➤ Print. In the Save As dialog box, enter a name for the exported version of the file, and choose the format you want to export to from the Format list before you choose OK to actually save the file. For more information on importing and exporting files, please refer to Chapter 33.

Using Fancy Sheet Feeders

WordPerfect generally assumes that your printer is using the standard sheet feeder that comes with that printer. If you buy an optional, more extravagant sheet feeder, you need to tell WordPerfect once you've installed that sheet feeder.

To do so, choose File ➤ Select Printer and highlight the WordPerfect printer driver for the printer you've added the new sheet feeder to. Then choose Setup.

Click the Sheet Feeder button (if it's available), and choose your sheet feeder from the list that appears. Choose OK twice, and when you return to the Select Printer dialog box, choose Select to activate the printer for which you've defined the sheet feeder.

Next, you need to create a paper size that takes advantage of the sheet feeder. To do so, choose Layout ➤ Page ➤ Paper Size. Then create or edit a paper size. While doing so, you can choose your sheet feeder from the Location drop-down list in the Paper Location section of the Create Paper Size dialog box. If you need additional help, please refer to "Creating a New Paper Size" in Chapter 8.

Using Fancy Output Bins

Depending on the capabilities of your printer, you can use commands under the Output Bin Options in the Print dialog box to control how pages come out of the printer.

1. Get to the Print dialog box (File ➤ Print or F5).

2. Choose Options, then, if the Output Bin Options are available, choose your options as follows:

> **Sort** Use this with the Output Bins option to print several copies of a document, each collated and fed to a separate bin.
>
> **Group** Use this with the Output Bins option to print documents grouped by page, where each page is stacked in a separate output bin (copies are not collated).
>
> **Jogger** If your printer can jog (offset) the output pages left or right, select this option to have each copy printed in a separate stack.
>
> **Output Bins** If your printer has multiple output bins, use this option to specify where to send the print job.

3. Choose OK to return to the Print dialog box. Then choose other options as appropriate, or Print to start printing.

Adding a Printer

If you buy a new printer, or decide to use somebody else's printer to print your documents, you need to first install the appropriate printer driver.

You can install the Windows printer driver, the WordPerfect printer driver, or both.

Installing a Windows Printer Driver

If you work exclusively in Windows, you might need to install only the Windows printer driver for your printer. You use Windows to install Windows printer drivers. But you can get to the appropriate dialog boxes without leaving WordPerfect. Here's how:

1. Gather up your original Windows 3.1 floppy disks.

2. In WordPerfect, choose File ➤ Select Printer ➤ Add Printer ➤ Windows.

3. In the Printers dialog box that appears, choose Add>>.

4. Under List Of Printers, click the name of the printer you want to install a driver for, then choose Install.

5. Follow the remaining instructions that appear on the screen.

The printer you installed will be available for selection in *all* your Windows applications, not just WordPerfect for Windows.

Installing a WordPerfect Printer Driver

There are several ways to install a WordPerfect printer driver. The easiest way, however, is to gather up your original WordPerfect for Windows floppy disks (particularly the disk(s) with printer drivers on them), and then follow these steps:

1. If you're in WordPerfect, save your work and exit to the Windows Program Manager.

2. In the Program Manager, open the WPWin 6.0 group, then double-click the WPWin6.0 Installation application.

3. In the Installation Type dialog box that appears, choose Options.

4. Choose Printers.

5. Specify the drive you'll be installing from. For instance, if you'll be installing from the printer drivers disk in drive A, enter **a:** under Install From. (You can leave the Install To setting at

C:\WPC20 unless you've stored your WordPerfect Corporation shared files on some other directory.)

6. Insert the Install 1 disk into drive A or drive B (as appropriate), then choose OK.

7. In the Printers list, choose the name of the printer for which you want to install a driver (by double-clicking), choose OK, and follow the instructions that appear on the screen.

8. When installation is complete, choose <u>C</u>lose, then choose <u>E</u>xit to return to Program Manager.

Remember, drivers that you install in this manner will only be available in WordPerfect...not your other Windows applications.

Expanding Your Font Collection

Your printer can print at least one font—and maybe quite a few fonts. But you can always expand your font collection to include dozens, even hundreds, of fonts, simply by purchasing those fonts from your local computer dealer or mail-order house.

There was a time when fonts were expensive, difficult to install and use, and just a big pain in the neck in general. But, since the introduction of Windows 3.1 and TrueType, Speedo, Type 1, and other *graphics fonts*, font management has become much simpler and less expensive.

A clear understanding of the differences between graphics fonts and printer fonts, however, is necessary to keep things simple. So let's start with a general discussion of the types of fonts available to you.

About Graphics and Printer Fonts

Basically, there are two kinds of fonts in the world today:

- **Printer Fonts**, the fonts of the 80s, were created for individual printers, mainly PostScript and LaserJet (PCL) printers. Built-in fonts, soft fonts, and cartridge fonts all fall into this category.

- **Graphics Fonts** are the fonts of the 90s. They work with any dot-matrix or laser printer that can print graphics. They work with both DOS and Windows versions of WordPerfect, they're scalable (they can be printed at any size), great-looking, fast, and (perhaps best of all) remarkably inexpensive. TrueType, Type 1, Bitstream Speedo, AutoFont, and Intellifont are all examples of modern graphics fonts.

The main difference between printer and graphics fonts is that with printer fonts, the *printer* handles all the behind-the-scenes jobs required to print the font. With graphics fonts, the *computer* handles those jobs. In general, graphics fonts are much easier to use than printer fonts.

Installing Graphics Fonts

Installing graphics fonts is generally a breeze, because Windows actually does most of the work. The exact steps you'd follow to install graphics fonts depends on which manufacturer produced those fonts. The fonts should come with some instructions. The general scenario goes something like this:

1. Copy the fonts to your hard disk, as per the font manufacturer's instructions. You should try to keep all fonts of a certain type in one directory. For example, all your TrueType fonts should go in one directory. All your Speedo fonts should go in another directory, and so forth.

2. Once the fonts have been copied to your hard disk, go to the Windows Program Manager, open the Main group, then open the Control Panel.

3. Open the Fonts application window, and click the Add button. You'll be taken to the Add Fonts dialog box shown on the next page.

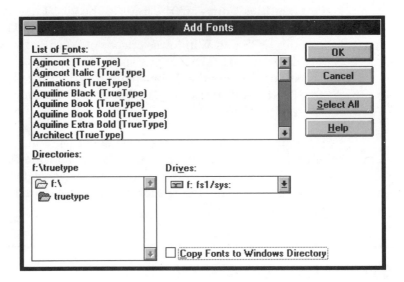

4. Near the bottom of the dialog box, choose the drive and directory that contains the fonts you want to install.

5. If you've already copied the fonts to your hard disk, you can deselect the Copy Fonts To Windows Directory option.

6. Select the font(s) you want to install by holding down the Ctrl key while clicking a font name (you can also just choose Select All to install all the fonts in the current directory).

7. Choose OK, and follow any instructions that appear on the screen.

When you're done, you can return to WordPerfect. The fonts you've selected should be available from the Font dialog box regardless of which printer driver you're using. (Unless you choose a printer that has no graphics capability, since graphics fonts require a graphics printer.)

For more information about selecting and using fonts (after you've installed them), refer to Chapter 6. For more information about installing TrueType and other graphics fonts, refer to your Windows documentation, or the documentation that came with the font(s) you've purchased.

Installing Printer Fonts

Printer fonts are destined to become a thing of the past. But you may have some favorite cartridges and/or printer soft fonts that you don't want to trash just because times are changing. There are three basic types of printer fonts:

- **Built-in (resident) fonts** are built into your printer and require no installation whatsoever. When you install the printer for use in WordPerfect, the built-in fonts are readily available in the font list.

- **Cartridge fonts** are stored in a cartridge that you can plug into a slot on the front of your printer, as per instructions in your printer manual. (Usually you need to turn the printer off before you insert the cartridge.)

- **Printer (non-graphics) soft fonts** are stored on your hard disk and *downloaded* (sent) to your printer as needed. Like cartridge fonts, soft fonts must be purchased separately.

In most cases, the font package will include specific instructions for installing the font with WordPerfect. Your best bet is to follow those specific instructions to a tee. Alternatively, you can follow the more general instructions in the sections that follow.

Copying Printer Soft Fonts to Your Hard Disk

If you're installing printer soft fonts, your first step will be to copy the soft fonts to your hard disk. You'll need to refer to the font manufacturer's instructions to find out how to do that. Typically, you'll run an installation program from the DOS prompt.

Also, be sure to follow any instructions specific to using the fonts with WordPerfect, particularly any instructions that refer to updating the WordPerfect printer .ALL file. The font names must be copied into the .ALL file before you can install them to your font list.

Keep track of which directory you copied the soft fonts to. If you've copied printer soft fonts to your hard disk in the past, use the same directory for any new soft fonts you install.

Updating the .PRS File

If you use a third-party program to update your printer .ALL file, you should update your .PRS file to be in sync with it. To do so, start from the WordPerfect document window and choose File ➤ Select Printer. Highlight the WordPerfect printer driver that you want to update, then choose the Update button. When updating is complete, choose Close.

Completing the Installation

Once you have your cartridge in hand, or your printer soft fonts copied to your hard disk, you can follow the steps below to update a WordPerfect printer driver to use those fonts.

WARNING If you're installing graphics fonts, such as TrueType or Type 1 (ATM), follow the instructions under "Installing Graphics Fonts" above, and ignore the steps below.

1. In WordPerfect for Windows, choose File ➤ Select Printer.

2. Highlight the name of the WordPerfect printer driver for which you are installing fonts, and then choose Setup.

NOTE If you chose a Windows printer driver rather than a WordPerfect printer driver in step 2 just above, you'll be taken to the setup dialog box for the Windows printer driver, not for the WordPerfect driver. To install fonts, see your printer manual. Or, choose Cancel, select the WordPerfect driver for that printer, and then choose Setup.

3. If you're installing printer soft fonts, choose Path and enter (or choose) the name of the directory that your soft fonts are stored on.

4. Choose Cartridges/Fonts.

5. Next to Font Source, use the drop-down list to indicate which type of printer font you want to install.

6. If you're installing a Cartridge Font or Print Wheel, choose the one you're installing from the Fonts list. If you're installing printer soft fonts, skip to "Installing Printer Soft Fonts" below.

7. Follow any instructions that appear on the screen, and choose OK and Close, as appropriate, to work your way back to the document window.

If you installed a cartridge font or print wheel, you should see it on the font list (Layout ➤ Font) whenever you're using the printer for which you've installed that cartridge or wheel.

Installing Printer Soft Fonts

Assuming you've completed steps 1 through 6 above, you should now be at a dialog box that looks something like Figure 10.2, though the list of soft fonts will depend on what printer you're installing fonts to.

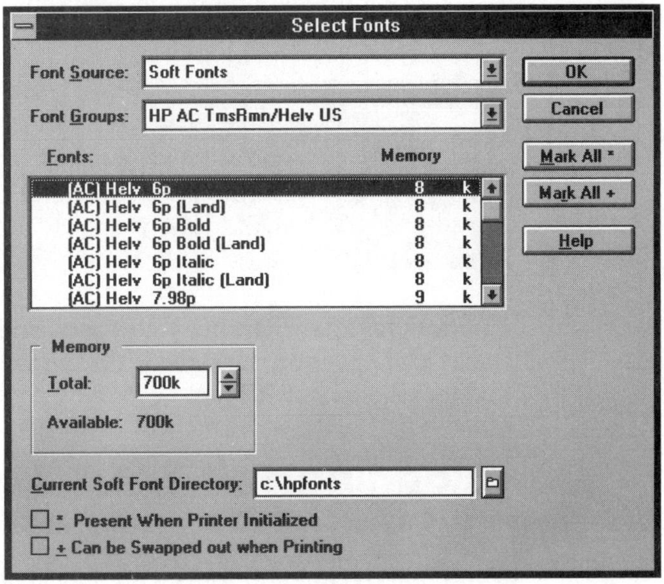

FIGURE 10.2

After opting to install printer soft fonts (not graphics fonts), the Fonts list displays all the supported soft fonts that are available for the current printer.

If (and *only* if) your printer has more memory available for soft fonts than is shown under Memory, you can change the Total setting to indicate how much memory you really have for soft fonts. (If you're not sure, leave the setting as is.)

Now, you can mark the soft fonts that you want to install in any of the following ways:

- Mark with an asterisk (*) any soft font that will already be in your printer when a print job begins. You can only mark as many fonts as will fit into available memory with the *. Thus, you might want to mark only your most frequently used fonts in this way. You can either type the * or choose the * option from the bottom of the dialog box.

- Mark with a plus sign (+) any printer soft fonts that you have installed on your hard disk, and want to be able to download to the printer "on the fly" as the document is being printed. You can type the + sign, or click the ± check box near the bottom of the dialog box.

- If your printer can swap fonts in and out of memory, you can mark fonts with both a * and a + (see your printer manual for more information on font swapping).

WARNING

WordPerfect can only *use* the fonts you've purchased and installed. It cannot *create* those fonts for you! Therefore, you shouldn't mark fonts that you don't own with * or +.

Choose OK after marking your fonts, and follow any additional instructions that appear on the screen. There may be a brief delay as WordPerfect updates the font .PRS file.

Downloading Soft Fonts You Marked with *

If you marked any soft fonts with only an asterisk (*), you must download them to your printer before using them to print a document. Otherwise,

WordPerfect will substitute a font that has already been downloaded, or some built-in font. Here's how to download those fonts:

1. Start at the document window and choose File ➤ Print and make sure the appropriate printer is selected. (If not, use the Select button to choose the printer you want to download fonts to.)

2. Choose Initialize, and follow the instructions on the screen.

WARNING If you forget to initialize the printer before printing a document that expects certain fonts to be in the printer, WordPerfect will substitute other fonts. You can cancel the print job (if it's a lengthy one), initialize the printer, then reprint the document to correct the problem.

Once the downloading is complete, the fonts will reside in the printer until you turn off the printer.

About the Printer .ALL and .PRS Files

WordPerfect stores most of the information about your printer(s) and fonts in two files, the .ALL file and the .PRS file. Understanding the roles played by these files can make getting along with printer fonts a little easier. (These files are virtually irrelevant when you're using the much simpler and more flexible graphics fonts described earlier in this chapter.)

The .ALL File

Information about all the printers in a particular category, and all the printer fonts available for those printers, is stored in a file with the .ALL extension, typically in your C:\WPC20 directory.

When you install third-party soft fonts (excluding graphics fonts), the installation procedure will usually require that you update the printer's

.ALL file. Otherwise, there'd be no way to select those fonts for inclusion on your font list.

Note that if you install third-party fonts to your .ALL file, then later replace the printer .ALL file (by reinstalling the printer driver from floppies), the new copy of the .ALL file won't include those third-party fonts. You'll need to reinstall those fonts to the .ALL file, per the font manufacturer's instructions, before you can make them available in WordPerfect.

The .PRS File

For each printer you install, WordPerfect creates a printer resource (.PRS) file and stores it in your WordPerfect Corporation shared directory (typically C:\WPC20). That file is automatically created from the .ALL file when you install a specific printer. The names and locations of any additional fonts (excluding graphics fonts) that you install for that printer are also stored in the .PRS file.

Note that if you reinstall the same printer driver from floppy disks, you'll lose any fonts and/or paper definitions you created for that printer driver. You'll need to go through the steps described in your fonts manual or earlier in this chapter to reinstall fonts. You'll also need to recreate any paper definitions using Layout ➤ Page ➤ Paper Size, as discussed in Chapter 8.

If You Lose Your Fonts…

The moral of the story, then, is don't go reinstalling your printer .ALL and .PRS files arbitrarily, or you may lose some of your printer fonts. If you do lose your printer fonts, first try updating your .PRS file, as described earlier under "Updating the .PRS File". If that doesn't work, you may need to reinstall all your printer fonts from scratch.

Understanding Font Substitution

Let's suppose you create a document using numerous fonts from your font list. Then, for whatever reason, you select a different printer. Since different printers will likely have different printer fonts, your document *may* call for fonts that the current printer *doesn't* have available to it. In such situations, WordPerfect must substitute the font you originally chose with some other font that *is* available to the current printer.

Two Names in One [Font] Code

When WordPerfect substitutes a font, it changes the [Font] code (visible only in Reveal Codes) to reflect the name of the font you had originally selected, followed by the name of the font that WordPerfect has chosen for *this* printer. That latter font is enclosed in square brackets. For example, the font code below indicates that although I originally selected CG Omega (W1) as the font, WordPerfect has substituted Corporate Mono because the Omega font isn't available in the currently selected printer. (This substitution also will be indicated in the Font area at the left side of the status bar.)

N O T E

If you choose File ➤ Select Printer and choose the original printer again, the substituted fonts will be removed from the document instantly. So when you print the document, you'll get your original fonts.

Preventing Font Substitution on Open

Normally, WordPerfect formats a document to match the currently selected printer. If you prefer that WordPerfect select whatever printer was in use when you last saved the document, follow the steps below:

1. Choose File ➤ Preferences, then double-click Environment.

2. Deselect (clear) Reformat Documents For Default Printer On Open.

3. Choose OK, then choose Close.

Of course, WordPerfect can only select the original printer if you've installed that printer for use with WordPerfect. If someone sends you a copy of a document that was created using, say, an Epson MX printer, and you don't have a driver for that printer installed, then WordPerfect has no choice but to format that document for the currently selected printer.

Understanding Automatic Font Changes (AFCs)

Let me clarify one thing: Automatic Font Changes (dubbed *AFCs* by WordPerfect Corporation) have nothing to do with font substitution. Font substitution involves multiple printers. AFCs involve font changes that WordPerfect makes within a document when you *don't* switch printers. WordPerfect would do that, for instance, if you assigned some *attribute*, such as boldface, italic, extra large, or subscript, and the currently selected font couldn't really display that attribute.

For example, suppose you have one Courier font, Courier 12 cpi. You tell WordPerfect to print some text in that font at Extra Large size. But WordPerfect can't make Courier 12 cpi any larger, because it's a nonscalable printer font that can only be displayed at 12 cpi. What does WordPerfect do? It checks to see if there is a similar font that *can* be displayed at an extra large size. If it finds such a font, it automatically changes to that font, so it can show your text in extra large size.

Changing AFCs

I'd be tempted not to even bother you with that preceding tidbit of information, were it not for the following fact: You can control exactly which font WordPerfect chooses when making these automatic font changes. Here's how:

1. Starting from the WordPerfect document window, choose File ➤ Select Printer. Highlight the name of the printer you want to change the AFCs for, and choose Select.

2. Choose Layout ➤ Font ➤ Font Map. You'll be taken to the Edit Printer/Document Font Mapping dialog box. Figure 10.3 shows this dialog box after I chose Automatic Font Change and selected Map Individual Styles to expand the left and right panels in the dialog box to include the Style and Size options.

3. Choose Automatic Font Change.

4. If you want to specify individual styles (such as Bold or Italic), or sizes, select (check) Map Individual Styles.

5. In the Printer Font area, choose the Font, Style, and Size you want to map. In the Automatic Font Change list, choose the attribute you want to map.

6. In the right-hand panel of the dialog box, choose the Face, Style, and Size you want to substitute for the printer font and AFC attribute you specified in step 5.

7. Choose OK twice to return to the document window.

FIGURE 10.3

The Edit Printer/Document Font Mapping dialog box lets you change WordPerfect's Automatic Font Changes (AFCs).

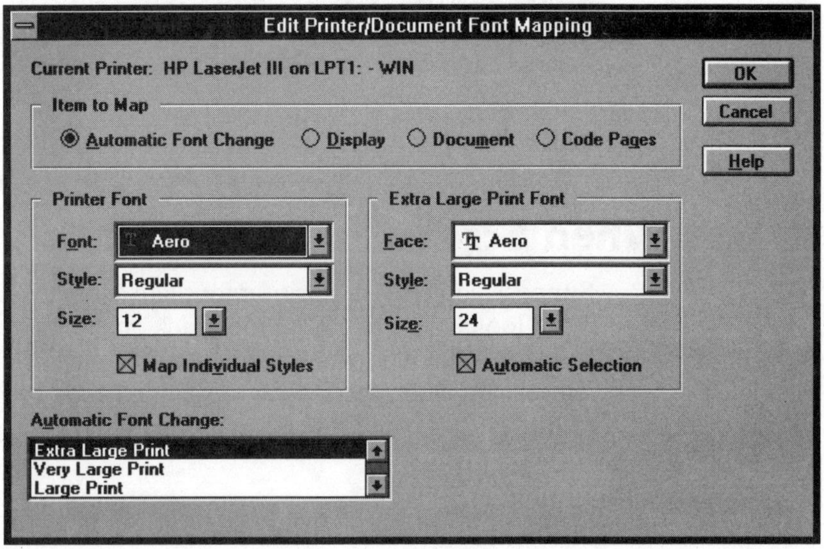

If you decide to return to the default settings later, repeat steps 1–3 above, select (check) the Automatic Selection option, and choose OK twice.

In the example below, I chose Automatic Font Change in step 2 and left Map Individual Styles deselected in step 3. Then I told WordPerfect that when I choose Extra Large with my Courier printer font, it should switch to the True Type Lucida Bright font.

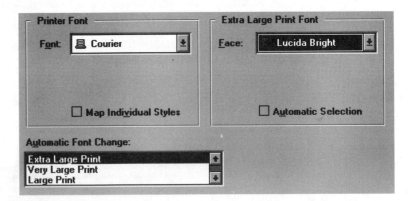

When Screen Fonts Don't Look Right

Suppose you choose a printer font like Albertus Extra and type some text, but it looks more like Aquiline Black on your screen. If you happen to notice the difference, you might say to yourself, "Hey! That's not the font I chose!" Yet when you look at the [Font:] code in Reveal Codes, it certainly indicates that you chose Albertus. So what gives?

Well, when you choose a *printer font* in your document, WordPerfect looks for the *graphics* font that best matches your selection, and displays *that* on the screen.

If you want to change the font that WordPerfect uses to represent your selected font, follow the steps under "Changing the AFCs," choosing Display in step 3. Select Map Individual Styles (if you wish), choose a Font, Style, and Size under Printer Font, then choose the Face, Style, and Size to use on the screen under Display Font.

NOTE For more advanced printer and font manipulation, you can purchase the optional "PTR Program" from WordPerfect Information Services (WordPerfect Corporation, Orem, Utah).

Upgrading Your Printer

If your printer isn't up to the job of producing professional looking documents like the ones you've seen in this book, you may need to upgrade to a fancier printer that has better resolution and more features. But before you rush out to buy just *any* expensive printer, here are a few words of advice.

When buying a printer, take along samples of what you'd like to be able to produce on your own, and ask the sales person to let you reproduce them on the machines you're interested in. Bring files that you've already created in WordPerfect (or "printed to disk" using the printer drivers for the printers you're interested in, as described earlier in this chapter), or bring examples of actual documents you want to emulate. If you don't get the quality you want, keep looking.

In this chapter you've learned how to get complete control over your printer, and, to some degree, over optional fonts. But as mentioned, any additional fonts that you purchase for use with WordPerfect will probably come with their own installation instructions. So be sure to check your font package for more specific information than I can give here.

In the next chapter, we'll start looking at some handy tools to increase your productivity and improve your writing.

CHAPTER

11

Auto-Checking Your Spelling

fast **TRACK**

When adding a word to a supplementary dictionary   400

> you can have Speller skip the word during spell checks, re-
> place it with another word, or set up a list of alternate words
> to choose from.

**To set up different or additional main and
supplementary dictionaries   405**

> choose Dictionaries from the Speller dialog box menu, then
> Main or Supplementary. Select a Language (to set up a new
> chain for that language, if necessary). Then Add, Create, or
> Delete the file names of dictionary files you want to use.

To edit a supplementary dictionary   405

> set up your chain of supplementary dictionaries (if necessary).
> Choose Dictionaries ➤ Supplementary from the Speller
> menus. If necessary, choose Language and select the diction-
> ary chain you want to use. Highlight the dictionary you want
> to change and choose Edit. Next, Add, Edit, or Delete words
> in the supplementary dictionary.

UNLESS you happen to be the local spelling bee champ, you'll probably need to use the dictionary to check your spelling from time to time. But you can put away your old paper dictionary. WordPerfect has a built-in dictionary that's much, much quicker.

About Speller

Before learning how to use Speller, you should understand a little bit about how it works. It's not smart. (Computers in general aren't smart, rating just above turnips on the IQ scale.) The Speller works by comparison only. That is, it simply checks words in your document against its own dictionary of about 115,000 words. If it can't find a word in its dictionary, it offers a list of alternative word choices.

It's important to understand that Speller knows nothing of context. For example, Speller wouldn't find anything wrong with this sentence:

Due u c what eye mien?

Because the words *Due*, *eye*, and *mien* are in the dictionary, along with single letters, like *u* and *c*, Speller finds no misspellings in the sentence. (However, the grammar checker discussed in Chapter 12 *can* help with these kinds of errors.)

Thanks to the blistering pace at which today's technology races along, it's quite likely that Speller won't find certain technical terms in your document. For example, Speller will assume that the medical term *adrenocorticotroph* (a pituitary hormone), or its acronym ACTH, is misspelled. Likewise, Speller may consider foreign words, like *lilangeni* (a word used in Swaziland), and proper names, like *Simpson*, as misspellings.

Those "so-called" misspelled words are really no problem. If Speller complains about a word that you know is spelled correctly, you can add that word to Speller's dictionary on the spot. That way, it will never again be considered a misspelling when you spell-check your document.

It Checks More than Spelling

While Speller is looking up words in its dictionary, it will also check for these other common errors:

- Typing the same word twice (*Look at the the moon*).

- Peculiar capitalization caused by pressing the Shift key too late, or for too long. For example, Speller would help you correct the capitalization errors in *LIghten Up on tHE sHIFt kEy*.

- Typing numbers instead of letters. For example, *1ike, I d0n't see the pr0blem* uses the number 1 for the letter L, and the number 0 for the letter O. (Computers hate it when you do that.)

When to Use Speller

You should use Speller just before you're ready to print a document or hand it over to someone else. After all, spell-checking takes only a few moments, and it's easy to do. What's more, it saves you the embarrassment of sending out a document that's loaded with misspellings, and it reduces the paper waste that occurs when you don't notice a mistake until the document is printed.

Using Speller

Using Speller is a breeze:

1. Move the cursor to wherever you want to start checking your spelling. If you wish, you can select a specific block of text to check.

2. Choose <u>T</u>ools ➤ <u>S</u>peller, or click the Speller button in the power bar, or press Ctrl+F1. The Speller dialog box will open, as shown on the next page. If you're in a hurry to get started, skip to step 5 now.

To start the Speller from outside of WordPerfect, open the WPWin 6.0 group window in the Windows Program Manager, then double-click the Speller icon. Your options will be similar to those described in this chapter, although some Speller features won't be available.

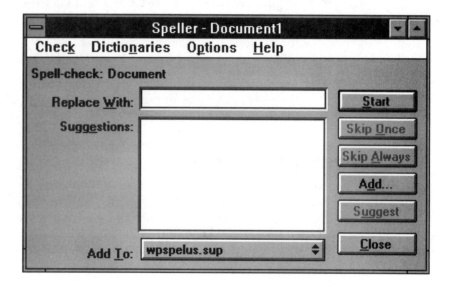

3. To tell Speller how much material to spell-check, pull down the Chec_k menu and choose an option. You can spell-check...

- The _W_ord, Senten_c_e, P_a_ragraph, or _P_age the cursor is on
- The entire _D_ocument (the default if you didn't select text in step 1)
- Everything from the cursor position To _E_nd Of Document
- The _S_elected Text only (if you selected text in step 1)
- The text in a _T_ext Entry Box
- A specified _N_umber Of Pages (when prompted, specify the number of pages to check starting from the current page, then choose OK)

4. To customize how Speller does its job, select or deselect items on the Options menu. (Perform this step repeatedly until you've set everything the way you want it.) Your selections will stay in effect through the current session and all future WordPerfect sessions (until you change the options again). Here are some explanations of the customization options:

Words With Numbers   Enables or disables checking for embedded numbers in words.

Duplicate Words   Enables or disables checking for double words.

Irregular Capitalization   Enables or disables checking for irregular capitalization.

Exhaustive Checking   Enables or disables searches for all possible suggestions in languages where limited suggestions are normally shown.

Auto Replace   If you deselect this option, Speller will prompt you before changing a word that you've previously designated as "auto-replace" (see "Changing a Supplementary Dictionary" later in this chapter). If you select this option, Speller will auto-replace without prompting first.

Document Dictionary   If you select this option, Speller *will not* stop at misspelled words that you previously added to the supplementary dictionary that's attached to the current document. If you deselect this option, Speller *will* stop at misspelled words that you previously added to this dictionary.

Beep On Misspelled   Enables or disables a beep sound when Speller finds a misspelled word. (If you're a bad typist or a rotten speller, turn this option off to keep your blunders a secret.)

5. When you're ready to start the spell check, choose <u>S</u>tart.

6. Once Speller gets going, what you do next depends on what Speller finds (if anything). I'll explain the possibilities in the next two sections.

7. When the spell check is complete, you'll be asked if you want to close Speller. Choose <u>Y</u>es to clear Speller from the screen, or choose <u>N</u>o to leave the Speller dialog box on-screen.

Figure 11.1 shows the screen after I started Speller in a document that has a misspelled word.

Anytime the Speller dialog box is open, you can suspend spell-checking and return to your document temporarily. Simply click in the document window and edit away (the Speller dialog box will remain on screen). When you're ready to resume spell-checking, click in the Speller dialog box, reset any options you wish, and choose <u>R</u>esume.

Of course, you can close Speller whenever you want by choosing <u>C</u>lose in the Speller dialog box. Any words that have been changed so far will remain changed.

FIGURE 11.1

When Speller finds a word that's not in the dictionary, it pauses and lets you decide what to do.

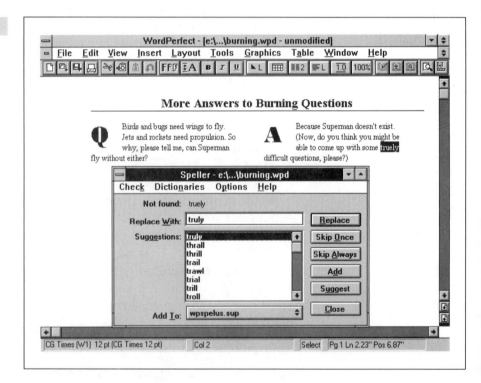

Correcting or Ignoring a Word Questioned by Speller

When Speller comes across a word that isn't in its dictionary, it will highlight the misspelled word, suggest correct spellings (if it finds them), and pause so that you can decide what to do next. Figure 11.1 illustrates how Speller handles the misspelled word "truely."

NOTE

The Speller dialog box will also resemble Figure 11.1 if Speller finds capitalization problems, words that contain numbers, or duplicate words.

Your options for handling misspelled words are listed below:

Replace   Replaces the misspelled word with the word in the Replace With text box. Use any method below to replace a misspelled word:

- If the word in the Replace With box is the one you want, choose Replace.
- Type the replacement word into the Replace With box, then choose Replace.
- Double-click the replacement word in the Suggestions list, or highlight the word and choose Replace.

Skip Once   Ignores the misspelling, this time only.

Skip Always   Skips the word here, and throughout the rest of the document.

Add   Adds the misspelled word to a *supplementary dictionary*, so that it's never counted as a misspelling again. By default, the word is added to the dictionary that's shown on the Add To pop-up list button. To add the word to a different supplementary dictionary, select the dictionary you want from the Add To pop-up list, then choose the Add button. There's more on supplementary dictionaries later in this chapter.

Suggest   Lets you look up a word in the main dictionary that matches a word or pattern. You can type the word or pattern into the Replace With text box; or highlight a word in the Suggestions list. Then choose Suggest to list the suggestions. See "Looking Up a Word" later in the chapter for more details.

Looking Up a Word

Here's how to use Speller to look up the spelling for a word you're about to type.

1. Position the cursor where you want the word to appear.

2. Start Speller (Tools ➤ Speller).

3. Type the word or word pattern you want to look up in the Replace With text box and choose Suggest. You'll see a list of words that are similar in pronunciation or construction to the word you typed. (The word you typed will appear in the list if it's in Speller's main dictionaries. Supplementary dictionaries are ignored.)

4. Next, you can do any of the following:

   • Copy one of the words from the list into your document. To do this, highlight the word you want in the Suggestions list, press Alt+W twice to select the text in the Replace With text box, and press Ctrl+C to copy the text to the Clipboard. Close the Speller dialog box, or click in the document window. Position the cursor where you want the word to appear, and press Ctrl+V to paste it in.

   • Return to step 3 and type in another word to look up.

   • Close the Speller dialog box.

TIP   If you just want to check the spelling of the word the cursor is on, start Speller, choose Check ➤ Word from Speller's menus, then choose Start.

Using Wildcards with Lookup

When you type a word into the Replace With text box in Speller, you can use the question mark (?) and asterisk (*) wildcards to stand for letters you're not sure about. Speller will scan the dictionary and look for any words that match the pattern of letters and wildcards you've specified.

Remember to choose the Suggest button after you type the word you're looking up.

The **?** wildcard stands for a single character in a word. For example, if you type **?ing**, Speller will show all four-letter words in its dictionary that end in *ing*.

The ***** wildcard stands for a group of any number of letters (from no letters to all the letters in the word). Typing ***ing** displays all words (of any length) that end in *ing*. This can be a real boon to poets searching for the perfect rhyme. But watch out! You can end up with a long, long list if you do this.

The ***** and **?** wildcards can appear anywhere in a word, and you can use **?** and ***** together to create a search. For example, the combination **i?p*** will find any word that starts with *i*, has a *p* in its third position, and ends with any combination of characters. As the example below shows, there are 515 such words!

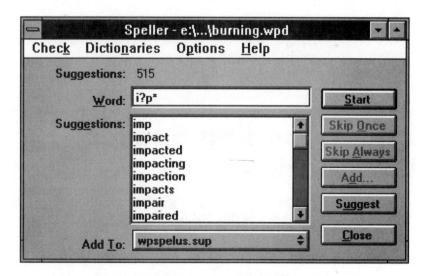

Disabling Speller

You can temporarily disable Speller and the other writing tools (Thesaurus and Grammatik) in any part of your document. This is particularly useful in passages that contain foreign words or technical terms that *you* know are correct, but that will give your writing tools fits. To disable the writing tools temporarily, follow these steps:

1. Move the cursor to where you want to disable spell-checking and grammar-checking. Or, select a block of text to limit your changes to that block.

2. Choose Tools ➤ Language.

3. Check the Disable Writing Tools box.

4. Choose OK.

WordPerfect will insert a hidden [Writing Tools:Disabled] code at the cursor location. You can delete this code if you change your mind later.

To enable the tools in another part of the document, move the cursor to where you want them to start. Repeat the steps above, except this time *deselect* the box in step 3.

Understanding Speller Dictionaries

When Speller is doing its job, it generally looks up words in three separate dictionaries in this order:

1. The main dictionary

2. The general supplementary dictionary

3. The document's supplementary dictionary

Each of these dictionaries is described below.

The Main Dictionary

The main dictionary is the one that contains the 115,000 or so words most often used in everyday English. This dictionary is stored on the WordPerfect shared programs directory—typically C:\WPC20—in a file named WP*xx*.LEX. The letters *xx* will be replaced by the abbreviation for the dictionary's language. For example, the main dictionary file is called WPUS.LEX in the United States.

The General Supplementary Dictionary

WordPerfect's general supplementary dictionary file has the file name WPSPEL*xx*.SUP. Again, the letters *xx* are replaced by the abbreviation for the dictionary's language. For example, the default supplementary dictionary in the United States is WPSPELUS.SUP. This dictionary is stored in the \WINDOWS directory (C:\WINDOWS).

The Document's Supplementary Dictionary

The document's supplementary dictionary (also called the *document dictionary*) is stored with the document. Initially, it's empty. However, each time you select Document Dictionary from the Add To pop-up list and choose Add during a spell check, WordPerfect stores the highlighted word in the document's supplementary dictionary.

You can speed up spell-checking by customizing your supplementary dictionaries to ward off spelling errors that you make often. We'll talk about that next.

Personalizing Speller

Once you understand the roles of the various dictionaries WordPerfect uses, you can further customize Speller. For example, if you often type *hte* instead of *the*, you can tell WordPerfect not to bother prompting you to correct this misspelling. Instead, when it finds *hte* it will automatically change it to *the*. It doesn't bother looking up *hte* in the main dictionary and presenting umpteen different suggestions. This simplifies and speeds up the spell-checking process.

Changing a Supplementary Dictionary

The best way to personalize Speller is to modify the supplementary dictionaries. Recall that the document dictionary or the general supplementary dictionary is updated automatically when you choose Add To, select the appropriate dictionary, and choose Add.

This technique of updating the supplementary dictionaries can't solve every problem, however. For example, if you tend to type things like *don;t* instead of *don't*, there is no way to tell Speller to change *don;t* to *don't* except by editing the supplementary dictionary yourself.

WARNING   If you want to include several supplementary dictionaries in this procedure, be sure to add those dictionaries to the *chain* first, as discussed later in this chapter.

To get started, you first need to follow the steps below.

1. Start Speller (Tools ➤ Speller).

2. Choose Dictionaries ➤ Supplementary to open the Supplementary Dictionaries dialog box shown in Figure 11.2.

3. Highlight the dictionary you want to change and choose Edit, or double-click the name. You can choose the document dictionary, the general supplementary dictionary WPSPELUS.SUP (in the United States), or any specialized supplementary dictionary that you've created. This opens the Edit dialog box shown in Figure 11.3.

FIGURE 11.2

The Supplementary
Dictionary dialog box
lets you add new
supplementary
dictionaries, delete
existing dictionaries,
and edit dictionaries in
a dictionary chain.
(There's more about
dictionary chains later
in the chapter.)

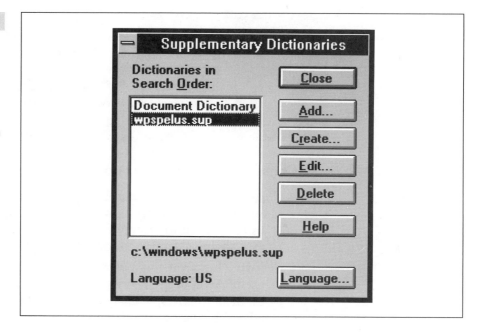

FIGURE 11.3

Use the Edit dialog
box to add, edit, and
delete words in a
supplementary
dictionary.

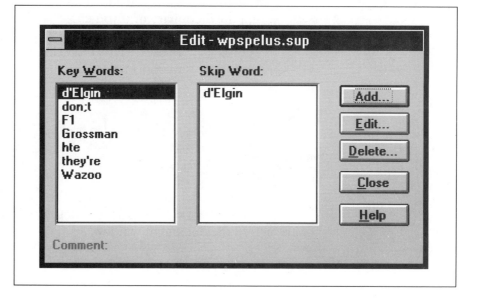

TIP As you scroll through the Key Words box, the title of the box to its right will indicate whether the highlighted word is to be skipped, replaced, or has alternates. The list at the right will show the word to be skipped, the replacement word, or the alternate words assigned to the word you've highlighted.

4. Choose any of the buttons below:

Add Lets you add words to skip, replacement words, and alternate suggestions to the dictionary. Words that you add will appear in the Key Words list in the Edit dialog box. (See the next section for details.)

Edit Lets you edit a word in the Key Words list. This is useful if you need to correct a mistake, add more words to a list of alternatives, or change a key word from one type to another. To change a word, highlight it in the Key Words list, choose Edit, make your changes, and choose OK.

Delete Lets you delete a word from the Key Words list. Use this option if you added an incorrect word while editing the dictionary or if you chose Add To accidentally during a spell check. To delete a word, highlight it in the Key Words list, choose Delete, then choose Yes when prompted for confirmation.

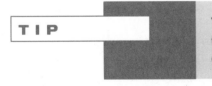

TIP To highlight a word in the Key Words list quickly, click in the list (or press Alt+W), then type the first few letters of the word you want.

5. When you're done editing the dictionary, choose Close until you return to the document window.

We'll look at ways to add words to the dictionary in the next section. But first, you should understand some basic concepts about how the supplementary dictionary works.

- During a spell check, lowercase letters in the supplementary dictionary are considered the same as uppercase, but not vice versa. For example, if you've added *dBASE* to your supplementary dictionary, Speller will accept dBASE or DBASE during a spell check. However, it will point out other capitalization differences, such as *Dbase, dBaSe, dBaSE,* and so on.

- WordPerfect will alphabetize your supplementary dictionary automatically, so you don't need to enter new words in any particular order.

- The automatic hyphenation feature (Chapter 16) uses the same *main* dictionaries as Speller. It doesn't look at supplementary dictionaries. When adding words to your supplementary dictionaries, *don't* type in hyphens, because they're treated as spaces during a spell check. For example, if you mistakenly add the word *Den-dro-bium* to your supplementary dictionary instead of *Dendrobium,* WordPerfect won't recognize the word *Dendrobium* as a properly spelled word during a spell check.

NOTE

Only the Spell-Hyphen Utility (purchased separately from WordPerfect Corporation) can add a hyphenated word to Speller's dictionary. This utility can also convert WordPerfect 5.x main dictionaries to WordPerfect 6 format, and transform WordPerfect 6 documents into supplementary dictionaries.

- If you want to add a hyphenated name, like *Grossman-Wazoo,* to the dictionary, just make two separate entries: one for Grossman and another for Wazoo. (You can do this by choosing Add To, choosing a supplementary dictionary, and choosing Add during a normal spell check.)

Adding Words to the Supplementary Dictionary

While you're in Speller's Edit dialog box (Figure 11.3), you can choose Add to add a new word to the dictionary. You'll see the Add Word/Phrase dialog box below, with the Skip option selected initially:

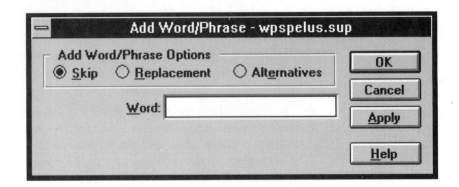

Here's how to use the Add Word/Phrase dialog box:

1. Select one of the options listed below:

    Skip   Lets you enter a word to skip. The Add Word/Phrase dialog box looks like the example shown above.

    Replacement   Lets you enter a word (such as *hte*) and its replacement (such as *the*). The Add Word/Phrase dialog box will look like the following one after you fill in the Key Word and its Replacement:

```
┌─────────────────────────────────────────────────────────┐
│ ▬    Add Word/Phrase - wpspelus.sup                      │
├─────────────────────────────────────────────────────────┤
│ ┌─ Add Word/Phrase Options ──────────────┐  ┌────────┐   │
│ │ ○ Skip   ◉ Replacement   ○ Alternatives │  │   OK   │   │
│ └─────────────────────────────────────────┘  └────────┘   │
│                                               ┌────────┐   │
│      Key Word: │hte                  │        │ Cancel │   │
│                                               └────────┘   │
│                                               ┌────────┐   │
│    Replacement: │the                 │        │ Apply  │   │
│                                               └────────┘   │
│                                               ┌────────┐   │
│                                               │  Help  │   │
│                                               └────────┘   │
└─────────────────────────────────────────────────────────┘
```

Alternatives   Lets you specify alternative choices for a word. The example below shows the Add Word/Phrase dialog box after entering a Key Word, a List Of Alternatives, and a Comment.

```
┌─────────────────────────────────────────────────────────┐
│ ▬        Add Word/Phrase - wpspelus.sup                  │
├─────────────────────────────────────────────────────────┤
│ ┌─ Add Word/Phrase Options ──────────────┐  ┌────────┐   │
│ │ ○ Skip   ○ Replacement   ◉ Alternatives │  │   OK   │   │
│ └─────────────────────────────────────────┘  └────────┘   │
│                                               ┌────────┐   │
│         Key Word: │they're          │         │ Cancel │   │
│                                               └────────┘   │
│       Alternative: │they're          │        ┌────────┐   │
│                                               │ Apply  │   │
│  List of Alternatives: │their        │        └────────┘   │
│                        │there        │        ┌────────┐   │
│                        │they're      │        │ Insert │   │
│                        │             │        └────────┘   │
│                        │             │        ┌────────┐   │
│                        │             │        │ Delete │   │
│                        │             │        └────────┘   │
│                        │             │        ┌────────┐   │
│ Comment:                               │       │  Help  │   │
│ │Check your grammar (and your grampa)│        └────────┘   │
└─────────────────────────────────────────────────────────┘
```

2. Fill in the dialog box as follows:

- **If you chose Skip** in step 1, type the word you want Speller to skip in the Word text box.

- **If you chose Replacement,** type the word you want Speller to replace in the Key Word box, then type the replacement word in the Replacement box. (If you've selected Options ➤ Auto Replace, the key word will automatically be replaced with the replacement word during a spell check. If you've de-selected Auto Replace, you'll be asked for permission to replace the word.)

- **If you chose Alternatives,** type the word for which you want to supply alternatives in the Key Word box. Type the next alternative in the Alternative box and choose Insert. Continue typing alternatives and choosing Insert until you've entered all the alternatives for this word. You can type in a comment in the Comment text box (the comment will appear above the list of alternatives during a spell check). If you want to delete an alternative word from the list, highlight the word in the List Of Alternatives and choose Delete.

3. Choose Apply. (Choose OK if you're editing an existing entry.)

4. Repeat steps 1–3 as desired.

5. Choose OK (or Cancel, if the text boxes are empty) when you're ready to return to the Edit dialog box.

Creating a Supplementary Dictionary

If you do a lot of word processing for various professions or special interest areas, you might want to create your own supplementary dictionaries. For example, you could create a supplementary dictionary of medical terms (named MEDICAL.SUP, for instance), or musical terms (named MUSIC.SUP).

Having separate, specialized dictionaries keeps each dictionary small. That, in turn, makes each one easier to manage. Also, the spell-checking process goes faster when you use a particular supplementary dictionary, as opposed to *all* your supplementary dictionaries.

To create a new supplementary dictionary, you simply add its name to a dictionary *chain* (see "Chaining Dictionaries" later in this chapter). Next, highlight the new dictionary name in Speller's Edit dialog box and choose Edit. Then choose Add and enter the new words as discussed just above.

Using Foreign-Language Dictionaries

If you write in a foreign language, or regularly use foreign words in your English documents, you might want to purchase a separate foreign-language module from WordPerfect Corporation. The documentation that comes with the package will include installation instructions.

NOTE Language modules are used to tailor many features, including date, sort, spell-checking, hyphenation, and thesaurus.

WordPerfect normally will use the language module that's listed on the outside of your WordPerfect package. If you've purchased and installed a foreign-language module, you can switch to it whenever you want by following the steps below:

1. Position the cursor where you want to begin using a different language dictionary. For example, press Ctrl+Home to use the new dictionary for the entire document. Or select a block of text to use the language in that block only.

2. Choose Tools ➤ Language.

3. Highlight the language dictionary you want to use and choose OK.

WordPerfect inserts a hidden [Lang:...] code at the cursor position. During a spell check, WordPerfect will switch to that other dictionary the moment it comes across this code. You can add as many [Lang:...] codes to your document as you wish.

Another alternative is to *chain* the dictionaries (see the next section). That way, you can use the English language dictionary and a foreign-language dictionary simultaneously. This would come in handy, say, if you're writing a tutorial on a particular language, and both English words and foreign words are dispersed throughout the document.

Chaining Dictionaries

If you want to use more than one main dictionary during a spell check, or you want to use (or create) specialized supplementary dictionaries, you need to *chain* those dictionaries. A chain is simply a list of dictionary files that Speller will search for words.

Suppose, for example, that you write articles for medical journals in both English and Spanish. You've purchased English and Spanish main dictionaries from WordPerfect Corporation, and you've set up some English and Spanish supplementary dictionaries that contain specialized medical terminology. Figure 11.4 illustrates this scenario.

Here, the main dictionaries are WPES.LEX (Spanish) and WPUS.LEX (English). I've chained two supplementary Spanish dictionaries, named WPSPELES.SUP and MEDICAL.SUP, and two supplementary English dictionaries, named WPSPELUS.SUP and MEDICAL.SUP.

When Speller sees the [Lang:ES] code for Spanish, it will use the Spanish main dictionary, the document's supplementary dictionary, and the two

FIGURE 11.4

The Speller uses dictionary chains to spell-check a document that is written in multiple languages.

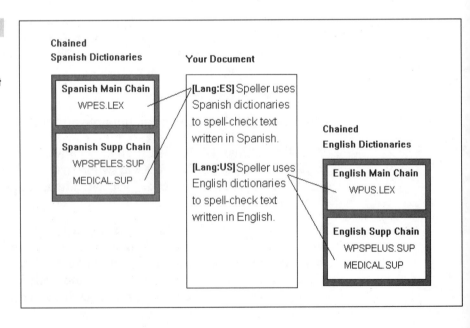

Spanish supplementary dictionaries. When it sees the [Lang:US] code for English, it will switch to the English main dictionary and the two English supplementary dictionaries (while continuing to use the document's supplementary dictionary). Supplementary chains and main dictionary chains are always searched in the order that the dictionaries are listed within the chain. For example, in the English supplementary dictionary chain, the WPSPELUS.SUP dictionary is searched before the MEDI-CAL.SUP dictionary, starting at the top of their respective chains.

T I P   You can reuse supplementary dictionaries in different chains, as I've done here with MEDICAL.SUP.

Setting Up a Dictionary Chain

Follow the steps below if you want to set up a dictionary chain or create new supplementary dictionaries.

1. Start Speller (Tools ➤ Speller), then pull down the Dictionaries menu in the Speller dialog box.

2. Do either of the following:

   - To set up or edit a main dictionary (.LEX) chain, select Main. The Main Dictionaries dialog box opens. This dialog box is similar to the example in Figure 11.2, except that it lists main dictionaries instead of supplementary dictionaries.

   - To set up or edit a supplementary dictionary (.SUP) chain, or create new supplementary dictionaries, select Supplementary. The Supplementary Dictionaries dialog box seen in Figure 11.2 opens.

N O T E   The currently selected language will appear next to the Language button in the Supplementary Dictionaries or Main Dictionaries dialog box.

3. If you want create or edit a *different* language chain (for example, the Spanish chain), choose Language. Highlight the language you want to use and choose OK (or double-click the language name). Make sure you choose a language for which you've already purchased and installed a dictionary.

4. Click in the Dictionaries In Search Order list, or press Alt+O.

5. Choose one of the command buttons described below:

> **Add or Create**   Lets you add an existing main or supplementary dictionary to the chain, or create a new supplementary dictionary. Highlight the place in the list the dictionary name should appear. (To add a dictionary name to the *end* of the chain, press Ctrl+End.) Choose Add or Create (Create is available only for supplementary dictionaries. Type (or highlight) the name of the dictionary you want to add, and choose OK. If the supplementary dictionary doesn't exist, WordPerfect will ask if you want to create it. Choose Yes to create the dictionary or No to enter a different name.

> **Delete**   Lets you delete a dictionary from the chain. Highlight the dictionary name you want to delete, and choose Delete, then choose Yes.

> **Edit**   Lets you edit an existing dictionary. Highlight the dictionary you want to change, and choose Edit. From here, you can Add, Edit, or Delete words as explained earlier in the section "Changing a Supplementary Dictionary."

6. You can repeat steps 3–5 as needed. When you're done making changes, choose Close until you return to the document window.

Here are some important points to keep in mind about chains:

- Speller will use all the dictionaries you've chained for the language that's currently selected, in the order you specified.

- You must *install* new foreign-language main dictionaries before adding them to a chain. (The foreign-language dictionary will come with installation instructions.)

- Don't mix main dictionaries in with supplementary dictionary chains and vice versa, or Speller won't work correctly.

- Deleting a dictionary name from the chain does not delete the dictionary file stored on disk.

- Spell-checking will take longer when you use multiple language dictionaries. If you no longer need to use a dictionary, you can delete it from the chain. (If you'll *never* need it again, you can also delete the dictionary from your hard disk.)

- If you move a dictionary to another directory or you change the dictionary file's name, you should delete the dictionary from existing dictionary chains, then insert it again and specify the new name.

Which Supplementary Dictionary Gets Updated?

The next time you spell-check a document, Speller will use the supplementary dictionaries you specified in the supplementary dictionary chain. When it finds a word that's not in *any* of the dictionaries, it will present the usual options to Skip <u>O</u>nce, Skip <u>A</u>lways, A<u>d</u>d, or S<u>u</u>ggest.

If you want to *add* the word in the Replace <u>W</u>ith text box to one of your supplementary dictionaries, you can open the Add <u>T</u>o pop-up list and pick whichever dictionary you want to add the word to. Then choose A<u>d</u>d.

In this chapter, you've learned about Speller, a tool that helps you make every document "word perfect." You've also learned how to customize Speller and create your own dictionaries of specialized terms. Now that you know how to chek the spelling in yur documint, therz no reezon to hav enny speling errorz in yer werk.

Next we'll look at Grammatik, a writing tool that checks your grammar and writing style. Grammatik may not turn you into an Abraham Lincoln or an Ernest Hemingway, but at least you'll be able to avoid writing documents that read like the fine print in an insurance policy.

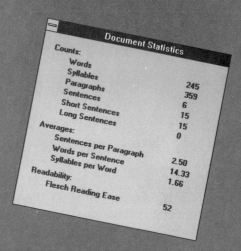

Document Statistics

Counts:
- Words
- Syllables
- Paragraphs — 245
- Sentences — 359
- Short Sentences — 6
- Long Sentences — 15

Averages:
- — 15
- — 0
- Sentences per Paragraph
- Words per Sentence — 2.50
- Syllables per Word — 14.33
- — 1.66

Readability:
- Flesch Reading Ease — 52

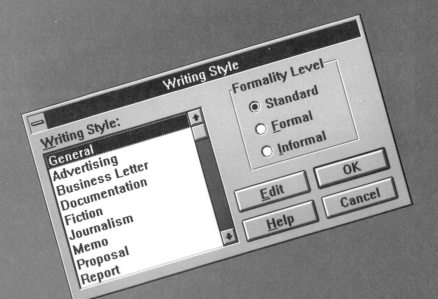

Writing Style

Writing Style:
- General
- Advertising
- Business Letter
- Documentation
- Fiction
- Journalism
- Memo
- Proposal
- Report

Formality Level
- ● Standard
- ○ Formal
- ○ Informal

Edit OK Help Cancel

CHAPTER

12

Auto-Checking Your Grammar

fast **TRACK**

To quit Grammatik and return to your document   416

choose <u>C</u>lose in the Grammatik dialog box, or answer <u>Y</u>es when asked if you want to close Grammatik after completing a grammar check.

When Grammatik detects a misspelled word you can   419

choose <u>S</u>kip to skip the word for now, Ignore <u>W</u>ord to ignore the word during the rest of the proofreading session, <u>A</u>dd to add the word to Grammatik's spelling dictionary, or <u>R</u>eplace to replace the word with a suggestion from the word list.

To replace a word or phrase with one that Grammatik suggests   419

double-click the word or phrase in the suggested word list, or highlight the word or phrase and choose <u>R</u>eplace.

To customize Grammatik   427

make selections from the <u>O</u>ptions menu in the Grammatik dialog box. You can customize existing writing-style rules or create styles of your own, select various formality levels, and control the proofreading mode.

PROOFREADING a document involves more than just checking your spelling and confirming that you've dotted all your *i*'s and crossed all your *t*'s. It also involves reading your writing to make sure that it's appropriate for your intended audience, gets the message across, and uses the mother tongue properly and with style. Grammatik (rhymes with *dramatic*) is a writing tool that can help you do all that.

What Grammatik Can Do for You

Grammatik can detect errors in spelling, grammar, mechanics, and style and suggest corrections or revisions. It can also display certain statistics about your document.

I assume you know what the term *spelling* means. However, the terms *grammar, mechanics*, and *style* might be unfamiliar, especially if you ditched English 101 during the first two weeks of class. Here are some decidedly nontechnical definitions:

Grammar   Refers to the rules for putting words together into proper (if not coherent) sentences.

Mechanics   Refers to boring stuff like capitalization, punctuation, spelling, and form (abbreviations, numbers, word division, etc.).

Style   Refers to clichés, jargon, wordiness, and other literary blunders.

By default, Grammatik uses rules for a *General* writing style and *Standard* level of formality to check your document (or selected text) for problems in spelling, grammar, mechanics, and style. When Grammatik finds a problem, it lets you make suggested replacements instantly, or provides diplomatic advice about how to make improvements. As you'll learn in this chapter, there are many ways to tailor Grammatik to your writing style and requirements.

WARNING

Grammatik sometimes finds trouble when everything is fine, or when you've intentionally broken a few time-tested rules. Your best bet is to heed Grammatik's advice when it makes sense, and ignore Grammatik when you think its advice is totally bogus.

Using Grammatik

Running Grammatik is much easier than writing a term paper. Just follow these steps:

1. Open the file you want to check. If you've made any recent changes, save them (<u>F</u>ile ➤ <u>S</u>ave).

2. If you want to check just part of the document, position the cursor where you want to begin. To check for problems in a block of text, select that block.

3. Choose <u>T</u>ools ➤ <u>G</u>rammatik, or click the Grammatik button (shown at left) in the power bar. You'll see the Grammatik dialog box shown at the top of the next page.

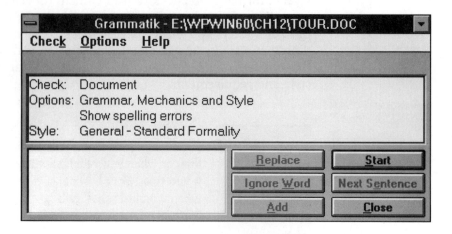

4. If you want to change the starting place for grammar checking or the amount of text that Grammatik checks, choose an option from the Check menu. You can check the Sentence or Paragraph the cursor is on, the entire Document, from the cursor to the End Of Document, or Selected Text (if you selected text in step 2).

5. If you want to change the grammar checking options, choose Options and pick any of the options listed below. You can repeat this step as necessary.

> **Writing Style**   Lets you choose (and edit) any of ten built-in writing styles and three formality levels. See "Customizing the Writing Style" later in the chapter for details.
>
> **Checking Options**   Lets you select (check) or deselect (clear) the options that can speed up the proofreading process a bit. The options are Check For Paragraph Errors, Ignore Periods Within Words, Suggest Spelling Replacements, and Start Checking Immediately. By default, all options are selected except Start Checking Immediately. If you select this option, proofreading will begin as soon as you choose Tools ➤ Grammatik or click the Grammatik button on the power bar.

NOTE Your changes to the <u>W</u>riting Style and <u>C</u>hecking Options remain in effect for this session and future sessions.

<u>R</u>estore Rule Classes   Restores any rule classes you turned off during interactive grammar checking. (More about this in a moment.)

<u>S</u>how Spelling Errors   When selected, spell checking is on. (This is the default.) When deselected, spell checking is turned off.

TIP Grammatik's spell checker can identify misspelled words, duplicate words, and capitalization errors. If you want to save some time and focus on writing problems only, run your document through Speller first (Chapter 11). Then fire up Grammatik and deselect <u>O</u>ptions ➤ <u>S</u>how Spelling Errors.

<u>G</u>rammar, Mechanics and Style   When selected, Grammatik checks for grammar, mechanics, and style problems. (This is the default.)

Grammar and <u>M</u>echanics   When selected, Grammatik checks for grammar and mechanics problems only.

S<u>t</u>atistics   When selected, Grammatik displays document statistics only. You'll see an example of statistics later in the chapter.

6. To begin checking your document, choose <u>S</u>tart.

7. Respond to the prompts on the screen by choosing appropriate buttons in the Grammatik dialog box. See "A Dramatic Grammatik Session" and Table 12.1, below, for details.

8. When the interactive checking is complete, Grammatik will ask if you want to close the Grammatik dialog box. Choose <u>Y</u>es to clear the dialog box from the screen and return to your document. Choose <u>N</u>o to leave the dialog box on the screen.

Here are some other things you can do with Grammatik:

- **To get help** while you're using Grammatik, choose options from Grammatik's Help menu or click the Help button if it's available. You can also click on underlined topics when they appear during proofreading (more on this later).

- **To exit Grammatik** at any time, choose Close or double-click Grammatik's Control-menu box. (The Grammatik dialog box will disappear.)

- **To move the Grammatik dialog box** so that you can see hidden parts of your document, simply drag the Grammatik title bar to a new spot on the screen. (Or, minimize the dialog box and drag the icon elsewhere on the screen. To restore the full dialog box, double-click the Grammatik icon.)

- **To suspend Grammatik temporarily** and return to your document, click in the document window. You can then edit the document as necessary. (The Grammatik dialog box will remain on-screen and the title bar will be dimmed.)

- **You can change the options** in the Check and Options menus whenever the Grammatik dialog box is visible on the screen.

- **To resume proofreading** after you've suspended Grammatik temporarily, click the Resume button in the Grammatik dialog box. Proofreading will continue according to the currently selected options in the Check and Options menus.

- **If you botch your proofreading** session and want to discard your changes, close the Grammatik dialog box, then choose File ➤ Close ➤ No from the WordPerfect menus. You can then open the original copy of your document (which you saved in step 1 above) and try proofreading again.

- **To save the changes in a different file** after proofreading is complete, close the Grammatik dialog box as described above, choose File ➤ Save As, type a new file name, and choose OK.

After you start the proofreading session, the buttons in the Grammatik dialog box will change to reflect the actions you can take at the moment. Table 12.1 summarizes these buttons. In the next section, we'll put the program through its paces so that you can see how you might use the buttons during a real session with Grammatik.

TABLE 12.1: Options Available during Interactive Checking

BUTTON	PURPOSE
Add	Adds the word to Grammatik's spelling dictionary
Close	Closes the Grammatik dialog box
Ignore Word or Ignore Phrase	Ignores the word or phrase for this proofreading session
Next Sentence	Doesn't make any changes and goes on to the next sentence
Replace	Replaces the problem word or phrase with one that Grammatik suggests and continues to the next problem
Resume	Resumes proofreading. Use this to resume proofreading after you've clicked in the document window.
Skip	Doesn't make any changes and goes on to the next problem
Start	Starts the proofreading session

NOTE: To disable checking for the current problem during the rest of the proofreading session, deselect the Rule Class check box. To restore rule-class checking for all rule classes that you've turned off during the proofreading session, choose Options ➤ Restore Rule Classes.

A Dramatic Grammatik Session

Now that you know your way around Grammatik, let's look at a quick interactive session with the program. Figure 12.1 shows a sample business letter named TOUR.DOC, which I'll use to demonstrate Grammatik. As you can see, this document has many problems.

November 9, 1993
Wanda Granolabar, Vice President
WANDOLA ENGINEERING CORPORATION
2230 Strappman Avenue
Strappman, CA 92147

Dear Ms. Granolabar:

Thank you for giving Hanley and me the opportunity to submit the attached proposal. It is always a pleasure doing business with your firm.

Every office facility that we design reflects our commitment to quality and excellence. Already this year we have won three awards. We pride ourselves on our ability to deliver well-engineered designs within budget constraints. We celebrated our ten-year anniversary last year, and haven't missed a single deadline yet. We are familiar with your staff's needs because we worked with you two years ago on the parking garage project. Hanley received an award for designing that interior.

Our Human Factors study report shows that the best use of office space is to divide the room into nine cubicles, four private offices, and two shared offices. Statistics suggest that most workers prefer private spaces that are close to the people they work with. The same principle applies to managers and chief executives. Our research shows that high-quality adjustable chairs and desks greatly reduce Worker Compensation claims for repetitive motion syndrome and similar problems, such as neck or back pain.

We have forwarded a copy of this proposal to your Operations Manager, W. B. Goode, as requested. Thank you for taking the time to review this proposal.

Sincerely,

M. Kim Cozee, Human Factors Consultant
Hanley Blake, Inferior Designer
PROFESSIONAL OFFICE DESIGNS

Checking the Document for Problems

Suppose you've just typed and saved the sample TOUR.DOC file and now you want to check it for spelling, grammar, and writing style problems. (Type this letter as shown and save it now if you'd like to follow the sample session on your own computer.)

With the document on screen, choose <u>T</u>ools ➤ <u>G</u>rammatik, then choose the <u>S</u>tart button to begin proofreading. Now follow the steps below:

1. The first problem Grammatik finds is the "misspelled" word *Granolabar*, which it highlights (see below). This word is okay (since it's somebody's name), so let's choose Ignore <u>W</u>ord to prevent Grammatik from bothering us about it again during this proofreading session.

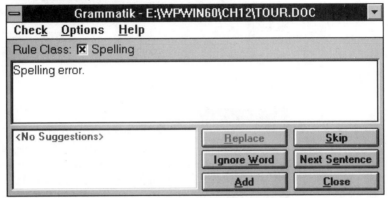

November 9, 1993
Wanda Granolabar, Vice President

NOTE Notice the *Rule Class* check box in the example above. You can temporarily turn off error checking for a particular rule class (such as spelling errors). Simply click in the *Rule Class* check box and choose OK. If you want to reinstate all the rule classes that you've turned off during the session, choose <u>O</u>ptions ➤ <u>R</u>estore Rule Classes ➤ <u>Y</u>es.

2. Grammatik makes two more stops at misspelled words: *WAN-DOLA*, and *Strappman*. Choose Ignore <u>W</u>ord at each stop.

3. Now Grammatik finds the grammar problem in the first paragraph and suggests replacing *I* with *me*, as shown on the next page. That's the right thing to do, so choose <u>R</u>eplace to replace the word and go on to the next problem.

Thank you for giving Hanley and I the opportunity to submit the attached proposal. It
is alway

Quality
this year
engineer
many ye
familiar
ago on t
Hanley,

Our Hu
the room
that mos
work wi

Grammatik - E:\WPWIN60\CH12\TOUR.DOC

Check   **Options**   **Help**

Rule Class: ☒ Pronoun Case

Prepositional phrases take object pronouns, not the subject pronoun I.

me

Replace	Skip
Ignore Word	Next Sentence
Add	Close

TIP

To display help about any underlined topic in the
Grammatik dialog box, simply click the mouse on
that topic. (The mouse pointer will change to a large
question mark whenever help is available for a topic.)
For example, you could click on *Prepositional phrases,
object pronouns,* or *subject pronoun* in the dialog box
above to get a definition of those terms. Press Alt+F4 to
close the Help window.

4. The next problem is the misspelled word *pleazure*. Grammatik will
   display a list of suggested replacements in the lower left corner.
   Choose *pleasure* by double-clicking it or highlighting the word and
   choosing Replace. Grammatik moves on to the next problem.

5. Grammatik finds another spelling error, *htat*, and suggests replacing it with *that*. Choose Replace.

6. Now Grammatik catches the incorrect use of *is* in the first sentence of the second paragraph ("Quality and excellence is reflected..."). Choose Replace to replace *is* with *are* and move on.

7. Our next stop is that dreaded bugaboo *passive voice*:

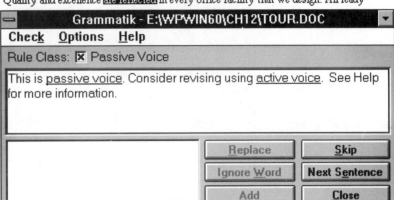

This requires a rewrite. Click in the document window and use your mouse, arrow keys, and other editing keys to change the sentence as shown below. When you're done making changes, click the Resume button to continue to the next problem.

Every office facility that we design reflects our commitment to quality and excellence.

8. Next, Grammatik chokes on *All ready* and suggests replacing it with *already*. Choose Replace to accept the suggestion and move on.

9. Our next stop is at the run-on sentence in the second paragraph (see Figure 12.1 and the example below):

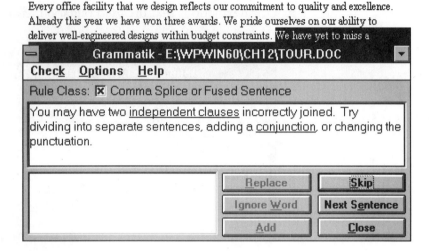

Every office facility that we design reflects our commitment to quality and excellence. Already this year we have won three awards. We pride ourselves on our ability to deliver well-engineered designs within budget constraints. We have yet to miss a

Grammatik - E:\WPWIN60\CH12\TOUR.DOC

Check   **Options**   **Help**

Rule Class: ☒ Comma Splice or Fused Sentence

You may have two <u>independent clauses</u> incorrectly joined. Try dividing into separate sentences, adding a <u>conjunction</u>, or changing the punctuation.

[Replace]   [Skip]

[Ignore Word]   [Next Sentence]

[Add]   [Close]

Click in the document window, rewrite the sentences as shown below, and choose Resume.

We celebrated our ten-year anniversary last year, and haven't missed a single deadline yet.

10. Next, Grammatik complains that our correction in step 9 introduced the word *haven't*, which might be too informal. That word seems fine (to me, anyway), so choose Skip to move on to the next problem.

11. Now Grammatik flags the cliché *due to the fact that* (in the next-to-last sentence of the second paragraph). It suggests replacing the cliché with *because*. Choose Replace to make the change and move on.

12. The next stop is in the last sentence of the paragraph, where Grammatik complains that *was given* is passive voice. Rewrite the sentence as shown below, then choose Resume.

Hanley received an award for designing that interior.

13. For some strange reason, Grammatik now complains that the blank line below the second paragraph should have more than one sentence. This complaint is bogus, so just choose Skip to go on.

14. Our next stops are at the numbers *4* and *2*, which Grammatik suggests replacing with *four* and *two*. Choose <u>R</u>eplace (twice) to accept each suggestion and continue.

15. Grammatik now objects to the wordiness of "Statistics indicate… in close proximity to…" in the third paragraph. It suggests replacing *in close proximity to* with *near* or *close to*. Double-click *close to* in the list of suggestions, or highlight it and choose <u>R</u>eplace.

16. Now Grammatik asks us to simplify the word *indicate* in the same sentence (notice that we've gone back a step here). It suggests that we change *indicate* to *show, say,* or *suggest*. Double-click *suggest*.

17. Our next stop, shown below, illustrates an important point: Grammatik isn't foolproof! Here it criticizes *principle* and suggests that we replace it with *principal*. That's clearly wrong in this context, so choose <u>S</u>kip to ignore the suggestion and move on.

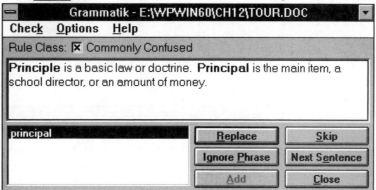

18. Grammatik has now recovered its smarts. It notices the misuse of *from* when we meant *form* in the sentence "According to our research…who suffer from a *from* of…." Choose <u>R</u>eplace to replace *from* with *form* and move on.

19. Next, Grammatik detects the double period (..) after the third paragraph. Choose <u>R</u>eplace to replace it with one period and continue.

20. In Figure 12.2, we've taken another step backward in the document; however, Grammatik's protest is right on! That convoluted Worker Compensation sentence really is long and difficult to understand. Click in the document window, revise the sentence as shown below, and choose Re<u>s</u>ume to continue.

FIGURE 12.2

Grammatik hates long, complex sentences.

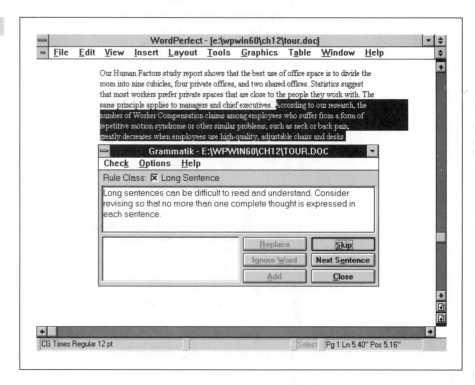

Our research shows that high-quality adjustable chairs and desks greatly reduce Worker Compensation claims for repetitive motion syndrome and similar problems, such as neck or back pain.

21. We get another bogus complaint about an empty paragraph that should have more than one sentence. Choose <u>S</u>kip.

22. Finally, Grammatik trips over the names *Goode* and *Cozee*, which are spelled correctly. Choose Ignore <u>W</u>ord to ignore each error.

23. We're done with the proofreading, but let's not stop quite yet. When Grammatik asks if you want to close the dialog box, choose <u>N</u>o.

24. Let's get some statistics for the revised document. Choose Options ➤ Statistics, then choose Start to display the Document Statistics dialog box.

NOTE

The Flesch Reading Ease score shown in the Document Statistics dialog box reflects the document's readability. The sample document's score represents six to ten years of schooling.

25. *Now you're done!* Click the Close button in the Document Statistics dialog box. You'll be returned to the Grammatik dialog box.

Figure 12.3 shows the revised letter. You might argue that the letter is still terrible. However, you'd probably agree that it's an improvement over the version shown in Figure 12.1. Still, it pays to have a human read through anything you're being judged on. There's no way a grammar checking or spelling program would know that a letter signed by an "Inferior Designer" is an embarrassment.

Now that you've seen Grammatik in action, you should have little trouble using its features.

Disabling Grammatik in Part of a Document

You can temporarily disable Grammatik at any time or for any portion of a document. Here are the steps:

1. If you're using Grammatik at the moment, choose Close to return to the document window.

2. Move the cursor to where you want to disable Grammatik, or select text to limit your changes to the selected block.

FIGURE 12.3

The letter after revising it with Grammatik's help. Compare this version with the one in Figure 12.1.

November 9, 1993
Wanda Granolabar, Vice President
WANDOLA ENGINEERING CORPORATION
2230 Strappman Avenue
Strappman, CA 92147

Dear Ms. Granolabar:

Thank you for giving Hanley and I the opportunity to submit the attached proposal. It is always a pleazure doing business with your firm.

Quality and excellence is reflected in every office facility htat we design. All ready this year we have won three awards. We pride ourselves on our ability to deliver well-engineered designs within budget constraints. We have yet to miss a deadline in our many years of operation, our ten-year anniversary was celebrated last year. We are familiar with your staff's needs due to the fact that we worked with you two years ago on the parking garage project. As you may recall, that interior, designed by Hanley, was given an award.

Our Human Factors study report shows that the best use of office space is to divide the room into nine cubicles, 4 private offices, and 2 shared offices. Statistics indicate that most workers prefer private spaces that are in close proximity to the people they work with. The same principle applies to managers and chief executives. According to our research, the number of Worker Compensation claims among employees who suffer from a from of repetitive motion syndrome or other similar problems, such as neck or back pain, greatly decreases when employees use high-quality, adjustable chairs and desks..

We have forwarded a copy of this proposal to your Operations Manager, W. B. Goode, as requested. Thank you for taking the time to review this proposal.

Sincerely,

M. Kim Cozee, Human Factors Consultant
Hanley Blake, Inferior Designer
PROFESSIONAL OFFICE DESIGNS

WARNING Disabling Grammatik also disables Speller and Thesaurus.

3. Choose Tools ➤ Language.

4. Select (check) Disable Writing Tools. WordPerfect will insert a hidden [Writing Tools:Disabled] code at the cursor location. You can delete this code if you later change your mind about disabling the tools.

To resume grammar and spell checking in another part of the document, move the cursor to that location (or select a block of text), choose Tools ➤ Language, and deselect Disable Writing Tools. WordPerfect will insert a hidden [Writing Tools:Enabled] code at the cursor location.

Customizing the Writing Style

As you know, different types of writing call for different styles and levels of formality. For instance, one writing style might work wonderfully in a pulp novel, but it wouldn't be at all appropriate for a technical report. You might want to choose a different writing style or level of formality if Grammatik's complaints about certain types of errors become annoying.

Grammatik offers ten built-in writing styles. Each style has a default formality level of Standard, Formal, or Informal. (In general, the less formal styles are more forgiving.) Grammatik will use the writing style you select for all future sessions, until you change the style again. You can also create and modify up to three custom styles of your own.

Follow these steps to select the writing style and level of formality you want to use:

1. From the Grammatik menus, choose <u>O</u>ptions ➤ <u>W</u>riting Style. You'll see the dialog box shown here:

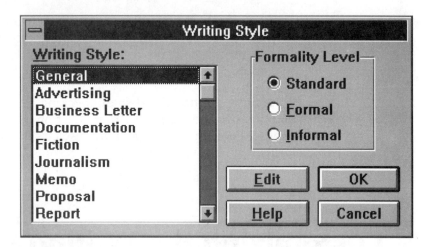

2. Highlight the style you want in the <u>W</u>riting Style list, then choose a Formality Level. (Custom styles that you've created will appear at the bottom of the <u>W</u>riting Style list.)

3. Choose OK.

If you're an English-language maven and love to tweak things, feel free to customize the writing styles. Here's how:

1. From the Grammatik menus, choose <u>O</u>ptions ➤ <u>W</u>riting Style.

2. Select the <u>W</u>riting Style and the Formality Level you want to change.

3. Choose the <u>E</u>dit button to open the dialog box shown in Figure 12.4.

4. Choose the general rule class you want (<u>S</u>tyle, <u>G</u>rammar, or <u>M</u>echanical). The dialog box will change to reflect the selected rule class.

FIGURE 12.4

You can use the Writing Style Settings dialog box to customize the writing style that Grammatik uses when it proofreads your documents.

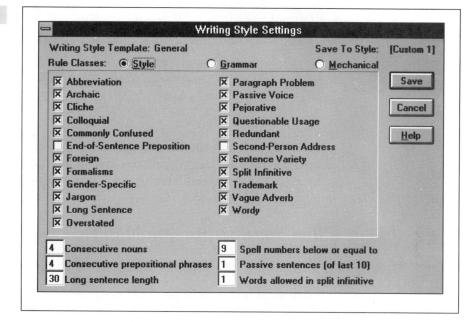

5. Use the check boxes to turn rule class checking on or off. Select an option (mark it with an ×) to turn it on; select it again (clear the ×) to turn the option off. You can also change the numbers near the bottom of the dialog box to control such settings as the number of nouns or prepositional phrases allowed consecutively, or the number of words in a "long" sentence.

6. Choose Save to save your changes as a custom style. Custom styles are named Custom 1, Custom 2, and Custom 3. If a custom style with that number already exists, you'll be asked if you want to overwrite it.

7. To select a writing style, highlight the style you want, and choose OK to return to Grammatik. To return to Grammatik without selecting a style, choose Cancel.

If you turn off Rule Classes during a proofreading session, Grammatik will ask if you want to save your changes to a custom style when the proofreading session ends. Choosing <u>Y</u>es will take you to the Writing Style Settings dialog box.

Need more help with Grammatik? Simply click the <u>H</u>elp button, choose options from the <u>H</u>elp menu, or click on an underlined topic when it appears in the Grammatik dialog box during proofreading.

This chapter covered Grammatik, which can check your document's spelling, grammar, and writing style. After you've used Grammatik a few times, you'll view your writing with a much more critical eye.

Now we'll move on to the Thesaurus, a tool that can help you find just the right *word* (term, expression, statement, or utterance) for any *occasion* (affair, circumstance, episode, happening, incident, or occurrence).

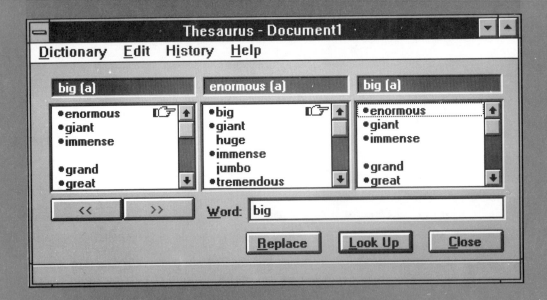

Finding the Perfect Word with the Thesaurus

fast

TRACK

HAVE YOU ever found yourself smack-dab in the middle of writing a sentence, only to discover that you're suddenly at a loss for words? Maybe you've already overused a word like *exciting* and want to try something spicier like *delightful, electrifying, exhilarating, inspiring,* or *thrilling.* Or perhaps you need a word that means the opposite of *arrogant.*

Even if you have the vocabulary of a verbal virtuoso, you'll appreciate the convenience of having an online thesaurus that not only suggests the right word to use but types it in for you as well.

Using the Thesaurus

To use the Thesaurus, just follow these steps:

1. Place the cursor on the word that needs a synonym or antonym.

2. Choose <u>T</u>ools ➤ <u>T</u>hesaurus, or press Alt+F1, or click the Thesaurus button (shown at left) in the power bar. The example below shows lists of suggested synonyms for the word *big.* Notice that the Thesaurus dialog box has three columns, each of which can contain synonyms and antonyms. The columns may show ways to use the word as an adjective (*a*), noun (*n*), or verb (*v*). If the word has any opposites, that group will appear near the bottom of the column, marked by (*ant*).

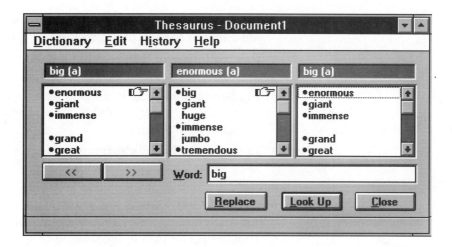

NOTE   You can also start the Thesaurus from outside of WordPerfect by double-clicking the Thesaurus icon in the WPWin 6.0 group window.

NOTE   If WordPerfect can't find a synonym or antonym for the word the cursor is on, the Thesaurus columns will be empty. You can type in another word and choose Look Up, or choose Close to return to your document.

3. Whenever a list of words appears in the Thesaurus dialog box, you can take any of the actions below:

- **To replace the highlighted word** in your document with a word from the Thesaurus, highlight or click on the replacement word in the appropriate list and choose Replace. You'll be returned to the document window.

- **To look up more synonyms and antonyms** for a word in the Thesaurus, double-click any bulleted word in the list (or highlight the bulleted word, then choose Lookup or press ↵). The bullet next to a word indicates that it's a *headword*, a word for which the Thesaurus has a synonym list. The new words will appear in their own column, with the headword you chose at the top of the column, above the word list.

- **To scroll up and down** within a column, click the scroll arrows or drag the scroll boxes.

- **To move the highlight up and down** within a column, press the ↑, ↓, PgUp, or PgDn keys. Or just click on the word you want to highlight.

- **To move the highlight from column to column**, press the → or ← keys, click in the column you want, or click the << or >> buttons in the dialog box.

- **To look up any word you want**, type it into the Word text box and choose Look Up or press ↵. You can then use the Thesaurus columns to look up more synonyms or antonyms for the word you typed in.

- **To close the Thesaurus** and return to the document window without making any changes, choose Close.

The next few sections describe other things you can do in the Thesaurus.

Viewing and Editing the Document from the Thesaurus

Sometimes, you might want to view or change your document without leaving the Thesaurus. If the Thesaurus dialog box is covering text in your document, you can drag its title bar to move it out of the way. Or you can click in the document window and edit normally. When you're ready to return to the Thesaurus, click on the Thesaurus dialog box.

Here's a trick for lazy typists who want to copy a word from the Thesaurus list into the document window.

1. Start the Thesaurus, then use the methods given earlier to locate and highlight the word you want to copy into your document.

2. From the Thesaurus menus, choose Edit ➤ Select All, then choose Edit ➤ Copy.

3. Position the cursor wherever you want the word to appear in your document, then press Ctrl+V to paste it in.

4. If you wish, click the Close button in the Thesaurus dialog box.

Reviewing the Lookup History

During a session with Thesaurus, WordPerfect keeps a history of the last several words you looked up. This history list is erased each time you start the Thesaurus. If you'd like to back up and start over at an earlier headword choice, choose History and select a word from the list that appears.

Choosing a Different Thesaurus

The default Thesaurus, named WPUS.THS, resides in the WordPerfect shared programs directory (C:\WPC20). You can buy and install foreign-language modules from WordPerfect Corporation. To use an installed foreign-language Thesaurus while you're in the Thesaurus dialog box, choose Dictionary ➤ Change Dictionary. Then type in or highlight the name of the Thesaurus file you want to use, and choose Select (or double-click the file name).

WordPerfect will switch to a foreign-language Thesaurus automatically whenever the cursor is positioned to the right of a [Lang] code in your document. To insert the [Lang] code, position the cursor where you want the foreign-language Thesaurus to kick in (or select a chunk of text that should use the foreign Thesaurus). Then choose Tools ➤ Language, highlight the language you want, and choose OK. See Chapter 11 for more about foreign-language modules.

You now know how to use the Thesaurus to help you find the right word for any occasion. In the next chapter, you'll learn how to use WordPerfect's automatic outlining and paragraph-numbering features.

PART THREE

Automating Your Work

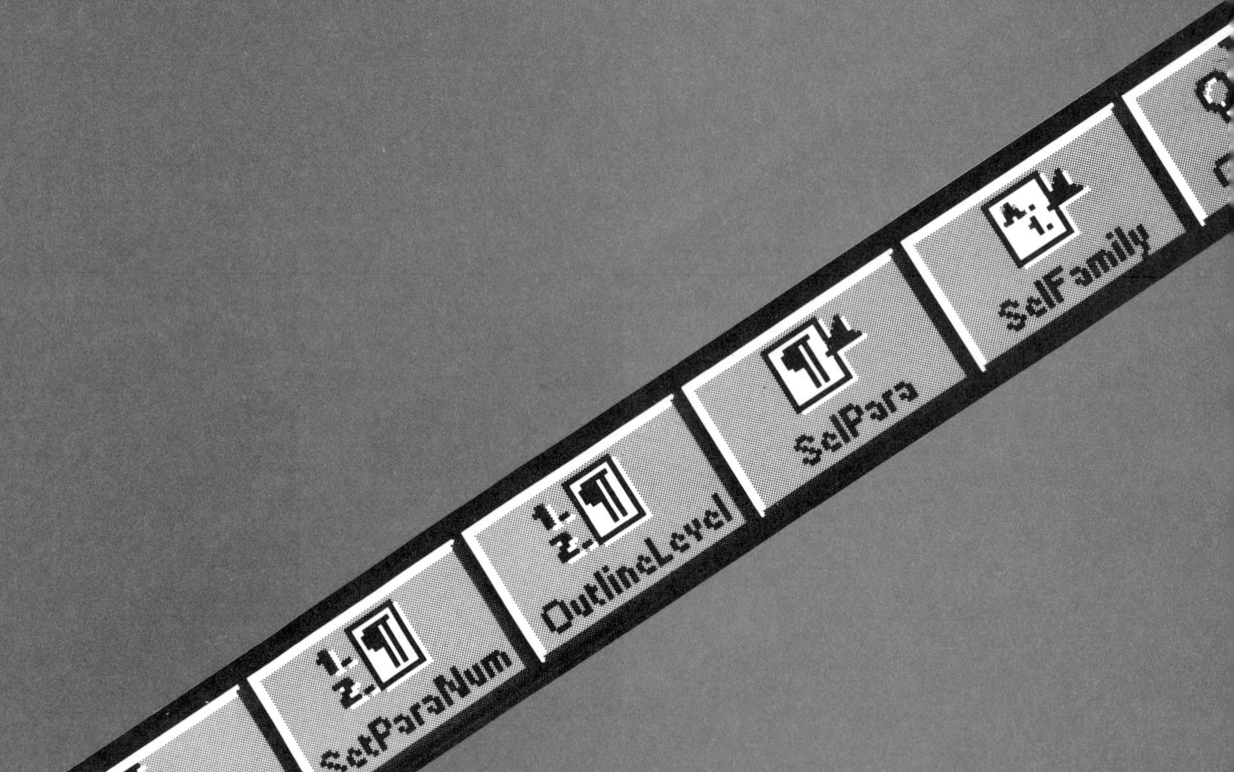
OutlineDef
SetParaNum
OutlineLevel
SelPara
SelFamily

CHAPTER

14

Automatic Outlining

fast TRACK

**To switch text between an outline level
and body text**   **461**

> move the cursor to the text you want to change and click the
> T button in the Outline feature bar (or press Alt+Shift+T) to
> toggle back and forth.

To change an outline level   **462**

> move the cursor to the beginning of the item. To demote the
> item, press Tab or click the → button in the Outline feature
> bar. To promote the item, press Shift+Tab or click the ← but-
> ton in the Outline feature bar.

To change an outline style (definition)   **463**

> move the cursor into the outline and choose a style from the
> Outline Definitions drop-down list in the Outline feature bar.

To hide or show an outline family   **464**

> move the cursor to the topmost item in the family. In the Out-
> line feature bar, click the − button (to hide) or the + button
> (to show).

To hide or show an outline level or all levels   **466**

> move the cursor to any item in the outline. In the Outline fea-
> ture bar, click the button for the level number you want, or
> click All to restore all levels to view.

To move an outline family   **469**

> move the mouse pointer to the level marker for the topmost
> level of the family you want to move, drag the marker to a new
> position in the outline, then release the mouse button. Or,
> click the ↑ or ↓ button in the Outline feature bar.

WE ALL learned in school that an outline is a great way to organize your thoughts before writing any large document. But we also learned (perhaps the hard way) that developing an outline by hand is often a trial-and-error effort and a messy job indeed.

WordPerfect's Outline feature makes it easy to modify and reorganize your outline to match your latest whim. Moreover, it renumbers every item in the outline automatically as you make changes, so you never have to do that job yourself.

In the next section, we'll look at basic outline concepts. Then we'll get to the nitty gritty of creating and managing outlines with WordPerfect for Windows.

NOTE

I'm using the term *outline* to refer to anything that WordPerfect should number automatically. The term *numbers* in this context refers to numbers, bullets, heading styles, roman numerals, letters, or any other character or appearance change that WordPerfect can display in an outline item.

Outlining in a Nutshell

Your outline can be as simple as a numbered list (1, 2, 3, 4, 5, and so on), or it can involve a hierarchical scheme with up to eight levels (for example 1, 1.1, 1.1.1, 1.1.1.1, and so on). The basic procedure for using WordPerfect's outlining feature is simple:

1. Move the cursor to where you want to begin the outline.
2. Begin (turn on) the outline and select a numbering scheme.
3. Type in your outline items.
4. End the outline.

With WordPerfect, you can change numbered items to a different numbering scheme with just a few keystrokes, and you can reorganize the outline just as easily. Each document can have as many different outlines and numbering schemes as you want.

About Body Text and Outline Levels

In WordPerfect parlance, the numbered items in an outline are called *outline levels*, and the "normal" unnumbered text is called *body text*. You can freely mix outline levels with body text in any outline. This combination style is common in contracts like the one shown in Figure 14.1, and it comes in handy for any documents in which you need to suspend numbering temporarily. In Figure 14.1, the paragraph that begins "The name of the Partnership" is body text; the remaining (numbered) items are outline levels.

About Outline Families

Most outlines consist of groups of related ideas, with each idea or topic placed on a level by itself. Ideas related to the topic appear one level below the topic as subtopics, or *daughters*, of the original topic. Topics at the

FIGURE 14.1

Two different outline numbering schemes. The sample contract combines numbered outline levels with unnumbered body text.

TO DO LIST (Paragraph Style)

1. Get up and do all the usual morning stuff
2. Drive to work
3. Take a coffee break
4. Do some work
5. Eat lunch
6. Do some work
   a. Finish that chapter on outlining
   b. Review contract
7. Go home
8. Eat dinner
9. Go to sleep

CONTRACT (Legal Style)

NOW THEREFORE, the parties agree as follows:

1 <u>**FIRM NAME AND PLACE OF BUSINESS**</u>

The name of the Partnership is DEWEY, CHEATHAM, AND HOWE, a California Limited Partnership ("Partnership")

2 <u>**DEFINITIONS**</u>

2.1 "Agreement" shall mean this Limited Partnership Agreement.

2.2 "Partner" shall refer to any one of the following persons or entities, and "Partners" shall refer to more than one of them.

2.2.1 "General Partner" shall refer to GONDOLA CLAPLOCK

2.2.2 "Limited Partner" shall refer to Trustor.

2.3 "Partnership" shall refer to the limited partnership formed under this agreement.

Outline level

Body text

Outline levels

same organizational level are called *sisters*. A topic and all of its subtopics are known as a *family*. This is illustrated in Figure 14.2.

Later in this chapter you'll learn how to hide, show, delete, move, and copy outline families.

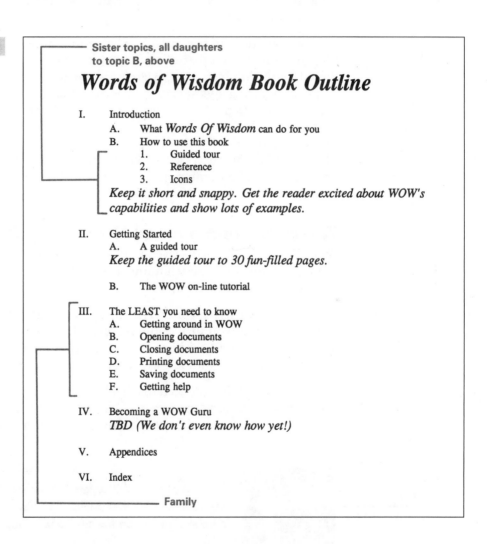

Sister topics, all daughters to topic B, above

Words of Wisdom Book Outline

I. Introduction
    A. What *Words Of Wisdom* can do for you
    B. How to use this book
        1. Guided tour
        2. Reference
        3. Icons
    Keep it short and snappy. Get the reader excited about WOW's capabilities and show lots of examples.

II. Getting Started
    A. A guided tour
    Keep the guided tour to 30 fun-filled pages.

    B. The WOW on-line tutorial

III. The LEAST you need to know
    A. Getting around in WOW
    B. Opening documents
    C. Closing documents
    D. Printing documents
    E. Saving documents
    F. Getting help

IV. Becoming a WOW Guru
    TBD (We don't even know how yet!)

V. Appendices

VI. Index

Family

About Numbering Schemes

A numbering scheme (or *numbering style*) is simply a way to number items. Figure 14.1 shows two different numbering styles: two levels used in a simple list and a more complex numbering scheme with three levels used in a contract.

The automatic number or style change that appears in your document depends on the number of times you indent before inserting the numbered item. (You can also assign a specific level number to an item.) In some numbering styles, each new level actually moves inward (indents) by a tab stop, as the "to do" list in Figure 14.1 shows. In other styles, the numbering changes to reflect the current indent level, but WordPerfect doesn't actually indent the numbered item. The contract in Figure 14.1 illustrates "unindented" levels. There, the numbers 1 and 2 are at the first indent level. The numbers 2.1, 2.2, and 2.3 are at the second level, and 2.2.1 and 2.2.2 are at the third level.

Automatic and Manual Numbering Styles

WordPerfect comes with seven built-in numbering styles. These are illustrated in Figure 14.3. Each numbering style falls into one of two categories: automatic or manual.

In the *automatic* style, WordPerfect inserts the next item number automatically, as soon as you turn outlining on and whenever you press the ↵ key at the end of a numbered line or paragraph. All the built-in styles, except the Headings and Numbers styles, are automatic.

In the *manual* style, you need to tell WordPerfect explicitly when you want to enter another numbered item. (*Counters*, discussed in Chapter 15, offer another way to number, or count, anything in your document.)

T I P

You can also use the Bullets & Numbers feature to set up a simple one-level outline that's marked with bullets, numbers, or roman numerals. See Chapter 5 for details.

FIGURE 14.3

Examples of
WordPerfect's built-in
numbering styles

BULLETS STYLE

● This is level 1
    o   This is level 2
        -    This is level 3
           ■   This is level 4
             *   This is level 5
               +   This is level 6
                  ●   This is level 7
                    x   This is level 8

HEADINGS STYLE

This is level 1

This is level 2

This is level 3

    This is level 4

      This is level 5

        This is level 6

          This is level 7

            This is level 8

LEGAL STYLE

1	This is level 1
1.1	This is level 2
1.1.1	This is level 3
1.1.1.1	This is level 4
1.1.1.1.1	This is level 5
1.1.1.1.1.1	This is level 6
1.1.1.1.1.1.1	This is level 7
1.1.1.1.1.1.1.1	This is level 8

FIGURE 14.3

Examples of
WordPerfect's built-in
numbering styles
(continued)

LEGAL2 STYLE

1   This is level 1
1.01   This is level 2
1.01.01   This is level 3
1.01.01.01   This is level 4
1.01.01.01.01   This is level 5
1.01.01.01.01.01   This is level 6
1.01.01.01.01.01.01 This is level 7
1.01.01.01.01.01.01.01   This is level 8

NUMBERS STYLE

1.This is level 1
  a.This is level 2
      i.This is level 3
        (1)This is level 4
          (a)This is level 5
            (i)This is level 6
              1)This is level 7
                a)This is level 8

OUTLINE STYLE

I.   This is level 1
    A.   This is level 2
        1.   This is level 3
            a.   This is level 4
              (1)   This is level 5
                (a)   This is level 6
                  i)   This is level 7
                    a)   This is level 8

PARAGRAPH STYLE

1.   This is level 1
    a.   This is level 2
        i.   This is level 3
            (1)   This is level 4
              (a)   This is level 5
                (i)   This is level 6
                  1)   This is level 7
                    a)   This is level 8

The numbering style you choose is completely up to you. It's easy to switch between different styles until you get the look you want. If the seven built-in styles don't suit your fancy, you can define new styles of your own. (Chapter 17 is devoted to matters of style, so look there to find out how to create your own outline styles.)

Using the Outline Tools

WordPerfect offers several tools to make outlining quick and easy. These include the Outline feature bar, keyboard shortcuts, and the Outline button bar. Once you've seen these features in action, you can decide which method works best for you. In this chapter, I'll focus on the simplest mouse and keyboard methods for each outlining task.

The Outline Feature Bar

The Outline feature bar, shown in Figure 14.4, provides everything you need to make automatic outlining a breeze. To display the Outline feature bar, choose Tools ➤ Outline. To hide the Outline feature bar, click the Close button on the Outline feature bar, or press Alt+Shift+C.

FIGURE 14.4

The Outline feature bar

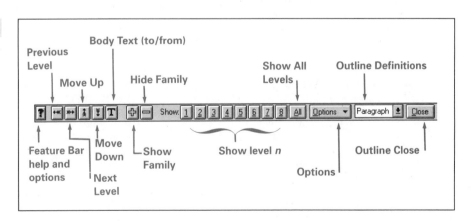

If you display the Outline feature bar for an outline, you'll see hollow *level markers* at the left edge of the document window (as shown below). The **T** marks normal body text, while the numbers mark the relative level number of each item in the outline. "Using the Outline Editor," later in the chapter, explains how to use these markers.

TO DO LIST (Paragraph Style)

1.	Get up and do all the usual morning stuff
2.	Drive to work
3.	Take a coffee break
4.	Do some work
5.	Eat lunch
6.	Do some work
	a.	Finish that chapter on outlining
	b.	Review contract

You'll learn more about each button in the Outline feature bar as you read through this chapter. But for now, you might want to take a quick look at Table 14.1, which summarizes each feature on the Outline feature bar.

TABLE 14.1: A Quick Guide to the Outline Feature Bar's Features, Buttons, and Keyboard Shortcuts

BUTTON NAME	BUTTON	KEYBOARD SHORTCUT	PURPOSE
Feature Bar Help and options	?		Provides menu options and lists keyboard shortcuts for many outlining features.
Previous Level	←	Tab or Alt+Shift+P	Promotes an outline item to a higher level.
Next Level	→	Shift+Tab or Alt+Shift+N	Demotes an outline item to a lower level.
Move Up	↑	Alt+Shift+U	Moves the current paragraph or selection up without changing its level.
Move Down	↓	Alt+Shift+W	Moves the current paragraph or selection down without changing its level.

TABLE 14.1: A Quick Guide to the Outline Feature Bar's Features, Buttons, and Keyboard Shortcuts (continued)

BUTTON NAME	BUTTON	KEYBOARD SHORTCUT	PURPOSE
Body Text	T	Alt+Shift+T	Converts body text to an outline item; converts an outline item to body text.
Show Family	+	Alt+Shift+S	Shows all members of an outline family.
Hide Family	–	Alt+Shift+I	Hides all but the main level of an outline family.
Show n	1, 2, 3, 4, 5, 6, 7, 8	Alt+Shift+n	Shows outline level n or higher, where n is the level indicated on the button. Excludes body text.
Show All Levels	All	Alt+Shift+A	Shows all outline levels, including body text.
Options	Options	Alt+Shift+O	Provides options for defining an outline, ending an outline, changing the level of an item, and renumbering an outline.
Definitions	Drop-down list		Lets you choose a different outline numbering style from a drop-down list.
Close Outline	Close	Alt+Shift+C	Removes the Outline feature bar from the screen.

Keyboard Shortcuts

For the keyboard addicts among you, WordPerfect offers many keyboard shortcuts for common outlining tasks. These are listed in the Keyboard Shortcuts column of Table 14.1 and in the **?** menu on the Outline feature bar.

The Outline Button Bar

You'll find convenient shortcuts for several tasks on the Outline button bar. To display the Outline button bar, follow these steps:

1. If no button bar is visible, choose <u>V</u>iew ➤ <u>B</u>utton Bar.

2. Right-click the button bar and select Outline from the Quick-Menu. You'll see the Outline button bar, shown in Figure 14.5.

TIP

You can move the mouse pointer to any button in a button bar or feature bar, then look to the title bar for a brief description of what the button does. I'll use the names that appear in the title bar when referring to specific buttons in the Outline button bar or feature bar.

FIGURE 14.5

The Outline button bar

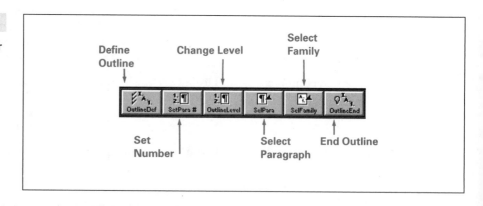

Creating an Outline

Now that you know something about the anatomy of an outline and what tools are available, you're ready to create an outline. Here goes:

1. Move the cursor to where the outline should begin.

2. Choose one of the following outlining methods:

   - If the Outline feature bar isn't visible, choose Tools ➤ Outline. An outline number will appear. Choose the outline style you want from the Outline Definitions drop-down list in the Outline feature bar. Skip to step 5 below.

NOTE   If the Outline feature bar is already on the screen when you're ready to start the outline, click the Options button, choose Define Outline, and continue with step 3 below.

   - Turn on the Outline button bar as described above, then click the Define Outline button. You'll see the Outline Define dialog box shown in Figure 14.6. Continue with step 3.

FIGURE 14.6

Use the Outline Define dialog box to begin a new outline and to select, create, and edit outline styles.

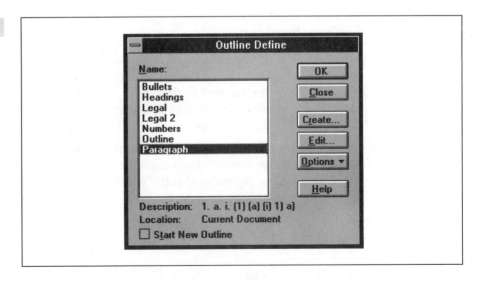

- Move the mouse pointer to the left margin of the document window (the pointer changes to an arrow), right-click the mouse, and choose Outline from the QuickMenu. When the Outline Define dialog box appears, continue with step 3.

3. Select (check) Start New Outline.

4. In the Name list, highlight the style you want and choose OK, or double-click the style name. An outline numbering character or other style change will appear on your screen.

5. To enter your text, do one of the following:

   - **To keep the item at the current level**, type the text for the item. The text can be one line or an entire paragraph.

   - **To demote the item** to a lower level, press Tab or click the → button in the Outline feature bar once for each level you want to move down. (You can have up to eight levels.) Now type your line or paragraph of text.

   - **To promote the item** to a higher level, press Shift+Tab or click the ← button in the Outline feature bar once for each level you want to move up. Type your text.

   - **To assign the item to a specific level number**, click the Options button in the Outline feature bar and select Change Level (or click the Change Level button in the Outline button bar). Type the level number you want (between 1 and 8), and choose OK or press ↵. Type your text.

6. After you've finished typing the item, you can enter another numbered item:

   - If you're using an **automatic style**, press ↵ to start the next item. WordPerfect will insert the next number (or style) at the current outline level. You can press ↵ more than once if you want to add blank lines between items and move the outline number down.

   - If you're using a **manual style**, press ↵ (as many times as you want), then click the T button in the Outline feature bar or press Alt+Shift+T. An outline numbering character (or style) will appear.

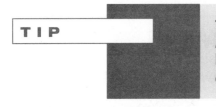

TIP   To turn off automatic numbering temporarily, press Alt+Shift+T or click the T button in the Outline feature bar. To turn the numbering on again, press Alt+Shift+T or click the T button again.

7. Repeat steps 5 and 6 as many times as you wish. (In the Reveal Codes window, each new outline item will appear between a pair of [Para Style] or [Para Num] codes.)

8. To turn off outline numbering, click the Options button in the feature bar and choose End Outline, or click the End Outline button in the Outline button bar. (If a leftover outline number appears above the cursor, press Backspace as many times as needed to remove it.)

NOTE   WordPerfect will end any previous outline automatically when you start a new outline.

You don't need to reactivate the Outline feature if you want to change your outline later. Simply move the cursor anywhere within the existing outline and make your changes. I'll talk about how to change the outline in just a moment. But first, you should know about a potential "gotcha."

Avoiding Number Style Pitfalls

If you chose the Number style for your outline, you might have noticed that WordPerfect doesn't insert an indent or tab after displaying the automatic number. You can still indent the text yourself. However, your first instinct—pressing the Tab key—wouldn't be right. That's because the Tab key demotes the numbering level; it doesn't indent. Here's what to do instead:

- Press F7 to indent the text (see Chapter 5). This is the best method for outline items that are longer than one line.

- Or press Ctrl+Tab to insert a tab.

Changing an Outline

Changing the outline is a cinch. Just follow these steps:

1. Move the cursor to the item you want to change. Or, if you want to change some feature that affects the entire outline (such as the outline style), move the cursor anywhere in the outline using one of the techniques below:

    - To position the cursor wherever you want it, click the mouse or press the arrow keys.

    - To position the cursor at the start or end of the current line, press Home or End respectively.

    - To move the cursor to the start of the next or previous outline item, press Ctrl+↓ or Ctrl+↑ respectively.

2. Click a button in the Outline feature bar, press a shortcut key, or click ? in the Outline feature bar and select an option from the menu.

That's all there is to it! If you're in an adventurous mood, go ahead and experiment with the Outline feature bar and shortcut keys (see Table 14.1 for a summary). If you're not feeling adventurous, or you're editing a document that you can't afford to mess up, please read on.

Adding Outline Items

Adding a new outline item is a lot like creating an outline item in the first place. First, move the cursor to the end of the line that will be *above* the new item. For instance, to add an item after section 2.2 of the contract shown in Figure 14.1, move the cursor after the period at the end of the sentence. Then...

- If you're using an *automatic* style, press ↵ (as many times as you want), then type your text.

- If you're using a *manual* style, press ↵ (as many times as you want), make sure the Outline feature bar is visible, then click the T button in the Outline feature bar or press Alt+Shift+T. Now type your text.

The new item will have the same numbering level as the one above it, and WordPerfect will automatically adjust any numbers below the item.

Deleting Outline Items

There are two ways to delete outline items: Use the usual methods for deleting text, or use the level markers in the Outline Editor to delete outline items or families.

The first method is best when you want to delete a topic that contains subtopics, but you *don't* want to delete the subtopics. Move your cursor to the beginning of the first line in the topic you want to delete (press Home or click at the beginning of the line). Then press Backspace to delete the outline number. Now delete the rest of the text for the item in the usual way (for instance, press Delete repeatedly or select the text and press Delete).

The Outline Editor is best for deleting the lowest-level item under a topic or for deleting a topic and its subtopics. (See "Using the Outline Editor," later in this chapter, for details.)

Switching between Outline Levels and Body Text

With just the few keystrokes shown below, you can instantly switch any text in your document between an outline level and body text:

1. If the Outline feature bar isn't visible, choose <u>T</u>ools ➤ <u>O</u>utline.

2. Position the cursor in the text you want to transform. (If you want to convert several outline level items to body text, select all the items you want to convert.)

3. Click the T button in the Outline feature bar (or press Alt+Shift+T) to toggle between outline level and body text.

If the current item is body text, WordPerfect will change it to outline level text. If the item is an outline level, WordPerfect will change it to body text. This is the quickest way to turn outline numbering off or on.

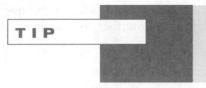

TIP You can also use these methods to suspend or resume automatic outline numbering when you're typing a new outline item.

Changing an Outline Level

It's not always easy to organize your thoughts in a logical manner. You'll probably need to rearrange the topics in your outline many times before your outline reaches the peak of perfection. Luckily, this is easy to do.

To change the level of an outline item, move the cursor to the *beginning* of the outline item (press Home or click your mouse on the outline number). Now proceed as follows:

- **To demote the item** to a lower level, click the → button in the Outline feature bar or press Tab once for each level.

- **To promote the item** to a higher level, click the ← button in the Outline feature bar or press Shift+Tab once for each level.

- **To move the item to a specific level number,** click the Options button in the Outline feature bar and choose Change Level (or click the Change Level button in the Outline button bar). Type the level number you want (between 1 and 8) and choose OK or press ↵.

WordPerfect will adjust the level number of the item you changed and will renumber the remaining items automatically.

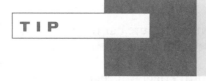

TIP You can place the cursor anywhere in the item if you aren't using Tab or Shift+Tab to demote or promote an item.

Changing the Outline Style

If you don't like the outline style, you can change it to another style. Here's how:

1. Place the cursor anywhere in the outline.

2. Click the Outline Definitions drop-down list in the Outline feature bar. Or, click the Define Outline button in the Outline button bar.

3. Highlight the style name you want and press ↵, or double-click the style name. You can choose any built-in style (see Figure 14.3) or any custom outline style that you've defined.

The outline style will change instantly. (This is almost too easy, isn't it?)

NOTE The outline style change will affect only the outline that your cursor is in. It won't affect the style of other outlines in your document.

Changing the Starting Number

Suppose your outline begins with number 1, and you want it to start with number 5 instead. You can change the starting number for any numbered level in your outline by following the steps below:

1. Position the cursor on the item you want to change. Usually this will be the first item in the outline.

2. Click the Options button in the Outline feature bar and choose Set Number. Or click the Set Number button in the Outline button bar.

3. Type the starting number you want. You must type Arabic numerals separated by commas, spaces, or periods. For instance, to start numbering a level 3 item at VI.C.7, you could type **6.3.7**.

4. Choose OK.

WordPerfect will change the starting number and renumber the remaining items in the outline. (You won't notice any change if you've chosen a non-numeric numbering scheme, such as bullets. However, if you switch to a numbered outline style, your new starting number will appear.)

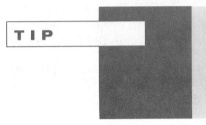

TIP

If your outline numbering seems "off" (perhaps some numbers are repeated), a stray [Para Num Set] code may be running loose. To solve this problem, turn on Reveal Codes (press Alt+F3) and delete the offending code.

Hiding and Showing Parts of the Outline

Recall that an outline *family* consists of a topic and any subtopics below it. Until now, only dedicated outlining programs allowed you to collapse (hide) or expand (show) different levels in an outline. One of WordPerfect 6's hottest new outlining features lets you collapse and expand the outline families, so you can focus on any level(s) of detail.

Figure 14.7 illustrates the effects of using these features on the outline shown in Figure 14.2. In the top example, I hid the family for items I, II.A, and III. In the middle example, I chose to show the items at level 1, then expanded item IV only. In the third example, I've shown only level 1 items.

The next few sections explain how to use the buttons on the Outline feature bar to collapse and expand outlines. Later you'll learn how to use the Outline Editor to do the job.

FIGURE 14.7

The sample outline in
Figure 14.2 in various
stages of collapse

Words of Wisdom Book Outline

I.   Introduction
II.   Getting Started
  A.   A guided tour
  B.   The WOW on-line tutorial

III. The LEAST you need to know
IV.   Becoming a WOW Guru
  TBD (We don't even know how yet!)

V.   Appendices

VI.   Index

Families for
items I, II.A,
and III are hidden.

Words of Wisdom Book Outline

I.   Introduction
II.   Getting Started
III. The LEAST you need to know
IV.   Becoming a WOW Guru
  TBD (We don't even know how yet!)

V.   Appendices
VI.   Index

This outline shows
level 1 items with
item IV expanded
to include body text.

Words of Wisdom Book Outline

I.   Introduction
II.   Getting Started
III. The LEAST you need to know
IV.   Becoming a WOW Guru
V.   Appendices
VI.   Index

This outline shows
level 1 items only.

N O T E

The outline collapse and expand features affect only the
outline that your cursor is in. They have no effect on
other outlines in your document.

Hiding and Showing Families

You can hide or show the daughters of any outline family. First, make sure the Outline feature bar is visible (Tools ➤ Outline). Move the cursor into the topmost item in the family that you want to work with. Then...

- **To hide (collapse) the family**, click the – button in the Outline feature bar (or press Alt+Shift+I). The daughter topics and any body text just below them will disappear from view.

- **To show (expand) the family**, click the + button in the Outline feature bar (or press Alt+Shift+S). The daughter topics will reappear.

- **To show all families** in the outline, click the All button in the Outline feature bar (or press Alt+Shift+A). This option instantly expands all families in the outline. It's especially handy when you're not sure whether or not you've collapsed parts of the outline.

N O T E

When you hide an outline family, WordPerfect inserts [Hidden Txt] codes into your document. The codes are removed when you show the outline family again.

Hiding and Showing Outline Levels

The show and hide options are useful for expanding or collapsing one family at a time. But suppose you want to view only the outline items at level 5 or above (that is, levels 5, 4, 3, 2, and 1). Or maybe you want to see just the items at level 1. This is easy to do:

1. Make sure the Outline feature bar is visible.

2. Position the cursor anywhere in the outline.

3. Click the numbered button in the Outline feature bar for the level you want (or press Alt+Shift+n, where n is the level number).

WordPerfect will instantly display only items that are at or above the level you selected.

Using the Outline Editor

Whenever the Outline feature bar is visible, you can use the *Outline Editor* to restructure outlines quickly and work with outline families. To activate the Outline Editor, choose Tools ➤ Outline. When you're finished using the Outline Editor, choose the Close button in the Outline feature bar, or press Alt+Shift+C.

As Figure 14.8 shows, the outline-editing tools appear at the left edge of the screen. The hollow numbers (*level markers*) mark the relative level of each

FIGURE 14.8

The outline from Figure 14.7 when the Outline feature bar is visible. The Outline Editor tools appear at the left edge of the screen. I selected a topic in the outline by moving the mouse pointer to the level marker and clicking.

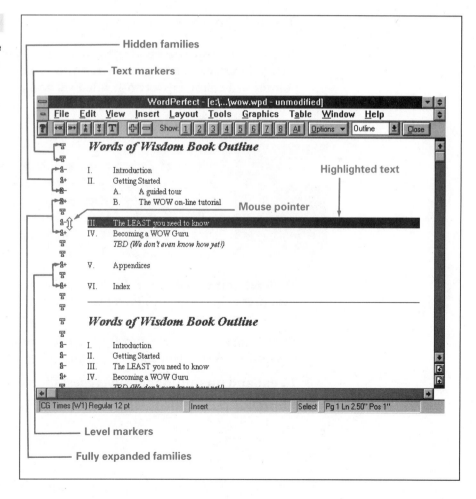

item within the outline. Minus (−) signs symbolize hidden families, plus (+) signs indicate fully expanded families, and hollow T symbols (*text markers*) denote body text.

T I P

If you can't see the outline-editing tools, try dragging the scroll box in the horizontal scroll bar to the left. To display the horizontal scroll bar, choose File ➤ Preferences and double-click Display. Then select (check) Horizontal, choose When Required, and choose OK then Close.

The Outline Editor tools make quick work of many outlining tasks:

- **To select an outline family,** move the mouse pointer to the highest-level marker or text marker that you want to select. The mouse pointer will change to a two-headed vertical arrow when it's properly positioned (see Figure 14.8). Now click the mouse.

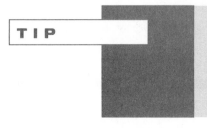

T I P

You can also use the Outline button bar to select outline items. To select one outline item, move the cursor to the item and click the Select Paragraph button. To select an outline family, move the cursor to the topmost item in the family and click the Select Family button.

- **To delete an outline family,** select it (as described just above), then press Delete. WordPerfect will delete the item and renumber the outline automatically.

- **To collapse an outline family,** move the mouse pointer to the topmost item that you want to collapse, then double-click.

- **To expand an outline family,** repeat the steps given just above for collapsing an outline family.

- **To move an outline family** to a new position in the outline, first select the family. Then move the mouse pointer to the topmost level marker in the family and drag the marker to its new position. As you drag the marker, a horizontal bar will indicate the new position of the family. When you release the mouse button, the family will appear at the new position, and the outline will be re-numbered automatically. As an alternative to dragging, you can select the family, then click the ↑ and ↓ buttons in the Outline feature bar (or press Alt+Shift+U and Alt+Shift+W) until you've placed the family where you want it.

T I P   You may find it easier to collapse a large outline family before you move it. After the move, you can expand the family again.

- **To copy an outline family** to a new position in the outline, collapse the family (if you wish), select the family, then choose Edit ➤ Copy or press Ctrl+C. Click in the outline where you want to place the copied family, then press Home twice. Choose Edit ➤ Paste or press Ctrl+V.

Remember that you can undo any editing mistake if you catch the problem immediately. Simply choose Edit ➤ Undo or press Ctrl+Z.

Creating Your Own Outline Style

Chapter 17 discusses WordPerfect styles, which are a great tool for using design elements easily and consistently throughout a document. Outline styles are just a special case of WordPerfect's general style features. You can define a new outline style for a single document, or you can store it in a library that will be available to any document you create. Once you've defined the style, you can use it as you would use any of WordPerfect's built-in outline styles.

If you're curious, here's a quick way to begin a new outline style:

1. Click the Define Outline button in the Outline button bar, or click the Options button in the Outline feature bar and choose Define Outline. You'll see the Outline Define dialog box (Figure 14.6).

2. To create a new outline style, choose the Create button. To change an existing style, highlight the style and choose Edit.

3. Define or edit the new style as explained in Chapter 17.

You've seen how convenient it is to create outlines, bulleted lists, numbered paragraphs, and other types of documents that present ideas in a hierarchical manner. In the next chapter, you'll find out how to number the lines in your document and set up counters.

Automatic Line Numbers and Counters

fast TRACK

You can use counters to number or count   **483**

> anything in your document. To reach the Counter Numbering dialog box, choose Insert ➤ Other ➤ Counter.

To create a counter   **487**

> position the cursor where you want to create the counter, and go to the Counter Numbering dialog box. Choose Create and then specify the counter name, number of levels, and numbering method.

To change a counter's value   **488**

> position the cursor where you want the counter code to change, then go to the Counter Numbering dialog box. Highlight the item you want to change, and choose Value, Increase, or Decrease.

To display a counter in your document   **488**

> position the cursor where you want the counter to appear, then go to the Counter Numbering dialog box. Choose Display In Document. Or, to increase or decrease the counter and display it in one step, choose Increase And Display or Decrease And Display.

CHAPTER 14 covered WordPerfect's powerful outlining features, which are great for creating simple lists and hierarchical outlines. In this chapter, I'll cover two more numbering features: line numbers and counters.

Line Numbering, Quick and Easy

WordPerfect can number every line in your document or just certain sections. Such formats are common in legal documents and in other documents that reference information by line number.

It's most common to print the numbers in the left margin of the document, as shown in Figure 15.1. However, WordPerfect lets you print the numbers anywhere on the page—even between columns in newspaper-style documents.

NOTE The vertical line between the line numbers and the text in Figure 15.1 is a graphic line. I placed it in a header that's printed on every page (see "Adding a Separator Line," later in the chapter).

Turning Line Numbers On and Off

You can add line numbers to a document in just a few steps:

1. Place the cursor where you want to start the line numbering.

FIGURE 15.1

Sample document with line numbers

```
 1   STEVEN C. SMITH
 2   53505 Orange Avenue
 3   Los Angeles, CA  90025
 4
 5   Telephone:  (123) 435-1200
 6
 7
 8   STEVEN C. SMITH, Complainant
 9
10
11
12
13              UNITED STATES OF AMERICA
14
15                    BEFORE THE
16
17       COMMODITY FUTURES TRADING COMMISSION
18
19
20
21   In the Matter of the Reparations   )   CFTC DOCKET NO. 90-S205
22   Proceeding Between:                 )
23                                       )   COMPLAINANT'S APPEAL
24   STEVEN C. SMITH                     )   INFORMAL DOCUMENT
25                                       )
26        Complainant,                   )
27                                       )
28   and                                 )
29                                       )
30   LEVER BROTHERS, INC.                )
31   and JOHN JONES                      )
32                                       )
33        Respondents.                   )
34        ─────────────────────────────
35
36
37                   INTRODUCTION

38      My Work Priority Policy - A prerequisite to other outside

39   involvement activities.  My work requires that I have no outside

40   interruption of any kind, except in an emergency.

41      As an introduction to any discussion of my undertaking with

42   others, including financial investments that could disturb me at

43   my work, except for emergencies, that the above policy be
```

-1-

2. Choose <u>L</u>ayout ➤ <u>L</u>ine ➤ <u>N</u>umbering. The Line Numbering dialog box, shown in Figure 15.2, will appear.

3. Select (check) Turn Line Numbering <u>O</u>n. Don't forget to check this box if you ever want to see any line numbers!

4. Select other options if you wish. Look to the sample page in the dialog box for a preview of the numbering options you've chosen so far. (I'll describe these options later.)

5. Choose OK to return to your document.

FIGURE 15.2

The Line Numbering dialog box

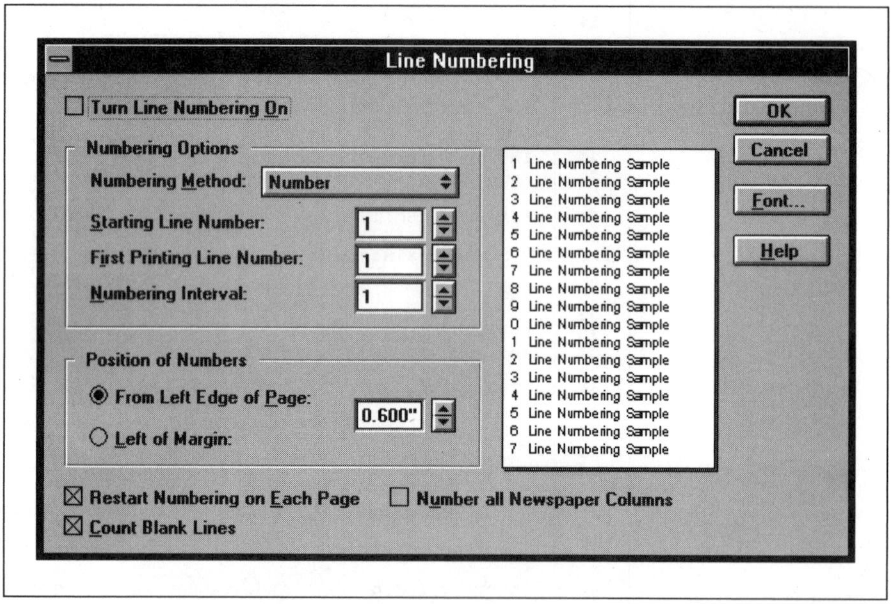

You'll see the line numbers as you type and when you print the document.

Turning line numbering off is as easy as turning it on. Position the cursor where you want line numbering to stop, choose <u>L</u>ayout ➤ <u>L</u>ine ➤ <u>N</u>umbering, deselect Turn Line Numbering <u>O</u>n, and choose OK. To turn off *all* the line numbering in your document, delete the [Ln Num:On] code in Reveal Codes.

What Counts as a Line Number?

WordPerfect usually counts blank lines when it numbers your document's lines. However, it doesn't count or number the following items:

- Lines in footnotes and endnotes (Chapter 31)
- Page headers and footers (Chapter 8)
- Lines that are left blank by your line-spacing setting (Chapter 5)

WordPerfect won't count any blank lines if you've deselected Count Blank Lines in the Line Numbering dialog box.

Changing the Line Numbering Format

You can change the appearance of line numbers when you turn on line numbering, or any time later, simply by choosing options from the Line Numbering dialog box (see Figure 15.2).

To change line numbering after the fact, proceed as follows:

1. Move the cursor to where you want the line number format to change. Usually this will be the first line-numbered paragraph in the document.

2. Choose Layout ➤ Line ➤ Numbering.

3. Make your changes in the Line Numbering dialog box, as described below. The sample page in the dialog box will reflect each change you make.

4. Choose OK.

TIP You can get to the Line Numbering dialog box and change the current line numbering format quickly by double-clicking the [Ln Num:On] code in Reveal Codes.

The Line Numbering dialog box offers the following options:

Numbering Method Lets you select the numbering method. Your choices are Number (1, 2, 3), Lowercase Letter (a, b, c),

Uppercase Letter (A, B, C), Lowercase Roman (i, ii, iii), and Uppercase Roman (I, II, III).

Starting Line Number   Lets you specify a starting line number. Regardless of the current numbering method, you should type the starting line number as an Arabic number (not as a letter or Roman numeral). This option is handy if you've stopped numbering lines in the middle of a page or document and you want to resume numbering later.

First Printing Line Number   WordPerfect usually starts printing line numbers at the spot where you turn line numbering on. This option lets you start printing numbers at a different line number. In the example below, I turned on line numbering at the beginning of the document and changed the first line number printed to 4. So, although line counting starts at the top, with line 1, WordPerfect doesn't actually begin printing line numbers until line 4:

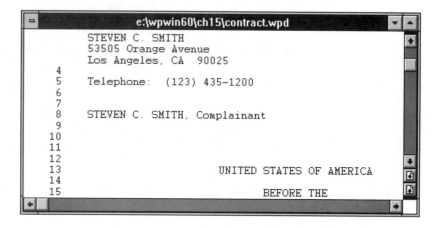

Numbering Interval   Sets the increment for the *printed* line number. When you set the option to 1 (the default), WordPerfect prints every line number. When you set it to 2, WordPerfect prints every other line number, and so on. This option does *not* change how the line numbers are calculated; it only changes how often WordPerfect prints the numbers.

From Left Edge of Page   WordPerfect starts measuring at the left edge of the page and then moves the line numbers right by the distance you specify in the Position Of Numbers text box.

Left of Margin   WordPerfect starts measuring at the left edge of the text and then moves the line numbers left by the distance you specify in the Position Of Numbers text box. This option is adjusted automatically when you number newspaper columns (see below).

WARNING

Don't place the line numbers between the page or column margins. If you do, WordPerfect is likely to clobber the text by printing line numbers on top of it (*not* good). Thus, if you have a 1" left margin, and the line number position is relative to the left edge of the page, you should specify a distance measurement that's less than 1".

Restart Numbering on Each Page   Determines whether line numbering will start anew on each page. When this option is selected (checked), numbering for each page restarts at the number specified in the Starting Line Number option (usually 1). When it's deselected, WordPerfect numbers consecutively from the previous page (thus, if the last line number on page 1 is line 7, the first line number on page 2 would be line 8).

Count Blank Lines   When this is selected (checked), WordPerfect counts and numbers the blank lines created by multiple hard returns. When it's deselected, WordPerfect counts and numbers only lines that contain text. (WordPerfect never numbers lines that are left blank by your line-spacing setting, as the numbering for lines 37–43 of Figure 15.1 shows.)

Number All Newspaper Columns   Select (check) this option if you want to number the lines in each newspaper column. To display the two-column newsletter in Figure 15.3, I turned on line numbering at the top of the document, and checked Number All Newspaper Columns. (See Chapter 27 for more about designing multicolumn formats.)

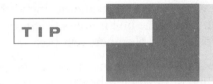

TIP

If you number all newspaper columns, WordPerfect automatically changes the Left Of Margin setting to 0.25" to avoid printing numbers over the text.

Font Lets you choose a different font, size, appearance, and color for the line numbers (see Chapter 6).

FIGURE 15.3

A document in two-column newspaper format with line numbering on for all newspaper columns

Adding a Separator Line

In Figure 15.1, I added a vertical line to separate the line numbers from the text on every page. This is actually quite easy once you know the secret I'm about to tell you (don't tell anyone else).

Simply place a vertical graphic line in a header that's printed on every page, like this:

1. Move the cursor to the top of the document (Ctrl+Home).

2. Choose <u>L</u>ayout ➤ <u>H</u>eader/Footer, select Header <u>A</u>, and choose <u>C</u>reate.

3. Choose <u>G</u>raphics ➤ <u>V</u>ertical Line (or press Ctrl+Shift+F11).

4. Choose <u>C</u>lose from the Header/Footer feature bar.

For a refresher on graphic lines, pop back to Chapter 6. Headers are covered in Chapter 8.

Counters

WordPerfect offers you many ways to number things automatically:

- Page numbering (Chapter 8)
- Footnote and endnote numbering (Chapter 31)
- Graphics box numbering (Chapter 25)
- Outline numbering (Chapter 14)
- Line numbering (Chapter 15)

You can also use *counters* to count or number anything in your document, including paragraphs, chapters, sections, graphics boxes, widget names—whatever! Counters can display numbers, letters, and roman numerals, and they can appear anywhere in your document. Each counter can have up to five levels.

WordPerfect provides two general types of counters:

User-defined counters Counters that you create. User-defined counters (henceforth called "counters") aren't updated and displayed automatically. Rather, you must tell WordPerfect exactly what values they should have and when to display those values. For example, you can tell WordPerfect to add 1 to (increment), subtract 1 from (decrement), or set a counter to a specific value.

You can also tell WordPerfect to display the current value of a counter, increment and display the counter, or decrement and display the counter. (Counters initially have a value of 1.) I'll explain the steps for creating, updating, and displaying counters later in the chapter.

Predefined system counters   Counters that WordPerfect uses to number graphics boxes automatically. We'll look at system counters next.

System Counters

In WordPerfect, you can use graphics boxes to store graphic images, text, tables, equations, charts, and drawings. WordPerfect can count and track five types of graphics boxes: Equation Box, Figure Box, Table Box, Text Box, and User Box. Each type of box is counted and tracked automatically, via system counters. (You'll learn all about graphics boxes in Part Seven of this book.)

Although system counters are similar to the manual counters that you can create, they do have the following special properties:

- System counters initially have only one level, though you can change this if you wish.

- WordPerfect automatically increments the *lowest level* of the appropriate system counter when you create a graphics box. For example, when you add a second Figure Box to your document, WordPerfect will increment the Figure Box counter to 2 automatically.

- The *highest level* of each type of system counter appears automatically when you add a caption to a graphics box.

- Graphics box captions (and the counters they display) are marked automatically for inclusion in lists. You just need to define the location and format of the graphics box list you want to generate, as described in Chapters 25 and 31.

Some Counter Examples

Figure 15.4 shows several counters in action. The relevant counter techniques used in this figure are explained on the following page.

FIGURE 15.4

Here I used counters to number section titles and figures, and to count fruits and vegetables.

15-1 Work Avoidance

Sometimes work avoidance is necessary to keep everyone on an even keel. For example, when your computer's mind is blown from working too hard, you're probably better off going to a movie. Let your PC play a video game for entertainment.

Figure 15.1 Poor PC

15-2 Work Enjoyment

When you return, you'll feel refreshed, and your computer will have had some time to cool off. Now you can go back to whatever you were doing with new zest and unstoppable enthusiasm.

Figure 15.2 Cool Fellow

15-3 More Counter Examples

Fruits	*Vegetables*
Apples	Carrots
Oranges	Celery
Pineapples	Tomatoes
Papayas	Lettuce

There are 4 <u>fruits</u> and 5 <u>vegetables</u> in this document. (Mushrooms *are* a vegetable, right?)

- I changed the default Figure Box counter to include two levels, and then I set the first level's value to 15.

- I displayed both levels of Figure Box counters in the paragraph titles (for example, *15-1 Work Avoidance*) and figure captions (*Figure 15.1 Poor PC*).

- I changed the default figure caption style to include the second-level counters. ("Using Counters with Graphics Boxes," later in this chapter, explains how to do this.)

- I set up two counters of my own—one for fruits and one for vegetables. Each counter has a single level.

- I incremented the Fruits counter before typing the *Oranges*, *Pineapples*, and *Papayas* entries in the table. I incremented the Vegetables counter before typing the *Carrots*, *Celery*, *Tomatoes*, and *Lettuce* entries. I displayed each counter in the last paragraph on the page, without incrementing the counters first.

Getting to the Counters Dialog Box

You'll find all the counter features in the Counter Numbering dialog box, shown in Figure 15.5. To open this dialog box, choose Insert ➤ Other ➤ Counter.

FIGURE 15.5

The Counters dialog box

Counter	Value
Equation Box	1
Figure Box	
Level 1	15
Level 2	4
Table Box	1
Text Box	1
User Box	1
Fruits	1
Vegetables	2

Definition: Create... Edit... Delete

Value: Value... Increase Decrease Display in Document Increase and Display Decrease and Display

Close Help

. Indicates System Counter

In Figure 15.5 you can see the five built-in system counters and the Fruits and Vegetables counters that I used in Figure 15.4. Notice that I added a second level to the Figure Box counter. This allowed me to create a two-level numbering scheme like the one used to mark figures in this book (for example, Figure 15.3).

Defining a Counter

To create a counter, follow these steps:

1. Choose Insert ➤ Other ➤ Counter. Then choose the Create button to open the Create Counter Definition dialog box:

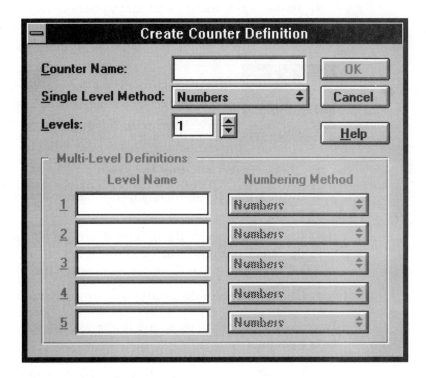

2. In the Counter Name text box, type a name of your choosing.

3. To define more than one level, choose Levels and type the number of levels you want. For example, the number *1.1.1* has three levels. You can define up to five levels.

4. Choose the numbering method you want from the <u>S</u>ingle Level Method or Numbering Method pop-up list buttons. The numbering methods are <u>N</u>umbers (1, 2, 3), <u>L</u>owercase Letters (a, b, c), <u>U</u>ppercase Letters (A, B, C), L<u>o</u>wercase Roman (i, ii, iii), and U<u>p</u>percase Roman (I, II, III).

5. Choose OK, then <u>C</u>lose to return to the document window.

Displaying and Changing a Counter

Once you've defined a counter, it's easy to change, delete, or display it in your document. Just follow these steps:

1. To display or change a counter, position the cursor to where you want the change to take effect or the counter to appear.

TIP If you need to get to the Counter Numbering dialog box often, add a Counter button to the button bar (as explained in Chapter 4).

2. Choose <u>I</u>nsert ➤ <u>O</u>ther ➤ <u>C</u>ounter.

3. In the C<u>o</u>unter list, highlight the counter or level you want to work with.

4. Choose as many of the options described below as you wish. Note that some options return you to the document window, while others leave you in the Counter Numbering dialog box.

5. Choose <u>C</u>lose (if necessary) to return to your document.

Here are the options you can use to change, delete, or display counters in your document:

<u>E</u>dit Lets you change the highlighted counter's name, number of levels, and numbering method.

De<u>l</u>ete Lets you delete a counter. You can use this option to delete only the counter itself, not an individual level. (Use <u>E</u>dit if you want to reduce the number of levels in a counter.) You can't delete a built-in system counter.

Value   Lets you set each level of the highlighted counter to a specific value.

Increase   Increases the highlighted counter value by 1.

Decrease   Decreases the highlighted counter value by 1.

Display in Document   Displays the highlighted counter at the cursor position.

Increase and Display   Increases the highlighted counter value by 1 and displays it in your document.

Decrease and Display   Decreases the highlighted counter value by 1 and displays it in your document.

When you define, display, and set counter values, WordPerfect inserts hidden codes in the document. You can see these in Reveal Codes, and you can use the techniques discussed in Chapter 4 to delete or move the codes as necessary. Table 15.1 summarizes the codes that will appear.

TABLE 15.1: Counter Codes

CODE	COUNTERS DIALOG BOX OPTION	DESCRIPTION
[Count Disp]	Display In Document or Increase And Display	Displays the counter number in your document
[Count Inc]	Increase or Increase And Display	Increases the counter number by 1
[Count Dec]	Decrease or Decrease And Display	Decreases the counter number by 1
[Count Set]	Value	Sets the counter to a new value

Counter Tips

Here are some tips for using counters effectively:

- Each counter begins life with an initial value of 1. Therefore, you should display at least one counter number before you increase or decrease it.

- When you increase, decrease, or set a value for a higher level of a multilevel counter, WordPerfect will automatically reset the lower levels to 1. Suppose you're using a three-level counter that currently has the values 3, 4, and 5. If you increase the first level to 4, the counter values will be 4, 1, and 1 the next time you return to the Counter Numbering dialog box.

- If you just want to count something without showing its value, increase the counter, but don't display it. Then, when you want to show the total, display the counter but don't increase it. The fruits and vegetables example in Figure 15.4 illustrates this use of counters.

Using Counters with Graphics Boxes

WordPerfect automatically increases the *lowest level* of the appropriate system counter when you create an Equation Box, Figure Box, Table Box, Text Box, or User Box. Moreover, the *highest level* counter for the box style will appear automatically when you add a caption to a graphics box.

When you change a system counter to use more than one level, WordPerfect doesn't insert those extra levels into captions automatically. However, it's easy to do this yourself if you know a bit about styles (Chapter 17) and graphics boxes (Chapter 25). Here's the simplest way to add a multilevel counter to graphic box captions:

1. Choose Layout ➤ Styles or press Alt+F8.

2. If you don't see a list of system styles (including BoxText, Caption, and so on), choose Options ➤ Setup, select System Styles, and choose OK.

3. In the Name list, highlight the numbering style for whatever type of box you want to change, then choose Edit. You'll see the Styles Editor dialog box, where you can make changes in the Contents box. The Contents box looks and works just like a Reveal Codes editing window.

N O T E

The caption numbering styles are *EquationNum* (Equation boxes), *FigureNum* (Figure boxes), *TblBoxNum* (Table boxes), *TextBoxNum* (Text boxes), and *UserBoxNum* (User boxes).

4. In the Contents box, position the cursor and type any text that should appear before the counter. Then choose Insert ➤ Other ➤ Counter, highlight the counter level you want to display, and choose Display In Document. (Because the Level 1 counter appears automatically in the caption number, you can start by inserting the Level 2 counter. Be sure to insert the level 2 counter to the right of the [Box Num Disp] code.)

5. Repeat step 4 until you've added all the counter levels and text you want.

6. Choose OK, then Close. New and existing caption numbers for the selected box type will have the numbering style you set up.

Repeat the steps above for each type of graphics box that has a multilevel counter. If you need more information, please see the chapters on styles (Chapter 17) and graphics boxes (Chapter 25).

Using Counters with Lists

WordPerfect automatically marks captioned graphics boxes for inclusion in Equation Box, Figure Box, Table Box, Text Box, or User Box lists that you define. However, counters that *you* create are not marked automatically. To include a user-defined counter and any surrounding text in a list, you'll need to select the counter and text, mark it, and assign it to a list. Chapter 31 explains how to do all these tasks (trust me, it's easy).

That about wraps it up for automatic line numbering and counters. In the next chapter, you'll learn about automatic hyphenation, a tool that helps you tighten loose lines and eliminate excess white space.

Auto-Hyphenating
Your Text

fast TRACK

To insert a hard hyphen **501**

press Ctrl+–. This prevents WordPerfect from breaking the word at the hyphen.

To insert a hyphenation soft return **502**

choose Layout ➤ Line ➤ Other Codes ➤ Hyphenation Soft Return [HyphSRt] and press ↵. WordPerfect will simply break the word at the location of the soft return (without adding a hyphen) if the entire word won't fit at the end of the line.

If a long word refuses to be hyphenated **504**

remove the [Cancel Hyph] code in front of that word in Reveal Codes.

To change the hyphenation zones **508**

choose Layout ➤ Line ➤ Hyphenation, type in the new Percent Left and Percent Right zone settings (in percentages) and choose OK. You can decrease the zones for more hyphens and tighter text, or increase them for fewer hyphens and looser text.

HYPHENATION lends a smoother, more professional look to your documents by tightening loose lines that contain too much white space. The first, fully justified paragraph in Figure 16.1 illustrates how a long word can cause a line to be very loose. That same paragraph looks much neater when a hyphen is added to the long word, as the second paragraph in Figure 16.1 shows.

FIGURE 16.1

A fully justified paragraph with and without hyphenation

Very long words like supercalifragilisticexpialidocious, of Mary Poppins fame, cause very loose lines (too much white space) if you leave them unhyphenated, especially when you squeeze them into tight margins.

Very long words like supercalifragilisticexpialidocious, of Mary Poppins fame, cause very loose lines (too much white space) if you leave them unhyphenated, especially when you squeeze them into tight margins.

You can hyphenate words in two ways: by inserting your own hyphens or by letting WordPerfect do it for you. You'll learn both ways in this chapter.

Hyphenating Text Automatically

To turn on automatic hyphenation, just follow these steps:

1. Move the cursor to where you want automatic hyphenation to begin, or to the start of the document (Ctrl+Home).

2. Choose Layout ➤ Line ➤ Hyphenation.

3. Select Hyphenation On and choose OK.

Helping WordPerfect Hyphenate a Word

Once you've turned automatic hyphenation on, WordPerfect will check for long words at the end of lines as you type new text or scroll through existing text below the cursor. When it finds a line where it can improve the spacing with a hyphen, one of two things will happen:

- WordPerfect will hyphenate the word without asking for your help.
- You'll hear a beep and a dialog box will appear, asking for your help in hyphenating the word (as discussed below).

WordPerfect uses the Speller dictionary to hyphenate words. If it finds a word that needs hyphenating in the dictionary, WordPerfect will hyphenate it accordingly. If the word isn't in the dictionary, WordPerfect will either leave that word unhyphenated or ask for your help. (See "Refining Automatic Hyphenation," later in this chapter, for information about controlling when WordPerfect asks for help with hyphenation.)

Suppose you type *supercalifragilisticexpialidocious* near the end of a line when auto-hyphenation is on. Since that word isn't in WordPerfect's dictionary, you'll see the Position Hyphen dialog box:

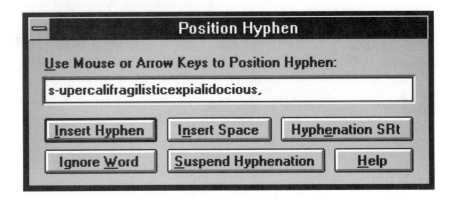

Now you can do any of the following:

- **To insert the hyphen where WordPerfect suggests** (between the letters *s* and *u* in this example), choose Insert Hyphen or press ↵.

- **To separate the letters with a space**, choose Insert Space.

- **To insert a soft return between the letters**, choose Hyphenation SRt.

- **To move the suggested hyphen** to the left or right, click the mouse where you want the hyphen, or use the ← key or → key to reposition the hyphen one character at a time.

- **To prevent the word from being hyphenated**, choose Ignore Word. The entire word will wrap to the next line, and WordPerfect will insert a [Cancel Hyph] code in front of the word. WordPerfect won't prompt you to hyphenate this word again, even if you change the text.

- **To turn hyphenation off for the moment**, choose Suspend Hyphenation, press Escape, or double-click the Control-menu box in the Position Hyphen dialog box. This is useful when you don't want WordPerfect to bother you with hyphenation prompts while you're scrolling through a document or checking your spelling.

Later in the chapter, I'll show you how to control hyphenation while you're typing your text (even when WordPerfect isn't prompting for your help).

Changing an Automatic Hyphen

Suppose WordPerfect automatically hyphenated a word in your document. Then, while scrolling through the document, you discover that you don't like the way WordPerfect hyphenated the word. To change the position of the hyphen when automatic hyphenation is still on, delete the hyphen WordPerfect inserted. You'll hear a beep, and the Position Hyphen dialog box will appear. Next choose one of the options discussed above to reposition the hyphen, insert a space or soft return, or prevent WordPerfect from hyphenating the word.

Turning Off Automatic Hyphenation

When you turn automatic hyphenation on, WordPerfect inserts a [Hyph:On] code into your document. Automatic hyphenation stays active for all text below that code to the end of the document, or until WordPerfect finds a [Hyph:Off] code, which turns hyphenation off.

There are two ways to turn off automatic hyphenation:

* Delete the [Hyph:On] code in Reveal Codes.

* Insert a [Hyph:Off] code where you want automatic hyphenation to stop. To do this, move the cursor to the right spot, then choose Layout ➤ Line ➤ Hyphenation, deselect Hyphenation On, and choose OK.

TIP

You can use Find and Replace (discussed in Chapter 9) to locate and remove the hyphenation codes discussed in this chapter.

The first method above turns off automatic hyphenation below the cursor, without removing existing hyphens. WordPerfect won't hyphenate the words again if you add or change text.

The second method leaves hyphenation on above the cursor, but turns it off for text below the cursor. This method is best when you want to hyphenate some, but not all, sections. You can turn hyphenation on and off in the document as often as you wish.

Hyphenating Text Manually

You can hyphenate words manually, without WordPerfect's help, at any time. However, there are a few characters you should understand—including hyphens, soft hyphens, hard hyphens, and dashes—before you try manual hyphenation.

Hyphen Characters

A *hyphen character* is just a normal hyphen (or minus sign), which you use to divide compound words like *forty-seven* and compound names like *Claplock-Strappman*. The word will be broken on this character only when the word is too long to fit on the current line, and the hyphen falls at the end of the line. In Reveal codes, the hyphen character appears as [- Hyphen].

Soft Hyphens

WordPerfect automatically inserts a *soft hyphen* when it needs to break a word at the end of a line. These are called "soft" hyphens because they remain dormant and invisible (except in Reveal Codes) when they're not needed for hyphenation.

You can type a soft hyphen yourself, even if WordPerfect isn't prompting you for hyphenation help. Here's how:

1. Move the cursor to where you want to insert the soft hyphen.

2. Press Ctrl+Shift+− (hold down Ctrl and Shift and type the hyphen). The soft hyphen will appear in Reveal Codes as [- Soft Hyphen].

Hard Hyphens

You can use a *hard hyphen* to keep text on either side of a hyphen together at the end of a line. For example, you might prefer that WordPerfect wrap a long name like *Smythe-Browne* to the next line, instead of breaking it after *Smythe-*. To add a hard hyphen, follow these steps:

1. Delete any spaces or regular hyphens between the words you want kept together. Then position the cursor where you want the hard hyphen to appear.

2. Press Ctrl+– (hold down Ctrl and type the hyphen).

TIP

You can also use a *hard space* to keep words together on one line. To enter a hard space, delete any regular spaces between the words, and position the cursor where you want the hard space to appear. Then hold down Ctrl and tap the spacebar (Ctrl+spacebar).

Dashes

People often use a *dash* character to show a sudden break in thought that interrupts the sentence structure, like this:

> Will he—indeed, can he—finish the book on time?

There are two types of dashes you can add: an *en dash* and an *em dash*. The exact appearance of these dashes depends on the font that's currently selected. In a proportional font, an en dash is the width of the letter *n*. An em dash is the width of the letter *m*. None of the dashes is ever used for automatic hyphenation. They're treated just like any other character.

To type an en dash or an em dash, you must use the Typographic symbol set in the WordPerfect special characters. The table below gives examples of the different dashes and tells how to type them into a document:

–	En dash	Press Ctrl+W, type **n-** or **4,33** then press ↵.
—	Em dash	Press Ctrl+W, type **m-** or **4,34** then press ↵.

Breaking Words without Hyphens

You can use a *hyphenation soft return* to break words at the ends of lines without inserting hyphens. The slash (/), en dash, and em dash are common replacements for a hyphen. For example, word combinations (like *and/or*) and funky compound words (like *Cattleya/Cymbidium/Dendrobium*) look much better if you break them into two lines at a slash, without adding a hyphen, like this:

> ...and funky compound words (like Cattleya/
> Cymbidium/Dendrobium)...

Suppose you're typing *Cattleya/Cymbidium/Dendrobium* while hyphenation is turned on and WordPerfect inserts a hyphen, placing *Cattleya/-* on the first line and *Cymbidium/Dendrobium* on the next line. You can delete the hyphen and break the words at the slash by following these steps:

1. Move the cursor to the hyphen, then press Delete to delete it.

2. When the Position Hyphen dialog box appears, move the cursor to where you want the word to break (after the first / in this example) and choose Hyphenation SRt.

You can also enter a hyphenation soft return when you type the words:

1. Position the cursor where you want to insert the hyphenation soft return.

2. Choose Layout ➤ Line ➤ Other Codes ➤ Hyphenation Soft Return [Hyph SRt] and press ↵.

Like the soft hyphen, the hyphenation soft return is invisible in the document window and remains dormant until WordPerfect needs it to break the word at the end of a line. In Reveal Codes, the hyphenation soft return looks like this: [Hyph SRt].

Temporary Soft Returns

The *temporary soft return* is a rather odd code that WordPerfect uses to break long words when automatic hyphenation is turned *off*. The code is invisible in the document window, but appears as a [TSRt] at the end of a line in Reveal Codes.

This code splits the word without hyphenating it. You'll never type this code yourself, and you don't need to worry about it until you start working with narrow columns of text (see Chapter 27).

Summary of Hyphenation Characters

Table 16.1 shows the various hyphenation characters available and summarizes the roles they play in breaking words at the end of a line. The table also shows the keys you need to press and the codes that appear in Reveal Codes for each type of hyphen.

TABLE 16.1: A Summary of Hyphens and Dashes

HYPHEN	DESCRIPTION	KEYSTROKE	CODE
Hyphen character	Permanent hyphen that you can use to break two words at the end of a line.	–	[– Hyphen]
Soft hyphen	Temporary hyphen that breaks a word only when necessary (Word-Perfect uses this during automatic hyphenation).	Ctrl+Shift+–	[– Soft Hyphen]
Hard hyphen	A hyphen that's never separated at the end of a line.	Ctrl+–	–
En dash	A dash that's never separated at the end of a line.	Ctrl+W **n-**	–:4,33
Em dash	A dash that's never separated at the end of a line.	Ctrl+W **m-**	—:4,34

TABLE 16.1: A Summary of Hyphens and Dashes (continued)

HYPHEN	DESCRIPTION	KEYSTROKE	CODE
Hyphenation soft return	Breaks words at a certain place without showing a hyphen.	Choose Hyphenation SRt in Position Hyphen dialog box, or choose Layout ➤ Line ➤ Other Codes ➤ Hyphenation Soft Return [HyphSRt] ➤ ↵ when typing a word.	[Hyph SRt]
Ignore Word	Wraps the entire word to the next line and prevents future hyphenation.	Choose Ignore Word in Position Hyphen dialog box or press Ctrl+/ when typing a word.	[Cancel Hyph]

NOTE: If you can't remember which character produces the hyphenation codes, choose Layout ➤ Line ➤ Other Codes, select the character you want from the dialog box, and choose Insert.

Taming Words that Refuse to Be Hyphenated

Sometimes a word simply won't hyphenate when you expect it to. This can happen if you previously chose Ignore Word when WordPerfect asked for help during automatic hyphenation, or you pressed Ctrl+/ while typing a word.

To hyphenate a word that stubbornly refuses to be hyphenated, turn on Reveal Codes and remove the [Cancel Hyph] code just before or within the word. If WordPerfect beeps and displays the Position Hyphen dialog box, just follow the usual procedure to position the hyphen and select the type of hyphenation you want.

Refining Automatic Hyphenation

You can customize the way WordPerfect carries out automatic hyphenation. Normally, WordPerfect's default settings will be perfectly fine, so feel free to skip the rest of the chapter if you're happily hyphenating your text already. However, the next few sections might be useful if you're a hyphenation techno-junkie or you want to refine automatic hyphenation further.

NOTE The Spell-Hyphen utility allows you to adjust the way words are hyphenated. You can purchase that utility separately from WordPerfect Corporation.

Choosing a Foreign Language Dictionary

The two-character language code (US in the United States) tells WordPerfect which dictionary you're using for hyphenation and spell-checking and which thesaurus to use. If you've purchased and installed a foreign language dictionary from WordPerfect Corporation, you can use that dictionary to hyphenate words as well.

To switch to a different language, move the cursor to where the new language should take effect (or select text to use the new language dictionary for a few paragraphs only). Then choose Tools ➤ Language, select a language, and choose OK.

You can use <u>F</u>ile ➤ P<u>r</u>eferences ➤ <u>F</u>ile ➤ Hyphenation to change the default location for the hyphenation dictionary. See Chapter 19 for details.

Choosing How Often You're Prompted for Hyphenation

The most convenient way to use automatic hyphenation is the default method, in which WordPerfect asks for help placing a hyphen only if it can't find a word in its dictionary. However, you can control when and whether WordPerfect prompts you for hyphenation help by following these steps:

1. Choose <u>F</u>ile ➤ P<u>r</u>eferences and double-click <u>E</u>nvironment.

2. Choose one of the following options from the Hyphenation <u>P</u>rompt pop-up list:

<u>A</u>lways   Stop and ask for your help every time a word needs to be hyphenated. Choosing this option will give you oodles of practice using the hyphenation feature and complete control over where words are hyphenated.

<u>N</u>ever   Never prompt to position the hyphen and always hyphenate according to the current hyphenation dictionary. Words that don't appear in the dictionary will be wrapped to the next line (and not hyphenated) if they're too long to fit on a line.

<u>W</u>hen Required   Ask for help in placing the hyphen only when the word isn't found in the current dictionary. This is the default setting.

3. Choose OK and then <u>C</u>lose to return to your document.

Your choice will affect automatic hyphenation in the current document and in all future documents until you repeat the steps above and choose a different prompt option.

Disabling the Beep

If the beep that precedes WordPerfect's hyphenation prompt is driving you nuts, turn it off. Choose File ➤ Preferences and double-click Environment. Deselect (clear) Hyphenation, then choose OK and Close. This will turn off beeping for the current session and all future sessions until you select (check) the Hyphenation box again.

Using Hyphenation Zones

WordPerfect uses *hyphenation zones* to decide when to break a word during automatic hyphenation. You can think of a hyphenation zone as the place on a standard typewriter where the bell sounds to let you know that you're nearing the end of a line as you type. Of course, WordPerfect doesn't sound a bell because it usually hyphenates automatically.

WordPerfect uses two zones to control hyphenation, one on each side of the right margin. However, you can't see the hyphenation zones on your screen. Figure 16.2 shows how these zones would look if they were visible. (The percentages shown in the figure are explained later.)

FIGURE 16.2

WordPerfect's hyphenation zones

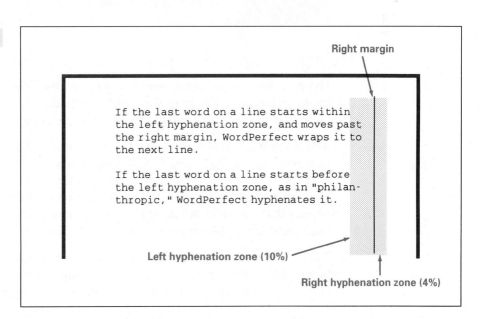

Right margin

If the last word on a line starts within the left hyphenation zone, and moves past the right margin, WordPerfect wraps it to the next line.

If the last word on a line starts before the left hyphenation zone, as in "philan-thropic," WordPerfect hyphenates it.

Left hyphenation zone (10%)

Right hyphenation zone (4%)

WordPerfect follows the rules below to decide whether to hyphenate a word when automatic hyphenation is on, or when you type a hyphen, soft hyphen, or hyphenation soft return character:

- Hyphenate the last word on a line if it starts before the left edge of or within the hyphenation zone and it extends past the edge of the hyphenation zone.

- Wrap the last word on a line to the next line without hyphenation if it starts before the left edge of the hyphenation zone, or if it starts within the hyphenation zone and is narrower than the zone.

The sample paragraphs in Figure 16.2 show how this works. Notice that the end of the first line in the first paragraph doesn't have enough room for the word "the" before the right margin. WordPerfect wraps it to the next line because it's narrower than the hyphenation zones. In the second paragraph, WordPerfect hyphenates the long word "philanthropic" because it starts before the left hyphenation zone and would extend past the right hyphenation zone if it were not hyphenated.

N O T E

Figure 16.2 is for illustration only. If you type the paragraphs shown, they may not be wrapped or hyphenated in the same way.

Changing the Hyphenation Zones

Hyphenation zones are measured as percentages of line length. This lets the hyphenation zone adjust to the width of the line. In addition, it simplifies matters when you create multicolumn documents with narrow columns.

The default left hyphenation zone is 10%, and the default right hyphenation zone is 4%. Each line is 6.5″ long when you print on standard 8.5″ × 11″ paper, with 1″ left and right margins and ten characters to the inch. With these facts in hand, some quick mental arithmetic (or a calculator) reveals that the default left hyphenation zone is 0.65″ long, and the default right hyphenation zone is about 0.26″ long.

These preselected hyphenation zones provide a happy medium between how tight the text is in justified paragraphs (or how much space is at the end of ragged-right lines) and the amount of hyphenation required.

However, you can change the sizes of the hyphenation zones to tighten the text further or loosen it a bit. Basically, it works like this: Smaller hyphenation zones produce tighter text and many hyphens. Larger hyphenation zones require fewer hyphens, but produce looser text.

To change the hyphenation zones, follow these steps:

1. Move the cursor to where you want the new hyphenation zones to start.

2. Choose Layout ➤ Line ➤ Hyphenation.

3. Type in new settings (in percentages) for either or both the Percent Left and Percent Right hyphenation zones.

4. Choose OK.

WordPerfect will use the new setting to prompt for hyphenation help when you type new text below the cursor position. Likewise, it will adjust existing text to comply with the new hyphenation zones when you scroll through text below the point where the new hyphenation zones begin.

If you change your mind about the new settings, you can return to the preset hyphenation zones. Simply go to Reveal Codes and remove the [Lft HZone] and [Rgt HZone] codes that you inserted earlier. When you scroll through existing text below that point, WordPerfect will readjust the hyphenation to the original settings, prompting for help when (and if) it needs it.

This chapter has covered hyphenation, a feature that smoothes out your text by using hyphens to break long words at the ends of lines. In the next part of this book, we'll look at ways to manage and simplify your work. We'll begin with *styles*, which make it easy to design a document to precise specifications and then change that design with just a few keystrokes.

PART FOUR

Managing (and Simplifying) Your Work

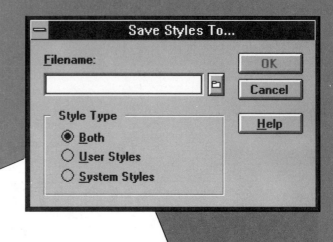

Very long words like supercalifragilisticexpialidocious, of Mary Poppins fame, cause very loose lines (too much white space) if you leave them unhyphenated, especially when you squeeze them into tight margins.

Very long words like supercalifragilisticexpialidocious, of Mary Poppins fame, cause very loose lines (too much white space) if you leave them unhyphenated, especially when you squeeze them into tight margins.

CHAPTER

17

Doing It with Styles

fast TRACK

To change an existing style   **531**

go to the Style List dialog box (Alt+F8), highlight the name of the style you want to change, and choose Edit.

A document can use styles   **534**

from the document's own style library, or from a default template, a supplemental template, or WordPerfect's built-in system styles. To specify the locations of template files, choose File ➤ Preferences ➤ File ➤ Templates.

To save the current library of styles to a style library file   **536**

go to the Style List dialog box and choose Options ➤ Setup. Under the Display Styles From options, check the style libraries you want to save, then choose OK. Choose Options ➤ Save As, enter the file name of the library you want to create (or replace), select which types of styles to save (user, system, or both), and choose OK.

To retrieve a style library file into the current style list   **538**

go to the Style List dialog box. Then choose Options ➤ Retrieve, specify the name of the style file, select which types of styles to retrieve (user, system, or both), and choose OK.

TO THE uninitiated, styles may seem like a peculiar, confusing topic that's best ignored. But ask anyone in the publishing biz, "What's the best thing about using a word processor?" My bet is that the answer would be "Styles!"

Why Use Styles?

A *style* is a predefined format for some design element of your document. A *design element* is anything that's repeated throughout a document. For example, the design elements in the sample newsletter shown in Figure 17.1 include article titles, bylines ("by" followed by the author's name), and the little sunshine character that marks the end of each article.

You might think of a style as your own custom hidden code. For example, WordPerfect has some simple codes, like [Ln Spacing] and [Font], which it inserts for you. It also has some paired codes, like [Bold], which are inserted when you boldface text. Your own hidden codes (styles) can contain any combination of virtually all the codes that WordPerfect has to offer. For instance, a style can define the font *and* the justification *and* the margins *and* whatever else you want in one fell swoop.

In the sample newsletter in Figure 17.1, I created a style to define the basic body text—that is, the column format and font of each article. I also created a style named Headline to define the appearance of each article title. Another style, named Byline, formats all the bylines (under the article titles). A third style, End Mark, defines the special character at the end of each article. (The last article continues onto the next page, which isn't shown; that's why it doesn't have an end mark.)

FIGURE 17.1

A sample newsletter that uses styles to define repeating design elements, such as article titles, bylines, and special characters at the end of each article

Byline style — Headline style

Headline style — End Mark style

THE VACATIONER

Vol. 1 No. 1   Travel fun for everyone   January

foreign lands. So relax, enjoy, and travel with us as we bring you a new issue every quarter of the year. ✿

CELEBRATE WITH US
by Jill Evans — Byline style

In honor of our newsletter's maiden voyage, we'd like to invite you to an Open House at 7:00pm on January 11 at our offices. Please dress casually or come in your most fashionable travel togs. If you miss this event, we'll see to it that your luggage ends up on the Space Shuttle. ✿

End Mark style

TROPICAL TRAVEL
by Elizabeth Olson

Travel to tropical islands is on the increase. In just the past four years, our tropical travel sales have tripled. That's really something in a recessionary economy! There's a good reason for these increases — tropical vacations are great

NEWSLETTER DEBUT
by Joan Smith

We're pleased to bring this first issue of our newsletter, *The Vacationer*, to our many loyal customers. The newsletter was inspired by your ideas and questions. You've asked us where to find the best travel fares, where to go for the person who has been everywhere, what to eat and how to eat it when visiting faraway countries. We've responded by creating this newsletter.

Here we'll bring you the latest news about great deals on vacations in exotic corners of our planet, fun places for inexpensive weekend getaways, and out-of-the-way spots you might never have thought to ask us about. We'll include handy vacation planning tips and introduce you to exciting foods, puzzling customs, and important laws you'll encounter during sojourns to

INSIDE...

Byline style — Headline style

Body Text style

NOTE You'll learn to create documents like the one in Figure 17.1 in Part Six of this book. However, you can start using styles with *any* document right now.

You can create as many different styles as you wish and give them names of your own choosing. Later, when you want to apply a particular style to something in your document, you just "turn on" the style. There's no need to go through all the steps required to change the font, the justification, the margins, and so forth, because all those things are already defined within the style.

The Real Beauty of Styles

The real beauty of styles is this: If you change your mind about the appearance of a certain design element, such as the headlines, you don't need to go through the document and change the font for every single headline one at a time. Instead, you just change the Headline style, in one simple action, and *all* the headlines take on the new look instantly. Make sense? You bet it does!

Better still, if you need to come up with another newsletter next month, your work will be much easier because you can use the same set of styles you used in this month's newsletter. No need to recreate all those styles! The consistency of styles applies not only throughout a single document; it actually carries over to other documents as well—be they monthly newsletters, chapters in a book, invoices, memos, or whatever.

Creating a Style

You create one style at a time, assigning each one a unique name. I'll give you the complete rundown below, including a lot of optional steps you might want to ignore until you get some practice with styles.

Assuming you're at a blank document window, or at a window that contains a document you'd like to create some styles for, here's what to do:

1. If you've already created a heading or paragraph that's styled the way you want the rest of them to be styled, move the cursor into the heading or paragraph.

2. Choose Layout ➤ Styles, press Alt+F8, or click the Styles button in the WordPerfect button bar (shown at left). You'll see the Style List dialog box shown in Figure 17.2. WordPerfect's built-in system styles and any styles that you've added to the current library may also appear in the list. (Don't worry if your list doesn't look like the example shown.)

3. If you want to choose which styles appear in the Style List, and specify where style changes will be saved, choose Options ➤ Setup, select the options you want from the Setup dialog box (Figure 17.3), then choose OK.

Here's a quick rundown of options in the Setup dialog box:

- *Display Styles From* options control which styles appear in the Style List. Styles from the Current Document and Default Template are usually selected automatically. If you also want

FIGURE 17.2

The Style List dialog box. Choose Layout ➤ Styles or press Alt+F8 to get here.

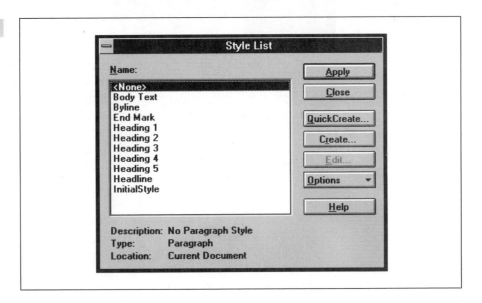

FIGURE 17.3

The Setup dialog box lets you choose which styles appear in the Style list and specify where style changes will be saved.

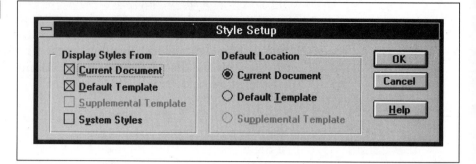

to include styles from your supplemental template, choose
Supplemental Template. To include built-in system styles, select
System Styles. (There's more about templates, supplemental
templates, and system styles later in this chapter.)

- *Default Location* options determine where WordPerfect saves
  your style changes. Normally you'll store style changes in the
  Current Document (the default setting). You can choose a
  different location if you wish.

N O T E

The options you choose in the Setup dialog box stay in
effect for all documents, until you change the Setup
options again or exit WordPerfect.

4. If you want to copy the basic formatting codes from where the
cursor is positioned into your new style, choose Quick Create.
(This is a handy alternative to filling in the style codes from
scratch.) When the Create Style dialog box appears, type in a
Style Name and Description, select a Style Type (either Paragraph
or Character), and choose OK. Your new style will appear in the
Style List (in alphabetical order). Skip to step 13.

5. If you want to create a style from scratch, choose C̲reate. Up pops the Styles Editor dialog box shown in Figure 17.4.

6. In the S̲tyle Name box, type a name for the style, up to 12 characters long, including blank spaces if you want them.

WARNING To prevent confusion, do not assign style names that are already used for other styles in other templates and documents.

7. In the D̲escription box, type a description for the style. (The description will appear near the bottom of the Style List dialog box when you highlight a style later.)

FIGURE 17.4

The Styles Editor dialog box

8. Choose one of the following style types from the Type pop-up list:

Character (paired)   Acts like a paired code in WordPerfect, formatting any number of characters between the [Char Style] codes. Use this style type to format selected text or text you're about to type, regardless of how long the text is or how many hard return ([HRt]) codes it contains. If in doubt, use a Character style rather than a Paragraph style. *Examples:* single special characters, formats of individual words or phrases, quotations containing hard returns.

Paragraph (paired)   As the name implies, this is useful for stylizing individual paragraphs, including single lines in an outline or list. When you activate a paragraph style, WordPerfect formats selected text or text in the paragraph that contains the cursor. *Examples:* headlines that word-wrap automatically, bylines, single-paragraph quotations.

Document (open)   This style has no "ending code." It's like a single code in WordPerfect, such as a code for line spacing, that once turned on, stays on until some other style (or code) takes over. *Examples:* the codes that set up the columns and font near the start of my sample newsletter (see Figure 17.1).

Table 17.1 summarizes the most important points about the three types of styles.

TIP   You can always change your mind about the style type later. If in doubt, try Character.

9. By default, pressing the ↵ (Enter) key turns on the same style again. If you want to control what the ↵ key does in a *Character* or *Paragraph* style, do one of the following:

- To have ↵ insert a hard return without turning off the style, deselect (clear) Enter Key Will Chain To. (This applies to Character styles only.)

TABLE 17.1: Paragraph, Character, and Document Styles Compared

TYPE	DESCRIPTION	START CODE	END CODE	USE TO FORMAT...
Paragraph (Paired)	Starts at cursor position, ends at the nearest hard return [HRt].	[Para Style]	[Para Style]	Short lines such as headings and bylines that end with a [HRt] code
Character (Paired)	Like paired codes, formats everything between the "On" and "Off" codes.	[Char Style]	[Char Style]	Any length of text, from a single character to many pages
Document (Open)	Applies from cursor to end of document, or next overriding code.	[Open Style]	(none)	Everything from the cursor down, such as a default font or columns

- To have ↵ move the cursor past a style and turn on another style, select Enter Key Will Chain To and choose <Same Style> from the drop-down list.

- To have ↵ move the cursor past the style, select Enter Key Will Chain To and choose <None> from the drop-down list.

- To have ↵ (for Paragraph styles) or ➤(for Character styles) move the cursor past the style, then turn on another style, select Enter Key Will Chain To and choose the style you want to turn on next from the drop-down list.

Table 17.2 summarizes how to turn off Character and Paragraph styles when typing new text. That table can help you decide how you want the ↵ key to behave. (You may want to ignore this option for now. You can always try it later, when you've experimented with styles a bit and are ready to fine-tune the role of the ↵ key for a particular style.)

TABLE 17.2:   How to Turn Off Character and Paragraph Styles When Typing New Text*

IF "ENTER KEY WILL CHAIN TO" IS...	FOR CHARACTER STYLE, DO THIS	FOR PARAGRAPH STYLE, DO THIS
Deselected (turned off)	Press →	Not allowed. Deselecting the Enter Key option changes the Paragraph style to a Character style.
<None>	Press ↵.	Press ↵.
<Same Style>	Press →	Choose Layout ➤ Styles (Alt+F8), then double-click <None>.
Another style in the list	Press ↵ to turn the style off and switch to the other style. Turn off the other style according to its "Enter Key Will Chain To" requirements.	Press *f*. to turn the style off and switch to the other style. Turn off the other style according to its "Enter Key Will Chain To" requirements.

* **NOTE:** You can't turn off Document styles, so those aren't included in the table.

10. If you want this style to activate some new format at its end, you can select Show 'Off Codes'. I'll talk about this option when I show you my sample styles later in this chapter.

11. Choose Contents when you're ready to define your format. Then select formatting features using the menus or the shortcut keys. As you make your selections, the appropriate codes are added to the Contents box. You can also do any of the following as you create or change your style:

- Type in any text or special characters (Ctrl+W) that you want WordPerfect to insert automatically.

- To delete a code, highlight it and press Delete, or drag the code out of the Contents box.

- To see how your style will look without the hidden codes, de-select <u>R</u>eveal Codes or press Alt+F3. When you want to see the codes, select <u>R</u>eveal Codes or press Alt+F3 again.

- To insert an existing style into the one you're creating (a style within a style, wow!), press Alt+F8, highlight a style in the Style List, and choose <u>A</u>pply. Now, any changes that you make to that other style will carry over into this style as well—not bad!

- To insert a page break [HPg] into the style, press Ctrl+⏎. To insert a hard return [HRt], press Shift+⏎. To insert a tab [Left Tab], press Ctrl+Tab.

12. When you're ready to return to the Style List dialog box, choose OK. Your new style will appear in the Style List (in alphabetical order).

13. If you want to return to your document, choose <u>C</u>lose. If you want to create another style, repeat steps 4–12.

Whew! Finally, you've created a style. Actually, it's a lot easier than these steps might make it seem, especially after you've done it a few times. Next, let's talk about how you can *use* the style you created.

Turning Styles On and Off

You can turn on (activate) any style in your Style List at any time. Just follow these steps:

1. First, decide what you want to apply the style to:

- To turn on a Paragraph or Document (Open) style for existing text, move the cursor to where you want to activate the style.

- To apply a style to a block of text, select that text.

- To apply the style to new text, position the cursor where you're about to start typing.

2. Choose <u>L</u>ayout ➤ <u>S</u>tyles, press Alt+F8, or click the Styles button in the WordPerfect button bar to open the Style List dialog box.

3. If you don't see the style you want, try choosing Options ➤ Setup. In the Setup dialog box, make sure you've selected (checked) the appropriate options under Display Styles From, then choose OK.

4. Double-click the name of the style you want to activate. Or, highlight the style name and choose Apply.

N O T E

Whenever you highlight a style in the Style List, its *Description* (if any), *Type* (Paragraph, Character, or Open), and *Location* (Current Document, Template, or Supplemental) will appear at the bottom of the dialog box.

That's all there is to it. You're returned to your document window, and the style codes (visible only in Reveal Codes, of course) are inserted into your document. The selected text, or the text you start typing, will be formatted according to the codes you defined in the style.

If you change your mind right away, you can choose Edit ➤ Undo or press Ctrl+Z to undo the change. If you change your mind later, after making other changes, just flip on Reveal Codes (Alt+F3) and delete the unwanted style code(s).

Turning a Style Off

There are several ways to turn off (deactivate) a style. Here are your options, assuming that you didn't change the Enter Key Will Chain To option when creating the style:

- If you selected text before choosing the style, the "style off" code will already be at the end of the selected text. Any text you type *between* those codes will have the new style. Any text outside those codes will not have that style.

- If you turned on a Character style before typing, just press → to move past the "style off" code and resume typing.

- If you turned on a Paragraph style without first selecting text, choose Layout ➤ Styles, press Alt+F8, or click the Styles button in the WordPerfect button bar. Highlight <None> and press ↵.

- If you activated an Open style, you really can't turn the style off, because it's a single code (like [Ln Spacing]). However, you can switch to a different style at any point in your document simply by choosing the new style you want.

You can also turn off a style by deleting its "style on" or "style off" code in Reveal Codes. Please refer to Table 17.2 for other ways to turn styles off.

Sample Newsletter Styles

In the next few sections, we'll take a quick look at the styles I used to format the newsletter back in Figure 17.1. You can use these styles as "food for thought" as you create styles of your own.

The Body Text Style

The columns and text of the articles in Figure 17.1 are defined in a Document (Open) style named Body Text. This Body Text style contains the codes listed under Contents, below:

Styles Editor

Edit   Insert   Layout   Tools   Graphics   Table

Style Name: Body Text   OK

Description: Columns and font for main body text   Cancel

Type: ☐ Enter Key will Chain to: Help

Document (open) ⬍   <Same Style> ⬍

Contents

Wid/Orph: On | Font Size: 12pt | Font: Times New Roman | Leading Adj | Just | Col Def | Col Bo

Here's how I filled in the Contents box:

- I chose Layout ➤ Page ➤ Keep Text Together ➤ Prevent The First And Last Lines Of Paragraphs From Being Separated Across Pages. This turned on widow/orphan protection.

- I chose Layout ➤ Font (F9) to define the typeface and size.

- I chose Layout ➤ Typesetting ➤ Word/Letterspacing ➤ Adjust Leading to reduce the leading between lines by −1p (see Chapter 28).

- I chose Layout ➤ Justification ➤ Left (Ctrl+L) to set left justification.

- I chose Layout ➤ Columns options to define two newspaper columns, with .35″ between columns and a "Column Between" separator line (Chapter 27).

The Headline Style

The article titles in Figure 17.1 are all formatted with a character style named Headline. That style contains the codes shown below:

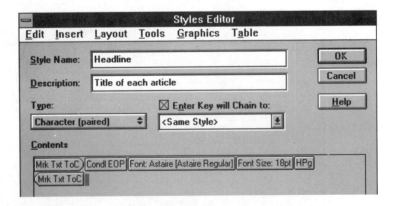

Before entering codes into the Contents box in the Styles Editor, I selected (checked) Show 'Off Codes'. This inserted the [HPg] codes you see in the example above. I used the Show 'Off Codes' check box here because this style uses a "Mark Text" code to identify the article title as a table of contents entry.

Here's what I did to enter codes into the <u>C</u>ontents box:

- I chose <u>L</u>ayout ➤ <u>P</u>age ➤ <u>K</u>eep Text Together ➤ <u>N</u>umber Of Lines To Keep Together, and I set the number of lines to 4. This keeps the article title, byline, and first two lines of article text together on the same column or page.

- I chose <u>L</u>ayout ➤ <u>F</u>ont (F9) and defined the typeface and size of the headlines.

- Next is the tricky part: I moved the cursor just before the very first code in the Contents box (Ctrl+Home, Ctrl+Home), then I pressed Shift+Ctrl+End to "select" the on and off codes. ([Select] appears as the first character in the Contents box.) Next I chose <u>T</u>ools ➤ Table Of <u>C</u>ontents and clicked the Mark <u>1</u> and <u>C</u>lose buttons in the feature bar at the bottom of the screen to mark the table of contents entry.

When I apply this style later, each headline will be between [Mrk Txt ToC] codes. So when I'm done writing, I can use the automatic referencing techniques described in Chapter 31 to have WordPerfect whip up a table of contents.

The Byline Style

The codes in my Byline style are shown below. These were added when I selected the Small <u>C</u>ap and <u>I</u>talic options from the Font dialog box (F9):

Notice that I didn't need to flip on the Show 'Off Codes' option here. In 99% of the cases, WordPerfect automatically puts the appropriate "off" code at the end of the style when it sees the "on" portion of a paired code. Similarly, when a style contains a [Font] code, WordPerfect "knows" to return to the original font at the end of the style. You don't need to put a specific font code at the bottom of the style.

About the only time you *do* need the Show 'Off Codes' option is when you're marking text within a style, as in the [Mrk Text ToC] example earlier. In that case, you must turn on Show 'Off Codes', then select all the codes, and mark the text.

You might also use the Show 'Off Codes' option when you want WordPerfect to do something special at the *end* of a style. For example, suppose you don't want WordPerfect to revert to the original font at the end of a style; instead, you want it to kick in some other font. Then you would turn on Show 'Off Codes' and put the second font code below the last [HPg] code. That activates the new font at the end of the style, instead of the beginning of the style.

The End Mark Style

The End Mark style is a Character style that contains just two codes: [Hd Flush Right] (Alt+F7) and the sun special character (Ctrl+W, character 5,6 from the Iconic symbols set). The codes are shown below:

Why bother to put these two simple codes in a style? Because if I decide to use some other character to end each article in place of the sun, I can simply change the End Mark style. No need to search for and replace the character throughout the entire document.

Changing an Existing Style

Let's say you've created some styles and applied them to your document. Now you want to change a style. That's easy:

1. Choose Layout ➤ Styles, press Alt+F8, or click the Styles button in the WordPerfect button bar.

2. If you don't see the style you want, choose Options ➤ Setup, check appropriate options under Display Styles From (see Figure 17.3), and choose OK.

3. In the Name list, highlight the style you want to change.

4. Choose Edit. The Styles Editor dialog box for the chosen style appears. You can change the name, description, type, codes, or any other characteristics of the style here.

TIP

For a really fast way to open the Styles Editor to edit a style that's applied to text in your document, turn on Reveal Codes and double-click the code for the style you want to change.

5. Choose OK (and Close, if necessary) to return to your document.

Any text in the document that's currently formatted with the style that you just modified will instantly reflect your changes. What a time-saver!

Deleting Styles

Your document's Style List might contain styles that you no longer need. Here's how to zap those unwanted styles:

1. Choose Layout ➤ Styles, press Alt+F8, or click the Styles button in the WordPerfect button bar.

2. If you want to specify which styles are deleted and where they're deleted from, choose Options ➤ Setup. You'll see the Style Setup dialog box shown in Figure 17.3. Then...

- Under *Display Styles From*, select (check) the styles you want to display in the Style List. If you want to delete styles from the current document only, deselect all the Display Styles From options, except C̲urrent Document.

- Under *Default Location*, choose the place where you'll be deleting the styles *from*. Normally, you'll choose C̲urrent Document, to delete styles from the current document only.

- Choose OK.

NOTE See "Displaying and Storing Styles," later in this chapter, for more information.

---

3. In the N̲ame list, highlight the style you want to delete and choose O̲ptions ➤ D̲elete. You can't delete system styles (though you can reset them to their default state, as I'll describe a bit later). You'll see this dialog box:

4. Now choose one of the following options, and then choose OK:

I̲nclude Codes   Deletes the style from the Style List, removes all style codes for this style from the current document, and deletes all hidden codes associated with the style. In other words, it cleans out the style name *and* its codes from the current document.

Leave Codes   Deletes the style from the Style List and deletes all style codes for this style from the current document. Use this option when you want to remove a style name from the style list, but leave its formatting codes and any text the Style contained in the current document.

When you're done deleting unwanted styles, choose <u>C</u>lose to return to the document window.

Technical Stuff about Styles

Any styles that you create generally are saved with the current document. In other words, when you close and save the document, all your styles are saved with it. You don't have to do anything special to save the styles, unless you want to make them available in *other* documents. In that case, you need to know some technical stuff about style libraries, templates, and supplemental templates.

NOTE   If you've had enough of styles for now, you might want to skip this section and try creating and using a few styles on your own. Then come back here to learn more.

About Templates

Templates are special boilerplate files (typically having the extension .WPT). These files set up the initial look of a new document and control which WordPerfect features are available to you. Templates can include anything that you'd normally add to a document, plus any collection of styles, macros (Chapter 18), abbreviations (Chapter 9), button bars, keyboards, and menus that you want. WordPerfect comes with many built-in templates. You can also create your own templates, if you wish (see Chapter 20).

Whenever you create a document, you're actually pulling the text, styles, and other features from a template file into a new document window. You can pick a specific template by choosing <u>F</u>ile ➤ <u>T</u>emplate (see Chapter 4).

If you don't pick a template, WordPerfect will use the default or standard template (C:\WPWIN60\TEMPLATE\STANDARD.WPT).

A *supplemental template* can be any secondary template that you use often, such as a standard company template stored on a network drive. If you specify a supplemental template file, you can use its styles and other features in your documents.

Choosing a Location for Your Templates

How does WordPerfect know where to find your default and supplemental templates? Easy. It looks at the file names and directories specified in File Preferences. To change the default location and names for templates, proceed as follows:

1. Choose File ➤ Preferences, double-click File, and choose Templates.

2. If you wish, you can specify the Default Directory and Supplemental Directory where templates are stored. You can also specify the name of your Default File and Supplemental File, as well as the Template File Extension that WordPerfect will use if you don't specify an extension when typing a template file name.

3. Choose OK, then Close to return to the document window.

About System Styles

WordPerfect uses *system styles* behind the scenes to control the appearance of graphics boxes, footnotes, and so forth. System styles are listed after you choose Options ➤ Setup, select System Styles, and choose OK in the Style List dialog box. They have names like BoxText, Caption, Comment, and so forth. Even though WordPerfect Corporation gave you all those system styles as a gift, you can still change them if you want. Use the same Edit command and techniques you use to edit your own styles. It's easiest to activate and edit system styles by going directly through the Style List dialog box.

Suppose you change a system style and later regret your change. Not a problem. Just highlight the style name in the Style List and choose Options ➤ Reset. WordPerfect will ask if you want to reset the style to its default state. If you choose Yes, the style will take on its original codes.

NOTE   Changes to system styles normally affect the current document only. You can, however, copy updated system styles to a template or save them in a style library for later use. You'll learn how later in this chapter.

About Style Libraries

A *style library* is a collection of styles stored on disk with its own file name (typically with the extension .STY). For example, I could save my sample collection of newsletter styles to a style library named NEWSLET.STY. Then, when creating future editions of the newsletter, I could just retrieve styles from that style library into the Style List of the new document I'm about to create. So there's no need for me to recreate the styles every time I write a new edition of the newsletter. I'll explain how to create a style library later in this chapter.

Displaying and Storing Styles

Normally, the Style List dialog box shows styles from your current document and template. Style changes are saved to the current document. You can change this by selecting options in the Setup dialog box shown in Figure 17.3.

To reach the Setup dialog box from the Style List (Alt+F8), choose Options ➤ Setup. Then...

- To choose which styles you want to display in the Style List, select (check) options under Display Styles From. Your options are Current Document, Default Template, Supplemental Template, and System Styles.

- To choose which file will be updated when you create, edit, or delete styles, select an option under Default Location. Your options are Current Document, Default Template, and Supplemental Template.

When you're ready to return to the Style List, choose OK.

Whenever you highlight a style name in the Style List, the Location information at the bottom of the dialog box will show where that style comes from. Be sure to look at the Location before you edit, copy, or delete a highlighted style.

Templates vs. Style Libraries

You might be wondering, "What's the difference between a template and a style library?" Good question. The most important differences are listed below:

- Style libraries typically contain styles only. Using the Options button in the Style List dialog box, you can retrieve styles from a style library into the current document, or save the current document's styles in a style library. You'll learn how in a moment.

- Templates can contain anything you'd put in a regular document, plus various elements that control WordPerfect's behavior. These "control" elements include menus, button bars, macros, abbreviations, keyboards, and styles. You can copy a style to the current template or to a supplemental template if you wish. You'll learn more about templates in Chapter 20.

If you've created a set of styles you often use for a certain type of document—such as an invoice, fax cover sheet, or newsletter—consider storing the styles in a template. Then, when you use the template to create a new document of that type, the styles will be available automatically.

Creating a Style Library

To create a style library, follow these easy steps:

1. If it isn't already open, open the document that contains the styles you want to save to a style library.

2. Go to the Style List dialog box (Alt+F8).

3. Choose <u>O</u>ptions ➤ <u>S</u>etup, and make sure <u>C</u>urrent Document and any other styles that you want to include in the library are selected (checked) under Display Styles From. Choose OK.

4. Choose <u>O</u>ptions ➤ Save <u>A</u>s. You'll see this dialog box:

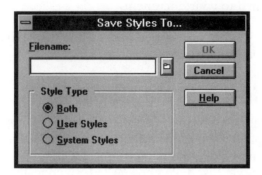

5. Type in a path (if necessary) and a file name (such as NEWSLET.STY) for your style library. If you prefer, you can use the button at the end of the <u>F</u>ilename text box to locate and fill in the file name and directory.

N O T E   It's a good idea to stick with a descriptive file name extension, such as .STY, when naming your style libraries. This makes the libraries easier to find later.

If you don't specify a directory, the styles will be saved in one of the directories listed below:

- Styles from your document or the default template are stored in the directory that contains the default template.
- Styles from the supplemental template are stored in the directory that contains the supplemental template.
- If you haven't specified a location for your default or supplemental template, WordPerfect will save the styles where the

WordPerfect application files are stored (typically C:\WPWIN60\).

6. Choose which set of styles you want to save. You can save Underline{U}ser Styles only (those you have defined), Underline{S}ystem Styles only (WordPerfect's built-in styles), or Underline{B}oth.

7. Choose OK to get back to the Style List, then choose Underline{C}lose to return to your document.

Your styles are now stored in the library style file under the file name and directory you specified.

Retrieving a Style Library

Style libraries from the template and supplemental template (if any) will be applied to your document so that they're ready for use every time you create a new document. You can view the styles in those libraries by going to the Style List dialog box (Alt+F8), choosing Options ➤ Setup, checking the Default Template and Supplemental Template options, and choosing OK. Once you see the styles you want in the Style List dialog box, you can use them as normal styles.

You can also retrieve styles from a style library that you saved earlier, or from any other WordPerfect document. Here's how:

1. Go to the Style List dialog box (Alt+F8).

2. Choose Options ➤ Retrieve to open the Retrieve Styles From dialog box. (Except for its title bar, this dialog box looks just like the Save Styles To dialog box shown earlier.)

3. Specify the name of the styles file or document that contains the styles you want. Or use the button at the end of the Filename text box to locate the file.

4. Choose which styles you want to retrieve, then choose OK. You can retrieve User Styles only (those you have defined), System Styles only (WordPerfect's built-in styles), or Both.

5. If any of the incoming styles has the same name as a style that's already in this library, you'll be prompted with

   Overwrite current styles?

6. If you choose No, only styles that don't have the same name as your current styles will be retrieved. If you choose Yes, all the styles from the other library will be retrieved, replacing any styles that have the same name.

7. The retrieved styles will appear in the Style List, along with any styles that were already there. If necessary, use Options ➤ Delete to delete any styles you don't want in this library. Then choose Close to return to the document window.

Copying Styles to a Template

Suppose you have some ideas for a great set of newsletter styles, and you want to store them in a template file. There are two ways to do this.

First, you can decide ahead of time where to store the styles. Follow these steps:

1. When you open the document, go to the Styles List dialog box (Alt+F8).

2. Choose Options ➤ Setup, and select Default Template (or Supplemental Template) as the default location for storing styles.

3. Create your styles as usual. Your new styles will be stored in the default template (or supplemental template) automatically.

To copy a specific style to the current document, default template, or supplemental template at any time, follow these steps instead:

1. Go to the Style List dialog box (Alt+F8).

2. Choose Options ➤ Setup. Select (check) the styles you want to display. Choose OK to return to the Style List.

3. Highlight the style you want to copy.

4. Choose Options ➤ Copy to open the Styles Copy dialog box.

5. Specify where you want to store the copied style. Your choices are Current Document, Template, or Supplemental Template.

6. Choose OK and respond to any prompts that appear.

Order of Precedence among Styles

If your document, templates, or WordPerfect system styles libraries contain duplicate style names, the style that is most specific to the current document will override the other styles. The precedence of styles is as follows: (1) styles in the document, (2) styles in the default template, (3) styles in the supplemental template, and (4) WordPerfect system styles.

For example, if the default template and supplemental template libraries each contain a style named Byline, then the style in the default template will take precedence. But if the document also contains a style named Byline, then *that* style will take precedence.

If you want a lower-precedence style to take effect, you can copy it from the lower-precedence library to a higher-precedence library. For instance, you could select and copy the Byline style from the template library to the document library. Just follow the Options ➤ Copy procedure described above. You could also delete the style from the higher-precedence library.

Styles are much easier to use than they are to explain. I hope this chapter has shed some light on the mysteries of styles, templates, libraries, and system styles. But experience is likely to be the best teacher when it comes to styles. (Don't forget, you can always press F1 for help or refer to your official WordPerfect documentation if you need more details.)

Now, on to another time-saver—macros!

CHAPTER

18

Saving Time with Macros

fast TRACK

To add a macro to the Tools ➤ Macro menu   **557**

choose the Menu button in the Record Macro, Play Macro, or Edit Macro dialog box. Click in the Available Macros list where you want the macro name to appear and choose Insert. If you wish, select the Location of the macro. Type the name of the macro you want to add in the Name text box, or highlight its name in the Macros In Template list. Choose Select.

To delete a macro from the template file or the hard disk   **562**

choose Tools ➤ Macro ➤ Edit or click the Macro Edit button in the Macros button bar. If you wish, select the Location of the macro. Type the macro name in the Name text box or highlight its name in the Macros In Template list. Choose Delete and Yes, then choose Cancel.

To edit an existing macro   **566**

choose Tools ➤ Macro ➤ Edit or click the Macro Edit button in the Macros button bar. If you wish, select the Location of the macro. Type the macro name in the Name text box, or highlight its name in the Macros In Template list. Choose Edit.

IF YOU'RE tired of choosing the same old sets of menu options or typing the same text over and over, then macros are for you. Macros automate mundane, repetitive jobs by letting you record all the keystrokes you need to do those tasks. Once they're recorded, you can just "play back" those keystrokes with a few mouse clicks or key-presses.

What Is a Macro?

In a sense, a *macro* is just a "large keystroke." By executing a single macro, you can perform the equivalent of many keystrokes or selections with your mouse.

For example, instead of retyping your company name and address over and over again in different documents, you can record the necessary keystrokes in a macro. Then, whenever you need to type your company name and address, you can just run the macro, which takes about 2 seconds flat.

Turning on the Macros Button Bar

The Macros button bar (shown below) makes using macros a breeze. To display this button bar, make sure a button bar is visible (View ➤ Button Bar). Now, right-click the mouse on the button bar and choose Macros from the QuickMenu that appears.

Recording a Macro

Recording a macro is easy. Here are the steps:

1. Choose <u>T</u>ools ➤ <u>M</u>acro ➤ <u>R</u>ecord, press Ctrl+F10, or click the Macro Record button on the Macros button bar. You'll see the Record Macro dialog box:

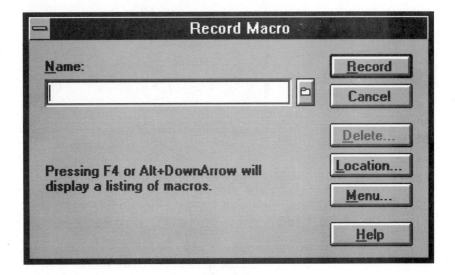

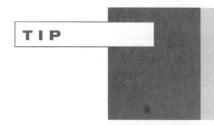
T I P

Many dialog boxes for managing macros have Delete, Location, Menu, and Help buttons. Delete lets you delete a macro. Location lets you choose the location of a macro. Menu lets you add macros to the Tools ➤ Macro menu. Help provides helpful information.

2. WordPerfect normally stores macros in a file on disk. To choose a different location, click the Location button. You'll see this dialog box:

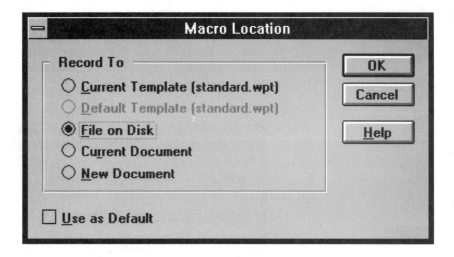

Your options are described just below. When you're done selecting options, choose OK to return to the Record Macro dialog box.

Current Template   Stores macro commands in the template you chose when you created the file. This is either the default template specified in File Preferences (typically C:\WPWIN60\TEMPLATE\STANDARD.WPT) or whatever template you selected after choosing File ➤ Template (see Chapter 4).

Default Template   Stores macro commands in the default template specified in File Preferences.

NOTE To change the default template directory location or name, choose File ➤ Preferences, double-click File, and select Templates.

File on Disk   Stores macro commands in a file on disk.

Current Document   Stores macro commands in the document you're editing now. You can use this option to add macro commands to a macro that you're editing (as discussed later).

New Document   Stores macro commands in a new document window.

Use as Default   Uses the selected location as the default for future macro record, play, and edit operations (available for the first three options only).

NOTE Macros stored in disk files can be run from *any* WordPerfect document. Macros stored in templates can be run only from documents that use those templates. You can, however, copy macros from one template to another (see Chapter 20). You can also save a template macro to a disk file (see "Saving and Compiling an Edited Macro" later in this chapter).

3. Choose a name for your macro, if necessary. How, or whether, you enter a name depends on your choices in step 2:

- If you're storing the macro in a File On Disk, enter a valid DOS file name into the Name text box (one to eight characters long, no spaces or punctuation). Or, to create a Ctrl+Shift+*key* macro, press Ctrl and Shift plus a letter (for example, press Ctrl+Shift+A). WordPerfect uses the default file extension .WCM for macros stored on disk, so you don't need to include a file extension.

- If you're storing the macro in a template, type any name you wish into the <u>N</u>ame text box. You can enter up to 31 characters, including blank spaces.

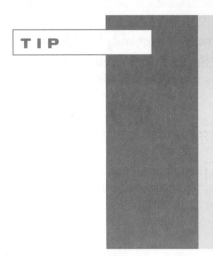

TIP

Ctrl+Shift+*key* macros offer the quickest way to run your macro later. They're stored on disk with names like CTRLSFTA.WCM (for the macro named by pressing Ctrl+Shift+A). If WordPerfect isn't already using a Ctrl+*key* combination as a shortcut for one of its own commands, you can assign one of your own. As long as you're using the standard <WPWin 6.0 Keyboard> keyboard, you can assign a key combination—for example, Ctrl+Y—as a macro name. To play back this macro, which will be stored on disk as CTRLY.WCM, you'd simply press Ctrl+Y. (See Chapter 20 for more about choosing a keyboard.)

- If you chose Cu<u>r</u>rent Document or <u>N</u>ew Document, you can't enter a file name now. However, you *will* need to save the file when you're done recording the macro (see step 8).

4. Choose <u>R</u>ecord.

5. If a macro with the name you've entered already exists, WordPerfect will ask if you want to replace it. Choose <u>Y</u>es to replace the existing macro, or <u>N</u>o to bail out and return to step 2.

6. Type the keystrokes you want to record, including any menu choices and keyboard shortcuts. The status bar will display the message "Macro Record" as a reminder that you're recording. Here are some things to keep in mind:

   - Macros record all text you type into the document, and most editing and cursor-movement keys you press (like ↵, ↓, ↑, and Backspace).

   - Macros record most commands that you can choose via the mouse or keyboard.

   - You can use your mouse to choose commands and use dialog boxes, but you *can't* use it to position the cursor or select text. To select text, use Shift+arrow keys, Edit ➤ Select, and other techniques discussed in Chapter 3.

7. When you're done recording, choose Tools ➤ Macro ➤ Record, press Ctrl+F10, or click the Macro Record button in the Macros button bar again. The "Macro Record" message will disappear from the status bar.

8. If you selected Current Document or New Document in step 2, you'll see a bunch of gobbledygook in the document window. (This computer flotsam is an assortment of macro programming commands, discussed later.) Choose Save & Compile from the Macro Edit feature bar. Type a name in the Name text box and choose Save. Finally, click the Close button on the feature bar.

Your keystrokes are recorded and stored in the location you specified in steps 2 and 3 (or 8) above.

Canceling Recording

Suppose you start recording a series of keystrokes or command selections, then make a mistake and want to start all over. You can't just press Escape, since WordPerfect would record that keystroke like any other.

Instead, you must stop recording keystrokes as though the macro were finished (press Ctrl+F10). Then start recording the macro from scratch, using the same macro name. WordPerfect will ask for permission before overwriting the faulty macro you just recorded. In this case, it's OK to overwrite the existing macro, so just choose Yes to proceed.

NOTE

As an alternative to starting over from scratch when you make mistakes, you can finish recording the macro (Ctrl+F10). Then you can open the macro, correct the mistakes, and save your changes. The only catch to this approach is that you'll need to know something about macro programming commands and programming in general. See "For Programmers and Power Users" later in this chapter.

Running a Macro

Running a macro is even easier than creating one:

1. If your macro works on a particular section of text (such as changing some text to uppercase or italicizing a word), move the cursor to where you want the macro to begin its action or select the text it will act on.

N O T E   The terms *run, invoke,* and *execute* all mean the same thing: to "play back" the keystrokes recorded in the macro.

2. If the macro is a Ctrl+Shift+*key* macro, press the Ctrl+Shift+*key* combination (for example, Ctrl+Shift+A) and you're done.

3. If the macro isn't a Ctrl+Shift+*key* macro, choose Tools ➤ Macro ➤ Play, press Alt+F10, or click the Macro Play button in the Macros button bar. You'll see the Play Macro dialog box:

Play Macro

Name:

[   ] [▢]   **Play**

    Cancel

    Delete...

Pressing F4 or Alt+DownArrow will   **Location...**
display a listing of macros.
    Menu...

    Help

4. If you want to choose the location where the macro is stored, click the Location button, select a location (Current Template, Default Template, or File On Disk), and choose OK.

5. Specify the macro name as follows:

   • If you selected File On Disk, type the macro name in the Name text box, or use the file folder button at the end of the text box to locate the macro.

   • If your macro is stored in a template, highlight or click on the macro name in the Macros In Template list.

N O T E The file folder button is available throughout WordPerfect to help you locate and manage files. (You can also press F4 or Alt+↓.) If you're an old Windows hand, you'll quickly figure out how to use this button. If you're new to Windows, you can look to Chapter 20 for help.

6. Choose Play.

WordPerfect replays all the keys you recorded when you defined the macro, then returns you to the document window. What you'll see in the document window are the *results* of the keys being played back, not the actual keystrokes.

N O T E You can also run a macro from the button bar or the Tools ➤ Macro menu, as I'll explain in a moment.

Stopping a Macro

If you've started a macro and want to stop it dead in its tracks (perhaps because you've run the wrong macro, or you didn't position the cursor properly before running it), press the Esc key (you'll have to be fast!). This will leave you at whatever point the macro was when you canceled it—

maybe in the document window, or perhaps at a dialog box or prompt. Since the macro will probably play back some keystrokes before the cancellation takes effect, you should look at the document and fix any unwanted changes that the macro made.

Let's Try It Out!

To get started with macros, try creating an easy one that transposes two characters. (This macro can be especially helpful if you consistently put your periods inside your parentheses, and discover later that many of your sentences should have the period outside the parentheses.) In any document window, type a sentence with some transposed letters, like this:

Where si hte cat?

Now, move the cursor between the *s* and the *i*, then do the following:

1. Start recording the macro (press Ctrl+F10 or click the Macro Record button in the Macros button bar).

2. Type **switch** to name the macro. (I'm assuming that you're storing macros in a file on disk.)

3. Choose Record. (If WordPerfect claims that there's already a macro named Switch, you may want to try a different name. In that case, choose No and type a different name.)

4. Now record your actions. First press the Del key to delete the second character.

5. Press ← once to move the cursor to the left of the letter *s*.

6. Choose Edit ➤ Undelete and then choose Restore when prompted.

7. Stop recording (press Ctrl+F10 or click the Macro Record button in the Macros button bar).

Now that you've recorded the keystrokes to transpose two characters, you can run that macro. For example, move the cursor between the *h* and the *t* in *hte*. Press Alt+F10 or click the Macro Play button in the Macros button bar, type the macro name (**switch**, in this example), then choose Play.

Bingo—the macro transposes the characters instantly. This macro will work with any pair of characters. Try it!

T I P   WordPerfect comes with several macros that you can use right away (see Table 18.1 at the end of the chapter). These macros can also serve as food for thought when you're trying to come up with ideas for your own macros.

Details, Options, and Alternatives

You now know about 95% of what most hot-shot macro mavens know. But, as with most WordPerfect features, there are plenty of additional details, options, and alternatives to ponder and play around with.

Recording a Temporary Macro

Some macros are handy for typing repetitive information in the current document, but they're not worth keeping for posterity. For this, you can create an *unnamed*, temporary macro that lasts through the current Word-Perfect session only. Any new temporary macro that you record will completely overwrite the old one. Temporary macros are lost when you exit WordPerfect.

To record a temporary macro, start as usual (for example, press Ctrl+F10). Now choose Record, record your keystrokes, then stop recording (press Ctrl+F10). To play back the macro, press Alt+F10 or click the Macro Play button in the Macros button bar, then choose Play.

Adding Macros to the Button Bar

Button bars (Chapter 4) offer some of the best shortcuts imaginable. You can even assign a macro to a button. Once you've done that, you simply click the button and the macro runs.

To add a button that runs a macro, follow these steps :

1. Choose File ➤ Preferences and double-click Button Bar, or right-click the current button bar (if it's visible) and choose Preferences from the QuickMenu. The Button Bar Preferences dialog box will open.

2. Now, do one of the following:

   - To create a new button bar, choose Create. In the New Button Bar Name text box, type a name for your button bar—up to 31 characters, including spaces. (If you wish, choose Template, select a template, and choose OK.) Choose OK to open the Button Bar Editor.

   - To change an existing button bar, highlight the button bar you want to change in the Available Button Bars list and choose Edit to open the Button Bar Editor.

3. Choose Play A Macro.

4. Choose Add Macro to open the Select Macro dialog box.

5. If necessary, specify the location of your macro. Choose Location, select a location (Current Template, Default Template, or File On Disk), then choose OK.

6. If the location is a file on disk, type the file name into the Name text box or use the button at the end of the text box (or press F4) to locate the file. If the location is a template, highlight the macro you want. Choose Select.

7. If you want, you can drag the new button to another spot in the button bar. If you need to delete a button from the button bar, drag the button below the button bar (the button will change to a trashcan icon), then release the mouse button.

8. Repeat steps 4–7 for each button you want to add. When you're done, choose OK to return to the Button Bar Preferences dialog box.

9. If you want to select the button bar you just created or changed, highlight it in the Available Button Bars list and choose Select. If you don't want to switch button bars now, choose Close. You'll be returned to the document window.

Adding Macros to the Tools ➤ Macro Menu

If you've perused the Tools ➤ Macro menu, you know that it's pretty short. Wouldn't it be nice to add your favorite macros to it? That's easy when you follow the steps below:

1. Go to the Play Macro, Record Macro, or Edit Macro dialog box (any one will work). For example, choose Tools ➤ Macro ➤ Edit or click the Macro Edit button on the Macros button bar.

2. Choose Menu to open the Assign Macro To Menu dialog box:

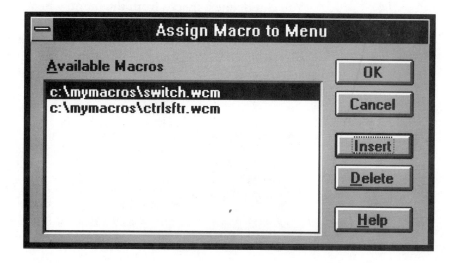

3. Highlight the place where you want the macro name to appear in the menu, then choose Insert. You'll see the Select Macro dialog box.

4. If necessary, choose Location, select the location where your macro is stored (Current Template, Default Template, or File On Disk), then choose OK.

5. If the location is a file on disk, type the file name into the Name text box or use the button at the end of the text box (or press F4) to locate the file. If the location is a template, highlight the macro you want. Choose Select. You'll be returned to the Assign Macro To Menu dialog box.

6. You can repeat steps 3–5 to add up to nine items. (Although the Tools ➤ Macro menu has room for up to ten macro entries, numbered 1 through 0, WordPerfect reserves one spot for the macro that you ran most recently. You're allowed to enter only nine items on your own.)

7. Choose OK then Cancel to return to the document window.

When you're ready to run your macro from the menu, choose Tools ➤ Macro. Type the number of the macro you want, or click the macro name. Your macro will run (just you *try* to catch it!).

As mentioned above, the macro menu can hold up to ten macro names. You can delete a macro from the menu whenever you're using the Assign Macro To Menu dialog box. To open the dialog box, do steps 1 and 2 above.) Simply highlight the macro name that you want to delete and choose Delete. (Deleting a name from the menu has no effect on the stored macro. See "Deleting a Macro Permanently," below, for more about deleting macros permanently.)

NOTE   You can also add macros to any other menus you want. To get started, choose File ➤ Preferences and double-click Menu Bar. From there, the steps are similar to adding buttons that play macros to a button bar. See Chapter 4 and the online help for more information.

Repeating a Macro

You can use the Repeat feature to play a macro as many times as you wish. Just choose Edit ➤ Repeat, type in the number of times you want to run the macro, and choose OK. Now run the macro as usual.

Remember that it may not always make sense to run a macro repeatedly. For instance, the SWITCH macro is meant to be run only once. Running it repeatedly will just flip two characters back and forth (though you *could* run SWITCH a bunch of times if you want to create movement or simple animation in your document).

Running a Macro when You Start WordPerfect

If you'd like to run a macro when you start Windows and WordPerfect for Windows, type the following command at the DOS prompt:

WIN WPWIN /m-*macroname*

In place of *macroname*, type the full path name of the macro you want to run (you can omit the .WCM extension). The macro must be stored in a disk file. For example, type

win wpwin /m-c:\mymacros\startup

TIP   Instead of typing the commands above, you can put them into a DOS batch program, then just run the batch program. Please see your DOS documentation for information about creating and running batch programs.

You can also run a macro when you start WordPerfect from Windows. To set this up, return to the Program Manager and click on the WPWin 6 icon in the WPWin 6 group window. Choose <u>F</u>ile ➤ <u>P</u>roperties from the Program Manager menus. The command in the <u>C</u>ommand Line text box starts WordPerfect for Windows (typically the command line starts with **c:\wpwin60\wpwin.exe**). Move the cursor to the *end* of the command line, press the spacebar, and type the following:

/m-*macroname*

Again, *macroname* is the path and file name of the macro you want to run whenever you double-click the WPWin 6 icon. After changing the command line, choose OK. The next time you start WordPerfect, your macro will run automatically.

Making a Macro Wait for You

Sometimes you might not want your macro to go through *all* the steps in a procedure from start to finish. Instead, you might want it to pause and wait for you to do something. For example, you might want the macro to get you to the Font dialog box, and then wait for you to pick a font. When you're done selecting a font, you might want the macro to proceed and type some text, or go on to some other dialog box.

Waiting at a Dialog Box

To make a macro pause at a dialog box, you need to tell it which dialog box to pause at while you're recording the macro. To do so, record the macro normally, but when you get to the dialog box you want the macro to pause at, select the check box in the upper-right corner of the dialog box, as in the example below:

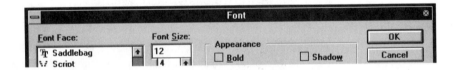

Note that this check box is visible *only* if you're recording a macro. (A few dialog boxes don't offer the check box at all.) You can then keep recording keystrokes and commands, go to other dialog boxes, select their check boxes to pause, and so on. When you're done and you've returned to the document window, stop recording the macro (Ctrl+F10).

When you play back the macro, it will stop at every dialog box you checked along the way. Make your selections in each dialog box, then choose OK or Close to leave the dialog box. The macro will continue with any additional actions you recorded.

Waiting for Text

You might want a macro to pause while it's typing some text, to give you time to type in some text of your own. For example, you might want a macro to type most of the text in a late payment reminder but pause and let you type in the exact amount owed.

Here's how to make a macro wait while you type in text:

1. Record the macro normally, and start typing whatever text you want the macro to type. (You can, of course, make any menu selections along the way, pause at dialog boxes, etc.)

2. When you get to a place where you want the macro to wait for you to type something, choose Tools ➤ Macro ➤ Pause or click the Pause button in the Macros button bar. The "Macro Record" message in the status line at the bottom of the screen will change to "Record Pause." (Now you can do anything you want in Word-Perfect without recording the keystrokes.)

3. When you're ready to record again, choose Tools ➤ Macro ➤ Pause or click the Pause button once more. The message in the status bar will change back to "Macro Record." (Behind the scenes, WordPerfect will insert a "PauseKey" macro language command into the macro.)

4. Type whatever remaining text you want the macro to type, or choose menu commands as usual.

5. When you're done, stop recording the macro (Ctrl+F10).

When you play back the macro, it will run up until it encounters the PauseKey command. At that point, you can type anything you want. When you're done typing, press ↵. The macro will pick up wherever it left off.

Where Macros Are Stored

Initially, macros that you save to a file are stored in the directory with the WordPerfect macros files (typically, C:\WPWIN60\MACROS). To avoid cluttering up that directory, you might want to store all your macro files in a separate directory, such as C:\WPWIN60\MYMACROS.

To tell WordPerfect where to store macros, choose File ➤ Preferences, double-click File, and select Macros. Then specify a Default Directory, a Supplemental Directory, or both. When you're done, choose OK then Close.

Here's how the directories work:

- If you leave the default directory blank, disk file macros will be stored in the supplemental directory.

- If you leave the supplemental directory blank, disk file macros will be stored in the default directory.

- If you leave both directories blank, disk file macros will be stored in the current directory.

If you change the location of your macro files, remember you can use the Windows File Manager or DOS to move all those existing .WCM files to the new directory.

Handy Macros that Come with WordPerfect

WordPerfect comes with many handy macros that are ready to run. You can run any of them with the Tools ➤ Macro ➤ Play commands, Alt+F10, or the Macro Play button in the Macros button bar. Table 18.1 at the end of this chapter lists the names of several of the supplied macros and describes them briefly.

Because WordPerfect Corporation often ships different macros with different interim releases of their products, the macros listed in Table 18.1 may be different from the ones available on your computer.

Deleting a Macro Permanently

Once a macro has outlived its usefulness, you can delete it permanently. Here's how:

1. Go to the Play Macro, Record Macro, or Edit Macro dialog box (any one will work). For example, choose Tools ➤ Macros ➤ Edit or click the Edit Macro button in the Macros button bar.

2. Choose Location, select the location where your macro is stored (Current Template, Default Template, or File On Disk), and choose OK.

3. If the macro is stored on disk, type the macro name or use the button at the end of the Name text box (or press F4) to locate the macro. If the macro is stored in a template, highlight the macro you want to delete.

4. Choose Delete. When asked to confirm the deletion, choose Yes.

5. Choose Cancel.

For Programmers and Power Users

For the rest of this chapter, I'm going to don my pointy programmer's hat and talk shop with the pros. If you're not a programmer or power user, feel free to skip the rest of this chapter. Everything you need to know about recording and playing back macros has already been covered. If you'd like to get a pointy programmer's hat of your own, look to the sources mentioned at the end of this chapter.

Converting Macros from WordPerfect 5.x

If you created macros with WordPerfect 5.1 or 5.2 for Windows or WordPerfect 6 for DOS, you may be able to convert them to run under WordPerfect 6 for Windows. Chances are, however, that you'll encounter a few bumps along the way because the macro programming languages in each version of WordPerfect are different.

N O T E   You can't directly convert WordPerfect 5.x for DOS macros to run under WordPerfect 6 for Windows. But if you have WordPerfect 6 for DOS and you're ambitious, you may be able to use the *MCV* program to convert the WordPerfect 5.x macros to WordPerfect 6 for DOS. Then you can follow the steps below to convert the converted macros to WordPerfect 6 for Windows. Whew!

Here's how to convert a macro:

1. Choose Tools ➤ Macro ➤ Edit, or click the Macro Edit button in the Macros button bar. You'll see the Edit Macro dialog box.

2. Choose Location, select File On Disk, and choose OK.

3. In the Name text box, type the full directory path and file name (including the file extension) of the macro you want to convert

(for example, **c:\wpwin\mymacros\bullet.wcm**). Or, use the button at the end of the dialog box to locate the macro.

4. Choose <u>E</u>dit. You may see a "Conversion in Progress" message. In a moment the macro programming commands will appear on your screen. (Don't worry about their meaning right now.)

5. Choose Save <u>A</u>s from the Macro Edit feature bar.

6. Type a valid DOS file name (one to eight characters, no spaces, punctuation, or extension) and choose <u>S</u>ave.

WARNING Be careful not to overwrite any existing macro file. If WordPerfect asks if you want to replace an existing file, choose <u>N</u>o, enter a different name, and choose Save <u>A</u>s again.

The conversion program will do its darndest to make the conversion and compile the macro so that you can run it later. If you're converting garden-variety recorded-keystroke macros, you might not have any problems. More sophisticated macros may not be so easy to convert.

If the macro converted without a hitch, you can click the <u>C</u>lose button in the Macro Edit feature bar to close the macro editing window. If any commands didn't convert perfectly, you'll see various error message dialog boxes. Figure 18.1 shows a typical example (friendly, isn't it?).

FIGURE 18.1

A typical error message that results when you try to convert a macro from an older version of WordPerfect for Windows to WordPerfect 6 for Windows.

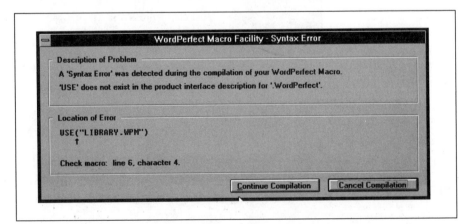

WordPerfect Macro Facility - Syntax Error

Description of Problem
A 'Syntax Error' was detected during the compilation of your WordPerfect Macro.
'USE' does not exist in the product interface description for '.WordPerfect'.

Location of Error
USE("LIBRARY.WPM")
    ↑

Check macro: line 6, character 4.

[Continue Compilation] [Cancel Compilation]

Write down the description of the problem and the location of the error (note especially the information at the bottom of the dialog box about which macro line and character to check). Then click one of the buttons listed below (as appropriate):

OK   Clears the message from the screen and continues.

Continue Compilation   Clears the message from the screen and continues compiling. (You'll learn about compilation later in this chapter.)

Cancel Compilation   Clears the message from the screen and quits trying to compile the macro.

Now you'll need to edit the problem commands to conform to the WordPerfect 6 for Windows macro language. Then compile and save your changes (until everything compiles successfully), and close the macro-editing window. (I'll explain editing, compiling, and saving changes in a moment.) If you haven't a clue about how to fix the macro right now, click the Close button in the Macro Edit feature bar. Just remember that you won't be able to run the macro until you fix the compilation errors.

What the Macro Really Records

When you record a macro in WordPerfect for Windows, you're actually recording *completed events*. That is, WordPerfect only records *completed* actions, such as choosing Layout ➤ Line ➤ Spacing, typing a number, and choosing OK. That series of menu choices would be recorded and put in the macro as a command that looks like this (if you set double spacing):

LineSpacing(2.0)

If you whip through a bunch of menus and dialog boxes without making any selections (or clicking the pause check box described earlier), the macro records nothing.

Opening and Editing a Macro

Macros are stored in standard WordPerfect documents. This makes them easy to edit, format, and print. (WordPerfect ignores formatting commands in macros, so feel free to make them pretty.)

Here's how to open any macro, whether it's one you recorded or one that WordPerfect Corporation has supplied:

1. Choose Tools ➤ Macro ➤ Edit, or click the Macro Edit button in the Macros button bar.

2. Choose Location, select the location where your macro is stored (Current Template, Default Template, or File On Disk), and choose OK.

3. If the location is a file on disk, type the file name into the Name text box or use the button at the end of the text box (or press F4) to locate the file. If the location is a template, highlight the macro you want to edit. Then choose Edit.

Figure 18.2 shows how the document window might look after you open the Switch macro presented earlier in this chapter. Notice the Macro Edit feature bar just below the button bar in the figure.

FIGURE 18.2

A macro opened in a document window, ready for editing

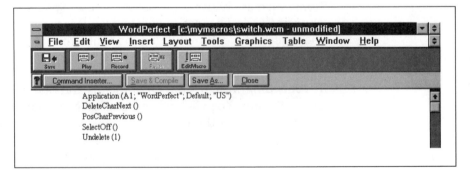

TIP

As shown in Figure 18.1, the macro compiler will reference line numbers when it detects compilation errors in your macro. To add line numbers to your macro, open the macro as described above and press Ctrl+Home to move to the top. Choose Layout ➤ Line ➤ Numbering ➤ Turn Line Numbering On, then choose OK. I'll discuss the macro compiler later in this chapter.

What's inside a Macro?

A WordPerfect macro generally consists of any combination of tokens, keystrokes, comments, and programming commands.

Tokens

A *token* represents an action. For example, FontDlg is a token that says, "Go to the Font dialog box." Tokens are usually shown in mixed case (for example, FontDlg and PrintDlg).

Keystrokes

When you're recording a macro, your *keystrokes* are recorded literally. Text that you type is placed in a Type ({"..."}) command. Other keys that you press are recorded as commands. For example, if you record the keystrokes to type *My dog has fleed* followed by a press of the ↵ key, the macro would record this:

```
Type({"My dog has fleed."})
HardReturn()
```

Comments

Comments are messages and notes typed by programmers into a macro. When WordPerfect *compiles* the macro (which I'll discuss later), it simply ignores the comments because they're for "human consumption only." Any line that starts with // in a macro is a comment.

For example, I could add comments to describe the SWITCH macro and explain what it's doing, like this:

```
┌─────────────────────────── e:\...\switch.wcm ───────────────── ▼ ▲ ┐
│ [?] [ Command Inserter... ] [ Save & Compile ] [ Save As... ] [ Close ]    │
│ Application (A1; "WordPerfect"; Default; "US")                          ▲ │
│ //      Switches two characters. To use it, position the cursor between   │
│ //      the characters you want to transpose, then run the macro normally.│
│ DeleteCharNext ()        //     Delete the character to the right of the cursor. │
│ PosCharPrevious ()       //     Move the cursor to the previous character.    ▼ │
│ SelectOff ()             //     Make sure Select mode is turned off.     ⬚ │
│ Undelete (1)             //     Undelete the most recent deletion.       ⬚ │
│ [◄]            [   ]                                                [►] □ │
└───────────────────────────────────────────────────────────────────────┘
```

Programming Commands

Many macros contain *programming commands*, which control how the macro executes. For example, the IF...ENDIF programming commands below allow commands between IF and ENDIF to execute if a certain *condition* is true:

IF(*condition*)
　　　　do these commands if the condition is true
ENDIF

The convention is to show programming commands in all uppercase, for example IF, ELSE, ENDIF, RETURN.

Adding Programming Commands to a Macro

To add a programming command to a macro, position the cursor where you want to insert the command. (If necessary, press ↵ to start the command on a new line.) Then, either type the command you want, using proper syntax (as in any programming language), or use the Command Inserter (shown below) to insert the command.

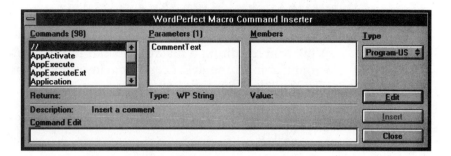

To use the Command Inserter, click the Command Inserter button in the Macro Edit feature bar. You'll be taken to the WordPerfect Macro Command Inserter dialog box. If necessary, choose the general Type of command you want, and then highlight a specific command in the Commands list. If you'd like to edit the command before inserting it into your macro, choose Edit to copy the command into the Command Edit text box, then edit the command as needed (be sure to follow the proper rules for the command you selected). When you're ready to put the completed command into your macro file, choose Insert. Choose Close to return to the macro editing window.

NOTE

WordPerfect comes with an online macros manual. To open it, choose Help ➤ Macros. Among other things, this manual describes each command and shows how to use it in a swatch of programming code. See "Learning More About Macro Programming" near the end of the chapter for details.

Adding Recorded Keystrokes to a Macro

While you're editing a macro, you can insert recorded text and tokens without going through the command inserter or typing commands manually. You'll love this time-saver:

1. Open the macro as described under "Opening and Editing a Macro."

2. Put the cursor wherever you want to insert some recorded keystrokes or tokens.

3. Choose Tools ➤ Macro ➤ Record, press Ctrl+F10, or click the Macro Record button in the Macros button bar.

4. Choose Location, select Current Document, and choose OK.

5. Perform whatever action(s) you want to record.

6. When you're done recording, press Ctrl+F10 again. The tokens and/or keystrokes required to perform your actions later are inserted into the macro at the cursor position.

N O T E   Some macro programming language commands can be added to a macro *only* by typing them in or by using the Command Inserter—they can't be recorded. Check the documentation in the online macros manual to see when a particular macro command is not recordable.

Saving and Compiling an Edited Macro

When you've finished editing a macro, you can use any of the following methods to save and compile it (compiling is discussed below):

- **To close the macro-editing window,** click the Close button in the Macro Edit feature bar, then choose Yes if you're prompted to save your changes. WordPerfect will compile the macro (if you've changed it since saving it last) and close the macro-editing window and feature bar.

- **To save, compile, and stay in the macro-editing window,** click the Save & Compile button in the Macro Edit feature bar. WordPerfect will save your latest changes and compile the macro.

- **To save and compile your changes in a new macro,** click the Save As button in the Macro Edit feature bar. You can select a different Location (if you wish), then specify a name for your macro and choose Save. You'll remain in the macro-editing window, but you'll now be editing the new macro.

T I P

To copy a template macro to a disk file, edit the template macro as described earlier in the chapter. When the macro-editing screen appears, click the Save As button on the Macro Edit feature bar, choose Location ➤ File On Disk, and choose OK. Finally, type a file name and choose Save.

About Macro Compilation

Whenever you create or edit a macro, WordPerfect *compiles* it once before running it. The macro also is compiled when you click the Save & Compile, Save As, or Close buttons in the Macro Edit feature bar.

During compilation, WordPerfect checks the macro for obvious errors and converts the tokens and programming commands to a language that the computer can interpret quickly. The compiled commands are stored in the .WCM file, along with the source code that you created. (The compiled commands are invisible to mere humans.)

Compilation Errors

Whenever you add or edit macro commands, it's possible that you'll make a mistake. (Unless you're superhuman, you can just about count on it.) If it's a syntax error or some other error that WordPerfect can detect while it's compiling the macro, you'll see a warning box like the one shown back in Figure 18.1. In that case, you can choose Continue Compilation to keep on going or Cancel Compilation to stop compilation immediately. (Don't bother trying to run the macro if it has compilation errors. You'll just get the same error message again until you either fix the problem or throw your computer into the nearest, darkest well.)

Runtime Errors

Sometimes a macro will compile correctly, but you'll get a *runtime error* when you run it. A runtime error often indicates that the problem isn't with the macro, but with the context you're trying to run it in. For example, if the macro is supposed to select a particular font, but you've selected a printer that doesn't have that font, the macro can't do its job. When you get a runtime error, don't go looking inside the macro right away. Instead, think about the job that the macro is supposed to do. For instance, you might need to select the appropriate printer, or position the cursor differently so the macro can do its job properly. Then run the macro again. If the macro still fails, the trouble is probably within the macro itself.

Learning More about Macro Programming

If you want to learn more about advanced programming commands and techniques, the first place to look might be WordPerfect's online macros manual. Just choose Help ➤ Macros to access it.

You can also learn by example. Run any one of the sample macros that came with your WordPerfect package to see what it does. Then you can open that macro file, as discussed earlier under "Opening and Editing a Macro," and use File ➤ Print to print a copy, see what's inside, and find out what makes it tick.

If you need more support than the online manual and sample macros offer, check your local bookstore for books on macro programming with WordPerfect for Windows. WordPerfect Corporation also offers a manual that deals *specifically* with the WordPerfect 6 for Windows macro language. You can purchase this manual from WordPerfect Corporation.

If you have no programming experience whatsoever and you want some real training, consider taking a programming course. Even an introductory BASIC course would be useful, because you really need to understand fundamental programming concepts, like syntax, looping, subroutines, and variables.

This chapter has taught you virtually everything you need to know about creating and running just about any WordPerfect for Windows macro imaginable. You don't have to be a programmer to create and use macros, but for those who *are* programmers and power users, WordPerfect offers a complete macro programming language.

Now I'll doff my programmer's hat, remove my pocket-protector, and tuck them away for the rest of this book. In the next chapter, we'll look at ways any average person with a nontechnical mind can customize WordPerfect.

TABLE 18.1: Macros that Come with WordPerfect for Windows*

MACRO NAME	WHAT IT DOES
Abbrev	Lets you work with multiple abbreviations. Similar to choosing the Insert ➤ Abbreviations command repeatedly (Chapter 9).
Adrs2mrg	Inserts (at the cursor position) merge data records from the online address book. Use the Adrsbook macro to create and manage the address book (Chapter 21).
Adrsbook	Lets you create an online address book. You can then use the Adrs2mrg macro to create merge records from the address book (Chapter 21).
Allfonts	Inserts samples of all fonts available for your printer into the current document (Chapters 6 and 10).
Capital	Capitalizes the first letter of the word the cursor is on, then moves the cursor to the next word (Chapter 3).
Clipbrd	Displays the contents of the Windows Clipboard (Chapter 3).

TABLE 18.1: Macros that Come with WordPerfect for Windows* (continued)

MACRO NAME	WHAT IT DOES
Closeall	Closes all open files at once, giving you a chance to save them if necessary (Chapter 4).
Ctrlsftf	Prompts for "FROM" and "TO" information and inserts it at the cursor position.
Dropcap	Creates a drop-cap graphic from the first character in the paragraph (Chapters 25 and 28).
Endfoot	Converts endnotes to footnotes (Chapter 31).
Expndall	Expands all abbreviations in the current document (Chapter 9).
Filestmp	Inserts a file stamp into (and creates, as necessary) a header or footer (Chapter 8).
Footend	Converts footnotes to endnotes (Chapter 31).
Fontdn	Decreases the font size by 2 points in selected text or text to the right of the cursor (Chapter 6).
Fontup	Increases the font size by 2 points in selected text or text to the right of the cursor (Chapter 6).
Gotodos	Opens a new DOS window. Running this macro is the same as switching to Program Manager, choosing <u>F</u>ile ➤ <u>R</u>un, typing **command**, and choosing OK.
Heading	In selected cells or rows of a table, lets you choose text color, fill, centering, locking, or header row (Chapter 7).
Linenum	Goes to a specific line and character number in a macro file (Chapter 18).
Pagexofy	Creates page x of y numbering (Chapter 31).
Parabrk	Places small, fancy, centered graphics on the line where the cursor is positioned; for best results, put the cursor on a blank line (Chapter 25).
Pgborder	Creates graphic page borders in many fancy styles (Chapters 6, 25, and 28).

TABLE 18.1: Macros that Come with WordPerfect for Windows* (continued)

MACRO NAME	WHAT IT DOES
Readclp	Reads aloud text from the Clipboard; requires ProVoice or Monologue voice software (Chapter 30).
Readfile	Reads aloud text from a saved text file, or plays a .WAV, .MID, or .AVI file; requires ProVoice or Monologue voice software (Chapter 30).
Readsel	Reads aloud selected text from the document; requires ProVoice or Monologue voice software (Chapter 30).
Reverse	Puts selected text in a graphics box. The text is white on a black background (Chapters 25 and 28).
Saveall	Saves all open documents (Chapter 4).
Sqconfig	Configures "smart quotes," like those used to typeset this book (Chapter 6).
Sqtoggle	Turns "smart quotes" on or off. (Smart quotes come in mirror-image pairs: the first one you type slants or curves automatically to the right as an open quote ("), the second slants or curves to the left as a close quote ("). This helps make it appear that the quotes enclose the text they surround.) Make sure smart quotes are OFF when you're doing macro programming! (Chapters 6, 18).
Transpos	Transposes the two visible characters to the left of the cursor; similar to the SWITCH example in this chapter, except that you place the cursor after the second of the two characters you want to transpose, instead of between them (Chapter 3).
Watermrk	Creates a text or graphic watermark from a variety of predefined phrases and logos (Chapters 8, 25, and 28).

*   *List may have changed since publication of this book.*

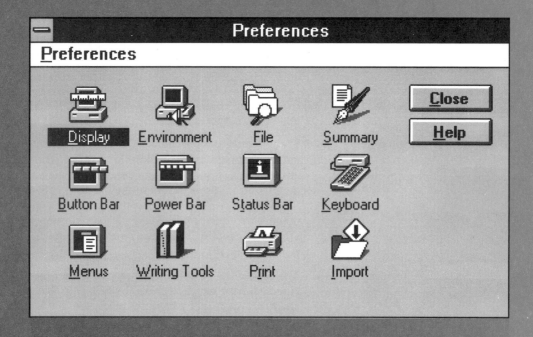

CHAPTER

19

Customizing
WordPerfect

To select or create a color printing and display palette   **596**

go to the Print Preferences dialog box and choose Define Color Printing Palette.

To set the initial style for the current document   **602**

choose Layout ➤ Document ➤ Initial Codes Style. As for any style, you can use the pull-down menus or shortcut keys to enter codes, and type any text you want. When you're done, choose OK.

To set the initial style for any documents created with a specific template   **603**

choose File ➤ Template and highlight the template you want to change. Choose Options ➤ Edit Template and click on the Initial Style button in the Template feature bar. Enter the codes and text you want, then choose OK. Choose Exit Template ➤ Yes to save your changes.

To set the initial font for the current document   **604**

choose Layout ➤ Document ➤ Initial Font or click the Initial Font button in the Font dialog box. Select the font face, size, and style, and choose OK.

WORDPERFECT'S behavior is easy to change if you don't like it. In fact, you can customize just about any WordPerfect setting to match your own requirements. Any settings you change will stay that way until you change them again.

Keep in mind that you don't *have* to customize WordPerfect at all. So if you're happy with the way WordPerfect is running now, skip this chapter and come back to it later when you do need to make some changes.

Incidentally, the easiest way to learn how to customize WordPerfect is to experiment. Be sure to watch the screen carefully for information about what to do next, and remember that the F1 key and Help button are always ready to assist you. For best results, jot down the original settings before you make a change, in case you don't like the result.

NOTE If you've made a hopeless mess of your default settings and saved the changes, you can reinstall all or part of WordPerfect to restore the defaults to their factory-fresh state. See Appendix A.

Using the Preferences Options

You'll typically use a "preferences" dialog box to customize WordPerfect. Not surprisingly, there are many ways to reach the preferences dialog boxes and many things you can do once you get there.

Here's a sure-fire way to open any preferences dialog box:

1. Choose File ➤ Preferences to open the Preferences dialog box shown below:

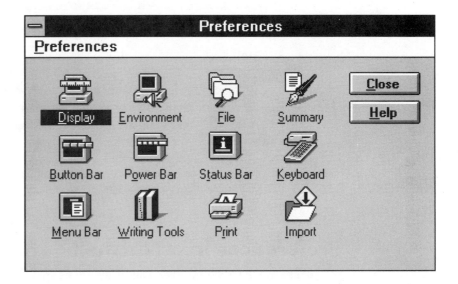

2. Double-click the icon for the preference you want to change, or highlight the icon and press ↵, or choose an option from the Preferences menu in the dialog box.

You can go directly to certain preferences dialog boxes by following these steps:

1. Move the mouse pointer to the button bar, power bar, scroll bar, status bar, or menu bar.

2. Right-click the mouse and choose Preferences.

You can also click on buttons in the Preferences button bar to go directly to a specific preferences dialog box. To display this button bar:

1. If no button bar is visible, choose View ➤ Button Bar.

2. Move the mouse pointer to the button bar and right-click.

3. Choose Preferences from the QuickMenu. You'll see the Preferences button bar shown below.

TIP

To find out what any Preferences button does, move the mouse pointer to that button. A short description will appear in the title bar at the top of the screen.

Once you've opened the Preferences dialog box you want, you can fill it in. When you're done, choose OK. If necessary, choose <u>C</u>lose to return to your document.

Preferences in a Nutshell

The next few sections explain why you might want to use each Preferences option and where you can find more information about it (or the features it controls) in this book.

Display Preferences

Display Preferences let you customize the appearance of the document window. Options include the following:

D<u>o</u>cument   Controls which features to show on the document window, including table gridlines (Chapter 7), Windows system colors, comments (Chapter 4), graphics (Chapter 25), hidden text (Chapter 6), and vertical and horizontal scroll bars (Chapter 2). You can choose the default units of measure for data entry, the status bar, and the ruler (Chapter 2), and can decide whether WordPerfect displays sculptured dialog boxes.

Show ¶   Controls which "invisible" symbols—including space, hard return, tab, indent, center, flush right, soft hyphen, advance, and center page—appear on screen (Chapter 4). If you can't see the symbols and want to, choose Y̲iew ➤ S̲how ¶ from the Word-Perfect menu bar. (The invisible symbols will appear in your document, but they'll never print.) To hide the symbols, choose V̲iew ➤ S̲how ¶ again. To have the symbols display in the future documents as well as the current one, select Sho̲w Symbols On New And Current Document in the Display Preferences dialog box.

View/Z̲oom   Controls the default view and zoom size (Chapter 4).

Reveal C̲odes   Controls the Reveal Codes font, size, color, window size, miscellaneous appearance options, and whether Reveal Codes initially appears in other documents (Chapter 4).

R̲uler Bar   Controls the behavior and appearance of the ruler bar, and whether it initially appears in other documents (Chapters 4, 5, 7, 27).

Merge   Controls the appearance of merge codes (Chapter 21).

Environment Preferences

Environment Preferences let you control these aspects of WordPerfect's behavior:

- User information displayed in comments and document summaries. User information includes user name, user initials, and the color used as a background for comment icons and boxes (Chapters 4 and 20)

- Hyphenation prompt (Chapter 16)

- Whether to confirm deletion of codes and stop the cursor at hidden codes (Chapter 4)

- Whether to confirm deletion of table formulas (Chapter 24)

- When warning beeps will sound (on error, when hyphenation help is needed, and/or when a find fails)

- Whether menus display the last open file names, shortcut keys, and help prompts (Chapters 2 and 3)

- Whether to take certain actions when you save or open a file. The options govern whether to save the workspace (Chapter 4), to set a QuickMark (Chapter 9), to reformat documents for the default printer when you open them again (Chapter 10), and to activate hypertext when you open a document (Chapter 30)

- Which *code pages* to use when opening or saving your documents. A code page is a table in the DOS or Windows operating system that defines which ASCII or ANSI character set is used in a document. Different languages may use different ASCII or ANSI character sets. You probably won't need to use the Code Page option unless you're working in a foreign language, or using files from a "foreign" computer system, such as the Apple Macintosh.

File Preferences

The File Preferences control default directory locations, file names, file extensions, and whether the QuickList is updated with changes to the default locations. These options are covered under "Organizing Your Files with File Preferences" later in this chapter.

N O T E   The QuickList gives you quick access to files and directories you use frequently. There's more about the QuickList in Chapter 20.

Summary Preferences

The Summary Preferences control default subject text and descriptive type on document summaries, whether to display descriptive file names in file management dialog boxes, and whether to create a document summary upon saving or exiting (Chapter 20).

Button Bar Preferences

You can use Button Bar Preferences to select, create, edit, copy, and delete button bars, and to customize the button bar appearance and position. Each button can execute a program feature, play a keyboard script, launch a program, or play a macro (Chapters 4 and 18).

Power Bar Preferences

Power Bar Preferences let you rearrange the power bar, select which buttons appear on it, reset it to the default buttons, and customize its appearance (Chapter 4).

Status Bar Preferences

Use Status Bar Preferences when you want to edit the status bar, select what information it shows, reset it to the default information, and customize its appearance (Chapter 4).

Keyboard Preferences

You can customize the behavior of keys on your keyboard, using Keyboard Preferences to select, create, edit, copy, and delete keyboards. You can have a key do nothing, display a text character, execute a program feature, play a keyboard script, launch a program, or play a macro. See "Customizing the Keyboard" later in the chapter for more details.

Menu Preferences

Menu Preferences let you select, create, edit, copy, and delete menu items and menus. Each menu item can execute a program feature, play a keyboard script, launch a program, or play a macro (Chapter 4).

Writing Tools Preferences

Writing Tools Preferences control which writing tools appear in the Tools menu. The writing tools are Speller (Chapter 9), Grammatik (Chapter 12), and Thesaurus (Chapter 13).

Print Preferences

Use Print Preferences to choose default print preferences for relative size of fonts (size attribute ratio), number of copies printed and how copies are generated, print quality, print color, whether graphics are printed, and the color printing palette used. (Chapter 10 covers most of these features.) Later in this chapter, you'll learn how to customize the color printing palette.

Import Preferences

Import Preferences control default import settings including delimiters for fields and records, characters used to enclose text strings, characters to strip during import, and the Windows Metafile conversion method (Chapter 33).

Organizing Your Files with File Preferences

DOS lets you divide your hard disk into separate drives, directories, and subdirectories. Each directory on a drive is like a separate file cabinet that contains its own set of files. Storing files in separate directories keeps your information organized and prevents individual directories from becoming cluttered with too many file names.

The File Preferences options let you specify a location for various categories of WordPerfect files, so that WordPerfect always knows where to store files as you create them, and where to look for files when you need them.

To set these options, choose File ➤ Preferences, and double-click File, or click the File Preferences button in the Preferences button bar. When the File Preferences dialog box appears (see Figure 19.1), follow the steps listed below.

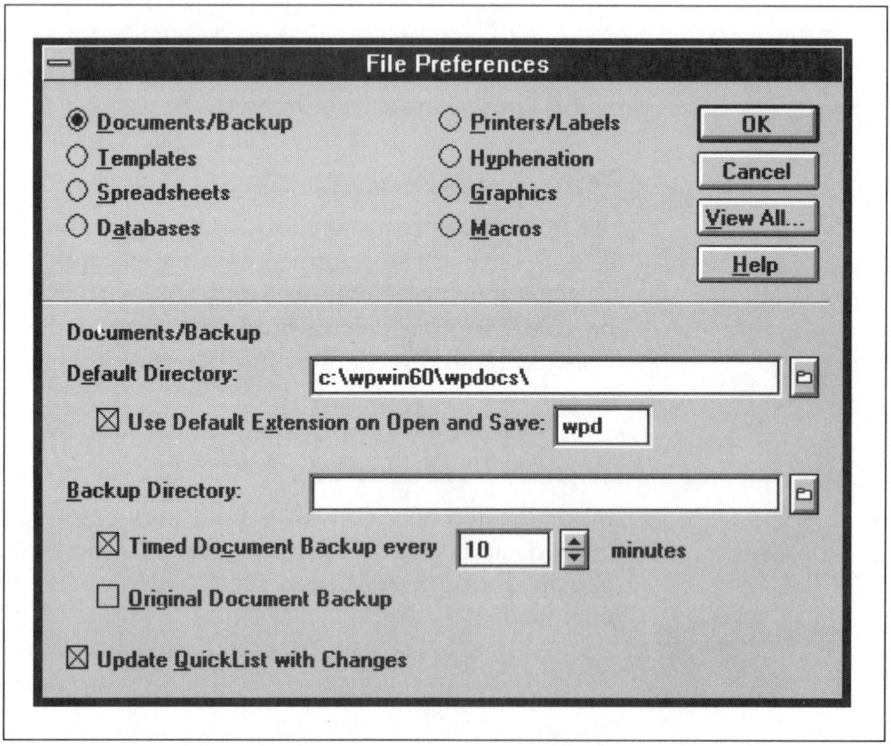

FIGURE 19.1

Use the File Preferences dialog box to tell WordPerfect where to look for and store various categories of files.

File Preferences

- ⦿ Documents/Backup
- ○ Templates
- ○ Spreadsheets
- ○ Databases

- ○ Printers/Labels
- ○ Hyphenation
- ○ Graphics
- ○ Macros

[OK]
[Cancel]
[View All...]
[Help]

Documents/Backup

Default Directory: `c:\wpwin60\wpdocs\`

☒ Use Default Extension on Open and Save: `wpd`

Backup Directory:

☒ Timed Document Backup every `10` ⬍ minutes

☐ Original Document Backup

☒ Update QuickList with Changes

1. Choose the category you want to change. The dialog box will change to reflect the selected category. Figure 19.1 shows the dialog box for the Documents/Backup category.

2. Fill in the dialog box as needed. Depending on the category you chose, you can provide some or all of the following information:

    Default Directory   The directory that WordPerfect will use unless you specify a different directory upon opening or saving a file.

    Backup Directory   The directory that WordPerfect will use for automatic backup files. (See "About Automatic Backup Files," below.)

    Supplemental Directory   A secondary directory that WordPerfect can search (see "About Default and Supplemental Paths," below).

    Default File   The file that WordPerfect will use unless you specify another file name when opening or saving a file.

    Supplemental File   A secondary template file that WordPerfect can search for styles.

    Label File   A file that WordPerfect will search for standard label formats.

    … **Extension**   A default extension for documents (usually *wpd*) or templates (usually *wpt*).

3. Repeat steps 1 and 2 for all the categories you want to change.

4. If you want to update the QuickList with your changes, select Update QuickList With Changes.

5. When you're done, choose OK (and Close, if necessary).

Keep these points in mind when you use the File Preferences options:

- When entering a directory name, type the drive letter and directory location using proper DOS conventions. For example, you could type **c:\wpwin60\mydocs** to specify the MYDOCS subdirectory of the WPWIN60 directory on drive C.

- When entering a file name, type the file name and extension using proper DOS conventions (for example, **standard.wpt**).

- When you can't remember the exact name of a directory or file, you can use the file button at the end of the text box to locate and fill in the name. The file button is discussed in Chapter 20.

- If you specify a nonexistent directory in the File Preferences dialog box, WordPerfect will offer to create that directory for you.

- After changing a directory location, you'll need to move existing files of that type to the new location if you want WordPerfect to find them in the future (see Chapter 20).

About Default and Supplemental Paths

You can specify a default directory path and supplemental directory path for many file categories, including templates and styles, spreadsheets, databases, printer drivers and labels, graphics, and macros.

You can think of the default location as the *first* place WordPerfect will look for information, and the supplemental location as the place where WordPerfect will look if it doesn't find what it's looking for in the default place. For example, suppose you've created a style named *Memo* in your default template. Your system administrator also has created a *Memo* style, but that one is in the supplemental template. Which Memo style will WordPerfect use automatically? You guessed it! The Memo style in your default template.

Here's what happens if you leave one or both of the default or supplemental directories blank in the File Preferences dialog box:

- If you leave just the default directory blank, WordPerfect uses the supplemental directory.

- If you leave just the supplemental directory blank, WordPerfect uses the default directory.

- If you leave both directories blank, Wordperfect uses either the directory that holds the WordPerfect application files (usually C:\WPWIN60) or the current directory. This depends on the category. WordPerfect uses the application directory for templates and styles, spreadsheets, databases, printer drivers, and label files. It uses the current directory for graphics and macros.

Speeding Up File Searches

WordPerfect searches for files wherever the File Preferences settings tell it to. If that directory contains hundreds of files, however, your computer may slow down considerably. You might be able to have your computer work faster if you heed this advice:

- Organize your hard disk into many directories with fewer files, instead of few directories with many files.

- Store WordPerfect's various categories of files in separate directories. (See the option buttons in Figure 19.1 for an idea of how to organize your file categories.)

About Automatic Backup Files

WordPerfect can make some limited file backups for you. To activate the automatic backup features, select (check) either (or both) of these options in the Documents/Backup File Preferences dialog box:

- **Timed Document Backup every ... minutes**
- **Original Document Backup**

A *timed document backup* saves the content of the active window (or windows) documents at regular intervals, as specified in the Timed Document Backup... text box. The default interval is every ten minutes. Timed backup files are deleted automatically when you exit WordPerfect normally. If the equipment or power fails, or you restart the computer accidentally before you've had a chance to exit WordPerfect, however, the timed backup files remain on disk and can prevent loss of work. When you start WordPerfect again after a failure, you'll have a chance to rename, open, or delete timed backup files that were saved before the shutdown. When you open a timed backup file, you can check to see if it is more up-to-date or is less damaged than the version you last saved, and use whichever file is more satisfactory. Timed document backups are stored in C:\WINDOWS as WP{WP}.BKn (where n is a document number from 1 to 9).

When Original Document Backup is selected, WordPerfect will automatically copy your original file to a file with a *.BK!* extension whenever you save changes to the original file. Suppose you've selected Original Document Backup and are editing a file named MYLETTER.WPD. When you save that file, WordPerfect will store the original (unedited) file as MYLETTER.BK! and the changed version in MYLETTER.WPD.

The original document backup can be helpful in those rare instances when your File ➤ Save trigger finger is a bit too fast and you save some bad changes accidentally. If, for example, you wanted to restore the previous version of MYLETTER.WPD, you could close MYLETTER.WPD (File ➤ Close) and open the backup copy in MYLETTER.BK! (File ➤ Open). Assuming that MYLETTER.BK! contains the information that you want to keep, choose File ➤ Save As, specify **myletter.wpd** as the file to be saved, and choose Yes when WordPerfect asks if you want to replace the existing MYLETTER.WPD file.

WARNING Automatic backups are *not* a substitute for saving your work regularly, exiting WordPerfect properly after ending a session, and making backup copies of important documents on separate disks. They're meant only to bail you out in case of emergency.

Customizing the Keyboard

WordPerfect comes with three built-in keyboard definitions: a keyboard for equation editing (Chapter 29), a keyboard that's compatible with DOS versions of WordPerfect, and the normal WordPerfect for Windows keyboard. You can use any of these definitions, or design custom keyboard definitions of your own. Procedures for selecting, creating, and customizing keyboards are similar to those for selecting and customizing a button bar or menu bar (see Chapter 4).

Changing the keyboard definitions can be hazardous to your sanity and make every shortcut key listed in this book seem totally wrong. To prevent confusion, Word-Perfect lets you set up and customize *new* keyboard definitions only. You cannot change the built-in keyboard definitions. If your shortcut keys don't seem to work as described in this book, make certain that you've selected the <WPWin 6.0 Keyboard> definition.

To select, create, edit, copy, or delete keyboard definitions, follow the steps below:

1. Choose File ➤ Preferences and double-click Keyboard, or click the Keyboard Preferences button in the Preferences button bar. You'll see the Keyboard Preferences dialog box shown below:

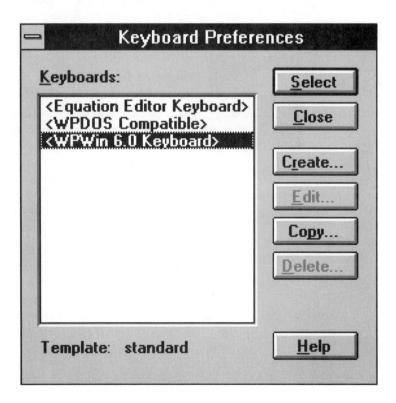

2. If you want to select, edit, or delete a keyboard definition, or you want to base a new keyboard definition on an existing one, highlight the definition you want. Then choose one of the buttons described below:

Select   Lets you select the highlighted keyboard. After choosing Select (or double-clicking the keyboard you want), you'll be returned to the Preferences dialog box or the document window.

Create   Lets you create a new keyboard definition that's based on the highlighted keyboard definition. To create a keyboard, choose Create, type in a name for the keyboard (up to 15 characters, including any spaces or punctuation that you want). If you want to store the keyboard with the default template or supplemental template instead of the current template, choose Template, select the template you want, and choose OK. Choose OK to continue with the steps given later under "Editing a Keyboard Definition."

N O T E

Keyboard definitions are normally stored in the current template (usually either STANDARD.WPT or the template you chose in the File ➤ Template command). See Chapters 4 and 20 for more about templates.

Edit   Lets you change the highlighted keyboard definition. After choosing Edit, continue with the steps given later under "Editing a Keyboard Definition."

Copy   Lets you copy an existing keyboard definition to a new one. To copy a keyboard definition, choose Copy. Choose the template you want to copy from, the keyboard(s) you want to copy, and the template you want to copy to, then choose Copy. You may be prompted to assign a new name to each keyboard selected. (When assigning a name, be careful not to overwrite an existing keyboard definition accidentally.)

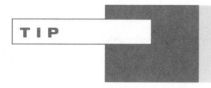

TIP To select more than one keyboard to copy, hold down the Ctrl key while clicking the keyboard names you want in the Select Keyboards To Copy list.

Delete Lets you delete the highlighted keyboard definition. After choosing Delete, choose Yes to confirm the deletion.

3. Repeat step 2 if you wish. When you're done choosing options from the Keyboard Preferences dialog box, choose Close as needed to return to the document window.

Editing a Keyboard Definition

After you use the Create option in the Keyboard Preferences dialog box to create a new keyboard definition, or highlight an existing definition and choose Edit, you'll see the Keyboard Editor dialog box shown in Figure 19.2.

FIGURE 19.2

Use the Keyboard Editor to define the behavior of keys on the keyboard

To use the Keyboard Editor, follow these steps:

1. In the Choose A Key To Assign Or Unassign list, highlight the key you want to define or change. To highlight the key, use any of the methods below:

   ● Click on the key name in the list (or use the arrow keys to highlight the key).

   ● Press the appropriate key on your keyboard.

   ● Click the appropriate key on the sample keyboard at the bottom of the screen.

   ● Type the first few letters of the key name.

2. Choose an action for the key, as follows:

   ● **To make the key "do nothing,"** choose the Unassign button.

   ● **To make the key activate a WordPerfect feature,** choose Activate A Feature, select a category from the Feature Categories drop-down list, then select a feature to execute from the Features list. Finally, choose the Assign Feature button.

T I P

As you highlight options in the Features list, you'll see a brief explanation of what each feature does just below the Assign Feature button.

   ● **To make the key type words or phrases,** choose Play A Keyboard Script. In the Type The Script This Key Plays box, type the text you want. The text can include normal keyboard characters and WordPerfect characters (Ctrl+W), but no formatting codes. When you're done typing, choose the Assign Script button.

   ● **To make the key launch a program,** choose Launch A Program, then click Select File, highlight or type in the name of the program you want the key to run, and choose OK.

   ● **To make the key play a macro,** choose Play A Macro. Click the Assign Macro button. In the Select Macro dialog box that appears, choose Location, select a location (Current Template, Default Template, or File On Disk) and choose OK. If the location is a file on disk, type a macro file name in the Name text box (or use the button at the end of the text box to locate the macro). If the location is a template, highlight the macro name in the Macros In Template list. Then choose Select. (See Chapter 18 for more about selecting and using macros.)

3. To display the highlighted key or key combination on the pull-down menus, select (check) Assignment Appears On Menu. (This option isn't available for unassigned keys.)

4. Repeat steps 1–3 as needed. When you're done customizing the keyboard, choose OK to return to the Keyboard Preferences dialog box.

5. If you want to use the modified keyboard now, highlight it and choose Select. Then choose Close (if necessary) until you return to the document window.

If you need more help, choose the Help button in the Keyboard Editor dialog box.

Customizing a Color Printing Palette

For you lucky dogs who have a color printer or monitor, WordPerfect provides *color printing palettes*. The color printing palettes let you group and name colors so that you can apply them to page elements very quickly, instead of having to select a custom color for every element. For example, you could create a "Cool Man Cool" palette with blues and greens, and a "Hot Chili Peppers" palette with bright reds, oranges, and yellows. Then, you'd just select the palette you want to use and pick colors from that palette for text, borders, shading, lines, and other elements in your document.

As usual, it's best to create new palettes of your own, rather than change WordPerfect's built-in palettes.

Color appears in printed documents only if your printer supports color printing and is currently set to print in color. To set your printer for color printing, go to the Print Preferences dialog box (File ➤ Preferences ➤ Print) or the Print dialog box (File ➤ Print). Make sure Print Color is set to Full Color. If you don't have a color monitor or printer, colors will appear in shades of gray, just like all the figures and graphics in this book.

Color palettes are stored in files with a .WPP extension, in the directories specified in File ➤ Preferences ➤ Files ➤ Printers/Labels.

You can select, create, and customize color palettes either from the Print Preferences dialog box or from any dialog box that offers a Palette button. I'll focus here on using the Print Preferences dialog box.

Selecting a Color Palette

To select a color palette, follow these steps:

1. Choose File ➤ Preferences and double-click Print, or click the Print Preferences button in the Preferences button bar.

2. Choose Define Color Printing Palette. You'll see the Define Color Printing Palette dialog box, shown in Figure 19.3.

To reach the Define Color Printing Palette dialog box quickly, press F9 and click the Palette button.

FIGURE 19.3

The Define Color Printing Palette dialog box lets you select, create, and edit color printing and display palettes.

Color wheel   Luminosity bar   Click on or select color(s) to change

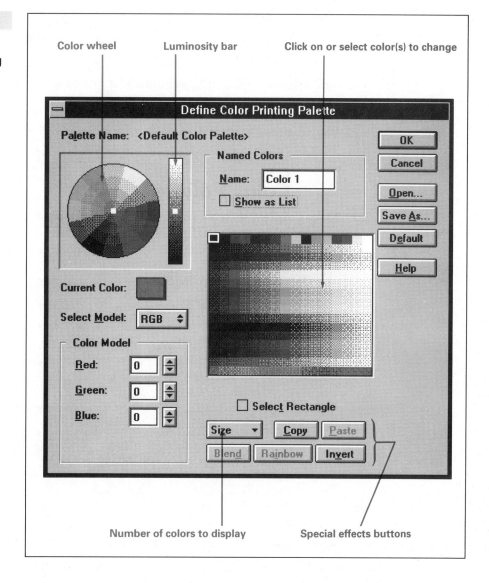

Number of colors to display   Special effects buttons

3. Choose <u>O</u>pen.

4. Highlight the palette you want and choose OK, or double-click the palette name.

5. Choose OK and <u>C</u>lose until you return to the document window.

You can choose a different palette whenever you wish. Any elements that you've already colored with another palette will stay the same color in your document, even if you change palettes.

Using a Color Palette

Once you've selected a color palette, you can use it to assign colors to any element in your document. For example, you might want to pick a Wild Strawberry color for new text that you type. Here are the steps to follow:

1. Select the palette that has the color you want, as described above.

2. Choose <u>L</u>ayout ➤ <u>F</u>ont or press F9 to open the Font dialog box. As shown below, all the color features are in the Color Options area of the dialog box.

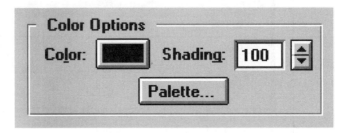

3. Click the Co<u>l</u>or button, then click the color you want.

4. To change the shade, choose Shading and enter a percentage of the selected color. Choose 100 to get the "pure" color shown in the Color button. Choose a smaller percentage to get a paler version of the selected color.

5. Choose OK.

The steps for coloring any element in your document are basically the same as those shown above. In step 2, however, you'll need to choose options for the specific element you're coloring. For example, you can color the vertical line between columns in a multicolumn document. Assuming you've already added the line, you could color it by choosing Layout ➤ Columns ➤ Border/Fill ➤ Customize Style. To choose a color for the border, click the Border Color button, then click on the color you want. To choose or change a color palette, click the Palette button.

Customizing a Color Palette

To customize a palette, follow the steps below:

1. Choose File ➤ Preferences, double-click Print and choose Define Color Printing Palette. Or, press F9 and click the Palette button. You'll see the Define Color Printing Palette dialog box shown in Figure 19.3.

2. If you want to customize a different palette, choose Open, highlight the palette you want, and choose OK.

3. If you want to select a color model, choose an option from the Select Model pop-up button. Your options are described below:

   RGB (Red Green Blue)   Uses the primary colors of light to define colors (this is the default setting).

   HLS (Hue Luminosity Saturation)   Defines colors in the context of your monitor, much like the hue, brightness, and contrast knobs adjust colors on a television. In the HLS system, Hue adjusts color, Luminosity adjusts the amount of white and gray, and Saturation adjusts the amount of color.

   CMYK (Cyan Magenta Yellow Black)   The same color model that print shops employ for color separations. The maximum settings for all colors produce black, while the zero settings for all colors produce white.

4. If you want to select the number of colors displayed at once, click the Size button and make a selection. You can choose 4, 16, 256, 512, or 1024 colors.

5. If you want to display the colors in a vertical list, select (check) Show As List. Here's an example of a list of colors (shown in black-and-white, of course, because this book is in black-and-white):

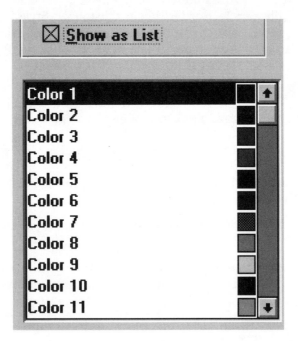

6. Select a color or rectangular area of color from the palette or list of colors in the middle of the dialog box. (You'll need to select a rectangular area to use the Blend or Rainbow buttons described in step 7.)

• **To select a single color,** click the appropriate color in the color palette or list.

• **To select a rectangle of colors,** deselect Show As List and select (check) Select Rectangle. Then drag your mouse through the colors in the center of the dialog box until you've outlined the area you want to work with.

7. Now, take some action:

- **To change a single color,** click the color you want in the color wheel, or drag the marker in the wheel to the color you want. To change the shade of the color, drag the luminosity bar up or down. Alternatively, you can set specific color values in the Color Model area of the dialog box.

- **To assign (or change) the** *name* **of a single color,** type the name in the Name text box.

- **To copy the selected color(s),** choose Copy. Next click on another color, or outline another rectangle in the color window, and then choose Paste to paste the colors into position.

- **To create special effects,** choose Blend (blends colors from the first to the last selected color), Rainbow (creates a spectrum effect from the first to last color), or Invert (inverts each selected color square; for example, white becomes black, blue becomes yellow). Blend and Rainbow work on rectangles. Invert works on rectangles and single colors. Try them!

TIP   If you make a mess of the color palette and want to start over, you can choose the Default button. This will reset the palette to its default settings.

8. Repeat any or all of steps 5–7 as needed. When you're done, do any of the following:

- **To cancel your changes** and close the dialog box, choose Cancel.

- **To save your changes** and close the dialog box, choose OK. When asked about saving changes permanently, choose Yes to update the palette file permanently, or No to make the changes last through the current session only.

- **To save the palette under another name,** choose Save As. In the Name text box, specify a descriptive name for the palette. In the Filename text box, specify a valid DOS file name (without any extension) and choose OK. Color palettes are assigned a .WPP extension automatically.

TIP — You can use file-management techniques covered in Chapter 20 to delete, rename, or copy palette files.

9. Choose OK and <u>C</u>lose as needed to return to the document window.

Changing the Initial Look of Your Documents

Every new document you create starts with an [Open Style:InitialStyle] code. This code formats the document with the *InitialStyle* system style for the template used to create the file. You can't delete this code, but you can customize the initial style. For example, you might want to set up different initial margins and justification, or choose a different font.

Changing the Initial Style for the Current Document

Follow these steps to change the initial style for the current document:

1. Choose <u>L</u>ayout ➤ <u>D</u>ocument ➤ Initial Codes <u>S</u>tyle. Or, turn on Reveal Codes (Alt+F3) and double-click the [Open Style:Initial Style] code at the start of the document.

2. In the Styles Editor dialog box, choose <u>C</u>ontents. Now use the pull-down menus and shortcut keys to add any formatting codes, text, graphics boxes, lines, styles, and whatever else WordPerfect offers. See Chapter 17 for other editing techniques you can use.

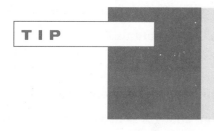

When you add a graphic to the InitialStyle, set the Contents option for the graphic to Image On Disk. This will make your documents smaller and conserve disk space. See Chapter 25 for more information about graphics.

3. When you're done, choose OK.

To return to WordPerfect's default settings for the current document, repeat step 1 above; then, in step 2, delete all the codes you added in the Styles Editor dialog box, and choose OK.

Changing the Initial Style for a Template

To change the initial style for a template, follow the steps below:

1. Choose File ➤ Template (Ctrl+T).

2. Highlight the template you want to change.

3. Choose Options ➤ Edit Template.

4. Choose the Initial Style button from the Template feature bar to open the Styles Editor dialog box. Make your changes as you would for any style and choose OK.

5. When you're done, choose Exit Template ➤ Yes.

Your changes will be reflected in any documents created with the template you chose in step 2.

Another Way to Change the Initial Style

You also can change the initial style for other documents by going through the Layout ➤ Styles commands below:

1. Choose Layout ➤ Styles (Alt+F8) to open the Style List dialog box.

2. Choose Options ➤ Setup to open the Setup dialog box.

3. Select (check) System Styles. If you want to save the style to a template, choose either Default Template or Supplemental Template. Choose OK.

4. In the Name list, highlight InitialStyle and choose Edit.

5. In the Styles Editor, make your changes as usual. When you're done, choose OK to return to the Style List dialog box.

6. If you want to copy the current styles to a style library file, choose Options ➤ Save As. Select System Styles (very important). Type a file name for your style library in the Filename text box and choose OK.

7. Choose Close to return to the document window.

If all this style and template stuff is still a complete mystery to you, please refer to Chapter 17 (styles) and Chapters 4 and 20 (templates).

Changing the Initial Font

You can add font codes to the Styles Editor dialog boxes described above. Alternatively, you can set initial fonts by choosing Layout ➤ Document ➤ Initial Font or by pressing F9 and then clicking the Initial Font button in the Font dialog box. Select a font face, size, and style, then choose OK.

Precedence of Initial Codes and Fonts

Now you might be wondering, "What if I change the initial style for the template and document, *and* the document initial font? Which settings will win the race?" Here are the rules that WordPerfect follows to decide the winners:

- Codes in your *document* override all equivalent codes in the template's initial style, the initial style for the document, and the document initial font.

- Codes in the initial style for the document override all equivalent codes in the initial style for the template and the document initial font.

NOTE You can also define initial fonts when you set up fonts for your printer. Please see Chapter 10 for more information on installing fonts.

Other Ways to Change Default Settings

If you think you've now learned everything about customizing WordPerfect, you're in for a little surprise. There are still a few more ways to personalize the program:

- You can choose options from the <u>V</u>iew menu to customize the appearance of the screen.

- Some dialog boxes include a *Setup* button or option that you can use to customize settings for certain features. For example, you can choose <u>L</u>ayout ➤ <u>S</u>tyles ➤ <u>O</u>ptions ➤ <u>S</u>etup to control how WordPerfect displays and updates the list of styles.

- You can customize styles (Chapter 17) or templates (Chapter 20) to control the appearance of nearly everything in a document, including lines, text, graphics, and borders.

- Want still more ways to tailor your system? Read the next section.

Customizing Windows

So what happened to the options for customizing such things as screen colors and mouse behavior? If you're looking to WordPerfect for these capabilities, I'm afraid you're barking up the wrong word processor. Look instead to applications in the Main group of the Program Manager.

Control Panel lets you customize the screen colors, desktop appearance, mouse behavior, and keyboard speed. You can use it to add and remove fonts, specify communications settings for serial ports, install and remove printers, customize various international settings, set the system date and time, specify settings for network connections, change MIDI settings, optimize Windows for 386 enhanced mode, install various drivers, and assign sounds to system events.

The *Windows Setup* application lets you inform Windows applications about the type of screen display, keyboard, and mouse you're using. You can also use Windows Setup to install certain applications and add or remove various Windows components (useful when disk space is at a premium).

For more about Control Panel and Windows Setup, please see your Windows documentation.

In this chapter, you've discovered dozens of ways to personalize WordPerfect for your own use. You could probably spend the rest of your life tweaking WordPerfect's behavior and appearance to the pinnacle of perfection. But surely you have more fun things to do with your free time, so let's move on to tools for managing your files.

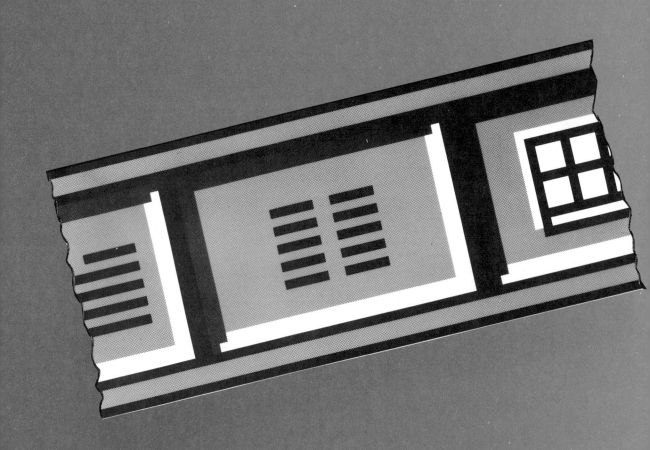

CHAPTER

20

Managing Your Files

f a s t TRACK

To save files under a different format   **627**

choose File ➤ Save (Ctrl+S) or File ➤ Save As (F3), type a file name, choose an option from the Format drop-down list, and choose OK.

To password-protect a file   **630**

select (check) Password Protect in the Save As dialog box.

To create a document summary   **633**

choose File ➤ Document Summary. Fill in the fields you want and choose OK.

To find out which files contain certain specific text   **638**

choose File ➤ QuickFinder, or choose the QuickFinder button in the Open File dialog box, or double-click the Quick-Finder File Indexer icon in the WPWin 6.0 group window of the Program Manager. Type the word, phrase, or pattern you want to search for, choose the location you want to search, and choose Find.

To select or manage templates   **648**

choose File ➤ Template (Ctrl+T). To use a template as the basis for a new document, highlight the template and choose OK. To create a new template, choose Options ➤ Create Template. To edit or delete a template, highlight the template you want and choose either Options ➤ Edit Template or Options ➤ Delete Template.

EVERY piece of information—be it a program, graphic, spreadsheet, database, or WordPerfect document—is stored in files on your computer's disk. The number of files can quickly mushroom into the thousands. Not surprisingly, finding and managing so many files can be a job in itself. You might need to delete old files to make room for new ones, copy groups of files to backup disks, or find a file whose name you've forgotten.

WordPerfect offers oodles of handy features for managing files. Of course, you needn't become an expert on every tool at once. Just experiment with the basics, and then try more sophisticated techniques when you need them. Remember that help for any feature is just a Help button or F1 keypress away.

Understanding File Lingo

Before trying out the file-management tools, you need to know some basic DOS terminology (aka *file lingo*). You'll find this kind of information in your DOS manuals, or in *Murphy's Laws of DOS* by Charlie Russel (SYBEX, 1993). In particular, you should understand these terms:

Drive This is where all files are stored. The first floppy drive is named A:, the second (if any) is B:. Hard drives are C:, D:, and so forth. A drive, also called a *disk drive*, is like a file cabinet.

Directory Each disk drive can be subdivided into numerous directories. Each directory can contain files and other directories (called *subdirectories*). For example, your WordPerfect program and its related files are usually stored on C:\WPWIN60 and C:\WPC20 (the directories named WPWIN60 and WPC20 on hard disk drive C:). A directory is like one drawer in a file cabinet.

File   This is a single document or program. File names can be up to eight characters long, and can be followed by a period and an extension of up to three characters. (In speaking to people about your files, you identify the period as a dot. A file with the name HANDOUT.WPD, for example, would be referred to in speaking as "Handout-dot-W-P-D.") A file is like a single manila folder in a file drawer.

Path   The combined drive and directory location of a file. The path specifies the exact route to take to find a particular file. For example, the path and file name

C:\WPWIN60\WPDOCS\HANDOUT.WPD

says, "Go to drive C:, then go to the directory named WPWIN60, then to the directory below it named WPDOCS, and then to the file named HANDOUT.WPD."

Subdirectory   A directory that's below another directory. The terms *directory* and *subdirectory* are used interchangeably.

Wildcard   A * or ?, used to represent unknown or unspecified characters. The * can match any character or group of characters. The ? matches any single character. Use wildcards in WordPerfect dialog boxes and DOS commands to select groups of files that match a certain pattern, as summarized in Table 20.1.

N O T E

Oddly enough, any characters that follow the * wildcard in either the file name or the extension are ignored. For example, the pattern CH*NEW.* is treated the same as CH*.*. Likewise, the pattern ABC.*X means the same as ABC.*.

TABLE 20.1: The DOS Wildcard Characters Used in File Names

WILDCARD	WHAT IT MATCHES	EXAMPLE	DESCRIPTION OF EXAMPLE
?	Any single character	a??.?	Any file name starting with "A" followed by two characters and a one-character extension, e.g., **abc.1**, **axe.z**
*	Zero or more characters	*.exe	All files with an EXE extension
		.	All files
		test*.*	All files that start with the letters "TEST"

Entering File and Directory Names

Many WordPerfect commands lead to dialog boxes that prompt for file or directory names. Examples include options on the File menu (Open, Save, Save As, and Preferences ➤ Files), options on the Insert menu (Spreadsheet/Database ➤ Import, Spreadsheet/Database ➤ Create Link, and File), and the Graphics ➤ Figure command.

When you know a file or directory name, you can simply type it into the appropriate field in a dialog box. Here are some techniques you can use:

- If you enter only the file name (for example, **mydoc.wpd**), Word-Perfect will store or look for the file on the default drive and directory. (As Chapter 19 explains, the File Preferences options control the default location for various categories of WordPerfect files.)

- If you enter a subdirectory name and file name (as in the name **wpfiles\mydoc.wpd**), WordPerfect will save the file or retrieve it from the named subdirectory of the current directory. You can create directories and change the current directory without leaving WordPerfect.

- If you enter a complete drive and path, such as the path name **c:\wpwin60\wpdocs\mydoc.wpd,** WordPerfect will save the file or retrieve it from that drive and directory.

TIP The characters .. (dot dot) refer to the *parent* directory that's just above the current directory. Thus, if the current directory is C:\WPWIN60\WPDOCS, ..\TEMPLATE would refer to C:\WPWIN60\TEMPLATE.

Locating and Managing Files

When you don't know the exact file or directory name you want, you can use the *file-management tools* and dialog boxes to find it and fill in the name for you.

Navigating the file system is easy. The first step is to go to any dialog box that offers file-management tools. Some commands—File ➤ Open, Insert ➤ File, and File ➤ Save As, for example—will take you directly to a file-management dialog box. Others—such as File ➤ Preferences ➤ File—use text boxes to prompt for file and directory names. These text boxes include a small file button (shown at left) that you can click to open a file-management dialog box.

TIP Instead of clicking the file button, you can move the cursor into the text box where the file button appears, and then press Alt+↓ or F4.

Not all file-management tools are available in every file-management dialog box. A surefire path to these tools is the Open File dialog box (File ➤ Open or Ctrl+O or F4) shown in Figure 20.1. Don't worry if your Open

File dialog boxes aren't the same as this one. You'll undoubtedly have different files and directories and may have chosen different Setup and QuickList options.

NOTE

The QuickList provides easy access to files or directories that you use frequently. By default, the file-management dialog boxes don't include the QuickList area shown in Figure 20.1. You'll learn how to display and edit the QuickList in a moment.

You can use any combination of the following methods to locate files and directories:

- **To list files on a different drive,** choose the drive you want from the Dri<u>v</u>es drop-down list.

FIGURE 20.1

The Open File dialog box provides all the file-management tools that WordPerfect offers. To reach this dialog box, choose <u>F</u>ile ➤ <u>O</u>pen, or press Ctrl+O. Other file-management dialog boxes are similar, though they may lack the Vie<u>w</u>, QuickFinder, <u>S</u>etup, or File <u>O</u>ptions buttons.

Open File			
Filename:	c:\wpwin60		OK
`*.*`			Cancel
dbqelbus.dll	**QuickList:**		View...
dbqelib.dll	Documents		QuickFinder...
dpengwin.dll	Macro Directory		
dplib.dll	Template File		File Options ▾
dplibus.dll			QuickList ▾
indblib.dll			Setup...
install.dat	**Directories:**		Help
install.exe	c:\		
inxbase1.dll	wpwin60		
inxbase2.dll	graphics		
pxengwin.dll	learn		
pxlib.dll	macros		
pxlibus.dll	template		
qelib.dll			

Total Files: 51
Total Bytes: 11,776,996

Dri<u>v</u>es: 59,472 KB Free
c: ms-dos_6

List Files of <u>T</u>ype: All Files [*.*]

- **To list files on a different directory,** double-click the directory you want in the <u>D</u>irectories list, or highlight the directory and press ↵.

- **To list files of a different type,** select List Files Of <u>T</u>ype and select a file type. Choose the top entry in the list (*.*) if you want to display all files.

- **To specify the drive, directory, and file type all at once,** type the full path name and wildcards into the File<u>n</u>ame text box (above the list of files) and press ↵. For example, typing **c:\wpwin60\wpdocs\e*.*** into the box would list all files in the \WPWIN60\WPDOCS directory on drive C: that start with **e**.

- **To quickly highlight an item in a list,** click in or tab to the appropriate list, then type the first few letters of the item name.

T I P

You can right-click the file list, <u>Q</u>uickList, or <u>D</u>irectories list to bring up a QuickMenu of options for that list. This method provides a handy alternative to selecting options from the File <u>O</u>ptions, Quick<u>L</u>ist, and <u>S</u>etup buttons in a file-management dialog box.

Once you've located the file you're looking for, you can double-click the file name, or highlight it and choose OK. If you're looking for a directory name, double-click its name in the <u>D</u>irectories list or QuickList instead. This closes the file-management dialog box and completes whatever operation brought you there (for example, a file will open or a text box will be filled in with a file or directory name).

Viewing Files without Opening Them

Sometimes you'll want to peek into a file without opening it first. The following steps can be a real time-saver:

1. Go to any file-management dialog box that has a Vie<u>w</u> button (for example, choose <u>F</u>ile ➤ <u>O</u>pen).

2. Choose Vie<u>w</u> to open the Viewer window.

3. Do any of the following:

- **You can maximize, restore, resize, scroll through, or close** the Viewer window as needed.
- **To see what's in a file,** click on the file name or highlight it in the file list. The file will appear in the Viewer window.
- **To see a whole slew of handy options,** right-click the Viewer window and choose the option you want. Here's an example of options that appear after selecting a WordPerfect file in the file list and right-clicking the Viewer window:

√ WordPerfect 6.0
Hex
Viewer Setup...
Document **S**ummary
√ **W**ord-Wrap
F**o**nt...   F9
Find...   F2

Easy-Does-It File Management

You don't have to go to the Windows File Manager or (horrors!) back to DOS to manage your files. All the file-management features you could ever want are available in WordPerfect.

NOTE If you're upgrading from an older version of WordPerfect for Windows, you may be wondering where the WordPerfect File Manager is. It's gone! In its place are the easy-to-use tools described in this chapter.

Follow these steps to manage your files:

1. Go to any file-management dialog box that has a File Options button (for example, choose File ➤ Open).

2. In the file name list, highlight (select) the file or files you want to work with. (I'll explain how to select more than one file in a moment.) If you want to delete a directory, highlight the directory in the Directories list.

3. Click File Options and choose one of the options listed below:

   Copy   Copies one or more files.

   Move   Moves one or more files to a new location.

   Rename   Renames one or more files.

   Delete   Deletes one or more files. As a shortcut to choosing File Options ➤ Delete, you can select the files you want to delete, and then press the Delete key.

   Change Attributes   Changes file attributes of one or more files. You can select or deselect Archive, Read-Only, Hidden, and System attributes.

   Print   Prints one or more WordPerfect files.

   Print List   Prints a list of the selected file names or the entire list of file names.

   Create Directory   Creates a new directory.

   Remove Directory   Deletes the current directory or whichever directory you specify.

4. Complete the dialog box that appears for the file-management option you chose.

Selecting Multiple Files

You can select and open multiple files, or use the file-management options described just above to manage several files at once. To begin selecting multiple files, click in the file list or press Tab until you reach the list. Then use the techniques below:

- **To select several adjacent file names with the mouse,** click the first file name. Then drag the mouse down through the list until you highlight the last file you want.

- **To select several adjacent file names with the keyboard,** move the highlight to the first file name you want to select. Hold down the Shift key and press ↓ until you highlight the last file name you want.

- **To select several non-adjacent file names with the mouse,** click on the first file name you want to select, then hold down the Ctrl key while clicking each additional file name you want.

- **To select several non-adjacent file names with the keyboard,** move the highlight to the first file name you want to select. Press Shift+F8 (the selection cursor will blink). Move the highlight to the next file name you want and press the spacebar (repeat this step to select additional files). When you're done, press Shift+F8.

- **To deselect multiple selected files,** click on any file name or press the spacebar.

- **To deselect one file without deselecting others,** hold down the Ctrl key and click on the file name you want to deselect. Or, press Shift+F8, highlight the file name you want to deselect, and press the spacebar.

TIP To open up to nine files at once, choose File ➤ Open (Ctrl+O), select the files you want to open, and then choose OK.

Tailoring the File-Management Dialog Boxes

The QuickList shown in Figure 20.1 is just one example of something you can do to customize the appearance and content of a file-management dialog box. There's much more, as the next several sections will reveal.

Get There Fast with the QuickList

The QuickList uses descriptive names for directories, files, or wildcards. These descriptive names make it much easier to locate directories and files that you use frequently. (After all, how easy is it to remember or type a ridiculous path name like c:\tax\year93\1993rtrn.wpd?) Many Quick-List directory entries are defined automatically when you use File ➤ Preferences ➤ File and select (check) the Update QuickList With Changes box (see Chapter 19). You can also define your own QuickList entries, as shown below:

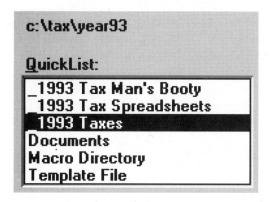

For example, if all your personal tax records for 1993 are stored in the directory C:\TAX\YEAR93, you could add a QuickList entry with a description of **1993 Taxes** for that directory. If you're working on your 1993 tax return (stored in the file 1993RTRN.WPD), you could set up a QuickList entry with the description **1993 Tax Man's Booty** and the path **C:\TAX\YEAR93\1993RTRN.WPD**. Now imagine that you also want a quick way to list Lotus 1-2-3 spreadsheet files stored in that same directory. You could set this description to **1993 Tax Spreadsheets** and the path to **C:\TAX\YEAR93*.WK1**. (Here, I've used a wildcard to stand for all files that have a .WK1 extension.) With a QuickList like this, there's no need to remember convoluted DOS path names or search through the drives and directories. (Dealing with your taxes will be your only worry now.)

Displaying the QuickList

To display (or hide) the QuickList, follow these steps:

1. Go to any file-management dialog box that offers a QuickList button. Our trusty File ➤ Open (Ctrl+O) command will do nicely.

2. Choose QuickList to open the QuickList drop-down menu.

3. Choose one of the options described below:

   > **Show QuickList**   Displays the QuickList and hides the Directories list.
   >
   > **Show Directories**   Displays the Directories list and hides the QuickList. (This is the default setting.)
   >
   > **Show Both**   Shows both the QuickList and the Directories list, as illustrated in Figure 20.1.

4. To return to the document window without making further selections, choose Cancel.

Using the QuickList

Once the QuickList is visible in any file-management dialog box, here's what you can do with it:

- Click a QuickList entry to copy its directory or file name into the Filename text box.

- If the QuickList entry points to a directory, double-click the entry to list file names in that directory.

- If the QuickList entry includes a wildcard, double-click the entry to list file names that match the wildcard.

- If the QuickList entry points to a file, double-click the entry to open, save, or select the file (depending on which dialog box you're using at the moment).

Editing the QuickList involves these easy steps:

1. Go to any file-management dialog box that has a QuickList button (for example, press Ctrl+O).

2. If you want to edit an existing item or delete an item from the QuickList, highlight the item in the QuickList first.

3. Click the QuickList button, then choose the option you want from the drop-down menu that appears. Your choices are:

> **Add Item**   Creates a new entry. In the Directory/Filename text box, enter the directory, path, or file name you want. In the Description text box, type the description for the entry. Choose OK.
>
> **Edit Item**   Edits the highlighted entry. Change the Directory/Filename and Description as needed, then choose OK.
>
> **Delete Item**   Deletes the highlighted entry.

4. If you see the message "*name* does not exist -- Use it anyway?" when you add or edit an entry, you can choose Yes to accept the entry or No to enter a new directory or file name.

5. Repeat steps 3 and 4 as needed. When you're done, choose Cancel to return to the document window.

The QuickList descriptions appear in alphabetical order. To put QuickList entries at the top of the list, just type a punctuation character in front of the description. In the sample QuickList shown earlier, I used an underscore in front the first three names to make sure those names will always be listed first.

Tailoring the File List Display

You can use the Setup button in a file-management dialog box to customize the appearance and sort order of the file list. Here's where the fun really starts ...and here's how to tailor the file list display:

1. Go to any file-management dialog box that offers a Setup button (for example, press Ctrl+O).

2. Choose Setup to open the Open/Save As Setup dialog box shown below:

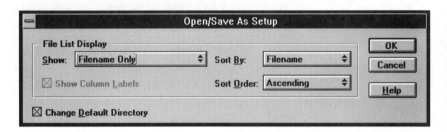

3. Choose any of the following options:

Show　Lets you display the Filename Only; Filename, Size, Date, and Time; Descriptive Name and Filename; or Custom Columns. If you choose either of the last two options, the dialog box will expand to include some speedup options. (See "About Speedup Files" and "Creating Custom Columns" for more about these options.)

NOTE　A *descriptive name* is a detailed name that can be longer than the document's DOS file name. You'll learn more about this topic in the later section on "Using Document Summaries."

Sort By　Lets you sort the file list by Filename, Extension, Size, Date/Time, Descriptive Name, or Descriptive Type.

Sort Order　Lets you sort files in Ascending (A-Z) or Descending (Z-A) order.

Show Column Labels　If you want to display the column labels in custom columns, select this option. To hide the column labels, deselect this option.

Change Default Directory　Select (check) this option to change the current directory whenever you switch directories in the Directories list box. Deselect the option to leave the current directory unchanged when you switch directories.

4. When you're finished choosing Open/Save Setup options, choose OK to return to the file-management dialog box. You can then choose other options in the dialog box, or choose Cancel to return to the document window.

About Speedup Files

When you elect to show the descriptive name or custom columns in the Open/Save As Setup dialog box, the dialog box expands to include two *speedup file* options. Speedup files save time by storing all descriptive name information in a separate file, rather than with the document summary itself (I'll discuss document summaries later in the chapter).

You can choose whether to create speedup files, and which directory they're stored in, with the options below:

Create Speedup Files   Select (check) this option if you want to create speedup files. Deselect it if you don't.

Directory   Specifies the directory for speedup files. If the directory doesn't exist, you'll be asked for permission to create it. (The default speedup directory is C:\WPSPEED.)

Creating Custom Columns

The file-management dialog box is pretty darn handy the way it is. But if you'd like to customize it with movable columns and other goodies, follow these steps:

1. Go to the Open/Save As Setup dialog box. For example, choose File ➤ Open ➤ Setup.

2. Choose Custom Columns from the Show pop-up list button.

3. Select (check) Show Column Labels. (You can deselect this later to hide the column labels and prevent accidental changes to the columns.)

4. Choose OK.

N O T E

Column Labels are the column headings that appear in the bar at the top of the file list.

The file-management dialog box will expand to resemble Figure 20.2.

Use the techniques below to organize the file list information:

- **To scroll to columns** that aren't visible at the moment, click the < and > buttons next to the column labels (the column-headings buttons) in the bar at the top of the file list.

- **To delete a column,** drag its column label above or below the column labels bar and release the mouse button.

- **To move a column,** drag its column label left or right and release the mouse button.

- **To adjust the width of a column,** drag the right edge of the column label button to the left (to narrow) or right (to widen).

FIGURE 20.2.

A file-management dialog box that includes custom columns

	Open File	
Filename:	c:\document	OK
		Cancel

QuickList:
_1993 Tax Spreadsheets
_1993 Taxes
Documents
Macro Directory
Template File
WPWIN 6 documentation

Filename	Size	Date	< >
abbrev.wpd	3,956	8/3/93	
abbrevi.wpd	12,158	8/20/93	
advanc.wpd	4,856	8/3/93	
advance.wpd	12,832	8/19/93	
append.wpd	9,998	8/19/93	
assoc.wpd	1,079	8/3/93	
backup.wpd	1,083	8/3/93	
barcod.wpd	6,371	8/3/93	
barcode.wpd	14,680	8/19/93	
baseline.wpd	10,801	8/19/93	
baslin.wpd	2,941	8/3/93	
bbared.wpd	7,207	8/3/93	

View...
QuickFinder...
File Options ▼
QuickList ▼
Setup...
Help

Directories:
c:\
document

Total Files: 250
Total Bytes: 5,157,416

Drives: 59,440 KB Free
c: ms-dos_6

List Files of Type: All Files (*.*)

- **To add a new column,** scroll to the blank space at the end of the column labels, or click any blank space that appears between buttons as a result of dragging column labels or reducing the width of a column. Now, right-click and choose an option from the Quick-Menu that appears. You can add columns to display Descriptive Name, Descriptive Type, Filename, Size, Date, Time, and Attributes. (See "Using Document Summaries" later in the chapter for more about Descriptive Name and Descriptive Type.) If necessary, drag the new column label to another position in the column label bar and adjust the column width as described just above.

Saving Documents

Two "save" options are available. File ➤ Save will save new documents or quickly replace the disk copy of an existing file with your on-screen copy. File ➤ Save As will also save new documents, but its main purpose is to let you *change* an existing document's name, format, or password. Figure 20.3 shows the Save As dialog box that opens whenever you choose File ➤ Save to save a new file or File ➤ Save As to save any file.

TIP

As added protection against power outages and other mishaps, WordPerfect can save your work automatically at timed intervals. See the section on automatic backups in Chapter 19.

The next few sections cover some things you might not know yet about the fascinating topic of saving files.

Exporting to Other Formats

WordPerfect normally saves files in its own WordPerfect 6 format. On occasion, you may want to use a different format, such as Microsoft Word for Windows or an earlier version of WordPerfect, so that you can change the file with a different word processor or text editor. To do this, choose

FIGURE 20.3

The Save As dialog box

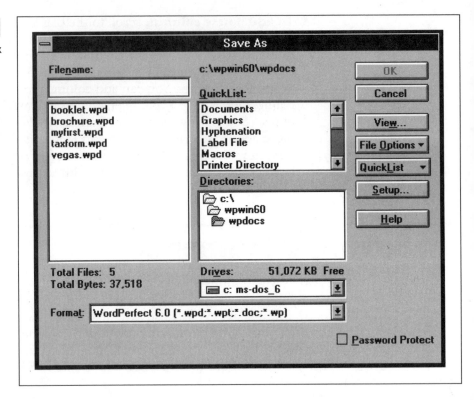

File ➤ Save As (or File ➤ Save for a new file) and supply a file name (if necessary). Select the file format you want from the Format drop-down list, then choose OK to complete the save.

N O T E

You can change the default save format from WordPerfect 6 to something else, though I don't recommend it. To do this, choose File ➤ Save As, choose the Setup button, and select a format from the Format drop-down list. Choose OK, then Cancel, to return to the document window.

To protect files from being damaged accidentally, WordPerfect displays a Save Format dialog box whenever you save a file to a format that's different from the one previously used to save that file. For example, you'll see the dialog box shown below if you open an ASCII Text file (such as \AUTOEXEC.BAT), then choose File ➤ Save to save it in WordPerfect 6 format:

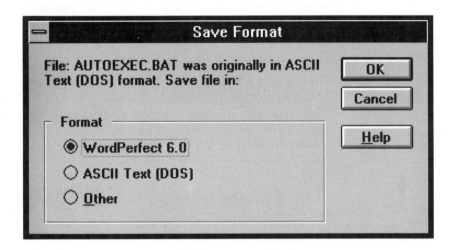

Choose the format you want from the options presented, then choose OK. You can choose Other from the Save Format dialog box to save the file in a format that's not shown in the dialog box. The Other option takes you to the Save As dialog box. From there, you can choose a new file name (if you wish), select a different format from the Format drop-down list, and choose OK.

WARNING

Do not convert crucial DOS system files, such as CONFIG.SYS or AUTOEXEC.BAT, to a different format. This can cause problems with your computer. If you change the format of a DOS system file accidentally, you should close the file, then open it again. Make sure there aren't any extra hard returns where you don't want them, then use File ➤ Save As and save the file in *ASCII Text (DOS)* format. If you accidentally convert a Windows .INI file to another format, close the file, open it again, then save the file in the *ANSI Text (Windows)* format.

Password-Protecting Files

Some documents contain sensitive information. If you're sharing your computer with other people, or you're using a network, you may wish to prevent others from viewing, printing, or changing that information. You do that by assigning a password when you save the file. Only people who know the password can use that document.

There's one catch, though. If *you* forget the password, you'll also be locked out of the document. So once you think up a password, write it down and store it in a safe place. (You might want to use the same password in all your documents to avoid confusion later.)

Follow these steps to add a password to your document:

1. Open or create the file, then choose File ➤ Save As (F3).

2. Type the Filename if necessary.

3. Select (check) Password Protect.

4. Choose OK. If you're asked about replacing the file, choose Yes.

5. When the Password dialog box appears, type the password you want to assign. (The characters you type will appear as a series of asterisks, so that nobody can see what you're typing.) Choose OK or press ↵.

6. When prompted to retype the password, type the password again to verify that you typed it correctly the first time, then choose OK or press ↵.

7. If you typed the same password both times, WordPerfect will accept it. Otherwise, you'll have to start over at step 5.

8. Close the file (File ➤ Close).

Opening a Password-Protected File

Whenever you open a password-protected document, you'll be prompted to enter a password.

Type the correct password (your typing will again appear as asterisks) and choose OK.

If you type the wrong password, you'll see an error message. Choose **OK** or press ↵ to clear the message, then retype the password correctly and choose OK. Or if you give up, choose Cancel to return to the document window.

Changing or Removing the Password

You can easily change or remove the password later, as long as you know the original password. First, open the file with File ➤ Open or with Insert ➤ File and enter the original password. Next, choose File ➤ Save As (F3).

- To remove the password, clear the Password Protect box and choose OK, then Yes, to confirm replacement of the file.

- To change the password, select (check) the Password Protect box, choose OK and Yes, then enter the new password as described earlier.

Incidentally, password-protecting a file only prevents people from opening, viewing, or changing the file through *WordPerfect*. It doesn't prevent anyone from using DOS or Windows, or the WordPerfect copy, move, rename, delete, and attribute commands on the file.

Other Save Options

A few save options are in the Environment Preferences dialog box. To reach this dialog box, choose File ➤ Preferences and double-click Environment (Chapter 19). The relevant options are discussed below:

Set QuickMark on Save   Determines whether a QuickMark bookmark is saved at the cursor location when you save a file (see Chapter 9). This option is normally deselected.

Reformat Documents for Default Printer on Open   Select this option to reformat documents for the selected printer when you open them (the default). Deselect this option to open documents with whatever printer was selected when they were last saved.

Code Page   You can choose the Code Page button if you need to specify an input and output code page to use when opening or saving WordPerfect documents. As explained in Chapter 19, you probably won't need to use this option unless you're working in a foreign language, or using files from a "foreign" computer system, such as the Apple Macintosh.

If you're using an additional language module or package language that has a *nonroman alphabet* (for example, Cyrillic, Greek, or Hebrew), you can use the Layout ➤ Document ➤ Character Mapping option to reduce the size of your document. After choosing this option, you'll see the Document Character Map dialog box. Select the character map for the language you're using and choose Apply. (Note that character maps are listed only for language modules that use nonroman alphabets.)

To change the character map for all new documents created with a particular template, edit or create the template as described later in this chapter, select and apply the character map you want from the Document Character Map dialog box, then exit the template and save your changes.

Opening "Non-6.0" Documents

Chapter 3 covered the basics of opening files with File ➤ Open (Ctrl+O) and combining files with Insert ➤ File. If you open or insert a document that was saved in any format except WordPerfect 6.0, you'll see a dialog box like this one:

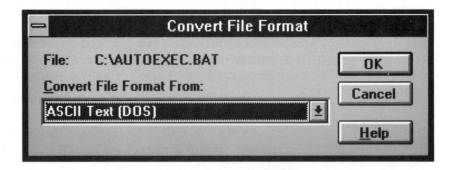

WordPerfect will take its best guess as to the original file format and will highlight that name in the list. If the format seems correct, choose OK to retrieve the document. Otherwise, open the drop-down list, scroll through it, and select the proper format. If WordPerfect has no idea what format the file is in, or you've tried to open a file that's in an unsupported format, you'll see an error message. Choose OK to clear the message and return to the Open File dialog box. Then try opening a different file.

Using Document Summaries

The file name assigned to a document when you save it is limited to the eight-character name, followed by the optional dot and three-character extension. This really limits how descriptive the file name can be.

One way around this problem is to add a *document summary* to your document. The summary lets you assign a more descriptive file name than DOS allows, provides a general overview of a document, and can help you organize and locate your files quickly. Often, you can find out what's in a document simply by taking a quick look at the document summary—no tedious reading required!

TIP   You can use QuickFinder to search for specific text and patterns in any document summary field. See "Find It Fast with QuickFinder," later in this chapter.

To create a document summary, follow these steps:

1. Open the document you want to summarize, or create a new document.

2. Choose File ➤ Document Summary. You'll see the Document Summary dialog box, shown in Figure 20.4.

3. To have WordPerfect fill in some fields automatically, choose Options ➤ Extract Information From Document. If your document

FIGURE 20.4

A Document Summary after extracting fields automatically. As indicated by the Revision Date, this file has been updated at least once.

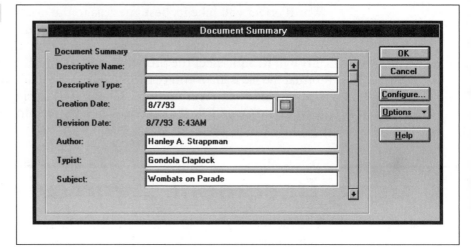

contains the word *RE:* followed by some text, Extract will copy the text after RE: as the Subject. (You can change the default subject text, as described later.) Extract will also copy a portion of text from the beginning of the document to the Abstract field.

NOTE

WordPerfect will automatically copy the Author and Typist fields from the most recent document summary you created or changed during the current WordPerfect session. If there is no previous document summary, WordPerfect will copy the text in the <u>N</u>ame field of Environment Preferences (<u>F</u>ile ➤ P<u>r</u>eferences ➤ Environ- ment) into the Author and Typist fields of your document summary.

4. Fill in the blank fields as you like, using the tips below as a guide:

- Use the vertical scroll bar to view additional fields.

- Type normal keyboard characters and WordPerfect characters (Ctrl+W) into any field. You can leave any field blank.

- Use the *Descriptive Name field* to assign a long (and descriptive) file name to the document. Use the Descriptive Type field to categorize the document (for example, **memo, chapter**, **report**, and **letter** might be useful Descriptive Type entries).

- The *Descriptive Name and Descriptive Type fields* will appear in the file-management dialog boxes if you've chosen to display them (see "Tailoring the File-Management Dialog Boxes" above, and "Tailoring the Document Summary" below).

- WordPerfect will fill in the *Creation Date and Revision Date fields* when you save the file. This information is based on the system clock, which you can set with the DATE and TIME commands in DOS or the Date/Time option in the Windows Control Panel. You can change the Creation Date if you like. (Try out the calendar button on the Creation Date field!)

- The *Keywords field* is useful for grouping documents by subject (separate each keyword by a space). For example, you could enter **wombat parade** into the Keywords field for the document summary shown in Figure 20.4.

- To view or change the *Abstract field*, scroll down to it in the list, click in the Abstract field, and edit normally.

5. When you're done changing the summary, choose OK.

WordPerfect will save the document summary the next time you save the document.

Document Summary Options

The Options button in the Document Summary dialog box offers the following features:

Print Summary   Prints the document summary fields.

Delete Summary from Document   Deletes the document summary from the document.

Extract Information from Document   Extracts document summary fields, as described previously.

Save Summary as New Document   Lets you save the document summary fields in a separate document file. If the file already exists, you can Overwrite it, Append it on a new page at the end of the file, or Cancel the operation. Append is useful when you want to store a collection of document summaries in a single file.

Tailoring the Document Summary

You can add and remove document summary fields, as appropriate for your own work. Starting from the Document Summary dialog box, choose Configure to open the dialog box shown in Figure 20.5.

Fields that are currently included in the document summary appear under Selected Fields. Other fields to choose from are listed alphabetically by field name in the Available Fields list. Customize the field lists as described below, then choose OK to return to the Document Summary dialog box.

- **To add a field** to the Selected Fields list, select (check) it in the Available Fields list.

- **To remove a field** from the Selected Fields list, click on it and drag it off the list, or deselect it in the Available Fields list.

- **To move a field** to a new position in the Selected fields list, drag the field to where you want it.

FIGURE 20.5

The Document Summary Configuration dialog box lets you choose which fields to include in the document summary.

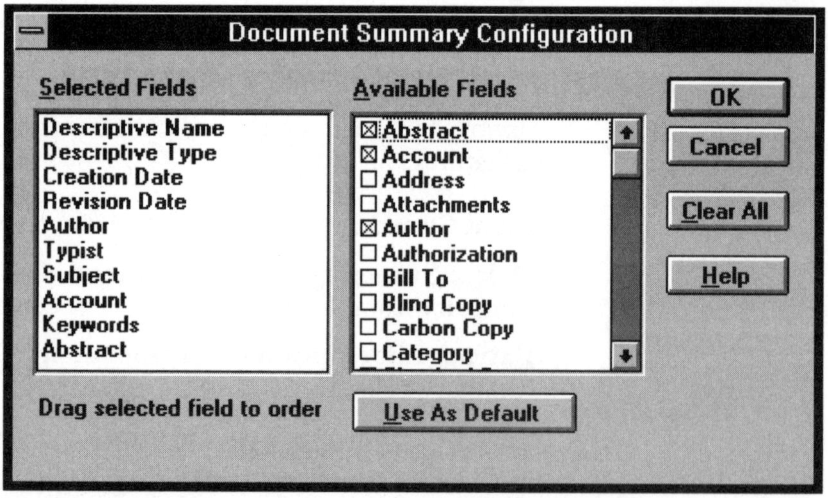

- **To quickly locate** a field name in the <u>S</u>elected Fields list, click in or tab to the list (or press Alt+S), then type the first letter of the field name. If there is more than one field that starts with that letter, you can continue typing the first letter until the field you want is highlighted.

- **To quickly locate** a field name in the <u>A</u>vailable Fields list, click in or tab to the list (or press Alt+A), then type the first few letters of the field name.

- **To remove all fields** from the <u>S</u>elected Fields list, choose <u>C</u>lear All.

- **To use the current <u>S</u>elected Fields list as the default** for other document summaries, choose <u>U</u>se As Default ➤ <u>Y</u>es.

To automate and further customize document summaries, follow the steps below:

1. Starting from the document window, choose <u>F</u>ile ➤ Pr<u>e</u>ferences and double-click <u>S</u>ummary. The Document Summary Preferences dialog box opens, as shown here:

2. Fill in, select, or deselect options as described just below:

- You can define the Default Subject Text (for example, **RE:**, **SUBJECT:**, or **TOPIC:**) and Default Descriptive Type (for example, **letter, invoice,** or **memo**). These will appear automatically when you create a new document summary.

- To automatically display descriptive names when you save or open documents, select (check) Use Descriptive Names.

- To automatically display the Document Summary dialog box when you save or exit a document, select (check) Create Summary On Save/Exit.

3. Choose OK, then Close, to save your changes and return to the document window.

Find It Fast with QuickFinder

Suppose you've created many documents and need to find all those that mention a fellow named *Willy O. Wontee.* This is clearly a job for *QuickFinder.* You can use QuickFinder to search through the current directory, disk, or subtree. Or, for blistering fast searches that will leave your computer breathless, search *QuickFinder indexes* instead (you'll learn how to work with QuickFinder indexes later in the chapter).

To find information quickly, you just tell QuickFinder where to look, what to look for, and send it on its way. Almost before you can blink, QuickFinder will present file names that match your search pattern. From there, you can use the standard tools to view, open, and manage the documents it found.

Starting QuickFinder

There are three ways to start QuickFinder:

- Choose File ➤ QuickFinder from WordPerfect's menu bar.

- Click the QuickFinder button in any file-management dialog box that offers it (for example, choose File ➤ Open or Insert ➤ File).

- Double-click the QuickFinder File Indexer icon in the WPWin 6.0 group window of Program Manager.

After choosing File ➤ QuickFinder, you'll see the dialog box shown in Figure 20.6. If you'd like to search the document summary fields, choose Options ➤ Summary Fields to expand the QuickFinder dialog box as shown in Figure 20.7. (Choose Options ➤ Summary Fields again to hide the summary fields.)

Searching with QuickFinder

Using QuickFinder to search for files is easy and fast. Here are the steps:

1. Start QuickFinder. For example, choose File ➤ QuickFinder.

2. Initially, QuickFinder will return all file names (*.*) that contain the text you search for. To limit the search to a group of files, type the pattern of file names in the File Pattern text box. To specify multiple file patterns, separate each entry with a space.

3. If you'd like to limit the results to files that were created or last changed within a certain date range, fill in the From and/or To text boxes. You can use the calendar buttons at the end of the From and To text boxes to locate and fill in dates quickly. If the From field is left blank, WordPerfect will return files that are as old or older than the To date. If the To date is left blank, WordPerfect will return files that are as new or newer than the From date.

FIGURE 20.6

The QuickFinder dialog box

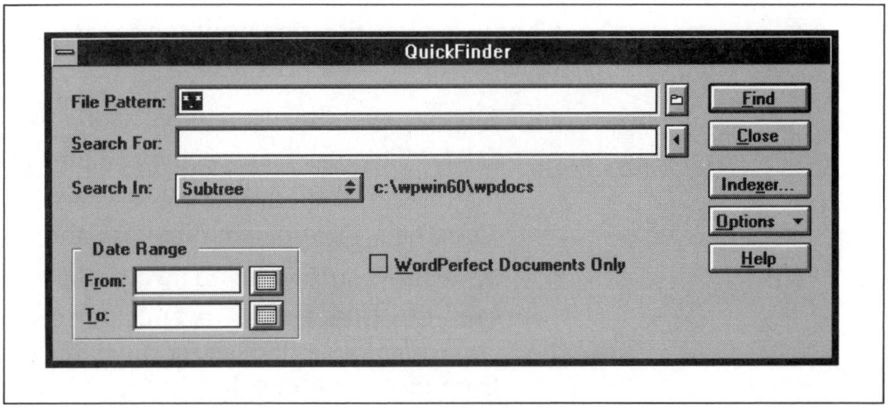

FIGURE 20.7

The QuickFinder dialog box after using Options ➤ Summary Fields to display Document Summary search fields

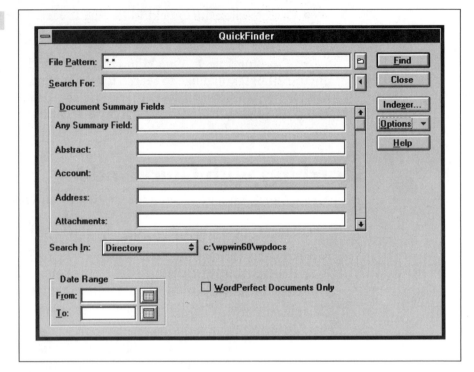

4. To limit the search to WordPerfect documents only, select (check) WordPerfect Documents Only.

5. If the option is available and you want to add the latest search results to the current search results list, select (check) Add Matching Files To Search Results List.

6. Choose the location you want to search from the Search In pop-up list button. Your options are:

> **Directory**   The current directory.
>
> **Disk**   The disk you specify. You'll be prompted to select a disk after choosing this option.
>
> **Subtree**   The current directory and its subdirectories.
>
> **Search Results List**   The current search results list.
>
> **QuickFinder Index**   A QuickFinder index. After choosing this option, select the index name you want from the drop-down list that appears. See "Creating and

Managing QuickFinder Indexes" later in the chapter for more about QuickFinder indexes.

NOTE If any indexed files have changed since the last time you updated the QuickFinder index you're searching, or you've added or deleted files in the index's list of directories and files, you should update the index before searching it. To update, choose Indexer, highlight the index you want in the Index Names list, choose Generate, and choose OK. When indexing is done, choose OK then Close.

7. In the Search For text box, type the word pattern you want to search for. (You can leave this option blank if you don't want to limit the search to specific text.) You can use the button (or press F4) in the Search For text box to display options for some fancier searches. Use the options to enter pattern operators in the search text, to limit the document components searched, to do a case-sensitive search, or to refine how close the matched words must be. (You can also type the fancy operators and options manually.) Table 20.2 shows the operators and some sample patterns.

8. Choose Find to start the search.

TABLE 20.2: Word Pattern Operators for QuickFinder[1]

OPERATOR	MEANING	SAMPLE WORD PATTERN	FINDS
" "	The phrase between the quotes	"just deserts"	Files with the phrase *just deserts*[2]
&	And—can also use the word **AND**	computer & "more productive"	Files with the words *computer* and *more productive*[3]
|	Or—can also use the word **OR**	"New York" | "New Jersey"	Files with the words *New York* or *New Jersey* or both sets of words[3]

TABLE 20.2: Word Pattern Operators for QuickFinder[1] (continued)

OPERATOR	MEANING	SAMPLE WORD PATTERN	FINDS
!	Not—can also use the word **NOT**	"New York"! "New Jersey"	Files with the phrase *New York*, but not the phrase *New Jersey*[3]
..	Followed by	"New York".. "New Zealand"	Files that contain both *New York* and *New Zealand*, with *New York* before *New Zealand*
?	Match single character	wombat?	Files with the word *wombat* plus a single character. Example: *wombats*
★	Match multiple characters	bar★	Files that have words starting with **bar**. Examples: *barb*, *barbarian*, *bark*

[1] You can type the pattern in uppercase, lowercase, or a mixture of both. The search will be case-insensitive, unless you click the button in the <u>S</u>earch For text box and choose Case <u>S</u>ensitivity ➤ <u>C</u>ase Sensitive.

[2] Place double quotation marks around phrases that contain the special operators (space & | - ? ★).

[3] The <u>C</u>loseness Of Words option on the <u>S</u>earch For text-box button determines where QuickFinder must find the words. For example, if the Closeness of Words is <u>L</u>ine and your pattern is *doris & ajar*, those two words must appear on the same line.

QuickFinder will search for all files in the selected location that contain the word pattern you entered, then it will display those file names in the Search Results window, as shown in Figure 20.8. You'll be astounded at how fast the search completes!

FIGURE 20.8

The results of a
successful search in
QuickFinder

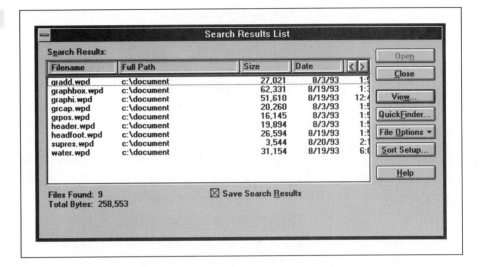

Here are some things you can do in the Search Results List dialog box:

- **To open files,** highlight the file (or files) you want to open, and choose Open.

- **To view a file** without opening it, choose View and highlight the file you want to see. Right-click the Viewer window for a list of handy options, including Find (F2).

- **To return to QuickFinder,** choose QuickFinder.

- **To perform file-management operations** on files, highlight the file (or files) you want to work with, choose File Options, and select the option you want (Copy, Move, Rename, Delete, Change Attributes, Print, or Print List). You can also right-click in the file list and select options from the QuickMenu that appears.

- **To sort the file list,** choose Sort Setup, select the By and Order options you want, and choose OK.

- **To rearrange the columns,** drag the column label buttons and add columns as described earlier under "Creating Custom Columns."

- **To save the search results list,** select (check) Save Search Results. The list will be saved when you return to QuickFinder or close the Search Results List window.

- **To return to wherever you came from** before opening Quick-Finder, choose <u>C</u>lose.

QuickFinder Search Options

The <u>O</u>ptions button in QuickFinder has some neat features for you to try:

Summary <u>F</u>ields   Expands the QuickFinder dialog box to let you search document summary fields. Choose the Summary <u>F</u>ields option again to hide the document summary fields.

Last Search <u>R</u>esults   Returns you to the last saved Search Results window (if one is available).

<u>C</u>lear   Clears all search criteria.

<u>L</u>oad Search Query   Lets you load a previously saved search query.

<u>S</u>ave Search Query   Lets you save a search query for later use.

<u>D</u>elete Search Query   Lets you delete a previously saved search query.

Managing QuickFinder Indexes

QuickFinder indexes are alphabetical lists of every word in the files and directories you specify. These indexes are stored in a highly compressed format that QuickFinder can scan almost instantaneously.

Although QuickFinder indexes contain alphabetical lists of words, they're quite different from conventional indexes like the one at the back of this book or the ones you can create with WordPerfect's automatic indexing feature (Chapter 31). For example, you can't look at a QuickFinder index directly, nor can you print it.

N O T E   QuickFinder indexes usually are stored in files with .IDX extensions in the C:\WPC20\QFINDEX subdirectory.

To manage QuickFinder indexes, start QuickFinder (for example, choose <u>F</u>ile ➤ QuickFinder), then choose Inde<u>x</u>er. If you're asked to specify a default directory for saving indexes, choose OK to accept the default index path, or type in another path name and choose OK. You'll see the Quick-Finder File Indexer dialog box shown in Figure 20.9.

If you want to work with an existing index, highlight it in the Index <u>N</u>ames list. Now choose any of the buttons listed below:

<u>G</u>enerate Lets you regenerate the highlighted index. You can up-date the index with new or modified files only, or reindex all the files defined for the index.

C<u>r</u>eate Lets you create and generate a new index. See the next section, "Creating or Editing an Index," for details.

<u>E</u>dit Lets you edit and regenerate the highlighted index. See the next section, "Creating or Editing an Index," for details.

<u>O</u>ptions Provides various options, listed below:

- **To get information about the highlighted index file,** choose <u>I</u>nformation.

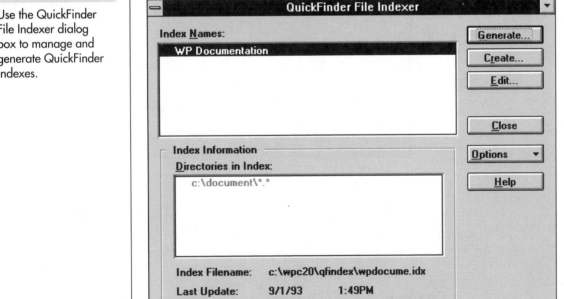

- **To delete, rename, or move the highlighted file,** choose <u>D</u>elete, <u>R</u>ename, or <u>M</u>ove (as appropriate).

- **To import an index from another location,** such as a network drive, choose Imp<u>o</u>rt. (You can search an imported index, but you cannot change it.)

- **To choose default settings** for new indexes or change the default location for index files, choose <u>P</u>references. The Preferences dialog box for QuickFinder indexes looks like this:

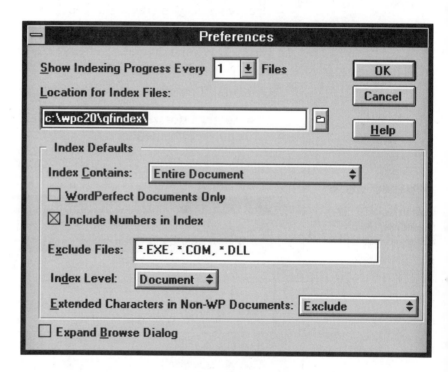

- **To get information about QuickFinder,** choose <u>A</u>bout.

When you're done using the QuickFinder File Indexer dialog box, choose <u>C</u>lose until you return to the document window.

Creating or Editing an Index

To create or edit an index, follow the steps below:

1. Go to the QuickFinder File Indexer dialog box. For example, choose File ➤ QuickFinder ➤ Indexer.

2. Now, do one of the following:

   - **To create a new index,** choose Create, type a name for the index (for example, **Office Memos**), and choose OK. The Create Index dialog box will appear. (This dialog box is similar to the Edit Index dialog box shown in Figure 20.10.)

   - **To edit an existing index,** highlight it in the Index Names list and choose Edit. You'll see an Edit Index dialog box, like the one in Figure 20.10.

FIGURE 20.10

The Edit Index dialog box

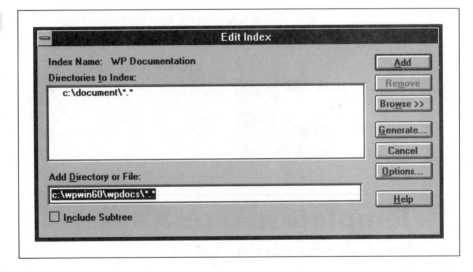

3. Use the methods listed just below to select the files and directories to include in the index definition:

   - **To add a file or directory** to the index, type the directory, file, or path name into the Add Directory Or File box (or use the Browse button to help you locate and fill in the name). If you want the index to include subdirectories of the path you entered, select (check) I̲nclude Subtree. Then choose A̲dd to add the path to the Directories T̲o Index list.

- **To remove a file or directory** from the index, highlight the name in the Directories T̲o Index list and choose Re̲move.

- **To set options for this index,** choose O̲ptions, fill in the dialog box, and choose OK. The Individual Index Options dialog box is similar to the Preferences dialog box shown in the previous section. For details about options in this dialog box, choose H̲elp.

4. Repeat step 3 as needed.

5. If you want to generate the index now, choose G̲enerate, specify whether to update the index with new or modified files, or with all files, then choose OK. When index generation is complete, choose OK to return to the QuickFinder File Indexer dialog box.

6. Choose C̲lose (or Cancel) as needed to return to the document window.

T I P

If you'd like WordPerfect to generate QuickFinder indexes for you automatically (even while you sleep), check out the KickOff application in Chapter 33.

Templates: Your Keys to Consistency

Templates are the greatest thing since sliced computer bits. Even more than styles, templates can create order and consistency in your word processing life. Every new document that you create is formatted according to an underlying template file. Templates establish the initial document text and they define the abbreviations, button bars, macros, menus, keyboards, preferences, and styles available to a document.

WordPerfect comes with several built-in templates, including the *standard* template you've probably been using all along. If WordPerfect's templates don't do the job for you, it's easy to set up new ones of your own.

Templates are ideal for fast-moving companies that use networks. The network administrator can change company-wide templates to match the latest corporate standard. Any new documents created with those templates will reflect the changes.

About Default and Supplemental Templates

When you create a new file via the File ➤ New command or by typing into an empty document window, WordPerfect automatically uses the *default template* defined in File Preferences. The default template typically is named C:\WPWIN60\TEMPLATE\STANDARD.WPT. You can also use a *supplemental template* that includes styles you might need often.

To specify (or change) the default template or supplemental template location, choose File ➤ Preferences, double-click File, then choose Templates. Fill in the default and supplemental directory and file names and the default template file extension (usually .WPT) as needed. When you're done, choose OK, then Close. (See Chapter 19 for more about Preferences.)

Choosing a Template for a New File

It's easy to create a new document with a nondefault template. Here are the steps to follow:

1. Choose File ➤ Template (Ctrl+T) to open the Templates dialog box shown below.

2. Highlight the template you want to use.

3. If you'd like to preview the text in the template, choose View. The Viewer window (described earlier in this chapter) will open.

4. To select the highlighted template, choose OK. Voila! A new document window will appear, and all text and objects defined for the template will be available to you instantly.

The quickest way to open a new file with a nondefault template is to press Ctrl+T and then double-click the name of the template you want.

Creating a Template

Creating a new template isn't difficult. However, to set up a full-blown template, you'll need to know something about styles (Chapter 17), macros (Chapter 18), abbreviations (Chapter 9), button bars (Chapter 4), menus

(Chapter 4), and keyboards (Chapter 19). If you don't know all that stuff, don't worry. You can start simple and refine your template later. Any new documents created with that template will have features from the revised template.

Follow these steps to create a new template file:

1. Choose File ➤ Template (Ctrl+T).

2. Choose Options ➤ Create Template to open the Create Document Template dialog box shown here:

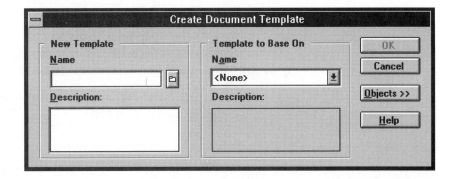

3. In the Name text box, type a name for the template. The name can have up to 25 characters, including spaces and punctuation.

WordPerfect will use the first eight characters of the template name to construct the template *file name*. Therefore, be sure that the first eight characters aren't used for other templates in the default template directory.

4. In the Description text box, type a description. (This description will appear at the bottom of the Templates dialog box when you highlight the template name.)

5. To base the new template on an existing template, choose an existing template name from the Name drop-down list at the right of the dialog box.

6. To preview the currently defined objects for the template, choose Objects.

7. Choose OK. A new window will open and the Template feature bar will appear. The completed template example in Figure 20.11 is named COMPUTER.WPT (shortened automatically from my entry of *Computer Commuter* in step 3). Because I based the template on an existing template, named *mileage*, it's already filled in with text styles and other attributes from the existing template.

8. Type or edit the template's text and choose options from the pull-down menus as for any document. You can also choose any of the Template feature bar buttons described below:

    ?   Opens other feature bars and provides an alternative to using feature bar buttons.

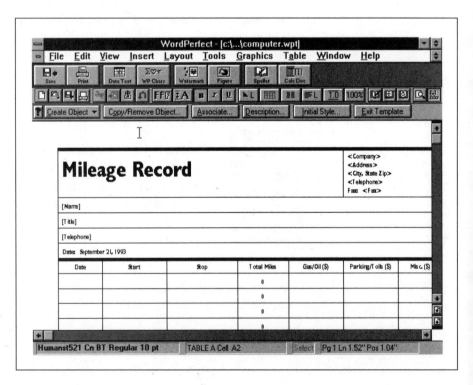

Create Object   Lets you create a new template object (Style, Macro, Abbreviations, Button Bar, Keyboard, or Menu Bar).

Copy/Remove Object   Lets you copy objects from a specified template to the current template, or remove objects from the current template.

Associate   Lets you establish a connection between a template object and various WordPerfect modes or features. You can also run (trigger) a macro that's stored with the template when certain events occur. For example, you could define and save a macro that displays some instructions. Then use Associate ➤ Triggers and set up a connection that plays back the macro whenever you create a new document with this template. (For more information on this topic, click Help or refer to the documentation that came with your WordPerfect for Windows package.)

Description   Lets you change the description for the current template.

Initial Style   Lets you define the initial style (Initial-Style) for documents created with this template (see Chapter 19).

9. When you're ready to save the template changes and return to the document window, choose Exit Template ➤ Yes.

Editing or Deleting a Template

Need to make a change to an existing template or get rid of an unwanted template? That's easy:

1. Choose File ➤ Template (Ctrl+T), and highlight the template you want to edit or delete.

2. Choose Options, then …

   • **To edit the template,** choose Edit Template. Continue with step 8 of the "Creating a Template" procedure above.

   • **To delete the template,** choose Delete Template ➤ Yes.

About Templates and Styles

Recall from Chapter 17 that styles can come from four different sources: the current document, the default template, the supplemental template, and WordPerfect's built-in system styles. Moreover, style changes can go to the current document, default template, or supplemental template. Sometimes all this can be downright confusing!

Suppose you define and save a template that includes a style named **Memo Heading**. You then make this template the new default template, via the File ➤ Preferences ➤ File ➤ Templates command. Now imagine that you use File ➤ Template to create a new file using this default template. Immediately, WordPerfect copies the template styles to the current document styles. If you apply the current document's Memo Heading style to text in the document, it will initially have the style defined in the template. However, if you (or someone else) changes the template's Memo Heading style, that change won't be reflected in your document. That's because document styles take precedence over template and supplemental template styles.

To make sure your documents always will reflect changes made to styles in their current and supplemental templates, follow these steps:

1. Open or create a document that uses the template you'll be working with.

2. Choose Layout ➤ Styles ➤ Options ➤ Setup to open the Setup dialog box for styles.

3. Deselect Current Document and select (check) Default Template (and Supplemental Template if you wish).

4. Choose Current Document as the Default Location.

5. Choose OK.

Now, if you need to change styles for the templates, close any open documents and go through the Template feature. That is, press Ctrl+T, highlight the template name, and choose Options ➤ Edit Template. Then choose Layout ➤ Styles (or press Alt+F8) and make your style changes normally. When you're done, choose File ➤ Save, then choose Exit Template from the Template feature bar. If you followed all the guidelines above, any documents created with the template will include the updated style and reformat instantly the next time you open them. (See Chapter 17 for more about Styles.)

About Templates and Macros

Like styles, macros can come from various sources, including the current template, default template, or a file on disk. If you record a macro to a template, any documents created with that template will inherit the macro automatically. Likewise, if you edit a macro that's stored in a template, any documents created with that template will inherit the changes as well.

To make WordPerfect look for and record macros in a template, choose Tools ➤ Macro and select Play, Record, or Edit. When the macro dialog box appears, choose Location, pick the template you want (either Current Template or Default Template), and select (check) Use As Default. Choose OK to save the location and Cancel to return to the document window. (See Chapter 18 for more about macros.)

This chapter has shown you many ways to use WordPerfect's file-management tools to locate and manage files stored on disk. As you've seen, your options are nearly limitless, far exceeding the capabilities of clunky old DOS and even the Windows File Manager. You've also learned how to set up QuickFinder indexes and templates.

Part Five, "Office Tools," is the next stop on our tour of WordPerfect. There, you'll learn about the many ways that WordPerfect helps offices run smoothly. I'll start by discussing form letters and mailing labels.

PART FIVE

Office Tools

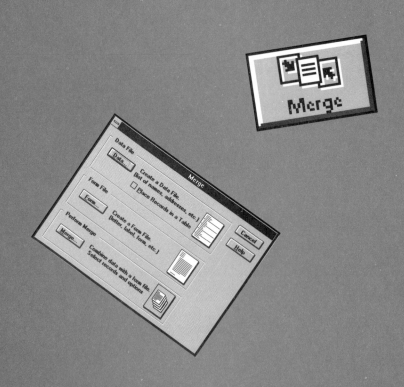

CHAPTER

21

Form Letters, Mailing Labels, and Other Merges

f a s t TRACK

● **To insert a merge field into the form**   **687**

click the Insert Field button in the Merge feature bar, position
the cursor in the form, and double-click the field name
you want.

● **To prevent blank lines resulting from empty fields**
in the data file   **692**

place a question mark (?) after the field name.

● **To insert a merge command into the form**   **693**

position the cursor where you want the command to appear,
click the Merge Codes button in the feature bar, highlight the
command you want, and choose Insert.

● **To prevent extraneous blank spaces caused**
by empty fields in the data file   **695**

use the IFBLANK...ENDIF and IFNOTBLANK...ENDIF
merge commands in your form.

● **To prompt for input from the keyboard**   **698**

position the cursor where you want the data to be inserted
during a merge, click the Keyboard button in the Merge feature bar, type a prompt, and choose OK.

● **To merge the data file and form**   **703**

choose Tools ➤ Merge ➤ Merge (Shift+F9,M). Specify the
names of the form file, data file, and output file, and choose OK.

F YOU ever need to produce mass mailings, multiple copies of a memo, or other multiple-copy documents, you're sure to love WordPerfect's *merge* feature.

For example, you might create a list of names and addresses of people to whom you send mail regularly. Later, you create a form letter, with placeholders for the recipient's name and address. Then you *merge* (combine) that letter with your list of names and addresses to create a personalized copy of the letter for everyone in the mailing list. While you're at it, you can print up mailing labels or envelopes.

The merge takes just seconds, and WordPerfect does all the work. Whether you have five or five hundred names and addresses, you need only type the form letter and your list of names and addresses *once* (though you'll need to update your list from time to time).

Your data isn't limited to names and addresses. You can type up your employee data, titles in your video or CD collection, research data, or anything else you can imagine. Once you've made the list, you can display it in any form you wish, without ever retyping anything.

Understanding Merge Files

Two files are usually involved in a merge:

Data File   A file that contains all the information that's unique to each document and that needs to be repeated on each document (such as names and addresses). It's easiest to create your data file first, though WordPerfect doesn't force you to.

Form File   A document (form letter, envelope, mailing labels, fill-in-the-blank form, directory, and so forth) that contains *merge codes* placed where information from the data file will appear.

NOTE   You can also get data right from the keyboard instead of from a merge data file. This is handy for "on-the-fly" data that isn't worth storing permanently in a data file.

Planning a Data File

A data file for a merge consists of *records* and *fields*. If you store this information in a table (as I recommend), it's easiest to think of each column in that table as a *field*, and each row as a *record*.

Figure 21.1 shows a simple data file stored in a table. I've defined five fields (columns): Name, Address, City, State, and Zip. The field names appear across the top row of the table. This data file contains ten records (rows), but could easily contain hundreds, even thousands, of records.

FIGURE 21.1

Sample data file, in table format, demonstrating *fields* and *records*

Fields

Name	Address	City	State	Zip
Sandi Fète	22 Beach St.	Eugene	OR	87654
Candy Mann	809 Circuit Ct.	Seattle	WA	43930
Doris Knight	Box 11	Boise	ID	74837
Willie Wanna	007 Bond St.	Yippi	OH	40394
Janet Green	543 Myrtle Ave.	Pleasant	VA	20394
Tony Buccio	Box 1234	Bangor	ME	01021
Mimi May Mee	812 Weasel St.	Anywhere	TX	39283
Daniel Tu	Route 22	Kazoo	KY	01234
Freddy Glassy	P.O. Box 228	New York	NY	52919
Wanda Granola	123 Oak Ln.	Leucadia	CA	91234

Records

TIP If your data file will contain more than a few hundred records, consider using an application such as dBASE, Paradox, or Access to manage the data. You can easily export data from a database file to a WordPerfect data file, then use WordPerfect to merge form letters, mailing labels, and so forth. See Chapter 33 for details.

Two Ways to Store Data

Once you've figured out what fields you want in your data file, you need to decide how to *structure* the data file. You have two choices:

Table Method   You can use a table to define the table structure, where each field is in a column, and each record is in a row, as in Figure 21.1.

Text Method   Alternatively, you can use text and merge codes, where each field ends with an ENDFIELD code, and each record ends with an ENDRECORD code, like this:

Sandi Fete**ENDFIELD**
22 Beach St.**ENDFIELD**
Eugene**ENDFIELD**
OR**ENDFIELD**
87654**ENDFIELD**
ENDRECORD

Besides the general appearance of the data, there are other differences between these two data file structures:

- The **table** method is limited to 64 fields (columns). The **text** method allows up to 255 named fields.

- The **table** method allows as many records as will fit in memory. The **text** method allows as many records as you wish, limited only by the amount of available disk space.

- WordPerfect takes longer to get around in a table than in a regular document. So for a huge data file (several thousand records), you might prefer the **text** method.

- The **table** method may lead to word-wrapping within the table. This won't be a problem if you just let WordPerfect handle the wrapping on its own (that is, you don't force the text to wrap a certain way by pressing ↵). WordPerfect will "unwrap" the line automatically when you merge it into your form.

- The **text** method is basically the same one used by earlier versions of WordPerfect. Therefore, if you already have data stored in a *secondary merge file* (the name for a data file in earlier versions of WordPerfect), you needn't bother converting that file to a table.

T I P

Unless your data file is (or will be) huge, you may prefer using the table method, simply because it's easier to work with records that appear in neat rows and columns.

Designing a Data File

The following tricks can help you design a flexible data file that you can reuse without ever having to retype any information:

- Use a separate field for every item of information you'll need in the merge. For example, if you send birthday cards to clients every month, include a field for the birth date. Add a field for fax numbers if you plan to create phone lists from your merge file.

- Every record must have the same fields, in the same order. For example, all records must have a Birth Date field if you want to store birth dates with *any* of the names and addresses in your data file—just leave the Birth Date field empty for people who won't be receiving birthday cards.

- The more fields you use for your data, the easier it will be to work with the file in the long run.

- Each field must have a unique name. For example, you can't have two fields named Address (though you *could* have one field named Address1 and another named Address2).

It's easiest to begin by listing all the fields you need. For example, you'd need a field in your data file for every blank in an income tax form that you're filling in with data.

In this chapter, I'll stick with the example of names and addresses in a data file, since this is such a common use for a merge. The example shown in Figure 21.1 is probably sufficient for a small data file. However, if you have many addresses, including some outside the United States, and want maximum flexibility in your data file, you might prefer setting up the fields shown in Figure 21.2.

FIGURE 21.2

A plan for fields in a data file that stores names and addresses for people within and outside the United States

Field Name	Stores
Hon	Honorific: Mr., Ms., Dr....
First Name	Person's first name
MI	Person's middle initial
Last Name	Person's surname
Dept/ Title	Department or title
Company	Company name
Address	Street address
City	City of residence
State/ Province	State or Province of residence
Zip/ Postal	Zip code or postal code
Country	Country (empty if USA)
Phone	Telephone number
New	✓ if new, No if old

In Figure 21.3 you can see a printed copy of some sample records that have the structure that was defined in Figure 21.2.

Hon	First Name	MI	Last Name	Dept/ Title	Company	Address	City	State/ Province	Zip/ Postal	Country	Phone	New
Mrs.	Janet	L.	Green	President	ABC Corp.	123 A St.	San Diego	CA	92000		(619)555-1023	No
Ms.	Wanda	B.	Granola	Accts. Payable	Logicon	P.O. Box 123	New York	NY	32555		(212)555-4049	No
Dr.	Janet	L.	Menezes	Botanist	Florália	Orquidários Ltda Box n 100541	Niterói	Rio de Janeiro		Brasil	55-21-555800	No
Dr.	Candy		Mann	Internist	Ono Pediatric Clinic	1101 Krager	Bangor	ME	02000-1234		(123)555-1234	No
	Cher		Bobo			3232 East Lake	Duarte	CA	92999		(213)555-3039	✓
				Sales Division	Doofdork Corp.	Box 1131	Lakewood	NJ	08701		(800)555-1030	✓
Ms.	Esther	C.	Clauser	Author		1101 Orchard St.	Nepean	ONT	K2E8A5	Canada	(613)555-4049	✓
Mr.	Stan	J.	Ramdrive	Clerk	Quark County Court	540 Grand Ave.	Orem	UT	84057		(800)555-4049 Ext. 323	✓
	Alberta	J.	Wein	Travel Agent	RSF Travel	12 Paseo Delicias	Saturn	FL	33431		(407)555-5052	✓

Why Four Fields for a Name?

Maybe you're wondering why I've split names into four separate fields, like this:

HONORIFIC	FIRST NAME	MI	LAST NAME
Dr.	Candy	Q.	Mann

I did this for several reasons. First, WordPerfect can sort (or alphabetize) the records based on any field. Thus, I could alphabetize all the records by last name (or last and first name, as in the phone book), as long as Last Name is in a separate field. (Chapter 22 discusses sorting.)

Second, by breaking the name into four separate fields, I can easily use any portion of a person's name when printing, and can arrange the parts of the names however I wish. For example, I could display Candy Mann's name in any of these formats when merging her record into a form letter:

Dr. Candy Q. Mann	Dr. Mann
Candy Mann	Mann, Candy Q.
Dear Dr. Mann:	Dear Candy:
Dr. Candy	Yo, Dr. Candy Q.

Granted, this many fields is probably overkill for a small mailing list of local names and addresses. But as you'll see, the technique can come in handy for larger applications.

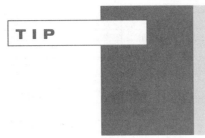

TIP

If you don't break names into separate fields, consider putting a field named Salutation into your data file structure. Then type into that field whatever you want to follow *Dear* at the top of a letter. For example, if the Name field contains *Ms. Jenny L. Sparta*, your Salutation field could contain *Ms. Sparta* or *Jenny*.

What's That "New" Field For?

The New field shown in Figure 21.2 is handy if you need to send a welcome letter or catalog to "new people" after adding them to the data file. You can just type some unusual character, such as a check mark, into that field (press Ctrl+W and choose a check mark or other unusual character). Later, you can isolate records that have a check mark in the New field, and print welcome letters and labels for those people only.

When you've finished printing the welcome letters and labels, use Replace (Ctrl+F2) to change all the check marks to *No* (or to nothing). That way, people who already have received welcome letters won't be included the next time you print those letters. But you'll still have their names and addresses on file for future mailings of other material.

Organizing the Fields

The order in which you list field names in the data file is not crucial, because you can display them in any desired order and format when you create the form. However, it does help to put them into some kind of naturally intuitive order—such as Name, Address, City, State, for instance—simply because you're less likely to make mistakes when typing data into the file. Similarly, if you'll be copying information into the data file from a paper form, it's best to order the fields as they appear on the form you're working with, since you'll naturally want to type them in that order.

Put Data into the Correct Field!

Although you can *define* field names in whatever order you wish, it's essential that you *type* the data into the correct field.

For example, if you type a zip code into the Last Name field, the computer won't say "Hmmmm, tried to trick me by typing that zip code into the Last Name field," and then correct the error. Nope, it's just going to put the zip code where you told it to: in the Last Name field. Because the computer does exactly what it's told, it's up to you to tell it *exactly* what to do. (Remember, computers have no brains whatsoever—on the IQ scale, they rate right up there with a blob of mayonnaise.)

Here's a true story about what can happen if you type the *right* information into the *wrong* field. Somebody, somewhere, has typed my name as "Author" into the Name field of a database. I now get mail that's addressed to "Author, P.O. Box 3384, etc." The letters start with "Dear Author:" and say things like "Author, it's your lucky day!" My name doesn't appear *anywhere* in this mail. Someone even sent me a personalized datebook that I could order as a gift for my friends. The cover announces, in gold embossed letters, "Compliments of Author."

Alphabetizing and Sorting

Whether you use the table method or text method to store your data, you can use WordPerfect's sorting features (Chapter 22) to instantly put the records in any order you want, whenever you want. For example, you can sort records into zip code order for bulk mailing. Then re-sort them into alphabetical order by name so you can print a directory or phone list.

Typing Dates and Numbers

If you include dates in your data file structure, follow a consistent format when typing each date. For example, **1/1/93** or **Jan 1, 1993**. You and I know that 1/1/93 means the same as January 1, 1993, but the computer doesn't know that. So be consistent when typing your dates. That way it'll be easier to isolate certain records later.

Similarly, when you type in numbers, follow a consistent pattern, such as *35,000.00* or *17,500.47*. In this example, I've used a comma separator, two decimal places (even if they're both zero), and no currency symbol for money items. (You can insert a currency symbol into the form letter, if you need it.) As with dates, this consistency will make it easier to isolate certain type of records later.

Creating a Data File

The *structure* of a data file refers to the quantity of fields and the name of each field—as opposed to the actual *data* (such as specific names and addresses) within the file. To create a data file structure, follow these steps:

1. In general, you should start from a new document window. (If you want to use text in the existing document or you forget to start a new document window, you'll have a chance to decide which window to use in step 6 below.)

2. If you'd like to allow for many fields in a table data file, you can reduce the margins (Chapter 5), choose a wide paper size such as Letter Landscape (Chapter 8), and pick a small font. To begin, choose Layout ➤ Document ➤ Initial Codes Style (Chapter 6). Then set 0″ margins (Layout ➤ Margins), and choose a landscape paper size (Layout ➤ Page ➤ Paper Size). You also might want to pick a small font, such as Arial 10 pt (Layout ➤ Font). Return to the document window when you're done.

3. To open the Merge dialog box (Figure 21.4), choose Tools ➤ Merge, or press Shift+F9, or click the Merge button in the WordPerfect button bar (at left), or click the Merge button in the Merge feature bar (described later in this chapter).

4. If you want to define a table merge data file, select (check) Place Records In A Table.

5. Click the Data button.

6. If the current document isn't empty, a dialog box will ask if you want to use the current document for your data file (Use File In Active Window) or open a new document window (New Document Window). Pick the option you want and choose OK.

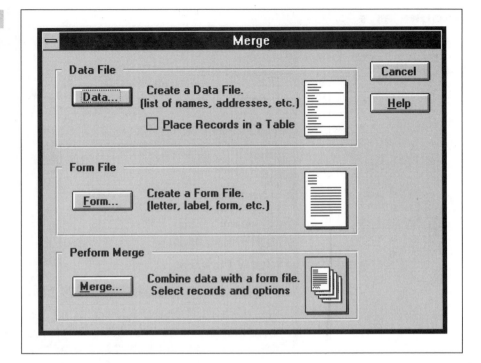

7. The Create Data File dialog box appears next (Figure 21.5).

8. In the <u>N</u>ame A Field text box, type a field name (up to 40 characters, including spaces if you wish), then choose <u>A</u>dd or press ⤶. (It
   doesn't matter whether you enter field names in uppercase, lowercase, or a mixture of both; it's all the same to WordPerfect. However, do be sure to add field names in the same order that data
   will be entered.)

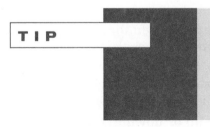

TIP

To make a field name wrap differently (especially useful
in tables), press the spacebar where you want the name
to break. For example, I put a space after the slashes in
Dept/ Title, State/ Province, and *Zip/ Postal* just to
control how the names wrap in the first row of the table.

FIGURE 21.5

The Create Data File
dialog box with eleven
fields defined

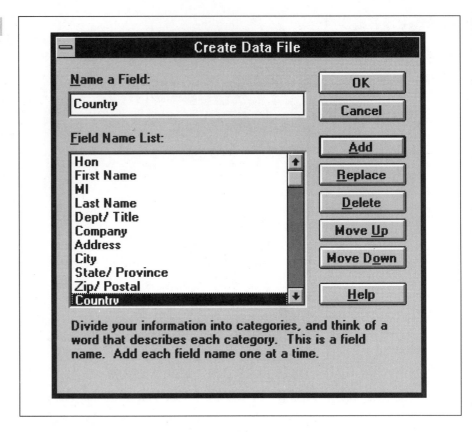

9. Repeat step 8 for each field you want to add. If necessary, you can reorder or rename fields in the Field Name list, as follows:

- **To add a new field name,** highlight the field that's just above the spot where the new name should appear in the Field Name List, type the name in the Name A Field text box, and choose Add.

- **To change a field name,** highlight the field you want to change in the Field Name List, type the new name in the Name A Field text box, and choose Replace.

- **To delete a field name,** highlight the field you want to delete in the Field Name list, and choose Delete.

- **To move a field name up or down in the list,** highlight the field you want to move in the Field Name list, and choose either Move Up or Move Down.

Figure 21.5 shows the first eleven field names from the sample structure presented earlier (Figure 21.2). (You can type in as many field names as you need—names at the top of the list will just scroll out of view.)

When you're done entering field names, choose OK. The Quick Data Entry dialog box will open. We'll look at Quick Data Entry next.

Entering Data Quickly and Easily

The Quick Data Entry dialog box makes entering data into a text or table merge data file unbelievably easy. (If you've used earlier versions of Word-Perfect and have previously avoided merges because data entry was such a pain, you'll truly be amazed at how easy it is now!)

You'll see the Quick Data Entry dialog box just after you finish defining fields for a new data file, and whenever you click the Quick Entry button in the Merge feature bar (you'll learn more about this feature bar later).

Figure 21.6 shows the Quick Data Entry dialog box after I entered some data and clicked the First button to pop back to my first customer record.

To enter your data, follow these steps:

1. For each field in a record, type the text or WordPerfect characters (Ctrl+W) you want, then press ↵ or click Next Field.

2. When you finish typing the last field in a record, press ↵ or choose New Record to create a new blank record automatically.

3. Repeat steps 1 and 2 as needed until you've entered all your records. To leave a field blank, simply press ↵ or click Next field without typing any text first. If necessary, you can use the data entry techniques described just below to correct mistakes.

   - **To move the cursor to a different field** in the record, click in the field you want, use the Next Field or Previous Field buttons, or press Tab or Shift+Tab.

   - **To enter more than one line of data** into a field, position the cursor where you want to break the line, then press Ctrl+↵. This is handy in an Address field, for example, where you might need to enter a second line for an apartment or

FIGURE 21.6

The Quick Data Entry dialog box makes data entry a snap.

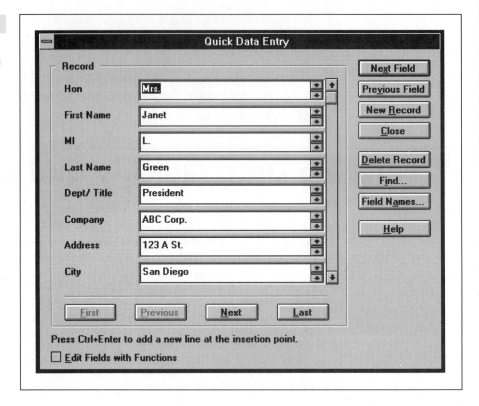

suite number. (You can use the ↑ and ↓ buttons on the field's text box, or the normal cursor positioning keys, to scroll to hidden lines of text.)

- **To insert a new record,** choose New Record and fill in the fields.

- **To bring hidden fields into view,** use the vertical scroll bar, then click in or tab to the field you want to change.

- **To go to another record,** choose the First, Previous, Next, or Last button as needed.

- **To go to a record that contains specific text,** choose Find. Type the text you want in the Find text box and choose Find Next or Find Prev. (See Chapter 9 for more about Find.)

- **To delete a record,** move the cursor into any field of that record and choose Delete Record.

- **To change fields that contain table functions**, select (check) Edit Fields With Functions and choose OK.

- **To use one of the writing tools**, position the cursor in the field you want to work with, right-click the mouse, and choose the tool you want. Your choices are Speller (Chapter 11), Grammatik (Chapter 12), or Thesaurus (Chapter 13).

- **To restructure the data file,** choose Field Names. There's more on this topic in the later section "Restructuring a Data File."

4. When you're done making changes, choose Close. You'll be asked if you want to save your changes to disk:

- **To save the changes now** (a *very* good idea), choose Yes, enter a valid file name, and choose OK. For example, you could name the file we've been working with here **customer.dat**.

- **To bypass the save operation now,** choose No. (You can save your changes later by choosing File ➤ Save or File ➤ Close ➤ Yes from the menu bar.)

5. The data file will appear in the document window with the Merge feature bar at the top. Now you can add or edit records in the data file, or move on to another merge operation. If you're done using the file for now, you can close it (File ➤ Close) and save any changes if prompted.

Figure 21.7 shows a *table data file* and Merge feature bar after entering some customer data. In Figure 21.8, the same file appears as a *text data file*. (The complete sample data file appeared earlier in Figure 21.3.) Notice the differences between the buttons at the left edge of the Merge feature bars and the format of the data in Figures 21.7 and 21.8.

FIGURE 21.7

A table data file and its Merge feature bar. Field names appear in a header row at the top of the table. Each field is in a separate cell. Each row is a record.

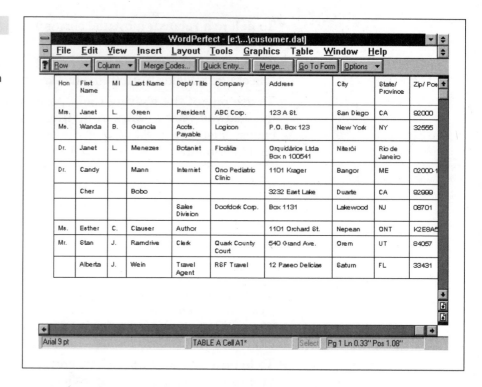

Hon	First Name	MI	Last Name	Dept/ Title	Company	Address	City	State/ Province	Zip/ Pos
Mrs.	Janet	L.	Green	President	ABC Corp.	123 A St.	San Diego	CA	92000
Ms.	Wanda	B.	Granola	Accts. Payable	Logicon	P.O. Box 123	New York	NY	32555
Dr.	Janet	L.	Menezes	Botanist	Florália	Orquidários Ltda Box n 100541	Niterói	Rio de Janeiro	
Dr.	Candy		Mann	Internist	Ono Pediatric Clinic	1101 Krager	Bangor	ME	02000-1
	Cher		Bobo			3232 East Lake	Duarte	CA	92999
				Sales Division	Doofdork Corp.	Box 1131	Lakewood	NJ	08701
Ms.	Esther	C.	Clauser	Author		1101 Orchard St.	Nepean	ONT	K2E8A5
Mr.	Stan	J.	Ramdrive	Clerk	Quark County Court	540 Grand Ave.	Orem	UT	84057
	Alberta	J.	Wein	Travel Agent	R&F Travel	12 Paseo Delicias	Saturn	FL	33431

TIP

To convert *any* WordPerfect table to a text data file, open the table file. If the top row doesn't contain field names already, add the field names across the top row. Now select the entire table (as described in Chapter 7), press Del, choose Convert To Merge Data File (First Row Becomes Field Names), and choose OK. Save the data file under a new name (using File ➤ Save As).

Remember, you can reopen a data file (File ➤ Open) whenever you want to add more records, delete records, correct misspellings, change an address—whatever. As you'll see, the Merge feature bar makes it easy to update data files.

FIGURE 21.8

A text data file and its Merge feature bar (in Draft view). Field names appear between FIELDNAMES...ENDRECORD codes. ENDFIELD codes separate each field within a record. ENDRECORD codes separate each record and are followed by a hard page break.

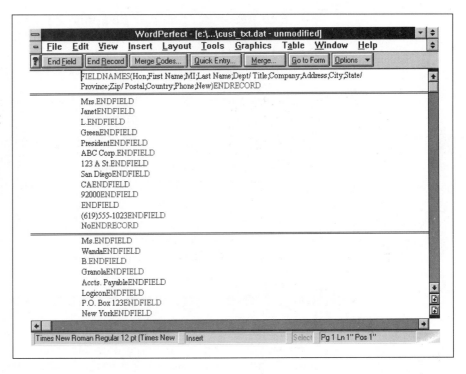

The Merge Data File's Feature Bar

The Merge feature bar provides all the buttons you'll need to manage table and text data files. You'll learn how to put these buttons to practical use a bit later. But for the curious (and impatient) among you, here's a quick summary of what each button can do:

Row   (Table data files only) Lets you insert or delete a row (record) in the table.

Column   (Table data files only) Lets you insert or delete a column (field name) in the table.

End Field   (Text data files only) Ends the data field at the cursor position. You can also press Alt+↵ to end a field.

End Record   (Text data files only) Ends the data record at the cursor position. You can also press Alt+Shift+↵ to end a record.

Merge Codes   Lets you insert merge codes (commands). We'll talk about merge codes later.

Quick Entry   Takes you to the Quick Data Entry dialog box described earlier in the chapter.

Merge   Takes you to the Merge dialog box shown in Figure 21.4.

Go To Form   Lets you switch to the form file associated with this data file. If no form file is associated with the data file yet, you can select or create one.

Options   Lets you Sort or Print the data file, control the appearance of merge codes (Display Codes, Display As Markers, or Hide Codes), and hide the Merge feature bar (Remove Merge Bar).

Adding, Deleting, and Renaming Fields

Suppose you've set up a merge data file (table or text flavor, it doesn't matter) and suddenly notice that you've made a typo in a field name, set up a useless field, put a field in the wrong spot, or forgotten to add a necessary field. Are you stuck with that bad arrangement of fields? No way!

To solve these problems painlessly, follow the steps below:

1. If the merge data file isn't already open, use File ➤ Open to open it. The document and Merge feature bar will appear on the screen.

2. Click the Quick Entry button in the Merge feature bar.

3. Choose Field Names to open the Edit Field Names dialog box shown in Figure 21.9.

4. Do any of the following as needed:

   - **To change a field name**, highlight it in the Field Names list, type a new name in the Field Name text box, and choose Replace.

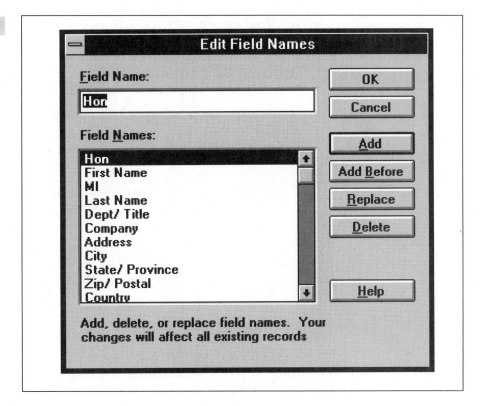

- **To add a new field,** highlight the position in the Field Names list where you want the field to appear. Type the new field name in the Field Name text box. Then choose Add (to add the new field below the highlighted field) or Add Before (to add the new field above the highlighted field). WordPerfect will insert a blank field at the appropriate spot in each record.

- **To delete a field,** highlight it in the Field Names list and choose Delete. When asked for confirmation, choose OK. The field will be deleted from all records in the data file.

5. When you're done, choose OK to return to the Quick Data Entry dialog box.

6. If you added any new fields, you can enter their data now. For example, click the First button (if you're not at the first data record), then move the cursor to the blank field in the first record, type the text for each blank field, and choose Next. Repeat this step until you've entered all the new data.

7. When you're done, choose Close and answer Yes to save your changes.

WARNING

If you change field names *after* creating forms, you'll also need to change the field names within the forms. If you delete a field from the data file, you'll also need to delete the reference to that field from any forms you've already created. Likewise, if you add fields, you may need to add references to those fields in your forms.

Other Ways to Restructure Data Files

The method discussed just above lets you restructure either type of data file—table or text—quickly, easily, and safely. However, you might wish to take the shortcuts described next.

If you just need to change a field *name*, you can edit the name in the document window:

- In a **table data file,** edit the appropriate field name in the top (header) row of the table.

- In a **text data file,** field names appear at the top of the document between FIELDNAMES...ENDRECORD codes. Each field name (except the last) *must be* followed by a single semicolon (;), as shown in Figure 21.8. If you mistyped a field name, just position the cursor within the erroneous field name and make your corrections. Be careful not to delete the FIELDNAMES command, ENDRECORD command, parentheses, or semicolons accidentally.

Adding and deleting fields (columns) in *table data files* is especially easy. Here's how to *add* a new column:

1. Position the cursor where you want a new column to appear.

2. Click the Column button in the Merge feature bar and choose Insert. An Add Field dialog box will appear.

3. In the Field Name text box, type a new field name.

4. Choose where you want to add the field. Your options are Before Current Field, After Current Field, or After Last Field.

5. Choose OK.

To *delete* a column from a table file:

1. Position the cursor in the column you want to delete.

2. Click the Column button in the Merge feature bar, choose Delete, then choose OK to confirm.

You can also select the column you want to delete, as described in Chapter 7. Then press Del and choose OK.

Editing, Adding, and Deleting Records

To make small changes to the contents of a data file, open the file (if it isn't open already), position the cursor, and make your changes using standard editing techniques. Remember to save your changes when you're done by choosing File ➤ Close ➤ Yes or File ➤ Save.

NOTE When editing a table, you can use any techniques described in Chapter 7 to change the table's appearance, column widths, and data formats. If the text is too small to see, use View ➤ Zoom to select a large magnification. You can also use any of the math features discussed in Chapter 24.

You can use either method below to add or delete *records* in a data file:

- Click the Quick Entry button in the Merge feature bar and use the buttons described under "Entering Data Quickly and Easily," earlier in the chapter. This is the safest way to make changes, and the easiest for most people.

- Add and delete records in the document window. The methods for doing this depend on whether you're editing a table data file or a text data file, as explained in the next two sections.

Adding and Deleting Records: Table Method

To *add* a new record (row) to your table, follow the steps below:

1. Position the cursor where you want the new row to appear.

2. Take either of the actions below:

   - Press Alt+Ins to insert a row at the cursor position. (If the cursor is in the last cell of the table, you can press Tab to add a new row to the bottom of the table.)

   - Click the Row button in the Merge feature bar and choose Insert. You can then choose Add Row Above Current Row, Add Row Below Current Row, or Add Row To End Of Table. Choose OK to add the row.

To *delete* a record (row):

1. Position the cursor in the row you want to delete.

2. Press Alt+Del to delete the row at the cursor position. Or click the Row button in the feature bar, choose Delete, and choose OK to confirm.

Adding and Deleting Records: Text Method

Quick Data Entry is, of course, the easiest way to work with text files. However, you can also use manual methods to add and delete records.

To *add* a record to a text data file, follow these steps:

1. Move the cursor to the end of the document (Ctrl+End), below the last page break.

2. You'll see the name of the field that WordPerfect is expecting you to type in the status bar at the bottom of the window. Type in your data (such as **Mr.**) and click the End <u>F</u>ield button in the Merge feature bar, or press Alt+↵.

3. Repeat step 2 until you've typed in a complete record. If you want to leave a field empty, click End <u>F</u>ield without typing anything first. Be careful to put the right data into the correct field—always look at the current field name before typing.

4. After typing in the last field and clicking End <u>F</u>ield, click End <u>Re</u>cord in the Merge feature bar, or press Alt+Shift+↵.

5. Repeat steps 2–4 to add as many records as you wish.

Be aware that this method of editing text data files has some disadvantages. First, you can easily forget to click End <u>F</u>ield when you want to leave a field empty. Second, you're unlikely to notice when you've made a mistake (WordPerfect won't complain). This can cause the wrong data to print when you merge the documents later. Luckily, you can always use Quick Data Entry to correct mistakes (as described earlier under "Entering Data Quickly and Easily"). You can also use the techniques listed below:

- **To insert a new empty field**, move the cursor to where the empty field belongs, at the beginning of a line. Now click End <u>F</u>ield in the Merge feature bar or press Alt+↵.

- **To join text** that you accidentally divided into two fields, delete the ENDFIELD code and hard return from the end of the first line that you want to join.

To *delete* a record in a text data table, follow these steps:

1. Turn on Reveal Codes (Alt+F3), and highlight the first character of the record you want to delete (just past the previous record's

[HPg] code). You can use Find (F2) to locate the record if need be.

2. Select all the text in the entire record up to and including the [HPg] code at the end. (The cursor in Reveal Codes will actually be on the first character of the next record.)

3. Press Del.

TIP   Choose Edit ➤ Undo (Ctrl+Z) or Edit ➤ Undelete (Ctrl+Shift+Z) if you delete a record by mistake.

Creating a Form File

You can create as many forms for a data file as you wish. Any form can use all the fields in the data file, or just a few (for instance, just the Last Name, First Name, and Phone for a phone list), in any order and as many times as you want. The basic technique is simple:

1. Start with a new document window. Or, if you have an existing file that you want to convert to a form file, open it (File ➤ Open) and position the cursor at the top (Ctrl+Home).

2. To open the Merge dialog box (Figure 21.4), use any of these methods: Choose Tools ➤ Merge, press Shift+F9, click the Merge button in the WordPerfect button bar, or click the Merge button in the Merge feature bar.

3. Choose Form.

4. If there's already information in the current document, you'll be asked if you want to use the current document (Use File In Active Window) or open a new one (New Document Window). Select an option and choose OK.

5. The Create Form File dialog box will open, as shown here:

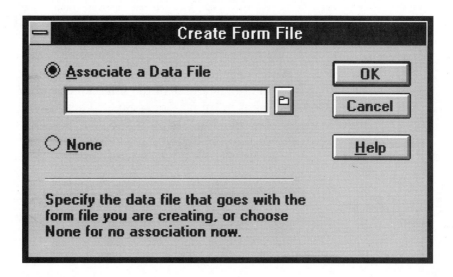

6. If you want to tie this form file to an existing data file, select <u>A</u>sso-ciate A Data File, type the data file's name and extension (or use the button at the end of the text box to locate the file, as explained in Chapter 20). If you don't want to associate a data file right now, choose <u>N</u>one. Then choose OK.

NOTE
Associate provides a handy way to assign a "default" data file to the form. If you don't associate a data file with a form, you can assign a data file name when you insert a field into the form later.

7. The document window will open and the Merge feature bar, shown below, will appear. We'll discuss each of these buttons in the following section.

8. To change the margins, paper size, font, or any other general formatting features of the final document, choose <u>L</u>ayout ➤ <u>D</u>ocument ➤ Initial Codes <u>S</u>tyle. Then choose your layout options, as described in Chapters 5–8. When you're done, choose OK to return to the document window.

T I P

If you'll be printing on letterhead stock, set the top margin large enough to make the letter text print below the letterhead.

9. Type the text for your form (for example, type **Dear** and press the spacebar in a letter salutation) until you come to a place where you want to insert a field from a data file, the system date, a merge code, or a prompt for data entry from the keyboard.

10. Choose a button from the Merge feature bar (as discussed below) and fill in any dialog boxes that appear.

11. Repeat steps 9 and 10 until you've finished typing your form.

12. Save your changes (<u>F</u>ile ➤ <u>S</u>ave or <u>F</u>ile ➤ <u>C</u>lose ➤ <u>Y</u>es).

T I P

If you give all your form files the extension .FRM, they'll be easy to recognize in the Open File and other file-management dialog boxes.

The Merge Form File's Feature Bar

Here's a quick summary of each button in the form's Merge feature bar. We'll take a closer look at many of these buttons in the sections that follow:

Insert Field   Inserts a field name and code at the cursor position. There's more about inserting fields in the next section.

Date   Inserts a DATE code at the cursor position. During a merge, this code will be replaced by the system date.

Merge Codes   Inserts merge codes (commands) at the cursor position. We'll talk about merge commands later.

Keyboard   Inserts a KEYBOARD code at the cursor position. During a merge, WordPerfect will pause at the KEYBOARD code and let you enter data. See "Getting Input from the Keyboard" later in the chapter.

Merge   Takes you to the Merge dialog box shown in Figure 21.4.

Go To Data   Lets you switch to the data file associated with the form. If no data file is associated yet, you can select or create one.

Options   Lets you control the appearance of merge codes (Display Codes, Display As Markers, or Hide Codes) and hide the Merge feature bar (Remove Merge Bar).

Adding a Field to a Form

When you're ready to tell WordPerfect where to insert text from the data file, follow these steps:

1. Click the Insert Field button in the Merge feature bar.

2. If you haven't associated a data file with this form, you'll see the message "No Fieldnames Or Records Were Found." Choose OK

to clear the message and display the Insert Field Name Or Number dialog box shown below:

Insert Field Name or Number

Field: [   ]   Insert

Type a field name or number, such as
"address," then choose Insert.   Close

(No data file associated or the data file   Data File...
does not contain records.) To associate a
file, choose the Data File option.   Help

3. To specify (or change) the data file associated with a form, click the Data File button in the Insert Field Name or Number dialog box, type in the name and extension of your data file (or highlight it in the file list), and choose OK. (Only one data file can be associated with a form at any given time. If the form contains fields from previously associated data files, those fields will be left blank during a merge.)

N O T E

If you haven't created your data file yet, that's no problem. Simply skip steps 3 and 4, and continue with step 5. When you get to step 6, type in the field name that you *will* use in the data file, or type a number that represents the *position* the field will have in the data file, then choose Insert.

4. If you associated a data file, the Insert Field Name Or Number dialog box will appear with the names of fields in the associated data file, like this:

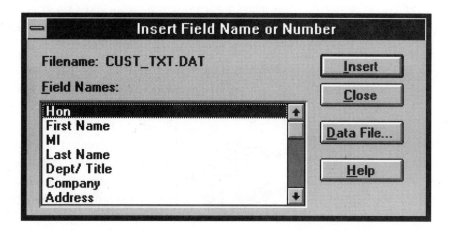

TIP

When entering many fields into your document, it's easiest to leave the Insert Field Name Or Number dialog box open (drag it out of the way as needed). When you're done using the dialog box, you can click its Close button.

5. Position the cursor where you want the field name to appear. For example, move the cursor to the space that follows the word **Dear:** in a salutation.

6. In the Insert Field Name or Number dialog box, double-click the field you want, or highlight the field name and choose Insert. (To quickly highlight a field name in the list, type the first few letters of the name.)

7. Repeat steps 5 and 6 as needed.

8. When you're done creating your form file, be sure to save it (File ➤ Save) and close it if you wish (File ➤ Close).

The example in Figure 21.10 shows the top portion of a form letter. The following steps show how I got this letter to its strange-looking state. (Trust me, this works perfectly when you merge it!)

- I used the Date button in the Merge feature bar to insert a DATE code that will be replaced with the system date when I do the merge.

- Each field name from the data file used in the letter is within a FIELD(...) code. Those codes act as placeholders that will be replaced by real data from the data file during the merge.

TIP

If you accidentally insert the wrong field into the form, you can change the text between parentheses in the FIELD(...) command to specify the correct field name.

FIGURE 21.10

The merge codes for printing a name and address at the top of a form letter

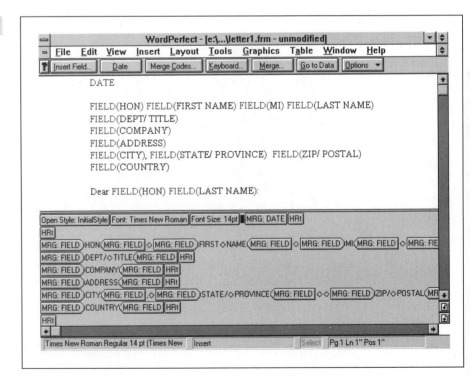

- Blank spaces appear between some fields (Hon, First Name, MI, and Last Name).

- I put a comma and blank space after the City field, and two spaces before the State field; so that line is printed in the familiar format:

San Diego, CA 91234

- I used the Hon and Last Name fields twice, once at the top of the inside address, and again in the salutation (next to *Dear*). You can refer to a field as many times as you wish in your form.

- I didn't use the Phone and New fields (you don't have to use all the fields).

So how will all of this look after I do the merge? Well, using a record from my sample CUSTOMER.DAT data file, most letters will be formatted like this:

April 26, 1994

Ms. Wanda B. Granola
Accts. Payable
Logicon
P.O. Box 123
New York, NY 32555

Dear Ms. Granola:

A slight problem may arise, however. In records where I've left the Hon, MI, Company, and Dept/ Title fields empty, WordPerfect will still print the hard return and any blank spaces surrounding the code. Thus, a printed name and address might end up looking like this:

Cher Bobo

3232 East Lake
Duarte, CA 92999

Dear Bobo:

You probably won't be happy with this result. Fortunately, this problem is easy to solve, as described in a moment. But first, a pause for a quick tip on reducing screen clutter.

Reducing Merge Code Clutter

All those merge codes cluttering the screen can become mighty confusing, and they'll make the document window wrap in awkward spots. To get a better idea of how the finished merge will look, click the Options button in the Merge feature bar, then choose either Display As Markers or Hide Codes. Your choice affects the document window only. You can still see all the merge codes in Reveal Codes (Alt+F3). To redisplay the codes, click Options and choose Display Codes.

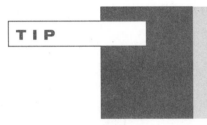

TIP To change the default appearance of merge codes, choose File ➤ Preferences and double-click Display. Choose Merge, pick the appearance you want (Display Merge Codes, Display Merge Codes As Markers, or Hide Merge Codes), then choose OK and Close.

Removing Blank Lines

If a field in a data file might be empty, *and* that field appears on a line by itself in your form, you can follow the field name with a question mark (**?**). This will prevent blank lines.

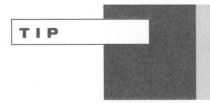

TIP Instead of putting ? next to the field name, you can just tell WordPerfect not to print blank lines in general when doing the merge. See "Handy Merge Options" later in this chapter to find out how.

Be sure to put the question mark just inside the closing parenthesis for the code. For example, this merge code:

FIELD(COMPANY?)

which looks like this in Reveal Codes:

[MRG:FIELD]COMPANY?[MRG:FIELD][HRt]

tells WordPerfect, "If the Company field *isn't* empty, print the company and a hard return. If the Company field *is* empty, don't print this line at all." Thus, if you were to insert question marks into our sample form letter like so:

FIELD(HON) **FIELD**(FIRST) **FIELD**(MI) **FIELD**(LAST NAME)
FIELD(DEPT/ TITLE?)
FIELD(COMPANY?)
FIELD(ADDRESS?)
FIELD(CITY), **FIELD**(STATE/ PROVINCE) **FIELD**(ZIP/ POSTAL)
    FIELD(COUNTRY?)

that record with all the blank fields would come out looking like this:

Cher Bobo
3232 East Lake
Duarte, CA 92999

Dear Bobo:

Almost perfect! Unfortunately, the blank spaces that follow the Hon and MI fields in the form still show up. And "Dear Bobo" isn't exactly an ideal salutation. These problems aren't solved by the simple ? option, because ? can only handle blank fields on their own line followed by a hard return ([HRt]).

We *could* make sure the HON field in *every* record of the table contains *something* (Ms., Mr., or the like). But this won't help with the middle initial. The real solution is *merge codes*, which help the form make semi-intelligent decisions when you do the merge.

In the next section, I'll show you how to add a merge code to your document. Then I'll explain how to use merge codes to make "smart" forms.

Adding a Merge Code

Here's the quickest way to add a merge code to your document:

1. Position the cursor where you want the code to appear.

2. Click the Merge Codes button in the Merge feature bar. This will open the Insert Merge Codes dialog box shown below:

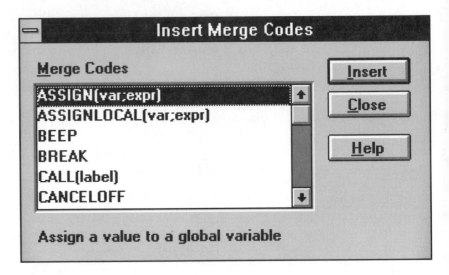

3. Highlight the command you want (you can type the first few letters of the command to highlight it quickly). A brief description of the highlighted command will appear near the bottom of the dialog box.

4. Double-click the command, or choose Insert to select it.

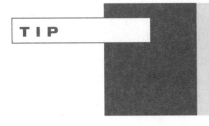

TIP

When entering many merge commands into your document, it's handy to leave the Insert Merge Codes dialog box open (drag it out of the way if it covers something you need to see). When you're done using the dialog box, you can click its Close button.

Removing Blank Spaces

You can use two pairs of merge commands (and they *must* be used in pairs) to control blank spaces in a merged form:

IFBLANK...ENDIF

IFNOTBLANK...ENDIF

The first command says, "If the field is blank (empty), print everything between here and the ENDIF command that follows." The second command says the opposite: "If the field is *not* blank (empty), print everything between here and the ENDIF command that follows."

WARNING

A field isn't "blank" if it contains even one single space. If your merge treats a blank field as though it *weren't* blank, you probably typed a space into the field. Open your data file, move the cursor to the offending field, turn on Reveal Codes, and delete the space (or whatever characters are there).

Note that all the codes, such as IFBLANK, IFNOTBLANK, and ENDIF, *must be* entered as merge codes. You can't simply type in those commands on your own.

Now, back to the original problem: If we tell WordPerfect to print First Name<space>MI<space>Last Name, and MI is blank, we end up with two spaces between the first and last names. To fix that, we can say "If MI is *not blank*, print MI followed by a blank space." That way, if MI *is* blank, neither the middle initial *nor* the blank space that follows it will be printed. However, you *must* remember to put the blank space that follows the MI field *inside* the ENDIF command. Why? Because anything to the right of the ENDIF command will appear, whether IFNOTBLANK was true or false. In other words, IFBLANK and IFNOTBLANK affect *only* text that comes *before* the next ENDIF command.

Suppose I modify the opening codes for my sample form letter as shown below.

IFNOTBLANK(HON)**FIELD**(HON) **ENDIF FIELD**(FIRST NAME)
IFNOTBLANK(MI)**FIELD**(MI) **ENDIF FIELD**(LAST NAME)
FIELD(DEPT/ TITLE?)
FIELD(COMPANY?)
FIELD(ADDRESS?)
FIELD(CITY), **FIELD**(STATE/ PROVINCE) **FIELD**(ZIP/ POSTAL)
    FIELD(COUNTRY?)

Now, even when I merge the record that has empty Hon, MI, Dept/ Title, and Company fields, I get the following clean result:

Cher Bobo
3232 East Lake
Duarte, CA 92999

Dear Bobo:

The first line in the merge file puts the Hon and MI fields, and the blank space that follows each field, into its own IFNOTBLANK...ENDIF codes. Thus, when merging a name that has a blank honorific and/or middle initial, the blank spaces that normally follow those fields aren't included.

This is close, but still not perfect—because *Dear Bobo* isn't exactly what we want.

Really Advanced Merge Codes

For the truly hard-core whizzes (and aspiring whizzes) out there, I'll mention that you can also use an ELSE command between the IF and ENDIF commands. Furthermore, you can nest the commands (put one IF...ENDIF pair inside another IF...ENDIF). Suppose you want to set up some fancy logic for the salutation of the letter, like this:

- Type **Dear** followed by a space.
- If the Hon and Last Name fields contain data, use those in the salutation (*Dear Ms. Bobo:*).
- If either Hon or Last Name is blank, test the First Name field. If it isn't blank, use it (*Dear Cher:*).
- If the First Name is also missing, just print "Valued Customer" (*Dear Valued Customer:*).

Why might the Last Name and First Name fields be blank? This can happen if records contain only a company name and address, and aren't addressed to a specific person in that company.

So, what would this fancy logic look like in the form letter? Figure 21.11 reveals all.

Now, for those who hate this kind of stuff (yes, you, with the digital clock that's been flashing 12:00 for years now), let me say that it's rarely necessary to use advanced merge commands. You can usually get by with simple FIELD commands, as long as your data file isn't too tricky, like Figure 21.1 earlier in this chapter.

Those who actually like this kind of stuff (with your clocks accurate to the second even during daylight savings time), please remember these points:

- You must use the Merge Codes button in the Merge feature bar to enter merge commands. You can't just type the commands into the document. (Each has its own special code that's visible only in Reveal Codes.)

Beginning of a form letter that uses advanced merge commands to control blank lines, blank spaces, and the appearance of the salutation (the text after *Dear* and before the colon)

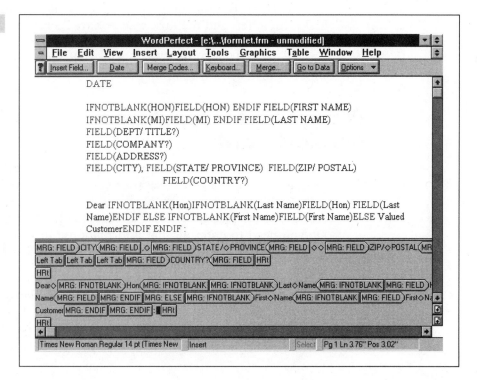

- Every IF... command *must* be followed by an ENDIF command. If you omit the ENDIF, the IF... affects everything to the end of the document, which can produce some *vErY wEiRd* results in your merge.

- To learn more about advanced merge commands, refer to the Appendices in the manuals that came with your WordPerfect package.

The sample forms later in this chapter illustrate some good ways to use advanced merge commands—many of which you can copy into your own forms. If something here sparks your curiosity, you can research it further in your official WordPerfect documentation, or in a book that specializes in advanced WordPerfect macro and merge programming techniques.

Saving Some Time and Trouble

If you've already set up one form letter with all the fancy merge codes you need, you can save yourself a bunch of time with this trick: Open the form letter, save it with a different file name (File ➤ Save As), then just change the text of the letter under the salutation.

You can also select the merge codes that format the inside address of your first form letter, and then use File ➤ Save As to save that block of text to a unique file name, such as MRGADDR.FRM. In the future, you can just insert your MRGADDR.FRM file into whatever form you're working on with the Insert ➤ File command.

Prompting for Input from the Keyboard

Here's something that anyone can use, even the technically timid souls among us. Suppose you've set up a data file that's just fine for 99.99% of your mailings to employees. Now, suddenly, you need to remind employees about their pledges to bring goodies to the company's annual potluck. Do you need to enter all that information into your employee data file? Absolutely not. You can enter it at the keyboard when the merge takes place.

Here's how to prompt for information from the keyboard:

1. Position the cursor in the form file, at the place where you want the typed-in data to appear during a merge. For example, put the

cursor after the last space in the phrase: **Thanks for agreeing to bring** |

2. Click the <u>K</u>eyboard button in the Merge feature bar to open this dialog box:

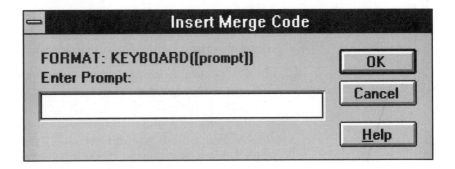

3. Type a prompt that will tell the user what to type in during the merge. Your prompt can include normal text and WordPerfect characters (Ctrl+W).

4. Choose OK.

WordPerfect will insert a KEYBOARD(...) command at the cursor position. The prompt you typed in step 3 will appear between the parentheses (You can edit this text if you need to change the prompt.)

Creating Envelopes

Creating envelopes for merged data is almost exactly as described in Chapter 8. The trick, however, is to create or open a form file *first*, and then create the envelope. Follow these steps:

1. Create a new form file (<u>T</u>ools ➤ <u>M</u>erge ➤ <u>F</u>orm), or open an existing form file (such as a form letter). Move the cursor to the end of the document if you opened an existing file (Ctrl+End).

2. Choose <u>L</u>ayout ➤ En<u>v</u>elope, or click the Envelope button in the WordPerfect button bar. Up pops the Envelope dialog box shown in Figure 21.12. This is the same dialog box you saw in Chapter 8,

with one important difference: It has a Field button at the bottom, which lets you insert merge data fields into the Mailing Addresses (or Return Addresses) area of the dialog box.

3. Fill in or select a return address (if necessary) and choose whatever Options you want (see Chapter 8).

4. Choose Mailing Addresses. (If you've already saved a mailing address that includes merge data fields, you can select it from the drop-down list below Mailing Addresses and skip to step 7.)

5. In the Mailing Addresses area, create or edit the mailing address. To add a field, position the cursor where you want the field to appear, click the Field button, highlight the field you want, and choose Insert. You can add punctuation (spaces, commas, and so on) between the fields and press ↵ to place a field on a new line. The fields will appear in the sample envelope area as you add them (see Figure 21.12). Repeat this step as needed.

6. When the mailing address is complete, choose Add so that you can use it for future mailings.

FIGURE 21.12

The completed Envelope dialog box. Notice the Field button, which lets you enter merge code fields into the address.

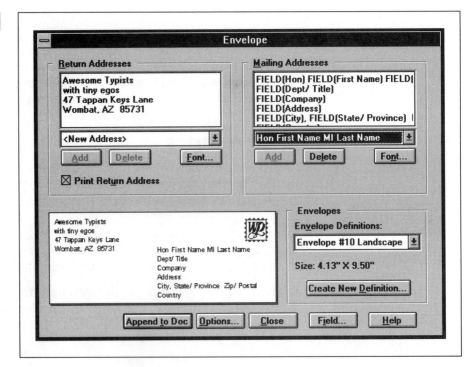

7. When you're done formatting the envelope, choose Append To Doc. WordPerfect will add your envelope format to the document. (If the document wasn't empty to start with, a hard page break will precede the envelope format.)

8. You can format the envelope further and refine the merge codes if necessary. When you're done, save the form file and close it (File ➤ Close ➤ Yes).

TIP   You can also use the Envelope button in the Perform Merge dialog box to define an envelope "on the fly," just before merging your form letter with your data file.

Creating Mailing Labels

As you learned in Chapter 8, mailing labels aren't a bit sticky to set up in WordPerfect. The secret to merging data onto labels is simply to create a new merge form and then set up your labels as usual. Here are the steps to follow:

1. Create a new form file (Tools ➤ Merge ➤ Form), as explained earlier in the chapter.

2. Choose Layout ➤ Document ➤ Initial Codes Style to open the Styles Editor (see Chapters 17 and 19).

3. Choose Layout ➤ Labels and select your label format by double-clicking, or by highlighting and pressing ↵.

4. If you'd like to center the labels vertically, choose Layout ➤ Page ➤ Center ➤ Current And Subsequent Pages, then OK. You can also choose a font in the usual manner (Layout ➤ Font).

5. Choose OK to save the style changes.

6. If you previously saved that MRGADDR.FRM file I mentioned earlier, use Insert ➤ File to retrieve it into the current document. Otherwise, you'll need to insert merge codes to define how you want to format the name and address.

N O T E If the address seems to extend past a page break, the codes may just be making it look that way. For a more accurate view of the actual height of the printed label, click the <u>O</u>ptions button in the Merge feature bar and select Display As <u>M</u>arkers.

7. When your label format is done, save and close it. Choose <u>F</u>ile ➤ <u>C</u>lose ➤ <u>Y</u>es, and enter a file name (such as LABELS.FRM).

T I P If the text doesn't align properly on the labels after you do the merge, change the margins in the label paper size (Chapter 8), instead of trying to fix the problem in the label form file.

Adding POSTNET Bar Codes to Labels or Envelopes

Chapter 8 explained how to place POSTNET bar codes on "normal" envelopes and labels. To print a POSTNET bar code on each merged label or envelope, follow the steps below:

1. Open your label or envelope form file and put the cursor wherever you want the code to appear.

2. Click the Merge <u>C</u>odes button in the Merge feature bar, highlight *POSTNET(string)*, and choose <u>I</u>nsert.

3. Place the cursor between the parentheses that follow the POST-NET command. Choose <u>I</u>nsert Field from the Merge feature bar, highlight the name of the field that contains the zip code (*Zip/ Postal* in my example), then choose <u>I</u>nsert.

You want the POSTNET(...) command to look something like this in the document window:

POSTNET(FIELD(Zip/ Postal**))**

and something like this in Reveal Codes:

[MRG:POSTNET][MRG:FIELD]Zip/ Postal[MRG:FIELD][MRG:POST-NET][HRt]

You may need to press ↵ before or after the POSTNET(FIELD (...)) code if you want the code to appear on its own line.

Running the Merge

Once you've created a data file and at least one form file, you're ready to merge the two. Proceed as follows:

1. In general, you'll want to start from an empty document window. However, it's perfectly fine if the current document is the form or data file you want to merge.

2. To open the Merge dialog box, use any of these methods: Choose Tools ➤ Merge, press Shift+F9, click the Merge button in the WordPerfect button bar, or click the Merge button in the Merge feature bar.

3. Choose Merge to open the Perform Merge dialog box shown below:

4. In the Form File text box, specify the form file. You can use the button in the text box (or press F4) to select a file on disk (Select File), the <Current Document>, or the <Clipboard>. If the current document is a form file, <Current Document> will be filled in automatically.

5. In the Data File text box, specify the data file. You can use the button in the text box (or press F4) to select a file on disk (Select File), the <None> (useful if all the input is from the keyboard), or the <Clipboard>. If the current document is a saved data file, its name will be filled in automatically.

6. In the Output File text box, specify the output file location. You can use the button in the text box (or press F4) to send output to the <Current Document>, a <New Document>, the <Printer>, or a file on disk (Select File). **Warning**: Never specify the same name for your output file as for the data file or form—you don't want to overwrite either of those with this third merged document.

NOTE

The <Printer> and Select File output options are useful if you're merging a huge data file and your computer doesn't have enough memory to complete the merge.

7. If you wish, choose the buttons described just below. Fill in the dialog boxes that appear and choose OK until you return to the Perform Merge dialog box. We'll talk more about these buttons later.

> **Select Records** Lets you choose which records will be included in the merge.
>
> **Envelopes** Lets you format envelopes "on the fly." After choosing this button, you can follow the basic steps described under "Creating Envelopes," earlier in the chapter. Choose OK (instead of Append To Doc) to return to the Perform Merge dialog box. (After you do the merge, the envelopes will appear at the end of the merged output file, after all the form letters.)

Options   Lets you customize the format of the output file and choose options for keyboard merges (more on this later).

Reset   Returns the Select Records, Envelopes, and Options settings to their previous values.

8. When you're ready to start the merge, choose OK.

A status message keeps you informed of WordPerfect's progress in the merge, and, after a brief delay, a new document containing all the merged data appears in the place you specified in step 6 (typically, your screen). If you sent output to the current document or a new document, the cursor will be at the *bottom* of the document. Each merged record usually will appear on a new page. You can use the Alt+PgUp key to scroll through each page, or press Ctrl+Home to jump to the top.

Figure 21.13 shows the results of merging my sample form letter with my sample data file.

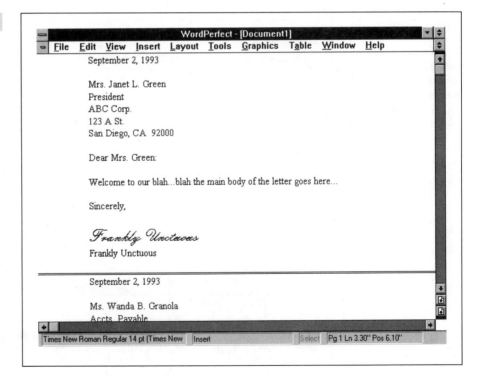

FIGURE 21.13

The first few lines of a letter, after merging my sample form letter form with my sample data file

From here, you can print the output file (if necessary, open the file first). If you sent the merge output to the current document or a new document window, you can save it (though saving isn't necessary because you can always do the merge again). If you do save the merge results, be careful not to overwrite the form or data file!

Responding to Prompts for Keyboard Input

If you entered KEYBOARD commands into your form file, the merge won't finish without your help. Instead, WordPerfect will display the first record, up to the KEYBOARD command, and will wait for you to type something (see Figure 21.14). Type as much text as you want (you can even insert graphics boxes, lines, and formatting codes). When you're done, click Continue in the Merge feature bar to continue the merge. You'll be prompted for more keyboard input until all the records have been merged.

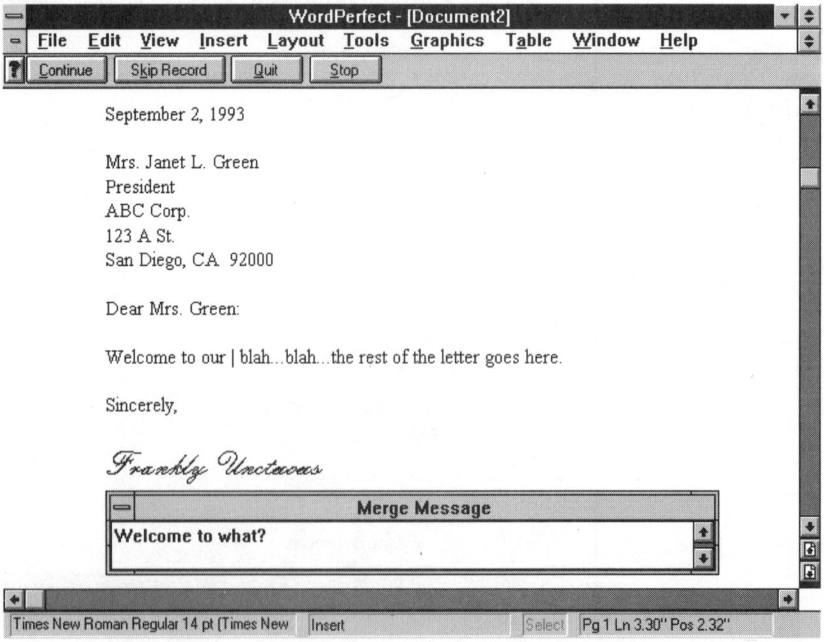

FIGURE 21.14

WordPerfect pauses at each KEYBOARD command during a merge and waits for you to type in missing information.

WordPerfect - [Document2]

File   Edit   View   Insert   Layout   Tools   Graphics   Table   Window   Help

Continue   Skip Record   Quit   Stop

September 2, 1993

Mrs. Janet L. Green
President
ABC Corp.
123 A St.
San Diego, CA 92000

Dear Mrs. Green:

Welcome to our | blah...blah...the rest of the letter goes here.

Sincerely,

Frankly Unctuous

Merge Message

Welcome to what?

Times New Roman Regular 14 pt (Times New   Insert   Select   Pg 1 Ln 3.30" Pos 2.32"

You can also use the feature bar buttons listed below to skip a record or stop the keyboard merge:

Skip Record   Skips over the next record without leaving the current one.

Quit   Includes the remaining text for the record, ignores further KEYBOARD commands, and stops the merge.

Stop   Stops the merge dead in its tracks, at the current position.

Handy Merge Options

Several merge options are available to you. To use them, click the Options button in the Perform Merge dialog box. You'll see this dialog box next:

```
┌─────────────────────────────────────────────────────────────┐
│ ─                    Perform Merge Options                    │
│  ┌─ Output File ──────────────────────────────┐  ┌────────┐  │
│  │                                             │  │   OK   │  │
│  │  ☒ Separate Each Merged Document With a Page Break      │  ┌────────┐  │
│  │                                             │  │ Cancel │  │
│  │  Number of Copies for Each Record:  [1  ] ▲▼ │  │        │  │
│  │                                             │  │  Help  │  │
│  │  If Empty Field in Data File: [Leave Blank Line ⬍]     │  └────────┘  │
│  │                                             │             │
│  └─────────────────────────────────────────────┘             │
│  ┌─ Keyboard Merge ───────────────────────────┐             │
│  │  Display Options:        [Hide Codes     ⬍] │             │
│  └─────────────────────────────────────────────┘             │
└─────────────────────────────────────────────────────────────┘
```

Here's what the options are for:

Separate Each Merged Document with a Page Break   During a merge, WordPerfect normally inserts a hard page break after every completed form. That's fine for form letters, envelopes, and labels, because you want each record to appear on a separate page or label. However, if you prefer to print the data as a list (without page breaks), you can deselect this option. (Deselecting this option is the same as adding a PAGEOFF merge code to the end of your form. Later in the chapter, you'll see an example that uses PAGEOFF.)

Number of Copies for Each Record   One merged form usually appears for each record in the data file. You can use this option to specify the number of times to produce a form for each record.

If Empty Field in Data File   WordPerfect usually prints a blank line in your document if it finds a blank field on a line by itself. You learned earlier how to control this behavior on a field-by-field basis, by putting a question mark (**?**) next to the field name. Alternatively, you can tell WordPerfect never to print blank lines for empty fields by choosing Remove Blank Line from the If Empty Field... pop-up list button.

Display Options   This pop-up list button controls the appearance of merge codes during a keyboard merge. Your options are Show Codes, Hide Codes, or Show As Markers.

Choose as many of the above options as you need (they'll be remembered until you exit WordPerfect or change them again). When you're done, choose OK to return to the Perform Merge dialog box.

TIP   To reset all the options quickly, click the Reset button in the Perform Merge dialog box.

Selecting Records to Merge

You don't have to produce a form for every record in your data file. Instead, you can choose the Select Records button in the Perform Merge dialog box. This opens the Select Records dialog box, where you can choose which records to include in the merge. Your selection options are as follows:

Specify Conditions   Lets you specify exact conditions for the merge (see Figure 21.15 and the next section). Choose OK after defining your condition(s).

Mark Records   Lets you mark specific records to include in the merge output (see Figure 21.16). To choose which field appears first in the list, pick a field name from the First Field To Display

FIGURE 21.15

The Specify Conditions option in the Select Records dialog box lets you specify exactly which records to include in the merge.

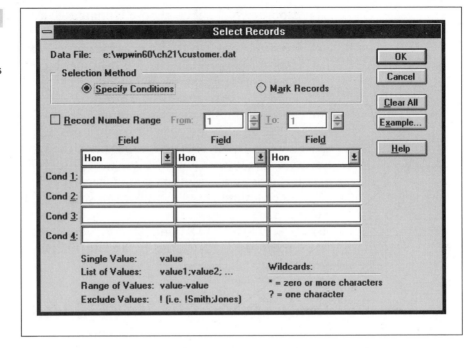

FIGURE 21.16

Records to include in the merge are checked. Only a portion of each record will appear in the Record List.

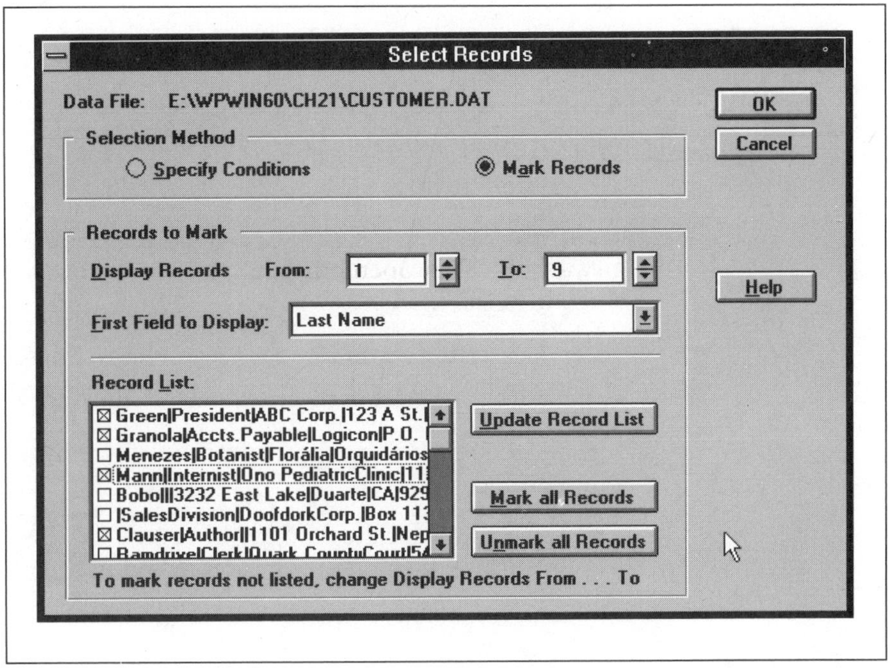

drop-down list, then choose Update Record List. To mark or un-mark all records at once, choose Mark All Records or Unmark All Records, respectively. To mark or unmark an individual record, click the appropriate check box in the Record List. Choose OK when you're done marking fields.

You can also limit the merge to a range of records from the data file. The merge will still obey any selection conditions or marking that you've chosen. However, it will only merge records in the specified range. To use this feature, select Record Number Range or Display Records From (depending on the Selection Method you picked). Then specify the "From" and "To" record numbers to include from your data file. For example, if the data file has 100 records, but you only want to merge records from the last 10, set "From" to **91** and "To" to **100**. If you're marking records, be sure to choose Update Record List to refresh the data shown in the Record List.

Defining Conditions for a Merge

If you choose Specify Conditions from the Select Records dialog box (Figure 21.15), you can define up to four conditions, each with up to three criteria. (Don't panic! I'll explain these murky concepts next.)

Defining Criteria

A *criterion* is basically a field name, followed by whatever it is you're looking for within that field. For example, the criterion

State/ Province
CA

means, "If this record has CA (exactly) in the State/ Province field, include it in the merge."

To enter a criterion, follow the steps below (these steps will be easier to understand if you refer to Figure 21.15 as you read):

1. Select a field from the Field drop-down list at the top of the column.

2. In the appropriate "Cond" box, type in whatever you want to find in this field, using options described in the next few sections. A

reminder of the special symbols you can use to define criteria appears at the bottom of the dialog box. These are summarized in Table 21.1. You can also click the Example button to see more detailed examples of valid criteria.

3. Define additional fields and conditions as needed. (If you've really botched your entries into the "Cond" rows, choose Clear All and retype the conditions you want.)

4. Choose OK when you're done entering criteria.

TABLE 21.1: Symbols You Can Use to Define Criteria for Selecting Records to Be Merged

CRITERION	DESCRIPTION	EXAMPLE
Single value	Only include records that have a specific value	**CA** (only records that have exactly *CA* in the field)
List of Values (;)	Only include records that have one of the listed items	**CA;AZ;TX** (records that have *CA* or *AZ* or *TX* in the field)
Range of Values (-)	Only include values within the specified range	**10,000.00-20,000.00** (from ten thousand to twenty thousand)
Any one character (?)	Only include records that have exactly one character in place of the question mark	**C?** (any record that starts with the letter *C* followed by one other character)
Zero or more characters (★)	Include any record that has nothing or *any* number of characters in place of the asterisk	**Jan★** (any record that starts with the letters *Jan*) Or **1/★** (any record that starts with *1/*)
Less than (<)	Only include records that are less than this value	**<N★** (any record that starts with a letter from *A* through *M*)
Less than or equal (<=)	Only include records that are less than or equal to this value	**<=8000** (any record with the value *8000* and below)

TABLE 21.1: Symbols You Can Use to Define Criteria for Selecting Records to be Merged (continued)

CRITERION	DESCRIPTION	EXAMPLE
Greater than (>)	Only include records that are greater than this value	**>8000** (any record with the value *8001* and above)
Greater than or equal (>=)	Only include records that are greater than or equal to this value	**>=8000** (any record with the value *8000* and above)
Excluded Values (!)	Only include records that *don't* have this value	**!CA** (all records *except* those that have *CA* in the field)

So why use rows and columns? Well, when you put two or more criteria on the same row (say, next to Cond 1), then *all* of those criteria must be true for the record to be included. For example, these criteria mean "Print the record *if* it has CA in the State/ Province field, *and* it also has a check mark in the field named New" (new customers in the state of California):

	Field	**Field**	**Field**
	State/ Province ±	New ±	Hon ±
Cond 1:	CA	✓	
Cond 2:			

Each Condition (Cond) row represents a "separate question." That is, Condition 1 poses one question, Condition 2 poses yet another question, and so forth. If any *one* of those questions proves true, the record *is* included in the merge.

In other words, there's an "and" relationship among criteria across a row, but there's an "or" relationship between the rows. If you're experienced with databases, you'll recognize this as the standard "QBE" (Query By Example) way of doing things. (Otherwise, you may be wondering if the person who thought this up lives on the same planet that you do.)

So now, let's take a look at the example below.

	Field		**Field**		**Field**	
	State/ Province	±	New	±	Hon	±
Cond <u>1</u>:	CA		✓			
Cond <u>2</u>:	NY					

In this example, WordPerfect will include a record in the merge if the record has *CA* in the State/ Province field and a *check mark* in the New field, OR it has *NY* in the State/ Province field (and I-don't-care-what in the New field). Boiling this down into English, these conditions say: "Include *new* customers in *California* and *any* customers in *New York*."

If you're not accustomed to using queries (which is what this "define conditions" operation really is), you may end up with some surprising, and seemingly incorrect, results in your merge. The next few sections may help you avoid some problems.

Case and Length Sensitivity

Queries are not *case sensitive*. That is, if you search for **CA**, records that have *CA*, *Ca*, *ca*, and *cA* in the field will match the criterion.

Queries that search for specific values are, however, *length sensitive*. That is, CA *won't* match *Cal* or *California* or *Cat*. You can use the ★ to overcome length sensitivity. For example, **CA★** will match *CA*, *ca*, *Ca*, *Cal*, *California*, or *Casbah*—anything beginning with the letters *ca*. The >, <, or <= criteria also ignore length sensitivity. Thus the criterion >**CA** won't match *A*, *ABC*, or *CA*. But it will match *Cat*, *Casbah*, *CB*, *ZORRO*, and so forth.

Isolating Records with an Empty Field

To isolate records that have nothing in a field, search for "less than any character," that is, **<?**. For example, if you've left the Country field empty for addresses within the United States, this criterion:

```
Country
<?
```

will pick out only the addresses within the United States (that is, records that have absolutely nothing, not even a blank space, in the field named Country).

To isolate records with nonblank fields (addresses outside the United States in my example), replace the **<?** condition with **>=?** (which means "greater than or equal to any one character").

Isolating Records within an Alphabetical Range

You can isolate records within an alphabetical range, such as "everyone whose last name begins with one of the letters *A* through *M*." To do this, set up your condition with the smallest letter first, followed by a hyphen, then the highest letter, followed by an asterisk. For example, this criterion isolates last names starting with any letter *A* through *M*:

> Last Name
> A-M*

If you forget the ending asterisk, you won't get names that begin with the letter *M*. Why? Because *M* followed by *anything* (as in *MacDonald*) is "larger than" the letter *M* by itself. **A-M** without the asterisk means "everything from *A* up to the letter *M* by itself."

TIP Try looking up *M* in the dictionary, where entries are alphabetized. You'll probably find that *M* by itself is the first entry. All other *M* words come after that, because alphabetically they're "larger than" the letter *M* by itself.

Isolating Records for a Specific Month

If you've typed dates into fields in a consistent format, it's easy to isolate records that fall within a range of dates. Suppose you've entered all dates in the format *month/day/year,* as in 1/1/94 and 12/31/94. You can isolate certain dates using these criteria:

1/*	Dates that start with 1/ (January dates)
*94	Dates that end with 94 (1994 dates)

| **1/*/94** | Dates in January of 1994 |
| **1/*;2/*;3/*** | Dates that start with 1/ or 2/ or 3/ (first quarter of the year) |

Likewise, if you type *all* your dates in the format *Month Day, Year,* you can easily isolate certain dates using criteria such as these:

Jan*	Dates that start with Jan (January)
***94**	Dates that end with 94 (1994 dates)
Jan*94	Dates in January of 1994
Jan*;Feb*;Mar*	Dates that start with Jan, Feb, or March (first quarter of the year)

Okay, let's say you *didn't* follow a consistent format when typing dates into a field—some are in 1/1/94 format, others in Jan 1, 1994 format, and still others in January 1, 1994 format. All is not lost, because this will still isolate all the dates in January of 1994:

    1/*/94;Jan*94

Nevertheless, you're better off if you stick with one format throughout your data file.

Isolating a Range of Zip Codes

When isolating a range of zip codes, you must watch for those zip+4 codes at the high end of the range. Suppose you want to isolate records that have a value between 92000 and 92999-9999 in the Zip/ Postal field. This criterion would do the trick:

    Zip/ Postal
    92000-92999*

The asterisk at the end ensures that you'll get zip codes such as 92999-0123 and 92999-9999 at the high end of the range.

Isolating an Area Code

If your data file contains a Phone field, and you've followed a consistent format when typing in phone numbers, you can easily isolate records within a certain area code. For example, if you typed all phone numbers in the *(xxx)xxx-xxxx* format, as in (619)555-1234, the following criterion will isolate records in the 619 area code:

    Phone
    (619)*

Isolating Records That Have Special Characters

As you've seen, my sample data includes a field named New. When typing new records into the data file, I use Ctrl+W to insert a check mark into this field to identify the record as a new one. Later, if I want to print welcome letters and envelopes for new customers only, I can define this criterion:

    New
    ✓

To type in the check mark, simply press Ctrl+W when it's time to enter the text of the criterion. Choose whatever character you've been putting into the New field to identify new records. Use the same code number, such as 5,51—even if the character looks different in the current font. Then perform the merge to print your letters, labels, or envelopes.

Once you've printed everything you need for new customers, you won't want them to keep on being "new." So, just open your data file (CUSTOMER.DAT in my example) and use Ctrl+F2 (Replace) to change all the check marks in the file to *No*, or nothing, or whatever.

Using an unusual character (check mark), rather than just *Yes* or *Y*, to identify new customers lets you do the replace with confidence. For example, if you tell WordPerfect to change all the *Yes* entries to *No*, a person named Yesyestowsky would have his/her name changed to Nonotowsky. And that would be a no-no.

Sample Forms

Now let's take a look at some sample forms that print data from the CUSTOMER.DAT data file. You can use these as food for thought when creating your own forms. I'll use some occasional graphics, which aren't discussed until Chapter 25, but these graphics are entirely optional.

NOTE Remember that you can't simply type merge codes in. You must use the Merge Codes button in the Merge feature bar.

A Form Letter

Figure 21.17 shows a form letter, based on fields from my CUS-TOMER.DAT data file. It uses the fancy IFNOTBLANK merge code described earlier in the chapter. (Obviously, the body of *your* letter will probably say more than this one does.)

FIGURE 21.17

A sample form letter with its own letterhead and signature (not shown)

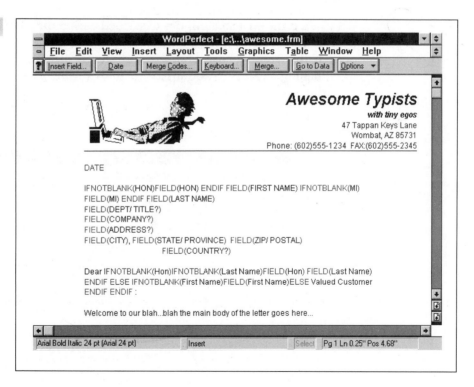

I used fonts and graphic images to create the letterhead. The signature (not shown) was scanned in and saved to a bitmap file. I then put that image in a graphics user box where I wanted the signature to appear. (Beats signing all those form letters!) Then I ran the merge as usual, specifying AWESOME.FRM as the form file and CUSTOMER.DAT as the data file. After the merge, the letterhead, inside address, salutation, text, and signature appeared on each letter automatically. I then printed the letters with the usual File ➤ Print command.

TIP

Remember to use the Image On Disk option (Chapter 25) when putting graphic images in a merge file, to speed things up and reduce disk consumption.

Envelopes

I used the basic techniques described earlier under "Creating Envelopes" to set up the envelope format shown in Figure 21.18. (In the Envelope dialog box, I chose Options and changed the Vertical Position for the mailing address to about 1.5″ to allow for the POSTNET code and multiline mailing address.)

FIGURE 21.18

Envelope format to print envelopes from my CUSTOMER.DAT data file

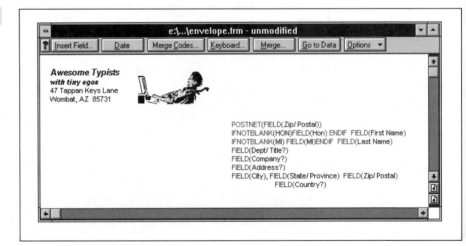

After choosing Append To Doc in the Envelope dialog box, I embellished the envelope with graphics and fonts, IFNOTBLANK...ENDIF merge codes to test for blank fields, question marks after field names to squeeze out blank lines, and the POSTNET(FIELD(Zip/ Postal)) command.

With the finishing touches complete, I chose File ➤ Close ➤ Yes to save and close the file (which I named ENVELOPE.FRM). I then used Tools ➤ Merge ➤ Merge, with ENVELOPE.FRM as the form and CUSTOMER.DAT as the data file. Figure 21.19 shows one envelope on the screen, as it appeared after the merge.

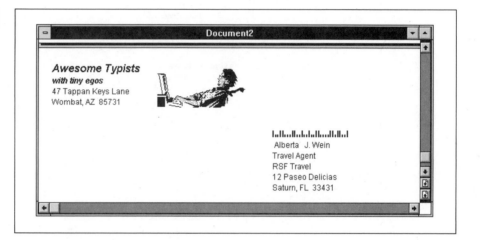

Merging to Columns: A Directory Listing

Figure 21.20 shows the sample data from my CUSTOMER.DAT file merged to a directory listing. I used two newspaper-style columns to create that example.

To create the form for the directory listing, I opened a new document window and chose Tools ➤ Merge ➤ Form. Then I used Layout ➤ Header/Footer to create a header (Chapter 8). To define columns, I chose Layout ➤ Columns ➤ Define ➤ Newspaper (or Balanced Newspaper) and defined the columns as described in Chapter 27.

FIGURE 21.20

A sample directory
listing created from the
CUSTOMER.DAT data
file using a merge

Customer Directory

Bobo, Cher
    3232 East Lake
    Duarte, CA 92999
    (213)555-3039

Clauser, Ms. Esther C.
    Author
    1101 Orchard St.
    Nepean, ONT K2E8A5
    Canada
    (613)555-4049

Doofdork Corp.
    Sales Division
    Box 1131
    Lakewood, NJ 08701
    (800)555-1030

Granola, Ms. Wanda B.
    Logicon
    Accts. Payable
    P.O. Box 123
    New York, NY 32555
    (212)555-4049

Green, Mrs. Janet L.
    ABC Corp.
    President
    123 A St.
    San Diego, CA 92000
    (619)555-1023

Mann, Dr. Candy
    Ono Pediatric Clinic
    Internist
    1101 Krager
    Bangor, ME 02000-1234
    (123)555-1234

Menezes, Dr. Janet L.
    Florália
    Botanist
    Orquidários Ltda
    Box n 100541
    Niterói, Rio de Janeiro
    Brasil
    55-21-555800

Ramdrive, Mr. Stan J.
    Quark County Court
    Clerk
    540 Grand Ave.
    Orem, UT 84057
    (800)555-4049 Ext. 323

Wein, Alberta J.
    RSF Travel
    Travel Agent
    12 Paseo Delicias
    Saturn, FL 33431
    (407)555-5052

The merge codes in my sample directory are shown in Figure 21.21. The trickiest part is the first two lines, which look like this (when not wrapped so tightly in the column):

```
IFNOTBLANK(Last Name)FIELD(Last Name), FIELD(Hon)
FIELD(First Name) FIELD(MI)[HRt]
ENDIF
```

(The hard return *[HRt]* at the end is visible only in Reveal Codes.) The next IF...ENDIF pair looks like this:

```
IFNOTBLANK(Last Name)[Hd Left Ind] ENDIF
```

FIGURE 21.21

The form file used to create the directory shown in Figure 21.20

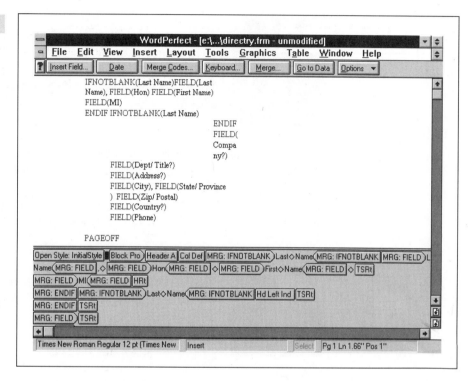

where, again, the *[Hd Left Ind]* code (inserted by pressing F7) appears only in Reveal Codes. This indents the Company name *only* if this record has a nonblank Last Name. That's why DoofDork Corp in Figure 21.20 is "outdented" like a person's name.

To prevent a person's name and address from being broken across two columns, I selected all the codes in the entire set, including the extra *[HRt]* code at the end (which serves as the blank line between names). Then I turned on Block Protect (Layout ➤ Page ➤ Keep Text Together ➤ Keep Selected Text Together On Same Page ➤ OK).

To prevent page breaks between records, I added a PAGEOFF code to the bottom of the form (click the Merge Codes button in the feature bar, type **P** to highlight PAGEOFF, and choose Insert and Close).

NOTE Adding a PAGEOFF command to the end of a form is equivalent to choosing the Options button in the Perform Merge dialog box and deselecting Separate Each Merged Document With A Page Break just before you start the merge.

Next I closed and saved the form (naming it DIRECTRY.FRM). Then, I merged the directory form with the data file as usual. After the merge, I sorted the entries into alphabetical order using Tools ➤ Sort (Chapter 22). Because this directory is formatted into paragraphs that end with two [HRt] codes, I could use Paragraph sorting *after* merging.

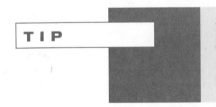

TIP You'll usually want to sort data file records *before* you do the actual merge. A quick way to sort the data file is to open it and choose Options ➤ Sort from the Merge feature bar.

I set up the Sort dialog box as shown below, then chose OK to sort the records:

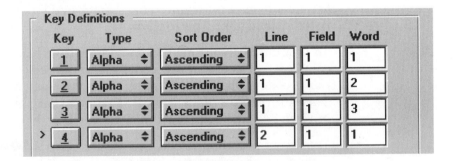

By the way, a hard return in the data file won't indent in the directory. Here, I had to manually indent the *Box n 100541* line in the Brasil address, shown in the second column of Figure 21.20, *before* printing the document.

Merging to a Table: A Phone List

Merging to a table is a bit tricky. Start the form as usual (Tools ➤ Merge ➤ Form) and create a two-row table that has as many columns as you want in the final output (I chose 2 columns for a two-column phone list and two rows to hold my merge commands). In the first cell (A1), use the Merge Codes button on the feature bar to select the LABEL(*label*) command, and make up a name (I used **Top Row**). In the second row (cell A2), insert a NEXTRECORD command followed by a GO(*label*) command, using the same label name you entered before (**Top Row** in my example). In a two-column table, the table would now look like this:

LABEL(TOP ROW)	
NEXTRECORD GO(TOP ROW)	

Now you can insert the FIELD commands into the top row (cells A1 and B1) describing what you want in each column. For example, in cell A1, these merge commands:

> **IFNOTBLANK**(Last Name)**FIELD**(Last Name), **FIELD**(First Name) **ELSE FIELD**(Company)**ENDIF**

will print the last and first name from the current record (or, if the Last Name field is blank, the company name). In cell B1, add the merge code FIELD(Phone) to display the phone number in that column. Then you can just close and save the form (I used the name PHONLIST.FRM).

LABEL(Top Row)IFNOTBLANK(Last Name)FIELD(Last Name), FIELD(First Name) ELSE FIELD(Company)ENDIF	FIELD(Phone)
NEXTRECORD GO(Top Row)	

Perform the merge normally, and it will create a table row for each record in your data file. After the merge is done you can customize the table to your liking, changing column widths, adding a header row, and so forth (see Chapter 7). You can also sort the table rows into alphabetical order (Chapter 22).

The example below shows the phone list after completing the merge, alphabetizing the rows, and changing the shading.

Name/Company	Phone
Bobo, Cher	(213)555-3039
Clauser, Esther	(613)555-4049
Doofdork Corp.	(800)555-1030
Granola, Wanda	(212)555-4049
Green, Janet	(619)555-1023
Mann, Candy	(123)555-1234
Menezes, Janet	55-21-555800
Ramdrive, Stan	(800)555-4049 Ext. 323
Wein, Alberta	(407)555-5052

Using "Old" Merge Files

Merge files created in an earlier version of WordPerfect are automatically converted to WordPerfect 6 format during the merge. Remember, though— once you've converted the files to WordPerfect 6 format, earlier versions (such as 5.1) can't open those files unless you first export the WordPerfect 6 file to 5.1/5.2 format using Files ➤ Save As ➤ Format. See Chapter 20.

We've covered merges in some detail here. There's lots more territory to explore in the Advanced Merge Codes area, for those who enjoy technical topics. To learn more, please dig into your WordPerfect manual and the Help screens. In the next chapter, you'll learn how to alphabetize (sort) a document.

22

Alphabetizing, Sorting, and Isolating Text

f a s t **TRACK**

To count backwards in a field, line, word, cell, or column   **748**

> use a negative number. For example, to use the last word in a field as the sort key, specify word –**1**.

To fool WordPerfect into sorting several words as one word   **749**

> enter a hard space (Ctrl+spacebar) between the words that you want to be treated as a single word.

To sort dates   **749**

> use forward slashes (/) or hard hyphens (Ctrl+hyphen) between the date's numeric month, day, and year (as in *12/7/93* or *5-2-94*). Then define three sort keys for each word in the date.

To isolate text   **752**

> first save your file under another name, since the isolated text will be only an incomplete version of the original file. Then follow the usual preliminary steps for sorting. Before choosing OK, define as a sort key the text that will identify records for selection. Type your selection criterion in the Select Records text box. Then choose OK. WordPerfect retains only those records that match your selection criteria.

NFORMATION is often much more useful when it's alphabetized, or *sorted*, into a meaningful order. This is especially true for any kind of tabular or formatted text, including merge data files. You might, for example, want to sort a list of names and addresses into alphabetical order by name. Or you might want to sort them into zip-code order for bulk mailing.

Occasionally you might also want to isolate (or *select*) certain types of information. For example, maybe you need to send a mailing to residents of a particular city or zip code, but not to everyone in your list. You use WordPerfect's Sort feature, described in this chapter, for all these tasks.

What You Can Sort

You can sort virtually any text that's organized into some consistent format of *records* and *fields*. The exact definition of record and field depends on what you want to sort. There are five different types of sorts to choose from:

Lines   Each record ends with a single hard return, and each field is separated by one tab code (Figure 22.1).

Paragraphs   Each record ends with two hard returns. The record can contain multiple lines, each ending with a single hard return. Each line can contain one or more fields separated by tab codes (Figure 22.2).

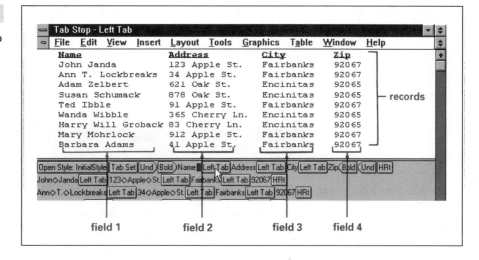

Table Rows   Works with any table, including those used as merge data files. Each table row is a record, and each column (cell) is a field (Figure 22.3).

Parallel columns   Each record is a row of text, and each field is a column (Figure 22.4).

Merge Records   Each record and field in the data file is also used as a record and field for sorting purposes (Figure 22.5).

Sorting Your Text

Once you have a basic idea of what kind of sort you need to do, the operation is straightforward:

1. Open the document you want to sort. If you want to sort only a portion of the text in the document, select that text. (It's not absolutely necessary to open the document you want to sort, but it's generally easiest that way.)

FIGURE 22.2

FIGURE 22.2

You'd use a Paragraph sort to alphabetize this information, where each "record" ends with two hard returns.

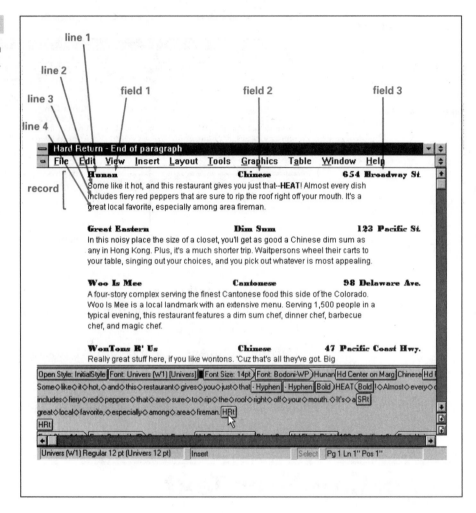

2. To play it safe, choose <u>F</u>ile ➤ <u>S</u>ave to save a copy of the document in its current state (just in case your sort doesn't turn out as planned).

3. Choose <u>T</u>ools ➤ Sor<u>t</u> or press Alt+F9 to open the Sort dialog box shown in Figure 22.6.

FIGURE 22.3

When sorting a table (even if it's a merge data table), each row is a record, each column a field.

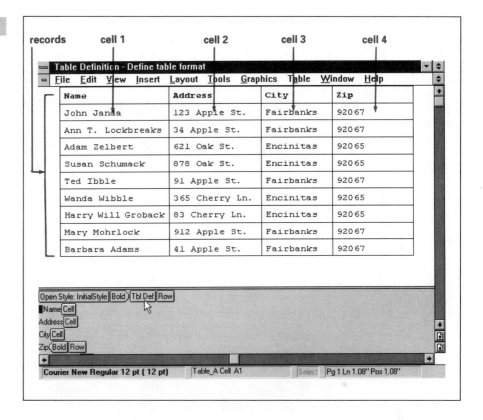

records   cell 1   cell 2   cell 3   cell 4

Table Definition - Define table format

File Edit View Insert Layout Tools Graphics Table Window Help

Name	Address	City	Zip
John Janda	123 Apple St.	Fairbanks	92067
Ann T. Lockbreaks	34 Apple St.	Fairbanks	92067
Adam Zelbert	621 Oak St.	Encinitas	92065
Susan Schumack	878 Oak St.	Encinitas	92065
Ted Ibble	91 Apple St.	Fairbanks	92067
Wanda Wibble	365 Cherry Ln.	Encinitas	92065
Harry Will Groback	83 Cherry Ln.	Encinitas	92065
Mary Mohrlock	912 Apple St.	Fairbanks	92067
Barbara Adams	41 Apple St.	Fairbanks	92067

Open Style: InitialStyle | Bold | Tbl Def | Row
Name | Cell
Address | Cell
City | Cell
Zip | Bold | Row

Courier New Regular 12 pt (12 pt)   Table_A Cell A1   Select Pg 1 Ln 1.08" Pos 1.08"

4. In the Input File text box, enter an input file name if you want to sort a disk file; or accept <Current Document> to sort the document that's currently open. If you've entered a file name and want to take a quick look at the input file, click the View Input File button in the Sort dialog box.

5. In the Output File text box, enter an output file name if you want to sort the output to a disk file; or accept <Current Document> to sort the output to the document that's open. Be careful! If you specify the name of an existing file, the contents of that file will be replaced with the results of the sort (previous information in the output file will be lost after the sort is finished).

FIGURE 22.4

Because I used parallel columns to create this document, I'd use a parallel column sort to alphabetize these records.

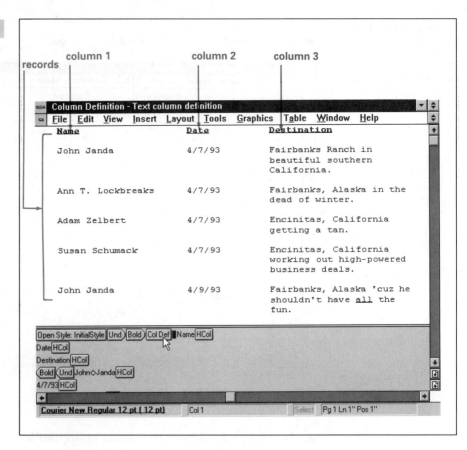

NOTE

In steps 4 and 5, you can use the button (or press F4) in the text box to search for and fill in a file name (Select File) or specify the current document (<Current Document>). After choosing Select File, use methods described in Chapter 20 to locate a file in the Select File dialog box, highlight the file you want, and choose OK to return to the Sort dialog box.

6. If the selected option under Sort By doesn't seem right for the type of sort you want to do, select the record type that fits. (Normally you won't need to fiddle with this, because WordPerfect will guess the record type correctly.)

FIGURE 22.5

When sorting a merge
data file (text type),
each data record and
field is also a sorting
record and field.

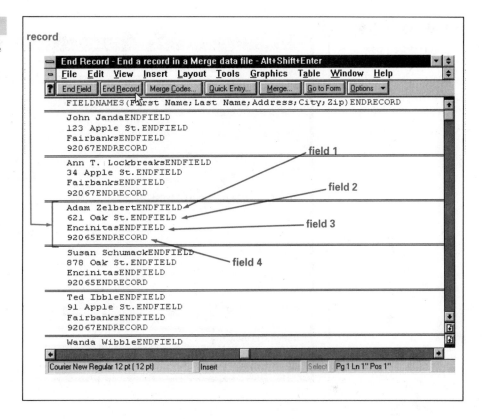

7. Define your sort keys (the text you want to base the sort on), as discussed under "How to Define the Sort Keys" in a few pages.

8. To sort uppercase letters ahead of lowercase letters, select (check)the Uppercase First check box (this would, for example, sort *Apple* before *apple*). If you don't select this option, lowercase letters sort ahead of uppercase letters (for example, *apple* before *Apple*).

9. When you're ready to begin the sort, choose OK.

WordPerfect will sort the text and return you to the document window. If you chose <Current Document> in steps 4 and 5, the text that's on your screen will now be sorted. If you chose a file name in step 5, you'll need to open the appropriate file to see the results of the sort.

FIGURE 22.6

The Sort dialog box

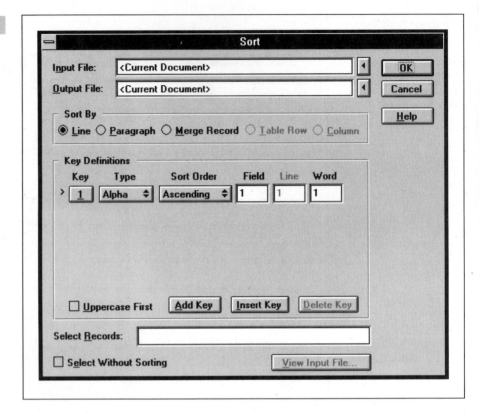

Undoing a Sort to the Current Document

If the sort results aren't what you expected and you sent the results to the current document, you can choose Edit ➤ Undo (Ctrl+Z) immediately to undo the sort. If you didn't discover the bad result until it was too late to undo, you can still recover. Just close the current (sorted) version of the document *without* saving it (File ➤ Close ➤ No). Then reopen the copy that you saved in step 2 above.

About Sort Keys

The key to successful sorting is properly defining the *sort key*. WordPerfect doesn't just intuitively "know" how you want your text arranged. You have to tell it exactly what information you want to base the sort on. In other words, you need to define the sort key(s).

Suppose you have a list of people's names in your document, as below:

Sandy Miller

Zeke Adams

Wanda Miller

Anna Zeeborp

Ted Goofenstein

Lee Miller

If you just sorted without first defining your keys, WordPerfect would sort the list by the first word in each row (record). Thus, your list would come out like this:

Anna Zeeborp

Lee Miller

Sandy Miller

Ted Goofenstein

Wanda Miller

Zeke Adams

This might not be what you had in mind. Now, had you told WordPerfect that you specifically wanted to sort these records (rows) by the second (or last) word in each row, the names would be alphabetized by that second word. In this example, each person's last name is the second word in the record. The result of such a sort, then, would be records sorted by surnames, as below:

Zeke Adams

Ted Goofenstein

Wanda Miller

Sandy Miller

Lee Miller

Anna Zeeborp

Sorts within Sorts

In this tiny list, the order of people with the same last name (for example, Miller) isn't terribly important. But in a larger list, you might want to alphabetize by first name within each last name—as in the telephone directory.

This is called a *sort within a sort* because you want to sort by first name *within* each last name. Here you must define two sort keys. The first sort key is each person's surname. The second sort key is each person's first name. Now the sorted output would look like this:

Zeke Adams

Ted Goofenstein

Lee Miller

Sandy Miller

Wanda Miller

Anna Zeeborp

Notice how the second sort key, each person's first name, acts as a tiebreaker. When several people have the same last name (Miller), their records are alphabetized by first name within that group (Lee Miller comes before Sandy Miller, which comes before Wanda Miller).

You can define up to nine sort keys in the Key Definitions area of the Sort dialog box (Figure 22.6). This gives you many flexible ways to organize your text. I'll show you some sample sorts in a moment, to shed more light on sort keys. But first, I'll digress for a moment and talk about other options you have while sorting.

Ascending vs. descending sorts When you're defining a sort key, you can choose between ascending order (smallest-to-largest, or A-to-Z) or descending order (largest-to-smallest, or Z-to-A).

Alpha vs. numeric sorts You can also choose between an alpha (normal alphabetical) or a numeric sort. In general, you want to use a numeric sort only when the field you're basing the sort on is a "true number," such as a quantity or dollar amount. Numbers that contain text and nonnumeric punctuation, such as part numbers (J-123), phone numbers ((415)555-1234), and zip codes (91234-4321), are best sorted as alphas.

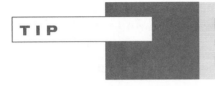

The Parts of a Sort Key Definition

As Figure 22.6 shows, each key definition is broken into parts. These "parts" will differ for the different record types, as described below:

- **Lines** are broken into Fields and Words.
- **Paragraphs** are broken into Lines, Fields, and Words.
- **Merge Records** (merge data files) are broken into Fields, Lines, and Words.
- **Table Rows** are broken into Cells, Lines, and Words.
- **Columns** are broken into Columns, Lines, and Words.

The "parts" of each key definition are numbered from left to right. In Figure 22.1, for example, the records are organized into lines. Some records include a first name, middle initial, and last name (as in *Ann T. Lockbreaks*), while others have just a first name and last name (as in *John Janda*). In this example, field 1 (Name) has two or three words, field 2 (Address) has three words, field 3 (City) has one word, and field 4 (Zip) has one word. Therefore, to sort the records in Figure 22.1 by first name, you'd type **1** in the Field box, and **1** in the Word box for the key you're defining.

If you want to number a specific part of the key definition from right to left (backwards), simply type a *negative number* in the appropriate text box. For example, to sort the name records in Figure 22.1 by *last* name, you'd enter **1** in the Field box and **-1** in the Word box for the appropriate sort key.

You'll see several more examples later in the chapter.

How to Define the Sort Keys

Once you've thought about how you want to do your sort keys, here's how to set them up in WordPerfect:

1. If you haven't already done so, complete steps 1–6 (listed earlier, under "Sorting Your Text") to get to the Sort dialog box. You'll be working in the Key Definitions list for the steps below.

2. If you want to *edit* a key or *delete* a key, you must select that key first. If you want to *insert* a new key at a particular spot in the Key Definitions list, you must select the place in the list where the new key will appear. To select a key, click anywhere in the key definition you want to select. Alternatively, you can press Alt plus the key number (as in Alt+2 to select the second key definition), or press Tab until you reach the key or "part" of the key that you want. The selected key will be marked with a **>** character in the Key column of the Key Definitions list.

3. Now, do any of the following:

   • To **add** a new key to the end of the list, choose <u>A</u>dd key.

   • To **insert** a new key at the selected position, choose <u>I</u>nsert Key.

   • To **delete** the selected key, choose <u>D</u>elete Key.

   • To **edit** the definition for the selected key, choose a sort Type (<u>A</u>lpha or <u>N</u>umeric) and Sort Order (<u>A</u>scending or <u>D</u>escending) from the pop-up list buttons (if necessary). Then, tab to or click on the "part" of the key definition you need to change and enter the number of that part into the text box. For example, to sort by the second word in the third field of a record, tab over to the Field box for the key you're changing and type **3**. Then tab over to the Word box and type **2**. For more information about defining the parts of a sort key, see "About the Parts of a Sort Key Definition" (above) and "Some Sorting Examples" (below).

4. Repeat steps 2 and 3 to define up to nine sort keys.

5. When you're finished defining your keys, choose OK to start the sort.

Some Sorting Examples

In the next few sections, we'll look at some examples of how to fill in the Sort dialog box for sorting lines, paragraphs, merge records, parallel columns, and table rows.

Sorting Lines

You should use the Line record type when your text is in a simple list format, and each line is broken by a single hard return ([HRt]) code, as in Figure 22.7.

Before choosing <u>T</u>ools ➤ So<u>r</u>t (Alt+F9) for the records shown in Figure 22.7, I selected all but the first line of the document. (That line is the heading for the list and I didn't want it to be sorted in with the names and addresses.) The sort key shown in the figure will sort the list alphabetically, in ascending order, by each person's last name. Notice that the first field in each line is a person's first and last name. The first word in each

---

FIGURE 22.7

Sort keys to sort alphabetically by last name

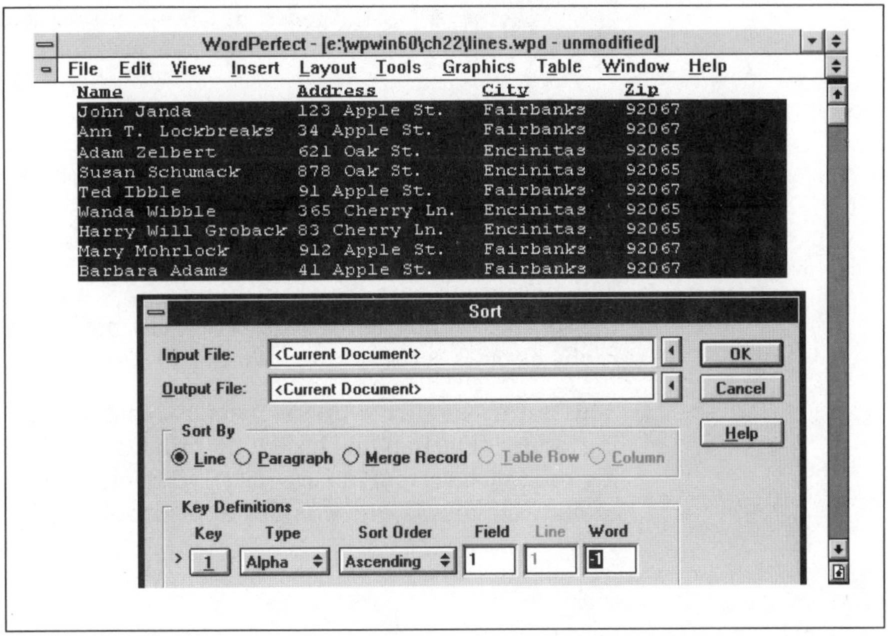

name is the person's first name, and the last word in each name is the surname (word −1).

Here are the keys for sorting this same list into zip-code order, then by
street name within zip code, and then by street number when several people reside on the same street:

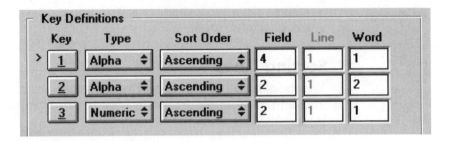

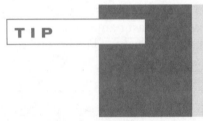

TIP

Use an alphanumeric key when sorting numbers that
include hyphens or other nonnumeric characters. For
example, you'd use an alphanumeric key to sort
extended zip codes (such as 94803-0011), foreign
postal codes, and telephone numbers.

Sorting Paragraphs

Paragraph sorts are good for—what else?—sorting a series of paragraphs.
Figure 22.8 shows the sort keys for arranging our restaurant reviews (Figure 22.2) by type of food, and then by restaurant name within type.

The paragraph sort shown in Figure 22.9 will group each paragraph in
the sample bibliography by author's last name. Notice that each bibliography entry is separated by two hard returns (that is, a blank line).

This is a tricky sort to define, because each paragraph starts with a hanging indent. The hanging indent command (Layout ➤ Paragraph ➤ Hanging Indent) inserts [Hd Left Ind][Hd Back Tab] codes before the first line
of text. Of course, these codes appear only on the Reveal Codes screen

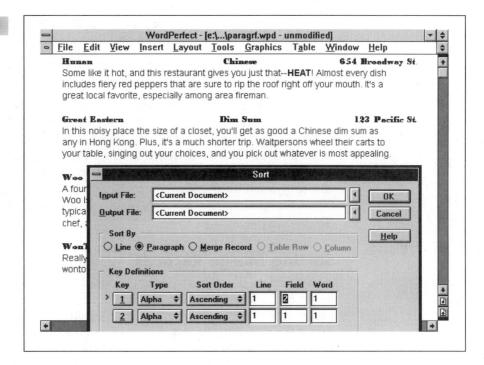

(not shown in the figure). For this example, in Reveal Codes the first line in the bibliography would begin like this:

[Open Style:InitialStyle][Hd Left Ind][Hd Back Tab]Gordon, Barbara, "Art . . .

In a paragraph or line sort, indent codes create new fields. So, although each author's name seems to be at the start of each line, we must define the sort key as field *3*, because the [Hd Lft Tab] and [Hd Back Tab] codes precede the author's last name. In other words, WordPerfect assumes that field 1 is to the left of the [Hd Lft Ind] code, and field 2 is to the left of the [Hd Back Tab] code—even though there is no text in either place. Therefore, field 3 (the author's name) starts at the right of the [Hd Back Tab] code.

Sorting Merge Records

A merge data file stores information used in form letters and other mass-produced documents. In Chapter 21 you learned that WordPerfect lets you create two types of merge data files: *Merge Record* (non-tabular text) and *Table*. Here I'll be talking about *merge record* merge data files. Recall that each field in a merge record file ends with an ENDFIELD code, and each record ends with an ENDRECORD code. If you want to sort a merge data file that's in Table format, simply open the file and sort it as a table, as described later under "Sorting a Table."

To sort a merge record file, make sure that the Sort By option in the Sort dialog box is set to Merge Record. Also remember that you only need to specify the line number for a sort key if a field contains more than one line of text.

The sort key for the merge record file in Figure 22.10 will organize the records into zip-code order (perhaps for bulk mailing). Field 5 identifies the zip code as the fifth field in each record (the name *John Janda* is in the first field).

FIGURE 22.10

This sort key will sort the sample merge record file by zip code.

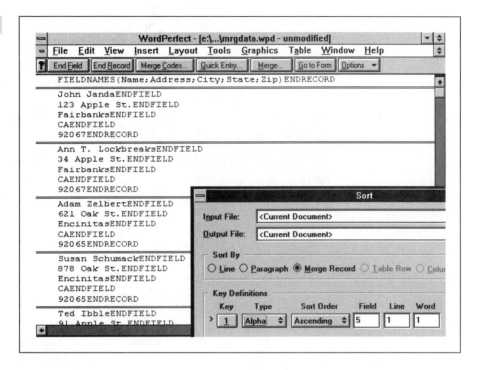

If you want to sort the merge record file into name order, like the telephone directory (by last name and then by first name within identical last names), you could define sort keys 1 and 2 like this:

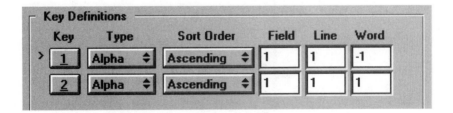

Sorting Parallel Columns

To format itineraries, scripts, and other text into parallel columns, you can use the Layout ➤ Columns ➤ Define ➤ Parallel (or Parallel w/Block Protect) command. (You'll read more about this in Chapter 27.) To sort a document that's organized into parallel columns, first move the cursor into the columns (if you want to sort all the rows), or select the rows you want to sort.

The sort keys in Figure 22.11 illustrate how to sort the sample itineraries shown at the top of the screen by each person's last name, and then by date (year, month, and day) for each person. This grouping tells you where everyone will be on any given date.

In this example, I selected all text except the heading line. The first key sorts by last name (word −1 in column 1). The dates in column 2 are divided into three words, separated by slash characters: The second key sorts the dates by year (word 3), the third key sorts the dates by month (word 1), and the fourth key sorts the dates by day (word 2).

FIGURE 22.11

These settings will sort text in parallel columns by the person's last name, then by date within the same last name.

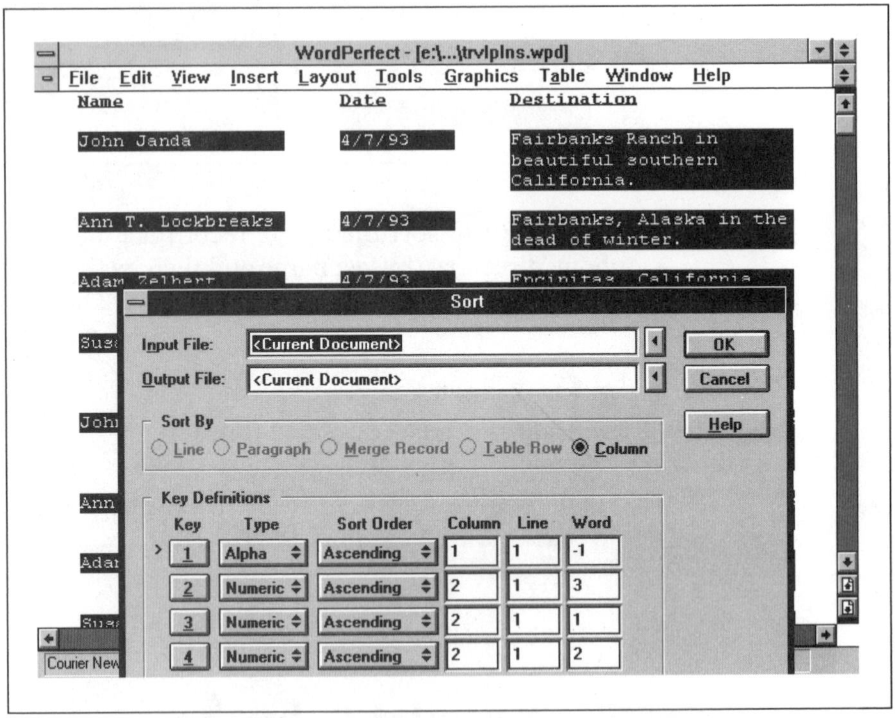

NOTE

For sorting purposes, you can use hyphen (Ctrl+hyphen) and slash (/) characters to divide numeric dates such as 4/7/93 into three words. "Sorting Tips and Tricks," later in this chapter, provides more information on sorting dates.

Sorting a Table

As with parallel columns, table sorts must start with the cursor in the table. To sort the entire table (except for header columns), simply position the cursor anywhere in the table. Or, if you want to sort just a portion of the table, select (block) the rows you want to sort, as shown in Figure 22.12. Then choose Tools ➤ Sort, make sure the Sort By option is Table Row, and pick the sort options you want.

FIGURE 22.12

This sort key organizes table rows in descending order from largest to smallest percentage of change (cell 4, the % Change column).

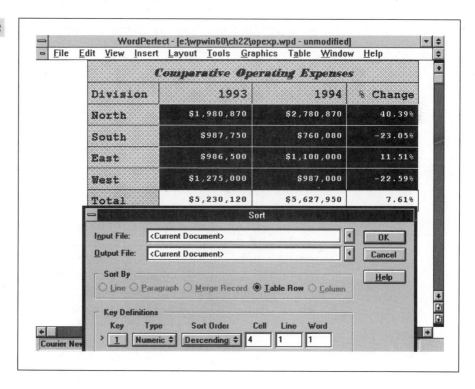

The settings shown in Figure 22.12 will sort the selected rows into descending order from largest to smallest percentage of change (cell 4 of the table).

Here are some points to remember about sorting tables:

- Generally, you don't want to sort column headings, table titles, subtotals, or totals. So be sure to select only the rows that you do want to sort. (WordPerfect won't sort table header rows, so you don't need to worry about sorting them accidentally. By the way, the first row of a Table merge data file is automatically created as a header row.)

- Try to avoid including rows with more, or fewer, cells than other rows in the sort. For example, if the sort in Figure 22.12 included the "Comparative Operating Expenses" row at the top of the table, that row's position after sorting would be unpredictable.

- The table's horizontal lines are sorted with their rows, so you may need to fix the line styles after sorting.

Please see Chapter 7 if you need more information about creating and using tables.

Sorting Tips and Tricks

No, this section isn't about sorting your tips and tricks. It's about tips and tricks for sorting. Here are some suggestions that can help you design successful sorts—the first time, every time.

Counting Backwards

The default numbering order for fields, lines, words, columns, and cells is left to right and top to bottom. In a sort key, word 1 is the first word in a field, word 2 is the second word, and so on. However, you can use a negative number in a key to count from right to left or bottom to top. You saw how this backwards-counting trick can help you sort lists that include three-word names such as *Hanley Allen Strappman* and two-word names such as *Gondola Granolabar* by last name. (If you missed that trick, see "Sorting Lines" earlier in this chapter.)

Sorting Several Words as One

Suppose you're sorting a list of names that includes *Harry Durante III* and *Victoria de la Rosa*. An ordinary sort by last name, using word −1 in the sort key, would list these names in the order

Harry Durante III
Victoria de la Rosa

which is backwards. The records end up in this order because *III* sorts before *Rosa*, since *I* is before *R* in the alphabet.

You probably want *de la Rosa* to appear before *Durante III*. To solve this problem, you must fool WordPerfect into thinking that Durante III and de la Rosa are both one-word last names. It's easy: Just place a hard space (Ctrl+spacebar) between *Durante* and *III*, and between each of the words in *de la Rosa*. Now the sort keys will correctly alphabetize *de la Rosa* ahead of *Durante III*.

Sorting Dates

You can sort dates by remembering that WordPerfect recognizes forward slashes (*/*) and hard hyphens (created with Ctrl+hyphen) as word separators. Just use either of these characters to divide dates into "words" that are the month, day, and year. Then define a separate key for each word.

Suppose you enter a list of dates in the form *07/29/93* or *07–29–93* (with hard hyphens, *not* regular hyphens). To sort these dates in year/month/day order, just set up three *numeric* sort keys and perform a line sort. Define key 1 (the year) as word 3, key 2 (the month) as word 1, and key 3 (the day) as word 2.

Be sure to use *numeric* sort keys for each part of the date. That way, the sort will work properly whether the dates include or omit leading zeros in any position. For example, the dates 7/4/93, 07/02/93, 7/01/93, and 07/5/93 will sort just fine—in the order 7/01/93, 07/02/93, 7/4/93, and 07/5/93—if you define each sort key as numeric. However, if you use alphanumeric sort keys for each word, the list will sort incorrectly as 07/02/93, 07/5/93, 7/01/93, and 7/4/93.

Sorting Codes and Table Lines

WordPerfect sorts codes along with any line that it moves, which can disrupt formatting such as bold and italic, and fonts. Your best bet is to use Initial Codes Style (Chapter 19) to keep as many formatting codes out of the document as you can. If that doesn't do the trick, avoid doing any fancy formatting until after the sort is complete.

You may also need to change a table's line styles after sorting, because table lines are sorted with their rows. (Chapter 7 explains how to create tables and customize their appearance.)

Changing the Sorting Language

One language's alphabetical order can be another language's alphabetical chaos, if the alphabets of the two languages are different. Fortunately, you can easily sort text according to the conventions of another language. First, move the cursor to where you want the new language sort order to kick in, or select a block of text. Then choose Tools ➤ Language and select the language you want.

Troubleshooting Sorts

If your sorted text doesn't come out in the order you expected, or if the sort order appears to be random, look for these sure causes of bad sorts:

- You may have defined the wrong text as the sort key. Or you used the wrong sort type (numeric instead of alphanumeric, or vice versa). This is probably the most common error.
- You haven't handled tabs and indents properly (see the suggestions in the section just below).
- You didn't choose the correct record type for the sort. Remember, sorting will work correctly *only* if you assign the proper record type—Line, Paragraph, Table Row, etc.
- Your records aren't structured uniformly. For example, the Name field of one record contains Address data in another record.
- You forgot to choose OK after defining the sort keys.

NOTE Some text is impossible to sort simply because it isn't arranged in any kind of field-and-record order.

Troubles with Tab Stops

Tab stops can pose special problems. Always remember to account for tabs and indents between fields in a line or paragraph, keeping in mind that *every* tab or indent defines a new field. For example, if you've indented the first column of text, that text is in field 2, the next field is field 3, and so forth. (The bibliography example in Figure 22.9 illustrates how to handle field numbering when tabs and indents appear at the beginning of a line.)

Another problem can occur if you don't define tab stops before typing text. For example, in the first of the two records shown below, the address is in field 3 because it's preceded by two [Lft Tab] codes. But in the second record, the address is in field 4 because it's preceded by three [Lft Tab] codes.

John Jones[Lft Tab]   ABC Corporation[Lft Tab]   123 Apple St.
Nancy Wilcox[Lft Tab] XYZ Co.[Lft Tab][Lft Tab]   345 Oak St.

To fix this problem, you must first redefine the tab stops so that you need only one tab code to separate each column of text (see Chapter 5). Then remove any extra tab codes so that text aligns properly in each column. When that's done, you can define your sort keys and perform the sort.

Isolating Information

In Chapter 21 you learned how to select (or isolate) certain records to include in a merge. You can do the same thing with any text by defining selection criteria in the Sort dialog box.

There is one very important difference between isolating records in a merge and isolating records in a sort. When you define selection criteria for a merge, WordPerfect just *excludes* records that don't meet your selection criteria. But when you define selection criteria for a sort, as explained in a moment, WordPerfect actually *deletes* the information that doesn't match your selection criteria. In fact, this difference is so important that I've devoted the entire next section to it.

Warning! WordPerfect Deletes when It Selects!

Let's suppose you have a list of 500 names and addresses in a WordPerfect document. You use the Sort dialog box to isolate addresses in the lovely city of Cucamonga. When the selection is done, you have a list of, say, 50 Cucamonga residents. Then you print that list.

If you now *save* the list under the same file name, that list of 50 will *replace* your original list of 500—meaning you just sent 450 names and addresses to permanent data heaven. Gone. Unrecoverable. If you didn't do it on purpose, it's a real shame.

Therefore, I strongly suggest that *before you use record selection in the Sort dialog box,* you open the document you plan to select from and immediately use File ➤ Save As to save this copy under a different file name. If you do that before you even get to the Sort dialog box, you don't have to worry about forgetting to later. So even if you do save the document with only selected records in it, you won't overwrite your original copy.

Steps for Isolating Text

The steps for isolating text are exactly the same as steps 1–6 under "Sorting Your Text" earlier in this chapter. In the Sort dialog box, you can still define any sort keys, if you want to put the text in some kind of sorted order.

You also must define as a sort key any text that you want to base a selection on, even if you don't need to sort on that field. For example, if you want to alphabetize a mailing list by name, but include only Cucamonga residents in the list, you must define the people's names as the sort key(s), then also define the city as a sort key. Be sure to place the keys you'll actually sort on *first* in the list of sort keys.

Once you've defined all your sort and selection keys, stay in the Sort dialog box and start defining your *selection criteria.* Just choose Select Records in the Sort dialog box to put the cursor in the Select Records text box. The available selection operators will appear on the status bar at the bottom of the screen, as shown below.

Select Records:		
☐ Select Without Sorting		View Input File...

Operators: |(OR) &(AND) = <> > < >= <=

You can type a selection criterion using the general format

KeyNumber Operator Value

KeyNumber should be the word *key* followed by the number of the sort key that represents the text you want to search. The *Operator* is one of the Selection Operators shown in the status bar and summarized in Table 22.1. The *Value* is what you want to search for. For example, if you chose the City portion of text as the third sort key, you'd type in your selection criterion like this:

key3=Cucamonga

TABLE 22.1: Selection Operators and How They're Used

SYMBOL	PURPOSE	EXAMPLES
=	Selects records that have *exactly the same* information in the indicated key.	**key3=92123** selects only the records in the 92123 zip code.
<>	Selects records that *do not match* the information in the indicated key.	**key3<>92123** selects only the records that *aren't* in the 92123 zip code.
& (AND)	Selects records that meet conditions of *both* keys. You can use the character & or the word AND for this operator.	**key3=92123 and key1<>Smith** selects every record in the 92123 zip code *except* those where key 1 is Smith.

TABLE 22.1: Selection Operators and How They're Used (continued)

SYMBOL	PURPOSE	EXAMPLES
| (OR)	Selects records that meet the conditions of *either* key. You can use the character | or the word OR for this operator.	**key1=Smith or key2=Arizona** selects any records that include Smith in key 1 or Arizona in key 2.
>	Selects records that have values *greater than* the information in the indicated key.	**key4>4700** selects any records where the value in key 4 exceeds 4700.
<	Selects records that have values *less than* the information in the indicated key.	**key4<4700** selects any records where the value in key 4 is less than 4700.
>=	Selects records that have values *greater than or equal to* the information in the indicated key.	**key4>=4700** selects any records where the value in key 4 is greater than or equal to 4700.
<=	Selects records that have values *less than or equal to* the information in the indicated key.	**key4<=4700** selects any records where the value in key 4 is less than or equal to 4700.
g	Global key that means "any key."	**keyg=45** selects records that have the value 45 in any key.
( )	You can use parentheses to change the selection order (see "Refining Your Selection Criteria with Parentheses").	**key3=92123 & (key1=Jones | key1=Smith)** selects any Jones or Smith who lives in the 92123 zip code area. Without the parentheses, this would select any Jones living in the 92123 zip code, and all Smiths.

Once you've finished defining your selection criterion (or multiple criteria, as I'll discuss in a moment), choose OK to get the job done.

Remember, WordPerfect will still *sort* on any sort keys you've defined. In addition, it will *isolate* records for which you've defined selection criteria.

> **T I P**
>
> If you'd like to isolate records without sorting them first, select (check) the Select Without Sorting option in the Sort dialog box. This can speed up the selection operation on a large data file. After you've isolated the records you want, you can sort them if necessary.

Figure 22.13 illustrates a sort key that will sort a list of names and addresses in zip-code order (key 1, field 4, word 1), then by street name (key 2, field 2, word 2), and then by street number (key 3, field 2, word 1). If this list included several people at each address, the list would also be

FIGURE 22.13

Sorting records that don't include Schumack by zip, street name, and street number

sorted by last name (key 4, field 1, word −1). You could add a fifth key, field 1 and word 1, to further sort by first name within the same last name. Thanks to the selection criteria in the Select Records box (*key4<>Schumack*), the sort will retain only those records that don't have Schumack as the last name.

Using AND and OR

The AND and OR operators can be a bit difficult to master if you're human (like most people) and don't have the mind of a computer programmer. Fortunately, if your first attempt doesn't do the trick, you can just choose Edit ➤ Undo or press Ctrl+Z to undo your selection. Then choose Tools ➤ Sort again, adjust your criteria, and choose OK to see the improved results. Let's take a quick look at some of the AND and OR traps that might trip you up.

Creating AND and OR Criteria

When combining selection criteria, don't forget to use all three elements—key numbers, selection operators, and search values—on *both* sides of the & (AND) and | (OR) combination characters. For example, you might think that WordPerfect is smart enough to read

    key1>=92000 AND <=92999

as "zip codes that are greater than or equal to 92000 AND less than 92999." But that's simply not the case, because (as everyone knows) computers have the IQ of turnips. Instead, this is interpreted as "zip codes that are greater than or equal to 92000 and who-knows-what is less than or equal to 92999."

The same rule holds true for the OR combination operator. Suppose you want to send letters to people in Georgia, Alabama, and Florida, and you've already defined the state field as sort key 1. You actually want to delete all records *except* those with GA, AL, or FL in the state field. But if you incorrectly enter the selection criterion as *key1=GA|AL|FL,*WordPerfect will return a completely empty file because *nothing* matches this criterion. The proper way to enter this selection criterion is

    key1=GA | key1=AL | key1=FL

Don't Use AND When You Mean OR

It's also important not to confuse the AND and OR operators, because they don't always represent your intent as you might express it in English. Consider the example of the mailing to residents of Georgia, Alabama, and Florida. You might think that this selection criterion will do the trick:

```
key1=GA & key1=AL & key1=FL
```

In English this says, "Keep only those records that have GA in the state field, *AND* AL in the state field, *AND* FL in the state field." WordPerfect, however, interprets this as "Keep records that have GA AL FL in the state field." A single record couldn't possibly have all three states in its state field, so the results of the selection would be no records at all.

Remember that you aren't asking a question in English when you define selection criteria. Instead, you're setting up a screen, or filter, through which some records will pass and some won't. WordPerfect will compare each record, one at a time, with your selection criteria. It retains the record if it can answer Yes to *all* the criteria joined by the AND (&) operator in your selection criteria for that record. Likewise, it retains the record if it can answer Yes to *any* of the criteria joined by the *OR* (|) operator in your selection criteria for that record.

Refining Your Selection Criteria with Parentheses

When selection criteria become rather complicated, you must be careful about how you combine the AND and OR operators. Suppose your document contains (among others) a field for the state where each person lives and a field for each person's credit limit. You then decide to write a form letter to all the names in Georgia, and to just the people in Florida whose credit limits are $500 or greater, informing them that you've raised their credit limit by $1,000 (perhaps because their swamp land has just been declared a national treasure and its value has increased). This requires a selection criterion that combines AND logic and OR logic. You must isolate *all* people who live in Georgia and *only* those in Florida who have credit limits of $500 or more.

If you're not careful in a situation like this one, you may end up creating an ambiguous selection criterion. Imagine that you've already defined the first sort key as the State field, and the second sort key as the Credit Limit field. You might compose the following selection criterion (though it isn't correct):

    key1=GA|key1=FL&key2>=$500

Selection criteria are evaluated from left to right unless you use parentheses to change the order. Therefore, WordPerfect will interpret the above criterion as "Select records that have GA or FL in the state field. From that list, select records where the credit limit is greater than or equal to $500." The selection result will include only those people in Georgia and Florida whose credit limits are $500 or greater. However, this doesn't do the job, since you want to include *everyone* in Georgia, regardless of their present credit limit.

To avoid potential confusion with such complicated selection criteria, you can use parentheses to control how WordPerfect interprets your criteria. The correct criterion for our Georgia/Florida example,

    key1=GA|(key1=FL&key2>=$500)

says that, to avoid being deleted, a record must have GA in the state field (so all Georgians will be selected), *OR* it must have FL in the state field and have a value that's greater than or equal to $500 in the credit limit field. This resolves the ambiguity and ensures that *all* Georgians (with any credit limit at all) and *only* those Floridians with credit limits of $500 or more will remain after the select operation is finished.

Making Global Selections

The key name *keyg* allows you to search *all* the sort keys for a specific value. Suppose you create a merge record file that includes both a business address and a home address for each person. To mail letters to everyone who has either a home or business address in New York, define both the home and business state fields as sort keys. Then specify **keyg=NY** as the selection criterion. This will delete all records except those with NY in either the home or business state field.

Now you know everything there is to know about sorting and selecting text in your WordPerfect documents. In the next chapter, I'll focus on two extremely useful office tools: WordPerfect's fax and mail features.

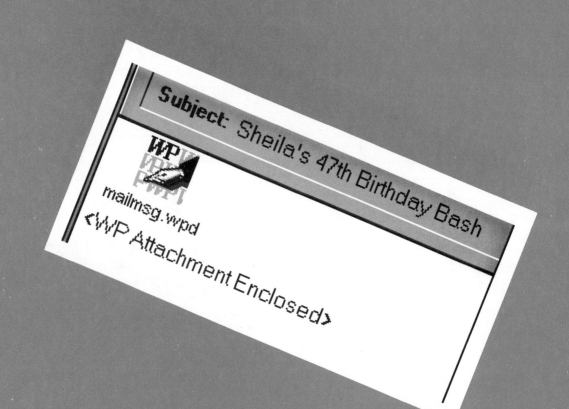

CHAPTER

23

Sending Faxes and Interoffice Mail

f a s t TRACK

● **To send a WordPerfect document as a mail message**   **767**

your network mail program must use the Lotus VIM or Microsoft MAPI protocol.

● **To send a document as a mail message**   **768**

connect to your network and then start WordPerfect. Open the file you want to send as mail and choose File ➤ Mail.

WORDPERFECT 6 for Windows is truly an application of the nineties, because it lets you take advantage of the latest in business communications, including faxes and interoffice mail. It's important to understand that WordPerfect doesn't have its own built-in fax and mail capabilities. Instead, it provides access to whatever fax and mail capabilities are already installed on your computer.

There are dozens of brands of fax boards and electronic mail software. Thus, in this chapter, I can only give you the general guidelines for using those programs from WordPerfect. Once the mail or fax program "takes over," you'll need to follow instructions in the documentation for your particular hardware and software.

Sending Faxes from WordPerfect

Sending a fax from WordPerfect is a lot like printing a document. The difference is that the document is printed on someone else's fax machine, instead of on your printer!

Before sending a fax, you must properly install the fax hardware and software on your computer, according to the manufacturer's instructions. Be sure to install any Windows fax drivers, so that you'll have access to your fax board whenever you're in Windows and WordPerfect for Windows.

Sending a Fax

Once you've gotten your fax equipment squared away, sending a Word-Perfect document as a fax is easy:

1. Start WordPerfect as usual, then create or open the document you want to send.

2. Choose File ➤ Select Printer. Assuming you've correctly installed your fax hardware and software, you should see a driver for that fax board, as in Figure 23.1, where I'm using Intel's Satisfaxtion boards and FAXability software.

3. Be sure to double-click the driver name, or highlight that name and choose Select before leaving the Select Printer dialog box.

4. If you want to send a block of text, select that text now. If you want to send just a single page, move your cursor anywhere on that page. Choose File ➤ Print.

5. Make any choices as to how much you want to print in the Print dialog box, as discussed in Chapter 10.

6. Choose Print to send the fax.

At this point your fax software should kick in and request the additional information needed, such as the name and phone number of the recipient. Figure 23.2 shows an example, using the dialog box that appears on my computer.

At this point, you need to follow the instructions for your particular fax software to send the fax. After the fax is sent, you can close the fax program's dialog box (if it stays open) to return to WordPerfect. If you have any problems sending the fax, you'll need to refer to your fax board's documentation, not WordPerfect's documentation, for advice.

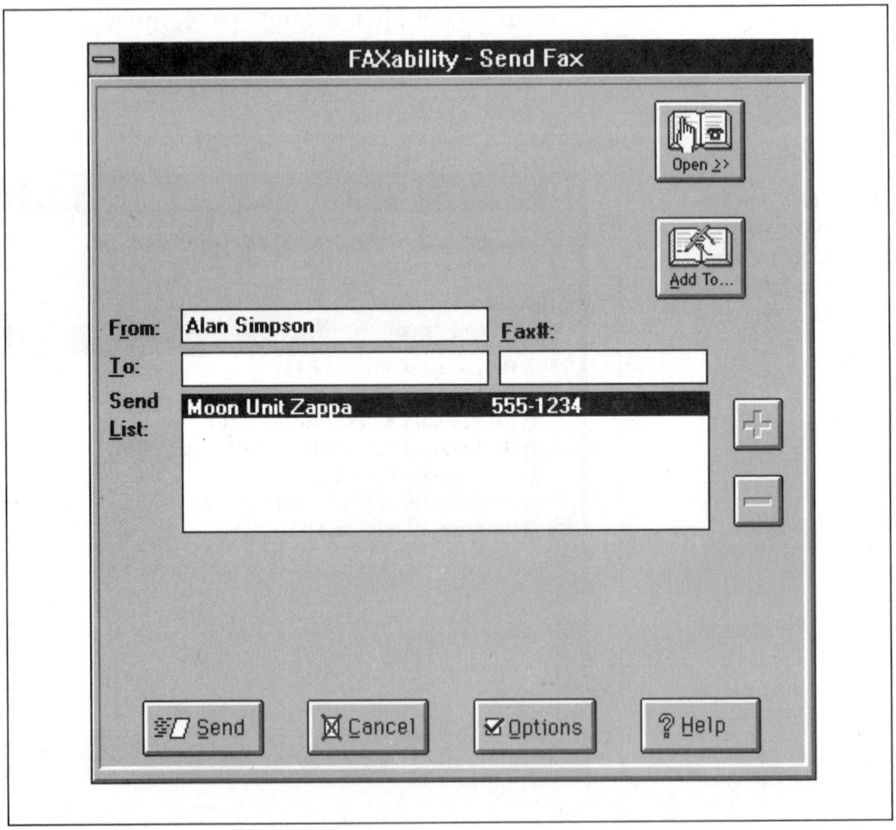

FIGURE 23.2

When you "print" to a fax board, the board's software should automatically take over, as in this example.

Sending Mail from WordPerfect

A *network* is a collection of cables and other hardware, plus the appropriate software, connecting two or more computers. In addition to sharing resources like printers and disk drives, some network users can send electronic messages from one PC to another. Electronic mail, or *e-mail* for short, travels rapidly, doesn't need to be printed before it's read, and can easily be incorporated into reports and other documents.

NOTE You cannot use WordPerfect's mail features unless your network uses the Lotus VIM or Microsoft MAPI protocol.

WordPerfect's mail feature hooks into your network mail program, so that you can send documents without ever leaving WordPerfect. You can use any features that your network mail program offers to route e-mail to specific people, reply to messages, and manage messages. (The only restriction is that your network mail software must fall into one of two mail protocol categories: Lotus *VIM* or Microsoft *MAPI*.) Typically, the e-mail software will alert the recipient automatically when mail arrives.

I'll assume your network is already up and running and that you're connected to it. (If you're not sure how to connect to your network, please ask your network administrator for help.)

What You Can Send as a Message

Your mail message can be a saved WordPerfect document—including formatted text, graphics, embedded objects (Chapter 33), and anything else WordPerfect can create. Alternatively, you can select text from a new or saved document and send that. The factoids below will help you decide whether to send the whole document or selected text only.

If you mail the entire document...

- The WordPerfect document will appear in the mail message as an embedded WordPerfect for Windows icon.

- You should save the document and make sure it has a .WPD file extension before sending it. This associates the WordPerfect for Windows application with the icon.

- Recipients can read your message only if they can run WordPerfect for Windows from their workstations.

- To read the message, recipients must double-click the icon embedded in the mail message. This starts WordPerfect for Windows and opens the message in a document window.

If you select text and then mail it...

- The text will appear in the mail message without any special formatting, and without graphics or other embedded objects.

- The recipient doesn't need WordPerfect for Windows to read the message.

Sending Your Mail Message

To send a document as a mail message, follow these steps:

1. Connect to the network and make sure the e-mail software is accessible on your computer. (See your network administrator if you need help with this.)

2. Start WordPerfect as usual.

3. Open the document you want to send as mail (File ➤ Open), or create a new document and save it (File ➤ Save). If you want to send a block of text, select that text now.

4. Choose File ➤ Mail to connect to your network's e-mail program.

5. The remaining steps will depend on the e-mail program that's on your network. Typically, you'll need to sign on to the mail program, specify who should receive your mail message, and then send the message.

Let's look at a quick scenario on a Microsoft Windows for Workgroups network. Recently I wrote a memo in WordPerfect for Windows and saved it with a wildly imaginative name, *mailmsg.wpd*. Next I chose File ➤ Mail to bring up the dialog box shown in Figure 23.3. I responded by typing my secret password, twisting my decoder ring three times to the right, and

FIGURE 23.3

The Windows for Workgroups Mail Sign In dialog box.

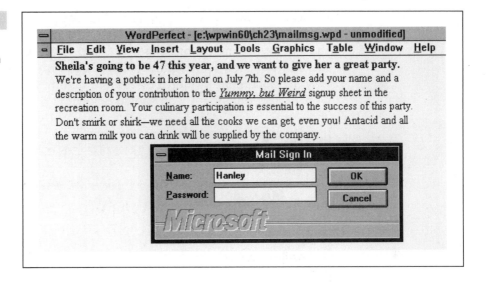

choosing OK. This brought me to the next dialog box, which lets me specify the recipients and send the message. Figure 23.4 illustrates this dialog box after I filled in the To, Cc, and Subject information. Moments after I clicked the Send button, my message arrived at workstations in *Gondola's Workgroup*.

Each receiving workstation beeped when my message arrived. Hungry for gossip, my first recipient dropped what she was doing in her spreadsheet

FIGURE 23.4

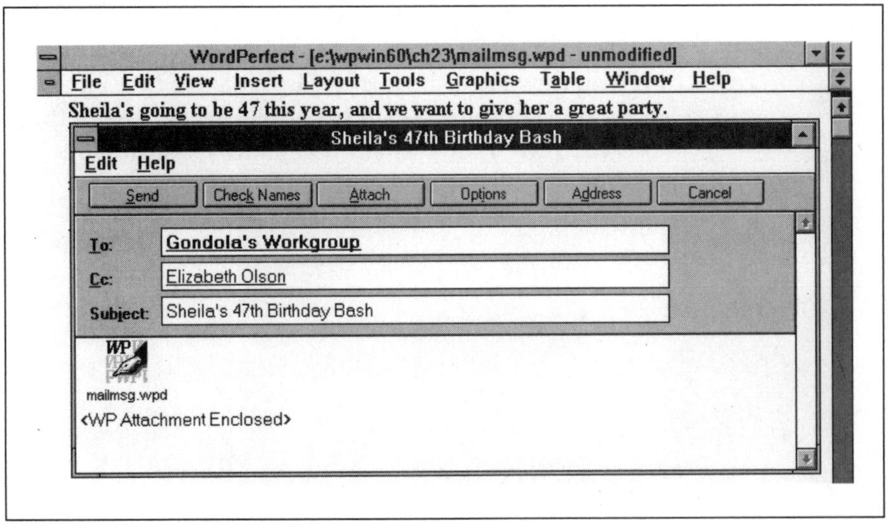

The Windows for Workgroups Mail Send Note dialog box after I filled in the To, Cc, and Subject information. The next step is to click the Send button.

application, switched to Program Manager (by pressing Alt+Tab as needed), and double-clicked the Mail icon in the Main group window. She then typed her e-mail password and chose OK. Next, she double-clicked her Inbox folder and double-clicked my message to open it. To view my document in WordPerfect for Windows, she double-clicked the WordPerfect document icon shown below:

Subject: Sheila's 47th Birthday Bash

mailmsg.wpd

<WP Attachment Enclosed>

Of course, the actual procedures for using mail may be different on your network. However, you've probably figured out that sending mail from WordPerfect is easy, convenient, and fun. Surely it beats the old "sneakernet" method of putting information on a floppy disk and walking it over to someone else's computer!

You now know how to set up and use the fax and mail features, which let you communicate with people in the next office or around the world. Next, we'll look at another handy tool for the office: WordPerfect's impressive ability to do math in tables.

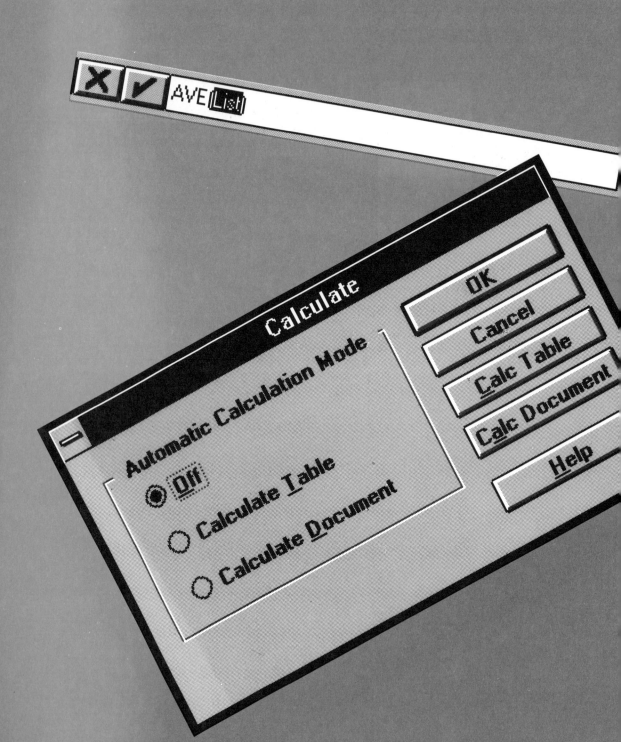

CHAPTER

24

Perfect Math with Spreadsheets

fast **TRACK**

● **To put numbers into an existing table**   **777**

type the numbers into their cells in the document window.

● **To display the Table Formula feature bar**   **778**

choose Table ➤ Formula Bar, or move the cursor into the table, right-click, and choose Formula Bar from the Quick-Menu. You can use the Table Formula feature bar to enter formulas and functions into table cells and floating cells.

● **To put a formula or function into a table cell**   **780**

select (check) Table ➤ Cell Formula Entry. Move the cursor into the cell where you want the formula, and enter the formula (or function). The formula results will appear when you move the cursor to another cell. To resume normal data entry, deselect Table ➤ Cell Formula Entry. You can also use the Formula Edit text box in the Table Formula feature bar to enter formulas and functions.

● **To enter a table function by choosing it from a list**   **784**

turn on the Table Formula feature bar and move the cursor to the cell where you want to enter the function. Click the Functions button, highlight the function you want in the Functions list and choose Insert. Fill in any options required for the formula and click the Insert (✓) button in the feature bar.

To point to a cell or range instead of typing it yourself

turn on the Table Formula feature bar. Position the cursor in the Edit Formula text box where you want to enter a cell or range (or select text in the box to replace that text). Then click on or select the table cell or range you want in the formula (or click on a floating cell).

You can use the +, =, or * shortcut functions, and the Sum button

to calculate a subtotal, total, or grand total, or to sum cells above or to the left of the current cell (respectively).

If the result of a calculation in your document looks wrong

you may just need to recalculate. Choose Table ➤ Calculate from the menu bar, then click Calc Table or Calc Document. Or, click the Calculate button in the Table Formula feature bar.

To add a floating cell to your document

position the cursor where you want the floating cell to appear (outside of any table or floating cell). Then choose Table ➤ Create ➤ Floating Cell ➤ OK and enter your formula. To edit the floating cell later, turn on Reveal Codes (Alt+F3), move the cursor between the [Flt Cell] paired codes, and make your changes. Floating cells can contain formulas, functions, references to table cells or ranges, and references to other floating cells.

DO YOU ever need to set up invoices, financial statements, and other documents that require both the complicated calculations that spreadsheets can do and the fancy formatting that WordPerfect is so good at? If so, you've come to the right place.

WordPerfect offers spreadsheet tools that let you perform math calculations right in your formatted documents. These tools are so powerful and easy to use that you're unlikely to ever need a standalone spreadsheet application for most of your work!

If you do have spreadsheets stored in other spreadsheet applications (such as PlanPerfect, Lotus 1-2-3, Excel, or Quattro Pro), don't worry. You can easily import or link existing spreadsheets into your WordPerfect documents with just a few quick keystrokes. I'll cover this topic in Chapter 33.

Now perhaps you've heard the famous adage "One graph is worth a thousand spreadsheets." Well, even if you haven't, you can see that it's true when you use WordPerfect's Chart feature to display tabular data graphically—as a pie, bar, line, area, scatter, hi-low, or whatever type of chart you desire. You'll learn how to create charts in Chapter 26.

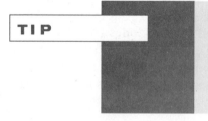

TIP

For quick "throwaway" calculations, you can use the Windows Calculator. To run it, switch to Program Manager (Ctrl+Esc) and double-click the Calculator icon in the Accessories window. Your Windows documentation explains more about using Calculator.

What the Spreadsheet Can Do for You

WordPerfect's built-in spreadsheet features are similar to widely used spreadsheet applications such as Lotus 1-2-3, Excel, and Quattro Pro. So if you're familiar with spreadsheet basics and WordPerfect tables, you'll have no trouble mastering WordPerfect's spreadsheet tools.

You typically start by creating a table, as explained in Chapter 7. You can then place your numbers, formulas, and functions right in the table's cells, using the normal document window. Or, you can use the Table Formula feature bar to make certain formula-entry jobs easier.

NOTE

In this chapter, I'll assume that you already know the basics of creating, formatting, and editing tables (as discussed in Chapter 7), and that you've already created a table to hold your numbers and calculation results. That way we can focus here on the mathematical aspects of tables.

Later in this chapter you'll learn about a unique WordPerfect feature called "floating cells." You can put floating cells anywhere in your document (*except* a table) to store numbers and perform calculations.

Entering Numbers, Formulas, and Functions

Entering a number into a table cell is easy. Position the cursor in the appropriate table cell, and type the number just as you would type any text. The number can contain decimal points, comma separators, and a leading dollar sign if you wish. For example, **1000**, **1,000**, **1,000.00** and **$1,000.00** are all valid ways to type in the number one thousand.

To enter a negative number, precede it with a minus sign (or hyphen), or enclose the number in parentheses. For instance, these are all valid ways to express negative one thousand or minus one thousand in cells with an accounting or currency type: **–1000**, **–1000.00**, **$–1,000.00**, **(1,000)**, or **$(1,000.00)**.

WordPerfect offers two ways to enter formulas and functions—the Table Formula feature bar and Cell Formula Entry mode. You can use either or both methods as you please. I'll explain how to use each method next.

N O T E   The general techniques for entering formulas and functions are the same. So I'll usually lump formulas and functions together by using the term "formulas." The later section, "Entering Functions," covers special topics that apply to functions only.

Using the Table Formula Feature Bar

The Table Formula feature bar, shown in Figure 24.1, offers convenient tools for creating and inserting formulas into tables and floating cells.

FIGURE 24.1

The Table Formula feature bar

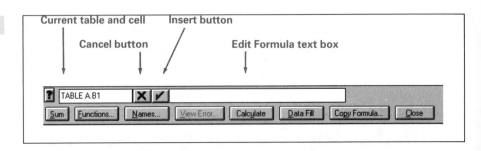

To display this feature bar, choose Table ➤ Formula Bar; or move the cursor into a table, right-click, and choose Formula Bar from the Quick-Menu that appears.

When you're ready to enter a formula into a cell, turn on the feature bar and follow these steps:

1. Position the cursor in the cell where you want the formula to appear.

2. Click in the feature bar's Edit Formula text box (the message "Formula Edit Mode is On" will appear next to the text box).

3. Type your formula, including numbers, operators, cell references, and math functions, as discussed later in the chapter.

4. When you're satisfied with the formula, press ↵ or click the Insert button (✓) in the feature bar. (To cancel the entry, click the Cancel button (✗) in the feature bar.)

WordPerfect will display the results of your formula instantly.

If you need to change a formula later, click in the cell where you want to make your change. Then click in the Edit Formula text box and use normal editing techniques to change the formula. When you're done, press ↵ or click the Insert button in the feature bar.

TIP

To quickly delete formulas from table cells, select the cell(s) and press Del.

Other buttons in the Table Formula feature bar offer data entry shortcuts and quick access to frequently used operations. These buttons are described briefly below, and discussed in more detail later in the chapter:

Sum (or Ctrl+=) Calculates the sum of cells above or to the left of the current cell.

Functions Lets you insert a function by selecting it from a list. See "Entering Functions."

Names Lets you name tables, floating cells, cells, ranges, columns, and rows. You can then use the names in formulas and functions, and can jump to any named area. See "Naming Cells."

View Error Displays a brief description about an error in the current cell. Calculation errors appear as two question marks (??) or the word **ERR** in a cell.

Calculate Recalculates all the tables in the current document. See "Recalculating Your Formulas."

Data Fill   (or Ctrl+Shift+F12) Lets you automatically fill selected cells with formulas or data. See "Filling in Data Automatically," later in the chapter.

Copy Formula   Lets you copy formulas from cell to cell. See "Copying Formulas."

Close   Closes the Table Formula feature bar.

Using Cell Formula Entry Mode

When *Cell Formula Entry mode* is active, you can simply position the cursor in a cell, and type in whatever formula you want. For example, you could move to cell E2 and type **C2*D2** to multiply the value in cell C2 by the value in cell D2. Similarly, you could position the cursor in a cell and type in the function **UPPER(A3)** to convert the value in cell A3 to uppercase letters. WordPerfect will display the result instantly, as soon as you move the cursor out of the cell. A handy shortcut indeed!

To activate Cell Formula Entry mode, choose T̲able and select (check) C̲ell Formula Entry from the menu.

Here are some points to remember about Cell Formula Entry mode:

- Only formulas that you type *after* activating Cell Formula Entry mode are affected. This mode has no effect on previously typed formulas.

- This mode doesn't recognize cells that are formatted with a Text number type. (See Chapter 7 and "Formatting Numbers and Calculated Results," later in this chapter, for more about formatting numbers.)

- You can use Cell Formula Entry mode whether the Table Formula feature bar is visible or not.

To turn off Cell Formula Entry mode, choose T̲able and deselect C̲ell Formula Entry. When this mode is off, any text typed into a cell is treated simply as text—not as a formula to be calculated.

NOTE If you try to change an existing formula while editing a table, WordPerfect will ask if you want to replace that cell's formula. If you choose Yes, the formula will be replaced with the text or formula you typed. If you choose No, your entry will be deleted and the original formula will remain. To turn off the prompt about replacing cell formulas, choose File ➤ Preferences ➤ Environment and deselect Confirm Deletion Of Table Formulas.

Using Arithmetic Operators and Precedence

You can use any combination of the following arithmetic operators in the formulas you enter:

OPERATOR	MEANING	EXAMPLE
^	Exponent (raise to a power)	3^2 (result is 9)
–	Negation	–3*6 (result is –18)
( )	Change the order of precedence (used for grouping)	(3+5)/2 (result is 4)
*	Multiplication	4*5 (result is 20)
/	Division	10/2 (result is 5)
+	Addition	10+15 (result is 25)
–	Subtraction	53–10 (result is 43)

TIP WordPerfect offers additional arithmetic and logical operators. You can find out about those in the documentation that comes with your WordPerfect package.

Formulas in WordPerfect follow the standard *order of precedence*. That is, calculations are performed in the order listed in the table above: first exponentiation, then negation, then multiplication, and so forth. So the result of this formula

10+5*2

is 20 (5 times 2 is 10, plus 10 makes 20). The result *is not* 30 (10 plus 5 is 15, times 2 is 30).

When entering formulas, you can use parentheses to group the parts of the formula you want to calculate first. WordPerfect always works from the innermost parentheses outward, just as in standard mathematics. Thus, the result of this formula

(10+5)*2

is indeed 30, because the parentheses force WordPerfect to perform the addition before the multiplication.

You can nest parentheses in a formula. This allows you to perform complex calculations within a table. For example, if cell A1 contains the COST of an item, A2 the SALVAGE value of that item, A3 the useful LIFE in years, and A4 the current PERIOD, then the formula

(A1-A2)*(A3-A4+1)/(A3*(A3+1)/2)

calculates the current depreciation using the sum-of-the-year's-digits method. However, it would actually be easier to enter this formula as the function *SYD(A1,A2,A3,A4)*. I'll discuss functions next.

TIP

You can name cells or ranges to make formulas more understandable. For example, you could name cells A1 through A4 *Cost, Salvage, Life*, and *Period*. Then you could enter the SYD formula as *SYD(Cost,Salvage,Life,Period)*. See "Naming Cells," later in the chapter.

Entering Functions

WordPerfect offers nearly 100 functions to do fancy calculations that would otherwise be difficult or impossible with simple arithmetic operators. You can enter a function in either of two ways:

- If you know the exact format of the function you want, you can type it into a cell (if Cell Formula Entry mode is active) or into the Edit Formula text box.

- If you can't remember all the rules for entering a particular function (and who among us can?), you can click the Functions button on the Table Formula feature bar for help.

When you click the Functions button, a list of available functions appears, as shown below:

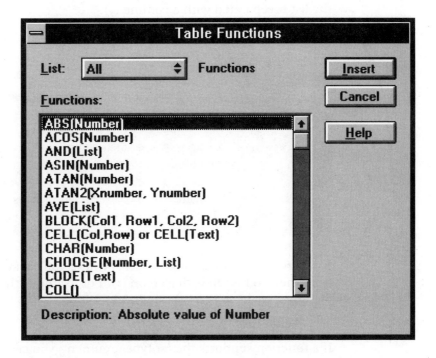

Most functions start with a brief name, such as SQRT (for square root), and are followed by parentheses and *arguments* (defined below) that the function expects to find in the parentheses. As you scroll through the Table Functions list using ↑ and ↓, you'll see a brief description of the currently highlighted function near the bottom of the dialog box.

The *arguments* are what the function bases its calculation on. An argument can be a number, cell address, list, or text, depending on the function's requirements. For example, the result of the formula below is 9, the square root of 81:

SQRT(81)

This next formula means "display the square root of whatever number is in cell A1":

SQRT(A1)

The following formula uses the AVERAGE function to compute the average of a *list* of numbers (10, 15, 25, and 16). Notice that each item in the list is separated with a comma (,).

AVE(10,15,25,16)

WARNING

Do not enter commas as separators when typing numbers into a list in a function. For example, suppose you want to average the numbers 1000 and 50. If you mistakenly enter the number 1000 as *1,000* in the formula *AVE(1,000,50)*, you'll end up with a result *of 17* (1+0+50 divided by 3). The proper way to enter this formula is *AVE(1000,50)*, which gives the result *525* (1000+50 divided by 2).

A list might also be a range of cells, where you separate the starting cell from the ending cell with a colon (:). For example, this formula averages the numbers in cells A1 through A4:

AVE(A1:A4)

If a function supports the *list* type argument, you can mix and match arguments. For example, the formula below averages the contents of cells A1 through A3, cell B1, and the number 15.5:

AVE(A1:A3,B1,15.5)

To enter a function into a cell (or floating cell) with the help of the Functions button in the Table Formula feature bar, follow these steps:

1. Turn on the Table Formula feature bar (Table ➤ Formula Bar).

2. Position the cursor in the cell where you want the function to appear.

3. Click the Functions button in the Table Formula feature bar.

4. To limit the list to certain types of functions, choose an option from the List pop-up button. Your options are All (all functions), Arithmetic, Calendar, Financial, Logical, Miscellaneous, and Text.

5. In the Functions list, highlight the function you want. You can use the mouse or PgUp, PgDn, ↑, and ↓ keys to highlight the function, or type the first few characters of the function name.

6. To select the highlighted function, double-click the function, choose the Insert button, or press ↵.

7. The selected function now appears in the Formula Edit Text box, with its first argument highlighted, like this:

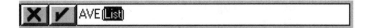

8. Between the parentheses, type or edit the arguments for the function, or use *pointing* (described shortly) to select the cell or range of cells you want to use as the argument. The AVE(*List*) function expects a list, so you could type in a list of numbers to average, like this:

AVE(15,27,36.5,91)

Or you might type in or point to a range of cells. For example, this formula tells the table to average all the numbers in cells A2 through A10:

AVE(A2:A10)

NOTE   When entering a text argument for a function, be sure to place quotes around the text. For example, to convert *give me an upper* to uppercase, use the function UPPER(*"give me an upper"*).

9. After completing your formula, press ↵ or click the Insert (✓) button in the feature bar. The formula result will appear in its cell.

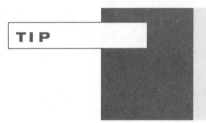

TIP

The functions used in WordPerfect are virtually identical to those used in spreadsheet applications. You can find out more about a math function by looking up the function in your spreadsheet documentation or WordPerfect documentation.

Pointing to Cells or Ranges

You can use your mouse to *point* to cells or ranges for an easy, more visual alternative to typing cell addresses into a formula. Suppose you want to average all the numbers in cells A2 through A10 in a table. Here's how to do that using the AVE(*List*) function and pointing:

1. Turn on the Table Formula feature bar (T̲able ➤ Fo̲rmula Bar).

2. Move the cursor to the cell in which you want to put the formula. (For this example, I moved the cursor to cell B6.)

3. Choose F̲unctions and select your function. I'll use AVE(*List*) here. The argument (*List*) to the AVE function will be highlighted automatically.

4. With the argument selected, simply click on the cell you want to insert in the formula, or drag your mouse pointer through the range of cells. Figure 24.2 shows the screen after I highlighted cells B2 through B5.

NOTE

If you click somewhere else, or highlight a different range, that cell or range will appear in the Edit Formula text box.

FIGURE 24.2

The screen after highlighting cells B2 through B5

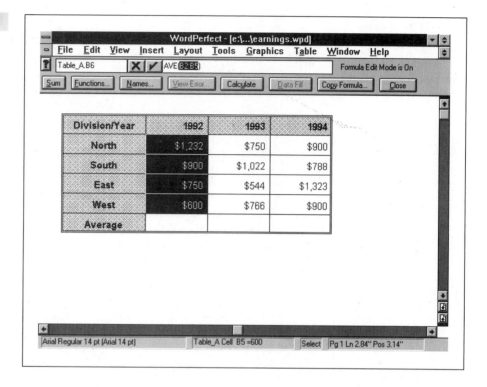

5. If you want to point to other cells, ranges, or floating cells, or enter an arithmetic operator or other text into the formula, click in the Edit Formula text box again. Now position the cursor in the box, type in text (if necessary) and repeat steps 4 and 5 until you've completed the formula. (For this simple example, I went directly to step 6 because I only wanted to enter one range and no other text into the formula.)

6. To put the formula into its cell, click the Insert (✓) button in the feature bar or press ↵.

In Figure 24.3 you can see the results of using pointing to enter the formula AVE(B2:B5). Notice that the cursor position and cell contents appear both in the feature bar and the status bar. (In this example, the true average of 870.5 was rounded up to $871. See "Fixing Rounding Errors" near the end of this chapter for information about rounding.)

The screen after using Point Mode to enter arguments for the AVE formula

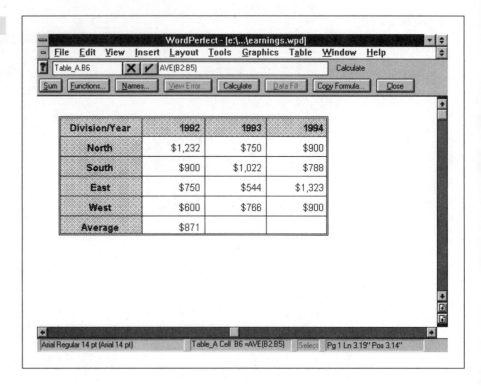

Formatting Numbers and Calculated Results

You can tailor the alignment and appearance of numbers and calculated results. Start by highlighting the cell or cells you want to change. Then…

- To change the alignment, choose Table ➤ Format ➤ Cell. Or, right-click the table and choose Format from the QuickMenu, then choose Cell. Pick the options you want from the Alignment area of the Format dialog box, and choose OK.

- To change the number format, choose Table ➤ Number Type ➤ Cell. Or, right-click the table and choose Number Type from the QuickMenu, then choose Cell. Select the number type options you want, and choose OK.

See Chapter 7 for more information about formatting tables.

Locking Formula Cells

You can lock any cell in a table to protect it from change or erasure. When a cell is locked, the cursor will jump right over it. This prevents you from typing text or other numbers into a cell accidentally.

If a locked cell contains a formula, it will still be recalculated when you recalculate the table.

To lock a cell, follow these steps:

1. Move the cursor to the cell you want to lock, or select the range of cells you want to lock.

2. Choose Table ➤ Format from the menu bar or press Ctrl+F12. Or, right-click and choose Format from the QuickMenu.

3. Choose Cell (if necessary).

4. Select (check) Lock and choose OK.

To unlock a cell or cells, select the cell(s), and repeat steps 2 and 3. Next, uncheck the Lock box and choose OK.

Calculating Totals and Subtotals

You can use the three special function characters listed below to calculate subtotals, totals (the sum of all the subtotals above the current cell), and a grand total (the sum of all the totals above the current cell).

+	Subtotal
=	Total
★	Grand Total

To enter one of these characters, simply type it into the cell if Cell Formula Entry mode is active, then move the cursor to another cell to see the result. Or, type it into the Edit Formula text box in the Table Formula feature bar and press ↵. This is much faster than typing a lengthy formula when you want to add a column of numbers.

NOTE The subtotal (+), total (=), and grand total (*) functions are initially set to zero and are reset to zero each time you display their contents. If you simply want to sum a column of numbers, use the subtotal (+) function, or the SUM function (described later in this chapter).

Figure 24.4 shows a table that uses the subtotal (+), total (=), and grand total (*) special functions. I entered the dollar amounts for new and used car sales, and formatted the numbers as Currency, with zero digits, as described in Chapter 7. (I also removed and changed many of the table lines in that example, using techniques discussed in Chapter 7.)

Quickly Summing a Row or Column

The Sum button in the Table Formula feature bar offers a quick way to add up a column or row of numbers. Here's how to use it:

1. Turn on the Table Formula feature bar (Table ➤ Formula Bar).

2. Position the cursor where you want the sum to appear:

   • **To sum a column,** place the cursor in the cell just below the last number in the column.

   • **To sum a row,** place the cursor in the cell just to the right of the numbers you want to add up. (Note that the cell above the cursor cannot contain a number or formula that yields a numeric result; otherwise WordPerfect will sum the column instead of the row. The cell above the cursor can, however, contain text, or be blank.)

3. Click the Sum button in the Table Formula feature bar, or press Ctrl+=, or choose Table ➤ Sum. The sum of the row or column will appear instantly.

In Figure 24.5, I used the Sum button to calculate column and row totals quickly. The labels in the figure point to the cells the cursor was in when I clicked the button.

FIGURE 24.4

A sample document
using the special
subtotal (+), total (=),
and grand total (*)
functions

First Quarter: Eastern Division

New Cars	$22,500,000	
Used Cars	$7,500,000	
Subtotal	$30,000,000	← + (subtotal)

First Quarter: Western Division

New Cars	$18,500,000	
Used Cars	$9,500,000	
Subtotal	$28,000,000	← + (subtotal)
Qtr 1 Total	$58,000,000	← = (total)

Second Quarter: Eastern Division

New Cars	$21,750,000	
Used Cars	$9,675,000	
Subtotal	$31,425,000	← + (subtotal)

Second Quarter: Western Division

New Cars	$16,000,000	
Used Cars	$8,775,000	
Subtotal	$24,775,000	← + (subtotal)
Qtr 2 Total	$56,200,000	← = (total)

Grand Total	$114,200,000	← * (grand total)

FIGURE 24.5

You can use the Sum button in the Table Formula feature bar to quickly add up numbers in columns and rows.

	JAN	FEB	MAR	TOTAL	
New Cars	$8,000,000	$8,000,000	$6,500,000	$22,500,000	← Sum
Used Cars	$1,500,000	$2,000,000	$3,500,000	$7,000,000	← Sum
TOTAL	$9,500,000	$10,000,000	$10,000,000	$29,500,000	← Sum
	↑ Sum	↑ Sum	↑ Sum	↑ Sum	

NOTE

Clicking the Sum button is exactly the same as inserting a SUM(...) function into the cell.

Excluding Cells from Calculations

The subtotal, total, and grand total operators and the Sum button base their calculations on all the numbers in the column (or row). If any cell contains a number that you don't want included in the calculation, you must allow for this. Otherwise, you'll get an incorrect result for the calculation. For example, if the heading of a column is the year 1994, you won't want to add the number 1,994 to the column total.

To exclude a cell from a calculation, move the cursor to the cell that you want to exclude from the calculation (or select a block of cells, if you wish). Then right-click and choose Format (or choose Table ➤ Format from the menus). In the Format dialog box, select Cell ➤ Ignore Cell When Calculating, then choose OK. You won't see a change right away. But when you recalculate the table, as discussed in the next section, Word-Perfect will ignore the cell or cells you designated.

Recalculating Your Formulas

If you've entered a formula into a cell and then add or change some numbers, the results may come out wrong. This happens because WordPerfect doesn't ordinarily recalculate tables on the fly—it usually does so only when you tell it to. (You can change this behavior, as you'll learn in a moment.)

If the Table Formula feature bar is visible, you can quickly recalculate all the tables in the document by clicking the Calculate button. If you want even more control over recalculation, follow the steps below:

1. Choose Table ➤ Calculate to open the Calculate dialog box shown here:

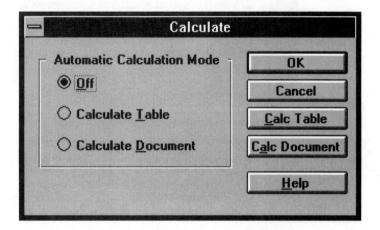

2. To change the automatic calculation mode, choose one of the options below:

> **Off** Turns automatic recalculation off (this is the default setting).
>
> **Calculate Table** Automatically recalculates the table the cursor is in whenever you make any change to a cell and move the cursor to another cell.
>
> **Calculate Document** Automatically recalculates all tables and floating cells in the document whenever you make any change to a cell and move the cursor outside that cell.

3. To recalculate *without* changing the automatic calculation mode, choose one of the following buttons:

> **Calc Table** Recalculates the table the cursor is in.
>
> **Calc Document** Recalculates all tables and floating cells in the document.

4. Choose OK.

Assuming that no errors exist in your formulas, your calculations will now be correct.

TIP

Automatic recalculation can slow you down, since Word-Perfect must stop to calculate the effects of every change you make to a cell. Therefore, if you don't need to see accurate calculation results after each change, turn automatic recalculation Off. Then, when you need to view the updated results, choose Calc Table or Calc Document (or click the Calculate button in the Table Formula feature bar).

Changing or Deleting a Formula

If your calculation results are wrong even after you've recalculated the entire table or document, the formula itself is probably incorrect. Similarly, if you add or delete table rows and columns, or you move or sort the contents of cells in the table, you may need to adjust cell references in your formulas accordingly.

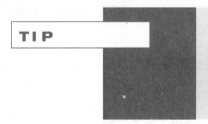

TIP

To see the formula in any cell, just move the cursor into the cell. The current table and cell address (or named cell reference) and formula will appear in the status bar at the bottom of the screen. This information also will appear in the Table Formula feature bar.

To change a formula, follow these steps:

1. Move the cursor to the cell that contains the formula you want to change.

2. Use either of the methods below to make your change:

   • If the Table Formula feature bar is visible, click in the Edit Formula text box. To delete the formula, select the text and press Del as usual. To change the formula, use standard editing techniques or the same methods you used to create the formula. When you're done making changes, click the Insert (✓) button in the feature bar or press ↵.

- If Cell Formula Entry mode is active, you can select the text in a cell, retype the formula, and move the cursor to another cell.

3. If necessary, recalculate the table as described above.

Copying Formulas and Data

When you want several cells to perform similar calculations, you can enter the first formula and then copy it to cells in adjoining rows or columns. Like most spreadsheet programs, WordPerfect will automatically adjust the references in the copied formulas to reflect the pattern of the original formula. For example, suppose you copy the formula SUM(B2:B5) over to columns C and D. The copied formulas in cells C and D will be SUM(C2:C5) and SUM(D2:D5), as demonstrated in the example below. Each formula automatically sums up the numbers in its own column.

	1992	**1993**	**1994**
North	$1,232	$750	$900
South	$900	$1,022	$788
East	$750	$544	$1,323
West	$600	$766	$900
Total	$3,482	$3,082	$3,911

↑	↑	↑
SUM(B2:B5)	SUM(C2:C5)	SUM(D2:D5)
(Original)	(Copy)	(Copy)

To copy a formula, just follow these steps:

1. Turn on the Table Formula feature bar (Table ➤ Formula Bar).

2. Move the cursor to the cell that contains the formula you want to copy.

3. Click the Copy Formula button in the Table Formula feature bar, or choose Table ➤ Copy Formula from the menu bar. This opens the Copy Formula dialog box, shown below.

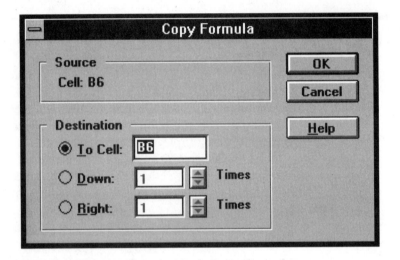

4. Choose whichever option best describes what you want to do:

   • To copy the formula to a specific cell, choose To Cell and specify the cell address where you want to copy the formula.

   • To make multiple copies down, or to the right of, the current cell, choose Down or Right and specify the number of times to copy the formula.

5. Choose OK.

Now scroll through the copied cells and look to the status bar at the bottom of the screen. You'll see that each copy has been adjusted to reference its own row or column.

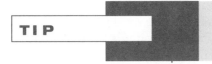

TIP

You can also use the Data Fill feature, described later in the chapter, to copy a formula.

Preventing Cell Adjustment in Copied Formulas

You learned in the previous section that cell addresses are adjusted automatically when they're copied. These addresses are called *relative cell addresses* because they're adjusted relative to their original home base.

Sometimes, however, you won't want WordPerfect to adjust cell addresses when you copy formulas. Cell addresses that aren't adjusted are called *absolute cell addresses*. To enter an absolute cell address, simply enclose the cell address within square brackets, like this: **[B6]**. If you only want to prevent a column adjustment, enclose the column letter in brackets, this way: **[B]6**. Similarly, to prevent only the row adjustment, enclose the row number in brackets, like this: **B[6]**.

Now let's look at a practical example in which absolute cell addresses are not only useful, but essential. Suppose you run a startup book publishing company that pays royalties to its authors. You've set up the (teeny) spreadsheet illustrated in Figure 24.6 to show Book Title (column A), Gross Sales (column C), Royalties To Author (column D), and Net To Company (column E) for each book you publish.

FIGURE 24.6

A spreadsheet to calculate royalties. The Royalty To Author formula in cell D2 is C2*[B5]. The brackets around cell address [B5] prevent Word-Perfect from adjusting that address when the formula is copied down to cell D3.

Book Title	Gross Sales	Royalty To Author	Net To Company
Taming Your Computer	$350,000	$45,500	$304,500
Taming Your Wombat	$45,000	$5,850	$39,150
Total	**$395,000**	**$51,350**	**$343,650**
Royalty Percent: 13%			

The Royalty Percent paid to the author (13%) is in cell B5. Because you always want WordPerfect to look in B5 for the royalty percentage, you must enclose that address in brackets when using it in a formula that you'll be copying later. Here are the calculations you'd enter for the book *Taming Your Computer* in row 2:

- In cell C2 (Gross Sales), enter **$350,000**.

- In cell D2 (Royalty To Author), enter the formula **C2*[B5]**. This is Gross Sales * Royalty Percentage.

- In cell E2 (Net To Company), enter the formula **C2-D2**. This is Gross Sales – Royalty To Author.

Now copy the formula in cell D2 down to cell D3. When the copy is complete, the formula in cell D3 will be **C3*[B5]**—just what you want. Finally, copy the formula in cell E2 down to cell E3. This result will be **C3-D3**.

N O T E If you add or remove rows or columns, WordPerfect will automatically adjust formulas to allow for the inserted or deleted cells—even if you've used absolute cell addresses.

Filling In Data Automatically

You can use a fancy feature called *data fill* to copy a formula or text, or to fill in a pattern of incrementing values across a row or down a column. Data fill is a terrific time-saver! Here's how to use it:

1. Establish the pattern you want, as described just below:

   - **To establish an incrementing pattern** with Roman numerals, days of the week, months of the year, or quarters: Type the starting value in the *first* cell of the range. *Examples:* **II** (Roman numeral 2), **Saturday** (day of the week), **February** (month of the year), **Qtr1** or **Quarter1** (quarter of the year).

- **To establish an incrementing pattern of numbers**, or a decrementing pattern of numbers, Roman numerals, days of the week, months of the year, or quarters: Type values into the *first two* cells of the range. *Examples:* To increment numbers by 20, starting at 100, type **100** in cell A1 and **120** in cell A2. To decrement the numbers by 20, starting at 100, type **100** in cell A1 and **80** in cell A2.

- **To repeat a single number, text value, or formula**: Type the value into the *first* cell of the range. Formula cells will be adjusted automatically, unless you use absolute cell addresses as described in the previous section.

2. Select the cell(s) you entered in step 1, plus any cells that should continue the pattern.

3. To fill in the data, choose T_able ➤ Data _Fill from the menu bar, or press Ctrl+Shift+F12. You can also click the _Data Fill button in the Table Formula feature bar, or right-click the selected cells and choose D_ata Fill from the QuickMenu.

The selected cells will instantly continue the pattern established in step 1 above, replacing any previous values, formulas, or text in the selected cells.

Figure 24.7 illustrates the beauty of data fill. In the top table, I typed the values **abc**, *3*, **Monday**, and **January** into cells A1 through D1, respectively. In cell E1, I entered the text function **UPPER(C1)**. This converts the contents of cell C1 to uppercase. To repeat the pattern in cell A1 in the rest of column A, I selected cells A1 through A4 and clicked Data Fill in the Table Formula feature bar. I used the same select-and-fill techniques to fill in columns B, C, D, and E. Notice how WordPerfect automatically generated the days of the week and months of the year in columns C and D!

TIP

Data fill usually replaces existing data in the cells you select. If it doesn't, select the cells (except for the cells that contain the pattern you want to repeat) and press Del. Then try the select-and-fill procedure again.

I used a similar technique to fill in the lower table in Figure 24.7, selecting rows instead of columns. To begin, I entered **100**, **June**, and **iv** in cells

FIGURE 24.7

Two tables after I used Data Fill to generate data automatically. WordPerfect generated the data for all cells, except those shown in boldface type.

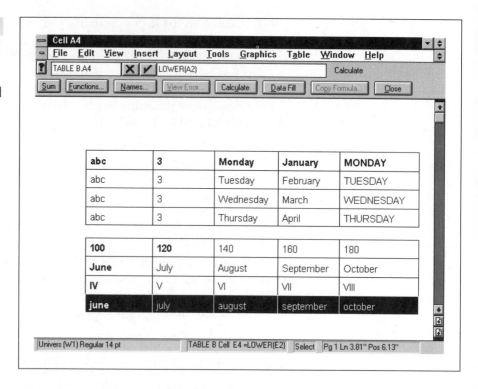

A1 through A3. I also entered **120** in cell B1, because I wanted to increment the numbers in the first row by 20. Cell A4 contains the text function **LOWER(A2)** to switch the contents of cell A2 to lowercase. Then, to fill in row 1, I selected cells A1 through E1 and clicked Data Fill. I used the same trick to fill in rows 2–4. Figure 24.7 shows the screen after I clicked Data Fill to fill in the selected cells in row 4.

Naming Cells

You can name a cell or any group of cells in your table. Once you do, you can use that name, instead of the cell addresses, in your formulas.

To name a cell or range of cells, follow the steps below:

1. Move the cursor to the cell you want to name, or select the range of cells you want to name.

2. Click the <u>N</u>ames button in the Table Formula feature bar, or choose T<u>a</u>ble ➤ <u>N</u>ames from the menu bar. You'll see the Table Names In Current Document dialog box shown below.

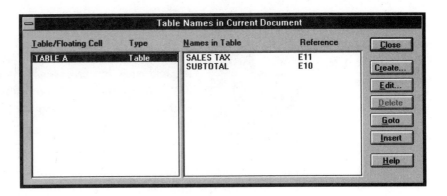

3. Choose C<u>r</u>eate to open the Create Name dialog box shown here:

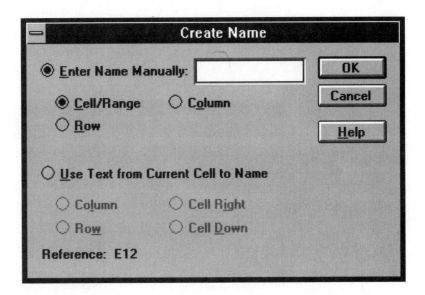

4. Select Cell/Range (the default), Row, or Column, and type the name you want in the Enter Name Manually text box. The name can include letters, numbers, and spaces, but it must begin with a letter or underscore (_).

NOTE

Instead of naming the cell or range manually, you can use text from the current cell to name the current column (Column) or row (Row), the cell to the right of the current cell (Cell Right), or the cell below the current cell (Cell Down).

5. Choose OK or press ↵. The new name will appear in the Names In Table list (this list is sorted alphabetically by name).

6. Choose Close to return to your document.

The example in Figure 24.8 shows part of an invoice (or receipt) that uses formulas and named cells. Notice the function, SUM(E2:E8), the two named cells (*Subtotal* and *Sales Tax*), and the formulas to calculate the subtotal and sales tax amounts.

FIGURE 24.8

The formulas in this table make it easy to type an invoice or receipt. You just fill in the blanks and recalculate the table, and WordPerfect does all the math.

ID	Description	Qty	Unit Price	Ext. Price	
A-100	Microwave Rice	2	12.50	25.00	← C2*D2
B-200	Wangdoodle Chips	2	7.99	15.98	← C3*D3
C-300	Vermicious Knid	5	1.99	9.95	← C4*D4
				0.00	← C5*D5
				0.00	← C6*D6
				0.00	← C7*D7
				0.00	← C8*D8
PLUCKY'S			Subtotal	50.93	← SUM(E2:E8) Name: Subtotal
			Sales Tax	3.95	← .0775*Subtotal Name: SalesTax
			Total	$54.88	← Subtotal+SalesTax

To calculate the total for the order in cell E11, move the cursor to that cell, then use one of the techniques below:

- If Cell Formula Entry mode is active, you can type the formula into the cell, using the cell names instead of cell addresses. For example, you could type **Subtotal + Sales Tax** and move the cursor to another cell to see the calculated result.

- If the Table Formula feature bar is visible, you can type the formula **Subtotal + Sales Tax** into the Edit Formula text box and press ↵.

- You can also position the cursor where you want a named cell or range to appear in the Edit Formula text box. Then click the Names button in the feature bar, and double-click the name you want (or highlight the name and press ↵ or click Insert).

WARNING

Be sure to turn off Cell Formula Entry mode before typing text that's the same as a named cell or range. Otherwise, WordPerfect will display the *value* of the named cell or range, instead of the text you want. In Figure 24.8, for example, the titles "Subtotal" and "Sales Tax" in column D are the same as named cells. I had to turn off Cell Formula Entry mode before typing those titles.

You've already learned how to define named cells or ranges. The steps below show you how to insert a named cell into the Edit Formula text box, edit or delete a named cell reference, or jump to a cell reference:

1. Turn on the Table Formula feature bar (Table ➤ Formula Bar).

2. If you want to insert a named cell reference into a formula, position the cursor at the proper spot in the Edit Formula text box or select text in the Edit Formula text box if you want to replace that text.

3. To open the Table Names In Current Document dialog box, click the Names button in the Table Formula feature bar or choose Table ➤ Names.

4. Highlight the reference you want in the Table/Floating Cell list and the Names In Table list. Then do any of the following:

- **To insert** the highlighted name or reference at the cursor position in the Formula Edit text box, click Insert or press ↵ (or double-click the name).

- **To edit** the highlighted name or reference, choose Edit, make your changes in the Edit Name/Reference dialog box that appears, and choose OK.

- **To delete** the highlighted name or reference, choose Delete.

- **To move the cursor to the cell** referenced by the highlighted name, choose Go To.

When you're done with the Table Names In Current Document dialog box, choose Close, if necessary.

TIP

Formulas can reference named cells or ranges from tables or floating cells located *anywhere* in your document. For example, the formula *Table B.A3 * Table A.Subtotal* multiplies the value in cell A3 of Table B (Table B.A3) by the value in the cell named Subtotal in Table A. If you omit the table name in a cell reference, as in *Table B.A3 * Subtotal*, the current table is assumed.

Using Floating Cells

Suppose you want to put calculations right into your document text, without using tables. That's easy to do with *floating cells*. A floating cell is simply a pair of codes that holds whatever formula or number you want. Floating cells can contain any formulas, text, or numbers that table cells can, and they can reference table cells and other floating cells. You can name a floating cell if you wish, or use the name that WordPerfect assigns automatically when you create the cell.

The example in Figure 24.9 contains floating cells that store total work hours, an hourly rate, and a tax rate. Other floating cells in the document reference these numeric cells to compute the subtotal, sales tax, and grand total the customer owes. In the figure, I've underlined everything that's in a floating cell. The Reveal Codes portion of the screen shows [Flt Cell] codes that mark floating cells. The cursor is positioned in the floating cell that computes the grand total amount (notice the information shown in the feature bar and status bar).

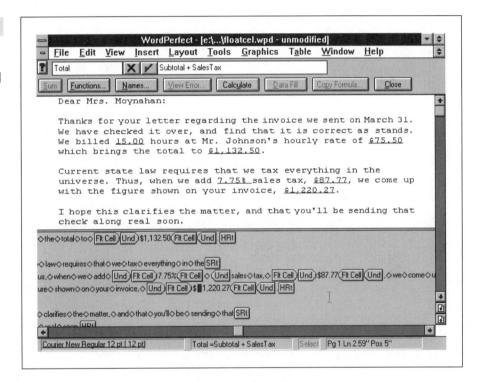

FIGURE 24.9

A document that uses floating cells to calculate an order total

Table 24.1 describes in detail the numbers, formulas, cell names, and format used in the example in Figure 24.9.

TABLE 24.1: Formulas and Cell Names Used in the Sample Document Shown in Figure 24.9

VALUE SHOWN	CELL NAME	FORMULA OR VALUE	NUMBER TYPE
Hours	Hours	15	Fixed, 2
Rate	HourlyRate	75.50	Currency, 2
Subtotal	Subtotal	Hours*HourlyRate	Currency, 2
Sales Tax Rate	TaxRate	7.75%	Percent, 2
Sales Tax	SalesTax	TaxRate*Subtotal	Currency, 2
Invoice Total	Total	Subtotal+SalesTax	Currency, 2

Here's how to create a floating cell:

1. Turn on the Table Formula feature bar or Cell Formula Entry mode.

2. Move the cursor to where you want to put the floating cell (anywhere *except* inside a table or floating cell).

3. Choose Table ➤ Create ➤ Floating Cell and OK.

4. Type the formula, number, or other data that belongs in the cell, using techniques discussed in this chapter. You can use the Functions, Names, and Calculate buttons and the Table Formula feature bar as necessary. To format the number in the floating cell, choose Table ➤ Number Type (or press Alt+F12) and complete the dialog box as you would for a table cell.

5. When you're done editing, you can recalculate the formulas in the document, if necessary.

WARNING

Floating cells that are supposed to have numeric values should contain numbers and formulas. Extra spaces, text, or codes may throw the calculations off.

Changing a Floating Cell

Because floating cells have no frames to distinguish them from other text in your document, you might accidentally type right over a floating cell. This can yield strange results when you recalculate your document. To avoid confusion, keep these tips in mind:

- When your document contains floating cells, leave Reveal Codes (Alt+F3) on, so you can see the codes that start and end the floating cell.

- To type information into a floating cell, move the cursor between the [Flt Cell] codes. Then use the editing techniques described in this chapter to fill in the cell.

- To delete a floating cell, first delete the [Flt Cell] code in Reveal Codes, then delete the leftover text that was previously between the [Flt Cell] codes.

After changing the contents of any floating cell, you can recalculate all the floating cell and table cell formulas throughout the document with the usual Calculate button or Table ➤ Calculate ➤ Calc Document commands. (Or, if the Calculate Document automatic calculation mode is on, WordPerfect will recalculate the values when you move the cursor out of the floating cell.)

Fixing Rounding Errors

If anything will drive you crazy about using computers, it's those pesky calculation errors in which totals are off by a penny or so. These *rounding errors* happen because, behind the scenes, the computer carries out decimal places to about 15 places of accuracy. When you display the result of such a calculation, it's sometimes rounded off more than it should be.

Here's what you can do about it:

1. Move the cursor to where the wrong result appears or select a range of cells to fix.

2. Choose Table ➤ Number Type or press Alt+F12.

3. Select <u>C</u>ell, C<u>o</u>lumn, or <u>T</u>able, depending on how many cells you want to fix.

4. Choose a numeric format other than General. (If not all the "problem" cells use the same number type, you'll need to repeat steps 1–5 for each group of cells that needs fixing. Then do step 6.)

5. Choose C<u>u</u>stom and check the <u>R</u>ound For Calculation box. Choose OK twice to return to your document.

6. Recalculate the table or document if necessary.

If that doesn't do the trick, you can use the ROUND(*Number,Precision*) function instead. You need to round the results of all calculations that contribute to the faulty total. Choose the ROUND(…) function from the Table Functions dialog box described earlier. Enter the formula to round and the number of decimal places of accuracy as arguments. For example, the formula **ROUND(C2*D2,2)** rounds the results of multiplying the contents of cells C2 and D2. Any totals based on those rounded calculations will be accurate to two decimal points.

In this chapter, you've learned how to use WordPerfect's spreadsheet and floating cell features to perform math calculations that rival those of sophisticated spreadsheet applications. In Part Six, you'll explore WordPerfect's desktop publishing and graphics capabilities. These topics are sure to dazzle the socks right off your feet.

PART SIX

Desktop Publishing

WordPerfect
Clip Art

Third-Party Clip Art

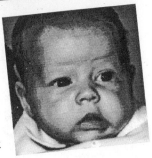

Scanned Photo
or Video Frame

DOS Screen Capture

Windows Screen
Capture

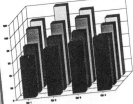

Business Chart

Scanned Signature

Special Character

Keycap

CHAPTER

25

Dazzle 'Em with Graphics

f a s t TRACK

● **To put text or a table in a box**   825

> right-click the box and choose Content, or choose Content from the Graphics Box feature bar. Use the pop-up list next to Content to choose Text. Answer Yes if prompted, then choose Edit and type in or create your text or table using the standard WordPerfect techniques. When you're done, choose Close from the feature bar or click in the document window.

● **To change a graphics box's attachment point**   826

> right-click the box and choose Position, or choose Position from the Graphics Box feature bar. Under Box Placement, choose an anchor, then use options under Position Box to position the box in relation to the anchor point. Choose OK.

● **To size a box precisely**   830

> right-click the box and choose Size, or choose Size from the Graphics Box feature bar. Use the Width and Height options to specify the box dimensions, then choose OK.

● **To determine how text flows around (or through)**
a box   831

> right-click the box and choose Wrap, or choose Wrap from the Graphics Box feature bar. Choose a Wrapping Type and a Wrap Text Around option, then choose OK.

NOTHING spruces up a drab document like pictures. You can add virtually any type of graphic to your documents, from pre-drawn clip art and business charts to scanned photos. Figure 25.1 shows some examples.

Graphics Boxes

Adding graphics is basically a matter of positioning a *graphics box* in the text, then filling the box. WordPerfect offers eight different styles of graphics boxes: Figure, Text, Equation, Table, User, Button, Watermark, and Inline Equation.

WordPerfect uses these different types of boxes for two reasons: 1) They make it easy to put all types of elements in their own boxes, and 2) They make it possible to automatically number different styles of boxes independently. For example, in this book we put all captioned figures in one style of box (Figure box), all tables in another style of box (Table box), Notes, Tips, and Warnings in yet another style of box (Text box), and all uncaptioned graphics in still another style of box (User box). Only figures and tables are numbered in this book, and they're numbered independently of one another. By providing different styles of boxes, WordPerfect lets you create your own documents in a similar manner.

WordPerfect Clip Art

Third-Party Clip Art

Scanned Photo or Video Frame

DOS Screen Capture

Windows Screen Capture

Business Chart

Scanned Signature

Special Character

Keycap

Figure 25.2 shows examples of some empty graphics boxes with their default borders, shading, and caption positions. These are just the default styles—you can change the appearance and numbering system of any style of box to your liking.

FIGURE 25.2

Examples of empty graphics boxes with their default borders, shading, and caption positions

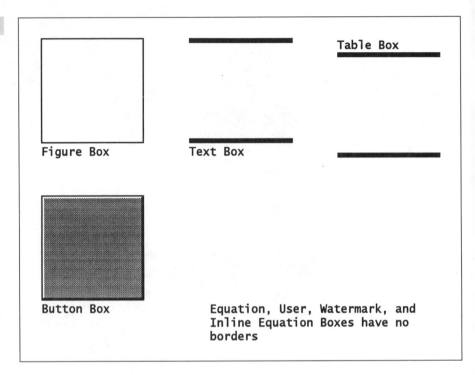

Figure Box

Text Box

Table Box

Button Box

Equation, User, Watermark, and Inline Equation Boxes have no borders

What Can Go in a Box?

Every box you create is empty initially. But you can fill any empty box with a graphic figure, a table, text, or an equation, as summarized below.

Graphic Images You can put virtually any image—a drawing, photo, or business chart—into a graphics box. You can use clip art that comes with WordPerfect (see Figure 25.3) as well as most third-party clip art. You can also create your own images using spreadsheet and graphics programs, screen capture programs, and scanners.

Some of the sample clip art that comes with WordPerfect. These images are copied to the C:\WPWIN60\GRAPHICS directory during normal installation.

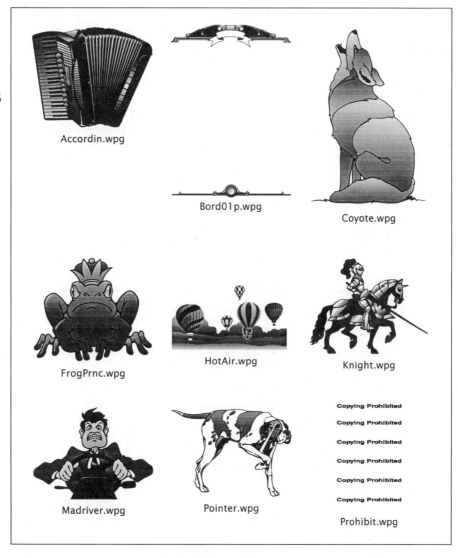

Accordin.wpg

Bord01p.wpg

Coyote.wpg

FrogPrnc.wpg

HotAir.wpg

Knight.wpg

Madriver.wpg

Pointer.wpg

Copying Prohibited
Copying Prohibited
Copying Prohibited
Copying Prohibited
Copying Prohibited
Copying Prohibited

Prohibit.wpg

Tables   You can put a table in a graphics box. The advantages of doing so are listed below:

- You can wrap text around the table.
- If the table is small enough to fit on one page, WordPerfect will not split the table across two pages.
- You can display two or more tables side by side.

- If you caption and number each table, WordPerfect can automatically renumber them for you if you change the order of the tables or add or delete tables in your document.

- You can automatically generate a list of captioned tables for your completed document (see Chapter 31).

Text A graphics box can contain text, using whichever fonts and printing features your printer offers. For instance, you can rotate text within a Text box so that it reads upside down. Text boxes are commonly used to display quotations, catchy phrases, and sidebars.

Equations As discussed in Chapter 29, a graphics box can also contain an equation. (You can skip directly to Chapter 29 if you want to add equations to your document.)

Creating a Graphics Box

To create a graphics box, follow these steps:

1. Move the cursor to where you want the graphic image to appear.

2. Choose Graphics, then…

- To create a Figure box and put a graphic image in it, choose Figure, then choose the drive, directory, and file name of the image you want to put into the box. Choose OK.

- To create a Text box and put text or a table in it, choose Text. Type the text or create the table that goes inside the box (you can also choose a font, justification, and other formatting options from the regular menus). Choose Close from the Graphics Box feature bar, or click in the document window (outside the text box), when you want to return to your document.

- To create some other style of box, choose Custom Box, the style of box you want to create, then OK. An empty box appears. You can choose Close from the Graphics Box feature bar, if you wish, and fill the box later.

Hidden Codes for Boxes

Unless you create an empty, borderless box, the box will be readily visible on your screen. In Reveal Codes, the box is represented by a [Box] code, which may be near the top of the document or current page, depending on where the box is *anchored* (you'll learn about anchoring later in the chapter).

Selecting a Box

Many operations that you do will require that you first select the box. To do so, click the box once with your mouse. Sizing handles will appear on the box.

In some cases, clicking the box won't do the trick. For example, if you're allowing text to flow through the box, as described later, clicking the box won't select it. But you can still select the box by right-clicking it and choosing Select Box from the QuickMenu. Or you can do as follows:

1. Move the cursor to just before (or above) the box you want to select.

2. Choose Graphics ➤ Edit Box or press Shift+F11 (or double-click the appropriate [Box] code in Reveal Codes).

3. If the Box Find dialog box appears, choose OK to select the next box.

The box will have sizing handles, and the Graphics Box feature bar, shown below, will appear near the top of the screen.

Here are some things to keep in mind:

- If you inadvertently selected the wrong box, you can choose <u>N</u>ext and P<u>r</u>ev from the Graphics Box feature bar to select the next or previous box.

- If you can't see the selected box with its sizing handles, you can use the scroll bars to scroll to the selected box.

- The Too<u>l</u>s button will appear on the Graphics Box feature bar only when you select a box that contains (or will contain) an image or image file on disk. You'll learn more about how to specify the contents of a box later in the chapter.

When you select a box as described above, the Graphics Box feature bar remains displayed until you click its <u>C</u>lose button. Clicking the <u>C</u>lose button also deselects the graphics box.

Tips for Using the Graphics Box Feature Bar

The Graphics Box feature bar offers the most convenient way to work with graphics boxes. For this reason, you might want to leave it on while you're working with graphics. Here are some additional tips for getting along with the Graphics Box feature bar:

- If the Graphics Box feature bar isn't visible, right-click a graphics box and choose <u>F</u>eature Bar from the QuickMenu. If right-clicking doesn't work, position the cursor ahead of the graphics box, press Shift+F11, and choose OK as described just above.

- If you forget what a button is for, move the mouse pointer to that button and look to the title bar for a reminder.

- If you want to do normal editing while the Graphics Box feature bar is on the screen, you first need to deselect the graphics box (if it's selected). An easy way to deselect a box and leave the Graphics Box feature bar visible is to click in the document window, outside the graphics box (the sizing handles will disappear). Now you can edit normally.

- When you're ready to hide the Graphics Box feature bar, click its <u>C</u>lose button.

What Happened to My Cursor Keys and Menus!?!

Once you select a box, any menu commands that are not relevant to graphics boxes will likely be dimmed and unavailable. Don't panic. To return to normal editing, click anywhere outside the graphics box to deselect it (so that it loses its sizing handles).

Moving and Sizing a Box with a Mouse

Once you've created a graphics box and returned to your document, you can easily move and size the box with a mouse. Select the box you want to size or move, so that its sizing handles appear on the box as in the example below:

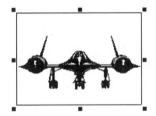

To move the box, move the mouse pointer anywhere within the box, so that it becomes a four-headed "move" icon. Now hold down the mouse button, drag the box to its new location, then release the mouse button.

To size the box, move the mouse to any sizing handle (the little dark squares on the box's border). The mouse pointer will change to a two-headed arrow when it's placed properly on the sizing handle. Then hold down the mouse button, drag the handle until the outline of the box is the size you want, and release the mouse button.

As an alternative to using the mouse method described above, you can size and position the box more precisely using menu commands and dialog boxes. I'll describe how as we go along.

Deleting a Box

To delete a box, select the box (by clicking once) and press the Del key. Or, locate the box's hidden code in Reveal Codes, and drag that code off the Reveal Codes screen. If you change your mind, you can use Edit ➤ Undelete (or Ctrl+Shift+Z) to undelete the box.

Editing a Box

There are several ways to edit a graphics box, as you'll see throughout this chapter. But for general editing, you just need to get to the Graphics Box feature bar, using whichever of the following methods is most convenient:

- Right-click the box you want to change and choose Feature Bar from the QuickMenu.

- Move the cursor just to the left of (or above) the hidden code for the graphics box you want to edit. Then choose Graphics ➤ Edit Box (Shift+F11), or double-click on the appropriate [Box] code in Reveal Codes. Choose OK. (If you select the wrong box, you can use the Next and Prev buttons on the Graphics Box feature bar to select another box.)

The box will be selected and (at least partially) visible on the screen.

TIP

There's also a Graphics button bar that offers shortcuts to some graphics commands. To display that button bar, right-click the current button bar and choose Graphics.

Filling a Box

As I mentioned earlier, a box can contain just about anything—including text, a table, a graphic image, or an equation. Equations are covered in Chapter 29. I'll talk about the other things you can put into a box in the sections that follow.

Adding a Picture

If you create an empty graphics box, or you decide to change the contents of an existing box to another graphic image, follow these steps:

1. Right-click the box and choose Content. Or edit the box and choose Content from the Graphics Box feature bar. You'll be taken to the Box Content dialog box shown in Figure 25.4.

2. Type the file name of the image you want to put into the box. Or click the file button next to Filename and choose the drive, directory, and file name for the graphic image, then choose OK.

3. Choose OK until you return to the document window.

FIGURE 25.4

The Box Content dialog box lets you fill a box or change its contents. Right-click the graphics box and choose Content to get to this dialog box.

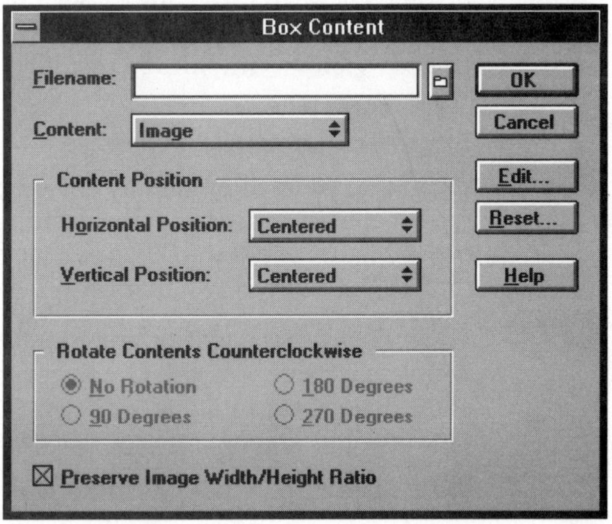

If you filled the box previously, you'll see a dialog box like this before you return to the document window:

Choosing Yes replaces the current box contents with the image you speci-fied. Choosing No leaves the graphics box unchanged.

Speeding Up the Screen

If your document contains lots of graphic images, editing might be slow and tedious because it takes the computer so long to redraw the images. To speed things along, choose View ➤ Graphics. The images inside boxes will disappear so you can concentrate on text and not be slowed down by the images. When you want to bring the images back out of hiding, choose View ➤ Graphics again.

But the Box Looks Empty!

If you retrieve an image into a box but the box appears empty when you return to normal editing, it may be that graphics viewing is turned off. Choose View ➤ Graphics to turn that feature back on.

Finding Graphic Files

If you find yourself frequently changing directories to locate a particular type of clip art, you can set the default location for graphics files to what-ever directory you want. Then, whenever you look for graphics files in the future, WordPerfect will first go to the directory you specified.

To change the location for graphics files, choose File ➤ Preferences and double-click File. Choose Graphics from the option button near the top of the dialog box, and type (or choose) the default directory for retrieving (and storing) graphic images. Choose OK and Close to get back to the document window.

Adding Text or a Table

Use any of the methods below to put text, a table, or both into a box:

- If the box contains text (or its Content is defined to contain text), double-click the graphics box. Or, right-click the graphics box and choose Edit Text.

- If the box contains an image (or its Content is defined to contain an image), right-click the graphics box and choose Content. Then use the Content pop-up list button to change the content to Text. If you're asked whether you want to delete the existing contents, choose Yes. Then choose Edit.

- If you can't click the box to select it, choose Graphics ➤ Edit Box (Shift+F11) or double-click the appropriate [Box] code in Reveal Codes and choose OK to select the box, as discussed earlier. Next, choose Content from the Graphics Box feature bar, and use the Content pop-up list button to change the image to Text. If you're asked whether you want to delete the existing contents, choose Yes. Then choose Edit.

If you're in Page view or Two-Page view, the cursor will move into the graphics box. If you're in Draft view, the cursor will move into a blank editing window. (On the blank editing window, the Text Box feature bar that appears has only one button, named Close.) Now you can type in your text, as you would in the normal document window. All the usual font, justification, and other options are available. If you want to create a table, choose Table ➤ Create (F12) and use the techniques discussed in Chapter 7 to create your table. When you're done filling the box, click outside the box (in Page or Two-Page view), or choose Close from the Text Box feature bar (in Draft view).

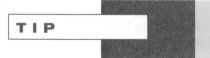

TIP   You can use WP Draw (Chapter 26) to combine text and graphics in a single graphics box.

If you forget that you're in a graphics box and start typing in text that belongs in the main part of the document, select and cut the text, return to the normal editing window, and then paste the text into the document.

Moving/Copying into a Box

If you've already typed some text or a table and you want to move it into a graphics box, select whatever you want to move or copy. (If it's a table, don't forget to include the [Tbl Def] and [Tbl Off] codes in the selected area.) Then choose Edit ➤ Cut (Ctrl+X) to move or Edit ➤ Copy (Ctrl+C) to copy the material to the Windows Clipboard. Create or edit the graphics box, and choose Edit ➤ Paste (Ctrl+V) to copy the Clipboard contents into the box. Then choose Close from the feature bar, or click in the document window, to return to normal document editing.

Anchoring and Positioning a Graphics Box

Though it's easy enough to position a graphics box by dragging it with your mouse, you may find that the box tends to move when you edit neighboring text. You may also find that it does *not* move in certain situations when you want it to. To solve the slippery box (or too-stubborn-to-budge) problem, you can *anchor* (or attach) the box to a page, paragraph, or character.

Anchoring is just one way to control a graphics box precisely. For those anxiety-driven perfectionists among us, WordPerfect also offers many ways to position a box exactly—down to about a hundredth of an inch, and relative to whatever the box is anchored to.

Here's how to anchor and position a graphics box:

1. Display the Graphics Box feature bar and select the graphics box as described earlier, or right-click the box. Then choose Position from the Graphic Box feature bar or QuickMenu. You'll be taken to the Box Position dialog box shown in Figure 25.5.

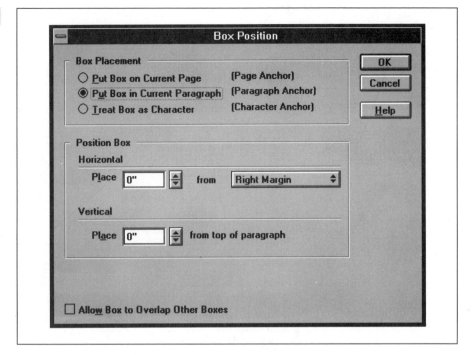

2. Choose one of the options listed under Box Placement, as described below. Refer to Figure 25.6 for examples of each type of box placement.

Put Box on Current Page (Page Anchor)   The box is anchored to the page, independent of surrounding text.

Put Box in Current Paragraph (Paragraph Anchor)   The box is anchored to the paragraph that contains its hidden code. The box "floats" with its paragraph, so that if you insert or delete text above the box, the box will move automatically along with its attached paragraph. (Example: A photo or diagram that needs to stay near its accompanying descriptive text.)

Treat Box as Character (Character Anchor)   The box is anchored to its neighboring character. If that character moves, the box moves too. (Example: An in-line equation or a small graphic symbol.)

FIGURE 25.6

A document with graphics boxes, explaining how each box is anchored to the document

Getting Anchored

SKIER

The skier on this page is in a User box. The box is anchored to the page, .25" from the top and left edges of the page, with Wrap set to No Wrap (Through).

CENTERED TEXT BOX

The Text box in the center of this page is anchored to the page, centered both horizontally and vertically. It's offset up 0.5" from the actual vertical center of the page. The border's Outside Space is about 0.04 inches.

TABLE OF CONTENTS

The Table of Contents is in a shaded Table box. That box is anchored to the page's Bottom and Right Margins. I manually typed the Table of Contents into that box. But you can use the Generate feature to create an automatic ToC in your document, then cut-and-paste that ToC into a graphics box.

COLUMNS

By the way, this document shows you newspaper-style columns. See Chapter 27 for information on columns.

DRAGON

The dragon image's User box is anchored to the left side of this paragraph, with Wrap set to Contour. It's offset down .32" from the top of the paragraph. The border's Inside Space is 0" all around. Outside Space is about 0.167 inches.

BUTTON BOX

The Button box below is anchored to this paragraph's left margin, and vertically offset down 0.3". Wrap is set to Largest Side. All border spacing is set to 0" except Outside Right at 0.04" to give a little space to the right of the box.

ALL THE REST . . . .

The rest of the graphics in this document are each anchored to a Character, centered on the Baseline.

I'm a Page Anchored Centered Text Box

Itsy Bitsy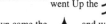

went Up the

spout. Down came the and washed

the out. Out came the and it

dried up all the   So the itsy bitsy

     went up the   again.

Note to Authors/Publishers of *Itsy Bitsy Spider*: If that's a copyright infringement, please don't sue. Thanks.

NOTE The *Paragraph* and *Page* anchors let you anchor the box so that it always floats with its neighboring text. The *Page* anchor affixes the graphics box to the page, so that changes to the surrounding text do not affect the placement of the graphics box.

3. If you want to move the graphics box slightly from its anchor point, choose options in the Position Box area of the dialog box. These options let you define the exact horizontal and vertical position of the graphics box, as described below:

- If you chose **Put Box On Current Page (Page Anchor)** in step 2, you can position the box in relation to the margins or page edges, or in relation to columns.

- If you chose **Put Box In Current Paragraph (Paragraph Anchor)** in step 2, you can position the box horizontally in relation to the left edge of the page, left margin, right margin, or center of paragraph. You can position the box vertically by specifying the distance between the top of the graphics box and the top of the paragraph.

- If you chose **Treat Box As Character (Character Anchor)** in step 2, you can position the box in relation to the baseline of neighboring text. Icons in the Box Position dialog box will illustrate your options.

NOTE When entering measurements, you can use inches or fractions of inches (for example, *1.25* for one and a quarter inches). You can also enter a measurement in points by following the number with a *p*. For example, *10p* is 10 points. WordPerfect will convert your entry to the default unit of measure, which usually is inches (see Chapter 2).

4. Choose OK to return to your document.

Remember that you can combine the mouse method of positioning a graphics box with the more precise method described above. For example, you can drag the box to its approximate position on the screen, then return to the Box Position dialog box and refine that positioning.

Sizing a Box Precisely

If dragging the sizing handles of a graphics box doesn't satisfy your need for exactitude, you can use the menus to size the box more precisely. Follow these steps:

1. Right-click the box and choose <u>S</u>ize from the QuickMenu. Or, select the box and choose <u>S</u>ize from the Graphics Box feature bar. You'll be taken to the Box Size dialog box shown below:

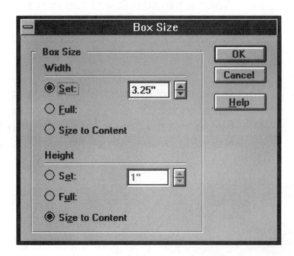

2. Notice that you can define both the width and the height of the box. Your options are as follows:

   Set Lets you specify the height or width in inches (or some other unit of measurement, such as *p* for points).

   Full Automatically sizes the box to the full width or height of the margins.

Size to Content   Adjusts the height or width of the box based on the box contents.

As usual, choose OK after making your selection(s).

Wrapping Text around a Box

You can choose how you want text to flow around a box. Figure 25.7 illustrates some examples. How your combination of choices will work out depends on how your graphics box is anchored and positioned. But it's easy enough to experiment and see what happens.

Here the Wrapping Type is set to Square, and the Wrap Text Around is set to Largest Side. When text reaches the bottom of the graphics box, like this, it wraps all the way back to the margin.

I'm a caption

The guitar is in a User Box, anchored to the center of this paragraph. Justification is set to Full. The Wrapping Type is set to Contour, and Wrap Text Around is set to Both Sides. The Outside Space around the graphics box is .02", which brings this contoured text in pretty close to the image.

NO WRAP (THROUGH)

Here the Wrapping Type is set to Contour, and the Wrap Text Around is set to Larger Side. I didn't change the default outside spacing, so this text doesn't wrap in as tightly as the example above.

To change the text flow and contour, follow these steps:

1. Right-click the box and choose Wrap from the QuickMenu. Or select the box and choose Wrap from the Graphics Box feature bar.

The Wrap Text dialog box, shown below, presents and illustrates your options.

2. After choosing your wrap options, choose OK.

3. Click outside the box or choose Close from the Graphics Box feature bar to deselect it.

Changing the Appearance of Boxes

As illustrated in Figure 25.2, different types of boxes initially have different default appearances and caption positions. Different types of boxes also have different default spacing measurements inside and outside the box. WordPerfect lets you change all those defaults to get a different look. You can change the style for one box at a time, or for all the boxes in a given category (for example, all the Figure boxes).

Changing the Appearance of One Box

To change the appearance of one box, follow these steps:

1. Right-click the box and choose Border/Fill from the QuickMenu, or select the box and choose Border/Fill from the Graphics Box

feature bar. You'll be taken to a dialog box like the one shown below.

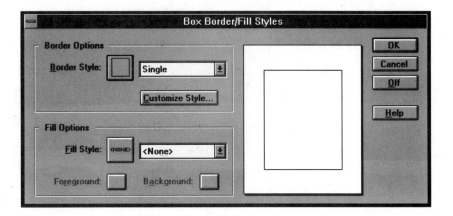

2. Choose the button next to Border Style to choose a border style from examples, or use the drop-down list to choose a border style by name.

3. If you want to fill the box with shading or a pattern, choose the appropriate pattern from the button or drop-down list next to Fill Style.

4. If you want to add a drop shadow or other special effect, choose Customize Style. You'll be taken to the Customize Border dialog box shown in Figure 25.8.

TIP

In Figure 25.8, notice that you can choose to modify any single line, or combination of lines, under *Select sides to modify*. You can also select Show Inside/Outside Spacing to see how your current Inside Space and Outside Space measurements will affect the spacing around the graphics box.

5. Choose your options, and then choose OK and Close as necessary to return to the document window.

6. Deselect the graphics box, if you're done changing it.

FIGURE 25.8

The Customize Border dialog box lets you define the border style, spacing, color, corners, and drop shadow for a graphics box.

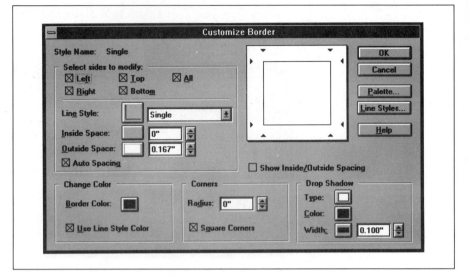

Figure 25.9 shows examples of graphics boxes with different border designs. Feel free to experiment to come up with whatever design best suits your needs.

Changing the Appearance of All Boxes

To change styles for all the boxes in a given category, such as all the Figure boxes, or all the Text boxes, proceed as follows:

1. Choose Graphics ➤ Graphics Styles from the menu bar. If that option is dimmed and unavailable, deselect the current box, then try again.

2. Under Style Type, choose Box. Then choose the type of box you want to redesign from the list of Styles.

3. Choose Options ➤ Setup, then choose whether you want to change the styles for the Current Document, the Default Template, or the Supplemental Template. These options are described fully in Chapter 17. (Generally, you'll want to change the styles in the current document only, so choose Current Document.) After choosing the option you want, choose OK.

FIGURE 25.9

Some examples of graphics boxes customized with drop shadows and other special features

Figure box with the default settings

Figure box with Thin Thick border lines

Figure box with inside spacing increased to .15" and a 50% Black drop shadow

Figure box with rounded corners set at 0.5" radius. and a 50% black drop shadow

4. Choose Edit. You'll be taken to the Edit Box Style dialog box shown in Figure 25.10.

5. Choose options from the Caption, Content, Position, and other buttons to define the default style for the type of box you selected in step 2. The box in the center of the dialog box shows an example of how your changes will look.

FIGURE 25.10

The Edit Box Style
dialog box lets you
change the style of all
the boxes in a given
category.

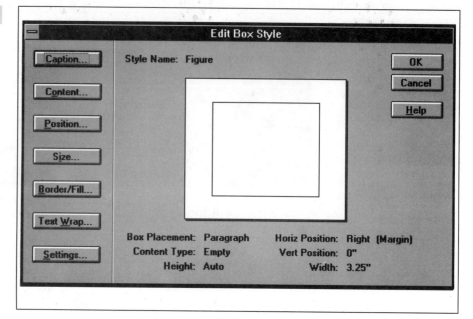

6. Choose OK and Close as necessary to return to the document
window.

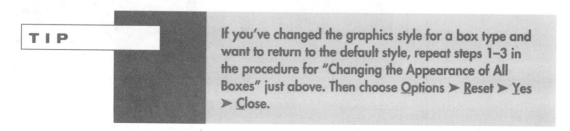

TIP

If you've changed the graphics style for a box type and
want to return to the default style, repeat steps 1–3 in
the procedure for "Changing the Appearance of All
Boxes" just above. Then choose Options ➤ Reset ➤ Yes
➤ Close.

If you chose Current Document in step 3, all the graphics boxes of the
type you chose in step 2 will change to reflect your new settings. Other
documents will be unaffected by these changes.

Spacing, Lines, Corners, Drop Shadows, and More

Several examples in this chapter illustrate graphic images with changes made to the default inside and outside spacing, corners, and so forth. If you want to change these features for your own graphics boxes, go through Border/Fill and Customize Style. That is, right-click the box and choose Border/Fill, or click the Border/Fill button in the Graphics Box feature bar. Or, if you want to change the spacing of all the boxes of a certain type, follow the steps under "Changing the Appearance of All Boxes." Choose Border/Fill in step 5.

Whichever route you take, you'll end up at the Box Border/Fill Styles dialog box. There, you can choose Customize Style to get to the dialog box that lets you select Sides To Modify. It also offers options for changing the line style, spacing, color, corners, drop shadow, and more.

If you're particularly interested in the spacing around the box, you can choose the Show Inside/Outside Spacing check box. Then, as you adjust the Inside Space and Outside Space using the spin boxes or buttons next to the spacing options, the spacing shows up as gray around the border of the sample box. As usual, choose OK and Close, as appropriate, to return to your document.

Changing the Box Type

Suppose you create a Figure box, and later you decide it should have been a Text box or a Table box (to match the style of other boxes in that category). Here's how to change a box type:

1. Right-click the box you want to change, and choose from the QuickMenu. Or, select the box and choose from the Graphics Box feature bar.

2. Choose the type of box you want to convert this box to, then choose OK.

The box will be numbered and styled like other boxes in that category.

Editing Graphic Images (The Easy Way)

WordPerfect offers a separate Draw application that lets you create drawings and edit existing images. This application is discussed in Chapter 26. But if you're as artistically impaired as myself, you'll probably be content to make changes that don't require any drawing skills. For example, Figure 25.11 shows a piece of clip art modified with the relatively simple tools I'll be explaining in this section.

1. Right-click the graphic image you want to change, and choose Image Tools from the QuickMenu. Or, select the graphics box and click the Tools button in the Graphics Box feature bar. The toolbox shown in Figure 25.12 appears.

2. If necessary, you can move the toolbox to a more convenient spot by dragging its small title bar.

3. Choose options as appropriate to get the desired effect.

T I P

Need a reminder about the purpose of a tool on the Image Tools toolbox? Just move the mouse pointer to the tool you're interested in and look to the WordPerfect title bar for an explanation.

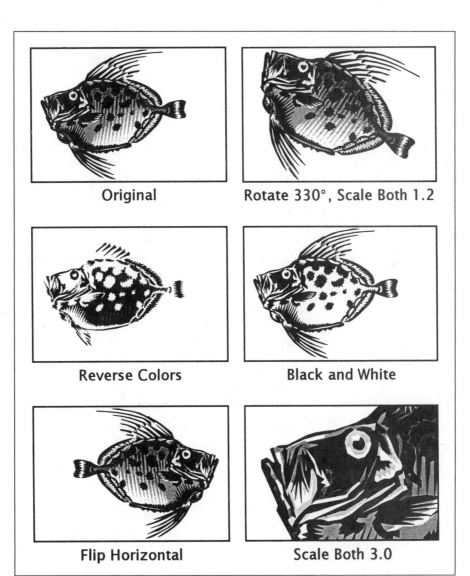

Original

Rotate 330°, Scale Both 1.2

Reverse Colors

Black and White

Flip Horizontal

Scale Both 3.0

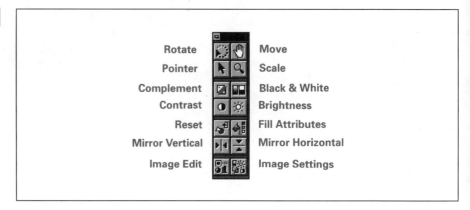

Here's a summary of how to use the tools:

Rotate After choosing this tool, drag the corner handles that appear to rotate the image within its frame. (The Rotate indicator in the status bar shows the current rotation.)

Move After selecting this tool, drag the image to any new location within its frame.

Pointer Choose this tool to disable the Rotate and Move tools and return to a normal mouse pointer.

Scale Use this tool to crop the image. When you choose Scale Image, you'll actually have three tools to choose from:

- The **Crop tool** looks like a magnifying glass. After choosing this tool, drag a frame around the portion of the image that you want to display in the frame. Then release the mouse button.

- The **Scroll Bar tool** (up and down arrows) displays a scroll bar that lets you scale the image larger or smaller within its frame.

- The **1:1 tool** restores the original dimensions of the image so that it fits within the box.

Complement   Reverses the colors of the image, like a negative.

Black & White   When you select this tool, you can choose the Black & White option to display the image in black and white. You can then select the Black & White tool again and set the black-and white-threshold. Any grays that are darker than the threshold you set will be changed to black. Any grays that are lighter than the threshold will be changed to white.

Contrast   After selecting this tool, choose a contrast from the examples shown.

Brightness   After selecting this tool, choose a brightness from the options shown.

Reset   This tool is the "undo" button for all changes you've made with the Image Tools so far.

Fill Attributes   Choose this tool to determine how the graphic image is to be filled: normal, transparent, or opaque white.

Mirror Vertical   Choosing this tool flips the image horizontally.

Mirror Horizontal   Choosing this tool flips the image vertically.

Image Edit   Takes you to WP Draw, which is described in Chapter 26.

TIP

If you get to WP Draw by accident, choose File ➤ Exit or press Alt+F4 and choose No (if prompted) to return to your document without saving any changes.

Image Settings   Takes you to the Image Settings dialog box shown below, where you can modify the image using settings and numbers rather than the mouse and toolbox.

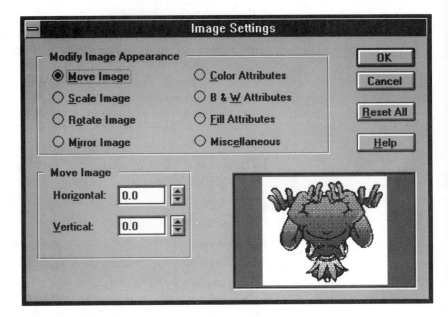

4. To close the Image Tools, use any of these techniques: Double-click the toolbox's tiny control-menu box (in the upper left-hand corner); right-click the graphics box and choose Image Tools again; click in your document (outside of the graphics box); or click the Tools button in the Graphics Box feature bar.

The easiest way to get the hang of the image tools is to play around with them a little. Have some fun. If you make a mess of things, you can always choose the Reset button to get the image back to its former self.

Rotating and Positioning Text in Boxes

If your graphics box contains text, you can rotate that text as illustrated in the example below. You can also align the text within its box.

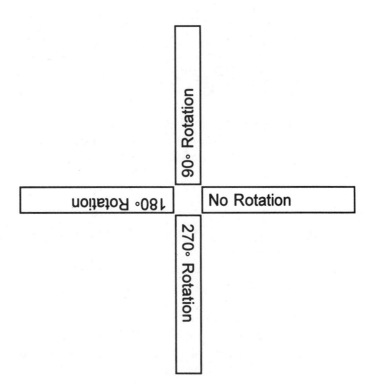

1. Right-click the graphics box that contains the text you want to rotate, and choose Content from the QuickMenu. Or, select the graphics box and choose Content from the Graphics Box feature bar.

2. If you want to change the position of the text within its box, choose appropriate options under Content Position.

3. If you want to rotate text, choose the degree of rotation. (The rotation is always measured in a counterclockwise direction.)

4. Choose OK when you're done.

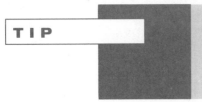

TIP For more flexibility in rotating and angling text, use the WP Draw application described in Chapter 26. For more precise positioning within the box, you can use the Advance feature covered in Chapter 28.

You may want to resize or reposition the entire box when you're done. Use the standard mouse or command button techniques described earlier in this chapter to do so.

Adding and Editing Captions

Captions are entirely optional, and certainly not all figures need captions. But WordPerfect lets you caption any graphic in any format you wish. As an added bonus, WordPerfect will automatically number the captions for you. The beauty of automatic numbering is that if you later insert, move, or delete a captioned graphic, WordPerfect will automatically renumber any other captions to reflect the change. This way, graphic numbering stays sequential throughout the document.

To add a caption to a graphics box, follow the steps below:

1. Right-click the box you want to caption and choose Create Caption (or Edit Caption to change an existing caption) from the QuickMenu. Or select the graphics box, choose Caption from the Graphics Box feature bar, then choose Edit.

2. Depending on the type of box you're working with, an automatic caption number may appear, followed by the cursor. Do any of the following:

   • To use the automatic caption number as is, skip to step 3.
   • To delete the automatic caption number and its leading text, press Backspace.

- To change the font or justification of the automatic caption number and the caption text, press Home ← to move the cursor in front of that number. Then choose your font or justification from the Layout menu, as usual. When you're ready to type the caption text, press End to move the cursor after the automatic number.

3. Press the spacebar or type a punctuation character (such as a colon or dash), then type your caption text.

4. Choose Close from the Graphics Box feature bar, or click in the document window, to deselect the box and return to normal editing.

Changing the Caption Position and Rotation

To change the position and rotation of the caption, follow these steps:

1. Right-click the box you want to change and choose Caption, or select the box and choose Caption from the Graphics Box feature bar. You'll be taken to the Box Caption dialog box.

2. Choose any of the options below to define the caption appearance. (The sample graphics box on the screen will reflect your selections, so it's easy to experiment.)

Side of Box   Choose which side of the box you want to put the caption on: Left, Right, Top, or Bottom.

Border   Choose where you want the caption to be placed, relative to the box border: Inside Border, Outside Border, or On the Border.

Position   Choose how you want the caption text aligned within the available space: Left, Right, or Center (if the caption is at the top or bottom of the box); or Top, Bottom, or Center (if the caption is on the left or right side of the box).

Absolute Offset   Specify how far you want to move the caption from its current position, as either a positive or negative measurement.

Percent Offset   Specify how far to move the caption from its current position as a percentage, from 0 to 100 percent of the width or height of the box. For example, if the caption is at the bottom left of the box, and you set Percent Offset to 25, the entire

caption will shift one quarter of the width of the box toward the right edge of the graphics box.

Caption Width Use options in this group to have WordPerfect determine the width of the caption automatically, to set a fixed width (in inches), or to set the width as a percentage (0–100) of the width of the box.

Caption Numbering and Styles To change the counter used for automatic numbering, choose the Change button next to Counter, and choose a counter. Note that the Initial Style and Number Style options don't change. They just provide information about which style is controlling the initial style and number style of the box. (I'll explain how to change those caption styles in a moment.)

Rotate Caption To rotate the text of the caption, choose one of the options under Rotate Caption.

Reset If you make a mess of things and want to start over from the initial style, click the Reset button. Choose OK when asked whether you're sure you want to delete the current caption (or choose Cancel if you change your mind about deleting it).

3. Choose OK when you've finished editing the caption appearance.

You can choose Close from the Graphics Box feature bar if you want to deselect the graphic, close the feature bar, and return to normal text editing. Or click in the document window to leave the feature bar on screen.

Changing the Caption Style

You can change the style of captions for all the boxes of a certain type. For example, initially all captions for Figure boxes start with **Figure** followed by the figure number (in boldface). But suppose you want the captions to be labeled *Fig. 1.1*, *Fig 1.2*, and so forth.

The procedure is basically the same as described earlier, in the section "Changing the Appearance of All Boxes." But here's a recap of the steps to follow, plus a few embellishments along the way:

1. If any graphics box is currently selected, click outside the box to get rid of the sizing handles (or choose Close from the Graphics feature bar, if the feature bar is visible).

2. Choose Graphics ➤ Graphics Styles.

3. Choose Options ➤ Setup and select the location of the styles you want to change. Your options are Current Document (which is probably what you want), Default Template, and Supplemental Template. Choose OK.

4. Under Style Type, choose Box.

5. In the Styles list, highlight the type of box style you want to change, then choose Edit.

6. From the Edit Box Style dialog box that appears, choose Caption. You'll be taken to the Box Caption dialog box. Notice that the Caption Numbering And Styles options all have Change command buttons next to them. Here's what to do next:

- **To change the counter used for the caption,** choose the Change button next to Counter, highlight the type of counter you want, and choose Select.

- **To change the font or general appearance of the caption,** choose the Change button next to Initial Style: Caption. Then choose the Edit button in the Style List dialog box that appears. Use commands from the Styles Editor menu bar to define a font, or any other attributes you want. When you're done, choose OK from the Styles Editor dialog box, then choose Close.

- **To change the first word or number of the caption,** choose the Change button next to Number Style:, then choose Edit. You'll see the current style displayed something like *[Bold]Figure [Box Num Disp][Bold]*. You can change the text (for example, change *Figure* to *Fig*), or delete/replace the [Bold] codes. You can also double-click the [Box Num Disp] code (if there is one in the current caption style), highlight a different counter, and choose Select. When you're done, choose OK from the Styles Editor dialog box, then choose Close.

7. Choose OK and Close until you return to the document window.

Deleting a Caption

If you want to delete the entire caption from a graphics box, right-click the box and choose Caption from the QuickMenu. Or, select the graphics box you want to change and choose Caption from the Graphics Box feature bar. Choose Reset from the Box Caption dialog box, and choose OK twice. You can deselect the graphics box if you wish.

Renumbering the Captions

Occasionally, you may need to change the numbering scheme of captions. For example, you might want to renumber Figures 5.1, 5.2, and so forth as Figures 5.10, 5.11, and so forth. To do so, proceed as follows:

1. If you want to renumber all the boxes in the document, move the cursor to the top of the document (press Ctrl+Home twice). If you want to renumber all the boxes from a certain place on, move the cursor to just before the hidden code of the first box you want to renumber.

2. Choose Insert ➤ Other ➤ Counter.

3. Select the type of box you want to renumber, then choose Edit. (You can also create your own counter style, as discussed in Chapter 15.)

4. In the Edit Counter Definition dialog box that appears, choose the Single Level Method pop-up list button and pick the numbering method you want (Numbers, Lowercase Letters, Uppercase Letters, Lowercase Roman, or Uppercase Roman).

TIP

You can also create a multilevel numbering scheme (for example, 5.1.1), by choosing the number of Levels to display, and then the numbering method to use at each level. You can then change the value of each level independently.

5. Choose OK.

6. Choose Value, enter the starting number you want, and choose OK.

7. Choose Close to return to the document window.

WordPerfect inserts a hidden [Count Set] code (or similar code) at the cursor position. Remember, only captioned graphics boxes beneath that code will be renumbered.

T I P

If you have problems with the caption numbering sequence, the [Count Set] code may be in the wrong place or is being overridden by a [Count Set] code that comes later in the document. You can use Reveal Codes (Alt+F3) and Find (F2) to seek out those codes. See Chapter 15 for more information on counters.

Generating a Figure List

You can automatically generate a list of all the captions for a particular type of box. For example, you can generate a list of all the figure numbers and captions. Here's how:

1. Move the cursor to wherever you want the list to appear in the document. For example, you might press Ctrl+End, then Ctrl+↵ to add the list to the end of the document.

2. Choose Tools ➤ List.

3. Choose Define from the List feature bar.

4. Choose Create.

5. Enter a name for your list (for example, *Figures*) and, if you wish, choose a Numbering Format from the buttons next to Position.

6. Under Auto Reference Box Captions, choose the type of box you want to generate a list for (for example, .Figure Box).

7. Choose OK, then choose Insert. You should see a << *List will generate here* >> indicator.

8. Choose Generate from the feature bar, then choose OK.

9. Choose Close to close the List feature bar.

If you want to generate lists for several types of boxes, repeat all the steps for each type of box you want to list.

If you add, change, delete, or move captioned figures, the list will *not* be updated automatically. However, you can update all the lists in your document by choosing Tools ➤ Generate ➤ OK. See Chapter 31 for more details.

Tying a Callout to a Box

When I say something like "See Figure 1.1" in this book, I'm using a *callout*. Presumably, there's a Figure 1.1 nearby for you to look at. Even though WordPerfect automatically renumbers graphics boxes as you shuffle them around, it doesn't automatically renumber the callouts. Thus, if you insert a figure above Figure 1.1, and Figure 1.1 becomes Figure 1.2, your text callout will still say "See Figure 1.1." Trust me: Readers don't like it when that happens.

To prevent that sort of mishap, you can use *automatic cross-referencing* to create a cross-reference in text to a particular graphics box's caption (counter) number. See Chapter 31 for details on cross-referencing.

Watermark Graphics

If you put a graphic image in a watermark, WordPerfect automatically centers it on the page, and prints it at a very high brightness so that text over the image can still be read easily. For example, the large computer in the middle of Figure 25.13 is a normal graphic image, in a watermark.

Here's how to create a watermark image in your document:

1. Move the cursor to the top of the document, or the top of the first page that you want the watermark to appear on.

2. Choose Layout ➤ Watermark.

3. Choose Watermark A. (Or, if you've already created a first watermark for this document and now want to create a second one, choose Watermark B.) Then choose Create.

4. If you wish, choose the Placement button on the Watermark feature bar, select which pages you want this watermark to appear on (Odd Pages, Even Pages, or Every Page), and choose OK.

FIGURE 25.13

The large computer in the middle of this letter is a watermark. The OK and Cancel buttons are button-box graphics boxes.

PC SUPPORT

Independent Support For Computing Professionals
P.O. Box 123
Mongoose, CA 91234
1-800-DNT-ASKM

It wasn't my idea

April 1, 1994

Wanda Bea Granolabar
1121 East Pickle St.
Burbank, CA 92123

Dear Ms. Granolabar:

Thanks for your letter dated March 1. Based on what you've told me, you made some menu selections, and a couple of changes to a dialog box. That's fine. Not likely to break anything. But, as a general rule, whenever you make changes to a dialog box, you must then "complete the dialog" to proceed. To do so, just click (using the left mouse button) either of these command buttons (on the screen) with your mouse pointer (that little thing that moves on the screen when you roll the mouse around):

OK Tells the program that you're happy with what you've done in the dialog box, and are now ready to proceed.

Cancel Tells the program you've got the willies about this dialog box, and would like to get outta here without saving any changes.

By all means, if we can be of any further assistance, please don't hesitate to call write.

Sincerely,

Willie Frank

Willie B. Frank
Vice President of Technical Details

5. Choose <u>F</u>igure and then select the drive, directory, and file name of the image you want to put in the watermark. Choose OK to return to the document window.

6. Choose <u>C</u>lose twice from the feature bars.

The watermark image shows up on the screen in Page and Two-Page views, but not in Draft view. You can type right over the image and add other graphics.

Editing a Watermark Image

Once you put a watermark image on the page, you cannot select or edit it in the usual manner (clicking or right-clicking). Instead, you first need to double-click its [Watermark] code in Reveal Codes, or choose Layout ➤ Watermark ➤ *A* or *B* ➤ Edit to get to the Watermark feature bar. Then you can edit the figure by turning on Reveal Codes (Alt+F3) and double-clicking the [Box] code in Reveal Codes, or by pressing Shift+F11 to select the graphic and display the Graphics Box feature bar. When you're done, choose Close twice to return to normal editing mode.

Button-Box Graphics

The Button box makes it easy for people who write computer documentation to create buttons that look like the 3-D buttons on computer screens. For example, in Figure 25.13 the OK and Cancel buttons are really just text displayed in a Button box. Here's a Button box with a graphic image in it:

To create a Button box, follow these steps:

1. Move the cursor to wherever you want to place the button, and choose Graphics ➤ Custom Box.

2. Double-click Button, or highlight that option and choose OK.

3. Size the box to whatever dimensions you want, either by dragging sizing handles or using the Size option on the Graphics Box feature bar. You can also reposition the image by dragging it or by choosing the Position command on the feature bar, as described earlier in this chapter.

4. To put text or a picture on the button, right-click the box and choose Content to get to the Box Content dialog box.

Now you can fill the box in the usual manner. To add a picture to the button, select the name of the graphic image to put on the button. Or, to put text on the button, choose Text from the Content button, then choose Edit. Choose fonts and justification, and/or type your text. When you're done editing, choose Close from the feature bar (if you're in Draft view), or click in the document window (if you're in Page or Two-Page view).

If you want to create additional buttons of the same size, select the Button box by clicking it once (so it has sizing handles) and choose Edit ➤ Copy (Ctrl+C). Then position the cursor and choose Edit ➤ Paste (Ctrl+V) as many times as necessary to create enough duplicate buttons. You can change the text on each duplicate button by right-clicking and choosing Edit Text, or by double-clicking the box.

If you need to space the buttons evenly on the page, consider putting each button into a separate table cell (see Chapter 7). Anchor each Button box to the current paragraph, so that each button sticks to its own cell.

Capturing Buttons

Another way to create buttons is to capture the screen that the button is on and save that screen capture to a file. (To capture the current screen, press the Print Screen, Alt+Print Screen, or Shift+Print Screen key on your keyboard—whichever key works.) Then edit the screen capture file, cropping out everything but the button, as shown below:

You can then retrieve the captured button into a graphics box anywhere in your document. See "Screen Captures," later in this chapter, for more information.

Using Keycap Fonts

If you write computer documentation, you might consider shopping around for a keycap font, like the one I used to create the image below. This is the easiest way to insert keycaps, because you just select the font and then type.

Putting Pictures in Tables

You can put a graphics box in a table cell. Just move the cursor to the cell you want to put the box in and create the box normally, as described earlier in this chapter. You should set the box's anchor to Put Box In Current Paragraph (Paragraph Anchor), so that it stays within the table.

To center the box horizontally within its cell, go to the Box Position dialog box and choose Center Of Paragraph under Horizontal. Then set the Place option to 0".

Conserving Disk Space

When you put a graphic image from your hard disk into a graphics box, WordPerfect usually saves a *copy* of that image in your document. If you're using the same image in many documents, you're saving that many more copies of the same image file. Not a good use of disk space.

You can avoid storing a copy of a graphic in your document by specifying the graphic as an "image on disk." That way, when you save the document, only the location and name of the image will be stored in the document, and the document will be smaller. Here's the steps to follow:

1. Right-click the graphics box and choose Content.

2. Use the pop-up list next to Content to change the box's content from the current setting to Image On Disk. If you're asked whether you want to delete the current box contents, choose Yes.

3. In the Filename text box, specify a graphics file name as follows:

   - To reuse an image that *doesn't have* a .WPG extension, change the extension to **.wpg**. This will convert the graphic to a format that WordPerfect can process quickly, and it will avoid clobbering the original graphics file.

   - To reuse an image that *does have* a .WPG extension, continue with step 4.

   - To use a different graphics file, type its name into the File-name text box (or use the file button, if necessary, to select and fill in the file name).

4. Choose OK. If you're asked about replacing the current file on disk, and you're sure the image is already a WordPerfect-format (.WPG) image, choose Yes, then choose OK. Otherwise, choose No, change the file name so that it has a .WPG extension, and choose OK.

5. If you're asked about deleting the current box contents, choose Yes.

6. If necessary, choose OK to return to the document window.

(*Warning:* WordPerfect will rely on the image file's name and location to display it. If you later rename the file or move it to another directory, WordPerfect won't be able to find it.)

If You Run Out of Memory...

If your printer runs out of memory while trying to print a complex document, first try printing one page at a time. That is, move the cursor to the page you want to print and choose File ➤ Print ➤ Current Page ➤ Print.

You can also reduce the amount of printer memory required to print your document by printing at a lower quality. For example, choose File ➤ Print ➤ Print Quality, choose Draft or Medium instead of High, then choose Print.

If you've supplemented your printer's built-in fonts with *soft fonts*, you may be able to conserve printer memory by reducing the number of soft fonts downloaded at one time. See Chapter 10 for more information.

Finally, if you don't need to print the graphics and want to print the text only, you can choose File ➤ Print, select (check) Do Not Print Graphics, then choose Print.

Tips for Building Your Art Collection

As I mentioned at the beginning of this chapter and illustrated in Figure 25.1, you can put a picture of just about anything in your document. WordPerfect can automatically convert and read graphic images in most of the common formats. Table 25.1 summarizes those formats.

As an alternative, many third-party programs can convert graphic images to and from WordPerfect format. Perhaps the most widely used program for this type of work is HiJaak from Inset Systems in Brookfield, CT.

About Imported PostScript Images

Imported PostScript Files (.EPS) generally don't appear on the screen. What does appear is the frame, and a message indicating that the box contains a PostScript image. However, when you print the document on a PostScript printer, the graphic will print correctly.

TABLE 25.1: Types of Graphic Images That You Can Read Directly into a Graphics Box

ABBREVIATION	TYPE
bmp	Windows 3.*x* and OS/2 Presentation Manager bitmap format
cgm	Computer Graphics Metafile
dfx	AutoCAD format
dhp	Dr. Halo PIC format
drw	Designer format
dxf	AutoCAD format
eps	PostScript and Encapsulated PostScript
hpgl	Hewlett-Packard Graphics Language plotter file
pcx	PC Paintbrush format
pic	Lotus 1-2-3 PIC format
pict	Macintosh PICT
tga	Truevision Targa format
tiff	Tagged Image File format
wmf	Windows Metafile format
wpg	WordPerfect Graphics format

Scanned Images and TV/Video Frames

You can display in your WordPerfect documents anything that you see printed on paper. You do this by *scanning* the image to a file. The image can be a photo, drawing, signature, company logo—whatever. As long as it's on paper, you can scan it to a file.

TIP

The better you can size and crop an image with your scanning software *while* scanning it (before saving the image as a file), the better it will look in your printed document. Messing with scanned images *after* scanning usually degrades the appearance of the image. The one exception is using photo retouching software, which is designed to improve scanned images.

To capture video images, TV screens, and so forth, you'll need to purchase additional hardware and software that's specifically designed for video. Check out your local Comput-O-Rama to see what's available.

Screen Captures

Another type of graphic that you can display in your WordPerfect documents is the "screen shot"—anything that's on your screen, captured to a file in some format that WordPerfect can import. If you need to capture many screens, your best bet would be to purchase a third-party program that lets you crop images and save them in a variety of formats. I used Collage Complete by Inner Media (Hollis, NH) for most of the Windows and DOS screen captures in this book.

For the occasional screen capture, you needn't spend the money on an extra program. Instead, use the built-in screen capturing abilities of Windows, as summarized below:

1. Get the screen looking the way you want. If you want to capture a DOS screen, you can exit to DOS using the MS-DOS Prompt icon in the Main group of the Windows Program Manager.

2. When the screen shows whatever it is you want to capture, press Print Screen (sometimes abbreviated as Prt Scrn or something similar). If you want to capture just the active window, press Alt+Print Screen instead. A copy of the screen or window is copied to the Windows Clipboard (though you won't notice anything right away).

3. If you used the MS-DOS icon to go out to DOS, type **exit** and press ↵ to return to Windows.

4. Work your way back to your WordPerfect document (for example, press Ctrl+Esc, highlight WordPerfect in the Task List, and choose Switch To).

5. Move the cursor to where you want the screen capture to appear, and choose Edit ➤ Paste. The image appears in a Figure box.

If you need to crop or modify the image before bringing it into your document, you can use Windows Paintbrush (if you don't have something better to work with). That is, complete steps 1–3 above, but instead of returning to WordPerfect in step 4, go back to the Windows Program Manager, open the Accessories group, then open Paintbrush. Maximize Paintbrush to full screen, and choose Options ➤ Image Attributes ➤ Default, and either Black And White or Colors. Then choose OK.

If you've captured a full screen, it might not fit into Paintbrush unless you "zoom out" first. That is, choose View ➤ Zoom Out.

To copy the image from the Clipboard into Paintbrush, choose Edit ➤ Paste or press Ctrl+V. If you zoomed out, you'll see only cross-hatching at first. Click any tool in the toolbox to the left (such as the scissors and square), then choose View ➤ Zoom In.

If you want to crop a portion of the image, use the Pick tool (scissors and square) to frame the section you want to save. Then choose Edit ➤ Copy To, and enter a drive, directory, and file name for the image portion you're about to save (e.g., C:\WPWIN60\GRAPHICS\MYFIG10.BMP). Then choose OK.

If you prefer to save the entire screen image, choose File ➤ Save. Specify a drive, directory, and file name, then choose OK.

TIP

For more information on the techniques summarized in this section, please refer to your Windows documentation.

When you've finished, you can choose File ➤ Exit to leave Paintbrush. Then work your way back to your WordPerfect document. To bring the screen image into your document, choose Graphics ➤ Figure, specify the drive, directory, and file name that you gave the image while saving it in Paintbrush, and choose OK.

Clip Art

Clip art images are small pieces of art often used to jazz up newsletters and other documents. Thousands of ready-to-use clip art images are available. Much of the clip art is free of copyright restrictions, so you can purchase it for a one-time fee, then use it freely in your work without paying a royalty to the artist.

WARNING

Don't assume *all* clip art is free of copyright. You cannot use copyrighted art without permission. Make sure you understand the terms of the licensing agreement before you buy.

Much of the sample clip art in this book is from the Presentation Task Force collection, published by New Vision Technologies in Nepean, Ontario, Canada. The beauty of this product is that the images are stored in CGM format, which works great in WordPerfect. And, it includes both a color copy and a black-and-white copy of every image in the collection. So if the gray shades produced by a color image don't quite fit the bill on your non-color printer, you can use the black-and-white version instead.

Many excellent clip art collections are available, as a trip to your local computer supermarket or a peek in a desktop-publishing magazine will prove. My own preference is to stick with vector (line) formats, particularly CGM. Bitmapped (dot) formats, like PCX, produce jagged edges and aren't as easy to manage with WP Draw and the WordPerfect Image Tools.

Business and Free-Form Graphics

You can create custom drawings and business charts using the Draw and Chart applications discussed in Chapter 26. Many spreadsheet and graphics programs also allow you to make charts and drawings. Specialized graphics programs are available for scientific, engineering, and other types of applications.

In general, once you create a chart or picture in one of these programs, you can easily "Save As" or "Export" the file to some format that Word-Perfect can read (as listed in Table 25.1). If the program you used to create the picture supports OLE, you can link or embed the picture in your WordPerfect document, as discussed in Chapter 33.

Special Characters

Don't forget that WordPerfect offers many special characters, including pointing hands, happy faces, musical notes, and so forth. Certain fonts, like PostScript's Dingbats, TrueType's Wingdings, and various keycap fonts, offer even more special characters. To use any one of those special characters as a graphic image, put it into a graphics box with the Content set to <u>T</u>ext. Set the font for the special character to an enormous size (say 360 points). You can then move and size that box in the usual manner and treat it as you would any other graphics box that contains text.

Fancy Text Shapes

You can use WordPerfect's TextArt application (<u>G</u>raphics ➤ Te<u>x</u>tArt) to pour text into fancy shapes like the ones shown below. You'll learn how to do this in Chapter 28.

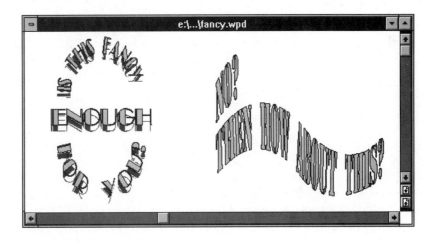

Adding graphics to your document is easy, once you've practiced the techniques a bit. In this chapter, we've covered all the basic techniques for adding, sizing, positioning, and controlling the appearance of graphics boxes. In the next few chapters, we'll look at more of WordPerfect's desktop publishing features, including more advanced techniques for using graphics boxes.

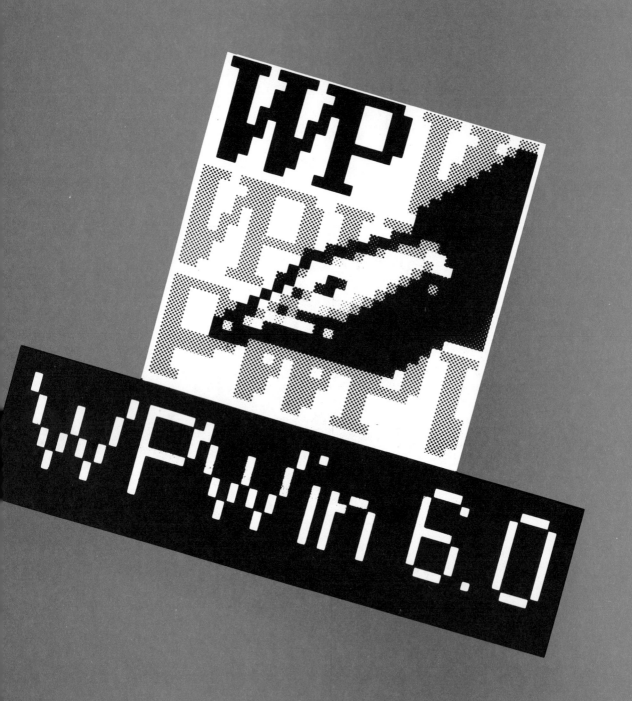

CHAPTER

26

Business Charts and Other Arts

f a s t *TRACK*

To create a chart   868

choose Graphics ➤ Chart or click the Chart button in the
WordPerfect button bar. Fill out the data portion of the screen
with the data you want to plot, and choose Redraw to see the
effects of your changes. When you're happy with the chart,
choose Return. You'll be returned to the document window
with the chart displayed in a graphics box. To create a chart
from a table in your document, position the cursor anywhere
in the table, then choose Graphics ➤ Chart.

To edit an existing chart   870

double-click the chart in your document. Or edit the graphics
box that contains the chart, using Graphics ➤ Edit Box ➤ OK
➤ Content ➤ Edit. After making your changes, click the Return button.

To annotate a chart   877

right-click the chart in your document, and choose WP 2.1
Chart Object ➤ Annotate. Use the tools available in WP Draw
to add lines, text, arrows, and graphics. Then choose File ➤
Exit and Return To… ➤ Yes to return to the document.

To start WP Draw   878

in order to create a new picture from scratch, choose Graphics
➤ Draw, or click the Draw button in the WordPerfect button
bar. To start WP Draw to edit an existing picture, double-click
the picture. Or choose Graphics ➤ Edit Box ➤ Content ➤
Edit from the menus to edit the graphics box that contains the
picture.

To insert a picture into WP Draw   **882**

choose the diamond-shaped Retrieve A Graphic tool, or choose
Draw ➤ Figure), then drag out a frame indicating how much
space you want the image to occupy. Or, choose File ➤ Insert
File. Choose the drive, directory, and file name of the graphic
image, then choose Retrieve.

To insert text into a WP Draw picture   **884**

choose the Text tool (with the uppercase *A* on it) from the tool
bar. Optionally, choose Text ➤ Font (or press F9), choose a
font face, font style, font size, appearance, and attributes, then
choose OK. Then, click where you want to start typing, and
type your text. Click the Select tool (at the top left corner of
the tool bar) when you're done.

To add arrows to a WP Draw picture   **886**

choose Attributes ➤ Line ➤ Arrowhead and choose the type
of arrowhead. Choose any other options you want, then choose
OK. Choose a line drawing tool from the toolbox, then drag
out the line you want to draw on your picture.

I N THIS chapter we're going to look at WP Draw and WP Chart. Draw is a general-purpose drawing program that you can use to create your own drawings, to obtain special effects with text, and to modify and combine existing clip art. Chart is a part of WP Draw that makes it easy to create bar graphs, pie charts, and other business charts. We'll start our discussion with Chart.

How to Create a Chart

You can use Object Linking and Embedding (Chapter 33) to display charts from spreadsheets, databases, and other programs in your Word-Perfect document. Or, as we'll discuss in this chapter, you can use the Chart feature of WP Draw to create a chart anywhere you wish in your document. Here's the basic procedure for creating a chart and putting it in your WordPerfect document:

1. Move the cursor to where you want the chart to appear in your document. Or, if you've already created a WordPerfect table in your document, move the cursor to any cell in the table.

2. Choose Graphics ➤ Chart, or click the Chart button (shown at left) in the WordPerfect or Tables button bar. You'll be taken to the Chart Editor feature of WP Draw.

3. For best results, click the Maximize button in the upper right corner of the WP Draw window. Then choose View ➤ Data And Chart from the WP Draw menu bar (if necessary).

Your screen will resemble Figure 26.1, where you can see some sample data plotted on a chart. Notice that the sample data at the top of the screen looks like a spreadsheet or table.

FIGURE 26.1

The Chart Editor in WP Draw lets you create business charts to put in your WordPerfect document.

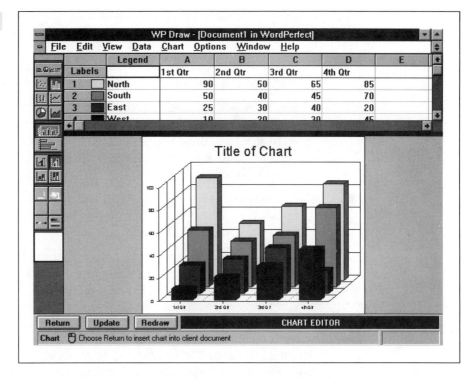

In Figure 26.1, the X-axis titles at the bottom of the chart appear across the Labels row of the data table (for example, 1st Qtr, 2nd Qtr, 3rd Qtr, 4th Qtr). Labels for the chart's legend (not shown in the figure) are taken from the Legend column in the data table.

TIP

When you create a chart from a WordPerfect table, labels for the chart's X-axis are taken from row 1 of the table, starting in column B (for example, from cells B1, C1, D1, E1, and so on). Labels for the chart's legend are taken from column A, starting in row 2 (for example, from cells A2, A3, A4, A5, and so on). You'll learn how to customize labels and display a legend later in the chapter.

4. To choose the type of graph you want (for example, pie chart, bar chart, and so forth), use commands on the Chart menu or click appropriate buttons in the tool palette. (To find out what a tool in the tool palette is for, move the mouse pointer to the tool you're interested in and look to the title bar for a brief description.)

5. Use standard editing techniques to change the titles and data presented in the data area until the chart plots the data the way you want it to. To make your changes appear on the chart, you must click the Redraw button at the bottom of the screen, or choose View ➤ Redraw, or press Ctrl+F3.

6. If you wish, use commands and techniques described under "Defining Your Data" and "Refining Your Chart" later in this chapter to make additional changes.

7. When you're happy with your chart, choose the Return button near the lower left edge of the screen. Or choose File ➤ Exit And Return To... from the WP Draw menu bar. Be sure to choose Yes when asked if you want to save your current changes.

The chart appears in a Figure graphics box. You can now use the standard techniques described in Chapter 25 to anchor, size, position, design, and caption the box to your liking. For example, you can right-click the chart in your document and choose Position, Size, and other options from the QuickMenu, to customize the chart however you want it.

TIP To reposition the tool palette on the screen, drag it by its title bar.

Editing a Chart

To change a chart that you've put in your document, use any of the methods below:

- Double-click the chart.
- Or right-click the chart and choose WP Chart 2.1 Object ➤ Edit from the QuickMenu.

- Or, choose <u>G</u>raphics ➤ <u>E</u>dit Box to get to the Graphics Box feature bar. If necessary, use the <u>N</u>ext and P<u>r</u>ev buttons in the feature bar to select the chart you want to edit. Then choose C<u>o</u>ntent (from the feature bar) ➤ <u>E</u>dit.

You'll be taken back to the Chart Editor, where you can make whatever changes you wish. When you've finished making your changes, choose Return or choose <u>F</u>ile ➤ E<u>x</u>it And Return To…. As usual, you'll be given the option to either save or discard your most recent changes.

TIP

The Chart Editor has its own button bar. To turn the button bar on and off, start from the Chart Editor and choose <u>V</u>iew ➤ <u>B</u>utton Bar or press F10. The button bar offers shortcuts for updating the chart in the document, returning to the document window, going to a particular cell, editing the selected cell, defining titles for the chart, defining the legend, and formatting labels for the chart.

Defining Your Data

Defining the data to plot in a chart is simply a matter of filling in the cells of the chart with the data you want to plot, and choosing Redraw or <u>V</u>iew ➤ <u>R</u>edraw (Ctrl+F3) to keep the chart in sync with the data.

Editing and Selecting Data

Here are some things you can do to simplify the job:

- **To focus on the data only,** choose <u>V</u>iew ➤ <u>D</u>ata Only. When you want to see the chart again, choose <u>V</u>iew ➤ <u>C</u>hart Only, or <u>V</u>iew ➤ Data <u>A</u>nd Chart. If you're viewing both data and chart, you can change the height of the data area by dragging the thick bar at the bottom up or down (see Figure 26.2).

- **To change or fill a cell,** click the cell you want, or move the highlight to the cell using the arrow, Tab, or Shift+Tab keys. To highlight a particular cell, choose <u>E</u>dit ➤ <u>G</u>o To Cell or press Ctrl+G, and type the cell address you want, as in a "regular" WordPerfect table.

FIGURE 26.2

Places to click in order to select data

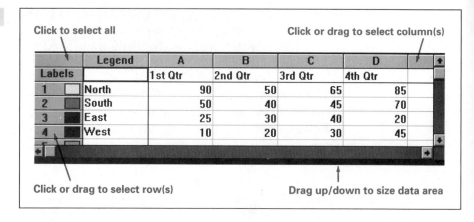

Then type and edit normally. (Alternatively, you can double-click the cell you want, or highlight the cell and press F11. Edit the data in the Edit Current Cell dialog box that appears, then choose OK to accept the changes.)

- **To select data within the table,** drag the mouse pointer through the cells you want to select, or hold down the Shift key while extending the highlighted area with the arrow keys.

- **To select an entire row or column,** click the row number at the left of the row, or the column title at the top of the column. You can select several rows or columns by dragging the mouse pointer through those row numbers or column titles.

- **To select all the data,** choose Edit ➤ Select All.

Inserting and Deleting Data

To insert rows and columns into the data, follow these steps:

1. Move the highlight to the place where you want to insert or delete a row or column. Then ...

   - **To insert rows or columns,** choose Edit ➤ Insert, then choose either Row(s) or Column(s). Specify how many you want to insert, and choose OK.

   - **To delete rows or columns,** choose Edit ➤ Delete, specify whether to delete Row(s) or Columns, how many you want to delete, and choose OK. (You can also delete rows or columns by selecting the ones you want to delete, choosing <u>E</u>dit ➤ <u>D</u>elete, then choosing OK.)

Be careful! There's no undelete or undo option for the <u>E</u>dit ➤ <u>D</u>elete command.

- **To empty some cells,** select the cells, column(s), or row(s) that you want to empty, and then choose <u>E</u>dit ➤ C<u>l</u>ear or press Del. Decide whether you want to delete the <u>D</u>ata, the <u>F</u>ormat (described in a moment), or <u>B</u>oth, then choose OK.

Remember that your changes won't be reflected in the chart until you choose Redraw or <u>V</u>iew ➤ <u>R</u>edraw (Ctrl+F3).

Transposing the Data

To *transpose* the data that you're charting so that rows become columns and columns become rows, follow these steps:

1. Move the cursor to any cell of the data being charted, then choose <u>E</u>dit ➤ <u>S</u>elect All. (Or, if you only want to transpose certain rows or columns, select those rows or columns by dragging or by using the Shift+arrow techniques discussed earlier.)

2. Choose <u>E</u>dit ➤ Cu<u>t</u>, or press Ctrl+X. (If you want to copy the transposed rows and columns elsewhere, choose <u>E</u>dit ➤ <u>C</u>opy or press Ctrl+C instead.)

3. Move the cursor to where you want the transposed data to appear. Usually, this will be the first (upper left) cell of the data being charted.

4. Choose <u>E</u>dit ➤ P<u>a</u>ste Transposed.

When you click the Redraw button, or choose <u>V</u>iew ➤ Redraw, the chart will reflect the new arrangement of your data.

Changing the Format or Appearance of Data

You can control the appearance of numbers and dates in the data portion of the chart. These changes will also carry over to the chart axis labels. To change the appearance of data:

1. In the data portion of the chart, select the cell(s) you want to reformat (or choose Edit ➤ Select All to set the format of all the cells).

2. Choose Data ➤ Format.

3. Choose either Numeric Format or Date Format, then choose the format you want.

4. Choose OK when you're done. Then choose Redraw to update the chart.

You can also change the width of the columns in the data area. To do so, select the column(s) you want to change. Then choose Data ➤ Column Width. Enter a value between 1 (narrow) and 30 (very wide), then choose OK. These changes have no effect on the chart—they just affect how much of the data you can see on the screen.

As an alternative to going through the menus, you can change column widths by dragging the separator line at the right of a column, next to the column label. This is the same technique you use to resize columns in "regular" WordPerfect tables (see Chapter 7).

Including/Excluding Data

Normally WordPerfect will attempt to plot all the data in the data area. If you want to exclude some data from the chart, follow these steps:

1. Select the row(s) or column(s) you want to exclude.

2. Choose Data ➤ Exclude Row/Col. If prompted, select either Row(s) or Column(s) and choose OK. The excluded data will appear dimmed in the data table.

3. Choose Redraw, or View ➤ Redraw, to check the results.

If you change your mind about excluding data, repeat steps 1 through 3 above, but in step 2 choose Data ➤ Include Row/Col.

Refining Your Chart

There are all kinds of ways to change the appearance of your chart while you're using the Chart Editor. You can use commands in the WP Draw menus, or equivalent shortcuts that appear on the tool palette. Feel free to experiment, because it's easy to undo any changes you make. Here are your options:

Chart ➤ type   To change the type of chart displayed, click the button in the tool palette that depicts the type of chart you want. (If you're not sure what the button is for, point to it with your mouse and look to the title bar for a description.) You can also choose Chart and pick a chart type. Or, choose Chart ➤ Gallery or click the Display Chart Examples button in the tool palette, highlight the type of chart you want, and choose Retrieve.

Options ➤ Layout   Lets you change the layout of the chart. For example, you can use the Layout options to explode a slice of a pie chart, as in Figure 26.3, and to add or remove the 3-D look.

FIGURE 26.3

A pie chart with an exploded slice and each series defined with patterns rather than colors. Use commands on the Options menu in WP Draw to make these kinds of changes to your chart.

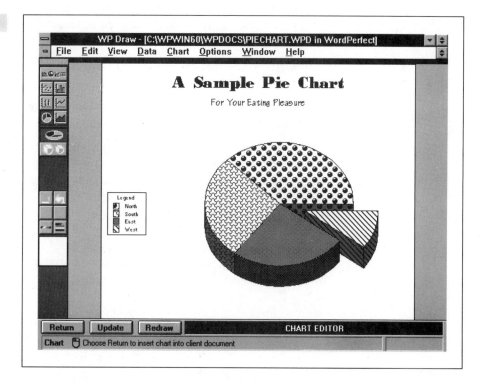

Options ➤ Series   Lets you select a series of data to change. Use the P̲revious and N̲ext buttons to switch among series, then use the Type, Attributes, and other options to customize the current series. You can also turn a color chart to black-and-white, as in Figure 26.3, by coloring and filling each series.

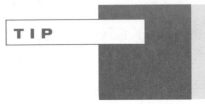

TIP

When using dialog boxes that change the appearance of the chart, you can click the Pre̲view button to see how those changes will look. To save the changes, choose OK. To abandon the changes, choose Cancel.

Options ➤ A̲xis   Lets you customize the X or Y axis of the chart.

Options ➤ G̲rid/Tick   Lets you customize the background grid on the chart.

Options ➤ F̲rame   Lets you customize the chart's background frame.

Options ➤ P̲erspective   Lets you change the angle from which you're viewing the chart, as well as to activate/deactivate a wireframe view.

Options ➤ T̲itles   Lets you change the main title, subtitle, and axis titles.

Options ➤ Le̲gend   Lets you hide/display a legend, and control the appearance and position of the legend.

Options ➤ La̲bels   Lets you create, hide, change, and control the appearance of data labels (which appear inside the chart) and axis labels (which appear outside the chart).

You can accomplish a lot by simply experimenting. Use the Pre̲view button (or Redraw button) to update the chart's appearance and see immediate results of your selection(s). If you need more information about a feature in the Chart Editor, you can turn to the options on the H̲elp menu or click the H̲elp button in any dialog box where it's available.

Annotating a Chart

You can annotate an existing chart by adding text, pictures, lines, and arrows. To do so, create the chart and exit WP Draw. Then, starting from the WordPerfect document window (*not* the WP Draw window), right-click the chart you want to change, and choose WP Chart 2.1 Object ➤ Annotate. You'll be taken to WP Draw without the Chart Editor. There, you can use the tools described in the rest of this chapter to further customize your chart.

For example, in Figure 26.4 I added two pieces of graphic clip art to the chart—one of the pigs and one of the speech bubble. I also added some text, which appears to be inside the speech bubble. The techniques I used to add the art and text are described under "Inserting a Picture" and "Adding Text" later in this chapter.

When you've finished annotating, choose File ➤ Exit And Return To ..., and be sure to choose Yes when asked if you want to save your current changes.

FIGURE 26.4

A sample chart annotated with some clip art and text via WP Draw

Some Charting Tips

Here are some tips you can use to get exactly the look you want in a chart. I'll assume that you've created the chart already, and have returned from WP Draw to the document window.

- **To put a frame around the box** that holds the chart, right-click the chart, choose Border/Fill from the QuickMenu, choose a border and fill style (or design a customized style), then choose OK.

- **To size and position the chart** in relation to other text in your document, right-click the chart and use the Position, Size, and Wrap commands on the QuickMenu (see Chapter 25).

- **To position the chart** within its graphics box, right-click the box and choose Image Tools from the QuickMenu. Then use the Move, Scale, and other buttons (described in Chapter 25), to control the size and appearance of the chart within its box.

Using WP Draw

WordPerfect Draw is a separate Windows application that came with your WordPerfect for Windows package. You can use Draw to create pictures, to edit existing clip art, to label pictures, and to enhance text.

Starting WP Draw

Use any of the following techniques to start Draw:

- If you want to create a new picture from scratch, move the cursor to where you want the picture to appear. Then choose Graphics ➤ Draw, or click the Draw button (shown at left) in the WordPerfect button bar.

- If you want to edit a picture that's already in a graphics box in your document, double-click that picture, or right-click it and choose Activate WP Graphic 2.1 Object.

- Or, to edit a picture in your document without clicking, choose Graphics ➤ Edit Box ➤ OK. If necessary, use the Next and Prev buttons in the Graphics Box feature bar to select the correct box.

Then choose Content from the feature bar, and Edit from the Box Content dialog box that appears.

You'll be taken to WP Draw, unless the picture you're editing is an OLE Object from some other application, in which case you'll be taken to that application rather than WP Draw. (See Chapter 33 for more information on OLE.)

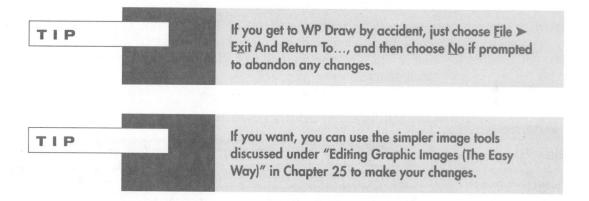

TIP If you get to WP Draw by accident, just choose File ➤ Exit And Return To..., and then choose No if prompted to abandon any changes.

TIP If you want, you can use the simpler image tools discussed under "Editing Graphic Images (The Easy Way)" in Chapter 25 to make your changes.

Setting Up the Draw Screen

When you get to Draw, you might want to try some of the following options to set the screen up to your liking:

- If the WP Draw window isn't full-screen, you can click the Maximize button in its upper right corner to expand it to full screen.

- To display or hide the Draw button bar, choose View ➤ Button Bar, or press F10.

- You can display or hide the ruler by choosing View ➤ Ruler (Alt+Shift+F3).

- To hide or display the background grid, choose View ➤ Grid (Alt+Shift+F8).

- To change the appearance of the background grid, choose View ➤ Grid/Snap Options and select your vertical and horizontal spacing, and the interval for the grid lines, and choose OK.

- If you want objects that you create in Draw to be aligned with the grid, choose <u>V</u>iew ➤ S<u>n</u>ap To Grid (Alt+F8). Selecting Snap To Grid a second time disables it.

- If you need some alignment guides, turn on the ruler. Then you can drag a horizontal guide down from the ruler on top, and drag a vertical guide from the ruler at the left. You can display as many horizontal and vertical guides as you need. To remove a guide, drag it off the drawing area.

Figure 26.5 shows an example of WP Draw open on the screen with the ruler, button bar, and grid turned on. In this example, I set the grid spacing to **.25″** and the interval to **1**. So, each grid line represents a quarter inch of actual drawing space.

FIGURE 26.5

The WP Draw window with the ruler, grid, and button bar turned on

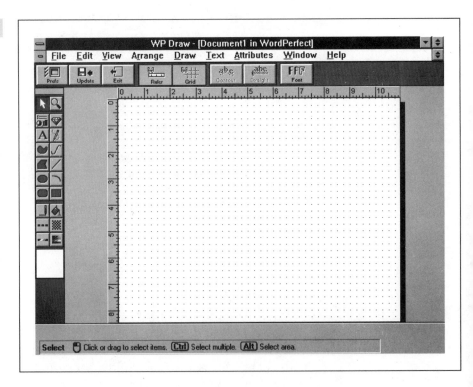

WP Draw Tool Palette

For future reference, Figure 26.6 points out the role played by each tool in the tool palette. Of course, you can just move the mouse pointer to any button, and look to the top of the screen for a description of what the button is for.

I should also point out that:

- You can reposition the tool palette by dragging its title bar.

- Once you select a tool (by clicking it), the status bar at the bottom of the screen describes how to use that tool, and lists optional keys you can use while dragging.

- When you finish using a tool and want to return to the normal mouse pointer, click the Select tool shown at the top left of the tool palette.

FIGURE 26.6

Buttons in WP Draw's tool palette. The role that each button plays appears at the top of the screen when you move the mouse pointer to a button.

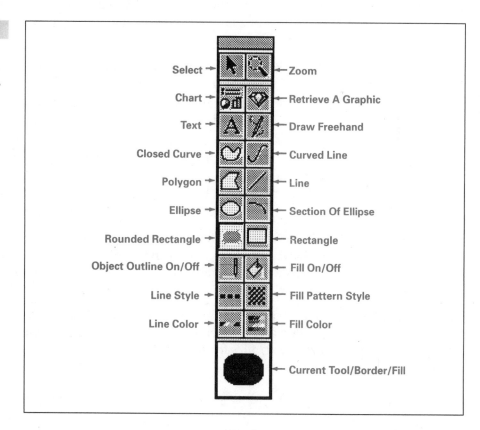

- Remember that in order to select an object to move, size, or change, you must first choose the Select tool, *then* click the object that you want to select.

- You can also choose drawing tools from the Draw menu instead of using the tool palette.

I'll talk more about selecting and changing objects as we go along.

Inserting a Picture

Instead of drawing freehand, you may just want to pull an existing picture into WP Draw. You can use either of the two methods below:

- If you want the incoming picture to fill the entire drawing area, choose File ➤ Insert File.

- If you want the picture to take up only a portion of the drawing area, select the Retrieve A Graphic tool (shown at left), or choose Draw ➤ Figure. The bottom of the screen explains what to do next. You can...

  - Click the mouse in the drawing area to size the image to a full page.

  - Drag a frame with the mouse to define a rectangular image of a particular size.

  - Hold down the Shift key while dragging to constrain the image to a perfect square of a particular size.

  - Hold down the Alt key while dragging to define the image size from the center. After outlining the size and shape you want, release the mouse button and any keys.

With either method, you'll be taken to a dialog box where you can choose the drive, directory, and file name of the picture you want to insert. Double-click the file name you want, or highlight the name and choose Retrieve.

In the example shown in Figure 26.7, I inserted two clip art files into the drawing area—the Thinker and a "thought bubble." These are two separate clip art files from the Presentation Task Force package.

FIGURE 26.7

Two separate clip art files inserted into the WP Draw drawing area using the Retrieve A Graphic button

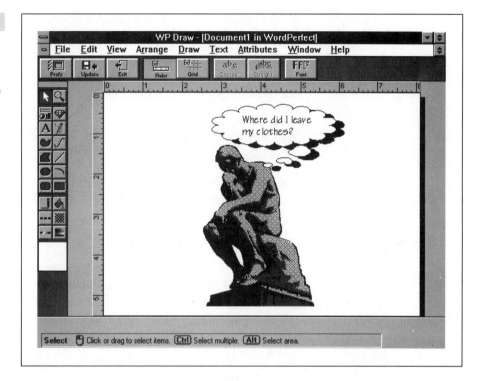

Each image is a separate *object* in the drawing area, which means I can alter, move, size, and position it independently. I'll discuss how under "Selecting and Editing Objects" later in this chapter.

Adding a Chart

You can create a chart while you're in WP Draw by following the steps below:

1. Choose the Chart tool in the WP Draw tool palette (see Figure 26.6).

2. Use the techniques described earlier under "Inserting a Picture" to define the size and position of the chart. Remember, you can click the mouse in the drawing area, drag a frame with the mouse, hold down the Shift key while dragging a frame, or hold down the Alt key while dragging a frame.

3. You'll be taken to the Chart Editor feature of WP Draw, where you can define the chart as described earlier in the chapter.

4. In the Create Chart dialog box that appears, choose the type of chart you want (Pie, Bar, Line, Area, Scatter, or Hi Lo), then choose OK. Or, choose Gallery, choose a chart type, and choose Retrieve.

5. When you're ready to return to WP Draw, choose File ➤ Close Chart Editor (or press Ctrl+F4).

If you need to edit the chart again later, start from WP Draw, then double-click the chart object (or right-click the chart and choose Edit Chart from the QuickMenu).

Adding Text

While you're in WP Draw, you can also add text to the drawing area. For example, I added *Where did I leave my clothes?* to the graphic image in Figure 26.7 using WP Draw. Here's how you can insert text into your picture:

1. Click the Text tool (shown at left) or choose Draw ➤ Text.

2. If you wish, choose Text ➤ Font (F9), and choose a font face, font style, font size, appearance, and any attributes that you want. Then choose OK.

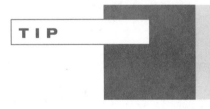

TIP　If you plan on reducing the size of your drawing in your document, you might want to select a large point size in WP Draw, because the text will shrink with the drawing. If in doubt, start with a size of about 36 points.

3. If you wish, choose Text and then other options as appropriate from the Layout, Justification, and other commands.

4. Click wherever you want to start typing the text, or drag out a box that frames the amount of space that you want the text to take up.

5. Type your text, then click the Select tool.

The text acts as a single object that you can size, position, and edit, as I'll discuss under "Selecting and Editing Objects" later in this chapter.

Freehand Drawing

You can use the drawing tools to draw any shape you want. The general procedure is as follows:

1. Click the tool you want to use in the tool palette, or choose a tool from the Draw menu. Now you have some choices to make:

   - **To control whether a closed shape will be outlined,** click the Object Outline On/Off button (shown at left) on or off. The affected tools will change their appearance in the tool palette.

   - **To control whether a closed shape will be filled with color,** click the Fill On/Off button (shown at left) on or off. The affected tools will change their appearance in the tool palette.

   - **To choose a line style, fill style, line color, or fill color,** click one of the last four buttons (shown at left) in the tool palette.

2. Look to the status bar for tips on using the currently selected tool. In general, you need to hold down the mouse button, drag out the line or shape you want, then either click or double-click.

3. If you're finished using the current tool, click the Select tool, or some other tool if appropriate.

The shape or line you drew becomes an object, just like text or a picture. You'll be able to use the techniques described under "Selecting and Editing Objects" later in this chapter to change that object if you wish.

Adding Arrows

You can use WP Draw to add arrows to a picture. This is very handy for creating labeled figures, like Figure 26.8. I put the text into the picture using the Text tool, and drew the arrows after adding arrowheads to the line tools. The computer is a clip art picture.

FIGURE 26.8

A clip art image with some labels and arrows added via WP Draw

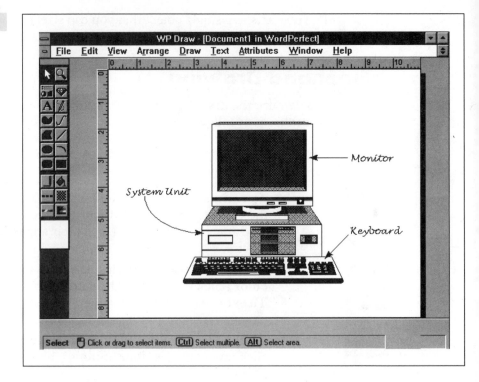

Here's how to draw arrows in your own pictures:

1. In WP Draw, choose Attributes ➤ Line.

2. Assuming you only want to add arrowheads to lines, leave the Apply To setting at Graphics Only.

3. If you wish, choose a Line Color, Line Width, and Style. (You can also click Fill and choose a fill pattern—though the fill will have no noticeable effect if you're not using a pretty thick line width. To return to the line options after choosing Fill, click Line.)

4. Using the pop-up list next to Arrowhead, choose where you want the arrowhead to appear: at the Beginning, Ending, Both Ends, or not at all (None).

5. Choose OK.

6. Select one of the line drawing tools shown at left.

7. Drag out the line then release the mouse button (the arrowhead will appear after you release the mouse button). If you're using the Curved Line or Line tool you'll need to double-click when you're done drawing the line. The arrowhead will appear at that time. Again, just look to the bottom of the screen for specific instructions.

If you're not pleased with the arrow, you can choose Edit ➤ Undo, then try again. Like everything else, the arrow is an independent object in the drawing area that you can select and change (or delete) at will, as I'll discuss next.

Selecting and Editing Objects

Once you get a picture, shape, text, or arrow on the screen, chances are you'll need to move it, size it, and make other corrections and refinements. The first step to doing so is to *select* the object you want to change or delete.

 To select objects, first click the Select tool (shown at left). Then use any of the selection techniques listed below to select the object or objects you want. (As you select objects, square sizing handles will appear around them.)

- **To select one object,** click it.
- **To select one or more adjacent objects,** drag a frame around the object or objects you want to work with.
- **To select multiple objects one at a time,** hold down the Ctrl key while clicking each item you want to work with.
- **To treat all objects as a single unit,** choose Edit ➤ Select ➤ All.
- **To deselect all selected objects,** click in an empty area of the drawing.
- **To deselect one object in a selected group,** hold down the Ctrl key and click on that object, or Ctrl+click the *unfilled* sizing handle for the object you want to deselect.

NOTE A single clip art file might consist of dozens of tiny objects. To work with the entire image at once, choose Edit ➤ Select ➤ All.

Once you've selected an object (or objects), you can do any of the following:

- **To move** the object, put the mouse pointer inside the sizing handles, and drag the object to its new location.
- **To size** the object, drag any one of its sizing handles.
- **To delete** the object, press Del.
- **To change** some attribute of the object, such as the font or fill, choose the appropriate tool or menu commands.

For example, suppose you select a text object. You can then choose Edit ➤ Edit Text (or double-click the object) to change the text. Or choose Text ➤ Font (or press F9) to change the font. Or choose Attributes ➤ Text to change the text attributes.

On the other hand, let's say you select a closed shape. If you then choose a fill color using the Fill Color tool (see Figure 26.6) the object will change to the color you chose. If the object doesn't change color, it may be that it has no fill. To fill an unfilled object, select it and click the Fill On/Off tool, then choose Fill Color.

TIP

You can double-click a text object to edit the text quickly, or double-click a graphics object to reshape it. As an alternative, you can select the object and then choose Edit ➤ Edit ... from the WP Draw menus.

In Other Words...

WP Draw works like most graphics applications. If you're new to graphics applications, the following points will make your work with WP Draw a little easier:

- If you *don't* select an object before choosing a tool and/or menu commands, those selections affect the *next* object you draw.
- If you *do* select an object (or objects) before selecting a tool or menu command, your choices will affect the currently selected object(s) only.

- You must choose the Select tool before you can select an object that's on the screen. If you choose the Select tool immediately after finishing with some other tool, you'll find it easier to switch between creating and editing objects.

- If you make a mistake and need to undo your most recent change, choose Edit ➤ Undo.

- If you're happy with the changes that you've made so far and want to update the document without leaving WP Draw, choose File ➤ Update ....

- If you want to clear all the objects from the drawing area in one quick step, choose File ➤ Clear (or press Ctrl+Shift+F4). Then choose OK to confirm the deletion.

- If you've really made a mess of things and want to abandon all changes that you've made since the last time you updated the drawing, choose File ➤ Exit And Return To ... and then choose No when asked about saving your changes.

You should practice creating, selecting, and editing some shapes, text, and pictures, just to get a feel for how you interact with WP Draw. You'll see that it's easy (and harmless) to explore all the tools, commands, and dialog boxes to see what kinds of images and effects you can create.

Saving a New/Modified Image

When you're finished with your WP Draw masterpiece, follow these steps to return to your document:

1. Choose File ➤ Exit And Return To...from the WP Draw menu bar.

2. If you want to save your current changes, choose Yes. To discard them, choose No.

You'll be returned to your document, and the image will be stored in a Figure box. You can then:

- Move and size the entire box by dragging (as discussed in Chapter 25).

- Change the anchor point, style, border/fill, wrap, size, or any other feature of the graphics box using the standard techniques described in Chapter 25. For example, you can right-click the image and choose a command from the QuickMenu, or you can right-click, choose Feature Bar to turn on the Graphics Box feature bar, and choose additional commands as needed.

- Use the image tools, discussed in Chapter 25, to size and position the image within its frame. Right-click the box and choose Image Tools to display those tools.

- To get back to WP Draw, double-click the picture, or right-click it and choose Activate WP Graphic 2.1 Object.

Arranging Objects

If you have two or more overlapping objects in the WP Draw window and want to put one in front of or behind the other, follow these steps:

1. Click one of the overlapping objects to select it. Or select several objects using Ctrl+click.

2. Choose Arrange from the WP Draw menu bar (or right-click the object), then choose one of the following commands:

    Front Moves the selected object(s) to the foreground.

    Back Moves the selected object to the background.

    Group If several objects are selected, combines those objects into a single object.

    Ungroup "Ungroups" selected objects that you previously combined using Group.

    Flip Left/Right Rotates the selected object(s) horizontally.

    Flip Top/Bottom Rotates the selected object(s) vertically.

Rotating Objects

To rotate one or more objects:

1. Use the Select tool in WP Draw to select the object(s) you want to rotate.

2. Choose <u>E</u>dit ➤ R<u>o</u>tate (or right-click the object and choose Rotate). Rotation handles appear around the object, as in the example below.

3. Drag any corner handle in any direction to rotate the object about its axis. To rotate in 45-degree increments, hold down the Shift key while dragging. To rotate a specific amount, right-click a corner handle, type in the angle you want (in degrees), and choose OK. To leave a copy of the unrotated image on the screen, hold down the Ctrl key while dragging. To slant the text and give it some perspective, drag one of the handles between the corners to the left, right, up, or down.

T I P

Whenever you're holding down the mouse button and a keyboard key at the same time, you need to release the mouse button *before* you release the keyboard key.

4. When you're done, you can click the Select tool, or some other part of the drawing area, to remove the rotation handles.

Special Effects

Applying special effects is simple and can actually be fun. Figure 26.9 illustrates some special effects you can apply to text and graphics in WP Draw.

1. In WP Draw, select the object(s) you want to apply the special effect to.

2. Choose <u>A</u>ttributes from the WP Draw menu bar, then choose one of the commands described below.

<u>C</u>olor   Lets you choose colors for the fill foreground, fill background, lines, or text.

<u>L</u>ine   Lets you assign attributes to text or graphic lines (or both), including a line color, width, arrowhead, and style.

<u>F</u>ill   Lets you change the fill type, color, and pattern for selected text, graphics, or both.

<u>T</u>ext   Lets you choose fill type, and outline color and width, for text only.

FIGURE 26.9

Examples of special effects applied to text in WP Draw

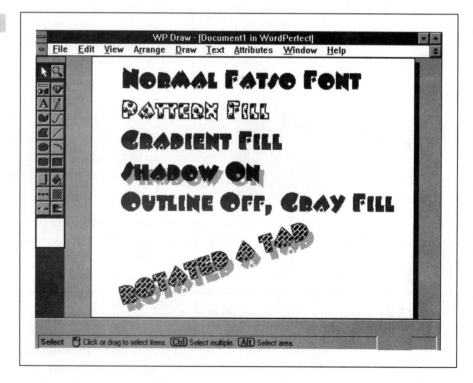

Shadow   Lets you turn shadowing and transparency on or off, and lets you choose a shadow color and offset.

Invert   Reverses the colors of the object.

Curving Text in WP Draw

You can use WP Draw to curve text to any shape in your drawing area. You can display the shape that the text is contoured to, as in the top half of Figure 26.10. Or, you can hide that graphic shape, as in the bottom half of that figure.

T I P   You can also contour text from your document around a graphic image. See "Wrapping Text around a Box" in Chapter 25 for details.

FIGURE 26.10

Curved text shown with, and without, the graphic shape that the text is contoured to

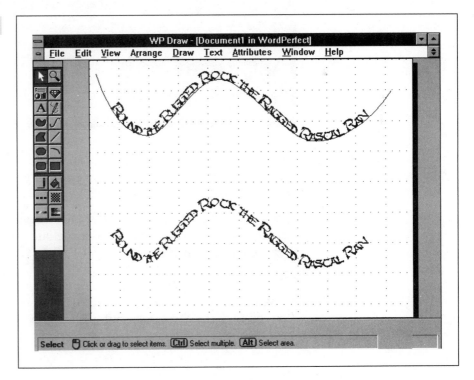

To contour text to a shape in WP Draw:

1. In WP Draw, use the Text tool to create the text you want to curve. (Choose the appropriate font, size, and so forth first, as described earlier in this chapter.)

2. Next, use any one of the drawing tools, such as Ellipse or Curved Line, to draw the shape that you want the text to follow.

3. Select the shape you just drew by clicking on the Select tool in the tool palette, then clicking on the shape.

4. Hold down the Ctrl key and click the text you want to curve, so that both the text and the shape are selected.

5. Choose Arrange ➤ Effects ➤ Contour Text, or click the Contour button in the WP Draw button bar. You'll see a dialog box like this:

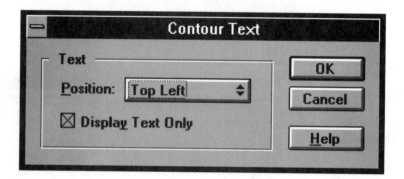

6. From the Position pop-up list, choose how you want to align the text with the shape.

7. You can use the Display Text Only check box to decide whether to display just the curved text, or both the curved text and the object that the text is contoured to.

8. Choose OK.

9. If you don't like the result, choose Arrange ➤ Effects ➤ Straighten Text, or click the Straighten button in the WP Draw button bar, to uncurve the text. Then try again starting at step 5.

N O T E Chapter 28 explains how to use the TextArt feature, which offers many quick and easy ways to add special effects to text.

For More Information

What you've learned in this chapter should be sufficient to get you started with Chart and Draw. You'll discover a lot more as you experiment on your own. If you need more information, you can:

- Choose Help or press Shift+F1 anytime you're in WP Draw.
- Or refer to the *WP Draw User's Manual* that came with your Word-Perfect for Windows program.

In the next chapter we're going to look at still more ways to control the appearance of your document, using WordPerfect's typesetting features.

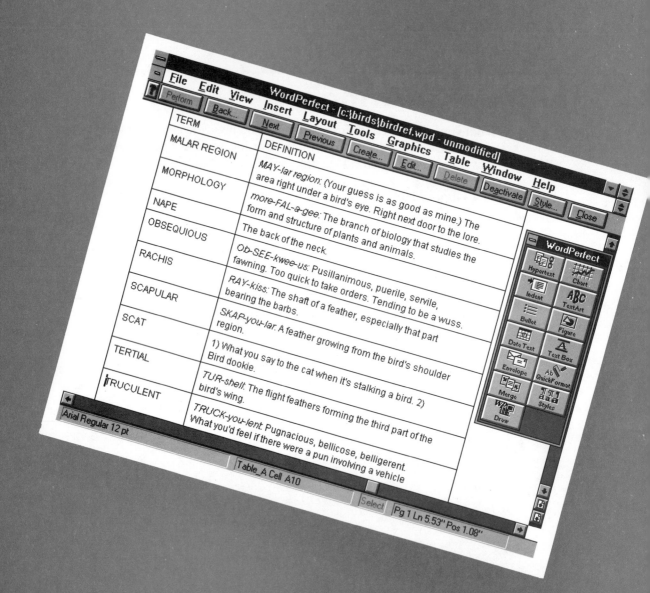

WordPerfect - [c:\birds\birdref.wpd - unmodified]

File **Edit** **View** **Insert** **Layout** **Tools** **Graphics** **Table** **Window** **Help**

Perform Back... Next Previous Create... Edit... Delete Deactivate Style... Close

TERM	DEFINITION
MALAR REGION	*MAY-lar region:* (Your guess is as good as mine.) The area right under a bird's eye. Right next door to the lore.
MORPHOLOGY	*more-FAL-a-gee:* The branch of biology that studies the form and structure of plants and animals.
NAPE	The back of the neck.
OBSEQUIOUS	*Ob-SEE-kwee-us:* Pusillanimous, puerile, servile, fawning. Too quick to take orders. Tending to be a wuss.
RACHIS	*RAY-kiss:* The shaft of a feather, especially that part bearing the barbs.
SCAPULAR	*SKAP-you-lar:* A feather growing from the bird's shoulder region.
SCAT	1) What you say to the cat when it's stalking a bird. 2) Bird dookie.
TERTIAL	*TUR-shell:* The flight feathers forming the third part of the bird's wing.
TRUCULENT	*TRUCK-you-lent:* Pugnacious, bellicose, belligerent. What you'd feel if there were a pun involving a vehicle

Arial Regular 12 pt

Table_A Cell A10

Select Pg 1 Ln 5.53" Pos 1.08"

WordPerfect

Hypertext Chart Indent ABC TextArt Bullet Figure Date Text Text Box Envelope Ab QuickFormat Merge Styles Draw

CHAPTER

27

Working in Columns

fast **TRACK**

To change or refine your columns

905

move the cursor just to the right of the [Col Def] code that defines the columns, or to wherever you want the changes to take place. Choose Layout ➤ Columns ➤ Define. Make your selections from the Columns dialog box, and choose OK.

To put a border around, or separator lines between, columns

906

move the cursor just to the right of the [Col Def] code, or to the page where you want the lines to begin. Choose Layout ➤ Columns ➤ Border/Fill. Design your borders and fill using the options presented, as well as the Customize Style button. Then choose OK as needed to work your way back to the document.

To define parallel columns

911

choose Layout ➤ Columns ➤ Define. Specify how many columns you want, the type of column (Parallel or Parallel w/Block Protect), and other options as appropriate. Choose OK when you're done.

To start a new column

913

while you're typing in parallel columns, press Ctrl+↵.

COLUMNS make a document more appealing because people prefer to read across short lines rather than across long ones. That's one of the reasons why newspapers, newsletters, and magazines use columns so often.

Newspaper Columns

Newspaper columns (also called *snaking columns*) organize your text like the text in a newspaper: Text runs down the leftmost column to the bottom of the page, wraps to the top of the next column, continues to the bottom of the page, and then wraps either to the next column or, if it has filled the last column on the page, to the leftmost column on the next page. Figure 27.1 shows a sample document with three newspaper-style columns.

Quick and Easy Columns

The quick and easy way to create newspaper-style columns, if you're using a mouse, is as follows:

1. If you've already typed the text that you want to put into columns, move the cursor to where you want to begin the columns. Otherwise, just move the cursor to where you plan to start typing text in columns.

2. If the power bar isn't visible, turn it on by choosing View ➤ Power Bar.

FIGURE 27.1

A sample document
with text in three
newspaper-style
columns

DOIN' NEWSPAPER COLUMNS

Newspaper columns like these are easy to set up. To create the columns, move the cursor to wherever you want the columns to begin. If the power bar isn't open, open it by choosing View ▸ Power Bar. Then click the Columns Define button shown below.

Drag the highlight to the number of columns you want, then release the mouse button.

TABLES

If you create a table while typing in columns, the table will automatically be sized within the column, like this:

If you want the table to be larger than that, put it in a graphics box, and position it wherever you want.

GRAPHICS BOXES

Graphics boxes are usually sized to fit within the columns, like this one.

I'M A GRAPHICS BOX ANCHORED TO THE CENTER OF THIS PAGE

If you want the box to be larger than the columns, and want text to flow around the box, anchor the box to the page, and size and position the box accordingly.

For example, to create the graphics box

at the lower right corner of this document, I used the Graphics menu commands to create the box, and anchored it to the right margin at the bottom of the page.

All the text in the columns flows around the box. The box doesn't move as you add or delete text, because it's affixed to the page, rather than to a paragraph or character. (See Chapter 25.)

SEPARATOR LINES

To create separator lines, use Layout ▸ Columns ▸ Border/Fill, as discussed in this chapter.

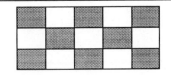

Figure 1. I'm a Figure box that's anchored to the bottom of the page, at the right margin.

3. Move the mouse pointer to the Columns Define button (shown at left) in the power bar, hold down the mouse button, and drag the highlight bar to select the number of columns you want.

4. Release the mouse button after highlighting your choice.

Any text below the cursor position will be formatted into however many columns you specified in step 3.

Defining Newspaper Columns without a Mouse

Instead of using the mouse and power bar, you can follow these steps to define your columns:

1. Move the cursor to where you want the columns to start.

2. Choose <u>L</u>ayout ➤ <u>C</u>olumns ➤ <u>D</u>efine. You'll see the Columns dialog box.

TIP To open the Columns dialog box quickly, double-click the Columns Define button in the power bar.

3. In the spin box next to <u>C</u>olumns, type or choose the number of columns you want (for example, **2** for two columns).

4. Under Type, choose the type of columns you want (<u>N</u>ewspaper or <u>B</u>alanced Newspaper). The sample page in the dialog box shows how a page will look with those columns.

5. Choose OK to return to your document.

Hidden Column Code

Regardless of which method you use to create a column, WordPerfect inserts a hidden [Col Def] code at the cursor position. All text *beyond* that code will be formatted into equal-width columns. Any paragraph-anchored boxes that are past the [Col Def] code will also be resized, if necessary, to fit within the columns.

Getting Around in Columns

Once you've defined your columns, you can type and edit normally. You can move the cursor to any place in your text simply by clicking wherever you want to make changes. In addition, you can use Alt+→ and Alt+← (on enhanced keyboards) to move the cursor across columns, and

Alt+Home and Alt+End to move the cursor to the top or bottom of the current column. You can also use Go To (Ctrl+G) to move the cursor within and between columns.

Forcing Text to Another Column

Naturally, WordPerfect will start a new column automatically when the current column is filled. However, you can force text from one column over to the next (or from the end of the last column on a page to the first column on the next page). To force text to another column, move the cursor to where you want to break to another column. Then insert a hard page break (press Ctrl+↵). Any text beyond the cursor will move to the next column, or the next page if the cursor is in the last column.

Deleting Columns

If you change your mind about the number or appearance of columns, the easiest way to "undo" the columns is by deleting the [Col Def] code in Reveal Codes. Edit ➤ Undo will also work if you use it immediately after creating the columns.

If you forced text to another column with Ctrl+↵ and now want to bring that text back to the previous column, turn on Reveal Codes, and then delete the [HCol] code that's forcing text to the next column.

Changing Newspaper Columns

By default, WordPerfect puts about half an inch of space between each column, and it doesn't place any borders around the columns. You can change all that, as well as the number of columns.

Changing Columns Interactively

You can change the width, gutter (the white space between columns), and other features of columns simply by dragging the markers on the ruler bar:

1. If the ruler bar isn't visible, choose View ➤ Ruler Bar or press Alt+Shift+F3.

2. As long as the cursor is within columns, you'll see the columns and gutter represented just above the numbers in the ruler bar, as in the example below.

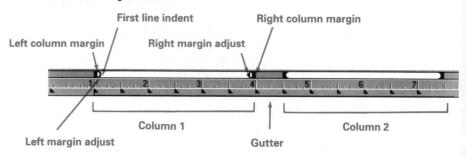

3. Make your changes as follows:

- **To change the first line indent**, left margin adjust, or right margin adjust, position the cursor where you want the change to take effect. Then drag the appropriate marker to a new position.

- **To change the location of the gutter**, drag the gray gutter space across the ruler bar.

- **To change the column margins** (which also will change the gutter width), drag the appropriate marker to a new position.

As you drag, vertical ruler guides will indicate the current position of the item you're changing. In addition, the right side of the status bar will show the item you're changing and its current position (for example, *Left Column Margin: 4.75"*). See Chapter 5 for more information about changing margins and indents.

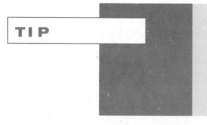

TIP

To turn the ruler bar guides on or off, right-click the ruler bar, and choose Preferences. Then, to turn the ruler guides on, select Show Ruler Bar Guides; to turn the ruler guides off, deselect Show Ruler Bar Guides. Choose OK when you're done.

If you don't like your changes, you can choose Edit ➤ Undo, as usual, to undo your most recent change. Or, if you dragged a marker that inserts a code, move the cursor to where you changed the columns, turn on Reveal Codes, and delete the [First Ln Ind], [Lft Mar Adj], and [Right Mar Adj] codes as appropriate. If you changed a width or a gutter location, you can use the method described in the next section to make refinements.

Sizing Columns Precisely

If the mouse and ruler bar techniques don't give you the exact column measurements you want, follow these steps:

1. Move the cursor back to where you first created the columns (just to the right of the existing [Col Def] code is ideal).

2. Choose Layout ➤ Columns ➤ Define, or double-click the [Col Def] code in Reveal Codes. You'll see a dialog box like the one shown in Figure 27.2.

FIGURE 27.2

The Columns dialog box lets you define or change columns. Use Layout ➤ Columns ➤ Define to get here.

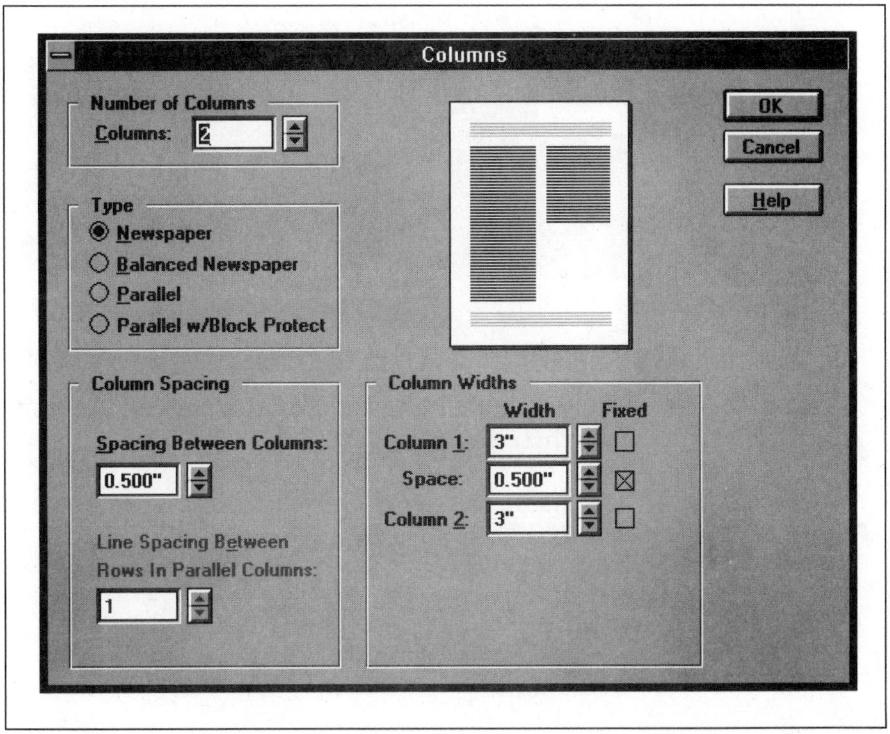

3. Make your changes from the options described below:

Columns   Use this spin box to define how many columns you want (up to 24).

Type   Lets you choose the type of columns: Newspaper, Balanced Newspaper (like newspaper, but with the columns adjusted to be equal in length; see Figure 27.3), Parallel, and Parallel with Block Protect (discussed later in this chapter).

Spacing Between Columns   Lets you enter the width of the gutter. For example, entering .25″ puts a quarter inch of space between the columns.

Column Widths   Lets you set the width and space between the columns individually. Choosing Fixed for a column or gutter ensures that its size won't change when you change the widths of other columns.

4. Choose OK after defining your columns to return to the document.

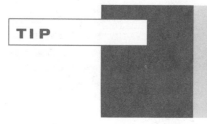

TIP

If WordPerfect ignores your column change, it's probably because the original [Col Def] code is canceling out the new one. Delete that old [Col Def] code. (You won't have to worry about this if you followed the advice in step 1 above.)

Customizing the Column Borders

You can easily place borders around, and shading within, columnar text with these steps:

1. Move the cursor into the columns, at whatever point you want borders and shading to begin.

FIGURE 27.3

A comparison of Balanced Newspaper, Newspaper, and "no" columns

Balanced Newspaper Columns

I chose Balanced Newspaper in the Columns dialog box, so that WordPerfect would make each column (roughly) the same height.

Notice that WordPerfect can't always make the columns the *exact* same height (as in this example). If the columns have an unequal number of lines, or some differences exist in font size within the columns, it might be impossible to align the lines of text in each column along the same baseline. But WordPerfect does as good a job as you could do manually.

At the end of this passage, I turned columns off using Layout ▸ Columns ▸ Off (or the Columns Off command on the Columns Define button of the power bar), before typing the text below.

No Columns

Now that I've turned the columns off (using Layout ▸ Columns ▸ Off), the text I type is back to normal. You can turn columns on and off at any time in your document. And you can use any variety of columns you wish.

Newspaper Columns

Before typing this text, I turned columns back on, but chose Newspaper instead of Balanced Newspaper columns. Here WordPerfect makes no attempt to equalize the height of the columns.

The text in Newspaper columns stays in one column until it the current column fills up and WordPerfect needs to start a new one. (I *could* force text to the next column by pressing Ctrl+↵ at the break.)

Now you can see the effects of filling up the first column as I blather along until I've typed enough text to start the next column. See?

2. Choose Layout ➤ Columns ➤ Border/Fill. You'll see the Column Border dialog box shown below:

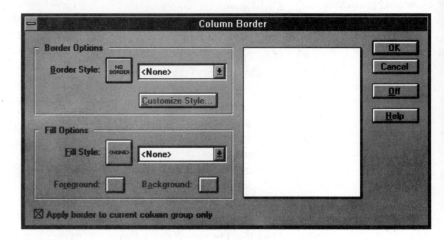

3. Choose options from the Border Options and Fill Options buttons or drop-down lists. You'll definitely want to give the following Border Options a try:

- **To place a vertical separator line between columns,** as shown in Figure 27.1, choose *Column Between* from the Border Style drop-down list.
- **To place lines around all sides of the columns and between columns,** choose *Column All* from the Border Style drop-down list.

TIP

To preview the effects of choosing Border Options or Fill Options, click on one of the drop-down lists next to the Border Style or Fill Style buttons. Then use your arrow keys (not the mouse) to scroll through the options. The sample page and the buttons in the dialog box will reflect the border style or fill style you've highlighted.

4. If you wish, you can choose a <u>B</u>order Style (other than <None>) and then choose <u>C</u>ustomize Style. This option lets you choose which sides to modify and to customize the line style, spacing inside and outside the columns, and border color. You can also use this option to add drop shadows to the columns. Choose OK when you're done customizing the style.

5. If you want the border settings to apply to the current group of columns only, select Apply Border To Current Column Group Only. To apply the settings to *all* borders below the cursor position, even if you turn columns off and back on again later in the document, deselect this option.

6. Choose OK to return to the document window.

Hiding Separator Lines behind Graphics Boxes

If you tried to reproduce the example in Figure 27.1, the vertical separator lines between the columns may have printed right through the graphics boxes. What a nuisance! Fortunately, this problem is easy to fix. The trick is to set the fill for the graphics box to something other than <None>. If you wish, you can also pick a different foreground color for the fill.

To prevent separator lines from printing through your page-anchored graphics boxes, follow these steps:

1. Right-click the graphics box you want to fill, then choose <u>B</u>order/Fill from the QuickMenu.

2. Select a fill style from the drop-down list next to the <u>F</u>ill Style button. I chose *10% Fill* in my example.

3. If you wish, change the Fo<u>r</u>eground color. I chose White for my example.

4. Choose OK.

The next time you print your document, the vertical lines won't print through any graphics boxes that you filled as described above. Instead, they'll stop at the top edge of the graphics box, and start again at the bottom edge of the box.

TIP In the graphics box at the lower-right corner of Figure 27.1, I moved the caption to *inside* the box. This prevents the vertical separator lines from printing through the caption.

Turning Off Newspaper Columns

To stop typing in columns and go back to the normal page format, follow the steps below:

1. Move the cursor to where you want to end the columns.

2. Choose Layout ➤ Columns ➤ Off, or select Columns Off from the Columns Define button in the power bar.

WordPerfect inserts a [Col Def:Off] code at the cursor position. Any text that you type below the cursor will not be put into columns. To reinstate the same columns later in the document, just choose Layout ➤ Columns ➤ Define, then choose OK. WordPerfect will remember your previous column settings.

Fixing Uneven Column Tops

If you create newspaper style columns and discover that the left column seems to start a little lower than the right column, it's probably because there's one or more [HRt] codes just after the [Col Def] code that turns on the columns. In Reveal Codes, you can delete the extra [HRt] codes next to or below the [Col Def] code to move that column up. Then, if you want to move all the columns down, move the cursor to the left of the [Col Def] code, and press ↵ as many times as necessary.

In other words, [HRt] codes above the [Col Def] code produce blank lines across the entire page. [HRt] codes below the [Col Def] code produce blank lines across the current column only. It all makes sense when you think about it.

Parallel Columns

In the olden (and less golden) days of WordPerfect, parallel columns were the way to go when you wanted to type text in a columnar format. Now, when you're working with a page or less of text, the Tables feature (Chapter 7) offers an easier way. But when you need to create a section that's longer than a page and has parallel (as opposed to "snaking") columns, the Parallel Columns feature is still the best alternative.

For instance, you might want to use parallel columns to create a section that includes a wide left margin used for margin notes, icons, or section headings. Figure 27.4 shows an example.

TIP   When using tables, processing slows down dramatically as the table grows. You can use parallel columns instead to create large, multicolumn tables.

Figure 27.4 nicely illustrates the difference between parallel and newspaper columns. Text doesn't "snake" from one column to the next. Instead, text and graphics in the left column align next to text and graphics in the right column. How well they stick together depends on whether or not you use *Block Protect*, which I'll describe in a moment.

Defining Parallel Columns

To set up your parallel columns, follow the steps below:

1. Move the cursor to where you want to begin the columns. This can be at the start of existing text that you want to format into columns, or where you plan to type new text.

2. Choose Layout ➤ Columns ➤ Define, or double-click the Columns Define button in the power bar.

3. Choose the number of columns you want.

FIGURE 27.4

Parallel columns, using the left column for margin notes, icons, and the start of section titles

THOSE WILD N' CRAZY PARALLEL COLUMNS

To create these columns, I put the cursor on this line and chose Layout ▸ Columns ▸ Define. I specified **2** columns and chose Parallel w/Block Protect as the column type. The first column is fixed at 1.5" wide, followed by .25" space, followed by a 4.75" wide column. Before typing this paragraph, I pressed Ctrl+← to move over to this column. At the end of this paragraph, I pressed Ctrl+← to move over to the left column.

Psssst: This is a margin note in the left column, with a User Box paragraph-anchored to the left.

Pressing Ctrl+← after typing the margin note, and resetting the font back to normal, brings me back over to here. Now I can start typing body text again. I pressed Ctrl+← after typing this paragraph to move back over to the left column, so I could put in the next margin icon.

Hot Tip!

After creating that margin icon as a User Box with the words Hot Tip! as a caption at the top of box, I pressed Ctrl+← to once again move over to this column. *The real hot tip here is*, when your document will contain repeating design elements, such as margin notes and margin icons, you should define each of those elements as a style (Chapter 17). That way, if you need to change all of them later, you need only change the style—once.

THIS HEAD HANGS INTO THE LEFT COLUMN

To make the heading above jut out into the left column a little, I just pressed Shift+Tab before typing the head.

4. Next, choose one of these options:

Parallel Text is split into columns, but no effort is made to prevent text in one column from ending up on a different page from text in the other column.

Parallel w/Block Protect Text in columns is protected, so that if text in one column is bumped to the next page, the text directly to the left or right will also be bumped to that page.

5. If you wish, you can choose any of the options described below to customize the appearance of the parallel columns:

- **To adjust the gutter space**, choose Spacing Between Columns and enter a measurement.
- **To set the number of lines between each row**, choose Line Spacing Between Rows In Parallel Columns and set the spacing you want. (The sample page in the dialog box changes to reflect your current choice.)
- **To define the column widths**, choose options from the Column Widths area of the dialog box (as described previously for newspaper-style columns).

6. Choose OK to return to your document.

Initially, any text you start typing will wrap within the first column.

Switching between Parallel Columns

As you're typing text into parallel columns, you can start the next column in the same way you do with newspaper columns. That is,

- To start typing in a new column, press Ctrl+↵.
- To move existing text over to the next column, move the cursor to the beginning of that text. If there are tabs, fonts, or other codes at the start of the paragraph, turn on Reveal Codes (using Alt+F3) and make sure the cursor is in front of any codes that you want to move over to the next column. Press Ctrl+↵.

Once you've typed text into parallel columns, you can use your mouse to click anywhere you want to move the cursor. Or, use the same keys you'd use in newspaper columns (Alt+←, Alt+→, Alt+Home, and Alt+End) to move the cursor from column to column and within columns.

N O T E If you pushed text into another column with Ctrl+↵ and want to bring that text back to the previous column, turn on Reveal Codes, and then delete the [HCol] code that's forcing text to the next column.

Turning Off Parallel Columns

You can turn off parallel columns in the same way you turn off newspaper columns. That is, move the cursor to where you want the columns to end, and choose Layout ➤ Columns ➤ Off. If you change your mind, choose Edit ➤ Undo or, if it's too late for that, drag the new [Col Def] code out of Reveal Codes.

Tables, Graphics, and Columns

When you create a paragraph-anchored graphics box or a table within columns, WordPerfect automatically sizes that object to fit within the column. On the other hand, if you put a graphics box within the columns and anchor the box to the page, the columnar text will automatically flow around the box. If you want columnar text to flow around a table, simply put the table in a graphics box that's anchored to the page.

For example, in Figure 27.1, the graphics box in the center of the page and the table near the lower-right corner of the page are both in graphics boxes that are anchored to the page.

The other graphics—the Columns Define button and man dying of boredom at his desk—are in graphics boxes that are anchored to their neighboring paragraphs. The smaller table isn't in a graphics box at all, and was automatically sized to fit within its column.

In the next chapter, we'll continue our exploration of WordPerfect's desktop publishing capabilities by looking at its typesetting features, and at special effects that you can create.

CHAPTER

28

Typesetting, Text Art, and Fancy Layouts

fast TRACK

To change the leading (amount of white space between lines)   **922**

> choose <u>L</u>ayout ➤ <u>T</u>ypesetting ➤ <u>W</u>ord/Letterspacing. Select the Adjust <u>L</u>eading check box. Then enter the leading adjustment next to Be<u>t</u>ween Lines, as either a positive or negative value in inches (for example, −0.28″) or points (−2p).

To change the line height (distance from baseline to baseline)   **924**

> choose <u>L</u>ayout ➤ Line ➤ <u>H</u>eight, then either <u>A</u>uto (the default) or <u>F</u>ixed followed by a measurement.

To change the horizontal spacing between words and letters   **924**

> choose <u>L</u>ayout ➤ <u>T</u>ypesetting ➤ <u>W</u>ord/Letterspacing. Then choose Normal (the printer manufacturer's suggested spacing), Optimal (WordPerfect Corporation's suggested spacing), or Percent Of Optimal. If you choose Percent of Optimal, then choose a percentage value (for example, 85 for tighter spacing, 115 for looser) or choose Set Pitch and specify a specific pitch.

To activate automatic kerning   **925**

> so that letters are tucked together a little closer, choose <u>L</u>ayout ➤ <u>T</u>ypesetting ➤ <u>W</u>ord/Letterspacing, then select the <u>A</u>utomatic Kerning check box.

**To change the spacing between characters
and words in fully justified text**   928

> choose <u>L</u>ayout ➤ <u>T</u>ypesetting ➤ <u>W</u>ord/Letterspacing, and
> then set the Word Spacing Justification Limits to new com-
> pression and expansion percentages.

**To advance text to a specific place on the page,
or in relation to the cursor position**   930

> choose <u>L</u>ayout ➤ <u>T</u>ypesetting ➤ <u>A</u>dvance, choose your ad-
> vance method and direction, and enter a measurement.

To embellish and shape text using TextArt   932

> choose <u>G</u>raphics ➤ Te<u>x</u>tArt. Type your text, and choose fonts,
> shapes, shadows, and so forth from the options presented. If
> necessary, use the Re<u>d</u>raw button to see the effects of your se-
> lections. When you're finished, choose <u>F</u>ile ➤ E<u>x</u>it & Return
> To WordPerfect.

**To display preprinted forms or other stock
on your screen**   945

> scan the form to a file. Then use that file as a full-sized graphic
> image on the page with Wrap set to No Wrap (Through).

To prepare a document for professional typesetting   949

> follow the typesetter's instructions for choosing a printer
> driver. Then use that printer driver to create the document
> and print the document to disk. The typesetter will need the
> copy of the file that you printed to disk.

MOST WordPerfect documents look like, well… WordPerfect documents. The reason is that most people just accept the default settings for spacing and measurement, and so their documents all have a certain generic look. For instance, Figure 28.1 shows a sample newsletter that looks, I guess you could say, "WordPerfecty."

FIGURE 28.1

A sample newsletter. Using the default standards that WordPerfect offers gives the newsletter a "WordPerfecty" appearance.

Ace In the Hole

The Joys of Writing

As every writer knows, good writing is accurate, succinct, truthful, and above all, a certain number of words. It's gotta be a certain length because 1) Production people have to fit it into some finite space and 2) Readers always peek ahead, and won't read it if they decide that it's too *many* words.

But word count isn't the only way to get text to fit on a page. You can use some of WordPerfect's typesetting features to squeeze a little more, or a little less, text on the page. And you can make the whole thing look less "WordPerfecty" in the process.

In this fake newsletter I changed several of Word-Perfect's default measurements. As you can see,

I'd Rather be Shopping

The Joys of Marriage

So anyway, there I was minding my own business, trying not to overhear the argument between my friend and his wife. Harte, the wife, says with dramatic exasperation: "Can't you see that Muriel is a flirt, that she's trying to steal you away from me, that she wants *my* lifestyle. Men…. You're all so blind, and so protective of these loose women."

David, the husband, twisted the cigar around in his mouth while considering Harte's statement. I thought he was going to agree, confess, or capitulate, to put an end to the argument. Instead, he blew out a big smoke ring and said "No, it's not about men. Women are just too quick to presume guilt."

What few people realize is that by simply changing some of the default settings, you can give your document a much different look and feel. For instance, Figure 28.2 shows the same newsletter as Figure 28.1 with some changes to the line spacing, character spacing, and other default settings.

FIGURE 28.2

The same newsletter shown in Figure 28.1 after changing some default measurements

Ace In the Hole

The Joys of Writing

As every writer knows, good writing is accurate, succinct, truthful, and above all, a certain number of words. It's gotta be a certain length because 1) Production people have to fit it into some finite space and 2) Readers always peek ahead, and won't read it if they decide that it's too *many* words.

But word count isn't the only way to get text to fit on a page. You can use some of WordPerfect's typesetting features to squeeze a little more, or a little less, text on the page. And you can make the whole thing look less "WordPerfecty" in the process.

In this fake newsletter I changed several of WordPerfect's default measurements. As you can see, there's much less white space, and more text.

Look better? I don't know. But it looks *different.* The thing is, you're not stuck with having all your WordPerfect documents look like WordPerfect documents. Play around. You can always change your mind and fix it later.

I'd Rather be Shopping

The Joys of Marriage

So anyway, there I was minding my own business, trying not to overhear the argument between my friend and his wife. Harte, the wife, says with dramatic exasperation: "Can't you see that Muriel is a flirt, that she's trying to steal you away from me, that she wants *my* lifestyle. Men.... You're all so blind, and so protective of these loose women."

David, the husband, twisted the cigar around in his mouth while considering Harte's statement. I thought he was going to agree, confess, or capitulate, to put an end to the argument. Instead, he blew out a big smoke ring and said "No, it's not about men. Women are just too quick to presume guilt."

Well, let me tell you, Harte wasn't about to buy that argument. And the scene that followed was not a pretty one. But since this little passage is entirely fictitious, and has absolutely nothing to do with WordPerfect typesetting features, I'll spare you the gory details.

The second example has a heavier look to it because there's less white space within the text. And as a matter of fact it is heavier (or denser), in the sense that the lines, letters, and words are packed tighter on the page. That's because:

- I removed two points of leading between lines, leaving less space between each printed line.

- I reduced the amount of space between characters.

- I altered the word spacing and letter spacing to tighten up text within each line.

- I used *kerning* to tighten up the gap between letters.

TIP

The text in Figure 28.2 uses Full justification (Chapter 5) as well as hyphenation (Chapter 16), to give a smooth right margin within columns, with minimal gaps between words and letters.

Now this might seem like a bit of overkill. But if you need to produce a flawlessly formatted newsletter, advertisement, or other document, you'll want to know how to use these typesetting features.

Perfecting Your Type

WordPerfect's typesetting features are all geared toward one goal—getting *exact* control of the placement of text on the page. The features are mostly bunched together on the menus under Layout ➤ Typesetting. But a word of caution before we proceed. Not all printers and fonts are created equal. There are few "absolutes" in this realm—sometimes you just have to play around and experiment to see how things will work with your current font and printer.

Changing the Space between Lines (Leading)

Leading (pronounced "ledding") is the amount of space between two printed lines. The more leading, the larger the white gap between one printed line and the next.

By default, WordPerfect adds two points of leading to proportionally spaced fonts and no leading to monospaced fonts. If you want to squeeze a little more text onto the page, you can always remove a little leading. Likewise, if you want to expand the text to fill out the page better, you can increase the leading a little. Here's how:

1. Move the cursor to wherever you want to start the new leading measurement, or select a block of text to change.

2. Choose Layout ➤ Typesetting ➤ Word/Letterspacing. You'll be taken to the dialog box shown in Figure 28.3.

3. Select (check) the Adjust Leading check box. Then, use the spin box next to Between Lines to enter a measurement: a positive number to increase the leading, or a negative number to decrease it. You can follow your entry with a **p** for points. For example, entering **-2p** would remove two points of leading. (Your entry will be converted to the default unit of measure—usually inches—automatically.)

4. Choose OK to return to your document.

FIGURE 28.3

The Word Spacing And Letterspacing dialog box lets you control spacing between letters, lines, and words. Choose Layout ➤ Typesetting ➤ Word/Letterspacing to get here.

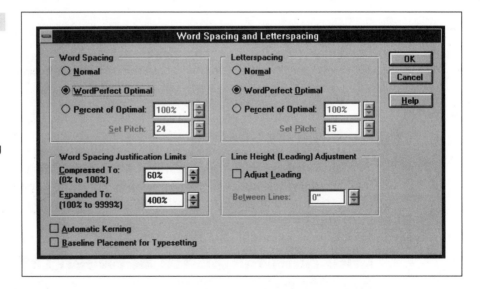

WordPerfect adds a [Leading Adj] code, and all subsequent text (or selected text) is reformatted accordingly.

Changing the Line Height

Another way to change the amount of space between lines is to switch to a fixed line height. Normally, WordPerfect determines the height of a line automatically based on the tallest font used in the line. But if you want to determine your own fixed line height, follow these steps:

1. Move the cursor to where you want to start the new line height, or select a block of text to change.

2. Choose Layout ➤ Line ➤ Height.

3. Choose Auto if you want WordPerfect to calculate the line height automatically (as it usually does). Or, choose Fixed, press Tab, and then enter a measurement in inches (for example, **.25**) or points (**12p**).

4. Choose OK.

TIP If you want to increase the spacing between lines, it's probably easiest to use Layout ➤ Line ➤ Spacing, which is discussed in Chapter 5.

WordPerfect will insert a [Ln Height] code (or a pair of [Ln Height] codes) into your document. If you did not select text, all text below the inserted [Ln Height] code will be affected by the change. If you want subsequent text to be printed normally, move the cursor to where you want to resume normal printing. Then repeat the steps to switch back to Auto line height.

Changing the Space between Letters and Words

WordPerfect also puts a little space between each printed character and between each printed word. There are no standards here—different fonts use different spacing. But you can tighten or loosen the space between characters, between words, or both, to squeeze more (or less) text across each line. Here's how:

1. Put the cursor wherever you want the change to take effect, or select the block of text you want to change.

2. Choose Layout ➤ Typesetting ➤ Word/Letterspacing.

3. To change the spacing between words, choose one of the following options under Word Spacing. If you want to change the spacing between characters, choose one of the same three options under Letterspacing:

> **Normal**   Uses the spacing the printer manufacturer thinks is best.
>
> **WordPerfect Optimal**   Uses the spacing that WordPerfect Corporation thinks is best (this is the default, and may be the same as Normal).
>
> **Percent of Optimal**   Use Percent Of Optimal to specify settings for tightening or loosening the text. After selecting this option, you can press Tab once and specify the spacing as a percent of the optimal setting, or press Tab twice and specify the spacing as a **Set Pitch**, in characters per inch. For example, if you choose Percent Of Optimal, press Tab, and type **75** (for 75%), the text will be 25% tighter than optimal. If you type **125** (for 125%), the text will be 25% looser than optimal.

4. Choose OK.

Kerning

Kerning provides another way to tighten up the space between letters. When kerning is on, small letters are "tucked under" large letters as space permits. Automatic kerning affects certain predefined letter pairs (depending on the font). It's especially apparent with large headline-style text. Figure 28.4 shows an example. In the first line the word *TuTu* is not kerned, and in the second it is kerned. Notice how the lowercase *u* tucks under each uppercase *T*. The third and fourth lines combine automatic kerning with other features that I'll describe a bit later.

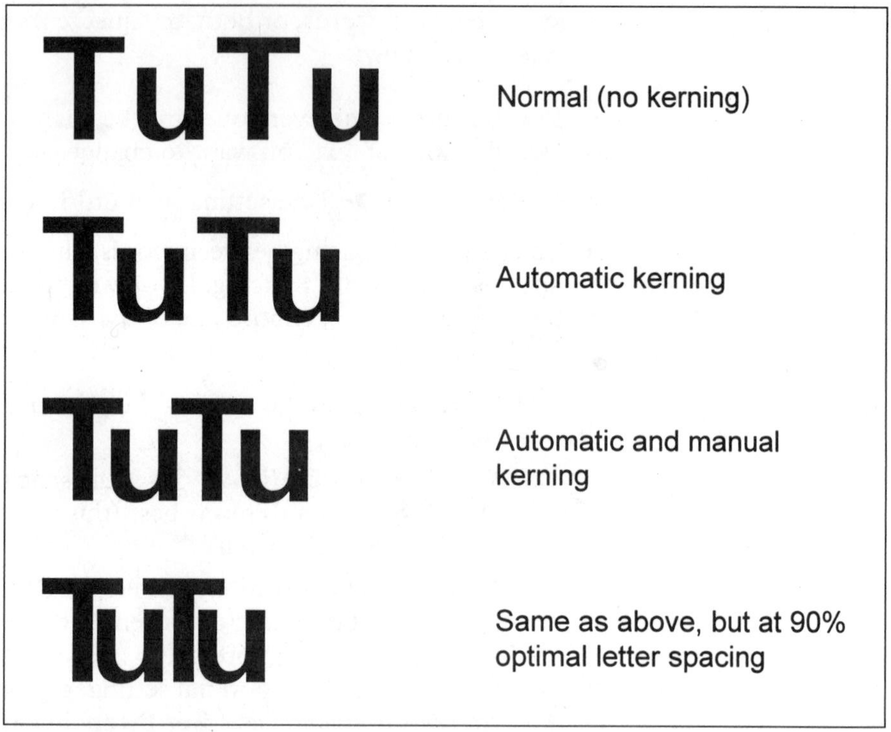

FIGURE 28.4

Examples of automatic kerning, manual kerning (using Advance), and both automatic and manual kerning combined with reduced letter spacing

TuTu — Normal (no kerning)

TuTu — Automatic kerning

TuTu — Automatic and manual kerning

TuTu — Same as above, but at 90% optimal letter spacing

To use automatic kerning, follow the steps below:

1. Move the cursor to where you want to activate kerning. Or, if you want to kern a portion of your text, select that text.

2. Choose Layout ➤ Typesetting ➤ Word/Letterspacing.

3. To turn kerning on, select (check) Automatic Kerning. To turn it off, deselect Automatic Kerning so the check box is cleared.

4. Choose OK.

WordPerfect inserts a [Kern:On] code where kerning starts and, if you selected text in step 1, a [Kern:Off] code where kerning ends. You can also end kerning at any point in your document by moving the cursor there and repeating the steps above, deselecting Automatic Kerning in step 3.

Manual Kerning

Notice that Figure 28.4 also shows an example of manual kerning, where I moved the second uppercase *T* 12 points to the left, thereby kerning that *T* over the first lowercase *u*. (Automatic kerning isn't quite so fancy.) To manually kern a pair of letters:

1. Put the cursor between the two letters that you want to change the gap between.

2. Choose <u>L</u>ayout ➤ <u>T</u>ypesetting ➤ <u>M</u>anual Kerning. You'll be taken to this dialog box:

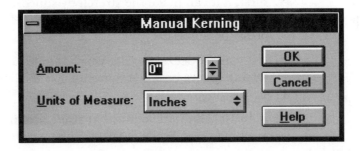

3. Optionally, choose an option from the <u>U</u>nits Of Measure pop-up list button.

4. Use the spin box next to <u>A</u>mount to increase or decrease the space between the two letters. (If the text you're kerning is underneath the dialog box, drag the dialog box by its title bar, to move it out of the way.)

5. Choose OK.

WordPerfect inserts a [HAdv:...] code (Horizontal Advance) that moves the text accordingly. If you change your mind about manual kerning, you can choose <u>E</u>dit ➤ <u>U</u>ndo, or drag the [HAdv] code off the Reveal Codes screen.

Just to show you the possibilities, the fourth *TuTu* in Figure 28.4 illustrates what happens after reducing the letter spacing to 90% Of Optimal (*after* kerning the letters manually).

Changing the Justification Limits

Though it sounds like a fancy legal term for a plea bargain, the *justification limits* really determine how much space WordPerfect puts between individual letters when fully justifying text across the margins. (To fully justify text, choose Layout ➤ Justification ➤ Full, or Layout ➤ Justification ➤ All, or equivalent justification in table cells.) Justification limits have no effect on left-justified, centered, or flush-right text.

When full justification is on, and WordPerfect is about to display a line that doesn't reach over to the right margin (with normal spacing), it must decide where to insert spaces to make the stretch. Here's how it works.

1. First, if it can make the stretch by squeezing one more word from the next line onto the current line, it does so (within the "compression limits").

2. If it can't squeeze another word onto the current line, it starts inserting spaces between the words on the line (up to the "expansion limits").

3. If it still cannot make the text stretch to the right margin after reaching those limits, it spaces the text evenly between characters.

By default, the most WordPerfect will compress text is to 60% of the current spacing. And the farthest it will expand text between words is 400% (four times the number of spaces between each word). After that, it starts spacing characters. Here's how you can change that:

1. Move the cursor to where you want to change the justification limits, or select a block of text. (Remember that this feature won't do anything unless the text is fully justified now or you add full justification to the text later.)

2. Choose Layout ➤ Typesetting ➤ Word/Letterspacing.

3. Choose a setting for Compressed To and Expanded To as described just below.

   - If you want to squeeze text a little tighter when necessary, *decrease* the Compressed To percentage.

   - If you don't want to compress text quite so much, *increase* the Compressed To percentage (for example, 100% means it can't get any tighter than its current tightness).

- If you want to put *more* space between words, and less space between letters when necessary, *increase* the Expanded To percentage (anything over 1000% is considered unlimited).

- If you want to put *less* space between words, and put more of the spacing between characters (to even out the spacing across the line), decrease the Expanded To percentage (100% would expand words and characters roughly the same).

4. Choose OK.

There are actually situations where these settings can be useful. For an example of compression, take a look back at Figure 28.2, where all the body text is fully justified within the columns. If I were to *decrease* the Compressed To percentage, WordPerfect might be able to squeeze even more text across certain lines. Then there would be even more room on the page, and the document would have an even heavier appearance. If I didn't allow WordPerfect to compress at all (set Compressed To to 100%), there would probably be more white space across some lines, and thus less text and a less heavy appearance.

Figure 28.5 shows a two-word title, *Make Spread*, with the justification set to All 2" left and right between margins. In the top example, I've minimized the Expanded To justification limit to 100%. Since WordPerfect can't stick all the space between the two words, it spreads the space throughout all the characters. In the bottom example, I maximized the Expanded To limit to 9999 (unlimited). Therefore, WordPerfect can (and does) put *all* the required extra spacing between the words only.

FIGURE 28.5

The top line has an Expanded To limit of 100%, so much of the spacing is between characters. The bottom line allows unlimited spacing between words.

Make Spread
Make   Spread

Baseline for Typesetters

WordPerfect also has a feature called *Baseline Placement For Typesetters*. I suppose this one is self-explanatory enough that I can skip it. (Just kidding.) But if you're not a typesetter yourself, *you* might want to skip to the next section.

A typesetter would probably notice that when you use a feature such as Advance to put text at a specific place on the page in relation to the edges of the page, the *baseline* of that text is roughly at the specified position—but as we know, "roughly" isn't always good enough.

If you need to ensure that the baseline of the text is precisely at the specified position, you need to

1. Choose Layout ➤ Typesetting ➤ Word/Letterspacing.

2. Choose Baseline Placement For Typesetters, then choose OK.

3. Switch to a fixed line height (Layout ➤ Line ➤ Height ➤ Fixed), set the line height you want, and choose OK.

Once you've done this, the first baseline on the page becomes the *top margin*, rather than the baseline of the first line of text on the page. Now, when you use a feature like Advance, the *baseline* of the advanced text will be exactly at the measurement you specified.

Positioning Text Exactly

The Advance feature lets you put your text *exactly* where you want it. It's sort of the laser-printing, obsessive-compulsive Word-Perfectionist's dream-come-true. Here's how to use it:

1. Move the cursor to just before the character or phrase that you want to reposition on the page.

2. Choose Layout ➤ Typesetting ➤ Advance. You'll see the Advance dialog box, as in the following example (which I've already filled in).

3. Choose the direction you want to advance the text. You can advance text relative to the cursor or to a specific position on the page.

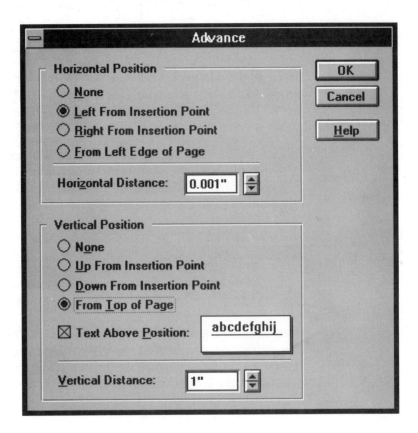

4. Type in the amount to move, either in inches (for example, **.0167**) or in points followed by a *p* (for example, **12p**).

5. You can repeat steps 3 and 4 to advance the text both vertically and horizontally.

6. Choose OK to return to your document.

WordPerfect inserts a code into the document that will tell WordPerfect how far (or where) to advance before displaying the next text.

Note that *all* the text to the right of the cursor is affected by the Advance. If you want to advance a small amount of text in some direction, you need to put the appropriate advance codes in front of the text you want to advance. Then, to get the cursor back to where it was, you need to advance back to the previous position.

For instance, suppose you move the cursor to the top of a page, and choose Layout ➤ Typesetting ➤ Advance ➤ From Left Edge Of Page, and set the Horizontal Distance measurement to 3.5″. Then you choose From Top Of Page, set the Vertical Distance measurement to .25″, and choose OK. Then you type **THIS IS WAY UP HIGH**. That text will be just below the top of the page, near the center of the page (horizontally).

To make any text after that phrase start at the "normal" margins, such as an inch down from the top and from the left edge of the page, you'd first need to put the cursor after that advanced chunk of text. Then use Layout ➤ Typesetting ➤ Advance to move the cursor 1″ from the top and left edges of the page.

TIP   You cannot advance text into a graphics box unless that box's Wrap option is set to No Wrap (Through).

Be aware that even with Advance, you still can't print within that roughly $\frac{1}{4}''$ of white space around the sheet. That dead zone is reserved for the rollers that move the paper through the printer. If the printer *could* print within the dead zone, the rollers would surely smudge the ink. Not good.

Using TextArt

WordPerfect 6 for Windows comes with a program called *TextArt* for adding special effects to your text. Using TextArt is quite easy and straightforward:

1. Move the cursor to about where you want to put the text art, and choose Graphics ➤ TextArt (or click the TextArt button in the WordPerfect button bar). You'll be taken to a dialog box like the example shown in Figure 28.6.

2. In the Enter <u>T</u>ext text box, type the text that you want to stylize (in Figure 28.6, I typed **WordPerfect is Hot!**).

3. Choose a font, justification, color, shape—whatever tickles your fancy.

4. Repeat step 3 until you get exactly the look you want. (In Figure 28.6 I used a Brush Script font, centered the text, and applied a checkered fill, a gray shadow, and a curved shape.)

5. When you're happy with your creation, choose <u>F</u>ile ➤ E<u>x</u>it & Return To WordPerfect. When prompted, choose <u>Y</u>es if you want to save your current changes.

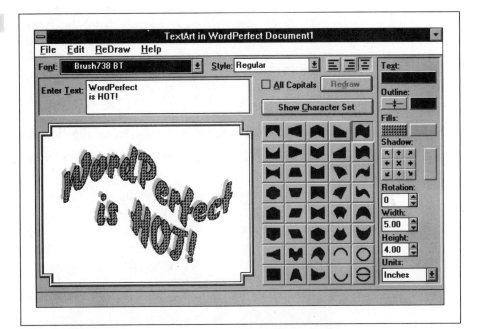

FIGURE 28.6

The TextArt dialog box lets you shape text, add drop shadows, and so forth.

TIP

If you'd like to save your work as you go, choose <u>F</u>ile ➤ <u>U</u>pdate WordPerfect from the TextArt menu bar. Then, when you're ready to return to WordPerfect, choose <u>F</u>ile ➤ E<u>x</u>it & Return To WordPerfect.

The embellished text is placed in a graphics box. You can size and position that box using all the standard techniques described in Chapter 25. If you want to change the graphic in TextArt, simply double-click the graphics box, or right-click the box and choose Edit TextArt Object from the QuickMenu.

N O T E   You can also use WP Draw to curve and embellish text. See "Special Effects" in Chapter 26 for more information.

By default, TextArt redraws the picture each time you make a change. This can be slow! If you want TextArt to redraw the picture only when you tell it to, choose Redraw ➤ Manual from the TextArt menu bar. With this setting, you'll need to click the Redraw button in the dialog box whenever you want to see an updated version of the art. To restore automatic re-draw, choose Redraw ➤ Auto from the TextArt menu bar.

Feel free to experiment and create your own unique designs. As in most Windows applications, if you change your mind after making a change, you can choose Edit ➤ Undo from the TextArt menu bar, or press Ctrl+Z, to undo that change.

T I P   For a quick reminder about how to use a tool or text box in TextArt, move the mouse pointer to the area you're interested in. A description will appear at the bottom of the TextArt dialog box. You can also choose Help from the menu bar. For help on a particular area of the screen, press Shift+F1 and click on the area you're curious about.

Sample Layouts

Now let's take a look at some sample desktop publishing layouts. I'll de-scribe the techniques used to create each one.

Overhead Transparencies, Posters, and Fliers

Creating full-page overhead transparencies, posters, signs, or fliers with WordPerfect is simply a matter of reducing the margins (if appropriate), switching to a landscape paper size (if appropriate), and centering text horizontally and vertically (again, if appropriate). Other than that, it's usually just a matter of using large fonts.

T I P

If you want to print on overhead transparencies, be sure to purchase the kind that will go through your laser printer. Avery makes some, and they're available at many office supply stores.

Figure 28.7 shows a sample flier that has a clip art border around its edge. The procedures used to create this document are summarized in the sections that follow.

FIGURE 28.7

A document with a clip art border all the way around

Graphic Border

The graphic border around the document is just a piece of clip art. Here are the basic steps you'd follow to add such a border to your own document:

1. If you'll be printing sideways (landscape), choose Layout ➤ Page ➤ Paper Size. Choose a paper size (for example, Letter Landscape), then choose Select.

2. Choose Layout ➤ Margins and set all four margins to the size you want. To use the smallest margins possible, enter **0** for each measurement, and WordPerfect will adjust your entries to account for the dead zone on your printer. Choose OK.

3. Choose Graphics ➤ Custom Box ➤ User ➤ OK. Then choose Content from the Graphics Box feature bar, and use the file button next to Filename to retrieve whatever graphic image you want to use as a border. Choose OK to return to your document.

4. Choose Position from the feature bar, then choose Put Box On Current Page (Page Anchor). Set the horizontal position to 0″ from Left Margin, and the vertical position to 0″ from Top Margin. Choose OK.

5. Choose Size from the feature bar, and set both the Width and Height to Full. Then choose OK.

6. Choose Wrap from the feature bar, then choose No Wrap (Through) so you'll be able to type within the border. Choose OK.

7. Choose Close from the feature bar.

Now the graphic border is surrounding the page, but you can type right over or through it.

Watermark

The ocean wave in the middle of the document is a piece of clip art displayed in a watermark. To create such a watermark in your own document:

1. Place the cursor on the page where you want the watermark to appear.

2. Choose Layout ➤ Watermark ➤ Watermark A ➤ Create.

3. Click on Figure in the Watermark feature bar, then choose the drive, directory, and file name of the image that you want to use as the watermark, and choose OK.

4. Once you've inserted the image, choose Close twice from the feature bars to return to normal document editing.

If you don't see the watermark on your screen, try switching to Page (View ➤ Page) or Two Page (View ➤ Two Page) view.

The Text

The rest of the document is simply typed onto the normal editing screen. *Sunset Stretch* is displayed in a font named Crazed, with the Shadow attribute turned on.

Solana Beach is in a graphics User box with Wrap set to No Wrap (Through). I anchored that box to the page, and dragged it into the position shown.

The next three lines are displayed in a font named Chili Pepper Bold, and the last four lines are in Lucida Handwriting font.

Tri-Fold Mailers

Figure 28.8 shows a sample blank tri-fold mailer. Figure 28.9 shows how that layout looks with some text added. In the sections that follow I'll briefly describe the commands I used to create each component of the layout.

The Panels

To create the three panels of the mailer:

1. Starting with a new document window, choose Layout ➤ Page ➤ Paper Size, highlight a landscape paper size (for example, Letter Landscape), then choose Select.

2. Choose Layout ➤ Margins and make all four margins small, such as .35″ each. Choose OK.

3. Choose Layout ➤ Page ➤ Subdivide Page, and set up three columns and one row. Choose OK.

TYPESETTING, TEXT ART, AND FANCY LAYOUTS

FIGURE 28.8

A sample tri-fold
brochure layout (blank)

Your Return Address
can go right
about here

FIGURE 28.9

The sample layout in Figure 28.8 with some text typed in

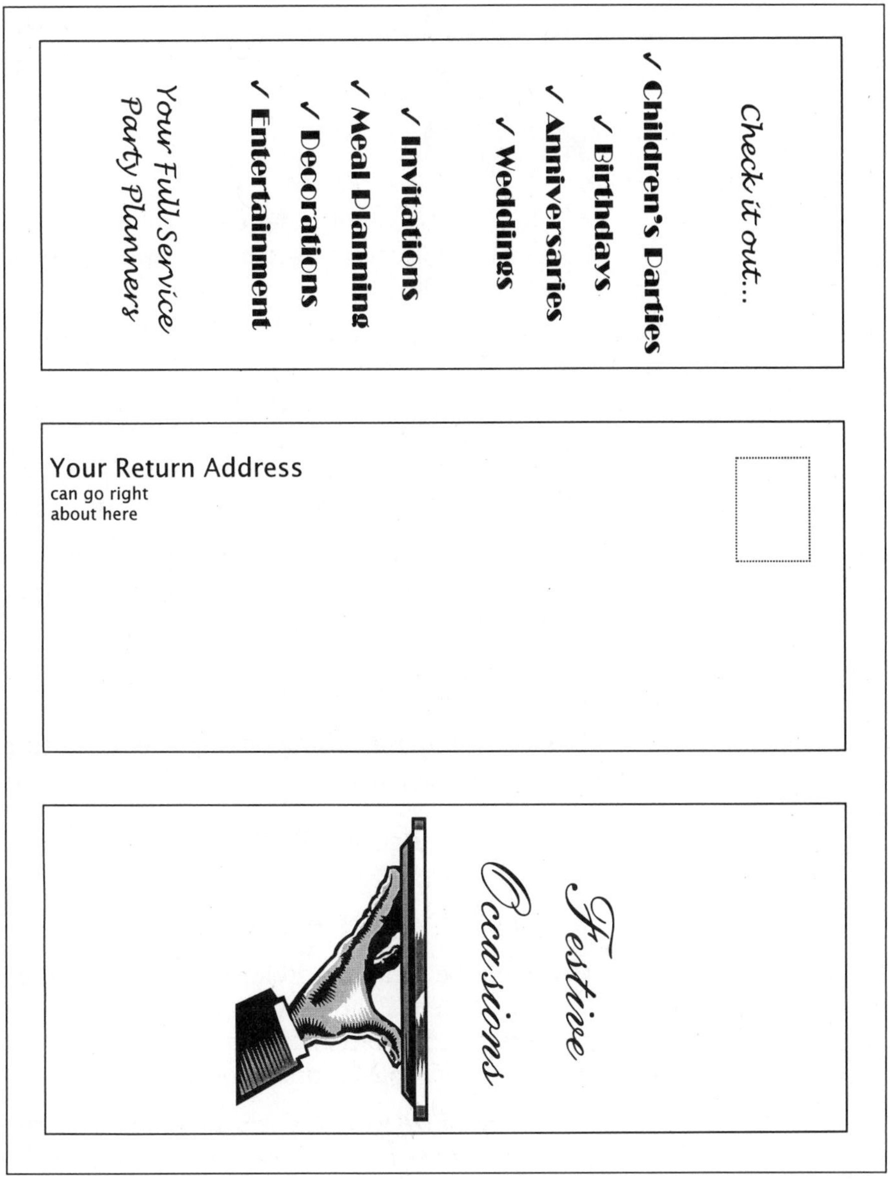

Check it out…

✓ **Children's Parties**

✓ **Birthdays**

✓ **Anniversaries**

✓ **Weddings**

✓ **Invitations**

✓ **Meal Planning**

✓ **Decorations**

✓ **Entertainment**

Your Full Service
Party Planners

Your Return Address
can go right
about here

Festive
Occasions

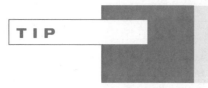

TIP

If you're going to print on preprinted tri-fold paper stock, as discussed near the end of this chapter, you can stop right here.

4. To put a border around each panel, choose <u>L</u>ayout ➤ <u>P</u>age ➤ <u>B</u>order/Fill. Choose a border style and, optionally, a fill style, then choose OK.

5. Press End, then press Ctrl+↵ twice.

After pressing Ctrl+↵ twice in the last step above, you can use the Alt+PgUp and Alt+PgDn keys to move the cursor from one panel to the next. The *Pg* indicator in the status bar actually reflects which panel you're in, rather than which physical page you're on.

If you want to see the panels as they'll be printed, use <u>V</u>iew ➤ <u>P</u>age or <u>V</u>iew ➤ <u>T</u>wo Page. (In Draft view, each panel will initially look like a separate page.)

Postage Stamp Spot

The place where the postage stamp goes is a little graphics box with a dotted line style for the frame. To create it:

1. Switch to Page or Two-Page view, then move the cursor to Page 2 (Pg 2).

2. Choose <u>G</u>raphics ➤ <u>T</u>ext.

3. From the Graphics Box feature bar, choose <u>P</u>osition ➤ <u>P</u>ut Box On Current Page (Page Anchor) and then set the horizontal position to .25″ from Left Margin, and the vertical position to .25″ from the Top Margin. Choose OK.

4. Choose <u>S</u>ize from the feature bar and set the Width to 1″, and the Height to 0.75″. Choose OK.

5. Choose <u>B</u>order/Fill from the feature bar, then choose Dotted from the drop-down list next to <u>B</u>order Style. Choose OK.

6. Choose <u>C</u>lose from the Graphics Box feature bar to return to normal editing.

Return Address

To get the return address in the middle panel, you'll need to put it in a graphics box and rotate the text sideways. Here's how:

1. Leave the cursor on Page 2 (Pg 2), and choose Graphics ➤ Text.

2. From the Graphics Box feature bar, choose Position, and then choose Put Box On Current Page (Page Anchor). Set the Horizontal position to 0.1″ From Left Margin. Set the Vertical position to −0.1″ From Bottom Margin. Choose OK.

3. From the feature bar, choose Content. Choose 90 degrees under Rotate Contents Counterclockwise, then click the Edit button.

4. Type your return address. You can use Layout ➤ Font (F9) to choose fonts before typing if you wish. Choose Close after typing the return address.

5. The text box you just created still needs some more editing, so click on it.

6. From the Graphics Box feature bar, choose Size and set both the width and the height to Size To Content. Choose OK.

7. Next choose Border/Fill from the feature bar and set the Border Style to Spacing Only. Choose OK.

8. Choose Close from the feature bar.

Now you can choose File ➤ Save, and save the layout now using any file name of your choosing. You may also want to print a copy of just the layout now, using File ➤ Print ➤ Print.

Filling It In

Now you can fill in the mailer as you see fit, using fonts, graphics boxes, whatever. Just be sure to keep an eye on the Pg indicator in the status bar to make sure you've positioned the cursor to whatever panel you want to type in, before you start typing.

Any page formatting that you use will be interpreted on a panel-by-panel basis. For example, if you center a graphic or text on the page, the item will be centered within the current panel, not the entire sheet of paper, so long as the cursor is past the [Subdivided Pg] code when you make your menu selections.

Newsletter with Vertical Masthead

There are as many different possible formats for newsletters as there are newsletters. Indeed, people have written entire books on the topic of newsletters. Figure 28.10 shows an especially fancy one (and one that might take some patience to create). It uses quite a few advanced features,

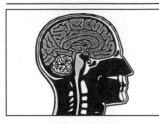

What Makes Us Human?

If you look around a town and a jungle, you'll see one difference between the humans and beasts. All the humans *have* things. None of the beasts do.

Everyone has things, from the lowliest beggar with the clothes on his proverbial back, to the kings and queens with near infinite amounts of stuff.

So ingrained into our being is this concept of ownership that we rarely notice it. For example, you probably didn't even flinch when I attributed "lowness" to the beggar, as though the person with the least stuff naturally *is* the "lower" or "inferior" of the two. We're used to assigning status based on amount of stuff owned.

And speaking of queens, have you noticed how just being the world's major heavy-hitting thing collectors has made the (otherwise powerless) British royals famous! You always see their faces in check-out stand tabloids. (Though I've often wondered if that's just to remind us that we, too, need to "pick up a few more *things*" while we're out.)

Whole countries are based on this thing-collecting thing. America is the envy of the world because it's based on an unspoken rule that says "You're

free to acquire as many *things* as you can in your lifetime. You just can't A)murder or B)deceive (too much) to get them."

For example, you can't walk over and kill your neighbor, then proclaim "all his things are now mine." If that were allowed, the US would have a population of one tough, ruthless dude. And he'd own *everything*.

You can't outright deceive to get things either. Like, you can't trick your neighbor into thinking he's signing an innocent petition, then say "Ha Ha I fooled ya. You just signed over all your earthly possessions to me."

Unfortunately, rules notwithstanding, some people are still just naturally better than others at acquiring things. Over time, those people end up having all the good stuff.

Fortunately, or unfortunately, depending on your own thing-collecting abilities, there is a group out there willing to say "OK, that's enough. You good thing-collectors have too much stuff now. Time to give some back and start over."

That group is called Democrats, and tends to come into power every 10 years or so, after the good thing-collectors have hogged up practically everything. (Apparently, there is no such group in Britain, where the same family has had all the good things for centuries. Maybe that's why our forefathers defected.)

Thing-ownership is so important that we even have legal means of deciding what happens to our things after we're dead. (Heaven forbid they give our ex-stuff to just *anyone*!) Though you may be gone, your will to own things lives on.

including rotated fonts, word and letter spacing, graphics, and graphic lines.

The Vertical Masthead

The first thing to create in this layout is the vertical masthead. Switch to Page view (or Two-Page view) and follow the steps below:

1. Starting with a new document window, choose Layout ➤ Margins. Set the left margin to 1.75", and the other three margins each to .5". Choose OK.

2. Choose Graphics ➤ Text.

3. From the Graphics Box feature bar, choose Position. Set the box placement to Put Box On Current Page (Page Anchor). Set the horizontal position to .5" From Left Edge Of Page, and the vertical position to 0" From Top Margin. Choose OK.

4. Choose Size from the feature bar. Set the Width to about 1.15", and set the Height to Full. Choose OK.

5. Choose Border/Fill from the feature bar, then select a Border Style (I chose Thin Right/Left in my example). Choose OK.

6. Choose Content from the feature bar, set Rotate Contents Counterclockwise to 90 degrees, then click the Edit button.

7. Now you can use Layout ➤ Font to choose a font (I used a Stencil typeface at 62 points). After choosing OK to leave the Font dialog box, choose Layout ➤ Line ➤ Center, and type your text (**Radical Rationalist** in my example).

8. Choose Close from the Text Box feature bar.

The exact size of the vertical masthead will really depend on the font you use within the headline. If the text doesn't fit at all, first try right-clicking the box and choosing Content. Set the Vertical Position to Top. Choose OK. (If you still can't get a decent fit, double-click the graphics box and try a smaller font.)

The Horizontal Headline

To create the horizontal headline, follow these steps:

1. Move past all the existing codes (press Ctrl+End then Ctrl+Home).

2. Use Layout ➤ Font to choose a font for the headline (I used a font named Fonture at 72 points).

3. Choose Layout ➤ Justification ➤ All.

4. Type the horizontal headline (**NEWS FLASH!** in my example).

5. Switch to a smaller font (choose Layout ➤ Font, and choose some 12 point font).

6. Press ↵ to move to the next line.

7. Choose Graphics ➤ Horizontal Line.

8. Press ↵.

9. Choose Layout ➤ Justification ➤ Full.

Now the cursor should be just under the horizontal headline, where you can define your columns.

The Columns

To set up the columns, proceed as follows:

1. Choose Layout ➤ Columns ➤ Define. Set the Spacing Between Columns to .25″, then choose OK.

2. To add a column border, choose Layout ➤ Columns ➤ Border/Fill.

3. From the drop-down list next to Border Style, choose Column Between.

4. Choose OK to return to the document window.

TIP   If the horizontal line under News Flash is too high or low, you can just drag it up or down to whatever position you want.

Now you can save and print the basic layout. To type text into the layout, move the cursor to the bottom (Ctrl+End), or wherever you want to start typing. Then choose your fonts, type your text, add graphics boxes if you like, and so forth.

NOTE The vertical separator line will extend only to the bottom of the current text and graphics in the column. To extend the line to the bottom of a "short" column, switch to Two-Page view (if you wish), move the cursor to the bottom of the column (press Alt+End), and then press ⏎ until the line reaches the bottom margin. If you press ⏎ too many times, and WordPerfect starts a new page, press Backspace until you delete the extra [HRt] codes.

Typing on Preprinted Forms

If you need to print on preprinted forms, you might want to put a picture of that form right on your screen, to make it easier to line up the text you type with the blanks on the form. To do so, you first need to beg, borrow, or rent time on a flatbed scanner, and scan a copy of the preprinted form to a bitmap or other file. While scanning, use your scanning software to size the entire image to the exact size of the form, say, 8.5 by 11 inches. Also, if you plan on printing with a laser printer or other sheet-fed printer, use your scanning software to crop out about $\frac{1}{4}''$ of margin around the form, to compensate for the $\frac{1}{4}''$ or so dead zone around the printed page. Save the scanned image as a bitmap (.bmp) or other WordPerfect-compatible file.

Be sure to keep track of the location and name of the file you scanned (for example, c:\images\taxform.bmp). Then, you can close your scanning program and run WordPerfect for Windows normally.

Once you've opened a document window, you can minimize the margins around the page, put a copy of the preprinted form in a graphics User Box, and size it to the page. Here's how to do all that:

1. Starting from a new document window, choose Layout ➤ Margins, and set all four margins to 0. (WordPerfect may increase your entries to accommodate the dead zone.) Choose OK.

2. To create a box for the scanned image, choose Graphics ➤ Custom Box ➤ User ➤ OK.

3. From the Graphics Box feature bar, choose Size ➤ Full ➤ Full ➤ OK. If you get a message indicating the box placement will change, just choose OK to proceed.

4. Using the feature bar again, choose Content, then use the file button next to Filename to specify the drive, directory, and file name of your scanned image. Then choose OK until you get back to the document window.

5. You should see the scanned image on your screen, as in Figure 28.11.

6. To make sure you can type over the image, choose Wrap from the feature bar. Then choose No Wrap (Through) from the Wrap Text dialog box, and choose OK.

7. Choose Close from the Graphics Box feature bar.

8. Use File ➤ Save to save what's on your screen as a WordPerfect document (for example, c:\wpwin60\wpdocs\taxform.wpd).

FIGURE 28.11

A scanned income tax form displayed in a graphics User Box in a WordPerfect for Windows document window

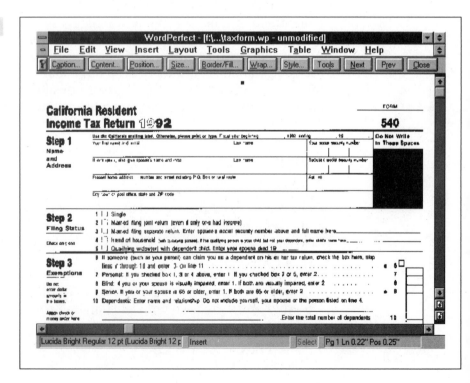

If you plan to print the text (but *not* the scanned image) from your document directly onto preprinted forms, follow these steps:

1. Print the document that contains the scanned image (don't bother filling it with text yet). Now, put the document that you just printed on top of the actual preprinted form, and hold both pages up to a strong light.

2. If the two images don't match exactly, you'll need to scale the image of the preprinted form on your screen to the actual printed form. To scale the image, edit the graphics box for the form (use Graphics ➤ Edit Box or Shift+F11 as discussed in Chapter 25). From the Graphics Box feature bar, choose Tools and then click the Image Settings button in the lower right corner of the tool bar. Choose Scale Image, set Both X & Y to 1.1, and choose OK. Choose Close from the Graphics Box feature bar.

3. Repeat steps 1 and 2 until the image on the screen exactly matches the printed form. In step 2, you can try other scaling values for Both X & Y (for example, 1.05 or 1.15).

Typing on the Form

When there's a preprinted form on your screen, your natural impulse will be to click wherever you want to type, and then start typing. But, because the page you're on is actually blank, it doesn't work that way. You need to use ↵ and Tab to move the cursor around, *unless* you do the following:

1. Turn off Graphics display (View ➤ Graphics) to prevent the graphic from being redrawn as you do the steps below. This will speed things up a bit.

2. Turn on Reveal Codes (Alt+F3), right-click the Reveal Codes screen, choose Preferences, select (check) Wrap Lines At Window, and choose OK.

3. Press Ctrl+Home, choose Layout ➤ Font (F9), choose the font settings for text that you'll be typing onto the form, then choose OK.

4. Press Ctrl+End to move the cursor to the bottom of the document, then press the spacebar until the [SRt] code appears at the end of the line. (Hint: You can use Edit ➤ Repeat to speed up the job of typing in a bunch of spaces. See Chapter 3.) Press Backspace as needed to delete the [SRt] code.

5. Select the entire first line, from the first space through the last space, and copy it to the Clipboard (Ctrl+C). Press Ctrl+End to deselect the text and move the cursor to the bottom of the document.

6. To fill the page with blank spaces, choose Edit ➤ Repeat, type **50** (or some number close to that), and choose OK. Press Ctrl+V to copy the text from the Clipboard to your document fifty times (or so). If necessary, press Ctrl+V a few more times, until you've filled the entire page with blank spaces. Each time you press Ctrl+V, watch the *Ln* indicator in the status bar to see how much of the page you've filled. If you paste beyond the current page (and a page break appears), choose Edit ➤ Undo, then press Backspace as needed until you delete the extra text.

7. Choose File ➤ Save to save the "skeleton" form with the blank spaces in it.

When you're ready to fill in the form with text, turn on Typeover mode (press Ins so that the *Typeover* message appears in the status bar), turn off Reveal Codes (Alt+F3), and turn the Graphics display back on (View ➤ Graphics). Now, press Ctrl+Home and fill in the form by clicking anywhere on the screen and typing the text. (Remember to stay in *Typeover* mode for best results.)

NOTE You may need to decrease or increase the leading (Layout ➤ Typesetting ➤ Word/Letterspacing ➤ Adjust Leading ➤ Between Lines) to make the text line up properly on the form. If necessary, add more blank spaces to the bottom of the document using the basic techniques given above in steps 4–6.

Printing the Form

After filling in the blanks on the form that's on your screen, you can print the document with, or without, the form.

- If you want to print just the text, load a preprinted form into the printer. Then choose File ➤ Print ➤ Do Not Print Graphics ➤ Print.

- If you want to print the form and the text you typed (on plain paper), print the entire document in the usual manner (File ➤ Print ➤ Print). Be aware, however, that this can be sl-o-o-o-w, and won't look as good as printing directly onto a preprinted form.

Preparing a Document for Typesetting

The term "professional typesetting" is a hard one to pinpoint these days, since desktop computers are quickly catching up to many of the high-end (and infinitely more expensive) typesetting machines. Nonetheless, if you don't have a fancy printer, you might want to get your local desktop publishing, typesetting, or prepublishing service bureau to print some documents for you.

The first thing you need to do is call that service bureau and tell them what you want to do (have them print fancy WordPerfect documents for you). If they can do it, ask them what it will cost so you don't die of fright when you get the bill. (You might want to shop around a little.)

Then ask them which printer driver you should use, ask about any font restrictions, what kind of file compression software they can work with, and whether you need to take any other special precautions to be sure the file will print successfully. For the sake of example, let's say they recommend that you use a PostScript printer driver, such as the Apple Laser-Writer IINT, and that your document should use only the built-in fonts for that printer.

Your first task is to install the printer driver for that printer, even though you, personally, don't have that particular printer attached to the computer. Unless the service bureau tells you otherwise, you can install either the WordPerfect printer driver or the Windows printer driver. See Chapter 10 and Appendix A for information on installing the WordPerfect driver. Or see your Windows documentation for information on installing the Windows printer driver. (Hint: For the Windows driver, open the Main group in the Windows Program Manager. Then open the Control Panel. Double-click Printers, then choose Add>>. Follow the instructions that appear on the screen.)

While you're installing the printer driver, you'll be prompted to choose the port that the printer is attached to. Choose the FILE or Prompt For Filename option, so that anything that's sent to that printer driver is actually sent to a disk file instead.

Once you've fully installed the printer driver you need, select that printer in WordPerfect. That is, start at the document window and choose File ➤ Select Printer, as discussed in Chapter 10. Once you've selected the printer, you can type, edit, choose fonts, and so forth normally.

You won't actually be able to print the document yourself, but you can see what it's going to look like in Page and Two-Page views. When you're happy with the document, save it as usual. Then print it to disk (choose File ➤ Print ➤ Print). When prompted, fill in a file name for the file you'll be creating (*don't* use the same name as the original document; save this as a separate copy). For instance, you might give this copy the name **MYFILE.EPS** (.EPS is the common extension for Encapsulated Post-Script files). Choose OK and wait a couple of minutes.

When WordPerfect seems to be finished, you can copy the file you just created (for example, MYFILE.EPS) to a floppy disk and bring it down to the printing service.

The one possible glitch might be that when you print to disk, the resulting file might be too large to fit on a floppy disk. You can use any combination of the following techniques to solve this problem:

- When printing to disk, print each page to a separate file.

- When you're done printing, use a file compression program to compress the finished files before copying them to floppies—but be sure to ask the service bureau if they have the same compression program, so they can decompress your files once they get them from you.

- Send the finished files to the service bureau by modem, rather than by floppy disk.

- You can also use a program like DOS's Backup (DOS 5 or earlier) or MSBackup (DOS 6) to split the large file into several separate files—but only if your service bureau can restore from the format you use.

For additional information, please talk to the folks at your service bureau.

Printing Color without a Color Printer

If you're happy with the quality of your printer, but you're looking to brighten up your documents with color, gold trim, or something nice like that, you might be able to use your own printer, even if it isn't a color printer. Just use paper that's already preprinted with fancy colored trim or background. To get started, contact one of the companies below and ask for a catalog:

Paper Direct

205 Chubb Avenue

Lyndhurst, NJ 07071

(800)-A-Papers (voice)

(201)507-0817 (fax)

or…

Premier Papers, Inc.

P.O. Box 64785

St. Paul, MN 55164

You'll be amazed at how many different kinds of paper you can run through your laser printer. Build up your clip art and font collections, and you'll be a veritable one-person publishing firm!

In this chapter we've looked at some of WordPerfect's most advanced features. If you have a high-powered printer, you can use these features to give your documents a more professional, polished look. Most people won't believe that you created them with WordPerfect! Next we'll turn to the Equation Editor, which makes it easy to set up complex equations.

CHAPTER

29

Set Up Equations in a Flash!

f a s t **TRACK**

To choose commands and mathematical symbols   962

double-click any command or symbol in the Equation palette. To use a different palette, select a palette from the pop-up list button above the Equation palette.

To change an equation   965

double-click the equation, or right-click the equation and choose Edit Equation from the QuickMenu. Or right-click the equation, choose Feature Bar, then use buttons in the Graphics Box feature bar to define the appearance of the equation.

To change the font of the equation   965

while you're in the Equation Editor, click the Equation Font button in the Equation Editor button bar, or choose Font ➤ Equation Font.

To change the appearance of all the equations in your document   965

choose Graphics ➤ Graphics Styles. Choose Options ➤ Setup ➤ Current Document, then OK. Highlight either Equation or Inline Equation, depending on which type of equation styles you want to change. Choose Edit.

FOR mathematicians, scientists, and other people who type mathematical or scientific documents, WordPerfect offers the Equations feature. This feature lets you type complex mathematical equations into a document and print them using all the special symbols and typesetting standards. Note, however, that the Equations feature does not *solve* the equations for you; it just lets you *enter* and *edit* them. A sample equation typed with WordPerfect is shown below:

$$\int_0^\infty x^{n-1}e^{-x}dx = \int_0^1\left(\log\frac{1}{x}\right)dx = \frac{1}{n}\prod_{m=1}^\infty\frac{\left(1+\frac{1}{m}\right)}{1+\frac{n}{m}}$$

By default, equations follow standard typesetting guidelines, where variables are printed in italics, and numbers and functions are printed in regular roman font.

Creating Equations

You can place equations in any of the eight types of graphics boxes discussed in Chapter 25, although it's often simplest to use *Equation boxes* for this purpose. The regular Equation box attaches the equation to a paragraph and displays the equation on its own line. If you want an equation to appear embedded as part of a line of text, use an *Inline Equation box* type—but be sure the equation you want to include will fit within the height of a single line.

WordPerfect offers a special Equation Editor for creating, editing, and previewing your equations. To add an equation to a document and access the Equation Editor, follow these steps:

1. If you've already typed some text in the document, move the cursor to where you want to place the equation.

2. Choose <u>G</u>raphics ➤ Equation, or click the Equation button (shown at left) in the Graphics button bar.

Figure 29.1 shows the Equation Editor. It's divided into three main sections, as illustrated in the figure.

- *The editing pane* in the top portion is used to type in and edit the equation.

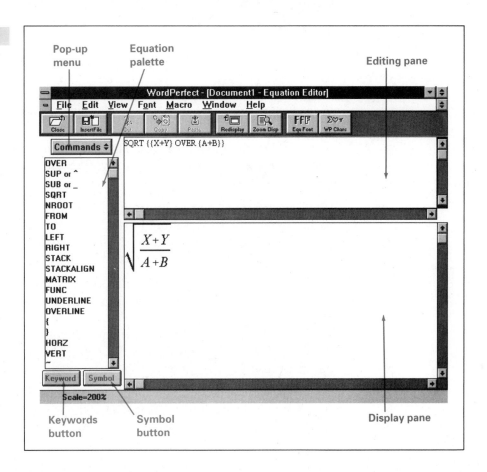

- *The display pane* in the bottom portion shows the equation graphically (much as it will be printed).

- *The Equation palette* on the left contains commands, symbols, and functions that you can insert in the equation instead of, or in addition to, typing them from the keyboard. The two buttons below the palette let you insert commands and symbols into the editing pane as either keywords or symbols.

TIP

The Equation Editor button bar offers handy shortcuts to choosing Equation Editor menu options. For example, clicking the Equation Font button is the same as choosing Font ➤ Equation Font from the menus. You can also right-click in the editing pane to open a QuickMenu of shortcuts.

Typing Equations

Typing and editing an equation in the editing pane is much like typing and editing any other text in WordPerfect. There are some differences, however. For the most part, you can type symbols and special operators either from the keyboard or from the various Equation palettes, as I'll explain a little later.

While the cursor is in the editing pane, you can use the usual editing techniques to modify the equation. For example, you can use your mouse and the ← and → keys to position the cursor. You can also use the Backspace and Del keys to delete characters and the Ins key to switch between Insert and Typeover modes.

To see a graphical representation of the equation you've typed so far, click the Redisplay button in the button bar, press Ctrl+F3, or choose View ➤ Redisplay. Then look at the display pane. If you'd like to zoom the image in the display pane in or out, click the Zoom Display button in the button bar or choose View ➤ Zoom Display. Then specify the zoom setting you want and choose OK.

TIP

You can also right-click the editing pane and choose Redisplay or Zoom whenever you want to refresh the display pane or zoom in or out.

When you're satisfied with the equation, click the Close button in the button bar, choose File ➤ Close, or press Ctrl+F4.

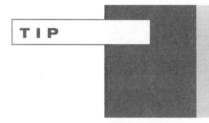

TIP

If you spend lots of time typing equations, you might want to use the Equation Editor keyboard. To switch keyboards, choose File ➤ Preferences, and double-click Keyboard. See Chapter 19 for more about changing keyboards.

Grouping Items within an Equation

When entering equations in WordPerfect, you should type them as you would read them aloud, and use *curly braces* { } to group items together. For example, the formula shown in Figure 29.1 could be spoken as "the square root of X + Y over A + B." This equation is expressed in the Equation Editor as

SQRT {{X+Y} OVER {A+B}}

Because everything to the right of the SQRT command must be under the radical, this entire portion of the equation is enclosed in curly braces. And because the entire X + Y portion should be placed over the entire A + B portion, these portions also are enclosed in their own set of curly braces. Figure 29.2 shows more examples illustrating the important role played by curly braces.

It's important that the curly braces *balance* in an equation. For example, if you have more open curly braces than closing curly braces, or vice versa, the grouping won't make sense. When you click the Redisplay button to view such a formula, you'll see the message "<<ERROR: Incorrect Syntax>>" in the status bar at the bottom of the screen, and the display pane won't be refreshed.

FIGURE 29.2

Using curly braces
in equations

SQRT X+Y OVER A+B

$$\sqrt{X} + \frac{Y}{A} + B$$

SQRT {X+Y} OVER A+B

$$\frac{\sqrt{X+Y}}{A} + B$$

SQRT X+Y OVER {A+B}

$$\sqrt{X} + \frac{Y}{A+B}$$

SQRT X+{Y OVER A}+B

$$\sqrt{X} + \frac{Y}{A} + B$$

SQRT {X+Y OVER A+B}

$$\sqrt{X + \frac{Y}{A} + B}$$

SQRT {{X+Y} OVER {A+B}}

$$\sqrt{\frac{X+Y}{A+B}}$$

NOTE

The same error message might appear if your equation
uses equation commands improperly, even though the
braces are correct.

Entering Spaces and Stacking Items in an Equation

Blanks entered with the spacebar are used to separate equation commands, but these blank spaces *aren't* part of the final equation. If you want to include a blank space in an equation, type a *tilde* (~) where you want the blank space to appear.

You can also insert a *thin space* (a quarter space) using the *backward accent* character (à). (It's on the same key as the tilde on most keyboards.) Use one accent to add a quarter space, two accents to add a half space, and so forth. The tilde and the accent appear only in the editing pane, never in the display pane or printed document.

Pressing ↵ while editing an equation moves the cursor to the next line, as in the normal document window. However, this doesn't insert a line break in the actual equation (it just gives you more room to type the equation and makes the editing pane easier to read). To *stack* items in an equation, you need to use STACK, STACKALIGN, MATRIX, #, or similar commands from the Equation palette.

Typing Numbers, Variables, and Operators

You'll need to type numbers and variables (such as X, Y, A, and B) directly from the keyboard. You'll also need to type the following operators and symbols, because they aren't on the Equation palette:

$$- + * / = < > ! ? \mid @ " , ;$$

NOTE   When typing a real number that contains a decimal point or negative sign, you must surround the number in curly braces.

Provided that you know the exact command to use, you can type commands like SQRT and OVER directly from the keyboard instead of choosing them from the Equation palette. You can type commands in either upper or lowercase letters, provided you know the exact command to use. Be sure to press the spacebar before and after the command keyword so that WordPerfect recognizes it as a command. Similarly, you can type special WordPerfect characters by pressing Ctrl+W or clicking the WP Character button in the Equation Editor button bar (see Chapter 6). However, when first learning to use the Equation Editor, you'll probably prefer to choose most commands and symbols from the Equation palette.

Using the Equation Palettes

You can choose commands or special symbols from the Equation palette anytime you're in the Equation Editor by following these steps:

1. In the editing pane, move the cursor to where you want to place an item from a palette.

2. If you wish, click the pop-up list button above the palette (initially this button is labeled *Commands*) and choose a different group of symbols or special characters from the menu shown here:

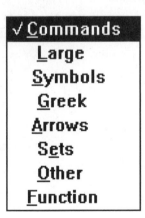

3. Click on or highlight the symbol or word you want in the Equation palette. Its name and a brief example of how to use it will appear at the bottom of the screen.

4. To insert the highlighted word or symbol into the editing pane, double-click it or press ↵. You can also insert the highlighted word or symbol by clicking the Keyword or Symbol button below the palette. The Keyword button inserts the highlighted word or symbol as a keyword. The Symbol button inserts the highlighted symbol as a symbol. (The equation will look the same in the display pane whether you choose Keyword or Symbol to put words and symbols into the editing pane.)

Remember, the equation won't be updated in the display pane until you click the Redisplay button or press Ctrl+F3.

Figure 29.3 shows several examples of equations created with the Equation Editor. Keywords in the examples that don't come directly from the Commands palette were chosen from other palettes. For example, AL-PHA, OMEGA, and THETA were chosen from the Greek palette; SUM and INT were chosen from the Large palette; INF and THEREFORE were chosen from the Symbols palette. Numbers, letters, and operators (as in **m + n = 0**) were typed directly from the keyboard.

The ways in which you can combine equation commands and symbols are nearly endless. When you're first learning, it may take some trial-and-error practice to get everything just right. You should build your formula gradually, pressing Ctrl+F3 (or clicking Redisplay) often to see how things are progressing. That way, you can correct mistakes and refine the equation as you type it. If you need additional help or information while you're in the Equation Editor, just press F1 (Help).

FIGURE 29.3

Examples of equation
commands and
symbols

BINOM ALPHA OMEGA	$\binom{A}{\Omega}$
SUM FROM {x=0} TO INF	$\sum\limits_{x=0}^{\infty}$
LEFT ({1^X} OVER m RIGHT)	$\left(\dfrac{1^x}{m}\right)$
LEFT DLINE MATRIX {a & b & c # x & y & z} RIGHT DLINE	$\left\|\begin{matrix} a & b & c \\ x & y & z \end{matrix}\right\|$
NROOT 3 {-{x OVER y}}	$\sqrt[3]{-\dfrac{x}{y}}$
tan ``THETA`=`{sin``THETA} OVER {cos``THETA}	$tan\,\Theta = \dfrac{sin\,\Theta}{cos\,\Theta}$
STACK {m+n=0 # m PHANTOM {+n}=2}	$\begin{matrix} m+n=0 \\ m=2 \end{matrix}$
LEFT. {X^1} OVER {Y_2} RIGHT LINE	$\left.\dfrac{X^1}{Y_2}\right\|$
SQRT {a^2 + b^2}``=c	$\sqrt{a^2+b^2}=c$
x SUB y SUP 1 (or x_y^1)	x_y^1
INT SUB 0 SUP INF	$\int_0^{\infty}$

Changing an Equation

After completing your equation and returning to the document window, the equation appears in a graphics box. You can edit the equation, if necessary, using the standard techniques used for editing any graphics box (see Chapter 25). For example, you can double-click the equation, or right-click it and choose Edit Equation from the QuickMenu.

Controlling the Appearance of Equations

You can control the caption, content, position, size, border and fill, wrap, or style of equations by editing a single equation's graphics box. To get started, right-click the equation you want to change, and choose Feature Bar. Then use the general techniques described in Chapter 25.

TIP

To change the *font* of a single equation from the Equation Editor, click the Equation Font button in the Equation Editor button bar (or choose Font ➤ Equation Font) and choose the font you want.

To change the appearance of *all* the equations in a document, start at the document window, deselect any selected graphics box, and follow the steps below:

1. Choose Graphics ➤ Graphics Styles (or click the Graphics Styles button in the Graphics button bar).

2. Choose Options ➤ Setup ➤ Current Document, then choose OK.

3. Highlight the type of box you want to change (Equation or Inline Equation), then choose Edit. You'll be taken to the Edit Box Style dialog box, shown in Figure 29.4.

4. Use techniques discussed in Chapter 25 to change the box style. When you're done, choose OK and Close to return to the document window.

FIGURE 29.4

Use the Edit Box Style dialog box to change the default caption, content, position, size, border and fill, text wrap, and font settings for all equations in the document.

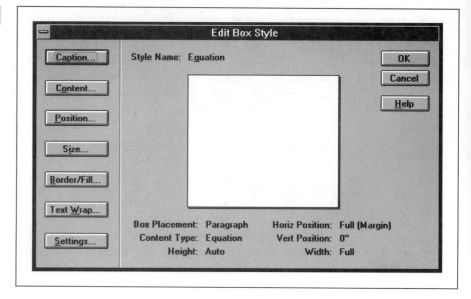

Your changes to the box style will affect all Equation boxes (or Inline Equation boxes) in the current document, *except* those that you customize individually using the Graphics feature bar or QuickMenu options, as described above. (You can customize individual graphics boxes before or after changing the overall box styles.)

If you want to return to the default system style for Equation boxes or Inline Equation boxes, follow the steps below:

1. Choose Graphics ➤ Graphics Styles.

2. Choose Options ➤ Setup ➤ Current Document, then choose OK.

3. Highlight the type of box you want to change (Equation or Inline Equation), then choose Options ➤ Reset ➤ Yes.

4. Choose Close to return to the document window.

As an alternative to changing the graphics box style in the current document only, you can change the box style for the Default Template or Supplemental Template. To do this, choose Graphics ➤ Graphics Styles ➤ Options ➤ Setup, select the location you want, and choose OK. Then highlight the box style you want to change. Finally, choose either Edit or Options ➤ Reset ➤ Yes. (For more about styles, see Chapters 17 and 25. For more about templates, refer to Chapter 20.)

Changing the Print Quality

Most equation characters are printed graphically. Therefore, if parts of equations are missing from your document, or are too rough, try changing the graphics quality just before printing the document. That is, start at the document window, choose File ➤ Print ➤ Print Quality, and choose a higher print quality.

Using the Same Equation in Multiple Documents

You can use the same equation in multiple documents simply by using standard copy-and-paste techniques to copy the equation's hidden code from one document to another. You can also save an equation in its own file, and retrieve previously saved equations into the Equation Editor by following these steps:

1. Open the graphics box that contains the equation you want to save in the Equation Editor (for example, by double-clicking the box). Or, if you want to retrieve a previously saved equation, create an Equation (or Inline Equation) graphics box in the current document.

2. If you want to retrieve an equation, position the cursor in the editing pane (where you want the retrieved equation to appear). Or, if you want to save a portion of the equation, select that text in the editing pane.

3. Choose whichever of the following options is appropriate:

   File ➤ Save As (or F3) Saves the equation, or a selected portion of the equation, in its own file.

   File ➤ Insert File (or the Insert File button) Retrieves into the editing pane, at the cursor position, an equation previously saved using Save As.

Saved equations are stored in *keyword* form, as normal WordPerfect text. For example, the equation shown in Figure 29.1 would be stored like this:

SQRT {{X+Y}} OVER {A+B}}

If you want, you can open and edit the saved equation file as you would any normal WordPerfect file (using the File ➤ Open command from the WordPerfect menus). However, it's generally easiest to use the File ➤ Insert File command described just above to bring the text into the editing pane of the Equation Editor, and then make your changes.

Equations are stored in graphics boxes, but they're unique because you use a special Equation Editor to edit and change them. In the next chapter, we'll look at two features—sound and hypertext—which you can use to create dazzling interactive multimedia documents.

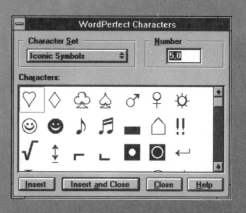

CHAPTER

30

Multimedia Mania with Sound and Hypertext

fast *TRACK*

Before you create a hypertext link   **986**

create the text you want the link to jump *to* and mark it with a named bookmark (Chapter 9). Or, create the macro that you want the hot spot to run (Chapter 18).

Once you've created the item you want the hot spot to link to   **986**

select the text in your document that defines the hot spot. Then choose Tools ➤ Hypertext and click the Create button in the Hypertext feature bar. Define the action and appearance of the hot spot in the Create Hypertext Link dialog box that appears and choose OK.

To activate hypertext in a document that contains links   **988**

choose Tools ➤ Hypertext. If the Activate button appears on the Hypertext feature bar, click it. Then just click any hot spot in your document to activate it.

To jump back to where you came from   **988**

click the Back button in the Hypertext feature bar.

To return to normal editing and deactivate hypertext   **988**

choose Tools ➤ Hypertext, then click the Deactivate button in the Hypertext feature bar. The mouse resumes its normal editing role.

WORDPERFECT 6 for Windows lets you design dazzling interactive documents for use right on the computer screen, instead of on paper. In addition to the usual text, graphics, and fancy fonts, interactive documents can incorporate *sound* and *hypertext*. These features make them exciting, informative, and much more fun to use than paper documents.

On a computer that can produce *sound*, you can add voice (such as spoken instructions, pronunciations, and greetings) to a document. In fact, you can add *any* sound, from bird calls to musical notes to zany cartoon-like sound effects.

Hypertext lets you put *jump words* and command buttons (collectively called *hot spots*) into your document. You can then assign an action such as "go to topic X," "open document Y," or "play macro Z" to each hot spot. The hot spot could jump to some related topic, display the definition of a term, play a sound clip, or even roll a movie across the screen. When the reader clicks a hot spot, its action is played out instantly.

Figure 30.1 shows a multimedia document that includes both sound and hypertext. The reader of this sample document could…

- Click on any bird command button to hear the bird's song.
- Click on an underlined bird name to jump directly to a description of that bird.

FIGURE 30.1

A sample interactive document. Clicking any bird button plays the bird's song.

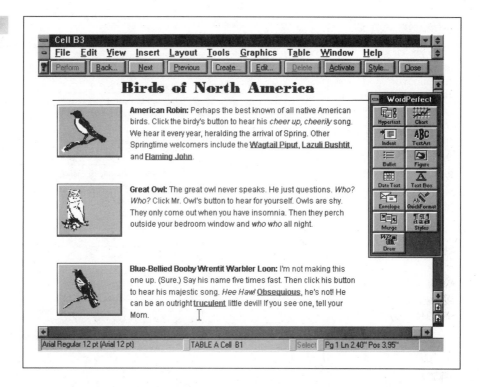

- Click on any underlined word to look up the definition for that term in a separate dictionary (see Figure 30.2), then click the <u>B</u>ack button in the Hypertext feature bar to get back to the birds.

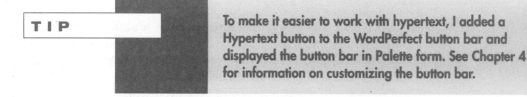

TIP

To make it easier to work with hypertext, I added a Hypertext button to the WordPerfect button bar and displayed the button bar in Palette form. See Chapter 4 for information on customizing the button bar.

Later in this chapter, I'll explain the techniques used to create that sample document. But first let's talk about the basic steps for adding sound and hypertext to your own WordPerfect documents.

FIGURE 30.2

When you click an underlined word like *obsequious* or *truculent,* you're taken to the dictionary entry for that word.

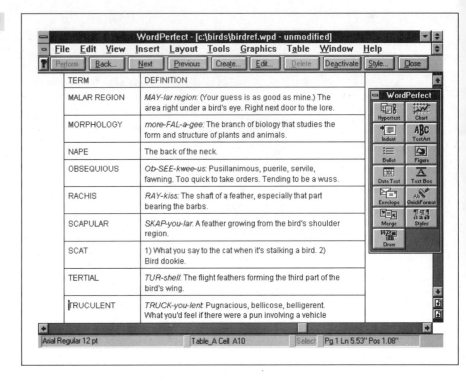

TERM	DEFINITION
MALAR REGION	*MAY-lar region:* (Your guess is as good as mine.) The area right under a bird's eye. Right next door to the lore.
MORPHOLOGY	*more-FAL-a-gee:* The branch of biology that studies the form and structure of plants and animals.
NAPE	The back of the neck.
OBSEQUIOUS	*Ob-SEE-kwee-us:* Pusillanimous, puerile, servile, fawning. Too quick to take orders. Tending to be a wuss.
RACHIS	*RAY-kiss:* The shaft of a feather, especially that part bearing the barbs.
SCAPULAR	*SKAP-you-lar.* A feather growing from the bird's shoulder region.
SCAT	1) What you say to the cat when it's stalking a bird. 2) Bird dookie.
TERTIAL	*TUR-shell:* The flight feathers forming the third part of the bird's wing.
TRUCULENT	*TRUCK-you-lent.* Pugnacious, bellicose, belligerent. What you'd feel if there were a pun involving a vehicle

Using Sound

Computers equipped with sound hardware can use WordPerfect's sound features. Your computer may already have multimedia capabilities, including sound, built right in. If it doesn't have built-in sound, you can buy and install a Sound Blaster card or an entire multimedia upgrade kit, including sound and a CD-ROM drive. Once you've added sound to your computer, you'll wonder how you ever lived without it.

Pssst!! Some Can Listen Too

Before I explain how to use sound, I'd like to tell you a little secret. Most systems equipped with a microphone can record sound. However, some can also listen to your voice and follow your commands. For example, my Microsoft Windows Sound System comes with a tiny microphone and a program named Voice Pilot. While I'm working, I can bark simple commands like "SAVE" or "OPEN" into the microphone. Windows obeys and does whatever I say. No need for messy mouse clicks or menu commands!

Pretty soon, I might even be able to teach my computer all the words I know. Then, I could have it type an entire document while my hands are tied behind my back. I just talk, and the computer types what I say. (Maybe I could convince the computer to type in my books while I loll around the pool. Hmmmm...)

This technology is still a little rough around the edges. But clearly there are many good things to come!

Getting Your System Ready for Sound

The next few sections outline the basic steps for getting your sound system up and running for use with WordPerfect.

Step 1: Install the Sound Hardware and Software

If your computer doesn't already have sound built into it, you need to purchase and install the appropriate hardware. Your sound system can be as fancy as you want. But a good, solid system with speakers, headphones, and microphones will probably run you about $250.00. (Yeah, I know, you already paid half/twice that. I'm talking ballpark figures here.)

Once you've laid out your hard-earned cash, you must install the sound device and its accompanying software so that it works on its own. The documentation from the manufacturer will explain exactly what's involved. You should follow those instructions to the letter. (Or even better, get someone else to do it for you.)

Most sound systems come with a test program. Be sure you can play sounds with that test program before you bother getting Windows and WordPerfect for Windows linked up to the sound system.

If you're using headphones, hold them away from your ears when you test a sound card. The volume might be high enough to damage your eardrums!

Step 2: Install the Sound Drivers for Windows

WordPerfect for Windows will use whatever sound drivers are installed in Windows. So once you've set up the sound card and tested it, your next task is to follow the manufacturer's instructions for installing the special driver programs that let Windows applications use your sound card. The general steps are listed below:

1. In the Windows Program Manager, open the Main group window, double-click Control Panel, and double-click the Drivers icon.

2. Add the new drivers to the Installed Drivers list.

3. Restart Windows.

Again, the manufacturer's instructions will tell you exactly what's required.

Step 3: Try It Out with WordPerfect for Windows

Now that you've installed your sound card and its Windows drivers, you're ready to try it out with WordPerfect for Windows. These steps are described next.

Adding a Sound Clip

Once you've installed your sound card, it's easy to add sound clips to your document. Here are the steps, starting from within WordPerfect:

1. Move the cursor to wherever you want to put the sound clip and choose Insert ➤ Sound ➤ Insert. You'll see this dialog box:

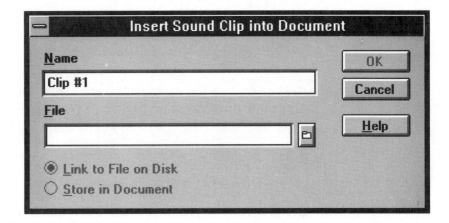

2. Choose File, then type the name of the sound clip file you want to add to your document, or use the button at the end of the text box to locate the sound clip file.

TIP

Use the QuickList (Chapter 20) to define a path for sounds, such as C:\WINDOWS*.WAV. Directories that are likely to contain sound files include the directory that your sound system software is on, C:\WINDOWS, C:\WINDOWS\SYSTEM, and C:\WINDOWS\SOUNDS. Sound files typically have a .MID or .WAV extension.

3. If you wish, choose Name and type in a brief description for the sound clip. That description will appear in the Sound Clips dialog box.

4. If you'll be using this document only on computer(s) that already have the sound clip on disk, choose Link To File On Disk to conserve disk space. If you're likely to distribute the document to people who might not have that sound clip on disk, choose Store In Document. A copy of the sound clip will be saved with the document (of course, this makes the document much larger).

5. Choose OK to return to your document.

The sound clip will appear in your document. In Draft view, it will appear in a shaded comment box, like this:

Sound: Robin

In Page or Two Page view, you'll see a little speaker icon at the left edge of the document window, like this:

In Reveal Codes, you'll see a [Sound] code. (The comment box and icons are never printed—unless, of course, there's some kind of magical paper that I don't know about yet.)

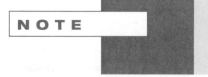

NOTE You can also use the *Object Linking and Embedding* techniques discussed in Chapter 33 to link and embed sounds into your document.

Playing a Sound Clip

You can use either of the methods below to play a sound clip:

- Click the sound icon or comment box.
- Choose Insert ➤ Sound or double-click a [Sound] code in Reveal Codes to open the Sound Clips dialog box, shown in Figure 30.3. Highlight the name of the sound clip you want to play, then click the Play button.

FIGURE 30.3

The Sound Clips dialog box for a document that already has some sound clips in it

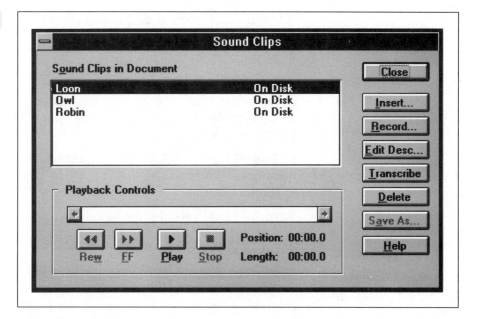

FIGURE 30.3

The Sound Clips dialog box for a document that already has some sound clips in it

NOTE

If you can't hear the sound, make sure your headphones and speakers are turned on and plugged in correctly. Then try playing the sound at a higher volume. If it still doesn't work, the culprit is probably the IRQ and Base Address settings. You'll need to determine the correct settings, then repeat step 2, "Install the Sound Drivers for Windows," described earlier in this chapter.

As Figure 30.3 shows, the Sound Clips dialog box includes several buttons along the right side. Here's what they do:

Close Closes the Sound Clips dialog box and returns you to your document.

Insert Lets you insert a new sound clip into the document at the cursor position. See "Adding a Sound Clip," above.

Record   Lets you record a sound clip to a sound file. See "Recording a Sound Clip," below.

Edit Desc   Lets you edit the description of the highlighted sound clip.

Transcribe   Lets you play the highlighted sound clip while typing in your document. See "Transcribing a Sound Clip," later in the chapter.

Delete   Lets you delete the highlighted sound clip from your document. (You can also delete a clip by deleting its [Sound] code in Reveal Codes.)

Save As   Lets you save the highlighted sound clip to disk. This option is available only for sound clips that are stored in the document.

Help   You guessed it! You can get help with using sound clips.

The Playback Controls buttons let you Rew (Rewind), FF (Fast Forward), Play, and Stop the sound. These controls work just as they would on a tape recorder or VCR. You can also use the scroll bar to position the sound clip at a certain spot and play it back from there.

When you're done using the Sound Clips dialog box, choose Close (if necessary) to return to your document.

Recording a Sound Clip

If your sound system can record sounds and you have a microphone, you can record sounds of your own. This might be handy if, for example, you want to put a personal message or instructions into a document. You can also add special effects to sound files, and you can combine several sound files into one (even if you don't have a microphone).

To record a sound, first make sure your microphone is properly connected to your sound device, according to the manufacturer's instructions. Then, follow these steps:

1. Place the cursor where you want the sound clip to appear in your document.

2. Choose Insert ➤ Sound ➤ Record to open the Windows Sound Recorder, shown in Figure 30.4. (Steps 3–11 just below refer to buttons and menu options in the Sound Recorder dialog box.)

NOTE

Sound Recorder isn't actually part of WordPerfect at all: It's an application that comes with Windows. The Record button in the Sound Clips dialog box provides a quick way to start Sound Recorder from within WordPerfect. For more information about using Sound Recorder, choose options from Sound Recorder's Help menu or consult your Windows manual.

3. If you want to add sounds to an existing sound file, choose File ➤ Open and select the file you want. Then position the scroll box where you want to insert the recorded sounds.

4. To start recording, click the Record button and speak your message or play the sound you want to record.

FIGURE 30.4

Sound Recorder lets you record your own sounds. You need a microphone and sound equipment with recording capability to use it. Choose Insert ➤ Sound ➤ Record to start this application from WordPerfect.

WARNING As you record, keep an eye on the length of your recording. The longer you record, the bigger the sound file you create. And big sound files gobble up disk space rapidly!

5. When you're done recording, click the Stop button.

6. To add sound effects, choose options from the Effects menu. You can increase or decrease the volume and speed, add echo, or reverse the sound (for some very weird effects, indeed).

7. To refine your sound clip further, choose options from the Edit menu. These options let you insert and mix other sound files with the file you're editing, and delete portions of the sound file.

8. To listen to your recording, choose the Play button.

9. Repeat steps 4–8 until you're satisfied with the recording.

10. To save your sound clip, choose File ➤ Save (or File ➤ Save As) and type a file name (e.g., **c:\windows\sounds\mysound.wav**).

11. To close Sound Recorder and return to WordPerfect, choose File ➤ Exit. (Don't forget this step. If you do, you'll end up with several copies of Sound Recorder running—one copy for each time you click the Record button in WordPerfect's Sound Clip dialog box.)

12. If you'd like to insert the sound clip into your document now, choose Insert and follow steps 2–5 under "Adding a Sound Clip." If you don't want to insert the clip now, choose Close to return to your document.

Transcribing a Sound Clip

You can type dictation from a recorded sound clip if you like. This is called *transcribing*. Here's how to do it:

1. Open the document that contains the sound clip you want to transcribe, then position the cursor where transcription should begin.

2. Choose Insert ➤ Sound, highlight the sound clip you want to transcribe, and click Transcribe. The Sound feature bar appears, as in the example below.

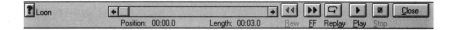

3. To start transcribing, click the <u>P</u>lay button. Then type *fast!* If necessary, use buttons on the feature bar to <u>R</u>ew (rewind), <u>F</u>F (fast forward), Repl<u>a</u>y the sound up to the last pause, <u>P</u>ause the sound, <u>P</u>lay the sound from the beginning or the last pause, or <u>S</u>top the playback. The scroll bar lets you position the sound clip at a certain spot for playback.

4. When you're done typing, choose the <u>C</u>lose button in the Sound feature bar.

Expanding Your Sound Clip Collection

Many freebie (public domain) sound clips are out and about on electronic bulletin boards. If you have a modem and know how to connect to the bulletin board, you can download these sound clips to your own computer.

If you don't mind spending some money (horrors!), you'll find plenty of sound clip collections advertised in computer magazines and catalogs. The collections probably will be listed under "multimedia" or "sound."

WARNING   Watch out! You'll need lots of disk space to store your sound clips.

Using Hypertext to Create Interactive Documents

Hypertext is a technique that lets you put *hot spots* into a document. It's totally independent of sound, so you can use it on any computer. Once you've put a hot spot in your document, you can assign an action to that hot spot. Specifically, you can link any phrase or term to a bookmark in the current document, to any part of another document, or to a macro (Chapter 18). When a reader clicks the hot spot, the action you assigned to it will be triggered instantly.

Before You Link Hypertext

Before you create hypertext links, you should create all the text, bookmarks, and any macros that you want to link to hot spots. That is, you want to...

1. Create the text that includes the hot spots you want to jump *from*. This is the document your reader will use initially.

2. Create the text (or document) that you want the hot spot to jump *to*. Then use Insert ➤ Bookmark ➤ Create (Chapter 9) to identify the text you want to jump to. Give the bookmark a descriptive name that will be easy to remember.

3. If you want the hypertext to run a macro, create and test the appropriate macro(s) (Chapter 18).

It's a good idea to put documents, macros, sounds, and clip art that make up the interactive document into one directory. For example, I put everything for my sample "Birds" interactive document in a separate directory named C:\BIRDS. Using one directory is easier than using the separate default directories for documents, graphics, and macros.

Creating Hypertext

Once you've created all your document(s) and any macros you want to activate with hypertext, you're ready to create a hypertext link. Here's how:

1. Select the text that you want to jump *from*.

2. Choose Tools ➤ Hypertext to open the Hypertext feature bar shown below:

3. Click the Create button in the Hypertext feature bar. This opens the Create Hypertext Link dialog box, shown in Figure 30.5.

4. Choose one of the Hypertext Action options listed below:

> **Go To Bookmark** Choose this option if you want to link to a bookmark in the same document. Then select the bookmark from the drop-down list.
>
> **Go To Other Document** Choose this option if you want to link to another document. Type in the document name, or use the button to the right of the text box to locate the document. To jump to a particular bookmark in that other document, choose the bookmark you want from the Bookmark drop-down list.
>
> **Run Macro** Choose this option if you want this link to run a macro. Then type the name of the macro, or use the button to the right of the text box to locate the macro.

5. To choose the appearance of the hypertext, select Text or Button. If you choose Text, the hypertext becomes a *jump word*. The jump word will be boldfaced, underlined, and displayed in a different color (usually green). If you choose Button, your hypertext will be inserted into a button graphic.

6. Choose OK to return to your document.

FIGURE 30.5

Use the Create Hypertext Link dialog box to define the action and appearance of a hypertext link.

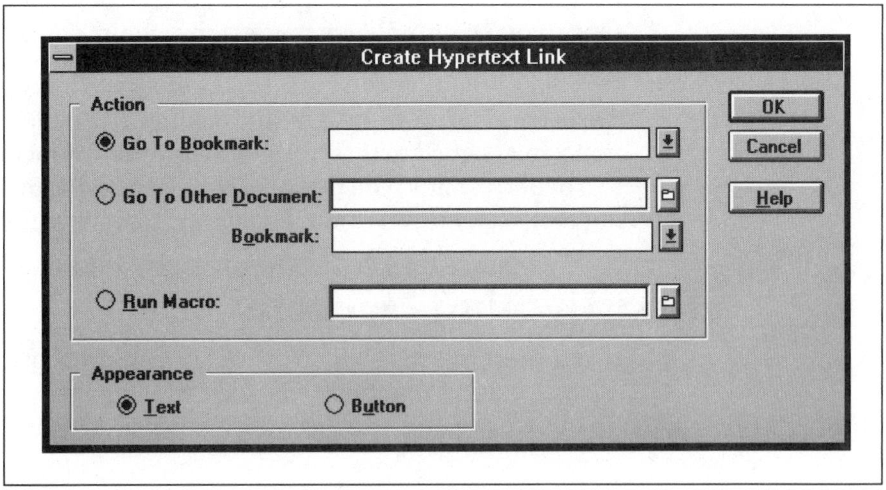

Create Hypertext Link

Action
- ● Go To **B**ookmark:
- ○ Go To Other **D**ocument:
- Bookmark:
- ○ **R**un Macro:

OK
Cancel
Help

Appearance
- ● **T**ext
- ○ B**u**tton

You can repeat the steps above to create as many links as you want. When you're finished creating links and making changes, save your document (File ➤ Save).

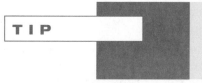

TIP The Hypertext feature bar provides all the buttons you'll need to use hypertext. Therefore, it's easiest to leave this feature bar on whenever you're working with hypertext.

Using Hypertext

When hypertext is *active*, you can click on the jump word or hypertext button to activate the link. When hypertext is *deactivated*, the mouse behaves normally; that is, clicking the mouse positions the cursor, selects graphics, and so on.

Follow these steps to activate hypertext:

1. If you haven't done so already, save your hypertext document.
2. Choose Tools ➤ Hypertext to display the Hypertext feature bar.
3. Look at the third button from the right in the feature bar. If it says "Activate," click the button to activate hypertext. If it says "Deactivate," hypertext is already active and you needn't do anything else.

Once you've completed these steps, the mouse changes its role. From now on, it will activate hot spots that you click.

To test and use your hypertext document, just click any hot spot. The action you assigned to that hot spot will be activated instantly. After jumping to a hypertext link, you can quickly return to the original hot spot by clicking the Back button in the Hypertext feature bar.

Deactivating Hypertext

If you want to edit a hypertext document and have the mouse resume its normal editing functions, click the Deactivate button in the feature bar (the button changes to Activate again). Now you can edit normally.

After deactivating hypertext, you can test your hypertext links without re-activating hypertext first. Move the cursor into a jump word or move the cursor just to the left of a hypertext button. Then click the Perform button in the Hypertext feature bar.

TIP You can also use the Previous and Next buttons in the feature bar to move the cursor to the previous or next hypertext hot spot. Then, jump to the link by clicking the hypertext hot spot (if hypertext is active) or by clicking Perform.

Changing the Default Behavior of Hypertext

By default, hypertext links are activated whenever you open a document. If you'd like to change this setting, choose File ➤ Preferences and double-click Environment. Then, to deactivate hypertext links, deselect the Activate Hypertext check box. To activate hypertext links, select this check box. Choose OK, then choose Close to return to your document.

Editing Hypertext

Once you've created some hypertext hot spots, you have several options for changing them:

- You can change the contents of the hot spot's jump word or button.
- You can delete the hypertext hot spot.
- You can change the action or appearance of the hot spot.
- You can change the style of jump words.

We'll look at each of these options next.

Changing the Contents of a Hot Spot

Follow these steps to change the text or graphics box shown in a hypertext hot spot:

1. Deactivate hypertext by clicking the De<u>a</u>ctivate button in the feature bar. (If <u>A</u>ctivate already appears in the feature bar, you can skip this step.)

2. Do one of the following:

   - To change a **jump word** (that is, a hot spot formatted as text), move the cursor into the hot spot you want to change. In Reveal Codes, the cursor should be between the [Hypertext] codes for the hot spot you want to change. Then edit the text normally, being careful not to delete the [Hypertext] codes.

   - To change the appearance of a **hypertext button**, use any of the techniques discussed in Chapter 25 for editing a graphics box. For example, you can right-click the button and choose options from the QuickMenu. You can also choose <u>G</u>raphics ➤ <u>E</u>dit Box (press Shift+F11), or you can just double-click the button.

Deleting a Hot Spot

To delete a hypertext hot spot so that it no longer jumps to a new place or runs a macro, follow the steps below:

1. Deactivate hypertext as described earlier.

2. Do one of the following:

   - If you're deleting the hot spot for a **jump word**, place the cursor anywhere in the jump word (between the [Hypertext] codes).

   - If you're deleting a hot spot for a **hypertext button**, position the cursor just before or after the button. In Reveal Codes, the button is marked by a [Box] code.

3. Click the <u>D</u>elete button in the Hypertext feature bar.

The jump word or button will remain in the document, but it will no longer behave as a hypertext hot spot.

You can also delete the hot spot for a jump word (text) by turning on Reveal Codes and deleting one of the [Hypertext] codes that surrounds the jump word.

Changing the Hot Spot's Action or Appearance

It's easy to change the action or appearance of a hot spot. Here's how:

1. Deactivate hypertext as described earlier.

2. Position the cursor within the text of a jump word or just before or after a hypertext button.

3. Click the Edit button in the Hypertext feature bar. This opens the Edit Hypertext Link dialog box, which is almost identical to the Create Hypertext Link dialog box shown in Figure 30.5.

4. Change the Action or Appearance options as desired, then choose OK.

Changing the Hypertext Style

By default, WordPerfect uses boldfaced, green, underlined text to identify jump words. If you'd like to use other formatting to make your jump words stand out, follow these steps:

1. Move the cursor anywhere in the document.

2. If the Hypertext feature bar isn't visible, choose Tools ➤ Hypertext.

3. Click the Style button on the Hypertext feature bar. This opens the Styles Editor dialog box, where you can change the codes that define the appearance of the jump word.

4. Edit the codes in the Contents area of the dialog box, as you would any style (see Chapter 17 if you need information about changing styles).

5. When you're done making changes, choose OK. The jump words in your document will reformat instantly.

The Sample Document

If you've read everything in the chapter up to this point, you may be wondering how I got from what's described here to command buttons with pictures of birds on them that you can click to hear a bird song. The secret is *macros* (Chapter 18). I'll run through the steps I went through to create the hypertext document shown in Figure 30.1. Once you've seen how it's done, you can try creating a similar document on your own.

The Initial Documents

I started out by creating a table (Chapter 7) with bird names in the left column and bird descriptions in the right column, as shown in Figure 30.6. The table is entirely optional. I just used it to set up the two-column format. I named this document BIRDS.WPD.

FIGURE 30.6

How my sample Birds hypertext document started out

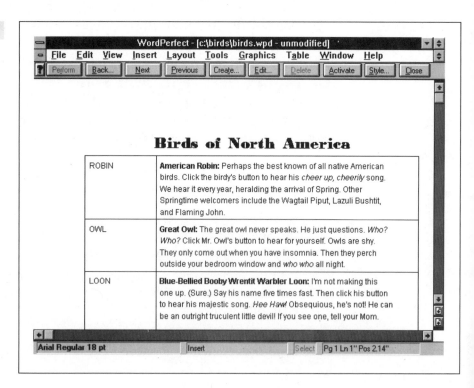

Though not shown in the figure, some of the entries have their own bookmark. For example, when I created the table row for Wagtail Piput (not shown), I added a bookmark (ingeniously named WAGTAIL PIPUT) to that table row. I created a bookmark entry for every bird that's cross-referenced from some other bird.

I also created the dictionary shown in Figure 30.2 as a separate document. It's just a standard WordPerfect document that uses the Tables feature to keep text aligned. What you can't see in the figure is the hidden bookmark that's next to each dictionary entry. For example, the hidden bookmark for the *Obsequious* entry is OBSEQUIOUS.

I saved the dictionary under its own file name, BIRDREF.WPD. I could just as easily have put the dictionary at the end of the original BIRDS.WPD document. Doing so would actually speed up the hypertext jumping.

The Sounds

Next, I spent months in the wild recording bird sounds for my document. (I knew you wouldn't believe that. Actually, I faked them with my own voice.) I probably could have scrounged some copyright-free prerecorded bird sounds. But since you can't hear the sounds anyway, my faked ones were fine for writing this chapter.

I inserted all the sounds at the *end* of the document. That is, if you were to scroll to the end of the BIRDS.WPD document, you'd see the sound clips stacked up looking something like this in Draft view:

Sound: Robin

Sound: Owl

Sound: Loon

Next, I hid those sound clips using Layout ➤ Font ➤ Hidden. That way, my readers won't ever see them unless they happen to be sneaking around with Reveal Codes turned on.

The Hypertext Jump Words

With documents created and bookmarks in place, my next job was simply to select a hot spot (for example *Wagtail Piput*) and create the hypertext link to the appropriate bookmark. I used the basic technique described earlier in this chapter, under "Creating Hypertext." I used the Go To Bookmark option for cross-references to the same document and the Go To Other Document option for references to the separate dictionary, BIRDREF.WPD. The appearance of all the hot spots in column B is Text.

The Macros

Next I needed a way to make hot spots play a sound. To do that, I set up three macros—one to play the LOON sound, one to play the OWL sound, and one to play the ROBIN sound. Unfortunately, the macro command that plays a sound isn't recordable, so I had to don my pointy programmer's hat and type those sound-playing macros from scratch. Fortunately, the macros use just two simple commands, which are easy to type.

Follow these steps to create the first macro, LOON.WCM, which plays the LOON sound:

1. Choose File ➤ New to open a new, empty document window.

2. Choose Tools ➤ Macro ➤ Macro Bar to display the Macro Edit feature bar.

3. Type the macro programming command shown below, and press ↵. This command specifies which application is used in the macro.

   Application(A1; "WordPerfect"; Default!)

4. Type the macro programming command shown below, and press ↵. This command tells the macro which sound clip to play.

   SoundClipPlayNext(Description:"Loon")

5. Choose the Save As button in the Macro Edit feature bar. In the Macro Save As dialog box, choose Location ➤ File On Disk ➤ OK (this is necessary only if the location isn't already set to File On Disk). In the Name text box, type the name of the macro you want to save (for example, **c:\birds\loon.wcm**), then choose Save.

To create the other two macros—OWL.WCM and LOON.WCM—you can take the shortcuts described below:

1. With the previously saved macro and the Macro Edit feature bar still on the screen, change *Loon* in the second line of the macro to **Owl**.

2. Repeat the Save <u>A</u>s command described in step 5 of the procedure given just above, substituting the new file name **owl.wcm** for *loon.wcm*.

3. Again, with the previously saved macro and the Macro Edit feature bar still on the screen, change *Owl* in the second line of the macro to **Robin**.

4. Repeat the Save <u>A</u>s command described in step 5 of the procedure given just above, substituting the new file name **robin.wcm** for *loon.wcm*.

5. Choose <u>C</u>lose from the Macro Edit feature bar. You'll be returned to whatever document you were working on previously, or to an empty document window.

Please see Chapter 18 and the "Online Macros Manual" (<u>H</u>elp ➤ <u>M</u>acros) for more information about macro programming.

The Sound Buttons

To create a sound button in the BIRDS.WPD document, I selected the text in column A for one row (for example, ROBIN). Then I chose <u>T</u>ools ➤ <u>H</u>ypertext and clicked the Crea<u>t</u>e button in the Hypertext feature bar. The action I chose was <u>R</u>un Macro, followed by the name of the macro the button should play (ROBIN.WCM). I chose B<u>u</u>tton as the Appearance, and then I chose OK to return to the document.

My ROBIN button ended up looking something like this:

> | ROBIN | **American Robin:** Perhaps the best known of all native American birds. Click the birdy's button to hear his *cheer up, cheerily* song. We hear it every year, heralding the arrival of Spring. Other Springtime welcomers include the <u>**Wagtail Piput**</u>, <u>**Lazuli Bushtit**</u>, and <u>**Flaming John**</u>.

With Hypertext active, I then clicked that button and, sure enough, it ran the macro and played the appropriate sound.

I relied on my Presentation Task Force clip art collection to come up with the picture for each button. To put the picture on a button, I first deactivated hypertext by clicking the Deactivate button in the Hypertext feature bar. Then I followed the steps below to size, position, and fill in the hypertext button:

1. I right-clicked the hypertext button (currently labeled ROBIN), and chose Feature Bar from the QuickMenu. This opened the Graphics Box feature bar.

2. I clicked the Size button in the feature bar, sized the button to my liking (1.45″ wide by 1″ high in this example), and chose OK.

3. I clicked the Position button in the feature bar, placed the box in the current paragraph at the left margin, and chose OK.

4. I clicked the Content button in the feature bar. In the Box Content dialog box, I chose Filename, retrieved the picture that I wanted to put onto the button, chose OK, and then chose Yes when asked if I wanted to delete the current box contents.

5. I clicked Close in the feature bar. This closed the Graphics Box feature bar and redisplayed the Hypertext feature bar.

The result is a button with a picture on it, as in the example below (and back in Figure 30.1).

 American Robin: Perhaps the best known of all native American birds. Click the birdy's button to hear his *cheer up, cheerily* song. We hear it every year, heralding the arrival of Spring. Other Springtime welcomers include the **Wagtail Piput**, **Lazuli Bushtit**, and **Flaming John**.

I repeated the basic steps given above for every entry in the first column of the table.

General Format

For the finishing touches, I set all the table lines to <None> (Chapter 7), set the table rows to a fixed height (about 1.5 inches), then saved and closed the file. To keep other people from messing up my document, I chose File ➤ Open, highlighted the BIRDS.WPD file, chose File Options ➤ Change Attributes, set its status to Read-Only, and chose OK. Then I chose Cancel. (See Chapter 20 for more about using file-management options in WordPerfect.)

For the ultimate in convenience, I added a Hypertext button to the Word-Perfect button bar (see Chapter 4). This way, my readers can activate hypertext by clicking the Hypertext button in the button bar and (if necessary) by clicking the Activate button on the Hypertext feature bar.

As you've seen, sound and hypertext add a new dimension to the author's craft. What's more, they're easy to use and a lot of fun. Keep in mind that because a hypertext link can run a macro, you can create a hot spot in your document to do virtually anything imaginable—not just jump to a bookmark or to another document.

Now we'll move on to Part Seven and look at tools for managing the big jobs and for sharing information with other Windows and non-Windows applications.

PART SEVEN

Managing the Big Jobs

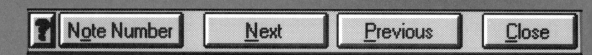

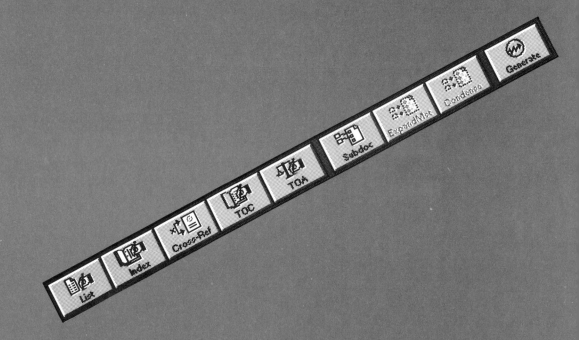

CHAPTER

31

Automatic Indexing
and Referencing

fast TRACK

To display the Generate button bar 1004

choose <u>V</u>iew ➤ <u>B</u>utton Bar (if necessary), right-click the button bar, and choose Generate. This button bar offers quick access to list, index, cross-reference, table of contents, table of authorities, and generate features.

To type a footnote or an endnote 1005

place the cursor where you want the note number to appear. Choose either <u>I</u>nsert ➤ <u>F</u>ootnote or <u>I</u>nsert ➤ <u>E</u>ndnote, then <u>C</u>reate. Type the text of your note. When you're done, click the <u>C</u>lose button in the Footnote/Endnote feature bar.

To edit an existing footnote or endnote 1008

place the cursor on the page that contains the note. Choose either <u>I</u>nsert ➤ <u>F</u>ootnote or <u>I</u>nsert ➤ <u>E</u>ndnote, then <u>E</u>dit (or double-click the [Endnote] or [Footnote] code in Reveal Codes).

To mark lists 1015

choose <u>T</u>ools, then select a list type (L<u>i</u>st, Inde<u>x</u>, Table Of <u>C</u>ontents, or Table Of <u>A</u>uthorities). The remaining steps depend on the type of list you're marking. Typically, you'll need to specify a list name (for lists), heading and subheading (for indexes), or short form name (for tables of authorities in which you've already defined the "long form"). Next, select the text you want to mark. Finally, click an appropriate Mark button in the feature bar.

To define the list location and format   **1023**

position the cursor where you want the list to appear. If you want to start the list on a new page, press Ctrl+⏎, and type a title or create a page header for the list. Choose Tools, select a list type, and choose Define from the feature bar. Complete the dialog box that appears. If necessary, adjust the starting page number of the document text.

To mark a cross-reference and target   **1030**

choose Tools ➤ Cross-Reference or click the Cross-Reference button in the Generate button bar. To mark the *target*, place the cursor at the target, click the Reference button in the feature bar and choose the type of target you want. In the Target box, type in a target name, then click the Mark Target button. To mark the *reference*, place the cursor where you want the reference to appear and type any introductory text. Select (or type in) the target name from the Target drop-down list. Click the Mark Reference button.

To generate lists and cross-references   **1035**

click the Generate button in the feature bar or Generate button bar, or choose Tools ➤ Generate, or press Ctrl+F9. Choose OK.

MANY documents require *references*, such as footnotes and end-notes, tables of contents, indexes, figure and table lists, cross-references, and more. As you'll see in this chapter, WordPerfect makes it easy to create and manage all these document references and, in true WordPerfect style, will automatically update them as you add, change, and delete text in your document.

All the features described in this chapter have their own feature bars, which make it easy to accomplish the task at hand. Chapter 4 covers the details of using feature bars, but for now you might want to keep these points in mind:

- You can quickly switch to another feature bar at any time. Simply right-click any feature bar that's visible and choose the bar you want.

- You can hide a feature bar at any time by clicking its Close button.

You can also use the Generate button bar shown below for quick access to the list, index, cross-reference, table of contents, table of authorities, and generate features covered here. To display the Generate button bar, choose View ➤ Button Bar (if necessary), right-click the button bar, and choose Generate from the QuickMenu.

Footnotes and Endnotes

Many scholarly, scientific, and technical documents use *footnotes* and *endnotes* to reference additional reading material or to provide parenthetical or related information that need not be included in the main body of the text. Footnotes appear at the bottom of the page, and endnotes generally appear at the end of the document.

Figure 31.1 shows a printed page with two footnotes at the bottom. The superscript numbers 1 and 2 in the body of the page are the note numbers that refer to these footnotes. Figure 31.2 shows the same parenthetical information, this time used as endnotes on the last page of the document.

NOTE Except for their positions when printed, footnotes and endnotes are virtually the same in WordPerfect, so from here on I'll just refer to both as *notes* and indicate any differences where appropriate.

Adding and Editing Notes

All notes consist of two elements: a superscript *note number* that appears in the text to alert the reader to the note, and the note itself. Typing a note is a simple procedure:

1. Move the cursor to where you want the note number to appear in the text (usually after the period in a sentence).

2. Choose either <u>I</u>nsert ➤ <u>F</u>ootnote or <u>I</u>nsert ➤ <u>E</u>ndnote, then <u>C</u>reate. You'll see the note editing window, a superscripted note number, and the Footnote/Endnote feature bar, shown below.

FIGURE 31.1

WordPerfect footnotes

Only two of Archie Medees' works on mechanics have been handed down to us. These are titled *On Why Mechanics Charge a Lot to Fix Our Cars* and *On Why Cars Have Top Speeds*. Both were published in 1955 by Clickety Clack Publishers, specialists on automotive matters. In *Why Mechanics Charge*, Medees dealt with mechanical price structures, which, along with the diminishing value of the dollar and the high price of fuel, serve to undermine the basic American freedom to drive cars as fast and as far as they want to. Archie Medees used the concept of the *center of gravity* to discuss these topics, but he never explicitly defined this notion.[1]

Great progress in the theory of mechanics followed Archie Medees time. In 1965 Johann Andretti proposed the principle of *virtual reality*[2] as the fundamental law of roadworthiness. The law states that

in roadworthiness, no work is needed to achieve an infinitesimal

displacement of a given mechanic's ability to mess up an engine.

---

[1] Many have speculated about why Archie Medees never defined the center of gravity. Most scholars believe that the concept had already been defined elsewhere, either by Archie or earlier writers. However, the real reason may be that the center of gravity has absolutely nothing to do with the topic that Mr. Medees was addressing.

[2] This principle is a well-known buzzword in the computer industry, but it applies to cars as well. People who drive them think the posted speed limit is virtually real--that is, they can define it to mean virtually anything they want.

FIGURE 31.2

WordPerfect endnotes

♫ **N O T E S**

1. Many have speculated about why Archie Medees never defined the center of gravity. Most scholars believe that the concept had already been defined elsewhere, either by Archie or earlier writers. However, the real reason may be that the center of gravity has absolutely nothing to do with the topic that Mr. Medees was addressing.

2. This principle is a well-known buzzword in the computer industry, but it applies to cars as well. People who drive them think the posted speed limit is virtually real--that is, they can define it to mean virtually anything they want.

3. Type the text of your note, just after the superscript note number that WordPerfect inserted automatically. You can use any of Word-Perfect's editing features, as usual.

4. Click the <u>C</u>lose button in the feature bar when you're done.

NOTE   WordPerfect comes with two macros that make it easy to convert all footnotes in your document to endnotes, and vice versa. The macro FOOTEND converts footnotes to endnotes. The macro ENDFOOT converts endnotes to footnotes. Chapter 18 explains how to run macros.

The notes will appear in Page or Two Page view, and whenever you print the document.

It's easy to edit the text of your note later. Follow the steps below:

1. Place the cursor on the page that contains the note.

2. Choose either Insert ➤ Footnote or Insert ➤ Endnote then Edit. Or, open Reveal Codes (Alt+F3) and double-click the [Footnote] or [Endnote] code that you want to change.

3. When prompted, type the number of the note you want to change and press ↵ or choose OK. A note editing window appears with the text of your original note.

4. Edit the note as you wish.

5. Click the Close button in the feature bar when you're done.

If you're using Page view, or Two Page view, there's another way to edit notes. Scroll down to the bottom of the page that contains the note (if you're changing a footnote), or to wherever the endnotes appear (usually at the end of the document). Now, click on the note you want to change, and edit normally. When you're done making changes, click in the document area, outside the note (or choose File ➤ Close). (The Footnote/Endnote feature bar won't appear automatically when you use this method to edit notes.)

Here are some tips you can use when you're editing a note in the note editing window:

• To add a space or indent after the note number, press the spacebar or use indenting techniques such as Tab, F7, and Ctrl+Shift+F7 (Chapter 5). You can also adjust the note's style, as described later in the chapter.

• To add space between notes, you can press ↵, or use the Options, described later, to add a uniform amount of space between notes.

• If you accidentally delete a note number while entering or editing a note, position the cursor where you want the note number to reappear, and click the Note Number button in the Footnote/Endnote feature bar.

• To switch to the editing window for the next or previous note, click the Next or Previous button in the feature bar.

The following tips can help you move and delete notes:

- To move the superscript note number from one place in your document to another, simply move the [Footnote] or [Endnote] code for that note. (See Chapter 4 for help on moving codes.)

- To delete a note, use Reveal Codes to locate its [Footnote] or [Endnote] code, and delete the code.

Renumbering Notes

Normally, the first note in a document is numbered 1, and any other notes are numbered consecutively and automatically whenever you create them. You can customize the note numbering method easily and change the starting note number anywhere in your document. Here's how:

1. Place the cursor before the first note that you want to renumber.

2. Choose either <u>I</u>nsert ➤ <u>F</u>ootnote or <u>I</u>nsert ➤ <u>E</u>ndnote, then <u>N</u>ew Number. The Footnote Number (or Endnote Number) dialog box appears:

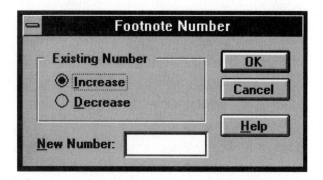

3. Choose one of the following options:

    Increase   Increases the next note number by one.

    <u>D</u>ecrease   Decreases the next note number by one.

    <u>N</u>ew Number   Restarts note numbering at whatever number you specify.

Choose OK. WordPerfect will renumber all notes from the cursor position to the end of the document.

TIP

If you need to change the note starting numbers in several files, try using the Master Document feature discussed in Chapter 32.

Changing the Format of Notes

Footnotes usually appear in the format shown in Figure 31.1. Endnotes usually are single-spaced, with a blank line between each note. You can change these defaults, as follows:

1. Move the cursor to where you want the new note format to take effect.

2. Choose Insert ➤ Footnote or Insert ➤ Endnote, then Options. The Footnote Options dialog box is shown in Figure 31.3. (The Endnote Options dialog box is similar, but has fewer options.)

3. Choose the options you want, and then choose OK.

The note formatting options are as follows:

Method   Which numbering method do you want (numbers, letters, roman numerals, or characters)?

Characters   Which character(s) do you want for character-style note numbering? You can type up to five characters or WordPerfect Characters (entered with Ctrl+W). WordPerfect will recycle and repeat each character in the list whenever it reaches the end of the list. To understand how this works, suppose you've entered the characters ★ and + in the Characters text box. In this case, the number for note 1 is ★, note 2 is +, note 3 is ★★, note 4 is ++, note 5 is ★★★, note 6 is +++, and so on.

FIGURE 31.3

The Footnote Options
dialog box

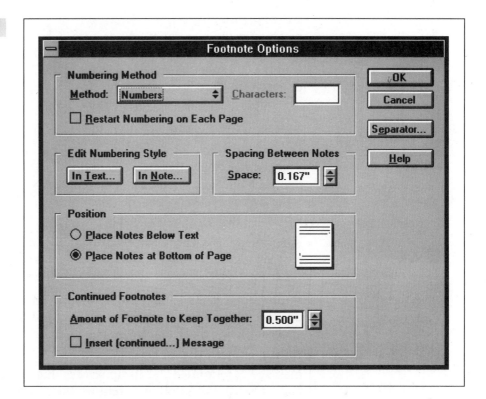

TIP

When you use characters to mark footnotes, it's best to restart note numbers on each page, to avoid long strings of characters. This way, your numbering characters will recycle on each page, starting again with one instance of the first character.

Restart Numbering On Each Page   Select this option to restart footnote numbers at 1 (or the first numbering character) on each page. Deselect the option to number footnotes consecutively.

Edit Numbering Style   What style do you want for the note number in the document text or note? Choose In Text or In Note (as appropriate) to open the Styles Editor dialog box for the note number. Change the style as described in Chapter 17, then choose OK. (See "Changing the Note Styles," later in the chapter, for more about customizing the note styles.)

Space   How much space do you want between notes?

Position   Where should footnotes appear on the page? Select Place Notes Below Text to place footnotes immediately after the text on a partially filled page. Select Place Notes At Bottom Of Page to place footnotes at the bottom of each page, regardless of whether the page is filled or not.

Amount Of Footnote (or Endnote) To Keep Together   For lengthy notes, how much note text do you want to keep at the bottom of a page before the text spills onto the next page?

Separator   What should the horizontal line that separates the document text from footnotes look like, and how much space should appear above and below the line?

Insert (continued…) Message   Select this option to print the message "(continued…)" for footnotes that continue to another page. Deselect this option to remove the continuation messages. Continuation messages appear as the last line of a footnote that's continued to the next page and as the first line of a footnote that's continued from the previous page.

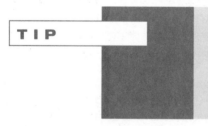

TIP   To change the language of the "(continued…)" message—perhaps to "(continúa…)" for a document in Spanish—move the cursor to where the language change should take effect, choose Tools ➤ Language, and select a language.

Where Endnotes Will Appear

WordPerfect endnotes are automatically numbered and placed at the end of a document by default. But you can place them anywhere you want, with these steps:

1. Position the cursor where you want the endnotes to appear.

2. To start endnotes on a new page, press Ctrl+↵. Create a page heading or type in a title, such as **The Living EndNotes**, if you wish, and press ↵.

3. Choose Insert ➤ Endnote ➤ Placement.

4. Choose one of the options below:

   Insert Endnotes At Insertion Point Inserts endnotes at the cursor position, and continues with consecutive numbering.

   Insert Endnotes At Insertion Point And Restart Numbering Inserts endnotes at the cursor position and renumbers any remaining endnotes, starting with 1.

5. Choose OK.

In Page or Two Page view, and in the printed document, you'll see the actual endnote text. In Draft view, the endnote text usually won't be visible (though you can turn on Reveal Codes to see the [Endnote] *codes*). If you used the Endnote Placement option, the endnote text will be marked in Draft view by a shaded comment box.

Changing the Note Styles

WordPerfect uses predefined *styles* to format notes and note numbers. You can customize these styles for the entire document, with the following steps:

1. Choose Insert ➤ Footnote or Insert ➤ Endnote, then Options.

2. To change the style of all the note numbers in the *document body*, choose In Text. To change the style of the text of note numbers and text in the *notes*, choose In Note.

3. Edit the style as you would any other style (see Chapter 17).

4. Choose OK twice.

TIP It's easy to indent text in the note or to display the note text in a different font. Just choose In Note in step 2 above, move the cursor past the codes in the Styles Editor (press Ctrl+End), then press Ctrl+Tab or Indent (F7), choose a font (F9) if you wish, and choose OK twice.

If you want to change the appearance of notes in future documents, you must copy the edited *system styles* to the *template(s)* used to create those documents (see Chapters 17 and 20). The system styles for note numbers in the document are named *Endn#inDoc* (endnotes) and *Ftn#inDoc* (footnotes). The system styles for the note text are named *Endnote* and *Footnote*.

TIP To change the appearance of just one note's text, use pull-down menus and other standard formatting techniques when you edit the note.

Automatic Reference Lists

A *reference list* is a list of items in a document and the page numbers on which they appear. WordPerfect documents can have four types of reference lists: *indexes*, *general lists* (useful for lists of figures and tables), *tables of contents*, and *tables of authorities* (bibliographies in legal documents).

You can generate lists in a single document, or use the Master Document feature (Chapter 32) to generate reference lists from multiple documents that are stored in separate files.

Here are the basic steps for creating any of these lists:

1. Display the feature bar for the list.

2. Mark all the items that belong in the list.

3. Insert a page break before (or after) the list and add a title or page header, if you wish. (Chapter 8 covers page headers and other page formatting techniques.)

4. Define the format and position for the list.

5. To ensure proper page numbering, adjust the page numbers for text above or below the list, if necessary.

6. Generate the lists and cross-references. To do this, click the Generate button in the feature bar or Generate button bar, or choose Tools ➤ Generate, or press Ctrl+F9. Then choose OK.

7. Click the Close button in the feature bar when you're done.

You can create the lists as you write the document or after the document is completed. I'll explain in detail how to mark items and define each type of list in the sections that follow. You'll learn more about generating and editing the lists near the end of this chapter.

Marking Table-of-Contents Entries

To mark entries for a table of contents (ToC), follow these steps:

1. Choose Tools ➤ Table Of Contents or click the Table Of Contents button in the Generate button bar. You'll see the Table Of Contents feature bar shown below:

2. Select the block of text that you want to include in the table of contents.

3. Click the "Mark" button in the feature bar to choose the indentation level you want for the selected text. There are five Mark buttons (Mark 1, Mark 2, Mark 3, Mark 4, and Mark 5), which

correspond to the five levels of indentation. The leftmost position in the table of contents is level 1. You might, for example, use level 1 for chapter headings, level 2 for main headings, level 3 for subheadings, and so on.

WordPerfect will mark the selected text with [Mrk Txt ToC] codes, which you can see in Reveal Codes (Alt+F3).

Figure 31.4 shows a sample table of contents, after marking the entries, defining the list, and generating it.

FIGURE 31.4

A sample generated table of contents

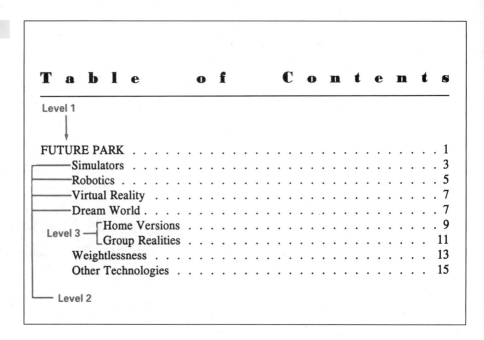

Defining a Table of Contents

Here's how to define the position and format of your table of contents:

1. Turn on the Table Of Contents feature bar (Tools ➤ Table Of Contents).

2. Move the cursor to where you want the table of contents to appear (press Ctrl+Home twice to start the table at the very top of your document).

3. To start the table on a new page, press Ctrl+↵. Press ↑ to move the cursor before the [HPg] code. If you wish, enter a title, such as **Table of Contents**, and press ↵.

4. Click the <u>D</u>efine button in the feature bar to open the Define Table Of Contents dialog box, shown in Figure 31.5.

5. If you wish, use the options described just below to customize the table. As you make changes, the sample page in the dialog box will reflect your choices.

FIGURE 31.5

The Define Table Of Contents dialog box

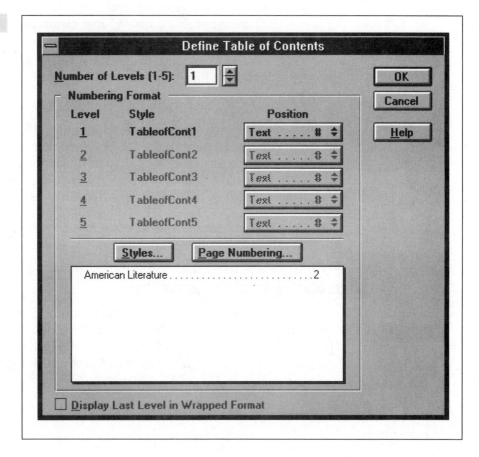

Number Of Levels How many levels do you want in your table of contents, in the range 1 to 5? Suppose you've marked chapter titles as level 1 and main headings as level 2. If you want the table of contents to include both levels, enter **2** as the number of levels. If you want to include only the chapter titles, enter **1** as the number of levels.

Numbering Format Where do you want to place page numbers in each level in the table of contents? Click the Position button for the level you want to change and choose one of the five numbering options.

Styles Lets you customize the appearance of the text in each table of contents level.

Page Numbering Lets you customize the page number format with text, page numbers, secondary page numbers, chapter numbers, and volume numbers.

Display Last Level In Wrapped Format Select this option to word-wrap the last level in the ToC if it's longer than one line.

6. Choose OK to return to the document window.

7. To ensure proper page numbering, move the cursor to the top of the first numbered page (the first page that follows the table of contents or any other front matter). Choose Layout ➤ Page ➤ Numbering ➤ Value, set the New Page Number to **1**, and choose OK twice (or OK then Close). See Chapter 8 if you need help.

You can now generate the table of contents and close the Table Of Contents feature bar if you wish.

Marking Index Entries

WordPerfect indexes offer two levels of index entries: the index *heading* (required) and the *subheading* (optional). In the example shown in Figure 31.6, the index headings are *Amusement, Questor, Robotics, Simulators,* and so on. Only the *Amusement* and *Robotics* headings have subheadings.

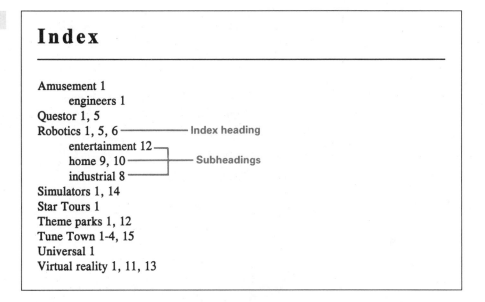

Follow these steps to mark your index entries:

1. Choose Tools ➤ Index or click the Index button in the Generate button bar. You'll see the Index feature bar shown here:

2. Select the word or phrase you want to include in the index.

3. To assign a heading for the selected text, click the Heading text box in the feature bar or select a heading from the Heading drop-down list. Edit the heading text if necessary.

4. To assign a subheading for the selected text, click the Subheading text box in the feature bar or select a subheading from the Subheading drop-down list. Edit the subheading text if necessary.

5. Click the Mark button in the feature bar.

Using an Index Concordance File

As an alternative (or supplement) to marking each index entry, you can create a *concordance file* that lists all the words you want to index. When you generate the index, WordPerfect will automatically create an entry for any word or phrase in your document that matches a corresponding entry in the concordance file. Each entry in the concordance file must end with a hard return ([HRt]) code.

By default, each entry in the concordance file is an index heading entry. If you want WordPerfect to match the entry both as a heading and a subheading, use the methods described just above to select the text and assign a heading and subheading to it. After creating your concordance file, save it as you would any other WordPerfect document.

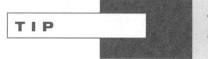

T I P

To generate the index faster, you can use Tools ➤ Sort to alphabetize the concordance file (see Chapter 22).

Defining an Index

You can define the location and appearance of your index by following the steps below:

1. Turn on the Index feature bar (Tools ➤ Index).

2. Place the cursor where you want the index to appear. (Press Ctrl+End to start the index at the end of the document.)

3. To start the index on a new page, press Ctrl+↵. Type in a title, such as **Index**, if you wish, and press ↵.

4. Click the Define button in the feature bar to open the Define Index dialog box shown in Figure 31.7.

5. Define the index format and concordance file (if you've created one), as described just below. As you make changes, the sample index in the dialog box will reflect your choices.

   Position   Where should the page numbers appear?

   Page Numbering   What should the page numbers look like?

FIGURE 31.7

The Define Index
dialog box

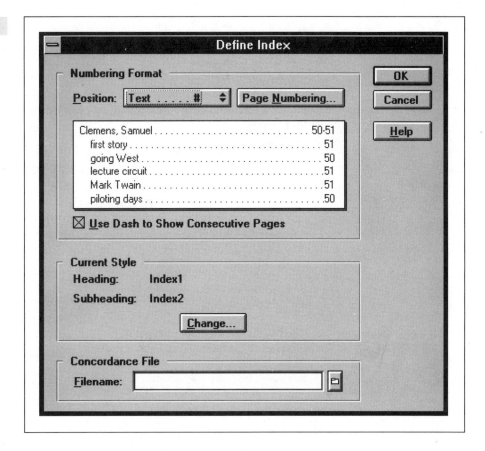

Use Dash To Show Consecutive Pages   Select this option to have WordPerfect list sequential page numbers as a range (for instance, 4–7). Deselect the option to print sequential page numbers separately (for instance, 4, 5, 6, 7).

Change   What style do you want for the index heading and subheading entries?

Filename   Lets you specify the concordance file name. Leave this blank if you're not using a concordance file.

6. Choose OK to return to your document.

You can now generate the index, and close the Index feature bar.

Marking List Entries

General lists show page numbers for items that don't necessarily fit into the index or table of contents format. For example, you might want to make a list of words or phrases as a glossary or make a list of books and articles as a bibliography. A general list can also contain references to graphics boxes.

Figure 31.8 shows a sample list of figure captions. (In this example, I tweaked the style to print a blank line between entries.)

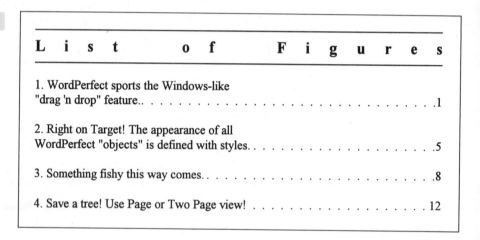

L i s t   o f   F i g u r e s

1. WordPerfect sports the Windows-like "drag 'n drop" feature.. 1

2. Right on Target! The appearance of all WordPerfect "objects" is defined with styles.. 5

3. Something fishy this way comes.. 8

4. Save a tree! Use Page or Two Page view! 12

Here's how to mark an item that you want to include in a list:

1. Choose <u>T</u>ools ➤ L<u>i</u>st or click the List button in the Generate button bar. You'll see the List feature bar shown below:

2. In the <u>L</u>ist box of the feature bar, type a name for the list or select a name from the drop-down list.

TIP   You can also retrieve list names and definitions from another document, as explained in the next section.

3. Select the text that you want to put in the list. You don't need to mark captions for graphics boxes. WordPerfect will do this for you automatically.

4. Click the Mark button in the feature bar.

Defining a General List

To define the location and format of a general list, follow the steps below:

1. Turn on the List feature bar (Tools ➤ List).

2. Move the cursor to where you want the list to appear.

3. To place the list on its own page, press Ctrl+↵. (If you're placing the list at the top of the document, press ↑ next to move the cursor before the [HPg] code.) Type a title for the list, such as **List of Figures**, if you wish, and press ↵.

4. Click the Define button in the feature bar to open the Define List dialog box shown below. (In this example I've already marked entries for a list named *Glossary*.)

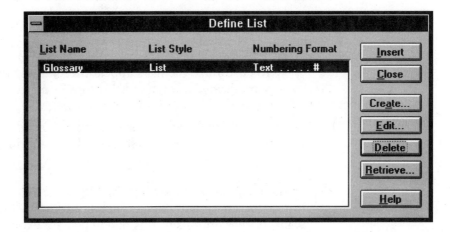

5. If the list you want to define appears in the Define List dialog box, skip to step 6. To create a list for captioned graphics boxes or any other list that doesn't appear, choose Create to open this Create List dialog box:

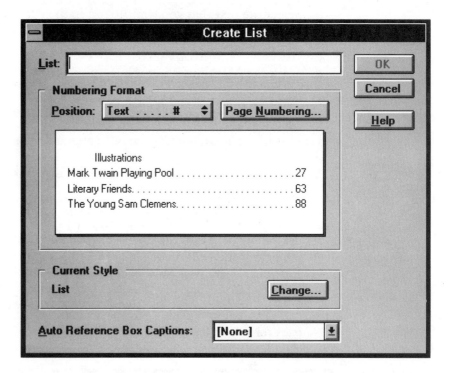

- In the List text box, type a name for the list (such as **Figures**).
- To customize the list's appearance, choose the Position, Page Numbering, and Change buttons as appropriate (these are the same as described earlier for indexes).
- To include graphics box captions in the list, choose a box type from the Auto Reference Box Captions drop-down list.
- Choose OK to return to the Define List dialog box.

6. In the Define List dialog box, highlight the list you want to place in the document and choose Insert, or double-click the name you want. (Other options in this dialog box are explained below.)

7. If you want a page break to appear after the list, press Ctrl+↵.

8. Repeat steps 2–7 for each list you want to define.

9. If you've placed the lists in the front matter, move the cursor to the first numbered page. Choose Layout ➤ Page ➤ Numbering ➤ Value and set the New Page Number to 1 (see Chapter 8). This step will ensure proper page numbering below the list. Choose OK twice or choose OK, then Close.

You can now generate the lists and close the List feature bar if you wish.

The Define List dialog box includes the options described below. Before you choose the Insert, Edit, or Delete options, be sure to highlight the list you want to work with.

Insert   Places the highlighted list definition in your document at the cursor position.

Create   Lets you create a new list, as described above.

Edit   Lets you change the format of the highlighted list and include graphics box captions in an existing list.

Delete   Deletes the highlighted list.

Retrieve   Lets you retrieve list definitions from another file.

Including Graphics Boxes in Lists

You don't need to mark graphics box captions if you want to include them in a list. If a box has a caption, WordPerfect will include it automatically in the general list defined for that box type. (Graphics boxes without captions won't be included in the list.)

Suppose you've added captions to several Figure boxes, using techniques discussed in Chapter 25. To create a list of figures for your document, follow the first four steps given just above. Next, choose Create and enter a name such as **Figures** in the List text box. Now select .Figure Box from the Auto Reference Box Captions drop-down list, and choose OK. When you return to the Define List dialog box, highlight the name of your list and choose Insert.

Marking Table-of-Authorities Entries

A *table of authorities* (*ToA*) is a list of citations in a legal document (see Figure 31.9). This table typically is divided into several sections, such as *Cases, Authorities, Constitutional Provisions, Statutory Provisions, Regulatory Provisions,* and *Miscellaneous.* Each section usually has a different format, which you can customize as needed (though you'll want to follow accepted legal practices to avoid strange glances from the legal community).

The document itself (typically a legal brief) generally contains two types of citations: a *full form,* which usually is the first reference in the document, and a *short form,* which is an abbreviated way to show all subsequent

FIGURE 31.9

A sample table of authorities

```
                    TABLE OF CASES AND AUTHORITIES

Cases                                                              Page

Association of General Contractors v.
City and County of San Francisco
      813 F.2d 922 (9th Cir. 1993) . . . . . . . . . . . .1, 9

City of Richmond v. Croson
_____ U.S. _____
109 S. Ct. 706
_____ L. Ed. 2d (1993)  . . . . . . . . . . . . . 1, 13

Fullilove v. Klutznick
      448 U.S. 488
      100 S. Ct. 2758
      65 L. Ed. 2d 902 (1993) . . . . . . . . . . . . 1, 13

Gregory Construction Co v. Blanchard
      691 F. Supp. 17 (W.D. Mich. 1993)  . . . . .1, 12, 14, 15

Jackson v. Conway
      472 F. Supp. 896 (D. C. Mont. 1993) . . . . . . . . 8, 11

London v. Coopers & Lybrand
      644 F.2d 811 (C.A. Cal. 1993) . . . . . . . . . . . 12

Authorities

California Rules of Civil Procedure
      Rule 58(a) . . . . . . . . . . . . . . . . . . 12

California Rules of Evidence
      Rule 704 . . . . . . . . . . . . . . . . . . . 40
```

references to the same authority. For each authority that you cite, you must complete these basic steps:

1. Use the full form procedure to mark the first citation of any authority, edit the text of the full citation (if necessary), and assign a "nickname" (the short form) to that authority.

2. Use the short form method to mark all remaining references to the same authority.

These basic steps are explained fully in the sections that follow.

After you've marked all the authorities, you can define the appearance and location of each section of the table and generate the entire table.

Marking the Full Form

Follow these steps to create and mark the full form citation for an entry in a table of authorities:

1. Choose Tools ➤ Table Of Authorities or click the Table Of Authorities button in the Generate button bar. You'll see the Table Of Authorities feature bar shown below:

2. Select the long form of the citation, as shown in Figure 31.10.

3. Click the Create Full Form button in the feature bar to open the Create Full Form dialog box.

4. In the Section Name text box, type a name for the ToA section, or select a name from the drop-down list.

5. In the Short Form text box, enter the short form "nickname" that you'll use to mark subsequent ToA entries for this authority. Be sure to assign a unique short name, since each short name will identify a separate authority.

FIGURE 31.10

A long-form ToA entry
selected in the
document window

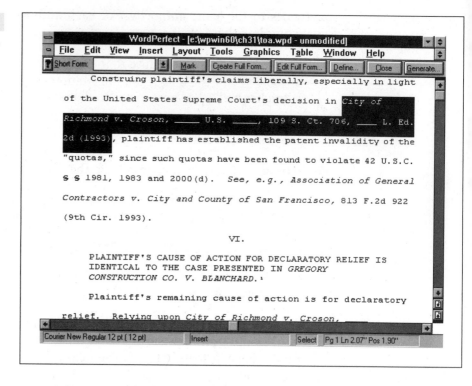

6. Choose OK. You'll see an editing window that contains the full-form text you selected in step 2 and the ToA Full Form feature bar shown below:

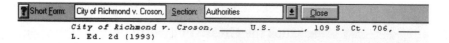

7. Make any of the changes described below.

- Use normal editing techniques and pull-down menus to edit and format the text of the full form citation as you want it to appear in the final table of authorities.

- To change the short form name assigned to the citation, edit the text in the feature bar's Short Form text box.

- To assign a different section to the citation, type a name in the feature bar's Section text box or choose a name from the drop-down list.

8. Choose the <u>C</u>lose button in the ToA Full Form feature bar.

If you need to update an existing ToA entry, click the <u>E</u>dit Full Form button in the Table Of Authorities feature bar, highlight the entry you want to change, and choose OK. Then repeat step 7 just above. When you're done, choose the <u>C</u>lose button in the ToA Full Form feature bar.

Marking the Short Forms

After marking the full form of the citation, use the short form procedure below to mark all subsequent citations of the same authority.

1. Turn on the Table Of Authorities feature bar (<u>T</u>ools ➤ Table Of <u>A</u>uthorities).

2. Select the short form for this citation from the <u>S</u>hort Form drop-down list in the feature bar.

3. Position the cursor just after the text you want to mark.

4. Click the <u>M</u>ark button in the feature bar.

5. Repeat steps 3 and 4 for each remaining short form of this citation in the document.

And that's the long and short (form) of it. Once you've marked the citations for one authority in a particular section, simply repeat the procedure to mark the full and short forms for each authority in the document.

Defining a Table of Authorities

You define a table of authorities one section at a time, like this:

1. Turn on the Table Of Authorities feature bar (<u>T</u>ools ➤ Table of <u>A</u>uthorities).

2. Place the cursor where you want the Table of Authorities section to appear (usually at or near the start of the document).

3. To insert a hard page break, press Ctrl+↵. Press ↑ to move the cursor above the [HPg] code. If you wish, type in a title, such as **Cases,** and press ↵.

4. Click the Define button in the feature bar. You'll see the Define Table Of Authorities dialog box. (This is similar to the Define List dialog box shown earlier in the chapter.)

5. Highlight the ToA section you want to define.

6. If you'd like to adjust the appearance of the highlighted section, choose Edit, and adjust the elements as needed. The options are similar to those described earlier for indexes. (If you need help with an option, click the Help button.) Choose OK when you're done changing the appearance.

7. In the Define Table Of Authorities dialog box, highlight the entry you want and choose Insert, or double-click the entry.

NOTE The Insert, Create, Edit, Delete, and Retrieve options in the Define Table Of Authorities dialog box work like the same-named options described earlier in the chapter under "Defining a General List."

8. Repeat steps 2–7 for each section in the ToA.

9. To ensure proper page numbering, move the cursor to page 1 (below the ToA and any other front matter), choose Layout ➤ Page ➤ Numbering ➤ Value, and set the New Page Number to 1 (see Chapter 8). Choose OK twice, or choose OK and then Close.

You can now generate the Table of Authorities and close the Table Of Authorities feature bar.

Cross-Referencing

You can use WordPerfect's powerful *cross-referencing* features to keep track of cross-references in your documents—such as "see Table 3.7 on page 14." And if the referenced page or table number changes—as is often the case—no problem! WordPerfect will update the cross-references automatically.

The item referred to is the *target* (in the above example, the targets are *Table 3.7* and *page 14*). The place where you mention the target is the *reference*. You'll have no trouble keeping these two terms straight if you remember that a *reference* always points to its *target*.

Generating cross-references involves two simple processes:

1. Set up the targets and references. You need to mark a target only once. Then, you can mark as many references to that target as you need.

2. Generate the cross-references.

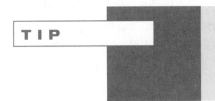

TIP You can define targets before references, or references before targets (WordPerfect doesn't care about the order). However, the instructions below assume you're defining the targets first.

Marking a Target

To mark a target, follow these steps:

1. Choose <u>T</u>ools ➤ Cross-Re<u>f</u>erence or click the Cross-Reference button in the Generate button bar. You'll see the Cross-Reference feature bar shown below:

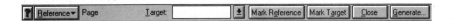

2. Move the cursor just past the target. If necessary, use Reveal Codes (Alt+F3) to help you position the cursor. (When marking a page-number target for a footnote or endnote, the cursor must be in the footnote or endnote.)

3. From the <u>R</u>eference drop-down list button in the feature bar, select the type of item you're targeting. Your options are <u>P</u>age, <u>S</u>econdary Page, <u>C</u>hapter, <u>V</u>olume, Paragraph/<u>O</u>utline, <u>F</u>ootnote, <u>E</u>ndnote, Caption <u>N</u>umber (for graphics boxes), and Coun<u>t</u>er.

4. In the feature bar's <u>T</u>arget text box, type a descriptive name for the target that will be easy to remember when you reference the target later.

5. Click the Mark T<u>a</u>rget button in the feature bar.

Marking a Reference

Here's how to mark a reference to a target in your document:

1. Turn on the Cross-Reference feature bar (choose <u>T</u>ools ➤ Cross-Re<u>f</u>erence).

2. Place the cursor where you want the reference to appear.

3. Type any introductory text and then enter a blank space, if necessary. For example, type **[see page** and then press the spacebar.

NOTE When generating references later, WordPerfect will automatically insert text from the caption number style of any graphics box. For example, if you mark Figure 1 as a target, WordPerfect will automatically insert the words *Figure 1* in the reference. Therefore, you don't have to include text from the caption number style in your introductory text.

4. In the <u>T</u>arget text box on the feature bar, type the target name (exactly as you specified it when marking the target), or select the target name from the <u>T</u>arget drop-down list in the feature bar.

5. Click the Mark R<u>e</u>ference button in the feature bar. *Don't worry if the reference appears as a question mark (?).* That character will be replaced by the correct reference when you generate the lists and references.

6. Finish typing any introductory text for the reference. For instance, to finish the example started in step 3, type a space and then **]**; the full reference will be **[see page 10]** after it's generated.

When you're done marking targets and references, you can generate the references and close the Cross-References feature bar.

Page X of Y Numbering

It's easy to define "page *x* of *y*" page numbering in your page headers or footers (where *x* is the current page of your document, and *y* is the last page in your document). For example, on page 30 of a 100-page document, your page header might say *Page 30 of 100*. If that document increased to 102 pages, WordPerfect would automatically adjust the header on page 30 to read *Page 30 of 102* the next time you generated lists and cross-references. In this example, the current page number would be the reference, and the last page of the document would be the target.

All this will become clearer as you follow the steps below:

1. Move the cursor to the end of the document (Ctrl+End).

2. To mark the target, choose Tools ➤ Cross-Reference. Choose the Reference button in the feature bar and select Page. In the Target text box, type an obvious target name, such as **LAST PAGE**. Click the Mark Target button.

3. Move the cursor to the very top of the document (press Ctrl+Home twice).

4. Choose Layout ➤ Header/Footer and follow the usual steps for creating a new header or footer (see Chapter 8).

5. In the header or footer editing window, move the cursor to where you want the current page number to appear. Type any introductory text, such as **Page** and a space.

6. Click the Number button in the feature bar and choose Page Number.

7. Press the spacebar, type **of**, and press the spacebar again.

8. To mark the reference, choose Tools ➤ Cross-Reference. From the Target drop-down list, choose **LAST PAGE**. Click the Mark Reference button, then click Close to return to the Header/Footer feature bar.

9. Finish typing the header or footer, and click the Header/Footer feature bar's Close button.

10. Generate the cross-references.

WARNING

If you add new text to the end of the document, be sure to place that text *above* the [Target(LAST PAGE)] code that identifies the last page number. Also, if you lengthen or shorten your document by a page or more, be sure to generate the cross-references again.

By the way, WordPerfect comes with a macro, named PAGEXOFY, that lets you create "page x of y" page numbering automatically. You might want to try it. (See Chapter 18 for information about creating and running macros.)

Using Styles to Mark Reference Entries

You can use the Styles feature (Chapter 17) to format and automatically mark entries for tables of contents and general lists. The trick is to include the marking codes right in the style.

To help you understand how this works, take a look at the steps below. These create a style that automatically marks chapter titles in a table of contents as ToC level-1 entries for a table of contents.

1. Choose Layout ➤ Styles ➤ Create and define a new Paragraph (or Character) style for the element you want to format, in this case the chapter titles.

2. In the Styles Editor dialog box, type a Style Name and Description. Select Show 'Off Codes'.

3. Choose Contents and enter the formatting codes you want.

4. Select (block) all the codes and text in the Contents area (above and below the [HPg] codes).

5. Choose Tools ➤ Table Of Contents. In the feature bar at the bottom of the screen, click the appropriate Mark button for this level (in this example, click Mark 1 for chapter titles). Click the feature bar.

6. Choose OK, then Close to save the style.

Use your new style to format the chapter titles. Then define the Table of Contents, as explained earlier in the chapter. To put on the finishing touches, generate the list as described next.

Generating and Editing Lists

Once you've marked your lists and cross-references, generating them is easy. In fact, you already know how:

1. Click the <u>G</u>enerate button in the feature bar or the Generate button bar, or choose <u>T</u>ools ➤ Ge<u>n</u>erate, or press Ctrl+F9.

2. If you wish, choose <u>O</u>ptions, select or deselect either of the options below, and choose OK.

> **<u>S</u>ave Subdocuments**   When this option is selected, WordPerfect saves changes to subdocuments of the master document being generated (see Chapter 32).

> **Build Hypertext Links**   When this option is selected, WordPerfect generates and saves hypertext links in your document (see Chapter 30).

3. Choose OK to start generating.

WordPerfect will generate all reference lists and cross-references in the document and will replace any previously generated reference lists with new lists.

WARNING   WordPerfect *does not* update the lists automatically when you change your document. Therefore, be sure to regenerate your lists after making changes.

If you decide to edit a generated list, pay special attention to the codes that define the list and its contents. You'll typically see codes like these after you generate a list:

[Def Mark][Gen Txt]…list goes here[Gen Txt]…

Each list begins at the [Def Mark] code that WordPerfect inserts when you define the list. The generated list appears after the first [Gen Txt] code and continues to the last [Gen Txt] code. Each time you generate a list, WordPerfect will completely replace any text between the sequence of codes shown above. You should, therefore, keep the following points in mind:

- Always place list titles and page headers *before* the [Def Mark] code. (Otherwise, they'll simply disappear—poof!)

- If you edit the generated list only, your changes will be lost when you regenerate the list. Therefore, it's best to edit your references within the main document, and then generate the lists anew.

In the next chapter, you'll learn about WordPerfect's Master Document feature, which makes it easy to assemble many small files into one big document for editing, formatting, list generation, and printing.

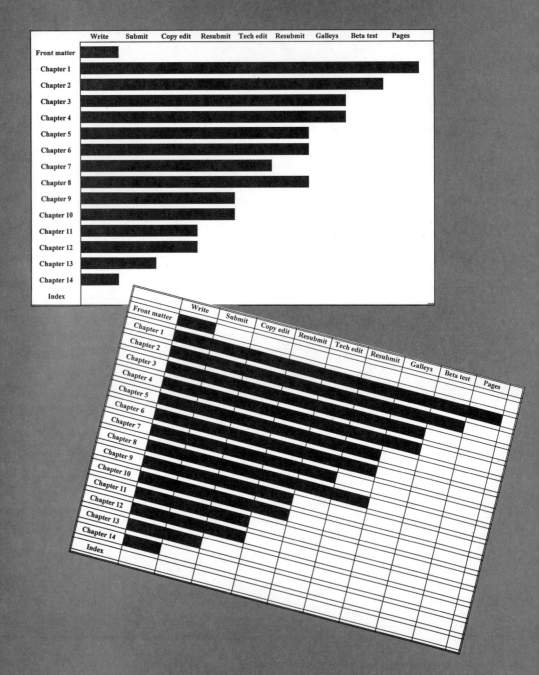

Using Master Documents to Manage Many Files

fast TRACK

**To condense a master document and save all
your changes**   **1050**

choose File ➤ Master Document ➤ Condense Master. Deselect
any subdocuments that you *don't* want to condense and save.
Choose OK.

To compare two documents   **1051**

open one of the documents to be compared. Choose File ➤
Compare Document ➤ Add Markings. Specify the document
you want to compare against the open document, select a
comparison option (Word, Phrase, Sentence, or Paragraph),
and then choose OK.

**To remove file comparison markings from
the current document**   **1053**

choose File ➤ Compare ➤ Remove Markings. Then choose
either Remove Redline Markings And Strikeout Text or Remove Strikeout Text Only, and choose OK.

IF YOU write large documents, such as books with several chapters or reports with many large sections, you'll undoubtedly find it easier to store each chapter or section in a separate file. This helps prevent any file from becoming so large that it's unwieldy to work with in a document window.

You can use WordPerfect's Master Document feature to *link* these individual files (called *subdocuments*) into one large *master document*. Then, when you want to assemble and work with all the subdocuments at once, you can *expand* the master document to its full size. After expanding the master document, you can generate lists and cross-references, print the entire document, and make global changes as necessary. When you're done using the master document, you can *condense* it back to its small size and save any subdocuments that you've changed.

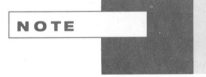

NOTE At the end of this chapter we'll look at Compare Document, a feature that shows differences between the current document and a document on disk.

Working with Master Documents

A master document is pretty much like any other WordPerfect document. And, like any other document, it can contain text and hidden codes. The only difference is that the master document contains links to other documents, called *subdocuments*. Each subdocument is also just a regular WordPerfect document that you've created and saved in the usual way.

WordPerfect doesn't enforce any hard-and-fast rules about what goes into a master document and what goes into a subdocument. In fact, it will gladly handle just about anything you throw at it (though it's not too keen on old cabbages). Nonetheless, you'll probably find master documents easiest to use if you stick to the general guidelines given in the two sections just below.

Structuring a Master Document

For best results, the master document should be a skeleton structure for your final document. It should contain only the bones and body parts listed below:

- Formatting codes and styles that apply to *all* subdocuments
- Links to each subdocument
- Titles and definitions for endnotes, tables of authorities, tables of contents, indexes, and lists

These additional tips will help you number pages, notes, boxes, and cross-references more accurately:

- If your final document will have front matter before page 1, move the cursor to the page that should be numbered as page 1 (*after* the table of contents and other front matter). Then choose Layout ➤ Page ➤ Numbering ➤ Value. In the New Page Number text box, type **1**, and then choose OK (or Close) until you return to the document window. This inserts a [Pg NumSet] code at the cursor position. Use additional [Pg Num Set] codes *only* if you want to interrupt the consecutive numbering sequence. For instance, if each section is numbered separately (1-1, 2-1, and so forth), you could restart the page numbering at the beginning of each section. (See Chapter 8.)

- To start each chapter or section on an odd-numbered page, include a [Force:Odd] code before each chapter. For example, if you've inserted each chapter as a subdocument, position the cursor before the chapter's beginning [Subdoc] code in the master document, then choose Layout ➤ Page ➤ Force Page ➤ Current Page Odd ➤ OK. (See Chapter 8.)

Structuring a Subdocument

Subdocuments should contain everything else needed to build the final document, including:

- Text and graphics for each chapter, section, etc.
- Formatting codes specific to each subdocument
- Marked text for cross-references, footnotes, endnotes, tables of authorities, tables of contents, indexes, and lists

Creating a Master Document

To create your master document, open a new document window and follow these steps:

1. Enter any codes or text that should appear before the subdocument link.

2. Position the cursor where you want to add the subdocument link.

3. Choose File ➤ Master Document ➤ Subdocument. Or right-click in the left margin area of the document and choose Subdocument from the QuickMenu.

4. Type the file name of the subdocument that you want to link, or use the file management tools (Chapter 20) to locate the file and fill in the text box. (The subdocument file doesn't have to exist at the moment.)

5. Choose Include. A comment box or icon will indicate the position of the subdocument within the master document, and a [Subdoc] code will appear in Reveal Codes.

6. To start the next document on a new page, press Ctrl+↵.

Repeat steps 1–6 for each subdocument you want to include in the master document, making sure to link the files in proper order (for instance, CHAP1.WPD, CHAP2.WPD, CHAP3.WPD, and so forth). When you're done, you'll see comments or icons in the document window for each subdocument, along with any hard page breaks you added, as shown in Figure 32.1.

FIGURE 32.1

Subdocuments in the
document window
(shown in Draft view)

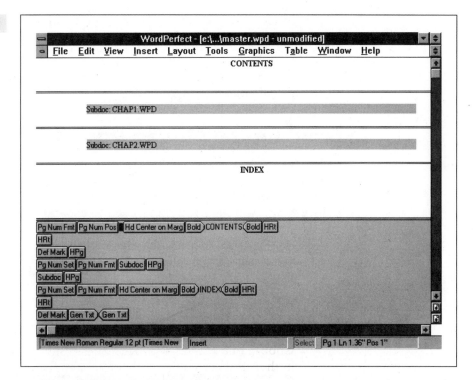

> **NOTE**
>
> In Page or Two-Page view, the link appears as an icon in the left margin area of the document window. In Draft view, the link appears as a shaded comment box. You can click the subdocument icon or comment to display the name of the linked subdocument.

Here are some tips for working with master documents:

- You can use a master document as a subdocument in other master documents. WordPerfect will automatically expand the file when you expand the master document that includes it.

- To delete a subdocument link from the master document, delete the [Subdoc] code in Reveal Codes (Alt+F3).

- To move a subdocument link to another place in the master document, move the [Subdoc] code, using techniques discussed in Chapter 4.

- It's easiest to move and delete subdocument links when the master document is condensed.

Expanding the Master Document

You can edit and save subdocuments individually, just like any other WordPerfect files. Often, however, you'll want to see and work with all your subdocuments at once. To do this, you need to *expand* the master document. Although you don't need to expand the master document to generate reference lists, you must do so for most other types of operations (for example, making global changes and printing).

Follow these steps to expand the master document:

1. Open the master document, and choose File ➤ Master Document ➤ Expand Master. You'll see the Expand Master Document dialog box, shown below:

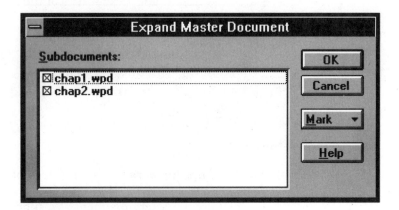

2. Initially, all subdocuments are marked for expansion. To unmark a subdocument (or to mark an unmarked subdocument), deselect or select the appropriate check box in the Subdocuments list. To mark or unmark all subdocuments at once, choose Mark ➤ Mark All or Mark ➤ Clear All.

   3. Choose OK.

Your retrieved subdocuments will appear as one large file on the document window, and you can edit this file as you would any other. Each subdocument is placed between a Subdocument Begin comment or icon and a Subdocument End comment or icon. In Reveal Codes, [Subdoc Begin] and [Subdoc End] codes surround the subdocument.

If WordPerfect can't find a document, a Subdocument Error dialog box will appear. You can handle this problem using any of the methods below:

- If the missing subdocument really does exist (but was named incorrectly in the subdocument link), type the correct name into the Subdocument Name text box (or use the file button at the end of the dialog box to help you locate the file), then choose OK.

- If you want to skip the missing subdocument and go on to the next one, choose the Skip button. After expansion, the expanded document will contain a [Subdoc] code for the missing file. You can delete the code (if appropriate) or restore the file to the correct location and expand the master document again.

- If you want to cancel expansion of the master document, choose Cancel.

Figure 32.2 shows a bird's-eye view of a master document after expanding it. (I chopped out some text and chose Draft view so you could see the entire document.)

WARNING   Don't delete the [Subdoc Begin] code or [Subdoc End] code in the master document, unless you want to break the links to a subdocument.

Generating References

Typically you'll *define* tables of contents, tables of authorities, indexes, and other automatic lists in the *master document*. You'll *mark* text for automatic lists in *subdocuments* (see Chapter 31). This way of organizing and marking lists will make the final document structure stand out clearly. It

FIGURE 32.2

A master document after expanding it (but before generating the table of contents and index)

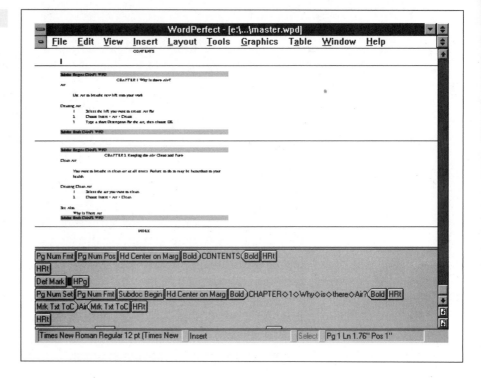

also will make the master document easier to manage, and the subdocuments easier to edit. (*WordPerfect* won't complain if you define lists in subdocuments and mark text in master documents—but *you* might get confused.)

When you're ready to generate the lists, follow the steps below:

1. Open the master document and expand it if you wish.

2. Choose <u>T</u>ools ➤ Ge<u>n</u>erate (Ctrl+F9).

3. Normally, WordPerfect will generate and update lists and cross-references in subdocuments automatically. If you don't want to update the subdocuments for some reason, choose <u>O</u>ptions, deselect <u>S</u>ave Subdocuments, and choose OK.

4. Choose OK to start generating the lists.

If you didn't expand the master document before generating the lists, WordPerfect will expand and condense subdocuments as needed, behind the scenes.

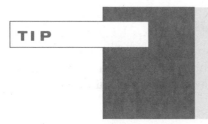

TIP

If page numbers or other automatic numbers in your generated lists aren't accurate, check to see whether any subdocuments contain codes that restart numbering incorrectly. Also, make sure that you've inserted hard page breaks whenever text needs to start on a new page.

Editing a Master Document

You can use any of WordPerfect's editing features to change subdocuments within the expanded master document. However, keep these points in mind:

- Any codes *outside* the [Subdoc Begin] and [Subdoc End] codes are part of the master document and will be saved in the master document only.

- Any codes *inside* the [Subdoc Begin] and [Subdoc End] codes are part of that subdocument and will be saved only in that subdocument when you condense the master document (see "Condensing a Master Document," later in this chapter).

- Changes made within a subdocument are saved *only* if you condense and save the subdocument (discussed later).

- As with single documents, later codes take precedence over earlier ones. For example, if you set the left and right margins to 2 inches at the top of the master document, all the subdocuments will have 2-inch margins, unless one of the documents contains codes that set the margins differently.

- Codes in subdocuments have no effect until you expand the master document. You won't know if the codes conflict until you expand the master document.

- When the master document is expanded, initial codes and styles in the master document take precedence over initial codes and styles in the subdocuments (see Chapter 19).

Printing a Master Document

To print the entire master document, expand it first, and then print as you normally do with File ➤ Print (Chapter 3). You can print the entire document, select multiple pages, or select text before printing, as for any other document.

Condensing a Master Document

Once you're done working with an expanded master document, you should condense it before saving it again. Condensing preserves disk space, ensures that your subdocuments are updated properly, and forces you to generate a fresh master document before printing and editing.

To condense a master document, follow these steps:

1. Choose File ➤ Master Document ➤ Condense Master. You'll see the Condense/Save Master Document dialog box:

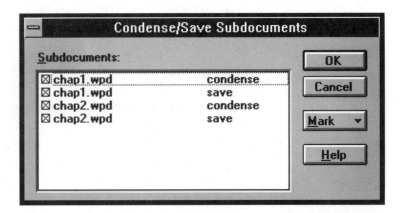

2. Initially, some or all subdocuments in the Subdocuments list are marked for condensing and saving. Here's how to change this:

   - To prevent any documents from being condensed, choose Mark ➤ Clear Condense. To mark all documents for condensing, choose Mark ➤ Condense All.

   - To prevent any documents from being saved, choose Mark ➤ Clear Save. To mark all documents for saving, choose Mark ➤ Save All.

- To mark or unmark individual files for condensing or saving, select or deselect the appropriate "condense" or "save" check boxes in the §ubdocuments list.

3. Choose OK to start condensing and/or saving.

WordPerfect removes condensed subdocuments from the master document, but retains the links to those subdocuments for future use.

Comparing Two Documents

Suppose you want to know what's different about two versions of a document, but you don't want to suffer through comparing them manually. This job is a piece of computer cake with WordPerfect's Compare Document feature.

WordPerfect can show differences between documents in three ways:

Added Text   Added text is placed between *redline* codes ([Redln]).

Deleted Text   Deleted text is placed between *strikeout* codes ([StkOut]), with lines drawn through the deleted text.

Moved Text   "THE FOLLOWING TEXT WAS MOVED" appears *before* text that you've moved, and "THE PRECEDING TEXT WAS MOVED" appears *after* text you've moved.

NOTE   WordPerfect will mark changes to footnotes, endnotes, and tables, but won't mark changes to graphics boxes, headers, footers, watermarks, and comments.

Follow these steps to compare two documents:

1. Open one of the documents that you want to compare. For added safety, make a backup copy of this document (Eile ➤ §ave As).

2. Choose File ➤ Compare Document ➤ Add Markings to display the Add Markings dialog box, shown here:

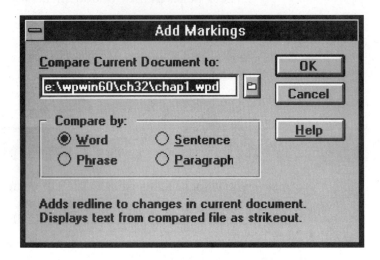

3. Initially the current file name is suggested in the Compare Current Document To text box, making it easy to compare the on-screen version with the saved copy of a file. If you wish, type a different file name.

4. Choose how you want WordPerfect to compare the two documents.

Word   Compares text word for word. A *word* is text that ends with a space, period, comma, colon, semicolon, question mark, exclamation point, hard return, or hard page break. (This is the default setting.)

Phrase   Compares the text sentence by sentence. A *sentence* is the text, phrase by phrase. A *phrase* is the same as a word, except that spaces *do not* end the phrase.

Sentence   Compares the text paragraph by paragraph. A *paragraph* is text that ends with a period, question mark, exclamation point, hard return, or hard page break.

Paragraph   Compares text that ends with a hard return or hard page break.

5. Choose OK to begin comparing the documents.

The comparison results will appear in the current document window. After looking at the results, you can remove the markings from the current document using any of these techniques:

- To remove all markings quickly, choose Edit ➤ Undo (Ctrl+Z) or File ➤ Close ➤ Yes. If it's too late for these options to work (because you've saved the document or done some other operation), choose File ➤ Compare Document ➤ Remove Markings ➤ Remove Redline Markings And Strikeout Text, and choose OK.

- To remove the strikeout text only, choose File ➤ Compare Document ➤ Remove Markings ➤ Remove Strikeout Text Only, and choose OK.

This chapter has shown you how to manage large documents that consist of smaller subdocuments and how to compare two documents. In the next chapter, you'll learn how to import and export information between WordPerfect and other programs.

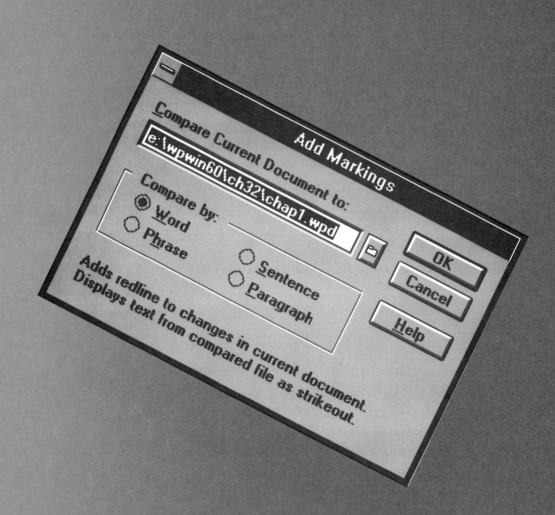

CHAPTER

33

Sharing Information with Other Applications

fast TRACK

To link an object created in another Windows application into a WordPerfect document   **1063**

switch to Program Manager, then open the server application for the object you want to link into your WordPerfect document. Create and save the file you want to link, or open an existing file. Select the object or portion of the object you want to link, then copy the selection to the Clipboard. Switch back to WordPerfect, and position the cursor where you want the object to appear. Choose Edit ➤ Paste Special, highlight the Data Type of the object you want to link, then choose Paste Link.

To embed an object created in another Windows application into a WordPerfect document   **1074**

choose Insert ➤ Object and double-click the server application you want to use. Create the object you want, choose File ➤ Update, then choose File ➤ Exit.

To launch any Windows application at a specified start time and repeat interval   **1083**

switch to Program Manager and double-click the Kickoff icon in the WPWin 6.0 group window. Use the Add button in the KickOff dialog box to specify which programs to launch, when to start them, and how often to repeat them. The programs will launch automatically in the future, as long as Windows and KickOff are running.

N THIS chapter, you'll learn the many ways that WordPerfect can interact with other programs and share information with them.

First, you'll learn about WordPerfect's automatic conversion features, which quickly convert files to and from WordPerfect format when you open or save the files.

Next, you'll discover WordPerfect's powerful abilities to import and link databases, spreadsheets, and comma-delimited text files into WordPerfect documents.

After that, you'll explore object linking and embedding, a feature that lets you combine objects created in other Windows applications with text and graphics in your WordPerfect document. You can even change those objects without leaving WordPerfect.

Finally, you'll look at the handy KickOff utility, which can launch any application automatically—even when you're miles away from your computer!

Converting Files

WordPerfect can automatically convert files from dozens of formats into WordPerfect format, and can save files to dozens of formats as well.

It's easy to convert a file that's in a "foreign" format to WordPerfect format. Just choose File ➤ Open or Insert ➤ File, specify the name of the document, and choose OK. If prompted, select the foreign format from the <u>C</u>onvert File Format From drop-down list or simply accept the suggested format (which is usually the one you want anyway), then choose OK.

NOTE Files created in version 5.0, 5.1, and 5.2 (5.x) of WordPerfect are automatically compatible with WordPerfect 6. You won't be asked to select a format when opening files in WordPerfect 5.x format.

Exporting is just as easy. Choose <u>F</u>ile ➤ Save <u>A</u>s, type in a document name, choose Forma<u>t</u>, specify the foreign format, and choose OK.

Please see Chapter 20 for more about opening and saving files.

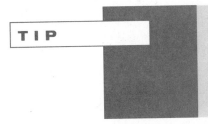

TIP The Viewer in file-management dialog boxes (discussed in Chapter 20) can display many types of files, including graphics files, word processing files, spreadsheets, and databases. The files may not look "perfect," but you can usually get a good idea of what's in them.

Keep the following points in mind when you convert files from one format to another:

- Your document won't always look the same after conversion. Therefore, you'll get the best results if you keep the formatting in files that you plan to convert as simple as possible.

- When WordPerfect formatting features aren't available in the program or format to which you're exporting, they usually are replaced by a space.

- When you choose <u>F</u>ile ➤ <u>S</u>ave, you'll usually have a chance to choose the format for saving files that were imported from a "foreign" format into WordPerfect.

- If you want to use WordPerfect files in older versions of WordPerfect—including WordPerfect 4.2, 5.0, 5.1, and 5.2—you'll need to convert them to the old version's format first. Just go through the usual File ➤ Save As steps, and select the appropriate "old" Word-Perfect format from the Format list.

- Special techniques for importing spreadsheets, databases, delim-ited-text files, and other objects created in Windows are described later in this chapter.

Choosing an Intermediate Data Format

If WordPerfect doesn't offer a way to convert a particular file directly to or from the WordPerfect format, try to find an *intermediate data format* that is common to both programs. The documentation that comes with the program will explain which formats the program can export. If those for-mats include one that WordPerfect can import, your problem is solved.

Many programs can export data in these formats:

- IBM DCA Final Form Text (FFT)
- IBM DCA Revisable Form Text (RFT)
- Navy DIF Standard
- ASCII Delimited Text (discussed later in this chapter)

WordPerfect 6 can handle all of these easily. And practically every pro-gram, including WordPerfect, can export and import ASCII text files. (Note, however, that ASCII files will have no formatting codes, just text.)

Using ASCII Text Files

DOS, Windows, and many application programs handle ASCII text files. You can edit and print these files from WordPerfect simply by opening them in ASCII Text (Standard) format. Here are some additional points to consider when you work with ASCII files in WordPerfect:

- You can use the > redirection symbol at the end of a DOS com-mand to send its output to an ASCII text file. For example, the command below sends output from the DIR command to a file named WPLIST.TXT:

```
dir *.wpd > wplist.txt
```

- Many programs let you "print" or save reports to disk in ASCII text format. These files often have the extension .PRN or .TXT.

- ASCII text files *aren't* converted automatically to WordPerfect 6 format when you save them. You'll be asked to specify the format you want.

- Beware of saving ASCII system files (files with .TXT, .BAT, .INI, or .SYS extensions) in WordPerfect format. Doing so can damage them and prevent your system from working properly (see Chapter 20 for more details).

Importing Spreadsheets and Databases

You'll be amazed at how easily you can import (copy) or link spreadsheets, database files, and ASCII-delimited text files into WordPerfect documents. You can even select which database fields to use and perform queries to isolate exactly the records you want. How's that for power?

Before we get into the exact steps for importing and linking data into your documents, let's take a quick look at some terminology and concepts you'll need to understand.

Importing and Linking Concepts

You should know the two important differences between *importing* and *linking* data:

- If you *import* the data file, subsequent changes made to the file in your application program *will not* be reflected in your WordPerfect document, unless you import the data file again.

- If you *link* to the data file, subsequent changes made to the file in your application program *will* be reflected in the WordPerfect document.

The section "Object Linking and Embedding" later in this chapter describes a more general way to link Windows objects into WordPerfect documents.

WordPerfect can import and link the following *spreadsheet* formats:

- PlanPerfect
- Lotus 1-2-3
- Excel
- Quattro Pro and Quattro Pro for Windows
- Spreadsheet DIF

And the following *database* formats:

- Clipper
- DataPerfect
- dBASE
- FoxPro
- Paradox
- SQL databases including DB2, Informix, Netware SQL, Oracle, SQL Base, SQL Server, Sybase, and XDB

If your favorite spreadsheet or database isn't listed above, but it can create ASCII-delimited text files, you're in luck because WordPerfect can read those files, too. The example below shows the first part of an ASCII-delimited text file.

```
"Date","Expense","Amount","Vendor"
"1/1/93","overhead","$1000","A.B. Properties"
"11/5/93","overhead","$566","Ace Power & Light"
"11/5/93","overhead","$600","Wheelin's Gas Co."
```

Typically, each field in a delimited file is separated by a comma, each record ends with a CR/LF (carriage return/line feed), and character strings (textual data) are enclosed in quotation marks. (Delimited files are sometimes called CSV—for Comma-Separated Value—files.)

You can import or link data into a WordPerfect table, text file, or merge data file. Here are some points to keep in mind about each type of file:

Tables   WordPerfect can import or link up to 64 columns (fields) into a table. Each field (or column) in the data file becomes a column in the table; each record (or row) of data becomes a row in the table. WordPerfect will do its best to preserve the original format of the data file. If you're using three-dimensional spreadsheets, you can bring in all the spreadsheets, or select which spreadsheets you want (each dimension will become a separate table). See Chapter 7 for more about tables.

Text Files   When you import or link data as text, each field (or column) in the data file is separated by a [Left Tab] code; each record (or row) of data appears on a separate line that ends with a hard return ([HRt]) code. WordPerfect does minimal formatting on the text.

Merge Data Files   In merge data files, each field (or column) in the data file ends with an ENDFIELD merge code; each record (or row) of data is followed by an ENDRECORD merge code. Chapter 21 covers merging.

Figure 33.1 shows my sample data file imported in Table, Text, and Merge Data File Format. Of course, you'd probably never use more than one formatting method in a single document, and your data files will be much larger; however, this example makes it easy to see the result of using each method.

Steps for Importing or Linking

To import or link a data file, follow these steps:

1. Position the cursor where you want the imported data to appear. This can be the normal editing window, a text graphics box, or any other text editing window—except for a style. Or, if you want

FIGURE 33.1

The data from my sample data file imported in Table, Text, and Merge Data format. I've hidden the bars (View ➤ Hide Bars) and increased the magnification (View ➤ Zoom) on the screen to make the imported data easier for you to see.

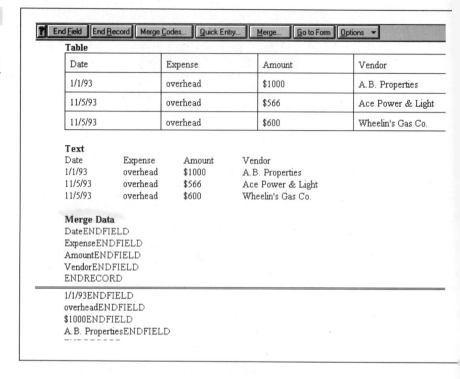

to limit the number of columns (fields) or rows (records) imported into a *table*, you can create your table first and then put the cursor in the table.

WARNING

Headers, footers, and some other WordPerfect substructures are limited in the amount of data they can hold. If you try to import or link too much data into a substructure, WordPerfect will bring in only as much data as will fit.

2. Choose <u>I</u>nsert ➤ Sp<u>r</u>eadsheet/Database.

3. Choose <u>I</u>mport (to import a copy of the data without a link) or <u>C</u>reate Link (to link to the data file). Depending on your choice, you'll see either the Import Data or Create Data Link dialog box.

4. In the <u>F</u>ilename text box, enter the name of the spreadsheet file you're importing or linking, then press Tab. You can use the button at the end of the text box to help you locate the file, as described in Chapter 20.

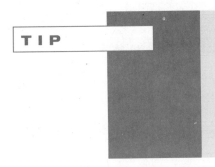

TIP

To define a default directory location for databases or spreadsheets, choose <u>F</u>ile ➤ Pr<u>e</u>ferences, double-click File, and select either <u>S</u>preadsheets or D<u>a</u>tabases, as appropriate. Fill in the D<u>e</u>fault Directory and Supplemental Directory (if you wish). When you're done, choose OK, then <u>C</u>lose. See Chapter 19 for more information.

5. If necessary, use the Data <u>T</u>ype pop-up list button to choose the type of data you're importing:

- **To import or link a spreadsheet,** choose <u>S</u>preadsheet. The dialog box will resemble Figure 33.2.

NOTE

If your spreadsheet is protected by a password, you may need to remove the password in the spreadsheet application before you can import it into WordPerfect.

FIGURE 33.2

This completed Create Data Link dialog box will link a spreadsheet named invoice.wk1 into a WordPerfect table.

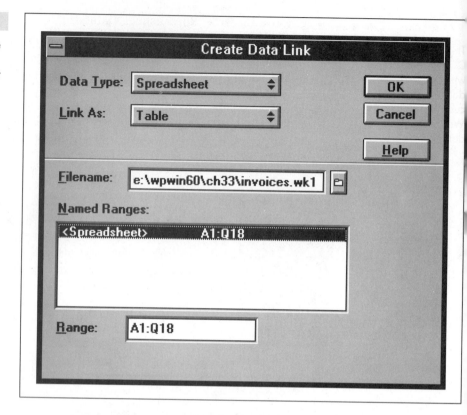

- **To import or link a database**, choose any of the database formats listed below the Spreadsheet option. The dialog box will resemble Figure 33.3.

- **To import or link a delimited text file**, choose ASCII Delimited Text. The dialog box will resemble Figure 33.4.

TIP

WordPerfect can automatically recognize the data type of most data files. Therefore, you can often skip step 5.

6. Use the Link As (or Import As) pop-up button to choose the format for the imported or linked data. Your options are Table, Text and Merge Data File.

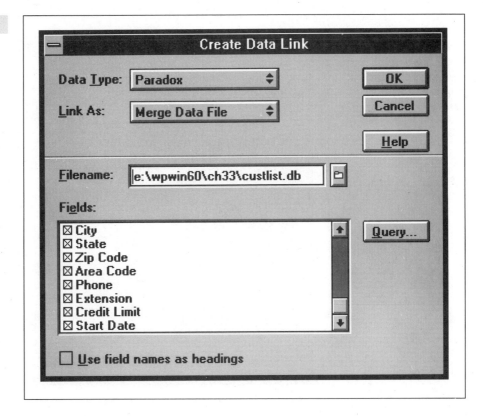

7. You can further tailor the imported or linked data if you wish (I'll explain your options in more detail later):

   - **For spreadsheets**, you can select a named range, or specify a range.
   - **For databases**, you can select (check) the fields you want and use field names as headings. You can also click the Query button to set up a query that limits incoming data to specific conditions in up to three fields.
   - **For ASCII-delimited text**, you can change the field and record delimiters, the characters that surround (encapsulate) strings of text, and the incoming characters to remove (strip).

8. Choose OK. After a brief delay, the data will appear in your document.

FIGURE 33.4

This completed Create Data Link dialog box will link a delimited text file named expense.csv into a WordPerfect text file.

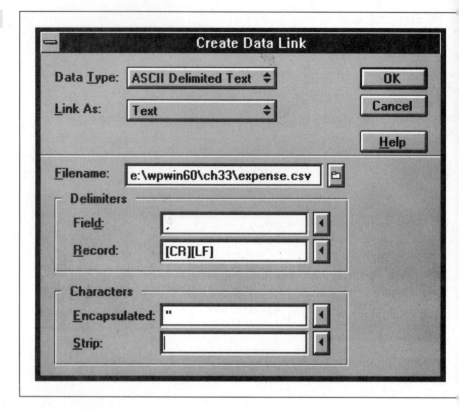

NOTE

Your selections in the Create Data Link, Edit Data Link, and Import Data dialog boxes are remembered until you change them again or leave WordPerfect.

If you linked the data, *link icons* or *comments* will surround the data. These icons and comments (referred to in this chapter as *messages*) show where the link begins and ends, but they're never printed. In Reveal Codes you'll see [Link] codes at the start and end of the linked data.

Spreadsheet Options

Figure 33.2 illustrated the Create Data Link dialog box for linking a spreadsheet. In step 7 of the importing/linking procedure above, you can type a range of cell *addresses* into the Range text box, or you can select a

Named Range that you've assigned within your spreadsheet program.

In a two-dimensional spreadsheet, the range extends from the upper-left cell to the lower-right cell. When typing a range, use a period or colon to separate the two range addresses, as in **A1.C10** or **A1:C10**. In a three-dimensional spreadsheet, each cell address also includes a letter followed by a colon, indicating which sheet the cell is from. Thus the range A1 to C10 in spreadsheet A is expressed as **A:A1.A:C10**.

A range name provides a shortcut method for referring to a range of cell addresses. For example, you could use your spreadsheet program to assign the name **TO_WP** to the range A1.C10. Later, when you link or import the spreadsheet to WordPerfect, you can select the name TO_WP from the Named Ranges list instead of typing the range as A1.C10.

N O T E WordPerfect imports or links only the *results* of spreadsheet formulas—not the formulas themselves. If you edit the data in WordPerfect, this has no effect on the underlying spreadsheet file. Likewise, if you try to recalculate the math after changing spreadsheet data in WordPerfect, nothing will happen, because the data doesn't contain any formulas.

Database Options

The dialog box in Figure 33.3 illustrates your options for specifying which fields and records you want to import or link from a database file. In step 7 of the import/link procedure, you can do any of the following:

- **To limit incoming data to specific fields**, select (check) or deselect field names in the Fields list. You can select or deselect a field by clicking on the field name you want (or by highlighting the field and pressing the spacebar). Deselected fields won't be brought into your document.

- **To use field names as headings**, select (check) Use Field Names As Headings. This option is particularly handy for tables in which field names appear as headings in the first table row, and for merge data files in which field names are enclosed between FIELDNAMES(...)ENDRECORD merge commands.

- **To limit incoming data to specific records**, click the Query button. The Define Selection Conditions dialog box will appear. Specify the conditions you want and choose OK. The example in Figure 33.5 shows selection conditions that will extract records of customers in Tucson, Arizona who have a credit limit of $5000 or more, and all customers in California.

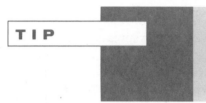

T I P

You define selection conditions for an import/link the same way you define them for a merge. See "Defining Conditions for a Merge" in Chapter 21 for more information.

FIGURE 33.5

The selection conditions shown here will extract records for customers in Tucson, Arizona who have a credit limit of $5000 or more, plus any customers in California.

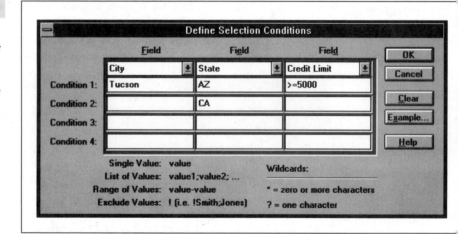

Delimited Text File Options

The import and link processes for ASCII-delimited text files are controlled by *delimiters* and *characters*. Figure 33.4 illustrates the default settings.

The *delimiters* tell WordPerfect what text separates each field and record. The *characters* tell WordPerfect what text surrounds (encapsulates) field data and what text (if any) should be removed (stripped) from the incoming data. WordPerfect will treat text surrounded by the encapsulating characters simply as text, and won't try to convert it to any special format.

The default characters will work for most delimited text files. If your files don't fit the standard, you can choose the Fiel<u>d</u>, <u>R</u>ecord, <u>E</u>ncapsulated, or <u>S</u>trip options in step 7 of the import/link procedure as necessary, then type the character or characters you want to use. You can enter keyboard characters, or press Ctrl+W and select a WordPerfect Character. If you want to use a tab, line feed, form feed, or carriage return as the character, click the button at the end of the appropriate text box and then choose the code you want.

TIP To set the default delimiters and characters for ASCII-delimited text files, choose <u>F</u>ile ➤ Pr<u>e</u>ferences and double-click <u>I</u>mport.

Fixing Imported Data

After you bring in data with many fields, the table or text columns might be too wide to fit between the current page margins. Cells in tables that extend beyond the right edge of the page will be invisible, and text imported as columns will wrap to the next line. To solve "too wide" problems like these, you can...

- Change the margins, font, and paper size (Chapters 5, 6, and 8).

- Adjust the width of the table's columns (Chapter 7).

- Remove extra tab codes and adjust the tab stops to bring text columns closer together and improve their alignment (Chapter 5).

Converting Imported Dates

Sometimes your imported or linked merge data files will end up with dates in the YYYYMMDD format, such as 19941115 (for November 15, 1994). To convert this YYYYMMDD format to a more readable one, such as 11/15/94, use the SUBSTR command in your merge form to isolate specific parts of the date. The SUBSTR command extracts a portion of a string from a larger string (called the *expression*), given a *start* position and a *length*.

Characters in a string are numbered from left to right, starting at 1. Therefore, the month number in a YYYYMMDD date starts at character 5 and is two characters long. The day starts at character 7 and is two characters long. The year starts at character 1 and is four characters long. The last two digits of the year start at character 3.

Now, let's assume that a field named **Date** in the merge data file contains a date in YYYYMMDD format. To show that date in MM/YY/DD format, you'd enter the series of SUBSTR commands that are shown next to "Date:" below.

Date: SUBSTR(FIELD(Date);5;2)/SUBSTR(FIELD(Date);7;2)/SUBSTR(FIELD(Date);3;2)

Entering those commands is a bit tricky, because you can't just type in **SUBSTR(FIELD(Date)...)** at the keyboard. Instead, you must enter appropriate merge codes and commands.

To start the document shown above, open a new document window, choose <u>T</u>ools ➤ M<u>e</u>rge ➤ <u>F</u>orm, type the name of the data file you want to associate with this form, and choose OK. This establishes your file as a merge form. Now, you can enter the first SUBSTR command:

1. Type **Date:** and press Tab.

2. Click the Merge <u>C</u>odes button in the Merge feature bar, then click the <u>I</u>nsert Field button in the feature bar. This will open the Insert Merge Codes and Insert Field Name Or Number dialog boxes, respectively. Now drag the dialog boxes to a convenient spot at the bottom edge of the screen.

3. Highlight the SUBSTR command in the Insert Merge Codes dialog box, and choose <u>I</u>nsert. An Insert Merge Code dialog box will appear.

4. In the Expression text box, type **X** (or any other letter); you'll replace this in steps 8 and 9.

5. In the Start text box, type **5**.

6. In the Length text box, type **2**.

7. Choose OK to return to the document window. (The Insert Merge Code dialog box will disappear; however, the Insert Merge Codes dialog box will remain visible.)

8. Move the cursor to the X in the SUBSTR command you just inserted (or to whatever character you typed in step 4) and delete it.

9. Double-click the DATE field in the Insert Field Name Or Number dialog box.

Now move the cursor to the end of the line and type a slash (/), which separates the month from the day. To enter the SUBSTR commands for the day and the year, just repeat steps 3–9. Adjust the Start value in step 5 and the Length value in step 6 accordingly. Type another slash at the end of the line, and repeat steps 3–9 once more (again adjusting the values in steps 5 and 6). When you're done, you can click the Close buttons in the Insert Merge Codes and Insert Field Name Or Number dialog boxes. Please see Chapter 21 to learn more about merging.

Managing Linked Data

WordPerfect offers several ways to control information in linked data files. I'll describe these next.

Changing Links

You can easily change the format or content of data links. For example, you can change linked data from a Table format to a Text or Merge Data file format. Or, you can link an entirely different file name or choose a different range of data. To change the link, move the cursor between the [Link] codes (or messages) of the link you want to change, then choose Insert ➤ Spreadsheet/Database ➤ Edit Link. (Or, open Reveal Codes and then double-click either of the [Link] codes for the link you want to edit.) The resulting Edit Data Link dialog box has the same options as Create Data Link (see Figures 33.2–33.4). Make your selections, as described previously in the chapter, and choose OK to update the link and return to your document.

Updating and Displaying Links

You can also control when links are updated and whether to display or hide the link messages. To use these options, choose Insert ➤ Spreadsheet/Database ➤ Options. When the Link Options dialog box appears, select or deselect the options below, then choose OK. Your settings remain in effect until you change them again.

Update On Retrieve   Select (check) this option if you want WordPerfect to update all linked data whenever you open the document. Deselect the option if you prefer to update links manually, as described just below.

Show Link Icons   Select this option to display the link messages. Deselect the option to hide the link messages.

If you prefer to update the links manually, choose Insert ➤ Spreadsheet/Database ➤ Update ➤ Yes. WordPerfect will refresh all the linked data in your document. (Any changes that you've made to information between the links will be lost.)

Deleting Links

You can delete links to a data file without deleting the actual data in your document. To do this, turn on Reveal Codes (Alt+F3) and delete one of the [Link] codes that encloses the linked data. This converts a linked data file to an imported data file, so that future changes made to the data file won't be reflected in your WordPerfect document.

Using OLE and DDE to Share Windows Data

You can use Object Linking and Embedding (OLE) and Dynamic Data Exchange (DDE) to combine graphics images, text, charts, spreadsheets, sound clips, video clips, and other Windows objects into a WordPerfect document or another Windows application. Once you've linked or embedded an object, you can view, play back, or change the object without having to switch back to the application used to create it.

Figure 33.6 demonstrates just how versatile this can be. Here I've inserted a graphic and a sound clip created by two other Windows applications—Paintbrush and Sound Recorder—into a WordPerfect document.

TIP You can also insert sound clips via WordPerfect's Insert ➤ Sound commands. See Chapter 30 for details.

We'll look at the specific steps for putting objects into WordPerfect files in a moment. But first, we need to cover some exceptionally weird terminology.

FIGURE 33.6

A graphic and a sound clip linked into a WordPerfect document

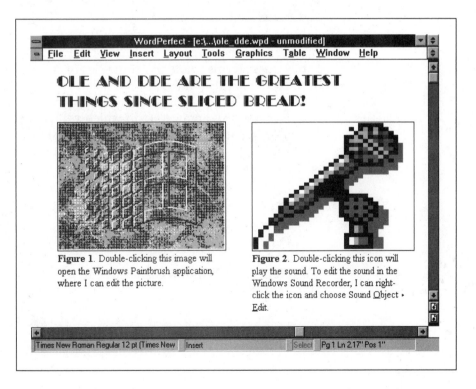

WordPerfect - [e:\...\ole_dde.wpd - unmodified]

File   Edit   View   Insert   Layout   Tools   Graphics   Table   Window   Help

OLE AND DDE ARE THE GREATEST THINGS SINCE SLICED BREAD!

Figure 1. Double-clicking this image will open the Windows Paintbrush application, where I can edit the picture.

Figure 2. Double-clicking this icon will play the sound. To edit the sound in the Windows Sound Recorder, I can right-click the icon and choose Sound Object ▸ Edit.

Times New Roman Regular 12 pt (Times New   Insert   Select   Pg 1 Ln 2.17" Pos 1"

About OLE, DDE, Clients, and Servers

OLE and DDE both are special techniques that let Windows applications exchange information with one another. The differences between OLE and DDE are rather subtle, but mainly have to do with how you edit linked information and when automatic updates take place. Nowadays, most Windows applications communicate via OLE. (If you're curious about the fine points of OLE and DDE, please see your Windows documentation.)

NOTE   DDE also provides a method called "DDE Execute" that allows Windows applications to communicate through their macros languages. For example, a WordPerfect macro could include DDE Execute statements to start Excel and copy certain spreadsheet cells to a WordPerfect table. See Help ➤ Macros for more information.

Applications that support OLE and DDE can be *servers*, *clients*, or both. I know these terms sound like some sort of curious business arrangement, but here's what they mean:

Server   An application in which you create information. *Examples:* Spreadsheet programs (such as Quattro Pro for Windows or Excel), graphics programs (such as Paintbrush or WordPerfect Presentations), sound programs (such as Sound Recorder), and word processing programs (such as WordPerfect for Windows).

Client   An application that can get data from a server and link server information into one of its own documents. *Examples:* Word-Perfect for Windows, Microsoft Word for Windows.

WordPerfect for Windows can act as an OLE server, an OLE client, or a DDE client.

About Linking and Embedding

When you *link* an object, the same information exists in two files: the server document and your WordPerfect document. When you change the information in the server, it automatically changes in WordPerfect also. This is similar to linking a spreadsheet, database, or ASCII-delimited text file.

Objects linked via *OLE* can be edited in either the server application or the client document. (Often, you can just double-click an object in Word-Perfect to open the server application and make changes.) To edit information that's linked via *DDE*, you must switch to the original document in the server application and then make your changes.

Embedded objects are copies of the original objects, much as imported spreadsheets, databases, and ASCII-delimited text files are copies. Embedded information exists independently in the server and client applications. Therefore, changes made to the object in the server application have no effect on the object in the client document—and vice versa.

Whether an object is linked or embedded depends on the commands you use to insert the object. The type of linking (OLE or DDE) depends on the data type you choose when you paste in the link.

Now, let's look at the steps for linking and embedding.

Linking an Object

To link an object from a server application into a WordPerfect document, follow these steps:

1. While WordPerfect is running, switch to Program Manager (Ctrl+Esc or Alt+Tab).

2. Open the server application for the object you want to link into your WordPerfect document.

3. In the server application, create and save the file you want to link, or open an existing file. (See your application's documentation for help on doing this.) Note that linking will work *only* if the object is

saved with a valid file name.

4. Select the object or portion of the object you want to link, then copy the selection to the Windows Clipboard (Edit ➤ Copy).

5. Switch back to WordPerfect (Ctrl+Esc or Alt+Tab).

6. Position the cursor where you want the object to appear.

7. Choose Edit ➤ Paste Special to open the Paste Special dialog box. A sample dialog box for a sound clip appears below.

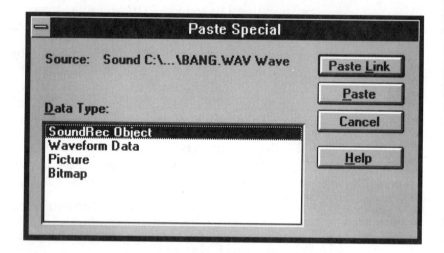

8. Highlight the Data Type of the object you want to link. (For example, to link a sound object, highlight SoundRec Object.) The Paste Link button will remain gray until you highlight an object type that can be linked. (Linkable formats typically are called "... Object." For example, "SoundRec Object" or "PBrush Object.")

9. Choose Paste Link. The linked object will appear in a graphics box. You can use techniques discussed in Chapter 25 to size, position, caption, and change the style of the linked graphics box.

NOTE Selecting Paste Link on a text format such as RTF will produce DDE links. Selecting Paste Link on an object or graphics format will produce OLE links. (If you choose the Paste button in the Paste Special dialog box, the object will be embedded, not linked.)

If you wish, switch back to the server application and exit the application (File ➤ Exit), then switch back to WordPerfect (if necessary).

If you later open a document that contains links to other files, you'll be asked for permission to update the links. Choose Yes to update the links, or No to skip the updates for now.

Embedding an Object

To embed an object into your document, follow these steps:

1. Choose Insert ➤ Object. The Insert Object dialog box will show a list of available server applications for your computer, as in the example below.

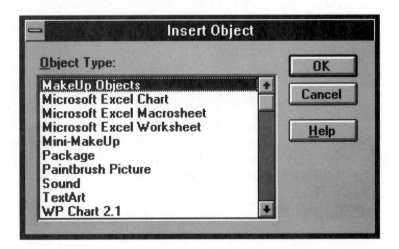

2. Double-click the Object Type you want (or highlight it and choose OK). The server application for the object will open.

3. Create the object (sound, Paintbrush picture, spreadsheet, chart, and so on).

4. Choose File ➤ Update to embed the object in your document.

5. Choose File ➤ Exit and answer Yes (if prompted) to close the application and return to your document. The embedded object will appear in a graphics box.

Viewing, Editing, or Playing Back Objects

It's easy to view, change, or play back linked or embedded objects. Here are the steps to follow:

1. Often you can just double-click an object to change it or play it back. If double-clicking doesn't do what you want, select (click on) the object, then...

   - Choose Edit ➤ ...Object from the WordPerfect menus.
   - Or, right-click and choose...Object from the QuickMenu.

   The exact wording on the menu and QuickMenu depends on the type of object you're working with.

2. For some objects (such as sound files), your menu or QuickMenu selection will lead to additional options such as Edit or Play. Pick the one you want.

3. If you chose an "edit" option, the application used to create the object will open. Make changes to the object as necessary (see the application's documentation if you need help). When you're done, choose File ➤ Exit ➤ Yes.

Changing and Deleting Links

Here's how to make changes to the links in linked objects:

1. Choose Edit ➤ Links to open the Links dialog box:

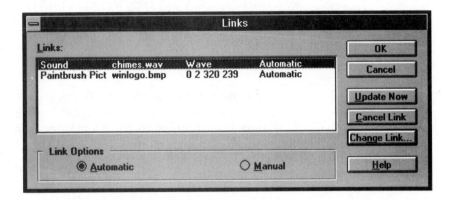

2. In the Links list, highlight the link you want to update, then...

- **To update the link** with any recent changes (including those made with Change Link), choose Update Now.

- **To break the link,** choose Cancel Link. The object will remain in the document. However, it won't be linked to the source file or application anymore.

- **To link to a different file name,** choose Change Link, and double-click the file you want (or highlight the file name and choose OK).

- **To change the link type,** choose Automatic or Manual. Automatic links are updated whenever the file changes. Manual links are updated only when you choose Update Now.

3. Choose OK to return to your document.

Sending WordPerfect Data to Other Applications

You can link, embed, or copy information from WordPerfect to other Windows and non-Windows (DOS) applications in several ways.

To send WordPerfect for Windows data to another *Windows application,* use either of the methods below:

- **Use normal copy and paste** procedures to paste text or graphics from a WordPerfect document into another Windows application. For example, to paste a graphic from WordPerfect into a Paintbrush document, select the graphic in WordPerfect and choose Edit ➤ Copy (Ctrl+C). Open or switch to Paintbrush, then choose Edit ➤ Paste.

- **Link or embed a WordPerfect document** into any OLE client. The procedures for linking and embedding WordPerfect documents into other client applications are often similar to the ones described here for linking and embedding from other applications to WordPerfect. However, you'll need to check the other application's documentation to be sure.

To paste *text* from WordPerfect for Windows into a *non-Windows (DOS) application,* follow the steps below:

1. In WordPerfect for Windows, select the text you want and choose Edit ➤ Copy (or Edit ➤ Cut).

2. Switch to Program Manager (Ctrl+Esc or Alt+Tab).

3. Use the standard double-click techniques to start your non-Windows application from Program Manager.

4. Press Alt+spacebar to put the application in a window.

5. Position the cursor where you want to paste the text.

6. Click the Control-menu box and choose Edit ➤ Paste to paste in the text.

7. Save your changes in the non-Windows application and exit the application in the usual way.

8. Switch back to WordPerfect for Windows (Ctrl+Esc or Alt+Tab).

Launching Programs Automatically

You can use KickOff, a handy little program that comes with WordPerfect, to launch any Windows application at a specified start time and repeat interval. Yes, this means you can start applications even while you're sleeping, working on your tan, or vacationing on the Riviera. Although KickOff is specially designed to automate updates to QuickFinder indexes, you can use it to launch any program at a specified time.

NOTE KickOff can launch programs *only* when it's running under Windows. To make KickOff run automatically (and be minimized) whenever you start Windows, start KickOff as described below, choose Setup, check the Start KickOff Minimized option, choose OK, then minimize KickOff. Finally, hold down the Ctrl key while dragging the KickOff icon from the WPWin 6.0 group window to the Startup group window.

Starting KickOff

Here's how to start KickOff:

1. Double-click the Kickoff icon in the WPWin 6.0 group window in Program Manager. (If you've already started KickOff, you can

switch to it using the standard Ctrl+Esc or Alt+Tab techniques.) The KickOff dialog box appears, as shown below:

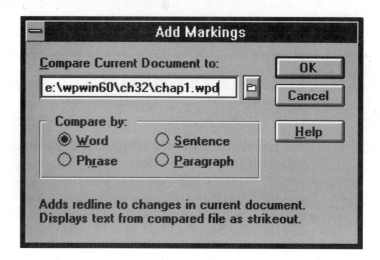

2. Choose any of the options below:

Add Lets you add a new event to KickOff's launching pad (see "Adding an Event to KickOff" below).

Edit Lets you change settings for an event. To edit an event, highlight the event in the Events list and choose Edit (or double-click the event you want to change). Edit the event as desired, then choose OK.

Remove Lets you delete an event from the list. To remove an event, highlight the event in the Events list, choose Remove, then choose Yes to confirm the deletion.

Setup Lets you customize KickOff's behavior. You can choose whether or not to start KickOff minimized, remove events after they finish running, disable old events that are past their date and time, or record any problems with launching a program in a log file named C:\WPC20\KICKOFF.LOG.

3. When you're done using KickOff, click its minimize button. (If you choose Close, KickOff will stop running and no applications will launch.)

Adding an Event to KickOff

Adding a new event to KickOff is easy. Just follow the steps below:

1. Choose <u>A</u>dd from the KickOff dialog box. You'll see the Edit/Add dialog box shown here:

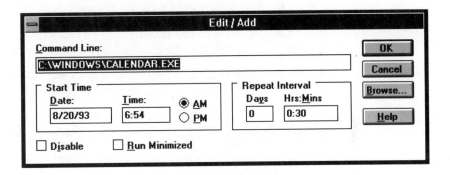

2. In the <u>C</u>ommand Line text box, enter the full command line for the program you want to run, or use the <u>B</u>rowse button to locate the program. For example, to run the Windows calendar, you'd type **c:\windows\calendar.exe** (or use <u>B</u>rowse to locate that program and fill in the path automatically).

3. Enter the starting <u>D</u>ate for the event.

4. Enter the starting <u>T</u>ime and choose the appropriate <u>A</u>M (midnight to a second before noon) or <u>P</u>M (noon to a second before midnight) setting.

5. To launch the program at regular intervals, enter the number of Da<u>y</u>s, or Hrs:<u>M</u>ins (hours and minutes), or both to repeat the launch. Here are some examples:

- Setting Da<u>y</u>s to 0 and Hrs:<u>M</u>ins to 00:30 launches at the specified date and time, then again every 30 minutes.
- Setting Da<u>y</u>s to 0 and Hrs:<u>M</u>ins to 12:00 launches at the specified date and time, then again every 12 hours.

- Setting Days to 1 and Hrs:<u>M</u>ins to 12:00 launches at the specified date and time, then again every day, at 12 hours from the specified time.

- Setting Days to 2 and Hrs:<u>M</u>ins to 00:00 launches at the specified date and time, then again every other day, at the specified start time.

6. To run the application minimized, select (check) <u>R</u>un Minimized.

7. To prevent the program from launching automatically until you clear the D<u>i</u>sable check box, select (check) D<u>i</u>sable.

8. Choose OK to return to the KickOff dialog box. The program you selected will appear in the E<u>v</u>ents list.

Launching QuickFinder from KickOff

To launch QuickFinder from KickOff, follow the general steps above for adding an event (be sure that you don't check D<u>i</u>sable in step 7). Use the following command line in step 2:

c:\wpc20\qfwin20.exe *options*

replacing *options* with any of the following:

/ra	Rebuilds all indexes listed in the QuickFinder Index Names list box.
/r-*long name*	Rebuilds only the index specified by *long name*
/ia	Updates all indexes with new or modified files
/i-*long name*	Updates the index specified by *long name with new or modified files*

To specify more than one index name, separate each name by a comma and a space, like this:

```
c:\wpc29\qfwin20.exe /r-document, customer
```

Please see Chapter 20 for more about using QuickFinder.

In this chapter you learned how to share information from other applications with WordPerfect, and how to export WordPerfect data to other Windows and non-Windows applications. You also learned how to use KickOff to launch programs automatically.

That's all folks!

APPENDICES

APPENDIX

Installing WordPerfect

THIS appendix summarizes hardware requirements and installation procedures for WordPerfect 6.0 for Windows. For more technical information, please refer to the appendices in your WordPerfect software documentation.

Hardware Requirements

You'll need the following hardware to run WordPerfect 6.0 for Windows:

- An 80386 SX or higher PC or PC-compatible computer with *at least* 8 MB of extended memory (WordPerfect *can* run in 4 MB, but will be very slow)
- DOS Version 3.0 or higher
- Windows Version 3.1 configured to run in 386 Enhanced mode
- A hard disk with at least 33 MB of available disk space for a standard (full) installation, or about 11 MB for a minimum installation
- Either a 3.5" (1.44 MB) or a 5.25" (1.2 MB) floppy disk drive
- At least a VGA graphics adapter and display
- A mouse (this is optional, but highly recommended)

Installing WordPerfect

Your best bet for installing WordPerfect 6.0 for Windows is to refer to the documentation that came with your WordPerfect program. This is especially true if you're a beginner or you're installing to a network. In general, the procedure goes like this:

1. Insert the WordPerfect 6.0 for Windows Install 1 disk in drive A or B.

2. Start Windows and go to the Program Manager.

3. Choose File ➤ Run from the Program Manager menus. In the Command Line text box, type **a:install** if you put the disk in drive A or **b:install** if you put the disk in drive B. Then choose OK.

4. Type your name in the Name text box. Then press Tab and type in your license number. (Your license number is printed on the Certificate of License that came with your installation disks.) Choose Continue.

5. When you see the installation options, choose the type of installation you want. Your options are:

> **Standard**   Installs the full program on your hard disk. For a first-time *non-network* installation, it's best to choose this option. This option requires about 33 MB of disk space.

> **Custom**   Installs only the WordPerfect files and utilities you specify and lets you choose the drive and directories to which you want to install. This option is useful if you need to reinstall part of the WordPerfect system.

> **Network**   Installs WordPerfect on a network server or workstation. You must choose this option to enable WordPerfect's network features. Install to the server first, then install to the workstation. Please see your WordPerfect documentation for more about network installations.

> **Minimum**   Installs the minimum number of files needed to run WordPerfect for Windows. Note that a Minimum installation won't install Speller, Thesaurus, QuickFinder, WP Draw, macros, graphics files, learning files, Help files, or any other nonessential files. This option requires about 11 MB of disk space.

> **Options**   Lets you install new or updated WordPerfect printer files, utilities, language modules, and TrueType fonts. This option also provides late-breaking WordPerfect product information.

6. Answer questions and respond to prompts as they appear on the screen.

7. When the installation is complete, and you're returned to the Windows prompt, remove all floppy disks from their drives and store them in a safe place.

Verifying the Installation

If you're a beginner, you might want to skip the rest of this appendix and proceed to Chapter 1. Otherwise, if you know your way around your system and want to verify your WordPerfect installation, do the following:

1. Starting at the Windows Program Manager, double-click the WPWin 6.0 icon in the WPWin 6.0 group window.

2. To verify your printer selections, press F5 S. You should see the names of all your installed printers. Choose <u>C</u>lose twice to return to WordPerfect.

3. To check out your font list, press F9. You should see your available fonts. Choose Cancel to return to your document.

NOTE For information on installing additional printers and fonts, see Chapter 10.

4. To try out various screen views, choose <u>V</u>iew, then choose <u>D</u>raft, <u>P</u>age, or <u>T</u>wo Page. You can learn about these options in Chapter 4.

5. If you want to exit WordPerfect and go back to Windows without saving anything, press Alt+F4.

Installing New Hardware

Suppose you install WordPerfect, then you get a new printer or graphics adapter. Or maybe you decide to add a fax board or a sound board to your system. WordPerfect for Windows can take advantage of hardware changes automatically. However, this can happen *only* after you complete the appropriate procedures to inform *Windows* of the change. Typically, this involves running the Windows Control Panel or Windows Setup applications in the Main group of the Program Manager. Please see your Windows documentation for details on installing new hardware.

If you specifically want to install new fonts, you can do so by starting the WordPerfect for Windows Install program (as described above). When you get to the installation options, choose Options then Fonts. See Chapter 10 for more details.

Tips for Conserving Memory

Windows manages the memory that WordPerfect for Windows uses. When you start Windows, you can choose About Program Manager from the Program Manager's Help menu to find out how much memory is available. Likewise, choosing About WordPerfect from WordPerfect's Help menu will show you the amount of memory and resources available to WordPerfect. The following tips can help you free up more memory for WordPerfect to use.

At the DOS prompt, before you start Windows...

- Reduce the FILES= or BUFFERS= command (or both) in your CONFIG.SYS file; however, don't reduce FILES= to less than 20. You'll need to reboot the computer after changing and saving CONFIG.SYS.

- Remove any RAM drives that you've defined.

- Remove any Terminate-and-Stay-Resident (TSR) programs from memory.

- If you're running DOS 6, use MEMMAKER to optimize memory usage.

Whenever you're using Windows...

- Reduce the number of programs currently running.

- Close any group windows that you're not using.

- Set the Windows desktop wallpaper option to None.

- Delete the Clipboard contents.

- Run non-Windows applications in a full screen, rather than a window.

- Minimize Windows applications to icons.

NOTE   You can find more information about memory management techniques in the documentation that comes with DOS and Windows.

Whenever you're using WordPerfect for Windows…

- Reduce the number of documents you have open.

- Use one of the built-in WordPerfect keyboards, such as <WPWin 6.0 Keyboard>, rather than a user-defined keyboard. (See Chapter 19.)

- Turn off hyphenation. (See Chapter 16.)

- Select a printer that uses a .PRS file with only a few fonts. (See Chapter 10.)

- Use fewer graphics boxes in your document. (See Chapter 25.)

Startup Switches

Normally, you can just start WordPerfect for Windows by double-clicking the WPWin 6.0 icon in the WPWin 6.0 group window. However, you can also use optional startup switches whenever you run WordPerfect with the File ➤ Run command in Program Manager. Here are the basic steps to follow:

1. Start Windows as usual and go to Program Manager.

2. Choose File ➤ Run from the Program Manager menu.

3. Type **wpwin**, followed by a space, followed by the startup switches you want. For example, you could type **wpwin /m-d:\wpwin60\macros\mystart.wcm** to start WordPerfect and run the macro named *mystart*. (There's more about startup switches just below.)

4. Choose OK or press ↵ to start WordPerfect with the options you specified in step 3.

Here are some of the optional startup switches you can use:

filename   Automatically opens the specified *filename* from the current directory. You can specify a complete path name, as in **wpwin d:\wpwin60\wpdocs\favorite.wpd**.

/D-*drive\directory*   Redirects overflow files and temporary buffers to a drive other than the default drive where the WPWIN.EXE file is located.

/M-*macroname*   Automatically runs the specified macro from the current directory. You can specify a complete path name, as in **wpwin /M-d:\wpwin60\macros\mystart.wcm**.

/NB   Disables the original backup option. (See Chapter 19.)

/X   Restores Preferences options to their default settings (for the current session only).

You can combine startup options, as in **wpwin /X /D-f:**, which temporarily restores all Preferences settings to their defaults and redirects overflow files to drive F.

To run startup options automatically when you double-click the WPWin 6.0 icon, you can type the **SET WPWIN=options** command at the DOS prompt, or place it in your AUTOEXEC.BAT file. Once you've done this, you can run WordPerfect for Windows with any of the options defined in the SET WPWIN= command simply by double-clicking its icon. For example, the following command would activate the /NB and /D startup options whenever you double-click the WPWin icon in the WPWin group window:

    set wpwin=/NB /D-f:

For more information about WordPerfect's optional startup switches, please refer to the Startup Options Appendix in the WordPerfect for Windows documentation.

APPENDIX

B

Summary of New Features: For Experienced Users

THIS appendix offers a quick overview of the hottest new features in WordPerfect for Windows. The material here is specifically written for

- People who are *considering* upgrading to 6.0 and want to know if it's worth the effort

- People who have upgraded to 6.0 already and want to find the good stuff in a hurry

What's Involved in Upgrading?

Before we get into specific new features, let's take a look at what's involved in upgrading to WordPerfect 6.0 for Windows.

How compatible is 6.0 with 5.x?   WordPerfect 6.0 will read any document created in WordPerfect 5.x for DOS or Windows. However, Version 6.0 has many new features not available in earlier versions. So once you save a document in WordPerfect 6.0, you can't open it in an earlier version of WordPerfect—*unless* you remember to save your 6.0 document specifically in WordPerfect 5.x format. This step is no trouble—it's just a simple menu selection—but, of course, any features that are specific to Version 6.0, such as hypertext or charts, won't carry down to the earlier-format file.

Macros created under WordPerfect 5.1 or 5.2 for Windows or WordPerfect 6.0 for DOS often will convert smoothly to run under WordPerfect 6.0 for Windows. You cannot, however, directly convert WordPerfect 5.1 for DOS macros to run under WordPerfect 6.0 for Windows. See Chapter 18 for more information.

What kind of hardware do I need for 6.0? I recommend that you have *at least* a 386 machine with a VGA monitor, 640 KB of RAM, and at least 8 MB of extended memory. I also recommend that you have DOS 5, DOS 6, or a third-party utility that can help you conserve memory. Plan on setting aside at least 33 MB of hard disk space if you want to install the whole kit and caboodle. You'll find the "official" hardware specifications in Appendix A.

How much trouble is the upgrade? No trouble at all. You put the Install disk in drive A or B, run the Install program, and follow the instructions on the screen. (See Appendix A.)

WordPerfect 6.0's Hottest New Features

For the remainder of this appendix, I'll summarize the hottest new features and point you to the chapters that discuss them. I'll categorize and alphabetize the main features, and I'll mark the start of each one with a Hot Stuff icon. That should help you find the features you're most interested in quickly.

HOT STUFF

Documents and Files

Improved File Manager, QuickList, and QuickFinder Streamlined file management tools make quick work of storing and finding files. You may never need Windows File Manager again (Chapter 20).

HOT STUFF

FAX and Mail

Fax If you have a compatible fax board, you can send a fax right from WordPerfect. No need to print the document first (Chapter 23).

Send Mail from WordPerfect If you have network e-mail that uses the Lotus VIM or Microsoft MAPI standards, you can send a document to somebody else without printing and without exiting WordPerfect (Chapter 23).

Formatting/General

Abbreviations Type shortcut words, symbols, or phrases into your document, then expand them automatically with the Abbreviations feature (Chapter 9).

Bookmarks You can find your place in a jiffy with the press of a key (Chapter 9).

Columns Working with columns is easier than ever, especially with the addition of optional built-in separator lines, borders, and Balanced Newspaper columns (Chapter 28).

Counters WordPerfect has always incremented counters for graphics boxes automatically. Now you can also create your own counters to count anything you want, then increment and decrement them manually (Chapter 15).

File and Path Names You can insert the current file or path and file name anywhere in your document. This is especially handy in headers and footers (Chapters 4 and 8).

Delay Codes You can define headers, footers, and other repetitive elements at the top of the document and then delay the codes so they don't print until you get to a specific page (Chapter 8).

Hidden Text You can make selected portions of your document invisible and view or display the hidden text at will (Chapter 6).

Initial Caps Quickly convert selected text to *UPPERCASE*, *lowercase*, or *Initial Caps* with Edit ➤ Convert Case (Chapter 3).

Labels, Envelopes, Pamphlets, and Booklets These are easier than ever to create (Chapter 8).

Outlines There's a special Outline feature bar that makes creating and editing outlines a snap. And the outlines are collapsible now (Chapter 14). You can also set up quick bulleted and numbered lists with the Bullets & Numbers feature (Chapter 5).

Find and Replace You can find, and optionally replace, *specific codes*—such as text in a particular font—throughout your document.

Graphics

Borders and Shading   Draw borders around pages and paragraphs, and shade them if you like (Chapter 6).

Contoured Text   You can now contour text around the image that's *inside* a graphics box, not just around the square box itself (Chapter 25).

Drop Shadows, Rounded Corners, Custom Lines   WordPerfect offers a host of predefined borders and lines to jazz up your documents. You can also customize borders and lines, set up rounded corners, and take complete control over the size, location, and color of drop shadows (Chapter 25).

Drawing, Charting, and TextArt   WordPerfect has full-featured drawing, charting, and text shaping packages built right in! You'll never need standalone applications for these jobs again (Chapter 26).

Watermarks   You can print a watermark (a faint background image) on every page of your text (Chapter 8).

Help

Coaches   These aids let you learn a new feature while you get some real work done (Chapter 4).

Find What You Need, Quickly   Help includes a Table of Contents, Index, "How Do I...?" list, Glossary, and jump words to help you find the information you need in a flash (Chapter 2).

Point-and-Click Help   Press Shift+F1, then click anywhere on a menu or dialog box to get help about the place you clicked.

Tutorial   Run the WordPerfect 6.0 tutorial right from your Help menu (Chapter 2).

Information Sharing

Import Databases and Spreadsheets   It's easy to import data from databases, spreadsheets, and ASCII delimited files into WordPerfect documents. You can link or import the data as a WordPerfect table, text file, or merge data file. Linked data is updated automatically if you change the underlying data file (Chapter 33).

Launch Applications Automatically The KickOff utility lets you launch applications anytime you want, and repeat the launch at specified intervals (Chapter 33).

Object Linking and Embedding WordPerfect supports Object Linking and Embedding (OLE) and Dynamic Data Exchange (DDE). These techniques let you put data created by other Windows applications into your WordPerfect documents. You can then view, play back, or edit the data without leaving WordPerfect. Changes to linked data are reflected in your WordPerfect document automatically (Chapter 33).

Interactive Documents

Hypertext Use hypertext to build instant cross-referencing capability into a document, just like the jump words in a Help screen. Jump to words, play sounds, roll a film clip—you name it. The capability is there (Chapter 30)!

Sound If you have a compatible sound card, you can make your on-screen documents talk, play music, or make any kind of sound you want (Chapter 30).

Macros

Macro Command Language For macro mavens, the macro command language offers the capabilities of a real programming language, and includes a command inserter to make programming jobs easier (Chapter 18).

On-line Macro Reference Extensive macro documentation is available on disk. Just choose <u>H</u>elp ➤ <u>M</u>acros (Chapter 18).

Mass Mailings/Merges

Envelopes Automatically create an envelope (with POSTNET bar codes!) for every form letter you print (Chapters 8 and 21).

POSTNET Bar Codes Automatically print a POSTNET bar code on every mailing label or envelope, to get your mail there fast (Chapters 8 and 21).

Quick and Easy Merges   Creating a merge data file and filling it with data is easier than ever before. When you reorganize or re-name merge fields, WordPerfect adjusts the data automatically (Chapter 21).

Store Merge Data in a Table   You can kiss goodbye those old "secondary merge files" with their weird coding. Now you can put merge data into a plain old WordPerfect table, making the whole job *much* easier (Chapter 21).

HOT STUFF

Math

Built-in Spreadsheet   The Tables feature is now a complete spreadsheet (you can even graph your data with the built-in Chart package). It's easy to do any kind of math, from financial calculations to trigonometry, and formula entry is easier than ever. You'll love the automatic Sum and Data Fill features (Chapter 24).

HOT STUFF

Printing

Create a Booklet or Pamphlet   You can subdivide pages and then print them as a booklet. When printing is done, just fold the pages in half, and the booklet is ready for binding. No need to figure out page numbering or reshuffle pages (Chapter 8).

No Need for Print Preview   What you see is what you get! You can view and edit your document at any magnification, and can even display and edit facing pages (see Screen/Interface below).

HOT STUFF

Screen/Interface

Power Bar and Feature Bars   Earlier versions of WordPerfect for Windows sported button bars, a ruler bar, and a status bar to make your on-screen life easier. A new *power bar* provides quick access to menu options. And when you perform certain tasks, *feature bars* appear automatically. Just click buttons in the feature bar to do any task quickly—no more scrounging around for the right menu options. The menu bars are customizable too (Chapters 4 and 20).

Double-Click Shortcuts   You can double-click certain hot spots on the screen, in the power bar, and in Reveal Codes, to go to relevant dialog boxes quickly (Chapter 4).

QuickMenu Shortcuts   Right-clicking the mouse on a screen hot spot or object brings up a context-sensitive QuickMenu of options for the area you clicked. No more searching through lengthy menus to find what you want (Chapter 2).

Three View Modes   You can work in any of three different view modes: Draft, Page, or Two Page. All are WYSIWYG (what-you-see-is-what-you-get), and you can make changes in any mode. You can also display or hide bars, Reveal Codes, graphics boxes, hidden text, and white-space symbols (Chapter 4).

What's It For?   Simply move your mouse pointer to a button, bar, menu option, or code. The WordPerfect title bar will tell you what that thing does.

Zoom   In Draft and Page view, you can zoom in for a close-up view or zoom out for an arm's-length view—even while editing your document (Chapter 4).

Spelling and Document Information

Auto-Replace   Automatically replace common misspellings, such as replacing *hte* with *the*, without being prompted (Chapter 11).

Dictionary Management   Design your own supplementary dictionaries and choose which dictionary will be updated with new words during a spell check. Your supplementary dictionaries can include words to skip, replacement words, and alternative words (Chapter 11).

Document Information   Get complete document statistics, not just a word count (Chapter 4).

Styles and Templates

Put *Anything* in a Style   Styles can now include columns, graphics boxes, and even other styles (Chapter 17)!

Quick Format   You can quickly copy formatting codes and styles from one paragraph to others with the QuickFormat feature (Chapter 5).

Style Libraries   You can store styles in the current document, the default template, a supplemental template, or a separate style library file. You can also change predefined system files (Chapter 17).

Templates   Templates define the initial appearance of new documents and the styles, macros, abbreviations, button bars, keyboards, and menus available when you edit them. Design your own templates or use one of many supplied with WordPerfect (Chapters 4 and 20).

Tables

Fancy Fills, Lines, and Drop Shadows   No need any more to put a table in a graphics box to get these special effects (Chapter 27).

Recalculate When You Want To   You can recalculate the current table or all tables in the document—manually *or* automatically (Chapter 24).

Spreadsheet   The built-in spreadsheet makes table math a breeze (Chapter 24).

WP
WPWin 6.0
WP
WPWin 6.0
WP
WPWin 6.0

APPENDIX

First Aid for Common Problems

THIS appendix is loaded with quick first-aid solutions for the most common WordPerfect problems and confusions. The solutions are categorized and alphabetized into these sections for easy reference:

- Document/File/Window Problems
- Formatting Problems
- Keyboard/Shortcut Key Problems
- Menu/Command Problems
- Mouse Problems
- Printer/Font Problems
- Screen Problems
- Startup Problems

The start of each section is marked with a First Aid icon.

How to Use This Appendix

Go to any section and browse through the problems explained in that section. Your problem may be covered and solved right there on the spot. If not, you can always get more in-depth information and help by looking up the appropriate topic in the index at the back of this book. (Or by pressing F1 in WordPerfect!)

Here I'll assume you already have your most basic skills down pat. If you don't, you'd do well to read Chapter 1 and browse through any unfamiliar topics in Part One, just to get your bearings.

First Aid

Document/File Problems

I Can't Find My Document

First of all, are you sure you *saved* the file before you exited WordPerfect and turned off the computer? If you don't know what I'm talking about here, see "Don't Shut Down Yet!" in Chapter 2.

If you didn't save your work before exiting WordPerfect, there's no hope of recovering it now. You can only open documents that you've saved and given a file name.

If you did save the document, but are just having trouble finding it, maybe (1)you're misspelling its name now, or (2) the file you're trying to open is not on the current directory, or (3) you or somebody else has deleted the file.

To start your search for the file, first click on File in the menu bar, then look beneath the Exit option for a list of the most recently edited documents. If you see the file you want to open, just click its name.

If that doesn't work, choose File ➤ Open as usual. Scan through the list of file names that appears. If you like, you can choose Setup ➤ Sort By ➤ Date/Time ➤ Sort Order ➤ Descending ➤ OK to put the names in date order, so that the most recently edited files appear near the top of the list. (You can also choose Setup ➤ Show ➤ Filename, Size, Date, Time ➤ OK to make it easier to find the file based on its editing date.

If the file is nowhere to be found in the current directory, try another directory and/or drive. You can view directory names and QuickList names by choosing QuickList ➤ Show Both while you're in the Open File dialog box. Then double-click any directory name to move to that directory. (The list of file names shows files on the current directory only.)

If you still can't find the file, you can use File ➤ Search in the Windows File Manager to search the entire disk. See your Windows documentation for more information on using the Windows File Manager.

Finally, it may be that you or someone else has deleted the document you're trying to open. If that's the case, you may not be completely out of luck. See "I Just Deleted My Document (or Reformatted My Disk)" later in this appendix.

It Says the Document Is "Read-Only"

If, when you try to open a file, you see the message indicating that the *document is in use or is specified as read-only*, it may be that you've already opened that document in this session. Choose <u>N</u>o, then choose <u>W</u>indow ➤ <u>C</u>ascade to neatly stack all your open document windows. If you see the name of the document you want to edit in a title bar, just click that title bar to start editing that document.

If you haven't already opened the file yourself, and are on a network, it may be that someone else on the network is currently editing that document. Your best bet might be to wait until that person is done, so you can open and edit the document yourself.

Another possibility is that the file really *is* read-only. To find out, leave the file closed (or close it), then choose <u>F</u>ile ➤ <u>O</u>pen again. Highlight the troublesome file name, then choose File <u>O</u>ptions ➤ Change <u>A</u>ttributes. If the Read-Only check box is checked, click it to clear it, then choose OK. You should now be able to open the file without getting the read-only message.

WordPerfect Just Up and Disappeared!

If it seems as though your entire WordPerfect for Windows application window has suddenly just disappeared, it might just be covered by some other window. Hold down the Alt key and press Tab until you get to the WordPerfect icon, then release the Alt key. Or, press Ctrl+Esc and double-click on WordPerfect in the Task List.

To simplify things, consider maximizing the window by clicking on the Maximize button in the upper-right corner of the WordPerfect window. To learn more about managing windows, see your Windows documentation or try the Windows Tutorial. (That is, go to the Windows Program Manager, and choose <u>H</u>elp ➤ <u>W</u>indows Tutorial from the Program Manager's menu bar. Follow the instructions that appear on the screen.)

My Whole Document Just Disappeared

Maybe it's just scrolled out of view. Press Ctrl+Home to scroll to the top of the screen.

If that doesn't bring it back, you may have accidentally created a new, blank document window (by choosing <u>F</u>ile ➤ <u>N</u>ew, or pressing Ctrl+N, or clicking the New Document button in the power bar). Choose <u>W</u>indow

➤ Cascade to look at all the open document windows. Then click the title bar of any window to see what's in that window.

If you still can't find the file, maybe you actually closed it. Use File ➤ Open to reopen the file. (See Chapter 3.)

I Just Deleted My Document (or Reformatted My Disk) by Mistake!

If you really did delete a file, or reformat a disk, WordPerfect won't be able to help you. If you're using DOS 5 or 6, or have a third-party Utilities program that can do the job, look up UNDELETE (if you deleted a file) or UNFORMAT (if you reformatted a disk) for help. You'll need to exit WordPerfect before you can use one of those programs.

First Aid

Formatting Problems

Boldface/Italics/Other Formatting Has Gone Too Far

If you turn on a feature such as Boldface or Italics, and then you forget to turn it *off*, the formatting feature will go on...and on...and on. Move the cursor to where the cursor begins, turn on Reveal Codes (Alt+F3), and delete the code that starts the format. Then select the text you really want to format, and choose the attribute or other feature. See "Revealing the Hidden Codes" in Chapter 4, and "Selecting (Blocking) Text" in Chapter 3.

WordPerfect Just Completely Ignored My Formatting Change

Chances are, there's some code right after the one you just inserted that's canceling out your new code. For example, in this pair of codes:

[Font: Script[Script Regular]] [Font: Perseus[Perseus Regular]]

the first code, which is supposed to switch to Script font, has no effect, because the code for Perseus font immediately cancels it out. Your task is to turn on Reveal Codes and seek-and-destroy (delete) the code that's canceling out the code you want. See "Revealing the Hidden Codes" in Chapter 4.

My Codes Just Up and Disappeared (or Moved)

WordPerfect 6.0 automatically moves and replaces certain formatting codes. So if the code you entered doesn't appear exactly at the cursor position, take a look at the start of the paragraph or the start of the page. Chances are that Wordperfect just moved the code to where it makes the most sense in the document.

Numbers (4488222) Are Appearing in My Document for No Reason

You're using the cursor-positioning keys with the Num Lock key turned on. Tap Num Lock (once only), then try those cursor-positioning keys again. You can then move the cursor over to the accidental numbers and delete them with the Backspace or Delete keys. See "Using Your Keyboard" in Chapter 2.

mY tEXT lOOKS lIKE tHIS

tAP THE cAPS lOCK kEY (oNCE oNLY) then try again. See "Using Your Keyboard" in Chapter 2.

First Aid

Keyboard/Shortcut Key Problems

My Keys Don't Work the Way You Say They Should

Are you sure you're using WordPerfect 6.0 for Windows? If so, choose File ➤ Preferences, then double-click the Keyboard icon. Highlight the <WPWin 6.0 Keyboard> option and choose Select, then Close. Now your keyboard should behave as described in this book.

My Cursor-Positioning Keys Don't Work

If you're using the keys on the numeric keypad, press Num Lock once. Then try again. If that doesn't cure the problem, perhaps text or a graphics box is selected. Click on any single character of text, then try again.

My Keyboard Just Beeps

Most likely, you're typing too fast for WordPerfect to keep up. Wait a few seconds, then try again.

If that doesn't work, it may be that text or a graphics box is selected. Click some "neutral" part of the document (any single character or blank space) and try again.

If that doesn't work, you may be "hung" due to a memory problem in Windows. Your only alternative might be to reboot (press Ctrl+Alt+Del), and follow the instructions that appear on the screen. If you have this problem often, you should remember to *save your work frequently* by using File ➤ Save or Ctrl+S. That way, if the computer does hang, you'll only lose the work you've done since the last time you saved your file.

First Aid

Menu/Command Problems

The Command I Need Is Dimmed

Commands are dimmed (grayed out) when they are not appropriate for the current context. For example, Edit ➤ Copy is available only when text is selected. Edit ➤ Paste is available only when there's something in the Clipboard to paste.

If a graphics box is selected, many commands will be dimmed. Try clicking some "neutral" part of the document (a single character), or select the portion of text you want to modify. Then try the menus again.

First Aid

Mouse Problems

Resurrecting a Dead Mouse

If your mouse doesn't work at all, it may not be properly installed for use in Windows. Check the documentation that came with your mouse for proper installation instructions.

My Mouse Buttons Are Backwards

If your left mouse button behaves as I've described the right mouse button, and your right mouse button behaves as I've desccribed the left, the button settings are reversed. Go to the Windows Program Manager screen and open the Main group. Then open the Control Panel and

double-click the Mouse icon. There you can "swap" the left and right mouse buttons by selecting or deselecting Swap Left/Right Buttons. You can also adjust the tracking speed, double-click speed, and so forth. (Choose Help if you need help.)

First Aid

Printer/Font Problems

My Printer Doesn't Do Anything

First look around the screen. If WordPerfect is waiting for you to respond to some question, do so.

Next, make sure you've selected the appropriate printer (File ➤ Select Printer), as discussed near the beginning of Chapter 10. Check to make sure the printer is plugged in (to the wall and the computer), turned on, and on line, according to the instructions in your printer manual.

If you're using a manual-feed paper size or paper type, the printer may be waiting for an envelope, sheet of labels, or whatever type of paper you chose. If there is a message window on the front of the printer, it will probably show you what type of paper it's waiting for. Insert the paper into the manual feed (usually on the top of the paper bin), until the printer pulls it in. You may have to feed each page manually.

If the printer still doesn't work, hold down the Alt key and press Tab until you get to the Print Manager, then release the Tab key. If the printer is stalled, you may be able to get it going again by highlighting the name of the document you're trying to print, then clicking the Resume button. See your Windows documentation for more information on using the Windows Print Manager.

Text Doesn't Align Properly on the Page

If you're using a dot matrix or other tractor-feed type printer, the paper may have been misaligned to begin with. You can change the left-to-right position of paper in the printer on most dot matrix printers. Read the first few sections in Chapter 10, and refer to your printer manual for additional information as necessary.

The Quality of My Printed Graphics or Text Is Awful

Try a higher print quality. See "Step 6: Tell It How to Print" in Chapter 10.

My Printer Runs Out of Memory

Try printing at a lower print quality, or reduce the number of soft fonts downloaded to your printer. See Chapter 10.

The Wrong Font Comes Out of the Printer

You've probably designed the document with one printer selected, and you're trying to print it with another printer. Use File ➤ Select Printer to display the list of installed printers. Double-click the name of the printer you used to create this document, then try printing the document again.

First Aid

Screen Problems

The Text Is Too Small or Large

You can choose View ➤ Zoom and change the magnification setting to increase or decrease the size of the text. To get an idea of how your complete page will look, you can then choose View ➤ Two Page. See Chapter 4 for more information.

I Don't See the Title Bar, Menu Bar, and Other Parts of the Document Window

Press Alt+Shift+F5, then switch to Page view (View ➤ Page). If that doesn't work, choose options from the View menu to indicate which bars and tools you want to see.

To change the default settings for some of those features, choose File ➤ Preferences, then double-click the Display icon. Choose Document and decide whether to turn the scroll bars on or off. Choose Ruler Bar to decide whether or not the ruler appears automatically on new and current documents. Choose OK, then choose Close.

First Aid

Startup Problems

It Says "Backup File Exists..."

From time to time, WordPerfect puts a copy of your current document on disk. When you save a file and exit WordPerfect properly, that temporary backup file is erased.

If you don't exit WordPerfect properly before turning off the computer, that temporary backup file is not erased. The next time you start Word-Perfect, it recognizes that temporary backup file is there, and asks if you want to open it, delete it, or rename it. In most cases, you'll probably want to choose <u>O</u>pen when you're prompted, to see what's in the backup file.

In the future, always remember to exit WordPerfect properly and save your work, as discussed under "Don't Shut Down Yet!" in Chapter 2.

APPENDIX

Hidden Codes
Revealed

CHAPTER 4 explains how you can use Reveal Codes (<u>V</u>iew ➤ Reveal <u>C</u>odes or Alt+F3) to view, move, and delete the codes that WordPerfect uses to format your document. Most of the codes are self-explanatory. For example, [Ln Spacing: 2.0] is the code that WordPerfect inserts when you change the line spacing to 2.

If you're not sure what a code is for, simply open Reveal Codes and move the mouse pointer to the code you're interested in. A description of that code will appear on the WordPerfect title bar.

TIP

You can often double-click a code in Reveal Codes to open a dialog box that lets you change whatever settings the code controls.

In this appendix, I'll cover some of the not-so-obvious codes, such as [TSRt], that seem to "just appear" in your document and aren't discussed elsewhere in this book. For a complete listing of codes, consult the Codes Appendix in the Reference manual that came with your WordPerfect package.

The [Dorm HRt] Code

The mysterious [Dorm HRt] *(dormant hard return)* code sometimes appears when the first line at the top of a page contains only a [HRt] (hard return) code. The code is "dormant" because WordPerfect assumes that you don't really want a blank line at the top of the page. If you add or delete text above the [Dorm HRt] code, and that line moves somewhere other than the top of a page, the code will revert to the regular [HRt] code.

The [Ignore:...] Code

The word Ignore at the beginning of a code indicates that the code no longer makes sense and is therefore being ignored. For example, suppose you have five tabs across a line. Then you change the ruler so that there are only four tab stops. The last Tab code on that line will probably have an [Ignore Tab] code in it, to let you know that the original Tab code is being ignored because it doesn't make sense.

If you change the ruler again, and insert five or more tab stops, the [Ignore Tab] is removed and the code takes on its original meaning.

[T...]: Temporary Codes

A *temporary code* is typically used to break text that won't fit within the margins or the current column. For example, if you're using narrow columns and you type a word that's wider than the column, WordPerfect will insert a temporary soft return [TSRt] code at the beginning of the word to ensure that it starts on a new line. If you later divide the wide word with a hyphen, or reduce its font size so that it fits within the space available, the temporary code will disappear.

Temporary codes also are likely to change if you change column widths, margins, and so forth.

The [Unknown] Code

An [Unknown] code indicates a code that was created in another version of WordPerfect or in another word processing program. WordPerfect can't interpret the code but leaves it in as an "unknown." If you convert the document back to the original word processor's format, that [Unknown] code will (usually) regain its original meaning.

GLOSSARY

I N addition to using the glossary provided here, you can look up words in the glossary that's built into WordPerfect. Here's how:

1. Choose <u>H</u>elp ➤ <u>C</u>ontents.

2. Click on *Glossary*.

3. At the top of the window, click on the button that represents the first letter of the term you want to look up.

4. Click the term you're interested in.

5. After reading the definition, you can repeat steps 3 and 4 to look up another term. When you're ready to return to your document, choose <u>F</u>ile ➤ E<u>x</u>it or press Alt+F4.

+ (as in Ctrl+Z or Alt+F5): Denotes a combination of keystrokes, meaning "Hold down the first key, and while holding the first key down, press the second key, then release both keys" (Chapter 2).

[…]: In a [Font] code, such as [Font:CG Omega (W1) [Corporate Mono]], indicates a font that WordPerfect has substituted for your original selection. WordPerfect does this only when you change printers and the current printer doesn't have the font you originally selected (Chapter 10).

⏎: The symbol used to indicate the Enter key; also called the Return key (Chapter 2).

➤: In this book, this symbol separates the commands or options that you select in a series. For example, "Choose <u>H</u>elp ➤ <u>A</u>bout WordPerfect" is a shorter way to say "Choose About WordPerfect from the Help pull-down menu" (Chapter 2).

.ALL file: A file that contains information about all the printer fonts and paper sizes for a family of printers (Chapter 10).

.INI file: A file that stores setup and startup information for Windows applications (Chapter 20).

.LEX file: A file containing the main Speller dictionary and hyphenation information (Chapter 11).

.PRS file: A file that contains information about a specific printer and its paper definitions. WordPerfect creates a .PRS file from a .ALL file when you select a printer (Chapter 10).

.WPG file: A file that contains a WordPerfect-format graphic image.

Abbreviation: A shortcut representation of a word or phrase. You can type abbreviations into your document and then expand them automatically (Chapter 9).

Alt: Abbreviation for the Alternate key; usually pronounced "allt," like the first three letters in the word *alternate* (Chapter 2).

Applet: An unofficial nickname used to describe any small specialized Windows application (program). For example, the Windows Clock, Calendar, Cardfile, Sound Recorder, and other accessories are often called "applets."

Argument: The number or text on which a *function* operates. In the function SQRT(81), for instance, SQRT() is the function, and 81 is the argument (Chapter 24).

Attribute: The way a font is printed, such as Boldface or Extra Large size (Chapter 6).

Baseline: The invisible line on which text is printed (Chapter 28).

Block: A selected chunk of text, or the act of selecting text. See *Select* in this glossary (and Chapter 3).

Bookmark: A place marker that you can put into your document in order to return to that spot quickly (Chapter 9).

Button bar: An on-screen display of buttons that you can click with your mouse, instead of going through the menus or pressing shortcut keys. You can customize WordPerfect's predefined button bars and create new ones (Chapters 4, 19).

Built-in font: A font that comes with the printer, and therefore need not be installed separately (Chapter 10).

GLOSSARY

Byte: Approximately one character of information; for example, the wor *cat* takes up three bytes of disk space.

Cartridge font: A collection of fonts stored on a cartridge that goes i a slot in the printer (Chapter 10).

Case-sensitive: Indicates that a function or application distinguishe between uppercase and lowercase. In a case-sensitive situation, "Smith, "SMITH," "smith," and "SmItH" would all be different. Most function and applications *are not* case-sensitive. However, WordPerfect's Abbrevia tions feature is case-sensitive, and you can perform case-sensitive Fin and Replace operations (Chapter 9).

Cell: In a table, the place where a column and row intersect. For exampl cell B2 is the intersection of column B and row 2 (Chapter 7).

Chart: A business graph created from data that's in a tabular format an stored in a graphics box (Chapter 26).

Check box: An option in a dialog box that can either be selected (con tains an ×) or deselected (is empty). To select or deselect the option, yo click it with the mouse or highlight it and press the spacebar (Chapter 2)

Click: Move the mouse pointer to the item, and then press and releas the mouse button—usually the *left* mouse button, but this is reversed o a left-handed mouse (Chapter 2).

Code: An item that is visible only in the Reveal Codes window, and dis played as text on a sculptured button or enclosed in a box. Codes contro document formatting. In this book, codes are enclosed in square bracket ([ ]) (Chapter 4).

Corrupted File: A file that can no longer be opened, or is incomplete because it has been damaged. To avoid corrupted files, don't turn off you computer until you've saved your work, exited all programs, and returne to the DOS command prompt (Chapter 3).

Counter: A feature in WordPerfect that counts or numbers things i your document. WordPerfect has built-in counters for each type of graph ics box. You can also create, update, and display counters of your ow (Chapter 15).

Ctrl: Abbreviation for the Control key; pronounced "control" (Chapter 2)

Current directory: The directory WordPerfect is currently using t store and search for files (Chapter 20).

Current document: When several documents are open on the screen, the current document is the one that's in the active window and may be covering other documents (Chapter 4).

Cursor: The (usually) blinking symbol on the screen that indicates where the next character you type will appear. In the document window, the cursor is a blinking vertical bar (|); in Reveal Codes, it is a small, non-blinking block; also called the *insertion point* (Chapters 2, 4).

Data file: Information that's used to "fill in the blanks" during a merge; for example, a list of names and addresses used for printing form letters and mailing labels (Chapter 21).

DDE: (Dynamic Data Exchange) A technique that lets you transfer, share, and update information in documents created by different Windows applications (Chapter 33).

Dead zone: An area around the edge of the page, about $\frac{1}{4}$-inch wide, where the print rollers touch the paper to move it through the printer. You can't print anything within the dead zone (Chapter 10).

Default: The setting or option WordPerfect uses if you don't make any changes on your own (Chapter 19).

Design element: Anything that's repeated throughout your document, such as section headings (Chapters 8, 17).

Dialog box: A box or window that appears on your screen and presents options for you to choose (Chapter 2).

Dimmed: A menu or dialog box command that's not relevant at the moment, and therefore can't be selected (Appendix C, Chapter 2).

Directory: A place on the disk (hard or floppy) where files are grouped together (Chapter 20).

Document: Any body of text or other information created with a computer program. Letters, essays, mailing labels, newsletters, and spreadsheets are all examples of documents (Chapters 2, 3, 33).

Document window: The part of the screen where you do your typing and editing; also called the *edit screen* or *editing screen* (Chapter 4).

DOS: (Rhymes with "floss") An acronym for *Disk Operating System*, the program that gets your computer running and controls the computer's operations. The DOS command prompt looks something like **C:\>** *or* **C>**

GLOSSARY

followed by a blinking cursor. You can run DOS commands and other programs from the prompt by typing a valid command and pressing ↵. For example, typing **ver** ↵ tells you which version of DOS you're using. Typing **win wpwin** ↵ starts both Windows and WordPerfect for Windows.

Dot leader: A line of dots that connects a piece of text with a page number or other information. To type the dot leader below, I pressed Alt+F7 twice, right after typing **Introduction** (Chapter 5).

Introduction...................12

Double-click: A technique that selects an option or highlights a word of text. This means, "move the mouse pointer to the item, and then press and release the mouse button twice, as quickly as possible"; double-clicking is usually done with the left mouse button (Chapter 2).

Drag: A technique that usually selects a block of text or moves or resizes a graphic. This means, "move the mouse pointer to the item, hold down the mouse button, move the mouse pointer to another location, and then release the mouse button"; dragging is usually done with the left mouse button (Chapter 2).

Drag-and-drop: A technique for moving or copying text with the mouse, where you place the mouse pointer on selected text, drag the mouse pointer to another location, and then release the mouse button to drop the selected text at that location (Chapter 3). Not to be confused with "dragon drops," which don't exist.

Draw: A full-featured drawing application that comes with WordPerfect. Use WP Draw to create your own pictures, enhance graphics that you've pulled into graphics boxes, and to annotate charts (Chapter 26).

Drive: Short name for *disk drive*, the place where files are stored (Chapter 20).

Driver: A small program that enables Windows or WordPerfect for Windows to communicate with a piece of equipment that's attached to your computer. For example, a *printer driver* helps WordPerfect send text and graphics to your printer correctly (Chapter 10).

Drop cap: A large capital letter at the start of a paragraph (Chapters 17 and 25).

Drop-down list: A list of alternatives available for a text box. To open a drop-down list, you click the downward-pointing triangle next to the text box. You can also press the ↓ key to open the list (Chapter 2).

Drop shadow: A darkened, offset patch behind a figure or text, used to give a raised or floating appearance (Chapter 25).

Dynamic Data Exchange: See *DDE.*

Editing screen: Same as *edit screen* and *document window*—the place on the screen where you type and edit text (Chapters 3, 4).

Extension: The optional suffix that follows a file name. The extension is preceded by a period, and is up to three characters in length. Example: In MYLETTER.WPD (pronounced "my letter *dot* w p d"), the extension is .WPD (Chapter 20).

Feature bar: An on-screen display of buttons that appears automatically when you use certain features. Buttons on the feature bar are specific to the feature you're using (Chapter 4).

Field: One column or type of information in a merge data file. Example: A data file of names and addresses usually has a field for name, a field for address, a field for city, and so forth (Chapter 21).

Figure box: A type of graphics box, typically used to hold graphic images (Chapter 25).

File: A single document or program stored on a disk (Chapter 20).

Flush right: Aligns the right edge of text with the right margin (Chapter 5).

Font: A combination of typeface, size, and any additional attributes (Chapter 6).

Footer: A section of text and/or graphics that's repeated at the bottom of every page (Chapter 8).

Form: The file used in a merge to fill out and format data from a data file; for example, a form letter (Chapter 21).

Function: In Tables math, a command that performs some action on a number or text. Example: The square root function SQRT(...) can determine the square root of any positive number (Chapter 24).

Function keys: The keys named F1 through F12 (or F1 through F10 on some keyboards) that appear across the top or at the left side of the keyboard (Chapter 2).

GLOSSARY

Graphics box: A container for storing a graphic image, table, or text in a document. Styles of graphics boxes include Figure box, Table box, Text box, User box, and others (Chapter 25).

Graphics font: A font that's stored on disk and can be used with any printer that prints graphics. Examples: TrueType, Speedo, and Type 1 (Chapter 10).

Gutter: The white space between columns in a multicolumn document (Chapter 27).

Hang/hanging indent: An "outdent" that reaches out into the margin, or sticks out from the rest of the paragraph (Chapter 5).

Hard return: An intentional line break that's inserted when you press ↵; appears as [HRt] in Reveal Codes (Chapters 1, 2, 3, 4).

Header: Text and/or graphics that are repeated at the top of every page (Chapter 8).

Hidden code: See *Code*.

Insertion point: See *Cursor*.

KB (or K or Kilobyte): 1,024 bytes, or roughly one thousand characters (see *Byte*).

Landscape: An orientation for printing in which the long edge of the page runs horizontally and printing appears between the short sides of the paper. Landscape is the opposite of *Portrait* (Chapter 8).

Leading: (Pronounced "ledding") The amount of white space between printed lines (Chapter 28).

Macro: A collection of actions that can be played back with a single keystroke or menu command (Chapter 18).

MB (or M or Megabyte): 1,024 kilobytes, or roughly a million characters (see *Byte*).

Memory: The chips in the computer hardware that store the program(s) and document(s) you're working on at the moment; also called RAM, for *Random Access Memory* (Chapter 2).

Menu/menu bar: The bar across the top of the screen that offers commands for you to choose (Chapters 2, 4).

Merge: To join data, such as names and addresses, from a data file to a form, such as a form letter or envelopes. Typically used for mass mailings (Chapter 21).

Mouse: A point-and-click alternative to the keyboard as a means to interact with a computer (Chapter 2, Appendix C).

Mouse pointer: The arrow or other symbol that moves on the screen when you roll the mouse (Chapter 2, Appendix C).

OLE (Object Linking and Embedding): A technique that lets you transfer, share, and update information in documents created by different Windows applications (Chapter 33).

Path: The location of a file; for example, **c:\wpdocs\myletter.wpd** refers to the file named MYLETTER.WPD on the directory named WPDOCS on drive C. The **c:\wpdocs** part is the path the computer needs to follow to get to the file (Chapter 20).

Point: In reference to *fonts,* a point represents about $\frac{1}{72}$ of an inch (Chapter 6). In reference to *the mouse,* to point means to move the mouse pointer so that it is touching the object (Chapter 2).

Pop-up: A list that pops up when you use certain buttons. If you click the button itself, you must then keep the mouse button depressed, highlight the option you want in the pop-up list, and then release the mouse button. If you choose the option and press the spacebar or Alt+↓, the pop-up list stays open until you make a selection (Chapter 2).

Portrait: The standard way of printing on the page, where text and graphics appear between the two long edges of the paper. Portrait is the opposite of *Landscape* (Chapter 8).

Power bar: An on-screen display of buttons that you can click to access commonly used file management, text editing, and text layout features in WordPerfect (Chapter 4).

Printer font: Fonts that are designed for use with a particular type of printer. Printer fonts include built-in, cartridge, and soft fonts (Chapter 10).

QuickFormat: A feature that lets you copy codes and styles from one place to another simply by clicking the mouse (Chapter 5).

QuickList: A list that lets you access files and directories without having to type a complete path name or file name (Chapter 20).

GLOSSARY

QuickMenu: A pop-up menu of options that are relevant to a particular object. To use a QuickMenu, move the mouse pointer to the object you want to work with, right-click the mouse to open the QuickMenu, then select an option by clicking the left mouse button (Chapter 2).

RAM: See *Memory*.

Read-only file: A file that can be viewed but not changed (Chapter 4, Appendix C).

Record: *In reference to merges,* a single row of information in a data table (used this way, "record" rhymes with "checkered"); for example, the complete name and address of one person in a mailing list (Chapter 21). *In reference to macros,* to save actions as you perform them, so that you can play them back again later (used this way, "record" rhymes with "I'm bored") (Chapter 18).

Reveal Codes: The window that lets you see WordPerfect's hidden codes (Chapter 4).

Right-click: This means "Move the mouse pointer to the item, then press and release the *right* mouse button." This is reversed on a left-handed mouse. Right-clicking opens a QuickMenu of options relevant to whatever you right-clicked (Chapter 2).

Right-justify: See *Flush right*.

Ruler bar: An on-screen representation of a ruler. The ruler bar lets you use your mouse to set up margins, paragraph formats, table columns, newspaper columns, parallel columns, and tab stops (Chapters 5, 7, 27).

Screen font: A font that's used to display text on the screen so that the text looks the way it will look when it is printed (Chapter 10).

Select: In reference to *documents,* the phrases *select text* and *select the text* refer to "blocking" or "highlighting" the text you want to work with, by dragging the mouse pointer through it or by using Edit ➤ Select, or F8 (Chapter 3). In reference to *a dialog box or menu,* select means to mark a check box with an ×, or mark a radio button option in a dialog box, by clicking the mouse or pressing the spacebar (Chapter 2). In reference to *sorting or merging,* selecting refers to the ability to isolate certain types of information, such as customers in the state of California, or in a certain zip code area (Chapter 22).

Sheet-feed: See *Tractor-feed*.

Shift: The key used to capitalize a single letter, or used in a combination keystroke such as Shift+F1 (Chapter 2).

Shortcut (key): An alternative to going through the menus and/or dialog boxes to get to a frequently used feature; often appears next to the command name in the menu, and often requires a *combination keystroke* (Chapter 2).

Soft font: A printer font (*not* a graphics font) that's stored on disk and *downloaded* (sent) to the printer when needed, or when the printer is initialized (Chapter 10).

Soft return: The [SRt] code that WordPerfect uses to break text at the right margin between words, rather than between characters. You can see [SRt] in Reveal Codes (Chapter 4).

Sort: To put text or numbers into a specific order, such as alphabetical or numerical (Chapter 22).

Specific codes: Codes with a specific setting, such as [Font:CG Times], as opposed to a general code such as [Left Tab] or [HRt] (Chapter 9).

Status bar: The bar that appears across the bottom of the screen. You can use File ➤ Preferences ➤ Status Bar to change the appearance of the status bar (Chapter 19).

Style: A set of codes that defines the format and appearance of a design element in your text, such as all the chapter titles or all the section titles (Chapter 17).

Style library: A collection of styles. You can store style libraries in the current document or template, a supplemental template, or any file (Chapter 17).

Supplementary dictionary: A dictionary that you can create and personalize with words and phrases that aren't found in the main dictionary (Chapter 11).

Tab: The key used to move to the next tab stop (Chapter 2), or the result of pressing that key (Chapter 5).

Tab stop: The place where the cursor stops when you press Tab, Indent, or any other key that indents or outdents. Use the ruler bar to change the tab stops (Chapter 5).

GLOSSARY

Template: Every new document that you create is formatted according to an underlying template file. Templates establish the initial document text and they define the abbreviations, button bars, macros, menus, keyboards, preferences, and styles available to a document (Chapter 20).

TextArt: A "mini" text enhancement application that comes with WordPerfect and that you can use to add an outline, fill pattern, shadow, or a shape to a text image (Chapter 26).

Text box: *In dialog boxes,* this is a box into which you enter information related to a selected option or command (Chapter 2). *In graphics,* this is the type of box used to display elements such as sidebars and quotations separately from the main text (Chapter 25).

Toggle: A key or option that turns a feature on and off every time you press the key or select the option. For example, each time you press it, the Insert key toggles between Insert and Typeover modes (Chapter 2).

Tractor-feed: A means of feeding paper into a printer by using paper that has perforations along its left and right edges. Tractor-feed is the opposite of *sheet-feed,* where individual, nonperforated sheets are fed to the printer from a bin (Chapter 10).

User box: A graphics box which, by default, has no frame (Chapter 25).

Watermark: Text or a graphic that's (usually) printed on every page, most often in a light shade of gray (Chapters 8, 25, 28).

Wildcard: A special character that stands for something else. For example, **?** stands for any single character, and ***** stands for zero or more characters (Chapter 20).

Window: A rectangular section of the screen that displays an application (program) or a document (Chapter 4).

Windows: The operating environment that you use to run WordPerfect for Windows. Windows is a graphical system that lets you run more than one application at a time, display several windows at once, transfer information between applications, and work with icons and menus instead of arcane commands (Chapters 1, 33).

Word-wrap: To end a line automatically by breaking it between two words rather than in the middle of a word. WordPerfect will automatically wrap a word when text that you're typing extends past the right margin (Chapter 3).

WYSIWYG: An acronym (pronounced "wizzy wig") that stands for "What You See Is What You Get." WordPerfect's Draft, Page, and Two-Page views all are WYSIWYG (Chapter 4).

Zoom: To increase or decrease the magnification of a document on the screen (Chapter 4).

INDEX

Note: Boldfaced page numbers indicate definitions of terms and principal discussions of topics. Italicized page numbers indicate illustrations.

H

new features for, 1104
layout. *See* formatting
Layout button bar, 145
layouts, desktop publishing. *See*
    desktop publishing layouts
leading, 918, **922–923**, 948, 1132
left justification, 151, *152*
left tab stops, 161, *162*, 163
Legal numbering styles, *451–452*
legends, 869, 876
length of graphic lines, 216
length-sensitivity, 713
less than symbols (<)
    in criteria, 711
    in isolating text, 753–754
letterheads
    delaying codes for, 296
    printing on, **303**
letters (alphabet), spacing
    between, **924–929**, *926*
letters (correspondence). *See*
    merges
levels
    in counters, 484, 487–491
    in outlines, 445, **447**, *448–449*,
        450–452
    changing, **463**
    collapsing and expanding,
        464–466, *465*, 468
    in entering items, 458
    markers for, 453–454, *454*,
        467–468
    in page numbers, 282
    in tables of contents, 1016,
        1018
.LEX files, 1127
libraries for styles, **535**, 1135
    creating, **536–538**
    retrieving, **538–539**

saving, **537–538**
Line button, 291
line numbering, 474, **476**, *477*
    format for, **479–482**, *482*
    lines counted in, **479**
    separator lines in, **482–483**
    turning on, **476**, **478**
Line Numbering dialog box,
    478–482, *478*
Line Spacing button, 145
linefeed settings, 146
Linenum macro, 574
lines (graphic), 187, **214–216**
    changing, **215–216**, **243–244**
    for headers and footers, 291
    height of, **924**
    joining, **241–242**, *242*
    in newsletters, 945
    in newspaper columns, *901*,
        908–910
    separator. *See* separator lines
    splitting, **243**
    in tables, **241–244**
    in WP Draw, 885, 892
lines (text)
    keeping words together on, **300**
    numbering. *See* line numbering
    sorting, 730, 739, **741–742**,
        742, 750
    spacing of, 121, **145–146**,
        922–923
    splitting, **76**
    in tables, 750
Link Options dialog box, 1074
links and linking, 1057
    changing, **1073**, **1081**
    in DDE, **1074–1076**
    deleting, 1045, **1074**, 1081
    vs. embedding, 1077

YOUR GUIDE TO A WORLD OF CONVENIENCE.

EASY ACCESS.

300 pp. ISBN:1189-0.

The *ABC's of Microsoft Access* is the perfect tutorial for any Access novice. This friendly, hands-on guide gives you the skill and confidence you need to get the most out of Microsoft Access.

Learn the basics of Access. In just a few minutes, you'll be able to get around in both Access and Windows, create your first database and get the information you need, when and how you need it.

Once you get a little experience, this step-by-step handbook will show how to create professional-looking reports with ReportWizard, generate mailing labels and work with all kinds of data.

SYBEX. Help Yourself.

2021 Challenger Drive
Alameda, CA 94501
1-800- 227-2346

SYBEX

YOUR GUIDE TO DOS DOMINANCE.

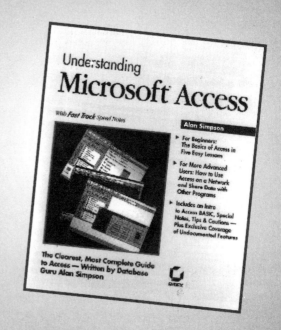

Alan Simpson's Mastering WordPerfect 6.0 for Windows Companion Disks

If you want to use the example documents presented in this book without keying them in yourself, you can send for the companion disks containing all the files (excluding the files that came with your WordPerfect package). You can use each file as it is, or as a starting point for creating your own document.

To purchase the optional companion disks, please complete the order form below and return it with your VISA or MasterCard number, a check, international money order, or purchase order for $20.00 U.S. currency (plus sales tax for California residents) to the address shown on the coupon. Or, we can bill you later.

If you prefer, you can return the coupon without making a purchase to receive free periodic newsletters and updates about Alan Simpson's latest books.

Alan Simpson Computing
P.O. Box 945
Cardiff-by-the-Sea, CA 92007
Phone (619) 943-7715   FAX (619) 943-7750

☐ Please send the companion disks for *Mastering WordPerfect 6.0 for Windows*.

☐ No disk thanks, but please send free newsletters from Alan Simpson Computing.

_____
Name

_____
Company

_____
Address

_____
City, State, Zip

_____
Country   P.O. Number (if applicable)

_____
Phone Number (Required for VISA/MC orders)

Check one:

☐ Payment enclosed ($20.00, plus sales tax for California residents), made payable to Alan Simpson Computing

☐ Bill me later   ☐ Bill my VISA or MasterCard

_____
Card Number   Exp. Date

Check one disk size:

☐ 5$\frac{1}{4}$-inch disk   ☐ 3$\frac{1}{2}$-inch disk

SYBEX is not affiliated with Alan Simpson Computing and assumes no responsibility for any defect in the disk or files.

FREE BROCHURE!

Complete this form today, and we'll send you a full-color brochure of Sybex bestsellers.

Please supply the name of the Sybex book purchased.

_____

How would you rate it?

_____ Excellent   _____ Very Good   _____ Average   _____ Poor

Why did you select this particular book?

_____ Recommended to me by a friend
_____ Recommended to me by store personnel
_____ Saw an advertisement in _____
_____ Author's reputation
_____ Saw in Sybex catalog
_____ Required textbook
_____ Sybex reputation
_____ Read book review in _____
_____ In-store display
_____ Other _____

Where did you buy it?

_____ Bookstore
_____ Computer Store or Software Store
_____ Catalog (name: _____)
_____ Direct from Sybex
_____ Other: _____

Did you buy this book with your personal funds?

_____ Yes   _____ No

About how many computer books do you buy each year?

_____ 1-3   _____ 3-5   _____ 5-7   _____ 7-9   _____ 10+

About how many Sybex books do you own?

_____ 1-3   _____ 3-5   _____ 5-7   _____ 7-9   _____ 10+

Please indicate your level of experience with the software covered in this book:

_____ Beginner   _____ Intermediate   _____ Advanced

Which types of software packages do you use regularly?

_____ Accounting	_____ Databases	_____ Networks
_____ Amiga	_____ Desktop Publishing	_____ Operating Systems
_____ Apple/Mac	_____ File Utilities	_____ Spreadsheets
_____ CAD	_____ Money Management	_____ Word Processing
_____ Communications	_____ Languages	_____ Other _____

(please specify)

Which of the following best describes your job title?

_____	Administrative/Secretarial	_____	President/CEO
_____	Director	_____	Manager/Supervisor
_____	Engineer/Technician	_____	Other _____

(please specify)

Comments on the weaknesses/strengths of this book: _____

_____

_____

_____

_____

Name _____

Street _____

City/State/Zip _____

Phone _____

PLEASE FOLD, SEAL, AND MAIL TO SYBEX

SYBEX, INC.
Department M
2021 CHALLENGER DR.
ALAMEDA, CALIFORNIA USA
94501

SYBEX

SEAL

Feature	How to Get There	Feature	How to Get There
Justification Limits	Alt+L TW, C or X	Object Link (create)	Select previously saved object in server, copy to Clipboard, switch t WordPerfect, press Alt+E S, highlight linkable format, press Alt+L
Kerning	Alt+L, TWA, or TM		
Keyboard Layout	Alt+F E Alt+K ↵		
Labels	Alt+L B		
Language	Alt+T L		
Leading Adjustment	Alt+L TWL ALT+T		
Left Justification (all lines)	Ctrl+L	Object Link (edit)*	Alt+E L
		Open Document	Ctrl+O or F4
Letterspacing	Alt+L TW, M or O or R	Outline	Alt+T O
License Number	Alt+H A	Outline (appearance)	F9 Alt+N
Line (graphic)	See Graphic Line		
Line Height	Alt+L LH	Overstrike	Alt+L TO
Line Numbering	Alt+L LN	Page Numbering	Alt+L PN
Line Spacing	Alt+L LS	Page View	Alt+F5
Links (DDE & OLE)	Alt+E L	Paper Size	Alt+L PS
		Paragraph Formatting	Alt+L AF
Links (spread-sheet & database)	Alt+I R E		
		Password Protect	F3 P
Lists	Alt+T I	Paste from Clipboard***	Ctrl+V or Shift+Ins
Macro (edit)	Alt+T ME		
Macro (macro bar)	Alt+T MM	Paste Special***	Alt+E S
		Path Name (insert in text)	Alt+I OP
Macro (play)	Alt+F10		
Macro (record)	Ctrl+F10	POSTNET Bar Code	Alt+I OB
Mail	Alt+F M		
Margin Release	Shift+Tab	Power Bar (customize)	Alt+F E Alt+O ↵
Margins	Ctrl+F8		
Master Document	Alt+F D	Power Bar (show/hide)	Alt+V O
Menus (customize)	Alt+F E Alt+M ↵	Preferences	Alt+F E
		Print Document	F5 or Ctrl+P
Merge Codes**	Alt+Shift+C	Print Quality	F5 Q spacebar
Merge Documents	Shift+F9	QuickFinder (indexer)	Alt+F Q
		QuickList (edit/display)	Ctrl+O Alt+L spacebar
New Document	Ctrl+N		
Object (edit)*	Alt+E O or double-click object	QuickMark (find)	Ctrl+Q
		QuickMark (set)	Ctrl+Shift+Q
Object (insert)	Alt+I J	QuickMenu	Right-click the mouse
		Redline	F9 Alt+R

*   Select text or object first
** If appropriate feature bar is visible
*** If information is on Clipboard